I YOU WE THEM

I
YOU
WE
THEM

WALKING INTO THE WORLD
OF THE DESK KILLER

DAN GRETTON

FARRAR, STRAUS AND GIROUX
NEW YORK

Farrar, Straus and Giroux
120 Broadway, New York 10271

Copyright © 2019 by Dan Gretton
All rights reserved
Printed in the United States of America
Originally published in 2019 by William Heinemann, Great Britain, as *I You We Them:*
Journeys Beyond Evil; The Desk Killers in History and Today
Published in the United States by Farrar, Straus and Giroux
First American edition, 2020

Owing to limitations of space, permissions acknowledgments can be found
on pages 1083–1084 and illustration credits can be found on pages 1085–1090.

Library of Congress Control Number: 2019955237
ISBN: 978-0-374-17437-8

Our books may be purchased in bulk for promotional, educational,
or business use. Please contact your local bookseller or the Macmillan Corporate
and Premium Sales Department at 1-800-221-7945, extension 5442,
or by e-mail at MacmillanSpecialMarkets@macmillan.com.

www.fsgbooks.com
www.twitter.com/fsgbooks • www.facebook.com/fsgbooks

1   3   5   7   9   10   8   6   4   2

For Corinne and Mark,
who gave us the most vivid maps,
and opened up limitless worlds of imagination.

For J. – who has walked this landscape with me.

'In a dark time, the eye begins to see . . .'

Theodore Roethke

'Once we accept, for a single hour or in a single exceptional case, that there can be something more important than sympathy for others, there is no crime against humanity that we cannot commit with a clear conscience . . . I was thinking about all those men – the superintendent, the convoy soldiers and all the others . . . most of them nice, kind individuals, who have turned into bad people only because of their official positions . . . These people . . . terrify me. And indeed they are terrifying people – more terrifying than any marauding gangster. *He* might feel some pity, but not these men: they've taken out insurance against pity . . .

'Imagine a problem in psychology: to find a way of getting people in our day and age – Christians, humanitarians, nice, kind people – to commit the most heinous crimes without any feeling of guilt. There is only one solution – doing just what we do now: you make them governors, superintendents, officers or policemen, a process which, first of all . . . allows people to be treated like inanimate objects, precluding any humane or brotherly relationships, and, secondly, ensures that people working . . . must be so interdependent that responsibility for the way they treat people never devolves on any one of them individually. Without these preconditions it would be impossible in our day and age to carry out atrocities like the things I have witnessed today.'

Nekhlyudov's reflections, in *Resurrection* by Leo Tolstoy

Contents

Author's Note

I You We Them: Journeys Beyond Evil is the first part of an ongoing exploration investigating the phenomenon of the 'desk killer' both in history and in our world today – the people who kill without ever leaving their offices, who rarely see the faces of their victims. This work is structured in two volumes: volume one, which you are holding in your hands, and volume two, which will be published in the near future. Each volume contains two books.

The four books were written and revised in four locations, beginning in 2006. Each place, by the sea, exerted its own influence on the writing, and, by chance not design, the beginning of each new writing phase, and each part, took place not only in a different location, but in a different season:

Volume One

Book One (Winter): East (Suffolk coast)

Book Two (Spring): West-south-west (Pembrokeshire)

Volume Two

Book Three (Summer): West-north-west (Traeth Bach)

Book Four (Autumn): West, west-north-west (Pen Llŷn)

For ethical, and sometimes more personal reasons, some names and identifying features in the text have been changed.

BOOK ONE

JOURNEYS INTO THE WORLD OF
THE DESK KILLER

Preface

First Day, White Page

January 2006, Suffolk

Why are we drawn back to particular places?

Since I was a boy I have been returning here. To this unremark-able stretch of shingle on the Suffolk coast – vast grey skies, the sea, usually a darker shade of grey. And undulating waves of peb-bles, interrupted only by tussocks of coarse grass, somehow hold-ing on against the bullying winds. We came here to fly kites once, but the wind defeated us, twisting the string into a dozen knots. I've brought many friends to this place over the years, trying not to build up expectations, wanting the peculiar force of the landscape to work on them wordlessly.

The twisting road that leads here is part of it. Arriving at night, as I did yesterday, it is like sinking into the beginning of a story, the story that captivated you as a child, that you would read again and again, because the absorption into that world was so entire that, momentarily, all else would fall away. Off the motorway. Over the estuary. Round the town that wants to be a city, with its scatter-ings of drive-through burger bars and superstores off the ring road. Onto a main road. The white lines finally fade. A long, straight stretch through woods of pine and silver birch. Through a last village. And then the little road, barely signed at all. The road where you never meet another vehicle. Driving in a trance now, slowing to twenty, fifteen miles per hour. A tunnel of trees. The right-angle bend sweeps round. The telegraph pole where the barn owl was. To the left, a final sway the other way, out into the open again, over a small, white bridge. Tall reeds now on both sides. And finally the road becomes a track, and the track ends at the blackness of the sea. As the engine fades the certainty of that soft roar of sea and wind. And a flickering understanding that the end and the beginning are the same.

*

I am sitting in the window of a small cottage that feels more like the cabin of a boat. In front of me a January sea, two upturned dinghies, a flock of birds I cannot identify flitting in crazed gusts, a red and white plastic bag cartwheeling just too fast for me to read the writing on it. Only two figures seen all day – a bearded man walking his dog, and now a distant figure, or rather a head and shoulders above the line of shingle, flying a huge, modern kite, purple and blue, that resembles a parachute. Having more success than we ever did.

And the paradox that despite the buffeting of the winds on all sides, I feel a sense of stillness for the first time in months. I always knew that the writing could only start here, and probably only at this time of year – the emptiness of January. Looking to the east, beyond the grey strip of the North Sea, which used to be known as 'the German Ocean'. And, in that sea, there still exist, in minuscule particles, the pulverised stones of Spandau prison dumped into these waters after its last prisoner died. All this time trying to understand violence, and its relationship to those who work at their desks, at their computers. Them. Us. You. Me. I reflect on the last decade of journeying and attempting to grapple with this subject. Ten years of visiting archives, walking through sites of extermination, reading interviews with survivors and perpetrators, and thousands of pages of testimony. And yet, as I begin to write, my screen is frozen. A white page. I'm rapidly trying to scan the multiplicity of images and sounds which inhabit me, searching for a way to begin. These understandings and experiences which have haunted me for years ... Voices, places, walks and faces jostle for attention as I write these words on a bitingly cold January day:

- 'It's hard to recognise, but it was here. They burned people here.'
- Zdzisław in his hut at Chełmno, fighting his personal battle against forgetting with the aid of handwritten pages that few will ever read.
- The minutes of the Wannsee Conference, the miraculous, single surviving document – one copy out of thirty.
- The killing of Ken Saro-Wiwa. The plumes of fire and smoke that have choked a land for over forty years. *And we have all let this continue.*
- Maria Saro-Wiwa singing the Ogoni anthem, in a broken voice, to a small crowd gathered by the Thames to remember her husband who died trying to save his land and people from being destroyed by oil.
- Saurer's corporate communications director protesting from her comfortable office, 'But we have nothing to do with that company now.'
- Talking to Gitta Sereny about Albert Speer, and that single line: 'I loved machines more than people.'
- Walking from Goethe's house, out of Weimar, over the Ettersberg and into the beech forest. '*Buchen-wald*'. You can walk it in an hour and a half.
- And Walter Stier, the railway official who timetabled the trains to Treblinka insists again, 'I just sat at my desk ... I was just a desk man.'
- Our fingers freezing in the snows of Monowice, trying to read Levi's words in the dying light.

All of these dancing in my head, defying me to begin without them.

PART ONE

Mapping the Past

1

Explorations: Maps and the Curiosity of a Child's Mind

A summer's evening, I'm five or six years old. It's terrible to have to go to bed when it's still light outside. Even more terrible when I can hear waves of music, laughter, the clink of wine glasses and the excited chatter of my parents and their friends, lapping up to the bedroom from below . . .

I can hold out no longer. I get out of bed, tiptoe out of the room I share with my brother, and go to the top of the stairs, which curve away to the sitting room downstairs. Through the bannisters I can see my father balancing a glass in one hand and a cigarette in the other, talking to two colleagues from the university – I notice the woman is wearing a long, swirly, purple and black dress, and she's smiling and smoking too, nodding vigorously. My mother is on the other side of the room, in her summery dress, light greens and blues that shimmer like water, she's slipping a record out of a paper sleeve, and lowering the needle. More music. This time, a thunderous bass, and drums, reverberating around the room, then African singers chanting. The one we love to dance to. I creep down five stairs, to the little landing. I now can see my glamorous London aunt is here too, and her American husband, pouring drinks. I didn't even know they were coming tonight. This gives me a chance . . . if I can just make her see me. But now she's sitting on the bottom stair, facing away from me, talking to somebody I don't know, and all I can see is the back of her head, and two, huge circles of silver earrings, which dance as she talks. I bump down the remaining stairs and tap her on the shoulder. I can still see her smile and surprise as she turns, 'Hello, little one! Up a bit late, aren't you?', but it's spoken softly, almost conspiratorially. 'I can't sleep, and . . . and I, I heard the music and . . .' But all of this is unnecessary with my aunt. She still remembers the unfairness of childhood, the restrictions, and she's always liked breaking the rules. I don't have to explain anything to her, I don't have to spell it out.

Curiosity. The intense absorption that children often have, quite instinctively. The fascination in the sensual world all around, the total concentration when playing. Didn't a philosopher once say that 'man is most nearly himself when he achieves the seriousness of a child at play'? And this seriousness seems inextricably linked to creativity, that intensity of concentration, an immersion in the present moment, which we all possessed as children, but which gets increasingly rare as we get older? This is not to see childhood as some kind of dreamland; we probably experience more shock and trauma in these years than in the rest of our lives put together. But there is a quality of seeing, a vivid intensity of living, which comes with being a child. And this is at the core, the origin, of who we are. The unfiltered mind. The lack of self-consciousness. And, at moments in our lives, we realise we can touch an energy that's still there, however deeply it's been buried.

*

From as far back as I can remember walking has captivated me – walking up mountains as a child, finding lakes, looking at maps, predicting what landscapes lie ahead; walking through forests, walking past skyscrapers, glimpsing oceans, dodging downpours; watching peregrine falcons electrify the skies, and foxes run the city streets at night. In the parched heat of an African summer or the raving winds of a Welsh winter, the action is the same. One foot in front of the other. Never knowing where you'll end up.

Most of my life I've lived in cities. There's something curious about the act of walking in cities – you don't really seem to notice the distance covered, at least not in the same way. This seems to be the inverse of the experience of walking in the countryside. I think it may be connected to how far ahead it's possible to see. When I was a child I knew it was exactly a mile and a half from the farmhouse in the bend of the river where I grew up to the nearest village, and I knew that it would take half an hour to walk. The walk was mainly downhill, across arable fields, and the church spire of the village acted like a lodestone, drawing you closer and closer, visibly reducing that mile and a half all the time, reeling you in. Walking in a city like London you can rarely see more than a few hundred yards ahead, so talk of miles becomes irrelevant, everything is about the marker points – the junctions where you turn, the shop you're heading to, the corner of the park. And, in this way, if you ever stop to calculate it, you'll find that in the course of a normal day you might have walked four or five miles without really noticing.

Walking in the countryside somehow seems a more self-conscious act. The very idea of 'going for a walk' is associated far more with the country than the city. I see people in Hackney taking their dogs for a walk in Victoria Park, but other people walking in the city nearly always appear to be *on their way* somewhere; it's functional walking, not walking for its own sake. Whereas to 'go for a walk' in the countryside seems eminently understandable. Yet rural walking comes with its challenges, the echoes of feudalism and privilege in the omnipresent signs, 'Private – Keep Out', 'Trespassers Will Be Prosecuted' – the kind of notices which so incensed the young poet John Clare when the early-nineteenth-century Enclosure Acts began to privatise the common land of his beloved Northamptonshire countryside. His freedom to walk 'free as spring clouds and wild as summer flowers, / Is faded all'. He complains that 'Fence now meets fence in owners' little bounds / Of field and meadow, large as garden grounds, / In little parcels little minds to please / With men and flocks imprisoned, ill at ease'. The paths he'd walked since childhood are blocked – 'Each little tyrant with his little sign / Shows where man claims, earth glows no more divine. / On paths to freedom and to childhood dear / A board sticks up to notice "no road here".'

It seems a curious anachronism that such signs, such patterns of land ownership, such remnants of authoritarian bossiness have survived in a society that now considers itself less deferential, more free. Perhaps that's why so many of us are drawn to the mountains and the coast – instinctively, so we may think, but there may be deeper impulses at work. Yes, an urge to have our horizons released by water or sky, but also a feeling that no individual there can really own the rocks or the earth we walk on. As another fine poet observed in Assynt: 'Who possesses this landscape? / The man who bought it or / I who am possessed by it? . . . this landscape is masterless . . .'

In the city there are far fewer no-go areas, so to the curious walker or explorer the vast lattice of streets, roads, lanes, mews and alleys are a continuous source of new fascinations. An immense democracy of discoveries. A spare twenty minutes in an unfamiliar part of London, even for someone who's lived there all their life, can reveal astonishing things. Last week I turned a corner in Kensington, not somewhere I often find myself, and an anonymous street emerged into a fine square of six-storey Victorian redbrick houses, like winter castles glowing, and at one end of the square I found a small, white Armenian church, which looked as if it had been airlifted from Yerevan and dropped there, almost by chance.

But it's our animal tracks in the cities that most fascinate me as I get older. In the countryside our walking is often determined by the route of a path, or the line of a lane, but in the city our choices are multiple and continuous. In one of the most vivid dreams I've ever had, I dreamt of recovering from a serious accident, and, in this liminal state between consciousness and unconsciousness, suddenly presented before me, superimposed on a vast map of London, were lines traced in pulsing multicoloured neon, of *every single street I'd ever walked down*. An explosion of wild colours triggering amazement and memories . . . How I'd love to see that map once again. And afterwards I thought about how miraculous it would be to see others' tracks of London. And then to colour-code these by time, so that you might realise that, eleven years before you met, you and your future lover happened to be walking down Charing Cross Road on precisely the same afternoon in February, separated by only a matter of yards. You both pause to look in bookshop windows, and then, most remarkably, both of you turn into St Martin's Lane, and, separated by less than a minute, take a shortcut through Goodwin's Court towards Covent Garden, before going your different ways and being swallowed up again by the city.

We all make our own paths in utterly various, and unpredictably anarchic, ways. If you asked a hundred people to walk across Soho from, say, Cambridge Circus to Oxford Circus, you would, in all likelihood, end up with dozens of different routes. And these choices would be as diverse as the human beings who made them – nostalgia to see the old café in Greek Street, a passion for vinyl leading to a Berwick Street record-shop diversion, a nervous visitor sticking to the safety of Shaftesbury Avenue, then up Regent Street . . . After a while, though, we begin to develop tracks, as surely as any fox does. We evolve our own favoured routes. Overleaf is one of mine – across Soho from a different direction – one that has been in my life for the last twenty-three years:

I first walked this particular zigzag in my mid twenties when I was sharing a flat in Charlotte Street with my Russian partner and a friend of mine (and later on, also with this friend's Czech partner). It was, technically, a one-bedroom flat, but at certain stages of life we seem able to be more flexible. We had the tiny bedroom at the back, with a window that looked towards Percy Street, and my friend had a futon in the small sitting room, which you had to walk through to get to the kitchen. The challenges of space and privacy were offset by being able to walk into Soho in three minutes, and to the British Museum in four.

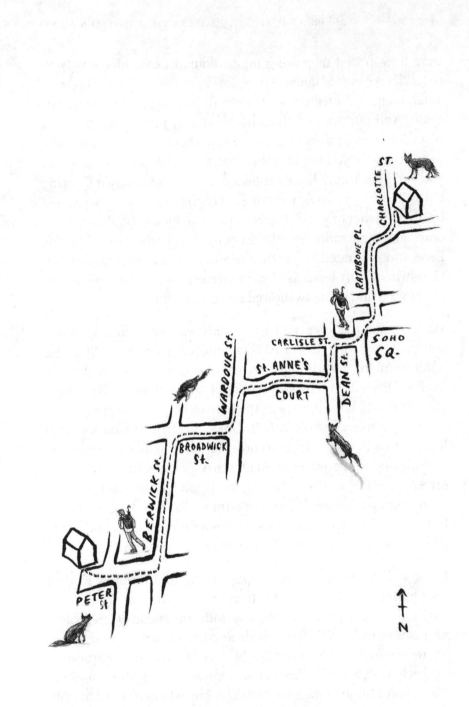

We became very popular for those two and a half years, with friends dropping by unannounced (that far-off era before mobile phones), for spontaneous gatherings, fuelled with takeaway retsina from the Venus Kebab House below – sometimes moving up onto the roof on summer evenings, which we made into a simple garden with a couple of trips to Columbia Road flower market. Chatter of voices and the scent of roasting meat and garlic floating up in waves from the streets below. And in the winter we had snowball fights high above Charlotte Street from our kitchen with the girls working in the offices of the sexual health clinic opposite.

At this time, Platform – the arts organisation I had started with a close friend some years before – hadn't yet established itself, and as there was only limited funding, I started teaching part-time at an adult education college in Soho to supplement my income. The students came from all corners of the world, some of them refugees, nearly all of them working (mostly in low-paid jobs) in London. I soon fell in love with teaching, which was relatively well paid in those days, and also the ethos of the place – because it was a state college the students got highly subsidised courses taught by extremely committed and well-qualified teachers (some of them also writers, musicians, journalists in their other lives). It was also a novelty to live so close to your workplace; when I started I realised the zigzag above was the most direct way there, and timed the walk at just under seven and a half minutes. This meant that if my afternoon class started at four o'clock, I could leave at ten to four, and just have time to do my photocopying before making my entrance, sweeping into the classroom with a theatrical flourish, already speaking to my gathered students as I was crossing the threshold … The classes soon developed a special energy, becoming much more than just a place of learning, rather an animated space where all of us shared our experiences, our political views, our memories – a place of real transformations and friendships.

More than twenty years on, so much in life has changed. Partners, friends, homes. Today I live in east London, in Hackney – a place that in my central London days I would have regarded with incomprehension, but which is now simply where I feel I belong. Platform has grown into a respected organisation of researchers, educationalists and activists, and has gained support for work examining the impacts of corporate power. And although I don't actually need to teach any more, I find it hard to stop altogether – it's a rather mysterious kind of addiction. And so, from time to time, I can still be seen making my darting fox-track through the city, though now it starts by emerging from the Central Line at Tottenham Court Road, fighting my way down Oxford Street for 300 yards before reconnecting with my zigzag route from over twenty years before . . . A very alert observer, positioned high in Soho Square, for the last twenty years, might have seen the same figure, walking very fast, cutting the corners off the square, almost every Tuesday and Thursday evening, before disappearing up Carlisle Street, and zigzagging into St Anne's Court . . . Walking from youth to middle age. Different coats over the years but the leather rucksack still the same, with the umbrella handle poking out the top.

To understand such continuity is simultaneously reassuring and disturbing. In many ways I feel the same as I always did, yet somehow the city confronts you – the same pubs, the same doorways, the same streets you first saw with the searching eyes of youth. Now these places are thick with memories and associations – not a street here or a pub that doesn't contain a past story. And catching a glimpsed reflection in a window I see reflected back a face I recognise, though more furrowed than I remember. The hardness of stone and steel in the city, its unforgiving fixity. The softness of a face, how quickly it can bruise, or crumple with a smile. And all of these people, rushing past me tonight with such animation, will be gone, like me, so quickly, in the vertigo of time. So a need to stop sometimes, to slow down, to look at things we never normally make time to look at. To raise eyes above, or below, the level of the street. To look back at ourselves from that reflection and ask about the things that get lost in the day-to-dayness of life.

*

Only a couple of days ago, coming up the steps from the Central Line platform at Tottenham Court Road, I saw something I'd never really looked at before. I paused, recognising the name of the little town stamped into the steel reinforcers on the edges of the steps. It was only a few miles from the house where I grew up:

FERALUN-BOWES-SCOTT &
WESTERN, HALSTEAD, ESSEX

Curious to have the name of a company marked permanently on the fabric of the city – hubris surely, with capitalism's continual process of extinction and reinvention? Then my eye caught another name, this time with a phone number, but it must be from many years ago because I noticed there was a digit missing in the code.

AATI LTD TEL. (0376) 346278

Some strange impulse makes me want to ring that number. Maybe for the simple reason that it exists. But also because hundreds of millions of eyes must have passed over this tiny corner of our city, yet I doubt if anybody has ever actually written down this number and phoned it. I have a feeling that a voice at the other end of the line might have something quite significant to communicate, perhaps a message from a different kind of underworld? Though, on reflection, the result would probably be far more banal, a recorded voice explaining to the caller that the number was no longer available . . .

*

A kind of assault.

That's the only way I can describe it.

A moment that changes the trajectory of your life.

It happened in a cinema in London, long ago. I was twenty-two years old. Watching one of the longest films ever made, certainly one of the most unforgettable – *Shoah*, a nine-and-a-half-hour examination of how the Holocaust was organised.

One section of the film disturbed me in a way I could not immediately understand. A voice was reading out an office memorandum, written by one bureaucrat to another. It slowly became apparent that the letter was explaining how a mobile gas chamber could be modified into a more effective killing machine. This was part of the document, as it was read out by the director, Claude Lanzmann, in the film:

> *Since December 1941 97,000 have been processed by the three vehicles in service with no major incidents. However, in the light of observations, the following technical changes are needed:*
> *1. The normal load is nine per square metre. In Saurer* vehicles, which are very spacious, maximum use of space is impossible. Not because of any overload but because loading to full capacity would affect the vehicle's stability.*
> *A reduction in capacity seems necessary. It must be reduced by one metre instead of attempting to solve the problem, as hitherto, by reducing the number of items loaded. That also extends the operating time, as the void must be filled with carbon monoxide. On the other hand, if the load space is reduced and the vehicle is packed solid, operating time can be shortened considerably. The manufacturers told us in discussion that reducing the length of the vehicle would unbalance it. They claim the front axle would be overloaded. But, in fact, the bal-*

---

* The story of the Saurer company appears in Chapter Five of Book One – 'The Town of Organised Forgetting'.

ance is automatically restored because the merchandise during the operation displays a natural tendency to push to the rear doors and is mainly found lying there at the end of the operation. So the front axle is not overloaded.

I did not know what to do with what I saw. I still don't really know. But the knowledge that a human being in an office somewhere wrote this to another human being in an office somewhere else terrified me. But more disturbing was the fact that memos like this are still being written in our world. The methods of killing may have changed, but the desk killers are still here – in fact they're flourishing, they're all around us. 'They', I say instinctively, because 'we' is too upsetting.

The comforting dividing line between those two small words . . .

*

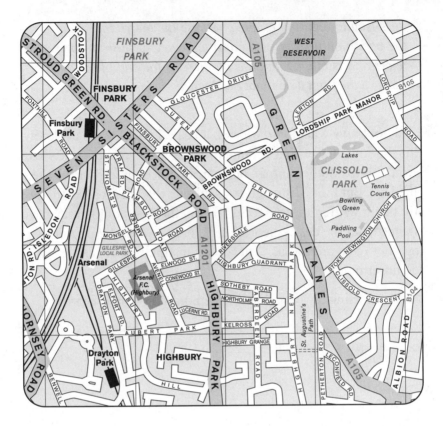

How to explain the fascination of the London *A–Z* for me as a young child growing up in the middle of Suffolk? More than fascination, more like an obsession. How I'd take the paperback, with its jaunty red, white and blue cover, from its place on the landing, and leaf through the cheap black and white pages almost furtively. Tracing with my finger the spaces between the football grounds that I recognised, and the very few parts of London that were known to me. So going from Uncle Ian's near Newington Green, across Petherton Road, up an alleyway, out at Highbury Hill, and then down to the Arsenal stadium. Arsenal, strange name, it didn't really seem to be a place. 'Tott-en-ham Hot-spur', I'd whisper the name to myself, full of something exotic, that curious second part – 'Hotspur'! No other team in the world could claim that . . . and their ground, 'White Hart Lane'. Look that up at the back. Page 52, square

E5. My finger negotiating the grids. There it is! Let's see if I could get from Highbury to there. I wonder how far it is? And what are the Seven Sisters? God, to have *seven* sisters – one is surely enough ... And then I'd suddenly be in central London, and lost entirely. Bewildered by the dipping and curving of the River Thames, and unable to find the place we reached on the boat to Greenwich ... my finger tracing north again, 'Kingsway' (but a long way from Buckingham Palace; strange name again), the British Museum – where we went to the Tutankhamen exhibition and had to queue for hours. University College, that's where Mark works, so what's his nearest Tube station? 'Euston Square'. Weird word, wonder how you say that? Ee-u-ston? Oo-ston?

And coming up to London in holidays, or at half-terms. Wired. Gripped. Greedily staring at everything, everyone, but trying not to show my fascination (which would mark me out as a visitor). My older brother was almost exactly the opposite; he seemed to turn a shade of sickly grey-green on his occasional excursions to the city, and visibly relaxed only when we were leaving. The train (change at Marks Tey for London) seemed to take for ever. 'Is it the next stop?' I'd ask Corinne, my long-suffering mother, again and again. But it was usually Shenfield or Ingatestone or Romford or Ilford ... Eventually those deep tunnels of brick arrived (with mysterious doors embedded in them, doors which I never saw a single person enter or emerge from). The darkness of 'Liverpool Street station' – again, what an odd name, hundreds of miles away from Liverpool, and not even facing in the right direction! Curious dark metal walkways over the platforms, then down a kind of tunnel, then right, past a war memorial built into the wall, blinking out into daylight, black taxi cabs with orange lights. We'd walk over to a smaller, older building, steps up to Broad Street station and the beginning of the line that took us round to Uncle Ian's (near Canonbury station). That was three, or maybe four stops round, in the trains with the heavy doors that made a reassuring sound when they swung shut, a kind of 'thunk'. But if you stayed on you could go all the way to Kew Gardens. That was where Borka ended; *Borka: The Adventures of a Goose with No Feathers*. My favourite book as a young boy, what

21

a subconscious impact it must have made on me! The sadness of being born with no feathers, of being teased by other geese. And then eventually, after all the other geese had left him behind when they migrated for the winter, he finds his happiness in London, with the other exotic birds living in Kew Gardens, including his special new friend Ferdinand. And how I loved to move from the purplish-browns of the Essex marshes and that sense of abandonment to the warmth of belonging, the burnt golds and rusty oranges of the city, repeating the story to myself. And vowing that one day I'd find my own Kew Gardens and my own Ferdinand . . .

It wasn't just the *A–Z* that captivated me. There was the shelf of books, halfway up the stairs on the landing, with gold and silver writing in capital letters on their spines that opened up worlds in my head. I would brush my hand over these spines as I'd go up the stairs, perhaps hoping that the mystical names would somehow penetrate the skin of my fingers and become a part of me. All these years later I can still see these books in my mind's eye: Freya Stark, *Beyond Euphrates* and *A Winter in Arabia*; Gavin Maxwell, *Lords of the Atlas*; Arthur Grimble, *A Pattern of Islands*; Elspeth Huxley, *The Flame Trees of Thika*; and Gerald Brenan, *South from Granada*. At the end of the shelf, as if keeping all the others upright, were the two green volumes of *Seven Pillars of Wisdom*, T. E. Lawrence – who, as I later found out, became better known as Lawrence of Arabia.

Like many children, I guess, I was mesmerised by maps – drawing them, creating imaginary islands, poring over the worlds conjured up by the black and white maps in *Swallows and Amazons* or *The Hobbit*, and then going back to the episode in the book and trying to reconcile the narrative with the distance and contours of the map. Occasionally I would find a discrepancy ('They couldn't possibly have sailed round that side of the island without being seen by the pirates!') and try to discuss this with my brother or sister, but neither of them seemed to be as bothered as I was by the lack of cartographic accuracy. The book that most bewitched me, though, was *The Ship That Flew* by Hilda Lewis. It had been my father's, and had his name, *Mark Gretton*, written inside in pencil, his handwriting barely recognisable, his familiar italics then only partly formed in that seven-year-old boy's hand.

Inside the front cover (terracotta, cloth) was a different kind of map, of a seaside town, not exactly bird's eye, but seen from above, at an angle: Radcliff-on-Sea. Everything was drawn in blue and white – the bandstand, the Marina Hotel and the cliffs beyond the town, and, beyond those, the house where the children in the story lived. Four of them, two girls, two boys (the eldest one Peter), and as the book opens all of them are gloomy. Their mother is seriously ill – a diabolically clever way to engage the child reader's heart – and Peter's father takes him aside to tell him that he needs to be very grown up, and not let on to his siblings the full extent of her sickness. And he wouldn't be able to take him to the dentist today, so here was two shillings and sixpence (the book was published in 1939, before the advent of the welfare state), he should go by himself, and with the shilling or so left over he could buy an ice cream, and still have money for his bus fare home.

Peter takes this, together with sixpence that he's saved up. So into Westhill he goes, to the dentist (the perfectly named Mr Frinton). He's brave, and feels quite grown up as he leaves, liberated by not being with his younger siblings for a change. This puts him in a more reflective mood than normal, more grown up, even the buildings of the little town seem subtly different. And then it happens – the moment of inexplicability. On his way down to the seafront to get his ice cream, he takes a 'narrow little street and rather dark, with old houses set close together. Peter was rather surprised. He didn't remember this street.' And I walked down this street with Peter so many times, thrilled at his perplexity in the face of this unfamiliar lane. He stops outside an old shop with a bay window, and his heart suddenly skips a beat – he's seen a beautiful ship, carved in wood, about as long as his hand. In the shop an ancient man with an eyepatch appears eventually, and, in response to Peter's enquiry about the carved ship, tells him that 'It would cost you all the money you have in the world – and a bit over.' Peter fishes in his pocket and takes out the shilling for his ice cream and bus fare home and his own sixpence. The ship is his. It doesn't matter about the ice cream or the bus fare, he's just so happy to have the boat, to feel it in his pocket. He decides to walk home along the shore, but has miscalculated the incoming tide. With growing horror he realises he's about to drown, and the water is licking at his feet, when suddenly as he says aloud 'I wish I could get home!' the boat reveals its true nature, and rapidly grows into a ship, big enough to step into. And soon he's flying, Radcliff behind him – the view inside the front cover of the book! And we're off . . .

That potent idea of the little street you've never noticed before – and will never be able to find again. And that the habitual could be transcended by taking a different turning. An astonishing moment for the child reading this. Of course, later when Peter tries to go back to the shop, to return the ship to the man – because clearly he can't have known about its magical properties – he's unable to find the little, winding street again. The imaginary Radcliff became more loved, more real, for me than any place I'd ever known. And I'd repeatedly follow Peter down the hill from the dentist, through those blue and white streets, imagining that winding lane appearing . . .

But there was one other map which intrigued me in a different way. This one was even less comprehensible than the A–Z, partly because it was hundreds of years old. And, unlike the map in *The Ship That Flew*, it was real. It was a map of Suffolk from the seventeenth century, drawn by a man with the evocative name of Abel Swale. It hung in a dark cloakroom near the front door of our house. And I kept looking at it, as if it would possibly reveal its secrets if I scrutinised it carefully enough. And maybe, in a way, it did. There were two places on this map that I was drawn to – the first, not surprisingly, was the place where we lived, the area around which had been shaded a faded yellow: Cow's Ford, the place where the animals used to cross the river, and the name that became so associated with my grandmother when we were growing up. The second place was far more mysterious. It was over on the coast – another country in my child's mind – and it was an extraordinary bent finger of land that was as close to being an island as it's possible to get.

I'd read the names of the nearby villages over and over again, repeating them as if to summon spirits. 'Ald-bor-ough' at the top, 'Or-ford' halfway down. And 'Bawdsey'. Over this area were the strange words 'Plomesgate Hun' – hun? Connected to hundred? But a hundred what? I would follow my finger down the sensuous curve of the River Alde, and then reach the most glorious point where the river was finally released into the sea. And how I wanted to be there, at that place! Even to a child's wild imagination the course of this snaking river seemed simply impossible. Surely the water would have broken through at some point? The narrowness of the land's neck was absurd. But the map was a map. It must be true. And I repeatedly traced my finger down that curve for years, and knew that one day it would be explored. Just as surely as finding my own Kew Gardens. And now, by this eastern shingle, I am here – the place where I'm starting to write this book.

2

Gitta Sereny, Albert Speer and the Desk Killer

Gitta Sereny. A name we will return to in the pages that follow. A name that you may already know. A writer who, perhaps more than any other, attempted to grapple with the concept that is usually, and lazily, reduced to the single word 'evil'. Virtually all of her work centres on the human necessity to understand how people can carry out appalling acts (they may not even see themselves as committing crimes), and can continue to live with themselves. And how they subsequently try to make sense of what they have done, and how it has shaped their lives, and the lives of others. Franz Stangl, the commandant of the Treblinka extermination camp; Albert Speer, Hitler's architect and subsequently minister of war production. Both responsible, directly or indirectly, for the deaths of hundreds of thousands of people. Sereny spends weeks, months, sometimes years, with her subjects. She goes through what happened, how it happened, why it happened. She's both extraordinarily patient and mercilessly relentless. She is more interested in understanding than judging. She rarely becomes angry. She leaves judgement up to her subject, when she senses the time is right for him or her to face their responsibility. And of course we as readers can ultimately

26

judge as well, but only when we've come through a process of what I now think of as 'Serenisation' – the understanding that's achieved through lengthy and empathetic exploration of a person – when a 'subject' stops being an object of condemnation and becomes a human being again.

I met her only once, in October 2004. We had a long conversation over coffee, in a break during a conference on 'The Psychology of Extermination', taking place at a college in Regent's Park organised by the psychotherapist Anthony Stadlen. I had made a contribution in which I described the research[*] I had started into the figure of the *Schreibtischtaeter* – that almost untranslatable German concept. I wondered if she'd considered why this concept had never found an English translation, 'desk killer' perhaps being the closest we could get to a synonym. And to what extent did she view Speer's fatal technocracy as falling into this category? Or did the process of psychological 'splitting', which she'd described so vividly in her book on him, actually hold the key to understanding the way the mind of the *Schreibtischtaeter* works – the way Speer seemed able to compartmentalise his work and ethics into different boxes? The session was coming to an end, she attempted an answer, but then rather generously said, 'But I don't think I've begun to answer your question, maybe we can continue our conversation in the break?'

She was shorter than I'd imagined, with the most expressive eyes, something birdlike in her manner, though not in the sense of fragile. A quick, darting intelligence, reflective, full of questions. She had little small talk, dived in straight away, wanting to know as much as possible about my research. We had an absorbing conversation, picking up references and shared understandings rapidly. At the end of our conversation she gave me her card and said, 'Well, you *must* come to supper. We've got a lot to talk about!'

---

[*] See chapter notes for a summary of this research.

I rang her the next day, and we had a longer talk. She agreed with my view that Speer sought safety in abstraction – systems, statistics, problems. And that although he was personable, even charming, this disguised an essential lacuna in him – an inability to fully understand the emotions of others, or indeed himself. And when confronted with the reality of pain or love he seemed to panic. There was an inability to face the human being. We talked about the moment in late 1943 when he visited the Dora weapons plant inside the Harz mountains, a place of utter degradation, where life expectancy for the slave labourers was often a matter of only days or weeks. Yes, you're right, it's extraordinarily significant, she said – it's one of the very few times in the war when he was directly confronted with the human cost of his directives from Berlin. And he could not look into the eyes of the slave labourers – *his* slave labourers. For this would mean acknowledging their humanity, and his own responsibility for their condition. The *Schreibtischtaeter* was out of his safe world of figures and abstractions, and suddenly that Olympian self-confidence was drained. He did not know where to look.

All of this horror is not so far away from our own times as we may like to think. The oil-company executives who rarely leave the cities, their carpeted, isolated existence which muffles any unwanted sounds or voices. The consultants who advise on 'restructurings' from their virtual worlds, who will never see the communities hundreds of miles away, devastated by their reports, for which they are richly remunerated. I asked Gitta her view about the psychological processes necessary to enable perpetrators like Speer, or our corporate executives today, to continue with their work. She was hesitant, and then wondered whether a lot is to do with seeing behaviour accepted by those around you. Think about how important it was for Stangl that some senior Catholics supported the supposed 'mercy killings' of Hitler's euthanasia programme. Yes, absolutely, and I then added the example of Eichmann at the Wannsee Conference, who, as we learn from Hannah Arendt, felt 'free of all guilt' because he'd heard senior figures in the Nazi government and civil service agree on the need for 'the final solution of the Jewish question' – as he put it, 'the most prominent people had spoken, the Popes of the Third Reich'.*

I told her about a piece of research I'd long wanted to carry out: to work together with an organisational psychologist to look at exactly this question, and to interview senior executives, perhaps from the oil industry or pharmaceutical companies or arms manufacturers, and ask them to reflect on how they are able to maintain their own values while continuing with their work (if indeed they have been able to). She seemed to be intrigued by this idea, but I also sensed a discomfort at moving from the historical examples we'd been discussing into our contemporary world. My thoughts triggered another memory for her, and she mentioned a speech she gave in Cheltenham some years ago, when she was pretty sure she addressed the question of how these conflicting forces interacted in Speer's career. She'd try to dig out her notes on this for when we met. We fixed a date for supper at her house in Warwick Avenue a few weeks later, in November.

Regrets, I've had a few. But this one still niggles away. She rang me a couple of days before we were going to have supper to say that she was in quite a lot of pain due to a medical condition, so could we rearrange our meeting? Of course, no problem. But then I was in America for two weeks with a colleague from Platform, giving the keynote lecture at a conference in Pittsburgh. And when I returned we had to deal immediately with a backlog of work, so anything non-urgent got pushed back to the new year . . . Before I knew it, months had passed, and the supper was not rescheduled. A couple of years later I saw her interviewed for a documentary about Diana Athill, who had been Gitta's editor (a brilliant one by all accounts), on her riveting and terrifying book about Franz Stangl (*Into That Darkness*). She looked much older and frailer, and again I thought

---

* *Eichmann in Jerusalem*, Hannah Arendt, Chapter VII, 'The Wannsee Conference, or Pontius Pilate.'

about getting back in touch, but didn't. It seemed that too much time had passed. Never mind, I'd send her a copy of my book when it was finally published.

Then, one day in June 2012, reading the *Guardian*, I turned a page and, with a stab of sadness, saw that she had died. Sadness that her fertile and remarkable mind was no longer in our world, but also a keen sense of loss at a conversation between us that had started, and now would never be finished. The obituary described her 'extraordinarily intense process of writing and researching' and her 'passion to understand and . . . intense moral commitment' which helped her to become such a formidable expert on the psychology of the Third Reich. But, however praising of her work, I didn't feel this account quite reflected the enormous influence that her books on Stangl and Speer have had. I've lost count of the number of people I've spoken to about these works, and how profoundly they have shaped their ways of thinking. They are some of the very few books that you could say are absolutely essential to our world; they should be required reading not only for all politicians, but for anyone seeking to understand power of any kind.

Yet, perhaps important conversations find their ways of continuing, even after death. More than twenty years since first reading her book on Speer, I still sense her, here at my shoulder, a companion in spirit on this journey.

*

There is a word, a German compound noun, which has been at the heart of my thinking and research over the last twenty years: '*Schreibtischtaeter*'.

'*Schreib*' (rhymes with 'scribe') means to write.
'*Tisch*' (rhymes with 'dish') is a table.
So '*Schreibtisch*' is a table that you write at, or work at – we could call it a desk.

'*Taeter*' (rhymes with 'later' or 'dictator') comes from the root '*tun*', to do, so a '*Taeter*' is a doer.

But the actions of a '*Taeter*' are not neutral – in fact, the way this word is used in Germany is nearly always pejorative. A '*Taeter*' does things that are either criminal – stealing cars, dealing drugs, etc. – (for instance, 'sex offender' in German is *Triebtaeter*) – or seriously disapproved of by many in society – killing animals, bullying people, extreme antisocial behaviour. Therefore, the closest translation we can get to this in English, I would say, is 'perpetrator'. So, if we put all this together:

> *Schreibtisch* + *Taeter* is a 'desk perpetrator' – i.e. a bureaucratic criminal.

However, this still doesn't quite convey the seriousness or weight of the word. The clear implication of '*Schreibtischtaeter*' from its early usage was somebody who killed from their desk – the figure who, by giving orders, uses paper or a phone or a computer to kill, instead of a gun. So, the term I will use in this work is 'desk killer'.*

It is extremely hard to pinpoint in history the exact first use of the term '*Schreibtischtaeter*' in German (or indeed 'desk murderer' or 'desk killer' in English), but the concept certainly gained widespread currency around the time of Adolf Eichmann's trial in Jerusalem in 1961. The word is often associated with Hannah Arendt's work, and her widely misquoted, and poorly understood, concept of 'the banality of evil', but, curiously, although she writes extensively about the *concept* behind 'killing from a desk', the phrases 'desk killer' or 'desk murderer' themselves do not appear anywhere in *Eichmann in Jerusalem*, published in 1963, two

---

* In the early stages of this research I used the term 'desk murderer'. However, it soon became apparent that many of the individuals who kill from their desks do not have the criminal intent to do so, therefore 'desk killer' is a more accurate term. Desk murderers do exist, but, thankfully, are very few in number. Desk killers, however, are all around us.

years after the trial. Arendt first uses 'desk murderer' in 1966, in the introduction she writes for Bernd Naumann's book on the Auschwitz trials in Frankfurt. And then, almost as if to make up for lost time, she uses the phrases 'desk murderer' and 'desk murder' no fewer than eight times in twenty pages. So it is clear that in the years between the Eichmann trial in 1961 and the publication of Naumann's book *Auschwitz* five years later, this phrase had become well known, and didn't require clarification in Arendt's introduction. To understand how much the concept had entered popular culture by this time, you only need to listen to Dylan singing 'Masters of War' in 1963 – 'Come, you masters of war, / You that build the big guns . . . You that hide behind walls, / You that hide behind desks.'

If there is a single individual responsible for inventing this term – or at least the concept behind the term – then I think it is Gideon Hausner, the leading prosecuting counsel in the Eichmann trial. Hausner, whatever his intellectual limitations and weakness for courtroom theatrics, made a remarkable speech, opening the prosecution on 17 April 1961, including these reflections on the changing nature of the figure of the 'killer' in society, and how the judicial process would also need to change to reflect these new developments: 'In this trial, we shall also encounter a new kind of killer, the kind that exercises his bloody craft behind a desk.' He then goes on to describe the power of Eichmann, the epitome of the desk killer, the bureaucrat who has no need to get his own hands dirty because, as he explains:

> it was his word that put gas chambers into action; he lifted the telephone, and railway trains left for the extermination centres; his signature it was that sealed the doom of tens of thousands . . . We shall find Eichmann describing himself as a fastidious person, a 'white-collar' worker . . . yet he was the one who planned, initiated and organized, who instructed others to spill this ocean of blood, and to use all the means of murder, theft, and torture . . .

His accomplices in the crime were neither gangsters nor men of the underworld, but the leaders of the nation – including professors and scholars, robed dignitaries with academic degrees, educated persons, the 'intelligentsia'. We shall encounter them – the doctors and lawyers, scholars, bankers and economists – in those councils which resolved to exterminate the Jews.

I also think it's possible that Hausner himself was influenced by an earlier piece of writing – which I first came across many years ago, at the very beginning of this research. It was written by C. S. Lewis during the war – *The Screwtape Letters* (first published in February 1942), a meditation on the nature of evil, conducted as a playful exchange of letters between a senior devil and a junior accomplice. Lewis writes this in the preface:

> I live in the Managerial Age, in a world of 'Admin'. The greatest evil is not now done in those sordid 'dens of crime' that Dickens loved to paint. It is not done even in concentration camps and labour camps. In those we see its final result. But it is conceived and ordered (moved, seconded, carried, and minuted) in clean, carpeted, warmed and well-lighted offices, by quiet men with white collars and cut fingernails and smooth-shaven cheeks who do not need to raise their voices.

Lewis's prescience is chilling. It is extraordinary to realise that at exactly the same moment that the printing presses were rolling with this book in January 1942, Eichmann and fourteen other men – the educated elite of the German civil service and security services – were meeting in an elegant mansion in Wannsee, Berlin, to co-ordinate 'the final solution of the Jewish question' – calmly organising genocide around a table in a pretty lakeside villa.[*]

---

[*] See Chapter Thirteen: 'The Doctors of Wannsee Meet in a Villa by the Lake'.

But the reason I have been haunted by this concept for most of my adult life is not primarily because of events that happened sixty or seventy years ago – it is because the desk killers have always been with us, and today are more numerous than ever. I've known one or two in my time, you might have met more. You can find people killing from their desks and their computers in the military, but also in the civil service. They might be in the oil industry, armaments, pharmaceuticals, but you can also find them in finance, insurance, politics or law. They rarely *intend* to kill, or injure, but their actions, combined with the vast and diffuse reach of government and contemporary corporate power, result in hundreds of thousands of deaths and devastated lives. And, as we race forward with ever more highly advanced technologies, it is inevitable that desk killing will become still more commonplace, because so many of the technologies now being developed only aid the process of what I would call 'distanced killing'.

Let me give you a single example of what I'm talking about. Unmanned aerial vehicles (UAVs), commonly known as 'drones', are now a central part of many countries' military and security forces; seventy-six nations around the world now have some type of UAV capacity. The market in drones is expected to rise from $5.9 billion to $11.3 billion in the next five years. This development has fundamentally altered the way wars are now being fought across the globe. Killers now do not even have to be on the same continent as those they kill. Most of the armed drones being used every day in Afghanistan and Pakistan are co-ordinated and flown from operators watching computer screens 8,000 miles away in the Nevada desert. Originally the vast majority of the drone operators were air force pilots, who may at least have had some experience of the reality of combat, but this is beginning to change as the technical demands alter, and younger operators are sought, the so-called 'PlayStation generation'. The terrifying extent of the desensitisation to killing can be seen in a recent advertising recruitment campaign for drone operators in the UAE:

Executive Solutions ME are currently recruiting UAE National
UAV Operators for an aerospace development project based
in Abu Dhabi.

This is an exciting opportunity to learn how to fly UAVs
(Unmanned Arial [*sic*] Vehicles)

And what was the very first question for potential applicants who
were going to be learning how to kill human beings from thousands of miles away?
'Do you enjoy playing computer games?'

*

In all of our lives over the last decades, just think about the staggering pace of technological change. So many rapid developments,
so many aspects that are liberating. Just in the years since I began
researching this work in the 1990s, I think back to the enormously
time-consuming nature of having to physically travel to archives all
over Europe, having to spend days and weeks accessing documents
– many of which are now available by travelling digitally in a fraction of a second, with a simple tap of a key on my laptop. There are,
undoubtedly, massive benefits for anyone interested in accessing
information. And the collaborative nature of some of this technology is also remarkable. So much so that it now seems impossible to
conceive of an era when we didn't have free access to information.

Many technological innovations have had profoundly positive
impacts on our daily lives – undeniably what could be called progress. But do we yet have the ability to assess the physiological and
psychological impacts of the technologies we're now becoming
dependent upon? And, crucially, does each element of these new
technologies bring us *closer* to each other or take us further away
from understanding others?

Not long ago, I had arranged to meet a friend at the Barbican, and as
it was a warm evening, I decided I'd walk from my place in Hackney. I

headed through the park, and out at the gate by the canal. As soon as I stepped on to the towpath, I was almost run down by a young guy on his bike, headphones on, clearly not in this world at all. And so many people walking along, looking down, eyes glued to their phones . . . Through Haggerston Park, a line that Speer used suddenly came to mind – how he used technology as a way of distancing himself from the realities of Nazism, as he wrote – what seemed to be 'the moral neutrality of technology' . . . And what did Hannah Arendt say, just before she died? The Sonning speech she gave in Denmark, where she predicted, with remarkable accuracy, so many developments now in our world – 'the threatening transformation of all government . . . into bureaucracies, the rule of neither law nor men but of anonymous offices or computers whose entirely depersonalised domination may turn out to be a greater threat to freedom . . . than the most outrageous arbitrariness of past tyrannies has ever been.' But has anything really been learnt, as we race ever faster into digital nirvana?

Through Old Street now, down the lane that runs past Bunhill Fields, where William Blake is buried. A friend has told me (and surely this cannot be true?) that the City of London, in its rapaciousness, is now wanting to build offices on top of this graveyard. I remembered his words about London: 'I wandered through each chartered street, / Near where the chartered Thames does flow. / And mark in every face I meet, / Marks of weakness, marks of woe.' Even in those days, everything 'chartered', everything commodified, all visible in the faces of the people he passed.

I continued on, down Bunhill Row, some fine, eighteenth-century buildings I didn't remember ever seeing before, and then a place that looked like a university halls of residence. Students padlocking their bikes to the railings. I walked on, and there to my left there was a long library with students working on their Sunday-night essay deadlines. I say 'library', but there are almost no books in this room at all. Just students, in rows, as if in some kind of digital factory, all gazing down at their screens, most with headphones on. Each person cut off entirely from their neighbour. All illuminated in their own digital worlds. The whole room a single blue glow.

*

In W. G. Sebald's final work, *Austerlitz*, the narrator Jacques Austerlitz recalls an inspirational history teacher from his school days, a man called André Hilary. Hilary's *pièce de résistance* is an extraordinarily detailed recreation of the Battle of Austerlitz in Moravia in 1805, involving meticulous descriptions of the weather conditions, the terrain, and portraits of all the senior officers. The boys are all deeply impressed by his performance and seemingly encyclopaedic grasp of the event. However, the narrator tells us, Hilary, like any truly creative teacher (or artist, for that matter), is never fully satisfied with his efforts:

> Hilary could talk for hours about the second of December 1805, but none the less it was his opinion that he had to cut his accounts far too short, because, as he several times told us, it would take an endless length of time to describe the events of such a day properly, in some inconceivably complex form, recording who had perished, who survived, and exactly where and how, or simply saying what the battlefield was like at nightfall, with the screams and groans of the wounded and dying. In the end all anyone could ever do was sum up the unknown factors in the ridiculous phrase, 'The fortunes of battle swayed this way and that', or some similarly feeble and useless cliché. All of us, even when we think we have noted every tiny detail, resort to set pieces which have already been staged often enough by others. We try to reproduce the reality, but the harder we try, the more we find the pictures that make up the stock-in-trade of history forcing themselves upon us: the fallen drummer boy, the infantryman shown in the act of stabbing another, the horse's eye starting from its socket, the invulnerable Emperor surrounded by his generals, a moment frozen still amidst the turmoil of battle. *Our concern with history is a concern with pre-formed images already printed on our brains, images at which we keep staring while the truth lies elsewhere, away from it all, somewhere as yet undiscovered.*

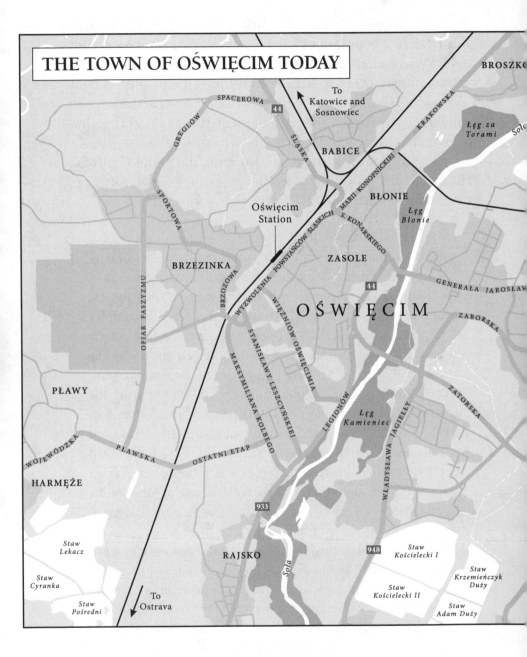

THE TOWN OF OŚWIĘCIM TODAY

SPACEROWA

To
Katowice and
Sosnowiec

44

BROSZKO

GRĘGLOW

ŚLĄSKA

KRAKOWSKA

Łęg za
Torami

Sol

SPORTOWA

BABICE

BŁONIE

MARII KONOPNICKIEJ

Oświęcim
Station

Łęg
Błonie

WYZWOLENIA POWSTAŃCÓW ŚLĄSKICH

S. KONARSKIEGO

BRZEZINKA

ZASOLE

BRZOZOWA

OFIAR FASZYZMU

44

OŚWIĘCIM

GENERAŁA JAROSŁAW

ZABORSKA

WIĘŹNIÓW OŚWIĘCIMIA

STANISŁAWY LESZCZYŃSKIEJ

PŁAWY

ZATORSKA

MAKSYMILIANA KOLBEGO

LEGIONÓW

Łęg
Kamieniec

WŁADYSŁAWA JAGIEŁŁY

WOJEWÓDZKA

PŁAWSKA

OSTATNI ETAP

HARMĘŻE

933

Staw
Lekacz

948

Staw
Kościelecki I

Staw
Cyranka

RAJSKO

Sola

Staw
Krzemieńczyk
Duży

Staw
Pośredni

To
Ostrava

Staw
Kościelecki II

Staw
Adam Duży

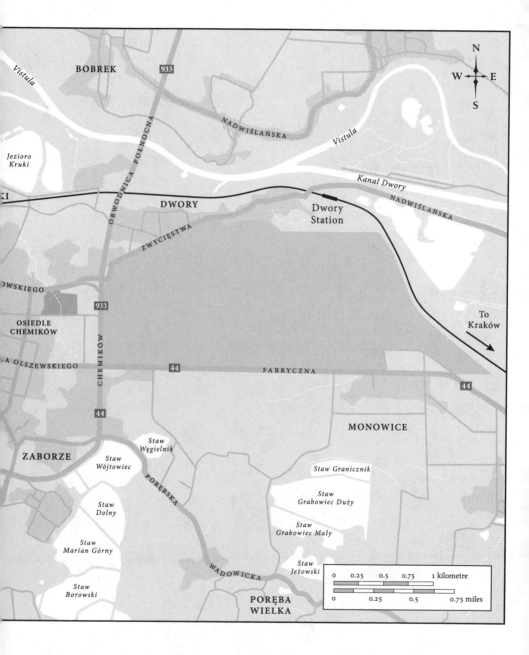

3

How We Look at History: A Moment at Liverpool Street Station

The layering of cities intrigues me more and more. The continual erasure of the past. This doesn't exist in the countryside in the same way. An entire village in Scotland may have been cleared, and the people forcibly removed to the coast or for emigration, but there remain ruined walls, or stones or humps of ground – like gums where teeth used to be – only serving to emphasise the disappearance. Or a farmer rips out a hedge between two fields, but, decades on, you can still see the ridge. You can detect what has gone before. In cities you have to rely on past maps, drawings, photographs. And our minds cannot keep the imprint of buildings in our memory for long, unless the structures were remarkable in some way. When new sites in the city are developed, and the demolition phase takes place, you notice the gap, but within days or weeks it's impossible to remember the buildings that existed before. Recently, as part of the Crossrail development, an entire block of Soho was suddenly not there any more. Having not been into the centre for a while, I was halted in my tracks by seeing the sky where buildings used to be. I knew that part well; my favourite Italian restaurant was at that end of Dean Street. No more. Gone within days. Yet now I cannot recall a single building or shop (apart from that restaurant) that stood there before. Wiped from memory.

Yet, despite this, there can still be a sometimes dizzying verticality of present and past together in the city. Even when hardly any physical trace of a building or a river remains. Take the River Fleet's course as an example: from the Vale of Health and Kenwood on Hampstead Heath, the two tributaries joining at Camden, just north of Hawley Road, and then following the curve of St Pancras Way, past Old St Pancras Church (or rather that should be the road following the course of the river), then between the two stations, snaking down one side of King's Cross Road (you can still see the water and hear it flowing under a grating at St Chad's Place), then crossing beneath Rosebery Avenue, flowing down Warner Street, the bottom of Herbal Hill, Saffron Hill and finally below Farringdon Road, and out under Blackfriars Bridge. Once you know it's there you can see it, it becomes part of your London – the great hill of Pentonville suddenly makes sense as one side of a valley, the twisting shape of the roads that cover the still-flowing River Fleet, which one day will emerge again, in all its curving beauty. When the sewers have collapsed, and the asphalt from the roads has been cracked by weeds, long after the last human beings have abandoned this city, the water will be flowing . . .

Other buried histories of the city remain more elusive, but equally powerful – Liverpool Street station, for example, my first portal into the city as a child, built on the remnants of the Bedlam lunatic asylum, one of the largest in Europe at the time. From old maps I've tried to trace the perimeter walls of the 'Hospital of St Mary of Bethlehem', as the asylum was officially known; they appear to run along London Wall on one side and Bishopsgate on the other, at almost exactly the spot where today the European Bank of Reconstruction and Development, the Royal Bank of Scotland and Deutsche Bank all have their London headquarters – some of the institutions that triggered the economic carnage of 2008. With this knowledge I often look at the manic flows of commuters today, and trains disgorging their daily offerings to the city, in quite a different way. The pinched faces, people so tightly wound up that the smallest, unintended slight can unleash a battery of aggression and rage. The supposed normality of this disturbs me more and more, just as surely as any visit to a psychiatric hospital would. Except there you might have a greater sympathy for the people. They at least have given up the pretences of the world – of performance, targets, deadlines.

There is so much that we still do not see. There are so many connections that we have not yet begun to make. Although they lie in front of us; we pass them every day on our way to work, on our way home. Only on a rare day does something make us stop. And for some unfathomable reason, on this particular day, we look up and notice what we've never seen before. This happened to me at Liverpool Street some time ago, stopping off one day on my way back to Hackney.

I must have walked past hundreds of times over the last twenty-five years or so, on my way home, or heading for the train that takes me down to Manningtree to see my family. That lulling familiarity of views accreted over three decades, so burnt into the memory that each place becomes a held image – the catacombs out of Liverpool Street, that narrowest of bottle openings where fifteen tracks momentarily shrink to half a dozen, often bringing trains to a halt tantalisingly close to their destination; Repton Boys Club, somewhere in the East End; the vast dull-green warehouse overhanging the canal as Bethnal Green turns to Bow; the old Bryant & May factory, standing high over the dual carriageway like some Victorian castle; now the Olympic site rising like a mirage just beyond; and then that strange hinterland of Maryland–Romford–Ilford, cemeteries and breweries; a kind of countryside arrives at Shenfield; Chelmsford – the Marconi factory now deserted; Witham, that oval of cricket pitch that seems impossibly English in the summer, when dotted figures in white are circled there, and others rest in the shade of chestnut trees; the kiosk with its old sign – 'The Times – get on to a train of thought'; Kelvedon, Marks Tey – the tiny local line that somehow survived Dr Beeching, curving temptingly away towards the Colne Valley and distant recesses of childhood. Smiling, remembering that we really believed it was called 'Mark's Tey' because that was where our father changed trains to go to work in London; almost home now, the stream with that odd concrete barrier, a tunnel of oaks, and Colchester arrives with what used to be several factory sheds – 'Woods of Colchester', now a Dutch-sounding name instead; the last miles between Colchester and Manningtree, a garden nursery, and then – that moment that still can thrill – as the whole valley of the Stour is revealed, the sheep kneeling in the meadows as they graze. The truth of summer. Coming home. The calming of the mind. And all the people that have greeted me here, at Manningtree station, over the years. My father's bearded face, my mother's smile and wave, nephews and nieces tumbling towards me gleefully . . .

I puzzle over the potential acuteness of looking, how we can really observe the most microscopic details at times. Taking in the tracery of veins on the underside of a leaf. Waiting for a friend in a crowded square and being able to recognise them hundreds of yards away, long before their face becomes visible. It must be the subconscious awareness of the way that she swings her arms when she walks. The thousand minute details we register when we love somebody, or when we are curious. But do we look as keenly at the city?

I don't have any difficulties distinguishing a beech tree from an oak, or identifying a barn owl's moth-like, flapping flight at dusk, but can I name the streets in London where the hedge funds are based? Or do I know what really happens in the Futures Exchange, or the difference between arbitrage, convergence trading and derivatives? All aspects of the financial world which have an enormous impact on our lives, yet which many of us have little real knowledge of at all.

Some years ago, on my way home, I got off the bus at Liverpool Street. I was trying to find a place that might repair my leather rucksack, an old-fashioned kiosk somewhere, and I thought of the little covered arcade that runs between Liverpool Street itself and Broad Street. There was a key-cutting place but they didn't do repairs and suggested somewhere else. I then walked across the 'Plaza' as it's

rather grandly called – the concrete square outside the front of the station, bordered on one side by an American burger chain. And suddenly I stopped, because a small monument had been installed there. The figure was a girl of around ten years old, a headband, sandals, standing awkwardly, a disconcerting stare, and around her in a glass case fragments of a life left behind – notes in a diary, an empty spectacles case, small black-and-white photographs showing grandparents, brothers. In this place of rushing for trains it seemed incongruous, an intervention of intimacy into a zone of speed and commerce. I searched for a title, an explanation, and eventually found a small plaque on the wall of the station behind:

FÜR DAS KIND ['FOR THE CHILD']
BY FLOR KENT

IN DEEP GRATITUDE TO THE PEOPLE OF
THE UNITED KINGDOM FOR SAVING THE LIVES
OF 10,000 CHILDREN WHO FLED TO THIS

COUNTRY FROM NAZI PERSECUTION ON
THE *KINDERTRANSPORTS* IN 1938–39

'WHOSOEVER RESCUES A SINGLE SOUL
IS CREDITED AS THOUGH THEY HAD
SAVED THE WHOLE WORLD'

DEDICATED BY THE CENTRAL BRITISH
FUND FOR WORLD JEWISH RELIEF
16 SEPTEMBER 2003

And reading this I remembered the epiphany that the elderly Jacques Austerlitz has in the old waiting room at Liverpool Street station:

And for the first time in as far back as I can remember I recollected myself as a small child, at the moment when I realised that it must have been to this same waiting room I had come on my arrival in England over half a century ago . . . I felt something rending within me, and a sense of shame and sorrow, or perhaps something quite different, something inexpressible because we have no words for it, just as I had no words all those years ago when the two strangers came over to me speaking a language I did not understand. All I do know is that when I saw the boy sitting on the bench I became aware . . . of the destructive effect on me of my desolation through all those past years, and a terrible weariness overcame me at the idea that I had never really been alive . . . I have no idea how long I stood in the waiting room . . . I realised then . . . how little practice I had in using my memory, and conversely, how hard I must always have tried to recollect as little as possible, avoiding everything which related in any way to my unknown past.

I looked at every detail of the memorial – trying to decipher the writing in the notebooks, take in every element of the photographs. I was very moved by the reality of these objects, far from the usual style of generic representation in such things.* And, possibly because of this, I sat down by the memorial, and it was only then that I noticed the logo of the Union Bank of Switzerland (UBS) looming on a building behind. I walked over and found that it was UBS's European headquarters, an unremarkable office block put up in the major redevelopment at Broadgate in the late 1980s. UBS, despite its problems since the financial crash of 2008, is still one of Europe's largest banks, with its most recent quarterly profits putting it in the top dozen European banking corporations. But what intrigued me most was the proximity of the *Kindertransport* memorial to the UBS headquarters, because, some years earlier, a security guard in Switzerland had made a startling discovery . . .

*

On 8 January 1997, Christoph Meili, a twenty-eight-year-old security guard, begins his evening shift at UBS's Swiss headquarters at Bahnhofstrasse 45 in Zurich. He's worked there for the previous eighteen months, and he's got to know the building very well. He starts his rounds that evening and notices something very curious, which he hasn't seen before, in the shredding room. There are two trolleys filled, in fact overflowing, with very old documents and books awaiting shredding. For a few minutes he continues his rounds, but he's still thinking about what he's seen, something troubles him, an instinct that makes him pause. There's been much recent discussion in the news about how victims of Nazism have been unable to claim back assets in Switzerland because of financial records being 'lost'. So he decides to return to the shredding room to look at these books in more detail. This is what he finds:

---

* Sadly, Flor Kent's original sculpture and installation is no longer outside Liverpool Street Station. The piece (together with the real objects and photographs) can now only be seen at the Imperial War Museum.

I saw two thick black-bound books, about A3 size, which had debit and credit columns. The years 1945–1965 was written on the cover. I opened one of the books and saw entries starting February 1945. Many German chemical companies. At that point, I recognized immediately that the entries starting February 1945 were still during World War II. Since there were many German firms, I looked at some of the entries more closely. I saw companies with names like: Lack und Farbenfabriken (IG Farben) Seifenfabriken, Bayerische Sodafabrik (BASF), etc. . . . I found many entries in the real estate column for 1930–1945. Additional entries were made there regarding bankruptcy auctions. The above books were divided in about five different categories: bonds, stocks, miscellaneous, real estate. Because of the sensitive dates, I ripped out the entire real estate part from both books. I replaced the books so that no one would notice anything. I brought the real estate pages and a book dated 1920–1926 to my locker in two trips. Finished my job dutifully and took the real estate pages home with me. There I inspected them with great curiosity.[*]

Meili lays out the pages on his kitchen table when he gets home. He wakes his wife, Giuseppina, who is also knowledgeable about history. And the more they study the papers, the more they realise the importance of these documents. Some are holding accounts for German companies which had worked hand-in-hand with Nazism, some even directly profiting from slave labour and extermination (such as IG Farben, Degussa and Degesch). Towards the end of the war corporate assets had been transferred to Swiss banks in an attempt to evade Allied confiscation. Other documents relate to the forced sale of real estate in Berlin – after the Nazis came to power they compelled Jews to sell property and other assets at well below the market rate. And here, in black and white, handwritten in fountain pen, in UBS bank ledgers, is evidence of all of these

---

[*] Taken from the transcript of Meili's testimony to the US Senate, 'Hearing on Shredding of Holocaust Era Documents', 6 May 1997.

crimes. Meili and his wife are both aware that only a few weeks earlier the Swiss government had established a historical commission to investigate Swiss collusion with Nazism,* and the legislation included an order specifically forbidding destruction of any documents from this period. Christoph and Giuseppina need time to think. They take the dog for a walk, and consider their options. Competing voices fight in their heads – 'It's not your responsibility, this is serious, take them back' – but another one, a stronger voice, prevails, compelling them to make these documents public.

But, before that, Meili has to be certain that these documents are being destroyed, meaning a crime is being committed, so he returns to work the next afternoon (Thursday 9 January), and goes straight to the shredding room, where he finds the two trolleys are now empty – all that remains are the covers of the books. But outside the room he finds two additional books, with information about loans to German companies from Swiss banks. He manages to smuggle these out of the bank, under his jacket, at the end of his shift.

The next day, Christoph phones the Israeli Embassy and tells them about the documents he's found. The embassy doesn't seem to share his sense of urgency, and, bizarrely, he's told to put the documents 'in the post'. Understandably, he doesn't want to do this, and now Giuseppina suggests giving them to a Jewish cultural organisation she's aware of, based there in Zurich. So, soon afterwards, Meili takes all the material to the Israelitische Cultusgemeinde Zurich (the ICZ), the largest Jewish organisation in the city, and hands it over to staff there. Werner Rom, the ICZ president, and Ada Winter, secretary general, immediately realise how serious the implications are and give the material to the Zurich police that same afternoon.

Nothing happens over the weekend, but on Monday a Jewish representative of ICZ visits Meili at his home and explains that the material has been handed over to the Swiss police. Meili is now very scared, but the man says, 'You're a smart guy, you'll be OK.'

---

* The Bergier Commission (Book One, Chapter Six – 'Saurer: A Coda').

The following day Christoph learns he's been suspended from his job at UBS. Also on Tuesday the 14th the local judge (former lawyer for the bank Credit Suisse) allows UBS to issue a statement about the incident, and then releases his own communiqué, stating that thanks to the full co-operation of UBS this matter has now been cleared up. Infuriated by this response, the ICZ call an immediate press conference, and from this point on Meili's discoveries become a global story. He is forthright about why he's done what he's done, explaining that his actions were not just for the Jewish community but also to safeguard the integrity of Switzerland, and the historical commission which had just been launched: 'The Swiss people should know their banks were involved with Nazi corporations.'

Initially Meili is treated as something of a hero in Switzerland, for exposing UBS's shocking behaviour. In the next days and weeks he and his family are besieged by international media at their little house just outside Zurich. The ICZ provide him with a lawyer to help him navigate the media storm and ongoing issues with the Swiss authorities. An American senator, Alfonse D'Amato, gets involved in the case and urges him to come to the US to testify before a Senate committee. UBS panic at how they are completely losing the battle of public opinion, and send their hapless president, Robert Struder, to the national TV studios to accuse Meili of simply being a publicity seeker. This strategy is, unsurprisingly, unsuccessful, not least because Meili and his family come across as very modest, model Swiss citizens, with strong religious and ethical convictions. But Struder's TV appearance backfires most spectacularly with his admission that UBS had indeed 'regrettably' shredded Holocaust-era documents – this understandably overshadows everything else, and feeds the growing media firestorm. And what is the response of the Swiss authorities to all of this? They launch a judicial investigation – not against UBS for their crimes, but against Meili for suspected violations on laws of banking secrecy! (No action was ever taken against UBS for destroying the wartime documents in the first place.)

The Swiss banks now move towards damage control, and offer to establish a $200 million fund for Holocaust victims affected by their actions. However, now things begin to get more complicated for Meili and his family – the US-based Anti-Defamation League arrive and present him with an award, and announce the establishment of a $36,000 legal defence fund for Meili, as well as a vast legal action against the Swiss banks. Although some of this seems positive at the time, the financial aspects soon begin to muddy the waters. Meili now reflects that 'What I did was not about money. It was about history and helping the poor people whose lives had been ruined by what these banks had done. But when money came into the picture, so did politics.'

The Swiss media then begin to turn on Meili and an ugly strain of antisemitism emerges; there are absurd stories about him being a Mossad agent, a gold-digger, a traitor. All of this begins to sour the atmosphere markedly. Family members and friends cut off contact, journalists follow Meili's children to school, taking pictures, and then come the death threats – one letter simply reading 'we will hunt you down'. Urgent action is needed. Meili and his family leave for the US at the end of April 1997, and on 29 July President Clinton signs an Act of Congress which grants Meili and his family political asylum in the US (reputedly the first Swiss nationals to be granted American asylum).

In January 1998 an action claiming $2.56 billion on behalf of Jewish Holocaust victims is filed against UBS and other Swiss banks involved in collaboration with Nazism. On 13 August 1998, a settlement is reached with the Swiss banks agreeing to pay a total of $1.25 billion in reparations. Significantly, the terms of this settlement are wider than originally anticipated, and specify that five categories of 'Victims of Nazi Persecution' will be eligible for compensation from this fund – Jewish, Roma, Jehovah's Witnesses, homosexuals and the disabled. Without Meili's ethical commitment and courage it is unlikely that such a resolution could ever have been reached. The former US undersecretary of commerce Stuart Eizenstat, who was a key figure in the negotiation of this settlement, describes in his 2009 book *Imperfect Justice* how critically important the 'Meili Affair' was in the Swiss banks' decision to participate in the compensation process for victims of Nazism. He wrote that Meili's actions 'did more than anything to turn the Swiss banks into international pariahs by linking their dubious behaviour during and after the war to the discovery of a seemingly unapologetic attempt to cover it up now by destroying documents'.

*

Back outside Liverpool Street station I look up at the UBS office windows and wonder if shredding machines are still being used by corporations, or whether more sophisticated ways of getting rid of 'difficult' information have now been developed. I also wonder how much of the $1.25 billion compensation actually came from UBS and Credit Suisse, and how much was paid by the Swiss government, i.e. the taxpayers. And I'd like to know whether the senior management of these banks today really have any understanding of the fatal role that their predecessors had played in the 1930s and 40s – essentially, as American diplomat Walter Sholes put it, being 'pro-fascist financial operators'. What does it actually mean to have helped the process of confiscation of Jewish families' assets from Germany? Or to have accepted massive transfers of funds from Nazi banks (at least $6 billion in today's money from the Reichsbank alone), and profits from German corporations across occupied Europe using slave labour? These columns of numbers in the ledgers Christoph Meili discovered in the shredding room at UBS are just as lethal as any gun.

UBS's connections with the Holocaust do not end there. UBS is also closely linked to IG Farben, the huge German chemicals conglomerate, without which Hitler could not have waged war.* In 1957–8, UBS became the majority shareholder in a company called Interhandel, which had originally been established in Switzerland

---

* I examine in detail IG Farben's collusion with Nazism and the operation of their Buna-Monowitz complex at Auschwitz in the next volume of *I You We Them*.

in 1929 as IG Chemie, a holding company for IG Farben – today broken down into its constituent companies, including BASF, Bayer, Agfa and Hoechst. IG Farben's largest industrial complex had been the vast Buna chemicals plant at Auschwitz, where tens of thousands of slave labourers died; a subsidiary company also manufactured the Zyklon B used in the gas chambers. After the war when IG Farben was broken up by the Allies, Interhandel was described as its 'prize asset'. So when UBS bought out the remaining shareholders in 1961 to gain sole control of Interhandel the bank developed immense financial power. The 1965 sale of the American company GAF (owned by Interhandel) netted UBS $122 million – equivalent to just under $1 billion today – and this further transformed UBS's equity base and allowed it to overtake Credit Suisse and Swiss Bank Corporation to become Switzerland's leading bank and one of the most powerful in Europe.

What part of this UBS building, what part of the company's value today, is connected to this other reality? And what part, along with hundreds of other corporations and banks and insurance companies, did UBS play in creating the conditions necessary for fascism to thrive? The results of which included, among millions of displacements and murders, the arrival of those 10,000 children, here at Liverpool Street in 1938 and 1939.

PART TWO

Walking Through Time

4

Journeys with J.

It happened in a matter of seconds. Halfway through university. An evening in late November. The end of 1983. And I knew, with an instantaneous certainty, that our lives would never be the same again. I can remember the room, the posters on the wall, the music that was playing. With absolute clarity. The moment before. Then, a whirlwind of energy coming up the stairs, I go out onto the landing and we see each other for the first time. The wild mop of hair, the strange, black Turkish jacket, DMs. We shake hands in mock formality, a moment of nervous laughter. It's hard to explain now, but these moments felt like finding a brother you never knew existed. We smoked and drank and talked and walked most of that night, to the Elm Tree, over Parker's Piece, Midsummer Common. But that was just what was expressed on the surface. Inside, something inexplicable had happened, and with a lightness and a depth simultaneously causing a kind of vertigo. As a great observer of such phenomena once said: 'We take almost all the decisive steps in our lives as a result of slight inner adjustments of which we are barely conscious.' There was a sense of vast possibilities opening up, whispering into the future. Of all that existed between the words we spoke that night.

Out of our coming together the organisation Platform was established – as a meeting place of art and activism. And it was born out of both of our individual instincts that something was missing in our culture – surely it must be possible to combine theatre and politics, to put art and research together? After all, think of the extraordinary explosion of agitprop art, cinema and theatre after the Russian Revolution, or what Brecht did in Germany in the 1920s and 30s. More recently, albeit more tamely, there were groups in Britain like Welfare State and 7:84 and Gay Sweatshop, who had tried to challenge the political consensus of the times by using cultural strategies, political theatre – but we wanted to take things further.

Our meeting couldn't have come at a better time in our lives. For the preceding three years my time had been completely taken up with anti-nuclear activism. At school I'd set up a Youth Campaign for Nuclear Disarmament group, and at Cambridge I helped to establish an effective student CND organisation. The early 1980s was a terrifying time to grow up. The Cold War was at its zenith, with extremely dangerous leaders on both sides of the Atlantic. The potential for nuclear war was real, and overshadowed everything.

In response to this, anti-nuclear activism grew rapidly – soon becoming a potent force, fuelled by the twin energies of moral outrage and the human instinct for survival. At this time I was driven by a kind of all-encompassing zeal which perhaps you can only live with when you're young. CND took up most of my waking hours, and I was at my happiest when expounding the message to agnostics or unbelievers, devouring the latest E. P. Thompson pamphlet, organising debates and demonstrations, breaking into American airbases at night (together with a future Archbishop of Canterbury, I seem to remember), bussing protesters to the site of the proposed cruise missile base at Molesworth. I used to cycle at furious speeds around Cambridge (symbolically perhaps, my bike possessed no brakes), between collecting leaflets from the printers, meeting college reps and planning the next protests.

My studies, naturally, took second place to all this. I did go, very occasionally, to lectures in the English faculty (those by Raymond Williams, Steven Heath, Geoffrey Hill and Lisa Jardine were among the few I made sure I attended). But, with the re-election of an extreme right-wing Conservative government in 1983, and the prospect of a renewed period of political gloom, I began to look for other outlets for my activism. I was elected to the Cambridge University Students Union in 1983, and had a year attending NUS conferences, but was never convinced by student politics. It seemed to be something of a dead end. Where was the *imagination*? Struggles over the wording of resolutions seemed limited – just students play-acting at Parliament, where indeed several of them ended up. So, by the end of 1983 I was desperately looking for another kind of politics. I had always loved theatre and film, and had done a lot of acting at school and in my first year at university. If only there was some way of fusing my political beliefs with art and theatre . . .

J's journey had been the inverse of mine. For the last years he'd immersed himself in experimental theatre. He'd had the good fortune to meet the wild impresario of the Scottish art world, Ricky Demarco, while still at school. Ricky had encouraged J. to bring his play to the Edinburgh Festival, where he'd met Joseph Beuys (who subsequently became a key influence), and had been introduced to the work of the great Polish director Tadeusz Kantor. But the group he'd established at school had fractured as people went to different universities, and besides, J. was beginning to tire of the self-referential little bubble of experimental theatre. Where was the engagement in wider society, in political issues? Especially issues of ecology that were becoming increasingly important for him? It's not hard to see why we fell upon each other like thirsting travellers finding water in the desert . . . the idea of each completing the other.

I should add here that although we were at university in politically turbulent times, and although the Thatcherite right were in the ascendancy, we were not remotely downhearted. There was a vigorous, well-supported left in Cambridge in the early 1980s – in fact, in some respects, the University Left of those days remains a model of how left and progressive forces can unite and work together effectively. Every Tuesday lunchtime we would meet in a long upstairs room at King's College – anything between thirty and eighty students, depending on what was happening. Labour students, liberals, independent socialists, Jewish and Palestinian activists, communists, gay and lesbian activists, environmentalists and anarchists, all sitting together once a week, happy to talk and campaign together in a non-sectarian way, regardless of our political differences the rest of the time. And every week, people would share news and we would determine what our common focus would be for the next seven days, and the University Left newsletter would be distributed to all college reps. Often there would be external speakers (in 1983 and 1984 during the Miners' Strike, many of these would be from 'Support the Miners'). After the 1983 election defeat for the Labour Party, and then the 1984 defeat of the Miners' Strike, there was also much discussion about the future direction of the left. The magazine *Marxism Today* enjoyed a brief success, and spawned discussion groups, and I recall excitedly crowding into the rooms of influential left professors and thinkers then teaching at Cambridge, such as Bob Rowthorn and Raymond Williams, once even hearing the great historian Eric Hobsbawm speak – who had written his seminal and prescient article 'The Forward March of Labour Halted?' a few years before.

But the figure who most inspired J. and me was a short, white-haired, seventy-year-old member of the English faculty, Margot Heinemann. Astonishingly, she was a living link to the Spanish Civil War – students would whisper to each other in her lectures that she had been the lover and partner of the poet and communist John Cornford, a hero of the civil war who had died fighting Franco and fascism in 1936, only twenty-one years old. Her lectures were remarkable – I can still remember her describing the brilliant, self-organised cultural and political initiatives of the south Wales valleys in the 1930s – 'Little Moscows' as they were called – work-ers' education at its finest, hundreds and thousands of women and men effectively organising their own kinds of universities and the-atres and concerts.

So you can imagine how thrilled we were when she not only came to the inaugural meeting of Platform in King's College, but at the end announced that our initiative to fuse theatre and politics was 'the most exciting thing that had happened in Cambridge politics for a generation'.

Over the next year or so, we developed Platform as a powerful force working on local issues – challenging the dominance of the university in decision-making, and then focussing on supporting a strike of cleaning staff at the local Addenbrooke's hospital. This was one of the early attempts by the Conservative government to start to privatise services that had been previously under NHS control, and we felt it would be the thin end of the wedge. In a matter of weeks we'd created a punchy piece of street theatre – 'Addenbrooke's Blues' – using music, satire and humour in equal measure. J., myself – and our comrades-in-arms Anna, Wes, Mel, Graham and Mark – developed a strong collective identity, sharing responsibility for researching, writing, performing and directing, which gave all of us a growing political confidence, which soon meant we had the courage to break out of the confines of the uni-versity. We got to know the workers on strike, and became even more appalled at how they'd been treated – the attempts of the cleaning contractors OCS to cut the hourly rates of this already extremely underpaid workforce. We performed our show on the picket line, and all over the city; hundreds of students and academics got involved as the campaign grew.

The strikers and the unions who represented them (then NUPE and COHSE) were soon asking us to support their fight by taking 'Addenbrooke's Blues' around the country to raise awareness. For the next few months our studies were left behind as the intoxication of political theatre and campaigning took over – the show became even punchier, media coverage and fundraising for the strikers increased, as we toured from the House of Commons (meeting Neil Kinnock and Michael Meacher* in the process), to the TUC education centre and numerous public meetings and events at hospitals affected by similar issues of creeping privatisation. Every performance would end with a rousing rendition of a song we'd adapted from the brilliant American singer and activist Phil Ochs:

> Here's to the land you've torn out the heart of,
> Mrs Thatcher find yourself another country to be part of!

The Prime Minister, unsurprisingly, did not take our advice. The Tory free-marketisation of Britain continued unabated, the Miners' Strike was defeated, the Addenbrooke's strikers eventually returned to work on only marginally improved pay and conditions. From a contemporary vantage point – and the inward-looking focus of today's identity politics – it would be easy to poke fun at the earnestness of a student political theatre collective fighting for social justice in the 1980s, and trying to change their small corner of the world. But this would be to miss the wider point, and the genuine radicalism of what was being attempted – the bid to break down the barriers which had always existed between the university and the city. To create a political solidarity across classes which had

---

* Neil Kinnock at this time was leader of the opposition Labour Party and Michael Meacher was the shadow health secretary.

always been taught to distrust each other. And, for a few weeks, as hundreds of students flocked to join the picket lines at Addenbrooke's, it felt as if we'd been part of something remarkable, and had glimpsed, even if for a moment, a future not based on greed and personal gain but on generosity of spirit and solidarity.

*

I've known J. for half my lifetime now. It is very hard to write about a friendship that has been such a central reality of life and is still evolving. And maybe harder still in our society that tends to find male friendship puzzling. J. has been my constant companion throughout these years, as we've made our own maps through unfamiliar territories together. And, after all this time, each of us is still curious about the other, needing to know what the other thinks, what they're experiencing. What Rilke writes about love – so far from that traditional romantic notion of love as being about fused identity – is something that I now recognise as true:

> The *being together* of two human beings is an impossibility . . . yet once it is recognised that even among the *closest* people there remain infinite distances, a wonderful coexistence can develop once they succeed in loving the vastness between them that affords them the possibility of seeing each other in their full gestalt before a vast sky!

When this is accepted I think real power can come from such an understanding – as somebody once sang, 'Let's be alone together, let's see if we're that strong.' And now, between J. and myself, curiosity and love seem to be bound together in an even greater closeness, in a way I didn't understand when I was younger, and I'm not sure I even fully understand today.

We've been walking together all this time. Walking has been perhaps our most fundamental way of being with each other. Our walks have changed in some ways, as we've changed, but some aspects remain constant. In the early years much of what we talked about were the challenges of working collectively (we'd set up Platform together when we were only twenty), what issues we should be focussing on, political events of the time, funding problems. Always having a vision of what the group could be, the influence it might have, if we got things right, if we got brilliant people to work with us. It was a mad time to be starting an avowedly political arts organisation – the mid-1980s, the high-water mark of extreme Thatcherism. The month we moved to London, the Greater London Council – perhaps the only coherent opposition in those days, led by Ken Livingstone – was abolished. Funding for what we wanted to do was non-existent; we'd have to start from scratch. We received a single, poignant letter, from the arts department of the GLC, saying, 'What you're wanting to do sounds excellent. It's just the kind of work we would have supported, but as you've probably heard, we're being abolished next month. Anyway, good luck!'

The first walk we did together was in summer 1985. We set off from the farmhouse in Suffolk where I'd grown up, with rucksacks and a tent – in those days we took an almost masochistic delight in having 'authentic' East German rucksacks (which had metal bars that cut into your back), but anyway, we didn't care, we liked the grey design. As we walked down the valley we could see my father working in the top field. He paused to wave at us, down on the lane below. A single image that is now cut into memory with an intensity that only comes with loss. For the next ten days or so we headed south, crossing into Essex at Manningtree, and then turning eastwards for the coast, which we followed round, up and down all the creeks and estuaries, skirting the Dengie Peninsula, and the mudflats all along that bleakly wonderful coast, ending up at Burnham-on-Crouch. It was this first experience that gave us such an appetite for doing further walking. And a plan began to dawn on us. What if we were to continue, for the rest of our lives, walking around the coast of Britain? We could do it in as many sections as we wanted, not necessarily sequentially following one section slavishly with the next. We could do whole weeks, or week-ends, when we had less time. And we'd simply follow the sea, or as close to it as we could get. And we'd always have to walk clockwise. (This last aspect we never really discussed, we never felt it worthy of discussion because it seemed instinctively so *right* to both of us to walk in this direction.)

And ever since then we've continued, usually doing a week or ten days every two years, but also doing quite a few shorter stretches every now and then. It's probably fair to say that we significantly underestimated the length of this challenge initially, but we now guess the total mileage (if you follow every river estuary and go round every peninsula of the mainland) to be approximately 7,500 miles. Of which, in our mid-forties, we've done about 1,375 so far. Not very impressive, as we'd be the first to admit. And we both realise that if we are to have any prospect of finishing, we're going to have to take it a bit more seriously. Having said that, to be fair to us, up to now we have been tackling some of the trickiest parts of the walk – one of the sections that is most vivid in my memory is the extreme north-west of Scotland, from Lochinver up to Cape Wrath. An experience of wilderness that I never expected on our supposedly overcrowded island, of being able to walk for almost two days, in the most remote part, and not see a single car. On another day being astounded to see, on the other side of the valley, an entire mountainside seeming to shift before our eyes – over a hundred red deer moving silently. An image of such timelessness, our century escaped us for those moments.

We've deliberately left the east coast and some of the south coast (to the east of Dorset) for our later middle age and old age, calculating that the mainly flat nature of these landscapes won't strain ageing limbs and muscles too much. The very final stretch we've planned for the Brighton seafront in about 2050, for two reasons: firstly, it was the place of our first public project after university; secondly, because it is tarmacked, and we rather like the idea of doing this final mile, as a race, in motorised wheelchairs . . .

*

Our first walk, in August 1985, ended rather unfortunately. J's girl-friend at the time had become dangerously ill, and so we had to rush back to London. The night before, our camping in Burnham-on-Crouch had coincided with a bikers' convention which involved motorbikes being driven as close as possible to people sleeping in their tents. Not content with causing such disturbance, when we returned, rather wearily, from breakfast the next morning we found all the guy ropes had been cut. After this episode we never bothered with tents again. There followed some glorious years of walking when we slept under the stars, simply stopping where we'd reached by dusk – in forests or by ruined priories or next to barns. All we used were sleeping bags inside 'survival bags' (basically giant orange bin liners). It was a romantic way of travelling, albeit one that left us wet with condensation every morning.

On only four occasions have we digressed from our coastal cir-cumnavigation: to walk across Germany, the south-western tip of Ireland, the Ardennes forest and the Swiss Alps. But we've always felt a trace of guilt about these wanderings away from the British coast, as if such walks, though enjoyable, were essentially taking us away from our ongoing odyssey.

Perhaps with the exception of that walk in Germany.

We'd come to the end of a period of intense work, culminating in a community performance event on environmental themes in Kemptown, Brighton, in the summer of 1987. We'd also spent a lot of time that year contacting groups and individuals in Germany who'd been connected with the artist and activist Joseph Beuys, who'd died the year before, and was now a key influence on our work. In the darkest days of those eighteen years of one-party rule in Britain – where the country became catastrophically divided, in a way I feel we've never really recovered from – we looked to the east for polit-ical hope, and progressive ideas, and we found much to admire in Germany. When the free-market ideologues were running rampant in Britain and the left was in a kind of shocked retreat, we found real food for thought and inspiration in Germany – particularly in the newly formed Green movement, and the realignment of the left.

In certain ways, the burgeoning 'red–green' alliances growing in Germany mirrored J.'s and my politics almost exactly: my strong commitment to the red – the independent, non-sectarian left, and J.'s passion for the green – ecological initiatives combined with more open forms of democratic practice.

So in the spring of 1987 we'd travelled to Kassel to meet people involved with the Free International University (FIU), which Beuys had co-founded in 1973 to encourage far greater participation in democracy, a radical challenge to the limits of our supposedly 'representative' systems. We were amazed to discover that an artist like Beuys could span the worlds of activism and education as well, and contribute significantly to national debates – so different to the far more limited reach of artists and writers in our own culture.

In spring 1987 in Kassel we stayed in the house of a former colleague of Beuys', the art historian and activist Rhea Thönges-Stringaris, who proudly told us that, some years before, she, Beuys and Petra Kelly had sat around the same table where we were eating and first discussed the idea of forming Die Grünen (the Green Party). It was a revelation to us that artists had been central to the creation of the most important political movement of our time. Rhea took us round Kassel and showed us the extraordinary *7,000 Eichen* ('7,000 Oaks') project that Beuys had begun five years earlier. As one of the most admired artists in the world at that time he'd been given an open brief at the Dokumenta festival in 1982 to create anything he wanted to, using any space within the Fridericianum, the main gallery in Kassel. But Beuys decided to do something remarkable: he turned his back on the safe, white spaces of the gallery and the art world and took his work across the streets of the city. He planted 7,000 oak trees in Kassel, together with 7,000 basalt pillars. As well as foresting an entire city, this would act as a kind of sculpture in time; when the oak saplings were planted the basalt pillars were the same height, but within a few years the young trees would dwarf the stone. There were also powerful historical dimensions to the work – Kassel had been heavily bombed in the war, and the oak leaf had been a Nazi symbol, so Beuys was reappropriating it quite consciously for the green movement. At a stroke he created a living sculpture of astonishing beauty and made one of the most powerful statements in the history of modern art.

Completely inspired, we hitched round Germany for two weeks (clockwise of course), south to Darmstadt, Göttingen and then Augsburg and Bavaria, west to Düsseldorf, first seeing the greatest collection of Beuys' work, including his early vitrine, *Auschwitz* – the disturbing and brilliant piece which contextualises all his subsequent work. Then meeting other former colleagues of his involved in remarkable experiments in local, economic networks and the campaign for *Volksentscheid* (direct democracy – government by the people directly, through the means of referenda). We ended in Düsseldorf, rather self-consciously leaving a hundred red roses for Beuys, outside the house of his widow, Eva, in Drakplatz, before meeting Johannes Stuttgen, who had worked closely with Beuys from the foundation of the FIU onwards.

We returned to London, vowing to start a Free International University in Britain, which we did – in the following year – transforming our shared terraced house in Brixton into a kind of international hothouse of continuous discussion, for seven days and seven nights – '168 hours for New Ideas', as we called it, rather portentously. The walls were turned into blackboards, bedrooms into performance spaces, a giant black banner proclaiming 'FIU London' was draped over the front of the house (complete with Beuys' favourite gold hare motif), and hundreds of people passed through in the course of the week, many from other parts of Europe. An oak tree was planted at the front of the house, with too little space to grow. But, in those heady days, the symbolism seemed far more important than practicalities.

In August 1987 – the same month that Rudolf Hess, the last relic of Third Reich madness, expired in Spandau prison – we returned to Kassel, after the Brighton project. It was the time of the next Dokumenta festival, and Rhea and her colleagues had the challenge of completing Beuys' *7,000 Eichen* without him. We helped out enthusiastically, and were impressed at the organisational beauty of the *Baumburo* (the Tree Office) from which the work was co-ordinated. Somewhere in our archive there are little black-and-white photos of us helping to plant some of the last of the 7,000 oaks. In these weeks we met some fascinating people, and were impressed by the refreshing lack of sectarianism that had so blighted the left in Britain – many in Germany seemed more relaxed about position-ing themselves broadly within a red–green spectrum. It was also exhilarating to be in a culture where people cared so much about art and ideas. And it felt important to be emissaries from Britain – to be showing that at least some spirit of internationalism still survived the meanness of the political climate there.

We began to conceptualise a line running from London to Kassel and then on into what was then East Germany, part of the Warsaw Pact, the target of our nuclear weapons, and the site of Soviet nuclear weapons. Mikhail Gorbachev had begun the process of glasnost but the terror of 'mutually assured destruction' was still the political orthodoxy, and President Reagan remained in power. We called the line 'West-Linie-Ost' and drew it onto maps in the most detailed way, coming up with a walk between Kassel and London that would embody our commitment to the links we'd created with the FIU. It would also be a line that we could extend, as Gorbachev's work unfolded, and take further east – over time – perhaps eventu-ally to an East Germany not hidden behind a wall.

That August we started the walk, with a series of explorations across Kassel, walking west to east, then east to west, following as closely as possible to our conceptual line. And then a circu-lar circumnavigation of the whole city – involving an exhausting thirty-five-mile walk, midday to midnight. As we walked, amazed at what such an arbitrary line revealed, we began to think about walking in a different way. Walking revealing what is hidden, walking that can connect things that are usually kept apart. On the outskirts of Kassel we came across shockingly poor housing estates, mothers pushing prams through broken glass, men with oily hands fiddling with the engines of battered-looking cars. About as far from the 'German economic miracle' as you could get. And, physically, to see the entire bowl of the city, shimmering before us in the heat haze, from the low hills around it, was so revealing – seeing how the River Fulda had completely determined the position of the city.

But as August ended these weeks of dialogue and experimentation ended too. And there was a sense of the honeymoon being over, we became more critical of what we perceived as the inward-looking nature of much of the FIU's discussion – ironic, we felt, in light of the 'International' in the middle of their name. And the heavy emphasis on theory rather than practice began to grate as well. We had been invited to do a final performance event at the Ottoneum museum on 28 August, and would be starting our walk back to England immediately afterwards. So we decided, in true Beuysian style, to make our farewell event as provocative as possible.

We started by taking a pickaxe to the concrete car park immediately outside the building, to create a garden where cars had previously parked. This delighted the younger members of the FIU but did not amuse others, including a red-faced official from the town hall. Our performance inside, using vast maps of the city, showing what we'd gathered from our weeks of urban walking, ended with us asking critical questions* of the hundred or so members of the FIU – which (in homage to Beuys) we chalked up on large blackboards at the back of the hall. This caused some consternation, with the audience divided between those who appreciated our questions and those who felt we'd overstepped the artistic line. Extremely heated arguments followed about the differences between German and British culture, some insisting that *Thought* must be considered firstly as a political *Action*, us saying that this surely doesn't preclude being involved in activism as well? The evening ended in further discussions with Rhea and others in a drab restaurant on Wilhelmsholer Aller, J. and I unsure about whether the cause of Anglo-German relations had been furthered by our intervention. But, as we left

---

* See chapter notes for details.

to start our walk, just after midnight, there were mostly affection-
ate goodbyes to the 'crazy Englanders'. A balmy summer night,
we walked towards the Herkules monument in irrepressibly high
spirits, relieved to be escaping, and reflecting on the consternation
we'd left in our wake with wry amusement. And then on, further
westwards, beyond the *Schloss*, and into the pine woods . . .

*

After the relentless discussion of the previous weeks we decided
we would experiment with walking in silence for the next days,
only speaking after dusk. Like a kind of balm. Letting birdsong
in, letting us be in the landscape, feeling the weather on our faces.
Not distracted by words. I would map-read up until we stopped
for lunch, J. in the afternoons until we stopped for the night,
usually in a wood just outside a village. So we developed a surprisingly expressive language of pointing, choices of way to go
reflected in eyebrows raised, tilted heads, enthusiastic or sceptical
noises made.

The vividness of the days that followed is intense. I've often thought
about the relationship of this silent walking to memory. I still have a
sense of the flow of the walk, like being able to follow the course of
a tributary all the way to the river, then to the estuary and out to
sea. All these years later I can still recall particular bends in the
road, lines of trees and church spires visible over brows of hills. I
have notes of this time from my journal as well. There is a temptation to edit out one's twenty-three-year-old self, the gawkiness of
some of the observations, the uncritical reading, but I'll resist – and
keep with the original words – because something developed in the
course of this walking, something connected to a fresh way of looking at the world around us.

29 viii: 87 (Saturday)

*Grey skies, pecking rain on the leaves above. As we'd decided,
we began this day in silence. Breakfasted well on yoghurts,*

bread, cheese, apples and 'studentenfutter' (fruit & nuts). Then our ritual of packing up (shaking our foil sheets, coiling our sleeping bags etc.) and off we went, me map-reading at first. Mist lurking below us blocking out any view of Kassel. The rain increased. Down a path between the pines – rain getting heavy, providing a heavier, soaking rhythm to the walking. Reassuring to see nettles here and the familiar pink of Himalayan Balsam. Began to move into a fluidity of walking, the sense of pacing, of the boots and the feet realising they've got another ten, twelve hours to go. Mist settled over the very lush pasture land – would you know this wasn't England? Superficially the road, the hedge, the oak saplings, the cows – we could be walking through the West Country, or even Suffolk. Intriguing how feelings towards J. can fluctuate even within the context of a silent walk, ranging from irritation at his gesturing towards a hovering hawk I've already seen, to a glowing warmth of brotherhood and shared vision.

Into a valley, down more wooded tracks. The rain continued so we stop at a gastubbe for some coffee. A soldier chats to the landlord at another table, and tries to persuade his daughter to eat her vegetables. Something very satisfying about just sitting and drying out, allowing the sweet taste of tobacco to mix with the warmth of the coffee. J. and I begin to communicate by writing on beer mats, though not sure if this undermines the idea of our silence.

Onwards, past a graffitied 'RAF' [Red Army Faction] logo. Extraordinary to think there is still an active, underground, armed, political group in W. Germany . . . The clouds began to move off fast as we walked into Habichtswald. Did a shop for the weekend here, and were surprised at the friendliness of the people in the supermarket – the manager giving us both little metallic badges and the cashiers smiling with curiosity at these strange Englanders, 'Fahren nach London?! Nein?!' V. sticky now, pack heavier than ever as we climbed southwards back into the forest and onto the Line. The first time when I stopped taking contemplative small steps – the sweat drenching my back utterly. Hit the main Kassel–Istha road that we'd driven down the other night and had lunch just beyond.

Crossed the Kassel–Dortmund autobahn – bit hairy! Climbed up to the top of the village of Burghasungen, old ochre-bricked, timber-framed barn in striking contrast to brutal redbrick of its new, neighbouring house. Three women walk though a rigorously neat cemetery. I remembered those lines from an old poem about 'here tulips bloom as they are told . . . [something?] an English unofficial rose'. Another stop for water . . . Then helping each other on with the rucksacks and following a stream through beech woods – sun burst through in the late afternoon as we skirted Isthaberg. Through a sea of wheat pockmarked with cornflowers and wild grasses, two, three buzzards wheeling overhead. This was the country of Martin von Mackenson, the farmer from FIU. Through Philippenberg, a one-lane village and every home a smallholding with a barn built into it. A father and baby setting off in a tractor; a woman cleaning a farrow; a man feeding grain through a machine. And as we walked through, several people stopped what they were doing and leant on their gates, stood in their doorways. A strong sense that we were the first outsiders to come through this village for days, weeks, possibly months. And again, good-humoured curiosity, questions thrown at us – ah walkers! Going to Wolfhagen, yes. Eventually London! . . . And smiling, on we walked, a breathtaking evening now, the rounded bergs in front of us looking very fine. Kept thinking about the village we'd just been through, so near to the city, yet what seems like a small farming/peasant community is still clearly surviving.

Down onto the Wolfhagen plain again, the familiar rivers of pylons beginning to dance towards the distant town. A farmer manoeuvres his tractor, farrowing the ploughed clods to break them down. He gets out of his cab. A shortish man, felt cap, rough-hewn face. 'Eng-land? Aaah! Wanderen. Heute von Kassel? Gut. Gut! Nach London?! Phew!' And then, fascinatingly, he asked us if we'd come to Kassel by Eisenzug ('iron train'). Words which make you aware of the distance, the experiential distance between people of the soil and people of the city. Through two more woods, perched on the summit of the rounded bergs; in the second one we decided to stay for the night, found a dry patch of pine needles, hung out our wet clothes, hid our packs and headed down to Wolfhagen for a beer and our reading. I knew what Wolfhagen would be like before seeing it. A new town, modern estates and factories. And not far wrong – a kind of East Anglian feel – the oh-so-quiet, small town in the countryside.

Beer and some Gulaschsuppe. Then outside, nearly dusk, a look at the fine old church, and then began to read aloud – Chatwin, The Songlines. The collision of aboriginal landscapes with middle Europe somehow wonderful. And the simple sound of our own voices after fourteen hours of silence, familiar and strange simultaneously. Soon too dark to go on, so we found a hotel and settled in a corner with two kanchens of coffee and the last of our Camels to smoke. Decided it was OK to talk now, after our reading, and climbed back up to the top of our berg, and, after a scare of not being able to find our place, eventually located our bags. Then a more extensive supper and soon snuggling into the warmth of our sleeping bags. J. saying that I'd talked in my sleep last night. What had I said? 'Something about "We've got six minutes to go! Just six minutes."' And then apparently I'd spoken in fluent Italian for a minute! Totally bizarre. But though funny it's also discomforting, any such subconscious revelation. Half hoped this would lead onto some talk about us. Suddenly felt very tender towards J. It would have been good to properly clear the air, get the tensions behind us. But the darkness of the night soon put us to sleep.

30 viii: 87:

Chill morning. Soon packed and off down the hill to Wolfhagen again, along that zigzagging way. Sunday morning and as we left the main road and Wolfhagen behind us, the regularity of the bells (one ring at quarter past, two at half past, etc.) began to fade. As if in response we started to sing our entire repertoire

*of English and Welsh hymns – 'Christ our Lord is Risen Today',
'Bread of Heaven', 'Jerusalem' – getting louder and louder the
further we got into the country.*

*Soon we came upon the 'restricted zone' we'd seen on the map.
'Gasterfelder Holz', and intrigued by the 'VORSICHT!' signs,
'ZONE MILITAIRE', 'Reichminister' this, 'Verboten' that. We
skirted the wood and the barbed wire. The site went on and on
. . . a fast forty minutes' walking and we were still adjacent to it.
I was walking at a real pace now, exhilarated by the quality of
the track, and the anticipation of the wild country in front of us
today. We followed the wood and the restricted zone round to the
right, and then we saw, through the trees, a whole series of what
looked exactly like missile silos – five, six, maybe eight in all. Sinister, partially covered, concrete silos. But all weirdly deserted,
not a single soldier or uniform in sight.*

Hotter now, short rest by side of the road. Water and cigarettes.

*Walking into Landau just before 1 p.m. – such an archetypically
German village – on a hill, the church nestling at the top,
surrounded by a cluster of solid, square-timbered houses.
Thought of Proust's description of the spires of, was it Martinville?,
and the optical illusion they gave. Intriguing with Landau,
approaching the village by a gentle hill – the spire slowly giving
way to a view of the entire village. Made me think of a camera's
eye – the quick, jerky movement of the walking body – how many
thousands of individuals over the centuries had experienced the
view we were seeing. It made me think of 'Heimat' – the concept
of one locality through different generations, political climates,
seasons. And imagining mercenaries approaching, peasants
armed with pitchforks, knives in the Thirty Years War – the
terror inspired by even a small group of strangers coming over
the brow of that hill.*

*Lunch in the shadow of the church. Then with the intensely sticky
midday heat I sleep for half an hour. Very hard to get walking
again, aware of a blistering heel on my right foot. Followed a*

Welsh-looking river out of the village. Poplars. Thought of an opening line to a story – 'He heard the poplars before he could see them.' Bluebells and harebells in the hedges here, surprised to see them so late in the summer. We moved up into the forest again – merciful shade. With our untutored eyes it's hard to be sure, but many of these pines and conifers looked more than half-dead, three-quarters of them bare in August. Many had dabs of white paint on them. Can it really be true that two-thirds of Germany's forests are dying due to acid rain? It would certainly help to explain the rise of Die Grünen here . . .

We took off right, deeper into the pines. Soft, needled track with smaller pathways every now and then beckoning us away from the main one. And the occasional hunting hide, on long, wooden legs . . . The power of the film, Shoah, still so much with me – the recurring, silent sweeps of camera down pine tracks, to make this landscape so sinister. The muffling silence of the woods (as Phil Ochs once sang – 'The fair trees of the forest have hid a thousand crimes'). The way that Chełmno and Treblinka were buried deep in the forest – few people would ever hear the screams.

And soon beech woods, more mixed woods, wider tracks. Spell-binding, utterly hypnotising walking in the afternoon light – flickering, strobing through the slanting trunks of the trees. My whole body seemed to be singing from within – a perfect harmony with this breathing wild. And all the time J. swinging along in front of me, and the smell of the woods, the heat, our male sweat, almost erotic now. Our imposed silence only adding to this – the proximity of the other, the wordless touch of bodies.

Just before we reached the River Twiste we looked back where we'd walked and, as far as we could see, green. Thick, cano-pied hillsides, lush valleys, totally tree-infested. This is one sort of landscape you could never see in England (acid-rain threat notwithstanding). On the outskirts of Twiste, in the shadow of a disused factory we rested, or rather, collapsed. Feet up on a wall in front of us (remembering my father's advice from his time in Korea, retold to us on Welsh mountain walks: lie back, let the blood flow from your bludgeoned feet). So close to J., hearing us breathing exactly together. Dirty, dusty, sweat-drenched, open shirts. Unspoken, unbreakable brotherhood.

Twiste – a disturbed town – the first we'd entered which clearly wasn't affluent. Here and there a battered-looking Ford Escort, young men walking around in cheap acrylics, ill-fitting, unfashionable. Quite shocking, coming from the modern super-affluent Germany we'd just been in. Marbled food halls and Mercedes with the latest catalytic convertors. This was going to be interesting. Tried to get something to eat in a very rough bar. Nothing doing. And all activity there (ten dirty-looking males sitting on bar stools) stopped completely while we asked. Seriously unfriendly. Back outside, a poster offering a 3 million DM reward for Baader–Meinhof and RAF terrorists, accompanied by intriguingly romantic mugshots of six of them, men and women.

Into another Kneiper for zwei grosse Bier. Half the town in there glued to the Rome athletics championships. We see an astonishing 100 metres, in which a new world record of 9.85 seconds is set by a Canadian I hadn't heard of, Carl Lewis only second. Food called, so we traipsed back to a stall we'd seen on the way in – 'Coca-Cola Grill'. Had two half-chickens, potato salad and chocolate milkshakes. Much needed.

Then, as it was getting dark, up via the church and war memorials to nearby woods. Remembering our last walk together, through Essex, and how we were struck by the war memorials and whole families being wiped out, but the whole thing seems even more catastrophic from this place. The remarkable thing here is that whereas in England the ratio of World War One dead to World War Two dead (seen on war memorials) is usually 3:1 or 4:1, here the numbers are more or less the same! The carnage of two total wars within thirty years. And never have I been more struck by the futility. All those children born in 1914, 1915, 1916, only to die twenty-five years later . . . Germany must still be traumatised. Not only to be held responsible for starting two world wars, not

only to have lost them both, not only to have had two generations
of young men virtually wiped out, not only to have experienced
pariah status after the last war, not only to have been despised
for not opposing twelve years of fascism, but to have been held
responsible for the most horrifically predetermined genocide in
world history. A vast load for any country to deal with. And it's
totally understandable that young people here today would still
feel that trauma, transmitted through the generations.

You might not be too surprised to learn that we didn't make it all
the way to London. In fact we only managed another two days,
forty miles or so – a combination of our money running out and
severely blistered feet. We left West-Linie-Ost at the point where
a stream (the Schwartmecke) crossed our track, and marked this
exact spot by burying two stones stamped with 'PLATFORM'
inside a Golden Virginia tin. A pledge that one day we would return
to continue our walk. And then we headed for the finely named
town of Bestwig, and a connecting train to Meschede and on to
Cologne and home from there. But, at least in our hearts, West-
Linie-Ost had been established as something real, and somewhere
in the forests of central Germany there still lies a rusting tobacco
tin with some curious contents...

*

In the thirty years of walking since this time we've never repeated
the silent way. In fact, rather the opposite. There was a period of
some years when the walking became focussed on very functional
matters – problem-solving, conversations about funding challenges, colleagues not getting on, or the future direction of our
work. It became a bit like moving our office outside, and whole days
would pass with us walking along glorious parts of the Scottish or
Welsh coast with our heads bowed down, furrow-browed. I would
joke with J. that there were probably eagles and otters dancing a
few yards away, but all we saw was the track and our boots as we
puzzled away at a problem.

But more often it's been a rich and diverse ecology of subjects as we walk. And it's hard to say where one matter starts and another ends. Some conversations continue for several days, with us layering back on ourselves, again and again. We rest on a gate and the song of a robin will trigger another thought. We come across the ruins of a croft, talk of the Highland Clearances and suddenly J. will then be telling me about a disturbing memory of a childhood holiday. The agreed pact of mutual forgetting in all families when things become too painful. More questions come up, as the bay stretches before us. The village must be what, four, five miles away? Shall we stay there tonight? (With the coming of early middle age B&Bs and rooms over pubs have tended to replace the joys of sleeping under the stars.) And in the hour and a half that follows, as dusk arrives, as the track curves down to the bay, I'll listen intently, ask another question, hear J.'s hesitation, but encourage him to go on. The call of an oystercatcher. I roll a cigarette. The track ends at a tarmacked lane, turn to the right. Our boots making a different sound, from the soft clumping of the track to the harder, ringing sound of the road. J. questioning me now – is he being too hard on his father? A hundred yards, a minute and a half of pause. Only the sound of the rucksack rubbing against the frame, and our boots. *I'm not sure.* Dark now, the edge of the village, the light of a pub.

And curious, in our still partly homophobic culture, that walkers are somehow given a kind of special dispensation. Two guys in tee-shirts and shorts arriving on a summer's night in the roughest of pubs, yet once you swing your rucksacks down, sweat staining your back, get your pints in, there's always a kind of respect, perhaps tinged with sympathy for carrying serious weight across this terrain in such heat. Could it be a long-buried folk memory of when pilgrims walked the land, getting fed and watered at inns along the way? Or travelling players, minstrels, clowns, the circus. The romance of these never quite extinguished by the Industrial Revolution and the move to the cities. The sense of absolute freedom, of carrying your life on your back, being able to stop or move on whenever you want.

The 'Map Ritual' then follows, as regularly as any religious rite. If J. is getting the first round I spread out my OS pink Landranger (one inch to the mile), and calculate how far we've come today. Depending on the terrain, the blister factor, whether it's the beginning or the middle of the walk, it will usually be between fifteen and twenty miles. And this will have involved walking as closely as possible to the sea, lovingly tracing each peninsula and headland, and only being forced inland occasionally by military installations or a river without a bridge. And the islands, always just out of reach, still captivating. The history always with us also, knowing that in the town we came through earlier that day a man was born in the late eighteenth century who became one of the most influential slavery abolitionists. Strange to think of growing up as a Quaker in that little farming town . . . And what did he witness as a child that first made him angry at his world, at injustice? We then discuss possible routes for the next day, both of us by now finely attuned to the codes of the paper and lines, allowing the flatness of the map to come alive. Instinctively visualising the loveliness of that piece of deciduous woodland, the steepness of that valley, the views from the little yellow road that runs along the shoulder of the hillside. If I'm getting the beers, when I get to our corner of the pub J. will have spread out *his* OS map – the orange Explorer (two and a half inches to the mile) – and he'll have found the parish boundaries, the tumuli and, most importantly of all, the exact boundaries of the watersheds, the rivers he loves more than anything else. The arteries of the earth. And then our talk picks up again, the flow returning. *You know what you were saying earlier reminds me of something I don't think I've ever told you before . . .*

Trust. Listening to each other. Things not even shared with lovers. Debilitating doubts, crises, fear at the prospect of fatherhood, grief of lost love, people we'll never see again. But being listened to. In the process of talking, something lifts. In the process of walking, something heals. And the rare equality that exists. One walk it's J. who's blocked in some way, impatient with himself; the next time it's me, perplexed, riddled with doubt. The patience with each other, though, the absolute belief that we'll come through anything. This comes from a long view of life. And knowing what we've already been through. Having seen each other fly, completely inspired at times, inspiring to colleagues, gripping audiences, and having also seen each other dulled and depressed, defeated by twists of fate and disappointment. This doesn't mean simply being kind or understanding – there have been many occasions when I've challenged J. to breaking point. And J. similarly with me can be remarkably stubborn, returning again and again to an issue I've been elusive on. Not letting me off the hook. And yes, there are times of being maddened, driven to rage, but these pass. And of course, knowing so much means we also know the exact spot of the exposed nerve, the point of weakness, and from time to time, whether consciously or not, these can be touched.

Of course there are sometimes walks where there's little intensity or tension or need to talk about anything in particular. There are, inevitably, longueurs – sections of landscape that do not thrill (treeless moorland I've yet to find appealing, for instance); there are times when we get bored by a subject, especially if it's something we've discussed many times before and are never going to agree on. Our response to these moments is usually to resort to a battery of accents – loud German, Aussie, South African being the most popular – scattering camp or obscene bursts of humour to the skies. Singing is always another possibility, or new forms of cockney rhyming slang, played as a kind of verbal tennis.

Most of all, though, with J. I return to that single word – curiosity. Our shared curiosity about the world, history, political change, revolution. Our curiosity about each other. But also, strangely often, knowing what's going through the other's mind before we speak. And, at the same time, being aware of the fundamental reality of existence – our unknowability. Even when we feel we've expressed everything. To the outside world we may seem astonishingly similar, yet in the vast majority of ways we remain mysteries to the other. And in this lies the fascination. Knowing that we see the world both as a unity and a fractured multitude. Often I'm sure of how J. will respond to something. But I also relish it when he throws me; I'm exhilarated at moving into unpredictable areas. Being made to look at somebody you love in a different way. Understanding that the temptation to possess another is really a way of keeping them in fixed positions, which may increase your sense of security but does nothing for the winged glory that love is. And still, after all these years, a sense that we cannot be complete by being alone. Love is about understanding what we lack. And being humble about that. 'I see that I must give what I most need.'

5

The Town of Organised Forgetting

22 August 2000, Arbon, Switzerland

It's taken thirteen years to get here. As our train edges round the lake, I reflect on this unhurried journey. J. and I are following the southern shore of Bodensee, 'Lake Constance' as the Grand Tour sightseers used to call it, and looking across to the other side and the low hills of Germany, where we'd travelled together many years before. J. is reading an account of the Huguenot refugees of St Gallen, the town where we've just changed trains, and their role in establishing the textiles industries that have dominated this part of Switzerland historically. I'm looking out of the window. Late afternoon, a lazy day at the end of August when the heat of the sun has died. Children cycling haphazardly between the shore of the lake and our slowly chugging train. Elderly couples sitting on benches under pine trees. And the little town of Arbon finally comes into view. Thirteen years since the epiphany of seeing Lanzmann's remarkable nine-and-a-half-hour film on the Holocaust, *Shoah*.

In January 1987, in my early twenties, I'd sat transfixed in the Curzon Mayfair cinema on consecutive afternoons, watching seemingly endless panning shots of Polish forests and trains and tracks and a sequence of devastated faces talking to the camera. It created its own mesmerising rhythm. There was a simplicity in the intent (to document testimony of perpetrators, survivors and witnesses), yet a complexity in the form (the disorientation of the changing seasons and geographical locations, the continual layering and over-layering of the narrative) which I found spellbinding. I have carried the faces and the memories of some of those interviewed with me through my life. In a strange reversal of what might be expected, these faces, seen for a matter of minutes on a screen, seem clearer to me now than that of my father. Simon Srebnik's bewildered expression on his return to Chelmno – 'Yes, it was here, they burned people here'; Filip Müller's eyes, darting in terror as he hears himself trying to find words for what it is not possible to find words for – working in the *Sonderkommando* at Auschwitz-Birkenau; and Jan Karski, poised, hawk-like, proud, his face suddenly crumpling recalling the Warsaw Ghetto, the assault of a memory he hasn't spoken of for more than thirty years – 'No, I don't go back.' In these testimonies there seems to be a quality of stillness, of allowing time between the words, that we almost never see in film. It is as close as you will ever come to witnessing, as tangible actions, the process of thought and memory. What rapid blinking can communicate, or a sudden glancing away.

But, of all the sequences in *Shoah*, the one that haunted me the most was the memorandum – the first part of which we saw at the beginning of this book. It had no narrative to it, it was not connected to a human being, just a disembodied voice reading a letter, a communication from one businessman to another. An interminable shot of industrial Germany, the Ruhr, wet roads, factories, cooling towers, and then a close-up image of the front of a truck. The camera focussed in further and further on a strange blue and white logo on the grill – 'Saurer' – a name I didn't know.

It transpired that the letter being read was a memorandum sent from one SS officer (with hellish irony a man named Just) to another, Obersturmbannführer Rauff, concerning how Saurer lorries might be adapted to gas people more rapidly, more efficiently. A piece of bureaucracy. A business transaction. The tone is pragmatic, almost bored. And in those few minutes in the Curzon cinema, though I didn't realise it at the time, something shifted within me. Instinctively I felt that the coldness and seeming banality of this document was more significant than all the accounts of the Holocaust I'd read before. Primarily because the language was so commonplace, it could have been a communication between departments of any corporation at any time over the last fifty years. In this moment I glimpsed something I later realised as a critical truth – the *modernity* of what we habitually think of as 'the Holocaust', a distant, historical event. No, the language, and therefore the psychology and the behaviour of the men who exchanged this memo, is entirely of our times. After this realisation it was impossible for me to think about those years as in the distant past, I was compelled by a sense of past and present colliding – of our absolute connectedness to this language and the terror it unleashed, and still unleashes today – because such memos are being written now as you read this page. The subject of the memos may change, but the result is still death on a massive scale. Memos by operators of drones in Afghanistan, memos by lawyers in Washington, memos by politicians trying to justify illegal 'interventions'. All today, still stamped 'Secret Business' at the top.

I've finally been able to find a copy of the original memorandum, including the underlinings made by Just.[*] It is noteworthy that only a single copy of this document was sent, reflecting the extreme secrecy of the correspondence with Rauff.

---

[*] The version of this document that Lanzmann includes in *Shoah* is considerably summarised, so I reproduce the full text here.

II D 3 a (9) Nr. 214/42 g.Rs.

·b-17-14

Berlin, den 5. Juni 1942

Einzigste Ausfertigung.

Geheime Reichssache!

I. Vermerk:

> Betrifft: Technische Abänderungen an den im Betrieb eingesetzten und an den sich in Herstellung befindlichen Spezialwagen.

Seit Dezember 1941 wurden beispielsweise mit 3 eingesetzten Wagen 97 000 verarbeitet, ohne daß Mängel an den Fahrzeugen auftraten. Die bekannte Explosion in Kulmhof ist als Einzelfall zu bewerten. Ihre Ursache ist auf einen Bedienungsfehler zurückzuführen. Zur Vermeidung von derartigen Unfällen ergingen an die betroffenen Dienststellen besondere Anweisungen. Die Anweisungen wurden so gehalten, daß der Sicherheitsgrad erheblich heraufgesetzt wurde.

Die sonstigen bisher gemachten Erfahrungen lassen folgende technische Abänderungen zweckmäßig erscheinen:

1.) Um ein schnelles Einströmen des CO unter Vermeidung von Überdrucken zu ermöglichen, sind an der oberen Rückwand zwei offene Schlitze von 10 x 1 cm lichter Weite anzubringen. Dieselben sind außen mit leicht beweglichen Scharnierblechklappen zu versehen, damit ein Ausgleich des evtl. eintretenden Überdruckes selbsttätig erfolgt.

2.) Die Beschickung der Wagen beträgt normalerweise 9 - 10 pro m^2. Bei den großräumigen Saurer-Spezialwagen ist eine Ausnutzung in dieser Form nicht möglich, weil dadurch zwar

keine

II D 3 a (9) NI. 214/42 GRS
Berlin, 5th June 1942
Only copy
Reich Secret Business

I. Note:

Conc.: Technical adjustments to special vans at present in service and to those that are in production.

Since December 1941, ninety-seven thousand have been processed, using three vans, without any defects showing up in the vehicles. The explosion that we know took place at Kulmhof* is to be considered an isolated case. The cause can be attributed to improper operation. In order to avoid such incidents, special instructions have been addressed to the services concerned. Safety has been increased considerably as a result of these instructions.

Previous experience has shown that the following adjustments would be useful:

1.) In order to facilitate the rapid distribution of CO, as well as to avoid a build-up of pressure, two slots, ten by one centimetres, will be bored at the top of the rear wall. The excess pressure would be controlled by an easily adjustable hinged metal valve on the outside of the vents.

2.) The normal capacity of the vans is nine to ten per square metre. The capacity of the larger special Saurer vans is not so great.† The problem is not one of overloading but of off-road manoeuvrability on all terrains, which is severely diminished in this van. It would appear that a reduction in the cargo area is necessary. This can be achieved by shortening the compartment by about one metre. The problem cannot be solved by

---

* Kulmhof was the German name for the Chelmno extermination camp in Poland.
† See chapter notes for more information.

merely reducing the number of subjects treated, as has been done so far. For in this case a longer running time is required, as the empty space also needs to be filled with CO. On the contrary, were the cargo area smaller, but fully occupied, the operation would take considerably less time, because there would be no empty space.

The manufacturer pointed out during discussions that a reduction in the volume of the cargo compartment would result in an inconvenient displacement of the cargo toward the front. There would then be a risk of overloading the axle. In fact, there is a natural compensation in the distribution of the weight. When [the van] is in operation, the load, in its effort to reach the rear door, places itself for the most part at the rear. For this reason the front axle is not overloaded.

3.) The pipe that connects the exhaust to the van tends to rust, because it is eaten away from the inside by liquids that flow into it. To avoid this the nozzle should be so arranged as to point downward. The liquids will thus be prevented from flowing into [the pipe].

4.) To facilitate the cleaning of the vehicle, an opening will be made in the floor to allow for drainage. It will be closed by a watertight cover about twenty to thirty centimetres in diameter, fitted with an elbow siphon that will allow for the drainage of thin liquids. The upper part of the elbow pipe will be fitted with a sieve to avoid obstruction. Thicker dirt can be removed through the large drainage hole when the vehicle is cleaned. The floor of the vehicle can be tipped slightly. In this way all the liquids can be made to flow toward the centre and be prevented from entering the pipes.

5.) The observation windows that have been installed up to now could be eliminated, as they are hardly ever used. Considerable time will be saved in the production of the new vans by avoiding the difficult fitting of the window and its airtight lock.

6.) Greater protection is needed for the lighting system. The grille should cover the lamps high enough up to make it impossible to break the bulb. It seems that these lamps are hardly ever turned on, so the users have suggested that they could be done away with. <u>Experience shows, however, that when the back door is closed and it gets dark inside, the load pushes hard against the door.</u> The reason for this is that when it becomes dark inside the load rushes toward what little light remains. This hampers the locking of the door. It has also been noticed that the noise provoked by the locking of the door is linked to the fear aroused by the darkness. It is therefore expedient to keep the lights on before the operation and during the first few minutes of its duration. Lighting is also useful for night work and for the cleaning of the interior of the van.

7.) To facilitate the rapid unloading of the vehicles, a removable grid is to be placed on the floor. It will slide on rollers on a U-shaped rail. It will be removed and put in position by means of a small winch placed under the vehicle. The firm charged with the alterations has stated that it is not able to continue for the moment, due to a lack of staff and materials. Another firm will have to be found.

The technical changes planned for the vehicles already in operation will be carried out when and as major repairs to these vehicles prove necessary. The alterations in the ten Saurer vehicles already ordered will be carried out as far as possible. The manufacturer made it clear in a meeting that structural alterations, with the exception of minor ones, cannot be carried out for the moment. An attempt must therefore be made to find another firm that can carry out, on at least <u>one</u> of these ten vehicles, the alterations and adjustments that experience has proved to be necessary. I suggest that the firm in Hohenmauth be charged with the execution.

Due to present circumstances, we shall have to expect a later date of completion for this vehicle. It will then not only be kept available as a model but also be used as a reserve vehicle. Once it has been tested, the other vans will be withdrawn from service and will undergo the same alterations.

II. To Gruppenleiter II D
SS-Obersturmbannführer Rauff
for examination and decision.
by order of
Just

What is it possible to say in the face of such words? What kind of numbing needs to have occurred for somebody to be able to write of men, women and children in this way – 'the load', 'the cargo'? There is only one moment when the memorandum writer, almost accidentally it seems, refers to human emotion and not machinery: 'It has also been noticed that the noise provoked by the locking of the door is linked to the *fear* aroused by the darkness' (my emphasis).

And how to connect these words with the individual deaths of 97,000 people over this six-month period? Soon, aided by the technical improvements suggested here, to become an estimated 300,000–350,000 deaths. Like killing every individual in a city the size of Nottingham or Hull, in ten of these Saurer lorries. This single memorandum should be a central image in our understanding of the Holocaust, because the vast majority of the mass murders were not 'spontaneous' shootings or pogroms – they were planned, timetabled, ordered, recorded methodically, currency and possessions of the victims catalogued obsessively, by an army of bureaucrats like Just and Rauff here, hundreds of thousands of them, who after the war melted back into German society, almost without trace.

So what of the sender and recipient of this memorandum? What do we know about these men? Very little about Willy Just, the author of these words. He was born in 1899, had served in the First World War, and then became a welder and mechanic, before joining the *Schutzpolizei*, the protective police department. He later moved to the Gestapo, and joined the SS in 1938, ending his career in Berlin in Amstgruppe II D (the Technical and Automative department of Himmler's RSHA, the Reich Main Security Office).[*]

More is known about his boss Walter Rauff, who was head of Amstgruppe II D at the RSHA and became a key figure in the development of the *gaswagen* as mobile gas chambers. But Rauff's mechanical innovation and redesign of lorries could not have happened without the prior expertise of several other specialists from scientific backgrounds. The original impetus that eventually led to the creation of the *gaswagen* derived from Himmler's concern that the *Einsatzgruppen* (mobile execution squads) mass shootings were having a demoralising effect on his men. After witnessing a mass shooting of Jews in Minsk in August 1941 Himmler had asked Dr Artur Nebe, his head of the *Reichskriminalpolizeiamt* (Reich Criminal Police), to come up with more efficient methods of mass killing. Nebe then turned to two chemists, who worked at the KTI (the *Kriminaltechnische Institut* = Criminal Technical Institute) in Berlin – Dr Walter Heess, who was the head of the KTI (and had gained his doctorate in chemistry in 1925), and his younger colleague, Dr Albert Widmann (doctorate in chemistry from the *Technische Hochschule* Stuttgart in 1938), who was a specialist in toxicology. Heess and Widmann had earlier been closely involved in advising on the most effective lethal chemicals to be used in the Nazi 'euthanasia' programme.[†] They (together with a third colleague, the chemist Dr August Becker – doctorate from the University of Giessen, 1933) recommended, and oversaw the use of, bottled carbon monoxide, which was then procured from BASF and used to kill patients at the six psychiatric hospitals across the Reich.

In September 1941, Dr Nebe asked Dr Heess whether he thought exhaust gas could be used for mass killings instead of bottled gas. Dr Heess and Dr Widmann then discussed this, rather bizarrely, according to Widmann's account, on a tube journey in Berlin –

---

[*] Information on Just from *Fateful Months* by Christopher Browning, chapter 3: 'The Development and Production of the Nazi Gas Van', note 33.

[†] The 'T4' programme will be explored in greater detail in Book One, Chapter Thirteen, 'The Doctors of Wannsee Meet in a Villa by the Lake'.

91

between Wittenberg-Platz and Thiel-Platz as he later recalled. Dr Widmann then travelled to Minsk, later in September, and oversaw the very first test of gassing human beings using exhaust fumes – five mental patients were killed in an airtight room, with exhaust from a truck outside pumped in using a hose. Building on the success of this experiment, Reinhard Heydrich, head of the RSHA, then turned to Rauff and asked him to design and develop a mobile *gaswagen*. Rauff did this relatively quickly, using five trucks ordered from Saurer in Switzerland, and then calling on the skills of Friedrich Pradel, head of the Security Police motor division, and his chief mechanic Harry Wentritt, whose workshop was located at the Security Police's headquarters at Prinz-Albrecht-Strasse in Berlin. Between the three of them, the *gaswagen* soon became a reality – Rauff's initial ideas being developed by Pradel and Wentritt, who customised the Saurer trucks by designing a U-shaped pipe that could link the exhaust to the sealed compartment at the back of the truck.

The historian Christopher Browning describes the moment that Wentritt drove the prototype grey Saurer truck to the courtyard of the KTI for testing in October 1941. Dr Widmann then gave the young chemists in his department a kind of seminar in the optimum way of killing human beings:

> Widmann . . . explained that through adjusting the timing of the ignition, one could maximise the amount of poisonous carbon monoxide in the exhaust. He also explained how to measure the carbon monoxide content within the sealed compartment . . . One of his men donned a gas mask and conducted the measurement.

Some days later, Dr Heess drove two of the young chemists who had witnessed this demonstration to the concentration camp at Sachsenhausen. There they found the Saurer truck again, surrounded by SS officers, and they watched as forty naked Russian POWs were led to the truck and locked into the rear compartment. The truck then drove for ten minutes or so, and Heess and his young students followed on foot. Groaning could still be heard, but after twenty minutes there was silence, and a check from the peephole in the driver's cab confirmed that all were now dead. Another test; another success for the chemists of the Reich.

Now full production of the *gaswagen* could go ahead – thirty trucks were ordered, larger ones from Saurer (which could take around fifty to sixty people), smaller ones from Opel and Diamond (for around thirty people). These trucks then were modified, under the supervision of Wentritt, and with the help of a Berlin company, Firma Gaubschat (which supplied sealed metal compartments that could fit inside the trucks). Within a matter of weeks, by 8 December 1941, the *Sonderkommando* under the command of Hauptsturm-führer Herbert Lange, had started killing Jews using the new *gaswagen*, at Chelmno. The vans (Saurers and Diamonds) were also sent to the Eastern Front, to the *Einsatzgruppen* operating in Riga, Vitebsk, Minsk and Moghilev – seen as timely Christmas presents by the unit commanders, who had been so concerned about the psychological traumas being suffered by their men in the process of mass shootings.

Later in the war, in 1942, Rauff led an *Einsatzkommando* in Vichy-occupied Tunisia, where he continued his work killing Jews and partisans. And had El Alamein not halted the Nazi forces in North Africa, Rauff would have brought his *gaswagen* to exterminate the Jews right across the Middle East. In 1943 he took charge of Gestapo operations in north-west Italy; he ended the war as an SS *Standarten-führer* (equivalent to colonel), and was arrested by the Americans in Milan in 1945, then transferrred to a camp in Rimini, from where he escaped. He managed to get to Rome, and was sheltered by Vatican officials until he was joined by his family. From here they sailed for Syria on fake Red Cross papers (an established procedure for many fugitive SS officers aided by the Vatican). From Syria, Rauff and family eventually made their way to South America. He ultimately found sanctuary in Pinochet's Chile, where he died on 14 May 1984.

I discovered that there had been a lengthy legal battle towards the end of his life, over his possible extradition and prosecution, but Pinochet continued to protect him. A friend passed on a documentary, *Images of Dictatorship*, which contains footage of the Nazi hunters Beate and Serge Klarsfeld chanting outside Rauff's house in Santiago in the early 1980s: '*Expulse der Nazi Rauff!*' Later there is footage of Rauff's funeral, with leather-coated thugs saluting as his coffin is lowered, '*Heil Hitler! Heil Rauff!*'

*

Because of the Ruhr background to the Saurer sequence in *Shoah* I had originally assumed that Saurer was a German company. However, Lanzmann told me, when we met some years ago, that they'd come across the Saurer lorry which appears in *Shoah* quite by chance. He'd been returning with his crew from filming in Switzerland one day, when they noticed the Saurer lorry driving behind them, and so they began to film it. Subsequently that footage was intercut with the Ruhr footage sequence to link it conceptually to Germany's military-industrial complex.

There was little information available on the company when I started my research in the mid-1990s. I telephoned the German Chamber of Commerce but drew a blank, I pursued business libraries and transport magazines, but found nothing. Finally, via a journalist at the *Financial Times*, I discovered that Saurer was in fact a Swiss textiles manufacturing business based at Arbon. They had diversified into lorry manufacture in the early part of the century, I was told, but had reverted to their core business of textiles machinery in the 1970s or early 80s.

Eventually I tracked down a Swiss phone number, made a call, and was eventually connected to a Herr Mickelson, the Saurer finance director and also, it seemed, the unofficial company historian. I explained that I was undertaking research into the vehicle manufacturing aspects of Saurer, and asked if a company archive existed. He sounded guarded: no, there isn't a formal archive, but he knows some of the history. Anyway, what particular angle of research was I pursuing? I muttered something about 'general' research and asked him some questions relating to when they started manufacturing vehicles. He told me that Saurer itself was founded in 1853 as an iron foundry just outside St Gallen, but soon after established itself in textile manufacture and moved to Arbon. The first cars were produced in 1898 and the last lorry in 1983. He told me that the lorries were produced in Arbon and at a subsidiary factory at Olten. Finally I asked whether they had exported many of the lorries and to what countries. There was another pause:

'What years are you referring to please?'

'Well, I'm quite interested in the period from the 1920s through to about 1950.'

Another pause. 'Just a moment, I have some papers here, but not very much for that time, only maybe ten or twenty sides.'

'Would it be possible for you to send me copies of what you have there?'

'But I need to know what kind of information you require.'

'Is there any information on exports during this period?'

'Almost nothing – there's just a couple of lines in an annual report saying that there is export to South America, Germany, England – that's all.'

At this stage I decided to be more direct, which was probably a mistake. 'I'd heard something about Saurer supplying lorries to the German government in the war years, but I don't know whether this is true. Could you shed any light on this?'

A sigh of exasperation. And Herr Mickelson's tone changed dramatically, suddenly impatient. 'Yes, well, this is what I thought you wanted from the beginning. I can't give you information on this. It's all currently being investigated by a federal commission in Bern. There's going to be a report on the war years. I can't tell you anything more.'

Afterwards I reflected on the conversation. The most intriguing aspect for me was that reference to the 'couple of lines in an annual report.' The invisibility of history, the hundreds of thousands of people who had been asphyxiated in Saurer lorries, reduced to this. In the weeks that followed I attempted to track down reliable information about Saurer's role in the Holocaust, but repeatedly met dead ends. The Wiener Library, usually such a fine resource, had nothing at all on Saurer, though it did hold some material on Walter Rauff. Frustrated by how little new information I had gleaned, I decided the only real option would be to go to Arbon directly and see what could be found on the ground.

And so now, a few months on, we're here – our little train rattling along by the lake towards a little town . . .

*

Yesterday was invaluable, learning some wider historic context about Switzerland and the war: we were staying in the little town of Neuchâtel with a former student of mine, an economic historian, who specialises in the relationship between Swiss regional and national banking. If this makes him sound dull I have done him a great disservice. He has an anarchist's quickfire wit and a bubbling energy. He was intrigued to hear about our research, and over the course of the day he gave us a detailed overview of Switzerland and the war years, and in particular the activities of the Bergier Commission, the government body that had been established in the late 1990s to investigate three main aspects of Switzerland's wartime role – banking (Swiss banks and their relationship with Nazi Germany); refugees and their wartime treatment by Switzerland (including the shameful story of the repatriation of refugees to Axis-occupied Europe); and Swiss industry in the war years, with a particular focus on the arms and chemical industries. He was able to give us mini biographies of all the historians on the commission, their past fields of study and even their political bias. He didn't know so much about Saurer, except that he thought the Swiss post office and some other government agencies used to use their trucks and lorries. They were supposed to be 'very reliable'.

J. is leaning out of the train window, and he shouts that we're finally arriving in Arbon. We get our rucksacks down and wait by the door. A slightly neglected feel to this northern part of the country. Far from the new buildings and affluence of the urban landscape we'd passed through earlier today, Zurich and Zug, the wealthy centre of Switzerland, this part looks down-at-heel in comparison, almost shabby. Something unreal about being here thirteen years after seeing *Shoah* and first hearing the words of that memorandum spoken. We're pulling into the station, not knowing what we're going to find. Not knowing if there will be any trace of the lorries, or the vehicle manufacturing. And then J. shouts to me to look – on the other side, just beyond the station:

That distinctive blue and white logo, with the strange gable and the little window. And on the other side of the station as we get off the train, these vast sheds, decaying, roofs caved in, and I know immediately, instinctively, that these were the assembly sheds, these were the buildings where the lorries had been manufactured. We walk down to the lake shore. There is a large bronze bust of Adolph Saurer, son of the founder of the company, Franz Saurer.

We look at a noticeboard nearby with information about the town, places of interest – one of these is the 'Oldtimer Museum', devoted to old Saurer vehicles, open once a week on Wednesday afternoons. This little town seems to be proud of its history.

We find a place to stay and begin to explore the building complex down by the station. We start to walk around it. We spot our first Saurer vehicle, an old army truck rusting in a car park, and walk round the back of these vast wooden sheds. We later learn that part of this was another textiles factory, Heine, which Saurer took over. Saurer itself had started at the little village of St Georgen, just outside St Gallen, and then moved its textiles business here in 1853. But the greater part of these buildings would have been used for the vehicle manufacturing. Eventually we come across a modern complex, adjoining the old assembly sheds – the new Saurer:

There are three flags – the Swiss, the local canton and, curiously, the Indian flag, Gandhi's symbol of liberation (we subsequently find out that Saurer now has substantial subsidiary companies based in India). We finish our circumnavigation of this complex at dusk – it's surprisingly extensive, it's taken us around forty minutes to walk around the perimeter. By the time we get back to the old town most of the restaurants have already finished serving, there's a melancholic emptiness here, but eventually we find a place off the little square and get some soup. Afterwards we wander down to the lake, expecting to find a bar, but there isn't anything. We sit on the wooden jetty looking over at the lights of southern Germany, remembering that mad tour of Beuys' former colleagues we made more than a decade ago, hitching, sleeping by autobahn service stations when we couldn't get lifts. J. reminds me of a lift we got with an Irishman chain-smoking joints and driving at 120 mph, which culminated in us smashing into the back of a Mercedes estate in the middle lane of the autobahn, and spinning wildly across three lanes of traffic, miraculously avoiding hitting any-thing else. Yes, that was certainly one of our nine lives gone . . .

But we also remember remarkable meetings with Johannes Stüttgen in Düsseldorf, with the political philosopher Rudolf Bahro in Augsburg, and with the pioneers of *Volksentcheid*, the movement for direct democracy – Wilfried Heidt and friends – just over the water there in Achberg. We're still not tired so we walk round the lake shore and eventually we do find a bar, a rather brash place by a small marina. Over whisky and cigarettes we reflect on what we've learnt this evening, and again on how physically being in a place gives you so much that you could never glean from libraries or archives. Only by being on the ground here and walking can you appreciate the sheer scale of the company in relation to this place These factories and assembly sheds, in their heyday, would have covered a third of the entire area of Arbon – creating a kind of 'Sau-rer Town'. What does such economic dominance do to the people reliant upon that company for work? How does it begin to affect, in numerous subtle ways, the whole culture of a community?

*

23 August 2000

Our *pension* is next to a church. Every quarter-hour throughout the night the bells rang, so we emerge this morning not in the best of moods. At breakfast we tell our host about the 'bells problem' – he seems rather amused but does agree to a change of room for this evening. Then we head for the town bookshop to get some local histories, on the way passing a model shop selling dozens of mini-ature Saurer vehicles. The man in the bookshop is very informative and tells us that over 3,000 people used to be employed at the ve-hicle plant, there was a huge fuss when it closed down in the early 1980s – most of the people in the town lost their jobs. Now only a fraction of that number remain, working on vehicle repairs. We discover that there are two distinct zones: the one at the heart of the old town, just under the castle walls, where the administrative headquarters have always been, and the one down by the station, where most of the manufacturing had taken place, mainly built in the 1920s – which we walked around last night.

We then head up towards the castle, and the administrative headquarters of the company, and suddenly I see something I never expected to see – coming down the hill towards us a working lorry with the unmistakeable Saurer logo on the front! I grab the camera and soon I'm snapping away like a crazed paparazzo.

The driver seems completely unfazed. J. goes up to talk to him – oh yes, there are many people who love these lorries. They may be twenty years old, but they're so reliable, still going strong. Would we like to see the other one he has in his garage? An even earlier model, and we're told to take a picture of the panel inside the door, apparently this is what lorry aficionados are most interested in.

Eventually we find the Saurer headquarters, a striking white art deco building of several storeys tucked down a lane beside the castle. Everything seems very sleepy in the August heat. We manage to access the downstairs lobby, and then climb up two flights of stairs and then along a corridor, nobody around. Finally we come upon two secretaries who seem surprised to see us. We explain we're doing some research into the vehicle side of Saurer, can we talk to anyone? They say Herr Mickelson would be the person but he's on vacation at the moment. What about other directors? No, nearly all of them are away. Then one of them says we could try talking to Herr Hess – he's the man who runs the vehicle repair section down near the station. They ring him and it's soon arranged, we can go down there straight away. On the way out we pick up copies of last year's Saurer annual report. Outside we walk past a frieze celebrating the three generations of the company's founders – Franz, Adolph and Hippolyt Saurer.

Herr Hess turns out to be a genial, moustachioed man in his fifties and tremendously knowledgeable and helpful about Saurer. He spends an hour or so taking us through the history of the company. It emerges that Saurer's vehicles are a part of Swiss national identity – they supplied the post office, the army, construction industry, and at peak production in the 1960s they supplied over 50 per cent of the Swiss truck market, employing, at the peak of production, 4,500 local people. Their key strength was in niche markets, often designing, for very specific needs, relatively small runs of trucks. They also were adept at franchising and joint ventures with other vehicle manufacturers round the world, for instance they had partnerships with Vickers-Armstrongs and Leyland in England. Hess confirmed that Saurer stopped manufacturing vehicles in 1983, but as everything was done on a twenty-year guarantee basis, there are still a few workshops, like the one we're in, which repair Saurer vehicles. At the end of our time, he proudly displays his drinks cabinet, branded under a sign that reads 'Saurer / British Leyland'.

Herr Hess also gives us two detailed books on the history of Saurer, which we don't have time to look at in detail yet because there are two museums we need to visit before they close. He has been delighted to talk to us, nobody has ever visited from Britain before, he presses other gifts on us before we leave – little Saurer lorry badges, a Saurer model truck, and even a Saurer ashtray and a Saurer cigar (which remains unsmoked in my flat to this day, in its silver and blue tube, proclaiming '30 Jahre Stark im Trend')

('Thirty Years On, Still Going Strong') to celebrate a partnership between Mercedes-Benz and Saurer.

We do further research at the local museum, and then, as it's Wednesday, we head for the 'Oldtimer Museum' – which is packed full of old Saurer trucks, engines and diagrams. Soon J. has befriended a young guy, Conrad, who's clearly obsessed by these lorries and is delighted to find kindred spirits. While they talk about engine sizes (J. doing a creditable impression of a lorry geek), I scour the museum for any reference to the war years or Saurer's role there. Predicatably there's almost nothing. An army truck from the 1940s is the closest in manufacturing date to the one we're researching. We look through a detailed book showing further models, trying to find the one that was used to customise the *gaswagen*, but with no success.

Tired now, we head back to the *pension*. While J. rests I switch on the TV to try and find coverage of an event that's happening not far from here this evening. The team I've supported since childhood, Leeds United, are playing 1860 Munich tonight, in a Champions League qualifying game. Leeds had only managed a 2–1 win at Elland Road, so tonight could be very tricky – I switch between a dozen channels, but eventually find what I'm looking for . . . Five minutes into the second half, a loose ball in the Munich penalty area, Alan Smith pounces. 0–1, Leeds. Now just to hang on till the end . . .

My tiredness has vanished, buoyed by the result, and we go out to eat, finding a much livelier place tonight, a kind of *Biergarten* on a terrace. We order large beers and fish from the outside barbecue and plan our final day of research here. I suddenly wonder why we haven't gone to the local paper. Surely they would know if this issue of Saurer and the *gaswagen* had ever been deemed newsworthy in the town? J. thinks it could be useful; we'll start there tomorrow morning.

We also examine the Saurer report we picked up earlier in the day, titled *What You Always Wanted to Know About Saurer: Facts, Figures and Analysis*. It's grey, red and white, innovatively designed, inside there's an A to Z consisting of all aspects of the company.

Starting with 'Acetate' ('Acetate fibers are man-made and obtained from cellulose acetate soluble in acetone. Characteristics: good temperature equalisation, silky handle, very good dimensional stability, fast drying properties, Application: furnishing fabrics') and ending at 'Zinser' ('Business unit of SaurerGroup which has its registered office in Ebersbach (D) . . . a leading company in the ring spinning system sector'). As well as sales pie charts, graphs of world market prices for cotton and wool and diagrams of the latest textile machinery, interspersed in these pages are informative historical entries on the 3,000-year history of 'Embroidery' and the 'Silk Road'. However, the other history of Saurer is virtually invisible, with only single paragraphs on 'Trucks' and 'Vehicles', despite the fact, as the text says, 'If one asks in Switzerland what is behind the name of Saurer, one obtains even today in most cases the answer "truck." '

Later we look at the two books that Herr Hess gave us. The first is extremely unusual – A3, beautifully produced and published for Saurer's centenary celebrations in 1953. It includes fifteen water-colours, aquatints and ink drawings of key figures and buildings in the company's history as well as high-minded essays from Dr Hans Sulzer, chairman at the time, and Albert Dubois, then managing director, which talk of the spirit of the company, 'the spirit of integrity and rectitude, the spirit of responsibility accepted by the employer towards his employees and his country':

> The Saurer centenary falls in a period of pronounced economic boom, with all the happy and less happy consequences this entails . . . Goethe has it that nothing is harder to bear than a succession of good days. If these words can be applied to industry, they are nowhere more apposite than in the case of the Swiss export industry.
>
> We shall never slacken in our endeavour to prove ourselves worthy of our company's past and to do our part in maintaining and fostering the worldwide renown of the Saurer name.

Turning the page we find the list of the board of directors and management in 1953, just eight years after the end of the war. We wonder at how the words written for the centenary would have struck these fifteen men.

Dr Hans Sulzer, Chairman
Albert C. Nussbaumer, Vice-Chairman
Albert Dubois, Managing Director
Charles Dechevrens
Professor C. August Hegner
Dr H. C. Paul Jaberg
Fritz Steinfels
Dr Heinrich Wolfer
Victor Diem, *Manager*
Werner Fleury, *Manager*
Adolf Haag, *Manager*
Rene Habs, *Manager*
Eduard Ruprecht, *Manager*
Otto Zipfel, *Manager*
Dr Robert Buchi, *Deputy Manager*

And whether any of them would have known that their 'neutral' Swiss company had supplied trucks to Germany in the war? Were any of these men involved in discussions with their neighbours across the lake about how these trucks might be adapted for their client's special purposes? Did any of them discuss how the 'reduction in the volume of the cargo compartment' might affect the stability of the vehicles? Were any of them in the meeting which explained to the SS that 'structural alterations (to vehicles ordered), with the exception of minor ones, cannot be carried out for the moment'?

The other book, *A Visit to the Saurer Works,* was published at the end of 1945, less than a year after its lorries were being used at Chelmno. The design and content of this book is revealing in two ways: first for what it tells us about Saurer's image and ambition, its sense of itself as a model industry in the vanguard of industrial design reflected in the elegant modernism of the book – fine black and white images of all aspects of the factories and offices of Arbon, showing the entire vehicle manufacturing process, juxtaposed with short texts; and second, to consider that this glossily produced book was being published only months after the end of fighting in the rest of Europe, and so demonstrates the flourishing economic health of Switzerland, which had prospered in the war years. Paper rationing, like the majority of other rationing, continued for many years in most of Europe.

The opening page shows a photograph of a Saurer engine, lit like a piece of sculpture, with these words above it, with their unsettling historical echoes:

DIE QUALITAT UNSERER ARBEIT MACHT UNS STARK UND FREI
('The quality of our work makes us strong and free')

The introduction states:

> SAURER have decided to publish this pamphlet not because there is any particular jubilee to commemorate, but because the up-to-date state of their works is deserving of being brought to the notice of a public beyond the circle of their esteemed clientele . . . Although SAURER vehicles ply the roads of practically every European country – thanks to its numerous licensees – thereby giving the name SAURER widespread diffusion and recognition, the works themselves are known to relatively few.

There follow images which celebrate the idealism of labour. There is a curious beauty and order in these photographs that seems to embody the belief in modernism and innovative industrial design – Saurer as a model factory at the cutting edge, excellent conditions for the workers, a dream of efficiency for the management.

This is the closest vehicle to the one used at Chelmno – a large capacity removal van.

Was this one of the men who were involved with discussions about the necessary 'technical adjustments' to the lorries in service at Chelmno? The need to reduce the lorry by one metre without changing the load capacity. A purely technical issue. And then, this man, or his colleagues, would have begun the problem-solving process. Drawings would be redraughted, scale models made, and then the new model would be created in the assembly sheds half a mile away next to the station. Perhaps one of the Saurer directors would have taken personal charge of this particular project? After all, the client could not have been more important, and if this contract went well, there would undoubtedly be greater orders from the Reich in the future . . .

*

24 August 2000

Our last day in Arbon. We start by visiting the local newspaper's office, as we discussed last night. And for the first time here we meet somebody who talks openly about Saurer and the war years – the bearded editor of *Tagblatt*, Enrico ('call me Rico') Berchtold, a chain-smoking, middle-aged man of wiry energy, the archetypal journalist. He tells us that there are 'two histories' of the town and its relationship to Saurer – one concerned with memory and one concerned with forgetting. The first was the social democrat one; there had been a workers' newspaper, the *Thurghau Arbeiter Zeitung*, which had always been anti-fascist and anti-Saurer, and it had done some research in the 1960s and 70s on Saurer's collaboration with Nazi Germany. Sadly this paper had folded in the 1980s and only an archive was left now. Most of the town is conservative, like his newspaper, Rico adds with an apologetic shrug, and historically it has been totally dependent on Saurer, and they simply pretend that nothing happened. A town that wants to eradicate its past. He bids us farewell, warmly shaking our hands and wishing us the best of luck. He seems like an island of conscience in a sea of organised amnesia.

We walk back to the Saurer head office, animatedly discussing what we've just learnt from Rico. I'm determined to see if we can't get to meet somebody senior in the company – surely there must be somebody not on vacation at the moment? By charming the two secretaries on the reception desk we manage, rather surprisingly, to get hold of the mobile phone number of the corporate communications director for Saurer, a Dr Lisa Kastelmann. A little later I call Dr Kastelmann, and she sounds a little surprised, but after trying to put me onto Herr Mickelson (I explain we've already tried to talk to him, but he's on vacation), she agrees to meet us an hour later. So, pretty wired and excited by now, we get a bite to eat, and plan our approach to this interview – this is going to require some careful thought. We then return to the office next to the castle, and head up the stairs again. This time I notice one significant sign that I hadn't seen before – a door labelled 'Archiv' – an intriguing detail, considering that Herr Mickelson had told me on the phone that there was no company archive.

We're shown into Lisa Kastelmann's office – white walls, black leather sofas, glass tables – inoffensive modern art. Lisa is mid-thirties, smartly dressed, looks slightly wary but trying not to show it: 'Hi, so you guys are from London, yes? I had some great times there. I did my MBA at City. And do you know the guys from St Luke's? They're really cool. We worked on some projects together. Anyway, so what kind of artists are you? For fame or for money?!'

'No, no,' I say, trying desperately to think of something that won't alarm her too much, 'we're environmental artists interested in education, and our organisation is currently doing work on certain companies in our society, especially looking at the relationship between the past and the present – you know, BP, Shell, Ford . . . also vehicle manufactuers, and we've heard a lot about Saurer, so that's what brings us here.'

We start off by discussing the annual report, hoping Lisa will relax more, after all this is her area of expertise. We compliment her on its innovative look and she says, 'Thanks, yes the design's smart, isn't it?' with an engaging bob of the head. We ask several detailed questions about Saurer's vehicle manufacturing period, but also about the company today, their employees, their expanding areas of production, textile machinery, their operations in India.

After fifteen minutes or so she's really warmed to us, she feels safe. And then I steer the conversation onto the history of the company. She provides a printout of the official company summary. I ask her about the 'difficult' history of Saurer. She looks blank. I show her the memorandum discussing modifications to the Saurer lorries. I've never seen somebody freeze in quite this way before. She scans the page. The silence in the office becomes very loud. I say, but you must know about this surely? She says no, she's never seen this before and then she gets defensive, angry. And she starts to question where are we coming from with all of this? What is our agenda? And then she says, rather foolishly, that she doesn't even know if this document is genuine. I tell her the document is quite well known, and features in an important film called *Shoah*. We can provide her with a copy and references as to the derivation of the document if necessary. And I repeat that we're interested in the relationship between the past Saurer and the present Saurer. There isn't any connection, she insists. And then she says that yes, Saurer has a history, of course, but they don't live on this history, they don't live in the past, like some companies, Levi's, Coca-Cola for example. They're not proud or hung up on the past. The employees are much more interested in what's happening right now. And at this moment, as she's speaking, my anger grows, and I think of something John Berger writes in the Historical Afterword to *Pig Earth*: 'The historic role of capitalism itself . . . is to destroy history, to sever any link with the past and orientate all effort and imagination to that which is about to occur.'

I also think of the distance – impossible to imagine – between this comfortable, light office, Lisa Kastelmann, her international friends, her worldly PR training and the barbarism of that memorandum, of the hundreds of thousands who choked to death in the back of perfectly designed Saurer lorries. Perhaps the engineers and the draughtsmen worked in this very building to discuss how the modifications might be made? Maybe Walter Rauff himself had lunch here one day with the Saurer directors. Did they toast the completion of the project with smiles and schnapps?

I tell Lisa that I disagree – how can a company go forward without reckoning with its past? And on a more practical level, has she not followed the work of the Bergier Commission? Have Saurer not been in contact with them already? She doesn't know – but she'll get back to us. And is she aware of the vast settlement that the Swiss banks had just had to pay out to Jewish groups? Over $1.25 billion? Yes, she was aware of this. She starts to take notes. J. asks about Saurer's risks and liabilities fund. How much has the company set aside for such contingencies? She doesn't know, she'll get back to us on this too.

Eventually we leave. She has regained her calm now. We say we'll be happy to share our research, if Saurer is willing to open up their archive. She tells us that she'll have to talk to the directorate about all of this. We get out of the building and out again into the pulsing heat of the August afternoon. J. jokes that he can hear the sound of shredding machines starting. I say they've had fifty years to do this, there's probably not much left, but no doubt there will be some phone calls being made this afternoon to Saurer directors lying on beaches around the Mediterranean or working in their gardens.

The power of a single piece of paper. The power to send a company scurrying. The power to destroy the distance between the past and the present. We shelter from the sun in a shaded café on the little square. A sense of exhilaration, but also now a wave of intense anger and sadness. Nothing remains of those 300,000 people apart from this single piece of paper. But, just for a moment, there is also a sense of representing in some way those men, women and children – or rather re-presenting them – as we've just tried to do in the Saurer offices. Fifty-nine years after they died in blackness and unimaginable panic, they were, momentarily, present again, in that airy office in this little Swiss town. The company being held to account. The past returns when it's buried with such contempt. The people are being spoken of once more. And in that very brief moment, they exist again. The company has to face them.

Before we leave the town we walk back down to the decaying assembly sheds where the Saurer lorries were manufactured. Climbing up to the broken windows, we look in and see that saplings are beginning to grow through the floors. Huge gaps in the roofs are letting the daylight in. There is something strangely hopeful about this reversion to nature. There seems to be a kind of truth here beyond all the offices and all the PR and all the technocracy and all the profiteering of corporations. All will end like this. With the ghosts of thousands of workers, the amnesia of corporations, sinking back into the ground, tree roots cracking the concrete.

Saurer: A Coda – 'The blind spot in the writing of history'

The Bergier Commission, also known as the 'Independent Commission of Experts', was established by Swiss government decree on 13 December 1996 to conduct a historical investigation into 'Switzerland throughout the years of National Socialist dictatorship in Germany and during the Second World War in general'. It was chaired by a distinguished Swiss economic historian, Professor Jean-François Bergier, and its panel of experts included Swiss historians and academics (Jacques Picard, Jakob Tanner, Georg Kreis), Swiss jurists (Daniel Thürer, Joseph Voyame), as well as US-based historians (Harold James, Princeton; Sybil Milton, Holocaust Memorial Museum), an IMF economist (Helen Junz), a Polish writer and diplomat (Wladyslaw Bartoszewski) and an Israeli historian (Saul Friedländer). The commission had a team of over forty researchers, advisors and translators, supported by an equivalent number of administrative staff, and in the five years of its existence it published twenty-five studies and reports, all building towards publication of its final report in 2002. The subjects investigated ranged widely, and you might have thought comprehensively, over the wartime role of Switzerland and its responsibility. Here is a selection of some of the reports published between 1997 and 2001 to give some sense of the scope of the commission:

- *Flight Assets – Looted Assets: The Transfer of Cultural Assets to and through Switzerland from 1933 to 1945, and the Problem of Restitution*
- *Companies and Forced Labour: Swiss Industrial Enterprises in the Third Reich*
- *Swiss Chemical Enterprises in the Third Reich*
- *The Swiss Armaments Industry and Trade in War Material during the National Socialist Period: Corporate Strategies – Market Trends – Political Control*
- *The Swiss Financial Center and Swiss Banks during the Nazi Period: The Major Swiss Banks and Germany (1931–1946)*
- *Dormant Accounts in Swiss Banks: Deposits, Accounts, and Safe-Deposit Boxes of Nazi Victims and the Problem of Restitution in the Post-War Period*
- *Switzerland and Gold Transactions in the Second World War*
- *Roma, Sinti, and Jenisch: Swiss Policy Regarding Gypsies in the Nazi Period*

At an early stage it became obvious that the original budget of 5 million Swiss francs was inadequate for the research needed, and in spring 1997 the Swiss government granted an additional 17 million Swiss francs to the project. Five years later, on 22 March 2002, the final report of the Bergier Commission was published in four languages. The report ran to 597 pages, and can now be read online, in its entirety, at www.uek.ch/en/.

In the introduction of the report I came across an intriguingly titled section – 'The blind spot in the writing of history', which perhaps could serve as an apposite epitaph for this particular commission. This section referred to Switzerland's original post-war positioning of itself as a 'victim of developments in world politics', and how this has now substantially changed. But not enough, because even in recent Swiss historiography, the passage continues:

the fate and the point of view of *the victims of the Nazi regime continued to be neglected* [my emphasis]. This has mainly to do with the fact that historical interest and enquiry in Switzerland have concentrated much more on the war and the war economy than on the Holocaust. This paradoxically reproduced an attitude in the public that had been prevalent already at the time: although as of 1942 people in Switzerland were able to obtain information about the mass crimes being committed in the territories under the Third Reich's control.

My hopes were momentarily raised that this report would finally deal fully with the involvement and collusion of Swiss corporations in the Holocaust. Perhaps then you can imagine my consternation when I turned to the index of this seemingly comprehensive report (costing a total of 22 million Swiss francs, and involving the combined labour of almost a hundred people, over five years), and found only a single reference to Saurer: 'Saurer, Adolph, AG, Arbon – page 202'. I turned to page 202 and what did I find on the subject of Saurer, the Swiss company which manufactured many of the *gaswagen*?

Nothing.

Or, rather, no words. Only a listing of the company's name, included in a table showing it to be the ninth-largest value exporter from Switzerland in the war years (buried between Vereinigte Pignons-Fabriken AG and Grenchen Autophon AG, Solothurn) with exports to Germany between 1940 and 1944 worth 4.4 million Swiss francs. Not a single word about what those exports were.

Table 2: Export permits issued for war material destined for Germany and other countries, 1940–4 (in million Swiss francs)

Company
    Value of exports to Gemany,
    other countries,
    (total)

Vereinigte Pignons-Fabriken AG, Grenchen
13.8
0
13.8

Aktiengesellschaft Adolph Saurer, Arbon
4.4
2.3
6.7

Autophon AG, Solothurn
6.4
0
6.4

How to communicate the meaning of those 4.4 million Swiss francs earned for Saurer's exports to Germany between 1940 and 1944? And all the terror that is hidden in those numbers?

*

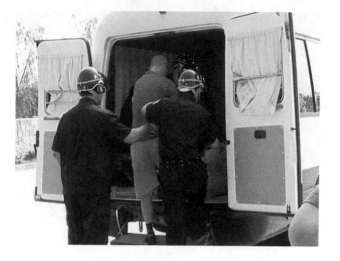

Walter Rauff's concept of a mobile van for killing did not end with the defeat of Nazism in 1945. Over the last fifteen years it has become the preferred method of execution in the People's Republic of China. Amnesty International has highlighted the use of 'execution vans . . . like specially outfitted ambulances to . . . carry out its exceedingly large number of executions. The method of killing in these vans is lethal injection, which has slowly but surely been replacing the firing squad as China's preferred means of execution, and both lethal injection and the vans are believed to faciliatate the widespread practice of harvesting organs of the executed prisoners.'

The *Irish Times* has reported that Jinguan Auto in Chongquing – a manufacturer of ambulances, police trucks and armour-plated limousines – has spotted a gap in the market, and is now selling execution vans to the Chinese government. Jinguan Auto's spokesman said 'each van was a refitted 17-seat passenger minibus, about seven metres long . . . the criminal is tied hand and foot to a stretcher, and a cocktail of lethal toxins is injected. There is a video monitoring system to ensure the execution complies with state rules.' The spokesman added, 'We have not sold our execution (vans) to foreign countries yet. But if they need one, they could contact our company directly.'

7

Interlude in Which We Meet a Figure We Will Be Returning to . . .
The Architect in London; First Trip

Falling through the cracks of history, the details that would tell us so much. The thirty-one-year-old man flying to London, his first time in Britain, another commission from the government in Berlin. Looking out of the window, and seeing, beneath the propellers, the fields of Kent almost ready for harvest, knots of woodland, clustered towns. Flying lower now, his architect's eyes noticing every detail of the church spires and even how the roof constructions differ from what he's known in Germany. July 1936. He sits back into his seat as the plane begins its descent, thinks back over the last four years, which have seemed unreal. Just four summers ago, his career drifting, almost no work, he and Margret about to leave for a months' canoeing in the East Prussian lakes. All packed and ready to go, the canoes already at the railway station. Then the phone call from Karl Hanke. The invitation to do the Gau Berlin HQ in Voss-strasse, but so rushed, weeks only to complete the refurbishment. Working eighteen-hour days, getting it finished on time, on budget. A sense of satisfaction but no more than that. Yet, in retrospect, that was the turning point . . . The following year, a week after the March elections, being invited to Berlin again by Hanke, again the

118

urgency in his voice. So driving through the night from Mannheim with Margret. The next day, meeting Hanke, being told that Goebbels wanted him to convert his new ministry building on Wilhelmsplatz. Within a few minutes, meeting Goebbels and being driven to the old Leopold Palace, walking through those rooms with him, as if in a dream. 'Light, that's what's needed here! Light and clear lines – you can get rid of all the stucco, all the heaviness . . .'. Again, working through the night, again finished within weeks.

The embassy car waiting as Albert steps down from the plane, and soon they're heading for Carlton House Terrace, London, only known from newsreels and photographs until now; he looks intently as the car sweeps along streets lined by plane trees, overtaking trams and the famous red buses. He asks the driver what the imposing buildings on the left are. Ah yes, of course – the Museum of Victoria and Albert, and there the Museum of Natural History. Large national flags decking the front – ah, the pure brilliance of flags! He smiles, remembering the famous Tempelhof Rally of May 1933, and all the fuss that had been made of him after that. But the idea was so simple! Just the platform, those three, huge flags behind Hitler and some clever lighting. The extraordinary reaction that followed – apart from his mentor Heinrich Tessenow, who, Albert flinches at the memory, thought it was 'showy, that's all'. Then being asked to design for the even bigger rally at Nuremberg. Completing the initial drawings and then being taken to Hitler's private apartment on Prinzregentstrasse in Munich for him to approve the designs. The first time he'd ever met the Führer. Hands shaking as he put the drawings down on the table. No eye contact. The pistol on the table. The curt 'Agreed', and then being ushered out. All over in a few minutes. The moments that change the course of a life, many lives . . . Now sweeping through Hyde Park Corner and along Piccadilly, Albert's mind replays the past.

The next promotion – being appointed to work as Paul Troost's liaison man in Berlin on the rebuilding of the Reich Chancellery – the most prestigious architectural project in Germany. Showing Hitler round the site on some days, but he was only one of several architects there, and very much the junior party. So the astonishment that day as Hitler turns to him and says: 'Come up and have lunch.' The next moments more like a dream. Protesting that his suit had got plaster on the sleeve, Hitler waving his concern away, 'We'll fix that upstairs.' Being taken into his private suite and given Hitler's own dark blue jacket, with the unique, golden party badge. Floating on air, walking into the dining room behind the most powerful man in the world, wearing his jacket. Goebbels appalled, asking what on earth he was up to. Hitler interceding with a smile, 'He's wearing my jacket.' And then sitting down next to this man admired more than any other in Germany, who had chosen him, the unknown young architect, as his sole conversational partner that day! The beginning of a kind of love . . . And only a year before, feeling like a nobody, barely employed in a provincial town, riddled with doubts about the career he'd chosen, diffident, still under the thumb of his father.

And now here he is – the famous young architect Speer, pulling up at the pillared London embassy in a limousine, being greeted by Ambassador Ribbentrop and his wife. Here to oversee the extension and refurbishment of the building in time for the coronation of the new King George VI. Germany starting an intensive diplomatic push with Britain, and the embassy must play its role, must impress.

During those summer days in London, Albert has more contact with Ribbentrop's wife than the ambassador, who's in a foul mood much of the time, furious with Foreign Minister Neurath back in Berlin interfering with what he sees as his role – diplomatic responsibilities in Britain. The architect's work is less than onerous, in part because Ribbentrop's wife already has employed an interior designer from Munich. Albert designs the central staircase, makes some other drawings to improve the windows, but he is more concerned at this time with messages coming from Berlin that Hitler is threatening to cancel the opening of the Olympic Games because of his anger over the 'modernist' design of part of the stadium – too much glass and concrete. There are daily phone calls, he makes suggestions about removing the glass and facing the concrete with stone; this could be done before the Olympics are due to open, as long as Hitler and the original architect approve the changes. A sense of the world now turning its eyes to Germany in a few weeks' time. A chance to demonstrate a vital country moving forwards. Albert feeling himself absolutely at one with the zeitgeist, and sensing that his star is still ascending . . .

PART THREE

The Violence of a Corporation

8

'Lord take my soul, but the struggle continues'

24 November 2006

J. and I are in a black cab speeding over Tower Bridge and through the City of London, heading for Clerkenwell, and the hotel where we're going to collect the renowned activist and writer Professor Angela Davis, who is on her first visit to London for many years to support our launch of the Living Memorial to Ken Saro-Wiwa and the Ogoni Eight at City Hall tonight. These are the kind of days we dreamed of when we started Platform, so we're high on adrenaline, hoping to make this evening as powerful as possible. It's the culmination to three years of work. Three years to make this happen, to move from just a thought in my head to material reality. But it's been much longer since we first heard about what was happening in the Niger Delta. The early 1990s, more than ten years now. When we first heard the name Ken Saro-Wiwa spoken, and first saw those images we couldn't believe – of vast plumes of fire burning continuously, in a land far away. And this being done by Shell, a partly British company. Shamelessly, at the end of the twentieth century.

*

What was it about this particular combination of environmental degradation and human rights abuses that so outraged us? To live as any kind of activist in our world, no – that's too specific, to live as any kind of half-aware human being in our world, is to live with knowledge of ongoing atrocities, torture, epidemics, poverty, starvation, extreme inequality, despoliation, pollution, and catastrophic, human-made ecocide. But this knowledge can lead to a kind of overload of information about suffering, which in turn may create what we could call 'digital paralysis' – where even to process the facts, let alone respond to them, is beyond the capacity of most people.

(At one point, perhaps the late fifteenth century, it may have been possible for an extremely long-lived, curious – and wealthy – individual to read everything that existed in print in their language. A gloriously mad, Borgesian thought. Closer to our own time, I heard Brian Eno on the BBC World Service a few years ago, saying that when he was a teenager in the 1960s, it would still have been theoretically possible to listen to every single recording ever made on vinyl in a particular musical genre, such as New Orleans jazz or Scottish folk ballads. Because the relatively expensive recording technologies meant that there were limits. Every single recording! I remember gasping with a kind of shocked delight hearing this. Today, of course, with the explosion in digital technology and distribution, there are limitless multitudes of music available, and though the liberation implicit in an infinity of music or books or anything seems alluring at first, I wonder if it isn't a little like the experience of looking at a summer night sky of stars in the mountains, far from any light pollution. You start staring in amazement, moving from one constellation to the next, astonished at the clarity of the Milky Way, at myriads of stars never seen before, and, after a while, a celestial dizziness descends, and soon an existential drunkenness takes over; all seems utterly pointless, what meaning does anything we do down here really have? All our loving and grieving and passion, all our work and striving and pain is, from the perspective of even the smallest, closest star, quite absurd. Less than absurd, simply of no consequence. Zero. To deal with this challenge of infinity we filter all the time. Many of us now spend most of our days staring at

computer screens. Or our mobiles. Or both. An enormous amount of mental energy is taken up with simply deciding what information to take in. We have all become filterers. This filtering now extends into all parts of our lives. We filter the news we receive, the entertainment we watch. We even filter our friends and families now. It's becoming a rare phenomenon to actually talk to a person on the phone. Why bother talking, when messaging or texting takes a fraction of the time? And this avoids the potential dangers of emotional involvement as well. Lives, like everything else, are now abbreviated, filtered.)

But, to return to Nigeria and Ken Saro-Wiwa – we were receiving the first news about Shell and the Ogoni in 1993 *before* the web really existed. That meant we actually had to read articles in the newspapers, and watch documentaries on Channel 4 and BBC2. We had to seek out the information ourselves, not simply type something into a search engine, and, as a result, what we learnt had a different quality to it. We would pass articles to each other, we would track down recordings of documentaries and then share them.

We found out that Nigeria had the seventh-biggest oil reserves in the world, that 95 per cent of its GDP came from oil, and yet the average income for the people living there was less than a dollar a day. We learned more about the history of the country – how in the 1670s the Royal African Company (backed by the English navy) began its trade in human slaves along the coast of what is now Nigeria. Vast profits from what has been called the 'Black Holocaust', which eventually claimed almost 40 million lives, returned to London, establishing the city as the financial and banking centre of the world. In the late nineteenth century, after the abolition of the slave trade, the Royal Niger Company (with its own substantial private army) moved into the lucrative palm oil market, in the process conquering territory far inland. In 1899 the British government revoked their charter, and established 'protectorates' (Niger Coast, Northern Nigeria and Lagos – which were later consolidated into 'Nigeria' by the British government in January 1914) in the territories which the Royal Niger Company had invaded. Lord Salisbury commended the founding directors for their work as 'pioneers of English civilisation in the dark places of the earth'.

As a natural extension to this unnatural relationship, British oil companies (the forerunners of today's Shell and BP) actively began prospecting for oil in Nigeria in the 1930s and 40s. The first major discovery came in 1956 at Oloibiri in Ijawland, and the first shipment of the high-quality oil, 'Bonny Light', left Port Harcourt in February 1958. Between then and today it is estimated that the Anglo-Dutch company Shell, the 'largest and most important oil company operating in the Niger Delta'*, has derived over £350 billion in income from Nigerian oil, while the average Nigerian annual earnings are around one billionth of that – £250 per year. We also found out that other oil companies had interests there – Chevron (American), Agip (Italian), Total (French) – and that the area where the majority of the oil reserves were – the Niger Delta, where the River Niger reaches the Gulf of Guinea on the west coast of Africa – was approximately 450 km long and reaching around 150 km inland. We learnt more about the process of oil extraction and the staggering levels of pollution. We saw photographs like this:

---

* Cited in Amnesty's 2017 report *A Criminal Enterprise? Shell's Involvement in Human Rights Violations in Nigeria in the 1990s*, page 18.

And this:

It was a process called 'gas flaring'. It was, we learnt, cheaper for the oil companies to release the gas (the by-product of drilling for oil) into the air – to burn it off like this, than to capture the gas or inject it back into the rock. This process was banned in most of the world, but apparently the oil companies thought it was acceptable to do it in this part of Africa. Even in the middle of villages and settlements. Twenty-four hours a day, 365 days a year, turning even the darkness to light. The effect of this was that the land immediately around effectively becomes 'carbonised' – burnt to a deep level and incapable of growing anything. The rate of respiratory illnesses in villages where flaring happened, not surprisingly, increased dramatically. Oil pipelines criss-crossed much of the Delta and spills and explosions were frequent. Hundreds have died from such accidents since oil was first exported. The resulting pollution has found its way into many of the waterways and mangrove swamps, and toxified what had once been rich fishing grounds.[*]

---

[*] A two-year study by the United Nations Environment Programme (*Environmental Assessment of Ogoniland*, published in 2011) found that 'oil contamination in Ogoniland is widespread and severely impacting many components of the environment', creating conditions so polluted, 'environmental restoration . . . may take 25 to 30 years' and cost up to $1 billion. It also found that many of the people living in the Niger Delta had been exposed to severe health risks for decades as a result of hydrocarbon contamination.

Why do Shell and other oil companies believe such behaviour is permissible? Whatever the reason, or reasons, the result has been a racism of thinking that has had lethal consequences for more than sixty years now. Nigerian governments (for much of this time a series of military juntas) must also bear their share of responsibility but we should remember that the international oil companies had been operating with impunity in Nigeria for thirty years before the country had its own government.

*

I never met Ken Saro-Wiwa, but his activism made an enormous impression on me and many thousands around the world. I feel I've been travelling with him, in some way, for the last twenty-five years. His writing and his interviews dance with a brilliant rage. His use of satire and irony is devastating but never loses touch with his humanity. As with so many of the most effective activists, he was never the dour puritan, but rather a man with enormous appetites for life. A wicked and irreverent laugh, a love of fine brandy and smoking, an intense curiosity about others. Full of inconsistencies? Maybe so. Like virtually all of us. He was an extremely successful businessman before he started writing, yet he sometimes described

himself as 'poor'; he railed against the inequities of British colonialism yet sent his children to English public schools. But, in the totality of his life, these are not important. What was extraordinary was
his ability to articulate the anger of his people, the Ogoni – a tribal
group of around 400,000 people in one of the areas of the Delta most
devastated by oil. Saro-Wiwa was able to bring to reality the spirit
that Brecht extols in his remarkable poem 'In Praise Of Doubt':

> But the most beautiful of all doubts
> Is when the downtrodden and despondent raise their heads
>   and
> Stop believing in the strength
> Of their oppressors.

Ken Saro-Wiwa helped the Ogoni people to realise the power that
they possessed. Together, over time, they simply stopped believing
in the oil companies' strength, and in the Nigerian government's
supremacy. This process took many years: in the late 1980s, Ken
gave up his very successful writing career (he wrote the novel *Sozaboy*, and *Basi & Company* – the most popular TV drama in Nigeria –
amongst many other works), and began to campaign strongly for
an end to the appalling treatment of the Ogoni, and what he saw
as their 'slow genocide' at the hands of the oil companies. In 1990
he established, together with a young lawyer, Ledum Mittee, and
other community leaders in Ogoni an organisation called MOSOP
(Movement for the Survival of the Ogoni People). In the same year
they published a small manifesto which had an enormous impact
across Nigeria – *The Ogoni Bill of Rights*. This spelt out the injustice that the Ogoni had experienced for the preceding thirty years
and their demands for radical reform and increased rights from the
Nigerian government, and an end to the 'complete degradation of
the Ogoni environment' by Shell and the other oil corporations.

He soon realised that to achieve change in his part of Nigeria, in
an increasingly globalised world, he needed to activate the engagement and concern of the international community. He began to get
the UN involved, he travelled to Geneva and New York and spoke

passionately to any group that would listen, often showing the footage of the devastation in Ogoni that he'd filmed himself. Audiences were stunned at first, then outraged that such things could be going on in the 1990s, and that Western oil companies were colluding so grotesquely in this. Ken, above all, was brilliant at articulating the responsibility of everyone in the West; having spent a lot of time in Europe he understood the power of saying to Westerners, 'This is being done in your name! Do you want this on your conscience?':

You have an atmosphere that has been poisoned by hydrocarbon vapour, carbon monoxide and carbon dioxide, and this flaring of gas has gone on 24 hours a day, 7 days a week, morning, noon and night, in sunshine and in rain, for 33 years! Now, the result of all this is you have acid rain all the time . . . this is an area of very heavy rainfall and so the acid rain gets back into the soil, and what used to be the breadbasket of the delta has now become totally infertile . . . Shell does not care, actually its habits are racist because they know what [they should] do. Why is it that it's only in Ogoni, in Nigeria, that they've flared gas for 33 years, sometimes in the middle of villages? Why is it that they do not care at all? . . . [that] Shell is able to get away with murder? They have destroyed the Ogoni people, they have destroyed other ethnic minorities everywhere they prospect for oil.

I'm trying to mobilise opinion, particularly in the West, among the shareholders of Shell, among the governments, the people of Europe, of Britain, of Germany, of France, of Italy, all those whose companies prospect for oil in Nigeria, [to get them] to realise that they are ruining the environment and dehumanising the people. So my mission has been to inform the West of the truth of what is happening in Nigeria, which has been hidden from them. I believe if the people knew what has been happening they'd do something about it, and stop this robbery and murder that is going on in broad daylight at the end of the 20th century. All the oil which is produced in Nigeria is bought by America, and the West and Japan. If they insisted – 'look we are not going to buy this oil unless you ensure that the environment is protected . . . that the people who live on oil-bearing land are not being dehumanised by the search for oil', then it would be a different story altogether. The Nigerian government couldn't continue to do what it is doing now. So the West has a big responsibility. The profits from oil come to Britain . . . it is . . . western credit that is keeping Nigeria alive . . . So [the West] has a moral responsibility to intervene in the situation.

In June 1993 he met Anita and Gordon Roddick, founders of the Body Shop and also, more significantly, activists with a global reach. Together they strategised campaigns, and dramatically improved the media profile of the campaign. Soon further documentaries were being made, more articles written in newspapers throughout the Western world; the Nigerian government and the oil companies began to feel real pressure for the first time. The skeletons were leaping out of the cupboards and beginning to dance. On 4 January 1993, the newly proclaimed 'Ogoni Day', 300,000 people came out onto the streets in an incredible demonstration of unity. Soon afterwards, Shell bowed to the inevitable and ceased all oil operations in the Ogoni areas – a staggering achievement for a people who'd always been taught they were a powerless minority in their own land. And all done using Gandhian principles of non-violent resistance, with women at the forefront of the fight. As with all such struggles, they cannot only be judged by the outcome – the political result – the process of such resistance involves the radicalisation of a whole community, people understanding that education is central to power, and that fighting for equality involves not just challenging the power of authorities but changing the power dynamics among those fighting too.

The implications for the oil companies and the Nigerian government of the Ogoni campaign were serious. If Saro-Wiwa's success was replicated in other regions of the Delta it would threaten the entire oil industry in Nigeria. Not just the lucrative profits for Shell, Chevron and the rest that would be lost, but the very survival of the military government, massively dependent on oil revenues, would be threatened. And Ken, ambitious as he was, and buoyed by the incredible success of getting Shell out of Ogoni, was now wanting to go further. Throughout 1993 the campaign grew, and the Nigerian military government began to panic. What could be done to stop the Ogoni campaign and get Shell back operating there?

In April the Nigerian State Security Service arrests Saro-Wiwa for the first time, but are forced to release him without charge a day later. In May, Shell executives meet government security officials to develop their shared understanding about the Ogoni situation. In June 1993 Saro-Wiwa is arrested again, and this time is imprisoned for a month on absurd allegations of causing electoral 'disturbances'. He used this time to write his book, *A Month and a Day*, which ends on this uncompromising note:

> I had been detained for a month and a day, during which I had witnessed the efficency of evil. In a country where virtu-ally nothing worked, the security services, armed with all the gadgets of modern invention, made sure that all orders were carried out with military precision. And the men were mar-vellously faithful to their instructions.

Finally he relates that he is told

> that on 15 July [1993] one hundred and thirty-two Ogoni men, women and children, returning from their abode in the Cameroons, had been waylaid on the Andoni River by an armed gang and cruelly murdered, leaving but two women to make a report. The genocide of the Ogoni had taken on a new dimension. The manner of it I will narrate in my next book, if I live to tell the tale.

In late 1993, following another coup, General Abacha seizes power and becomes President of Nigeria, and the crisis esca-lates further. Ever the brutal army bully, Abacha demands that more decisive action be taken against Saro-Wiwa and the leader-ship of MOSOP by whatever means necessary. On 30 April 1994, according to internal company documents, Shell Nigeria's new chairman Brian Anderson meets Abacha for the first time and stresses Shell's concern about 'the problem of the Ogonis and Ken Saro-Wiwa' – that they haven't been able to operate in Ogoniland for a year. Anderson leaves the meeting with the feeling that Abacha 'will intervene with either the military or the police'. Anderson later stated that he had made it clear to Abacha that he had asked Shell 'not to involve either body (military or police) during the recent problems for fear of escalation', as cited in Amnesty's 2017 report, *A Criminal Enterprise? Shell's Involvement in Human Rights Violations in Nigeria in the 1990s.*

But Abacha now turns to violent repression, sending the Rivers State Internal Security Task Force (ISTF), under the sociopathic Major Paul Okuntimo, into Ogoni. The raids by this mobile force create a wave of terror – Okuntimo's approach was to act by night, surround a town or village with his soldiers, then 'the machine gun with five hundred rounds will open up and then we are throwing grenades . . . and what do you think the people are going to do? We have already put roadblocks on the main road . . . so the option we made was that we should drive all these boys, all these people into the bush'. Witnesses later described how

> Troops entered towns and villages shooting at random, as villagers fled to the surrounding bush. Soldiers and mobile police stormed houses, breaking down doors and windows with their boots, the butts of their guns, and machetes. Villagers who crossed their path, including children and the elderly, were severely beaten, forced to pay 'settlement fees', and sometimes shot. Many women were raped.

An Amnesty International report from June 1994 estimates that thirty villages were attacked by ISTF at this time and 'more than 50 members of the Ogoni ethnic group are reported to have been extra-judicially executed'. By July, the Dutch ambassador told Brian Anderson that the army had killed some 800 Ogonis. According to the same report, Okuntimo is completely unrepentant, and stresses to the military authorities that 'Shell operations [are] still impossible unless ruthless military operations are undertaken.'

According to witness evidence given in US proceedings against Shell brought by Ken Saro-Wiwa's family in New York (settled by Shell in 2009 before trial), these operations were partly subsidised by Shell, paying what they call 'field allowances' for helping with supposed 'security' for their installations*. One of these payments was described as a 'show of gratitude and motivation for a sustained favourable disposition towards [Shell] in future assignments.'† Shell has denied providing logistical support and money to the Nigerian security forces but this is undermined by Okuntimo – by now promoted to lieutenant-colonel in recognition of his work with the ISTF – telling journalists quite openly in late 1995 (according to a report by *The Sunday Times*, 17 December 1995) that 'Shell contributed to the logistics through financial support. To do this, we needed resources and Shell provided these.' Speaking seventeen years later, the retired Okuntimo retracted this part of his original statement, while at the same time confirming that Shell had been secretly in touch with him throughout the mid-1990s, and encouraged him to take action in Ogoniland. Shell has said that there is a lack of any credible evidence in support of these allegations. It has also said that it spoke out frequently against violence and publicly condemned its use at the time.

But if Abacha's intention, through these vicious interventions by the ISTF, is to repress the opposition in Ogoniland, then his actions have precisely the opposite effect. More and more protest is created throughout the Delta, and, as news of the appalling rapes and killings emerges, there's a growing outcry internationally. On 21 May, Saro-Wiwa is on his way to address a rally in Ogoni, but is turned back at

---

* For a description of how Shell is alleged to have paid Okuntimo directly, in cash, see the evidence of Mr Ejiogu, in the *Independent*, 5 December 2010: 'Ken Saro-Wiwa was framed, secret evidence shows'.
† Quotation from Amnesty's 2017 report *A Criminal Enterprise?*, page 10.

a military checkpoint miles before his destination, and has to return home. The rally goes ahead without him, but culminates in a riot, and in the resulting chaos, four Ogoni elders, thought to be sympathetic to the military government, are killed. The Abacha regime sees an opportunity to frame Saro-Wiwa for 'incitement to murder' – even though he'd been miles away from the incident, travelling in the opposite direction – and Saro-Wiwa and fifteen Ogoni colleagues are arrested. During the same period Brian Anderson and other Shell executives again meet General Abacha and government officials.

Saro-Wiwa and his colleagues are imprisoned, without access to lawyers for nine months, and then put on trial, at a specially convened tribunal, in 1995. The trial is a farce, with clear manipulation of the court by the military government, including widespread bribery of the so-called 'witnesses' and no right of appeal. The few international legal observers allowed access agree that it is 'a kangaroo court' – the British lawyer Michael Birnbaum concluding that the trial is 'fundamentally flawed and unfair.'* On 2 November 1995 the inevitable verdicts are announced – Saro-Wiwa and eight of his Ogoni colleagues are sentenced to death.

At any time during the period between Saro-Wiwa's arrest in May 1994 and the tribunal verdict in November 1995, senior figures in Shell could have intervened to stop what was clearly a grotesque injustice. They could have intervened in many different ways – with the Nigerian government, with Abacha directly, through their excellent contacts at the oil ministry, through British diplomatic channels or by making public statements of concern. Given the vast power that oil companies have always had in Nigeria, it is highly probable that such intervention would have been effective. But their lack of action was lethal. Shell's chief executive at the time, Mark Moody-Stuart, repeatedly stated, as did the company as a whole, that intervention by Shell would not have been appropriate: 'the company does not get involved in politics' and it would be 'dangerous and wrong'. Yet, what had they been doing in

---

* See chapter notes for Birnbaum's further thoughts on the tribunal.

Nigeria – if not intervening dramatically in the country – for the previous fifty years? What exactly were Brian Anderson and his colleagues in Shell doing in those meetings with General Abacha and Nigerian government representatives on 5 August 1994, 16 March 1995 and 22 July 1995 – if not 'intervening'? The records of these meetings should be made public. It would be instructive to know exactly what was said at these meetings (particularly in regard to Saro-Wiwa's case) – and also to know which other senior figures in Shell were present at those meetings with Abacha. Some presumably who may have gone on to 'higher things' in their careers – both in the oil industry and in the world of politics.

Appeals did come, from the Pope and Nelson Mandela and some prominent Commonwealth leaders. Mandela made one of the most tragic mistakes of his life (as he later admitted), calling for 'quiet diplomacy' with Nigeria, the old African National Congress ally. But the efforts that did come, came too late, and were to no avail. On the morning of 10 November 1995, in Port Harcourt prison, Ken and eight of his colleagues were hanged. Ken was the first, crying out as he was led to the gallows, 'You can only kill the messengers, you cannot kill the message! You can only kill the messengers, you cannot kill the message! . . .' The first attempt did not work due to a mechanical problem with the gallows. Ken was taken down from the gallows while the executioners attempted to remedy the fault. A second time the noose was placed round his neck, and a second time the lever failed to work. Ken was marched out again. More repairs were done and eventually the lever mechanism began to work. Then the executioners decided to make him watch all of his friends die. First of all John Kpunien, the youth leader of MOSOP, then Dr Barinem Kiobel, the former commissioner of Rivers State, then, one by one, the remaining six men. And then they hanged Ken. His final words were: 'Lord take my soul, but the struggle continues.'

*

Five days later, it was announced that Shell and the Nigerian government were jointly launching a $4 billion liquefied natural gas venture in Nigeria. Brian Anderson stated that Shell 'remains firmly committed to the long term future of the country and its people'.

The nine men executed on 10 November 1995:

Baribor Bera

Saturday Dobee

Nordu Eawo

Daniel Gbokoo

Barinem Kiobel

John Kpuinen

Paul Levula

Felix Nuate

Ken Saro-Wiwa

J. and I were in Glasgow when we heard the news. Ironically, we had been speaking at a conference celebrating the legacy of Joseph Beuys – how art could play a vital role in social change. We were staying with a Basque friend of mine in his shared flat. J. had gone out to get milk. I still remember exactly where I was sitting, in the little kitchen at the table, when J. reappeared with a newspaper, and held out the front page, 'They did it. The fuckers did it.'

NIGERIA DEFIES WORLD WITH HANGING OF SARO-WIWA

I was uncomprehending. Like many others I'd thought the pressure being put on Nigeria would mean that they couldn't carry out the sentences. Something in me burned at that moment, like a fuse blowing. A deep and vivid sense of unfinished business, of rage. I knew that the spotlight would soon move away from Nigeria and Ogoni – with the media's habitually short memory span – but we would not. We would do exactly the opposite. We would never let this disgrace be forgotten. Nor the fact that none of this would have happened without the barbaric behaviour of an Anglo-Dutch oil company, over more than fifty years.

There was the predictable global outcry afterwards. Ken Wiwa (Saro-Wiwa's son) felt that Shell had been jointly responsible for the killing of his father – 'they didn't tie the noose around my father's neck, but without Shell's intervention and encouraging of the military government it would never have happened[*].' Even mild-mannered John Major managed to rise a little to the occasion and said that what Abacha had done amounted to nothing less than 'judicial murder'. Mandela, stung by his own catastrophic mis-reading of Abacha, succeeded in getting Nigeria suspended from the Commonwealth. Shell and the other oil companies shed some crocodile tears in public, while no doubt being mightily relieved that this particularly effective activist had been silenced.

---

[*] Quotation taken from *The Next Gulf* by Andrew Rowell, James Marriott and Lorne Stockman.

But these murders proved to be an astonishing watershed, as tens of thousands more activists joined campaigns against environmental devastation. In Platform we began our initiative, '90% CRUDE', in 1996, to investigate the culture, the psychology and the impacts of the oil industry worldwide. We started to take Ken's message all over the world: we organised conferences, created performances and published books and newspapers – all focussing on the nature of oil corporations and their responsibility, looking in detail at their global environmental and human rights impacts.

Returning from a conference in Pittsburgh in November 2003, I had an idea. Platform had given the keynote presentation on 'Art and Social Change' to a packed lecture theatre at Carnegie-Mellon University, and we ended, as we often did, with the filmed interview of Ken (the last he ever gave), speaking directly about the potential of art, at its most powerful:

> What is of interest to me is that my art should be able to alter the lives of a large number of people, of a whole community, of an entire country, so that my literature has to be completely different, the stories I tell must have a different sort of purpose from the artist in the Western world. And it's not now an ego trip, it is serious, it is politics, it is economics, it's everything, and art in that instance becomes so meaningful, both to the artist and to the consumers of that art.

On the plane back to London I'd been rereading his book *A Month and a Day* and, very tired and jet-lagged on the Piccadilly Line on the way home, I came upon this particular passage: 'this is why the Ogoni environment must matter more to me than to Shell International ensconced in its ornate offices on the banks of the Thames in London. But I cannot allow the company its smugness because its London comfort spells death to my Ogoni children and compatriots.'

It suddenly seemed obvious! Why not create a memorial to the Ogoni Nine in London, preferably outside the Shell Centre, unveiled in time for the tenth anniversary of the murders? I canvassed the idea with friends and colleagues, among them Anita and Gordon Roddick, and they put us in touch with Ken Wiwa and soon we were organising the first meeting under the banner 'The Struggle of Humanity Against Power is the Struggle of Memory Against Forgetting' (adapted from Milan Kundera's famous quotation), at Platform's workspace, next to the Thames near Tower Bridge. We were delighted by the response – many organisations sent representatives and we secured the involvement of directors at Greenpeace, Amnesty, Friends of the Earth and PEN.

We fundraised for the project, and, with the help of the curator David A. Bailey, we began to conceptualise the process we wanted for our memorial, and then, working with Platform colleagues Lorne Stockman and Jane Trowell, publicity materials for the campaign were designed – and the 'Remember Saro-Wiwa' campaign was up and running. We were determined the project would not be a conventional public art commission, but rather a 'living memorial' which would refocus attention on the ongoing environmental devastation caused by oil extraction in the Niger Delta.

144

A year later, in March 2005, we had the official launch, at a packed City Hall, hosted by the Mayor of London, Ken Livingstone, Ken Wiwa and Anita Roddick, where we called for submissions for 'a Living Memorial to Ken Saro-Wiwa and the Ogoni Eight'. Linton Kwesi Johnson, Kadija Sesay and Helon Habila read and performed their work, and William Boyd described his shock on hearing of the executions, and read one of the last letters he'd ever received from Ken in prison:

> I am bitter and I am dreadfully sad. Ken Saro-Wiwa, the bravest man I have known, is no more. From time to time, Ken managed to smuggle a letter out of prison. One of the last letters I received ended in this way: 'I'm in good spirits . . . There's no doubt that my idea will succeed in time, but I'll have to bear the pain of the moment . . . the most important thing for me is that I've used my talents as a writer to enable the Ogoni people to confront their tormentors . . . And it makes me feel good! I'm mentally prepared for the worst, but hopeful for the best. I think I have the moral victory.'
>
> You have, Ken. Rest in peace.

*

24 November 2006

In the taxi we remember the first articles we ever read about what had been happening in Ogoni, by Andy Rowell and John Vidal, seeing those first pictures thirteen years before, hearing the name 'Ken Saro-Wiwa' for the first time. And all that has come afterwards . . . the vow we made that morning in Glasgow. A long way travelled since. Clerkenwell Green. We've arrived. The taxi pulls up at the hotel, we take a deep breath. We ask the taxi to wait and head inside. I hear myself say to the receptionist: 'We're here to collect Angela Davis', and a minute or so later, the lift doors open, and walking towards us is a smiling woman in her sixties, that instantly recognisable face and hair, iconic of those years of revolutionary change – the Black Power movement of the early 1970s. She introduces us to her colleague and fellow academic Gina Dent, and the four of us then head back towards Tower Bridge in the taxi. She apologises for still being a little jet-lagged, wants to know more about the shape of the event tonight, quizzes us on 'Mayor Livingstone' and the current state of the left in Britain. Soon we're back at Tower Bridge and the Platform offices, and we're introducing Angela and Gina to our colleagues and Maria Saro-Wiwa, Ken's widow, and her son, Ken Wiwa.

I get another text from the mayor's assistant asking us when we will be arriving – at City Hall – the mayor and officials are all waiting outside. Well, it won't hurt for them to wait a little longer. We're walking under Tower Bridge now towards City Hall, I can see the winner of our Living Memorial to the Ogoni Nine, shimmering ahead of us – Sokari Douglas Camp's glorious 'battle bus' glinting silver in the night.

And there they are outside City Hall, Ken Livingstone and his deputy Lee Jasper and other officials waiting in a line, like nervous schoolchildren. I savour this moment, as we approach – politicians, for once in their lives, deferring to activists and artists. I introduce Angela Davis and Ken Wiwa to the mayoral group, flashes of cameras, official pictures taken.

There's an admiring inspection of the memorial, and then we're ushered inside City Hall, and whisked up to the seventh floor –

the mayor's inner sanctum. Assistants look up as we go past, we're guided into a room with a fine view of Tower Bridge below. There's a long table with nibbles laid out and glasses, we've got about half an hour before the event starts, and Ken Livingstone's in his hostly element now: 'Right, what will you all have to drink? Wine? Beer? Whisky? Rum?' Conscious of the event to come, we mostly ask for juices and water; this does not go down well with our mayor: 'God, I dunno what's happened to the left these days! Nobody drinks any more. Talk about the New Puritanism!' Soon he's deep in conversation with Angela about Chavez and Venezuela, J. and I are on the other side of the table talking to Lee Jasper, but I'm still finalising in my head what I want to say this evening.

In a few moments we're being taken down to the chamber. We emerge to a buzz of expectancy. City Hall is packed tonight. Three or four hundred people here. I'm sitting between Angela Davis and Ken Livingstone, there are our huge projections in green, black and white behind us, 'REMEMBER SARO-WIWA'. This campaign has come a long way from that moment on the Piccadilly Line three years ago. A time when the Ogoni struggle had almost been forgotten in our culture. Shell were beginning to breathe more easily, hoping that things had 'moved on' – to use that favourite phrase of corporations and politicians who rely on our short-term memory to get away with murder.

And now I can see Maria Saro-Wiwa smiling at me from the second row. How much I've learnt from her in the last years: the sorrow that she carries with her like a cloak, the permanence of grief, her absolute determination that justice for her people will come one day, that all the deaths will not have been for nothing, the tenderness of her love for her children and grandchildren. I can never forget what she'd told me the year before: that, just after Ken was killed, she gathered the whole family together to talk and to pray. She told them that she'd had a dream, and in this dream Ken had come to her and promised that 'a lion of justice will come to help you all in the future'. And then she thanked us for all that we had done, and all that we were planning to do. At the moments in the campaign when we've had major setbacks I've simply thought of Maria and what she and the family have been through. She has give us an incredible strength and inspiration. And I can guess what this memorial means to her, to the children, Ken, Zina and Noo, and to the wider Ogoni community, both here in London and in the Niger Delta.

Ken Livingstone is now introducing tonight's event and speaking about the formative influence of Angela Davis, and how he remembers as a boy, and a member of the Young Socialists, collecting money in south London for the imprisoned Black Panthers. I'm interested to hear him speak from the heart tonight about Ken Saro-Wiwa, and what his campaign for justice has given to the world. Then Angela Davis is given a rousing reception, and she's soon describing the electrifying impact of Saro-Wiwa's message, and the way it links to so many other struggles for self-determination. Much of what she says concerns the illusion of permanence which those in power try to create, but how shallow this illusion is. She quotes Brecht's comment that 'because things are the way they are, they will not stay the way they are', and then links this to her own experience of growing up in the most segregated city in America – Birmingham, Alabama – and not being able to go to the libraries and the museums as a girl. How her mother told her that change would happen, and it has – though, going back to Birmingham today, she still feels 'like a stranger to the city, because black people weren't allowed in the majority of areas' when she was a child. And, despite all the social advances, there are still huge legacies from centuries of such institutionalised racism and violence, the prison system in America being just one example – over 2.2 million people imprisoned, with a disproportionately high percentage of young African American men incarcerated.

She ends her speech by returning to the significance of Ken Saro-Wiwa in a global context. His exemplary activism and defence of his people are an inspiration, and today is still 'a beacon of light' for all struggling against racism and genocide. His insistence that art should play a crucial role in transforming the lives of people is very important as well because 'artists can encourage us to dream in a radically different way', and this is also the power of the Living Memorial that Sokari Douglas Camp has created.

After Angela's speech, we've organised for a section of Ken Saro-Wiwa's final interview to be projected on a large screen at the back of the chamber. I've seen this film so many times, but it has a visceral power tonight, as if he's speaking to us directly:

> To deny a people their right to self-determination for well on 100 years is to subject them to slavery.
> To take away the resources of a people and refuse to give them anything in return is to subject them to slavery.
> To take away the land of a people who depend solely for land for their survival, and refuse to pay them compensation is to subject them to genocide.
> I accuse the ethnic majority who run Nigeria of practising genocide against the Ogoni people. I accuse the oil companies who prospect for oil in Ogoni of encouraging genocide against the Ogoni people. I accuse Shell and Chevron of practising racism against the Ogoni people, because they do in Ogoni what they do not do in other parts of the world where they prospect for oil.

The film extract finishes. You can sense a collective drawing of breath right across the chamber. Then I can hear Lee Jasper, our chair this evening, introducing me, and I have one of those strange, disembodied experiences where you actually look down on yourself from outside your body. I see myself walking to the lectern, hear myself begin to speak. I start by taking issue with the title of the film extract we've just seen – 'Nigeria's Shame'; for surely the killing of Ken and his eight colleagues was just as much Britain's shame, the Netherlands' shame? For without Shell's devastation of the Niger Delta there would never have needed to be an environmental campaign in the first place. Then I gesture to the cityscape of buildings visible on the other side of the Thames from City Hall, and describe the even greater historic responsibility for providing the financing and organisation of the slave trade – Barclays' European headquarters, the Royal Bank of Scotland, Lloyd's of London. All of these pillars of the British banking and insurance industries, all of these founded upon wealth coming directly from the trade in human beings. And how much of our supposed 'civilisation' has come from centuries of what might be called 'successful violence' perpetrated by Britain? I talk about Ken's inspirational activism, celebrate Sokari's exceptional Living Memorial, and reflect on the role of art, quoting John Berger's magnificent words about how art sometimes has 'judged the judges, pleaded revenge to the innocent and shown to the future what the past has suffered, so that it has never been forgotten . . . the powerful fear art . . . when it does this . . . because it makes sense of what life's brutalities cannot, a sense that . . . is inseparable from a justice at last. Art when it functions like this, becomes a meeting place of the invisible, the irreducible, the enduring, guts and honour.'

There is an electricity in the air now. Ken Wiwa speaks, updating us on the situation in the Niger Delta today, and explaining how the memorial and our campaign are already having an impact – people in Nigeria, and in Ogoni, know that there is international solidarity and their struggle is not forgotten. J. makes his contribution, describing what he calls the 'carbon web' of the oil companies and their tentacular reach into our society, Baroness Lola Young then links the themes of the campaign to broader issues of anti-racism and equality, and at the end, Ben Okri's poem 'For Ken Saro-Wiwa' is read:

That he should be jailed / For loving the land / And tortured / For protecting his people / And crying out / As the ancient town-criers did / At the earth's defilement / Is monstrously unfitting. / And we live in unnatural times. / And we must make it Natural again / With our singing / And our intelligent rage.

There are then animated contributions and questions from people in the chamber, which end in a discussion about political strategy now, political strategies in the past. The South African boycott is mentioned, Lee Jasper asks the speakers for our thoughts on this, and any final ideas. I say that we need the spirit of the anti-apartheid movement, but we need to develop new strategies, new ways of resisting. But what we can take from those years, when some of us in this chamber used to gather on Fridays for the pickets outside the South African Embassy, is that a state that appeared to be immoveable suddenly crumbled. As Angela said this evening, what is perceived as permanent never is. As for a new strategy, what would happen if we got rid of that cliché 'corporate social responsibility' and started to talk instead about the *individual responsibility* of those working in corporations? If we started to hold the individuals within Shell to account? Those men and women who were in power at the time of the executions of Ken and his eight colleagues? What about starting to bring these individuals to justice?

I end by asking people to reflect on what oppressors always try to do – the attempt to silence the voices of truth, and the absurdity of this. They might just as well try to catch the air in their fingers. I tell the story of Osip Mandelstam, the great Russian poet who Stalin sent to the Gulag in Siberia, where he died in 1938 at the age of forty-seven. One of Mandelstam's last poems was not written down, but rather memorised by his fellow prisoners. These four lines are a precise reason why truth can never be silenced. And why Ken Saro-Wiwa, Baribor Bera, Saturday Dobee, Nordu Eawo, Daniel Gbokoo, Barinem Kiobel, John Kpuinen, Paul Levula and Felix Nuate will never be forgotten:

> You took away all the oceans and all the room,
> You gave me my shoe-size in earth with bars around it.
> Where did it get you? Nowhere.
> You left me my lips, and they shape words, even in silence.

Yes, the struggle is certainly continuing tonight – we can sense Ken looking down on us with that wild smile, chuckling away, and also Shell, just along the river, getting nervous that our campaign is beginning to gather strength and allies now . . . The event eventually ends with thunderous appreciation for Ken Saro-Wiwa, for the family, for the Ogoni.

Such evenings do not happen very often. When they do, we should use them like a battery for the times ahead, granaries for the winter to come.

9

From a Desk in Waterloo to a Cell in Port Harcourt

For a long time now an imaginary film has been playing in my head. And with the passing of time, this imaginary film becomes ever more vivid. The two main characters were born barely a year apart, in 1940 and 1941, both into relatively privileged families, the first in Sussex, England, the second in Bori, Nigeria. The first, after many years working in an oil company, rose to become a managing director in 1991; the second began his career as a teacher, later became a businessman, a writer and finally an activist. The film takes us inside their parallel experience of the same day – 10 November 1995:

The first man is in his fifties, tall, craggy, with thick eyebrows that give his face the appearance of a kindly owl. He wakes, as he always does these days, before the alarm can go off. The thick darkness of the Sussex Downs outside. Before dawn a silence that is total, apart from the almost imperceptible breathing of his wife. He gets out of bed gently, feet fishing for his slippers, careful not to wake her. He puts on his dressing gown, opens the bedroom door and makes his way to the bathroom across the landing. Already the day's business whirring through his head, picking up where it left off late last night – how to make sure everyone who matters is on board today? How to isolate the doubters? In all his years with the company these have been the hardest months. Fire fighting, that's what it's felt like. And as soon as he's finished, more smoke, more flames. Media requests coming through, questions which cannot be ignored. Then having to do interviews, and calmly repeat the company line about the important principle of non-intervention in the sovereign affairs of another country.

And seeing the sharp scepticism in the interviewer's eyes, more than the familiar arched eyebrows, more than the usual dance of knowing media performance. Oddly discomforting.

*

Waking to exhaustion. Surprise that sleep had come at all. Snatching at a dream, a fragment of a dream – a face now fading – he couldn't be certain. His son? His dead boy? Calling out to him, but the words were indistinct. And now other noises of nightmarish reality pounding the walls. Heavy doors closing. Harsh metallic echoes. Voices raised. Boots on concrete. Doors opening. Crackle of walkie-talkies. The hardest day may be here. '*And yet you will weep and know why*', this line from a poem learnt long ago in school, returns this morning. Strange the workings of memory. But he can't recall the next line . . . maddening. Shouting from Felix in the next cell. '*Teh! Teh!*' He will need courage for all of them today. He will first need to be their father. He glances at the jagged piece of glass that has served as a mirror these last months. The world sees Saro-Wiwa, the smiling, pipe-smoking leader. He sees Ken looking back, an exhausted man. Fifty-four, but looking older now. So the day has come. Suddenly, and with a sharpness of memory that ambushes him, he's back in the village where he was born, cooking with his grandmother, stealing the corn before it's cooked, she, playfully, rapping his hand with the long wooden spoon. Three, four years old? The breathtaking astonishment of life before we're conscious of it. Wild wanderings with the forests and the rivers and the birds. Sense of all unfolding, all in its inchoate and loveliest frenzy. All before you. His parents' words. Beeson and Mama. All before you.

153

Stop this. Almost out of time now. Even for remembering. The absurdity of this day. A sense of everything seen from a long way away, even himself. Looking down through the other end of the telescope. Small and overwhelmingly tired. From somewhere his brain has recaptured some of the lines from the school poem: '*It is the blight that man was born for . . . you mourn for. And yet you will weep and know why.*' Try to pray. Try to still the mind. But the film in his head plays on, relentlessly, to the end that disables other thoughts. He snatches at the white gown on the chair. Don't let them see any vulnerability now.

*

As this imaginary film plays again in my mind – the last day these two men shared on this planet – I wonder, if they could now break the barriers of time and space, what they might say to each other. Whether they might once have been able to go beyond their male roles as 'leaders', their public selves. Strangely, I can imagine them drinking whisky together, wryly smiling at the way fate brought their lives into conflict, the oil executive and the freedom fighter. But all such speculation is too late now. The imagined film becomes a documentary, the events as seen through witnesses' eyes:

> We were all peeping from the prison windows and every little space we could put our eyes. The place, the gallows, was very close to our block. We saw them coming out of the vehicle and listened in absolute horror as they were screaming, crying and shouting.
> It was an unusual day in Port Harcourt prison. Inmates woke to find they could not step outside as usual by 9 a.m. Their confinement was to drag on till 4.45 p.m. As early as 8 a.m., armed soldiers had effectively taken control of the prison yard, a scenario prison officials and inmates were unfamiliar with. Soon came a green van carrying coffins. Then a Black Maria, guarded by heavily armed soldiers, sped to a stop in front of the adjoining prison block. With their hands chained

to their backs and their legs secured in leg irons, out came Saro-Wiwa, world-renowned writer and minority-rights crusader, Barinem Kiobel, a commissioner in the Rivers State government, and John Kpuinen, youth leader of MOSOP. With them were Saturday Dobee, Paul Levula, Daniel Gbokoo, Baribor Bera, Felix Nuate and Nordu Eawo, relatively unknown youths whose death sentences had been confirmed by Nigeria's Provisional Ruling Council (PRC) despite international outcry and entreaties . . . They looked confused and alarmed, their eyes darting in every direction. They seemed taken by surprise. Though the PRC had confirmed the sentences forty-eight hours earlier, the news may not have reached them. They probably still hoped that pressure from the international community would pull them from the jaws of death.

It was too late. Saro-Wiwa . . . put on a brave face. He wore a locally made adire jumper. There was a diamond-studded watch with the UN logo on his wrist. He asked to be allowed to see his wife. Again it was too late. His guards said so. Saro-Wiwa seemed uncomfortable with the position of his hands, tied to his back. He beckoned a stern-looking warder nearby and asked that the grip of the handcuff be relaxed a bit to reduce the pain. But the warder taunted him instead. 'Relax wetin. Di place where you deh go, e no go pain pass that?' ('Will the gallows you are heading to not be more painful?') He tried to draw the attention of another guard. It was too late. A priest stepped forward to help him say his last prayers.

Then the rest of the Ogoni nine began to cry. Saro-Wiwa scolded them in a loud voice. 'Why are you people crying?' . . . Instantly they stopped. '*OK Teh, OK Teh*' (OK Sir). They were still treating Saro-Wiwa with respect even as they were about to die. Saro-Wiwa was the first to be marched to the gallows.*

*

---

* Testimony of Bariture Lebe and Popgbara Zorzor, of the Ogoni Twenty, interviewed in *Africa Today*, 'To Set the Captives Free', November 1998.

The second episode takes place the following day, 11 December 1995, and involves the man we've already met getting up in Sussex, the group managing director of Shell, coming into work. As he's driven into the Shell Centre in Waterloo – the rear entrance today, to avoid the fury of the protesters in York Road – I wonder if he's thinking about the events of the last days? Knowing what has happened, knowing that nine men are no longer alive. Did he allow himself to consider the role that his company had played in these events?

What kind of moral gymnastics would you have to do in your head to continue doing your job in such circumstances? How would it be possible? Especially if you considered yourself a person of conscience. And the man in question here thinks of himself in this way. His wife is a committed Quaker, she's been involved for many years in social campaigning, especially prison reform. I grew up with an enormous admiration for the Quakers, they were centrally important to the anti-nuclear movement of the 1980s. I loved the quiet steeliness of their activism, the gentle stubbornness of their non-violence, and though never a pacifist myself, I respected the courage that this belief engendered. Yet what a world away from non-violence now. Nine men, choking on ropes, the strands of which have been made from the collaboration between a military regime and the oil corporations.

Business as usual? Damage limitation? Crisis management? To be able to listen in to the conversations that happened that day between the group managing director and his investor relations team, and then between them and the major shareholders, the heads of the pension funds, would be to see inside the collective mind of desk killers. To be able to see the minutes of meetings that day on the top floor of the Shell Centre would be to momentarily glimpse the psyche of a vast corporation. People acting without any understanding of how others, 3,000 miles away, had been traumatised by their company's actions. As the share price was threatened across the world, the only thoughts in this building, 'the ornate offices on the banks of the Thames' as Ken had put it, would

have been how to deal with this crisis, how to make this nightmare go away, how to protect Shell's interests. Would some of the highest-paid legal minds in the country have already been working on the question of Shell's potential liabilities and exposure? Would emergency meetings already have been set up by the external relations team at Shell and J. Walter Thompson, their PR specialists? What line should they take in public? *'Deeply regret'* . . . *'tragic outcome'* . . . *'company's appeal for clemency'* . . . *'sad chapter'* . . . *'turn a new page'* . . . *'lessons learned'*? Would the legal team have checked all of this, making sure there was no wording that could be construed as constituting an 'apology', thus establishing some link of responsibility to what had happened in Port Harcourt?

*

'It is not our business to try and influence a trial . . . Our business is to continue the business of petroleum.'*

---

* Brian Anderson, Shell Nigeria managing director, speaking in 1996 about Shell's strategy of 'non-intervention' in the case of nineteen jailed Ogoni activists.

10

The Invisible Corporation

Part One: 25 St John's Lane, Thursday 15 April 2004

Although we cannot be sure about the events which took place in the Shell Centre on the day of the executions in Port Harcourt, we can be quite certain of what occurred on Thursday 15 April 2004, at 25 St John's Lane in the London offices of the solicitors Leigh Day. We know that on that day, Sir Mark Moody-Stuart (who by this time had left Shell, been knighted for his services to the oil industry, and was working as a non-executive director at the mining corporation Anglo-American) – arrived at these Clerkenwell offices and started giving his deposition as evidence in the case *Wiwa v. Royal Dutch Petroleum Company and Shell Transport and Trading Company* (Case 96 Civ. 8386 – KMW, in the United States District Court for the Southern District of New York). Judith Chomsky (of Ratner, DiCaprio & Chomsky) represented the plaintiffs, Tom Rafferty (of Cravath, Swaine & Moore) represented Shell, the defendants.

What I find remarkable is the fact that this deposition happened at all. That nine years after the executions, and three years after he left the company, the former head of Shell was compelled to spend a day in front of lawyers revisiting every detail of the events that occurred in 1995. Despite the vast amount of money that Shell paid its lawyers at the time, despite the supposedly 'world class' PR that the corporation employed (PR that seems to pride itself on 'making difficult issues go away'), Moody-Stuart was still required to appear at these solicitors' offices and spend a whole day answering questions.

We learn more from this deposition about Shell's direct communication with General Abacha during the trial of Ken Saro-Wiwa:

> MS CHOMSKY [representing the plaintiff, Wiwa]:
> Q: Do you recall receiving information from Brian Anderson [head of Shell Nigeria] that, based on his conversations with General Abacha, he concluded that Ken Saro-Wiwa would be found guilty?
> THE WITNESS [Mark Moody-Stuart]:
> A: 'No' is the answer, but I do recall occasions when Abacha expressed to Brian Anderson, from my memory, extreme irritation with the international outcry of Saro-Wiwa, etcetera. So I was certainly aware that General Abacha was aware of the progress of the trial of Saro-Wiwa, but not through any indication that he gave to Brian, or Brian gave to me, that he concluded that he would be found guilty. Not that I can recall.

Moody-Stuart attempts to explain the bizarre position Shell took in relation to Saro-Wiwa's trial. Firstly he states that they weren't able to judge the fairness of the trial because they didn't have the expertise to do so:

> A: . . . any criticism of political processes, I think, or involvement in politics, would certainly have been very strongly part of the, sort of, Shell DNA; that one didn't do it. There were two strong elements of them. The business principles were complex documents, but the common bits that people got – if you said to them, 'What are the Shell business principles?' people would say, 'We don't bribe people and we don't get involved in politics.' Within that framework, there would be scope for expressing statements, such as everyone has the right to a fair trial, but that is not a criticism of the trial that was going on . . . what would surprise me if there

had been a statement suggesting that the trial was not fair, because I don't think we were competent to judge that.

Then Moody-Stuart goes on to detail how the Shell legal team worked – but how, in this case, they were never asked to examine the Saro-Wiwa trial:

Q: Is there a legal staff within the service companies?
A: Yes.
Q: Within which service company is that legal staff? At this period in time, which is late 1995?
A: ... in London and The Hague. These are conjoined organisations with a single head. We spent some time in each. At that time, I think the head would have been Jack Schraven, but I'm not absolutely certain of that ...
Q: Was there any consideration given by the Committee of Managing Directors of asking the holding company legal staff to analyse the case against Mr Saro-Wiwa and his co-defendants?
A: No.
Q: Was there any consideration given by the Committee of Managing Directors in asking the SPDC (Shell Petroleum Development Company) to provide a legal analysis of the trial procedures involving the trial against Mr Saro-Wiwa and his co-defendants?
A: No.

But then, later in the deposition, he states that he and Shell knew about an international legal report strongly criticising the unsatisfactory nature of Saro-Wiwa's trial, yet he didn't feel the need to read the report himself, or for anyone at Shell to read it either:

Q: Were you aware of any independent legal organisations that evaluated the trial procedures of the trial involving Mr Saro-Wiwa and his co-defendants?

A: Yes. I believe the Bar Association in London – now whether this is part of the global Bar Association or not – I believe they had views on it and expressed views on it, that the trial was not satisfactory, according to the legal standards of this country.

Q: Were you aware that the British Bar Association . . . had issued a written report about the trial of Mr Saro-Wiwa and his co-defendants prior to Mr Saro-Wiwa's sentence?

A: I remember press reports. I certainly remember an utterance of some sort from the Bar Association. There was a particular individual,[*] whose name I've forgotten, who authored this report but I—

Q: Did you – I'm sorry, were you finished?

A: Yes.

Q: Did you read the report?

A: I would have read, I think, press reports of the report. I doubt that I would have read the report in its entirety.

Q: Did you ask anyone in the Shell group to read that report and report back to you what it said?

A: No.

And the notion that the executions came as a surprise is significantly undermined by this testimony below (which raises the question again – when Shell knew the executions were imminent why did they do so little to stop them going ahead?):

Q: Did there come a point in time, when your view, as to both the timing and imposition of the death sentence, changed?

A: Yes.

Q: How did that come about?

A: I think it was a message from Brian, which was something like three or four days, to my recollection, three or four

---

[*] Michael Birnbaum QC's highly respected report, 'Nigeria: Fundamental Rights Denied. Report of the Trial of Ken Saro-Wiwa and Others', had been published by Article 19 in association with the Bar Human Rights Committee of England and Wales and the Law Society of England and Wales in June 1995, five months before the executions.

days before the actual execution, Brian transmitting, I don't think necessarily in writing but certainly a message saying that, 'Look, contrary to what we had expected, it looks as though these folk are really getting wound up to carry out the execution.'

The deposition also reveals how Shell internally approached the public relations side of the unfolding Nigeria debacle by setting up a specific unit:

Q: After reviewing this document [exhibit 653], does it refresh your recollection that Mr Watts was appointed chairman of the Nigeria Group Crisis team?

A: No, not particularly, but, I mean, there was a great deal happening in Shell. The fact we were responding to the issue in a co-ordinated global way, yes, I certainly recall that, but the precise formulation of structure of the crisis team I don't recall. I should tell you that Phil Watts is a very systematic person and he thinks in very systematic ways. This is a classic piece of Phil Watts and something I respect greatly in him; he's a very systematic person, much more systematic than I am, who is much more cavalier about organisations and structures . . .

Q: I'd like to bring your attention to the letter from Mr Watts to Brian Anderson. It begins on the page Bates stamped 14016.

A: Yes.

Q: Do you see where it says, under a bolded section, it says 'The Message'?

A: Yes.

Q: It says: 'In the meantime, the crisis surrounding Nigeria needs to be effectively managed. To do so will require that throughout the Group wherever we are approached or taken to task regarding our actions and intentions in Nigeria, we convey a single, consistent message.'

A: Yes.

All of this material is important. Virtually every corporation lists 'transparency' at the top of their values, yet of course, unless legally forced to be so, corporations generally want to have their practices kept in the shadows as much as possible. (As I'm editing this, in August 2011, we have the current unravelling of News International, which, were it not for the exceptional journalism of the *Guardian* investigative team, would now be continuing to operate their criminality and phone hacking and bullying under a cloak of invisibility.) But I'm also struck by an 'elephant in the room' aspect to all of this – the way that lawyers' focus on the detailed and procedural aspects of a case can sometimes blind them, and consequently all of us, to the wider picture. Let us look at what is *not* discussed here. The lawyers can spend six or seven pages clarifying the smallest detail about whether or not a certain document was seen by x or y's department, yet at no point does anybody ask Moody-Stuart how he could justify the fact Shell continued to use gas flaring (in defiance of the UN, in defiance of international law) throughout the 1970s, 80s and 90s, when he occupied senior positions in the company. A case perhaps of not seeing the wood for the trees . . . And other words missing, in all of this forest of words? Not once here is Moody-Stuart asked about his own responsibility for the situation in Nigeria – or the collective responsibility of himself and his colleagues running Shell, all of them highly renumerated. And not once is he asked about morality or ethics. As for Shell, they decided that a public trial in New York of *Wiwa v. Royal Dutch Petroleum Company and Shell Transport and Trading Company* would not be beneficial for them. So on 8 June 2009, just days before the trial was due to start, they agreed to settle the case for $15.5 million, presumably to avoid further details of their environmental and human rights abuses coming out. This public humiliation didn't stop the Shell PR machine from trying to spin a different interpretation about such an obvious setback – the $15.5 milllion was being paid as a 'humanitarian gesture', and some of the payment would support an educational and social trust 'in recognition of the tragic turn of events in Ogoni land'* (which, naturally, Shell believed they had no

---

* 'Shell to Pay $15.5 Million to Settle Nigerian Case', *New York Times*, 8 June 2009.

responsibility for). Ken Wiwa stated his 'relief that we've been able to draw a line over the past. And from a legal perspective, this historic case means that corporations will have to be much more careful.'

But when corporations have behaved so egregiously, over so many years, flagrantly violating human rights and basic environmental considerations, it is difficult to 'draw a line over the past'. International court cases against Shell have continued, including an action taken by Esther Kiobel (wife of Dr Barinem Kiobel, one of the Ogoni men executed along with Ken Saro-Wiwa) in the US federal court in 2002, and another action, this time against Shell in the Netherlands, was initiated on 29 June 2017 by Kiobel, together with Victoria Bera, Blessing Eawo and Charity Levula (the widows of Baribor Bera, Nordu Eawo and Paul Levula of the Ogoni Nine). This case charges Shell with complicity in the unlawful arrests and detentions of the men, and complicity in the violation of their right to fair trials, and right to life.

There was further bad news for Shell in 2017 with the publication of a major report by Amnesty International titled: *A Criminal Enterprise? Shell's Involvement in Human Rights Violations in Nigeria in the 1990s*[*]. This report – the most detailed ever published on Shell's actions in Nigeria – was unambiguous. It investigated Shell's history in the Niger Delta, Shell's role in human rights violations in Ogoniland and finally it laid out the legal implications of the company's actions. Its conclusion states that:

'Shell repeatedly encouraged the Nigerian military and police to take action to deal with community protests when the company knew this put lives at risk. Even when the risks came to fruition, and hundreds of Ogoni women, men and children had been killed or assaulted, Shell went back to the military and asked for their engagement...

On several occasions Shell provided logistical assistance to military or police personnel – specifically transport. Without transporting

---

[*] *A Criminal Enterprise?* is available online at: https://www.amnesty.org/download /Documents/AFR4473932017ENGLISH.PDF

the military or police to areas where community protests were occurring, it is likely that the subsequent violence would not have happened. . .

Finally, Shell's relationship with the Nigerian authorities at the time gives rise to questions about its complicity or involvement in the violations and crimes. The company had significant access to senior figures, and was at times in daily contact with parts of the security services.'

The report's final recommendation is that:

'The governments of Nigeria and Shell's home states, the Netherlands and the United Kingdom, should investigate, with a view to prosecution, Shell and/or the individuals who were formerly in decision-making or supervisory positions within the company, for potential involvment in crimes linked to human rights violations committed by the Nigerian security forces in Ogoniland in the 1990s.'

Shell responded to the Amnesty report with a single-page letter. In this letter it stated that it had appealed to the Nigerian government to grant clemency to Ken Saro-Wiwa and his fellow Ogonis but to their 'deep regret' those appeals went unheard. Shell also stated that the company had not colluded with the military authorities to suppress community unrest, nor had it 'encouraged or advocated any act of violence in Nigeria.'

Part Two: Investigating 'the Shell DNA'

This pretty Victorian building, in St Helen's Place, just off Bish-opsgate, was the headquarters of Shell from 1913 until Shell-Mex House on the Strand was completed in 1932. It's only a stone's throw from Liverpool Street station and the *Kindertransport* memorial. And I find myself coming back to those words used by Moody-Stuart in the solicitors' office in Clerkenwell – 'part of the Shell DNA'. I've been thinking today, writing this, about going beyond the metaphor here. How do corporations actually evolve? What if we tried to look at them as living entities and not just sets of annual reports and figures? How do they learn and adapt? And how do patterns established in the past affect the growing organism today?

Sir Henri Deterding, born in the Netherlands in 1866, was chairman of Shell, and based here at St Helen's Place, and later at Shell-Mex House, from 1900 until his retirement in 1936. Thirty-six years at the top of the company, in the years that Shell truly established itself as a global entity, yet curiously he does not appear to be much celebrated in the official accounts of the company's history. Nor in wider British history, which is also surprising given his contribution to his adopted country. He was a central figure in the Royal Navy's transition from being coal-powered to oil-powered in the First World War, which Churchill and others believed contributed significantly to the Allied success – he'd helped to 'float the Allies to victory on a sea of oil'. Indeed, after the war, Deterding was even offered British citizenship – a rare honour for a foreign national – which he politely declined while agreeing to accept an honorary knighthood.

So why is Deterding almost invisible today? Surely his acknowledged financial brilliance, his drive and workaholism and his trenchant anti-leftist views would find many a sympathetic ear in the City of London and our tabloid media today? His brand of populist intolerance would no doubt find a warm welcome in many of the far-right movements now growing in the West. Here, for instance, are his views on the unemployed, from his autobiography written in 1934:

> Nature demands that every one of us shall work, and it strikes me as a criminal transgression of her laws, that . . . any healthy, able-bodied man should be able to live, except as a result of his own efforts. If I were dictator of the world – and please, Mr Printer, set this in larger type – I WOULD SHOOT ALL IDLERS AT SIGHT.

Anyway, on most days Sir Henri would have been chauffeured in one of his saloons from his grand residence near Windsor to St Helen's Place, going through financial papers and correspondence on the back seat. From the head office here, and his bank of telephones with all the latest communications technology, he made decisions and sent messages that had far-reaching implications all around the world – among these, exchanges with Churchill, in the years leading up to the First World War, on the issue of using Shell's oil to power the Royal Navy. And subsequently, in the 1920s and 30s, international communications with very different clients, and consequences.

Deterding had always been firmly on the right politically, but by the 1930s, as Anthony Sampson puts it, he became 'entranced with Hitler'. And with this growing admiration, so too a growing alliance developed between the National Socialists in Germany and the Anglo-Dutch oil company. The official Shell accounts often play down the significance of this relationship, but the historical record refutes this categorically. The Shell historians suggest that Deterding and Hitler never actually met, when we know that they did. They also minimise contacts between Deterding and other senior Nazis, which had been established for years. Shell also implies that there were no significant financial or oil deals done by Deterding and Shell to help the Nazis, when there is clear evidence to the contrary. Most strikingly, in the official Shell history[*] of the company, the historians, bizarrely, attempt to deflect responsibility for the co-operation with Nazism away from the company itself towards individuals – not only Deterding himself, but his German wife's 'political leanings' and his 'fascist' personal secretary are blamed for Shell's sympathetic treatment of Nazi Germany.

You could read the entire official Shell history of these years and not learn that Royal Dutch Shell was an influential member of the Anglo-German Fellowship. This body was incorporated in October 1935 (only a matter of weeks after the viciously anti-Semitic Nuremberg decrees in Germany had become law), to foster support in Britain for closer ties to Germany and Nazism. As the historian Ian Kershaw states, in *Making Friends with Hitler*, 'the organisation served largely as an indirect tool of Nazi propaganda in high places, a vehicle for exercising German influence in Britain'. Not

---

[*] *From Challenger to Joint Industry Leader, 1890–1939: A History of Royal Dutch Shell, Volume 1* by Joost Jonker and Jan Luiten van Zanden.

only did Shell have corporate membership of this body (along with companies such as Unilever, ICI, Tate & Lyle, Price Waterhouse and several leading banks), but Sir Andrew Agnew, general manager of Shell, was a prominent individual member of the organisation. From December 1935, right through until the outbreak of the Second World War, regular meetings were held in London, addressed by senior figures from the German Nazi government, such as Foreign Minister Ribbentrop and Himmler's adjutant Hajo Freiherr von Hadeln. Other influential members of the Anglo-German Fellowship included Montagu Norman, governor of the Bank of England; Frank Tiarks, Bank of England director, managing director of Schroders, partner in the Anglo-Iranian Oil Company (and member of the British Union of Fascists); and Geoffrey Dawson, editor of *The Times*.

The official Shell history, even more remarkably, fails to mention three critical meetings Deterding had between 1931 and 1933. The first two of these meetings took place with Dr Alfred Rosenberg, the notorious Nazi ideologue, leader of its Foreign Policy Office (later Reich minister for the Occupied Eastern Territories) and author of *The Myth of the Twentieth Century*, one of the most anti-Semitic texts ever written. Rosenberg was found guilty of war crimes and crimes against humanity at the first Nuremberg Trial after the war, and was one of ten senior Nazis executed in October 1946.

Deterding's support for Hitler and the *Nationalsozialistische Deutsche Arbeiterpartei* (NSDAP) began to grow in the early 1920s, primarily out of a shared, and extreme, hatred of communism. Shell had had substantial oil interests in Russia, Grosni, Miakop and Baku, all of which were nationalised by the Soviet Union following the Russian Revolution of 1917. This led Deterding to form common cause with all those who were anti-communist, so he followed the progress of Hitler and his burgeoning National Socialist movement in Germany with great enthusiasm, as well as creating alliances with White Russian organisations. In 1924 he married Lydia Pavlovna Koudoyaroff, the daughter of a czarist Tashkent general, herself a staunch anti-communist and activist for the White Russian cause. Deterding also supported uprisings against the communists, such as the Georgian rebellion of 1924, which revolt, the *New York Times* noted in September 1924, was 'being financed by . . . former proprietors of Baku oil wells'. Deterding also gave financial support to Ukrainian separatists, and was heavily involved in other anti-Soviet initiatives.

It was through this activity, according to his biographer and others, that Deterding first established links with Nazism. Dr Georg Bell, a German businessman, political agent and fixer, became one of Deterding's representatives, and attended conferences of the Ukrainian Patriots in Paris on his behalf (where Bell also represented Hitler). Bell, an extremely shady figure, was a close associate of Ernst Röhm (the senior Nazi who headed the SA, Hitler's militia), and also a friend of Rosenberg's; it was through Bell that Deterding began to channel financial support to the Nazis. One German source at the time reported that 'from the day of the Ukrainian Conference [in Paris in 1926], Deterding has been supporting Hitler with considerable sums of money (which found their way into the Hitler exchequer through Dr Bell)'. Dutch newspapers reported that Dr Bell had facilitated a donation of 'no less than four million guilders' from Deterding to Hitler, at a time when the Nazis were extremely short of funding. But soon the Deterding–Nazi channels were to become more direct.

On a chilly October afternoon in 1931, two men arrived by boat at the port of Harwich on a delicate mission – to develop closer ties between the Nazi movement and the British establishment. But this was no official trip, hence the low-key arrival, and the fact that the two men then made their own way to London on the boat train from Harwich. The first man was Dr Rosenberg, at this time a newly elected NSDAP Reichstag deputy, who the year before had published *The Myth of the Twentieth Century* about the 'degenerate' nature of the Jewish race. Accompanying him was an Anglo-German journalist and Nazi sympathiser based in Berlin, Baron Wilhelm de Ropp. They were met at Liverpool Street station by a contact of de Ropp's, Major Freddy Winterbotham, who had served with de Ropp in the RAF in the First World War. Winterbotham's first impression of Rosenberg was of 'a keen, intelligent and cheerful type . . . anxious to make a good impression and, above all, to talk about his beloved movement'. Rosenberg was taken to a luxury hotel, and then, over the next days – apart from an excursion into the Surrey countryside (where the Nazi was charmed by the manners of English country folk) – he was introduced to many key contacts in the British establishment.

As well as Deterding, the figures he met included Geoffrey Dawson of *The Times*, Lord Beaverbrook, owner of the *Daily Express* and the *Evening Standard*, Montagu Norman of the Bank of England and other top banking and financial representatives. The strategic aims of these meetings were clear – it wasn't simply a charm offensive to reassure opinion formers in Britain of the legitimacy of the growing Nazi movement in Germany, but there were also serious, practical outcomes. More favourable press coverage was certainly one of these, with Dawson subsequently keeping news of Nazi excesses in Germany out of *The Times*. But, more significantly, Rosenberg prepared the ground for Montagu Norman to make loans to a future Hitler government. Norman, a Germanophile since his student days in Dresden, was already well disposed towards Germany, feeling the Versailles Treaty and reparations demanded of Germany in the 1920s had been 'economic lunacy'. He was also, according to his biographer, 'full of contempt for the Jews', just like Rosenberg. No doubt the two men found plenty of common ground as they chatted in Norman's Threadneedle Street office; they also had a mutual friend – Dr Hjalmar Schacht, former president of the Reichsbank in Germany, a supporter of Hitler, and a prominent fundraiser for the Nazis.[*]

---

[*] With Hitler's accession to power in 1933, Schacht once again became president of the Reichsbank, and from 1934, also the minister of economics. In these capacities he and Montagu Norman negotiated critical loan arrangements for the Nazi government – deals which drew sharp criticism from some sources at the time. The *Daily Herald* wrote that 'Mr Montagu Norman's financial support for the Nazi regime raises questions of the utmost political importance'. And Norman's biographer, John Hargrave, later wrote that 'it is quite certain that Norman did all he could to assist Hitlerism to gain and maintain political power, operating on the financial plane from his stronghold in Threadneedle Street' (*Montagu Norman: A Biography*, 1967).

Norman also opened doors to Rosenberg on this trip. Through his agency Rosenberg was able to meet Frank Tiarks, another director of the Bank of England, but more importantly from Rosenberg's perspective, he was also managing director of the Schroders. Tiarks subsequently connected him to other senior representatives of this bank, including Baron Kurt von Schröder himself. Baron Schröder was a director of the Stein bank of Cologne too, and he was to become an important supporter of Hitler's, and fundraiser for the Nazis, as we learn from Professor Antony Sutton's *Wall Street and the Rise of Hitler*. And, through Baron Schröder's connections, the Stein bank later became a conduit for channelling financial support to Himmler's SS.

Given the 'under the radar' nature of Rosenberg's first visit to London, we only know some of the figures he met, and it is extremely difficult to quantify the amount of financial support raised. But Deterding's biographer quotes contemporary newspaper reports (in the *Daily Telegraph* and the Vienna *Arbeiter Zeitung*) that there had been a meeting in London between a major international business magnate and 'the Hitlerite leader Rosenberg', and that 'big credits for the Nazis followed'. That such support became public knowledge at the time can be illustrated by the fact that on Rosenberg's return to Germany, the Jewish Telegraphic Agency reported that 'it became a common taunt in the Reichstag to describe [Rosenberg] as a "tool of Deterding"' – so much so that one session had to be adjourned when Rosenberg threatened to 'box the ears of another deputy who had taunted him with the fact'. There were other reports in late 1931 and 1932 that Deterding had made a loan of between £30 million and £50 million to Hitler 'in return for a promise of a petroleum monopoly'. The respected journalist Louis Lochner, head of the Associated Press bureau in Berlin in the 1930s, put the figure lower, but wrote that 10 million RM had been contributed by Deterding to the Nazi cause.

Rosenberg's second visit to London, in May 1933, was a more official affair, as he was now head of the Foreign Policy Office for the new Nazi government in Germany. He had meetings with the

British Foreign Secretary, Sir John Simon, the minister for war, Lord Hailsham, and Roosevelt's representative, Norman Davis, so you might have expected him to be based at the German Embassy in Carlton House Terrace for the duration of his visit. But apparently not. We learn from a contemporary account that 'on 5th May 1933, Dr Rosenberg, the . . . official plenipotentiary of Hitler arrived in London . . . Before calling on the German Ambassador, Dr Rosenberg went to Buckhurst Park, Ascot, which is the home of Sir Henri Deterding. Only after this visit did he request the German Embassy to arrange an interview with the Foreign Office.' News of Rosenberg's visit was confirmed in the *New York Times* of 9 May 1933:

> During the weekend Germany's special envoy stayed at Buckhurst Park with Sir Henri W. A. Deterding, head of the Royal Dutch Company. With Dr Rosenberg's long-standing interest in Russia, it is assumed they discussed the Soviet oil monopoly. Sir Henri is bitterly hostile to the Soviet Government, owing to the confiscation of the Baku oil fields, which his company owned.

Two British newspapers, the *Evening Standard* and *Reynold's Illustrated News*, also reported Rosenberg's stay with Deterding, the latter commenting:

> In the light of the present European situation, this private talk between Hitler's foreign advisor and the dominant figure in European 'oil politics' is of profound interest. It supports the suggestion current in well-informed political circles that the big oil interests have kept closely in touch with the Nazi Party in Germany.

But the third documented meeting of Deterding and the senior Nazi leadership is the most remarkable of all. Especially as – if you were to believe Shell's historians – it never took place. The official Shell history asserts no fewer than three times that Deterding and Hitler never met. According to this 'history', Deterding 'sought an audience with Hitler' in March 1933, but was 'rebuffed'; 'the refusal to grant [Deterding] an audience with Hitler ... was motivated ... by keeping him firmly at arm's length'; and, of this supposed request to meet the Führer it asserts that 'Deterding was turned down without further ado' by the Reich Chancellery.

The reality could not be further from the truth. When Hitler came to power in 1933, the links between Shell and the Nazi leadership became even stronger, with a direct relationship soon established between Deterding and Hitler – prepared by Rosenberg's earlier visits and discussions. This new relationship is most vividly illustrated by the fact that we know that Deterding not only met Hitler, but stayed for four days at the Führer's private residence, his mountain retreat at Berchtesgaden, in 1934. Under the headline 'Reich Oil Monopoly Sought by Deterding', the *New York Times* of 26 October 1934 relates the following details of Deterding's visit:

> LONDON, Oct. 25 – It is reported confidentially from Berlin that the object of Sir Henry Deterding's recent visit to Chancellor Hitler at Berchtesgaden, where he stayed for four days, was to discuss the conditions for granting a monopoly to the Royal Dutch and Shell Companies of petrol distribution in Germany for a long period of years.

Such a length of stay at Hitler's personal retreat was quite exceptional, and only given to the closest of allies – Neville Chamberlain, by contrast, in September 1938, in talks to resolve the crisis in Czechoslovakia, received only a three-hour audience with the German leader on the Obersalzberg. Among other matters Hitler and Deterding discussed during their days together was a proposal for Shell to supply oil on credit to Germany for a year, and for the company to build a network of petrol stations (designed to be 'protected against air attacks') along the new networks of major roads and autobahns that were then being constructed all across the Reich. Deterding's discussions with Hitler were also reported in the *Montreal Gazette* (26 October) and the *Daily Gleaner* (29 October).

175

In the following two years, right up to his retirement from Shell, Deterding did all he could to personally ensure that the fascist governments in Germany and Italy would receive the most preferential treatment possible from his oil company. As well as the warm relations with Germany, Deterding also cultivated Mussolini, writing in his autobiography, *An International Oilman*, in 1934 that 'In Italy, not long ago, it fell to my lot to talk with Mussolini, a man who . . . has shown a driving force almost unparalleled in running a country . . . My talk with Mussolini proved that there were several points on which we saw eye to eye.' Such contacts were soon reaping dividends for Shell. An American newspaper ran a headline in September 1935, 'Europe's Oil Napoleon Seen Winner Over US Rivals for World Trade', and reported that Deterding and Shell had not been wasting any time over consolidating deals with the new political forces in Europe. It recorded that 'Shell has been awarded a monopoly to furnish fuel to Italy's armed forces during the coming Ethiopian struggle', and that 'huge importations of Soviet oil and by-products by Germany before Hitler's rise to power have been curtailed and . . . Sir Henri now enjoys a monopoly in the Nazi state'. This may have been an exaggeration, but there's no doubting the trajectory of Deterding's ambitions.

In 1934 the American consul in Hamburg reported back to the US government that not only had Deterding 'contributed fairly large sums to the National Socialist treasury before the advent of the Party into power', but he had also 'offered to supply the Reich with all their oil requirements in return for payment in blocked Reichsmarks'.* This tallies with the American foreign correspondent Edgar Mowrer's assertion in *Germany Puts the Clock Back* that there had been a pre-1933 agreement between Deterding and the Nazis. But by 1934 the co-operation between Shell and the new fascist government had gone to a different level altogether.

---

* Information on the consular briefings from *Doing Business with the Nazis: Britain's Economic and Financial Relations with Germany 1931–1936* by Neil Forbes, 2000.

We know that there was a further meeting between Deterding and Rosenberg in April 1934 to negotiate a new oil deal, with discussions continuing into May. Rosenberg wrote in his diaries that he had 'made a deal with Deterding in May 1934' – the deal was that the Shell Group would 'stock one million tons of oil products' in underground tanks which the company would build across the Reich. But Deterding wasn't satisfied with this; he saw Germany not only as an ally in the anti-communist cause, but as a huge potential market, and wasn't remotely put off by increasing evidence of the Nazis' brutality in dealing with their political opponents. He considered Hitler's bloody purge of June 1934 ('the Night of the Long Knives') as a necessary step, and expressed that it had only 'increased his respect and veneration for the Nazi leader'. There were more American consular reports the following year stating that Shell were aiming 'to obtain a monopoly in Germany' and that Deterding had agreed to a major oil loan to the German government, to facilitate this agreement – reports which Mowrer, at the Foreign Press Association, confirmed: 'In 1935 [Deterding] agreed to give Germany one year's oil supply on credit.'*

By 1935 Germany was increasing its rearmament programme, so when these deals became public knowledge there was understandable nervousness in the British government. The Foreign Office, and the British ambassador in Germany, Sir Eric Phipps, were asked to investigate the situation further, but details could not be verified. However, it seems that it was Deterding's proposed oil credit deal that was the final straw, and contributed to his stepping down as the head of Royal Dutch/Shell in 1936 at the age of seventy – no doubt British government pressure on the Shell board of directors in London playing a significant role in his resignation. In June 1936, Deterding moved with his new wife, Charlotte Knaack, and his young family to Germany,

---

* The oil loan is also confirmed by Anthony Sampson in *Company Man* – 'In 1935 he [Deterding] negotiated with the Nazis to give them a year's oil reserves on credit.'

formally relinquishing his position as chairman of the company on 31 December 1936.

In his last years Deterding could finally be completely open about his support for fascism. In December 1936 (when he was still Shell chairman), he donated 10 million guilders (40 million RM) to establish a fund for buying surplus food in the Netherlands and re-routing it to German consumers – the proceeds going to support the Nazi charity Winterhilfswerk. Goebbels noted approvingly in his diary on 12 January 1937 that 'Deterding has donated 40 million'. He also helped to finance a Dutch fascist organisation's newspaper in 1937, and gave Hitler a further large donation. All this from the man whom the official Shell history describes as holding 'few political convictions', a man who 'rarely mentioned fascism or Nazism in his letters'.

*

Much of what I have outlined above relates to Deterding's own contacts and relationships with senior Nazis and fascists, but we should also understand that, in the 1920s and 30s, to all intents and purposes, given the authoritarian nature of his leadership, Deterding and Shell were indivisible – one and the same entity. The British Foreign Office had made precisely this point back in 1927 when a worried diplomat had written: 'Sir Henri's word is law, he can bind the Board of Shell without their knowledge'. And so throughout this period we need to remember the fact that an Anglo-Dutch company was playing a critical role in supporting Hitler's rise to power, and then directly fuelling Germany's rearmament in the 1930s – between 1932 and 1938, British oil exports doubled, with a particularly steep increase in aviation fuel for Hermann Goering's rapidly developing Luftwaffe. There seem to have been no scruples whatsoever about dealing with a fascist government, no concern about the morality of aiding a dictatorship that had made its intentions clear in the first weeks it came to power.

COMMUNISTS TO BE INTERNED

First Camp in Bavaria To Hold 5,000 Men

(From our own Correspondent.)

BERLIN

The President of the Munich police has informed the press that the first concentration camp holding 5,000 political prisoners is to be organised within the next few days near the town of Dachau in Bavaria.

Here, he said, Communists, "Marxists," and Reichsbanner leaders who endangered the security of the State would be kept in custody. It was impossible to find room for them all in the State prisons, nor was it possible to release them. Experience had shown, he said, that the moment they were released they always started their agitation again. If the safety and order of the State were to be guaranteed such measures were inevitable, and they would be carried out without any petty considerations.

This is the first clear statement hitherto made regarding concentration camps. The extent of the terror may be measured from the size of this Bavarian camp — which, one may gather, will be only one of many.

The Munich police president's statement leaves no more doubt whatever that the Socialists and Republicans will be given exactly the same sort of "civic education" as the Communists. It is widely held that the drive against the Socialists will reach its height after the adjournment of the Reichstag next week.

MARCH 21, 1933

ABSOLUTE POWER FOR HITLER

Dictatorship Plans

(From our own Correspondent)

BERLIN

The Cabinet at its meeting this afternoon decided on the text of the Enabling Bill which it will submit to the Reichstag. If this bill is passed the Hitler Government will be endowed with absolute dictatorial powers — powers more complete than those enjoyed even by Stalin or Mussolini.

Within two months, as we can see here from this *Manchester Guardian* article of 21 March 1933, the Nazis had opened the first concentration camp at Dachau, just outside Munich, and started rounding up 'undesirable elements' such as trade unionists and socialists. In 1935, the year of the Deterding oil credit deal, the wildly anti-Semitic Nuremberg Laws were passed. So how does the historic Shell mantra – 'we don't interfere with national politics' – relate here? How would the inmates of Dachau, driven there in vans fuelled by Shell, have felt about this? Or Jews who'd had their businesses 'Aryanised' (i.e. stolen), and were forced into emigration, how might they have reflected on this Anglo-German alliance, this marriage of business and fascism?

It wasn't Shell alone – by 1938, with German war preparation now in full flow, Shell, Anglo-Persian (later BP) and Standard Oil (later

Exxon) were, between them, quite literally fuelling fascism – by supplying almost two-thirds of Germany's oil. How is it possible for us to appreciate the impact of such economically vital support? Without this oil how would the factories have met their growing demands? How could the autobahns have been built? How would the Luftwaffe have functioned? Yet this aspect of Germany's history – or rather, it should be said, this aspect of Britain's historical relationship with Nazi Germany – is hardly discussed at all. The vast power emanating from decisions made by Deterding and his friends from St Helen's Place in the heart of the City of London. Papers signed at desks. Ink lines and curves that meant wheels would move and armies could invade hundreds of miles to the east. We do not yet have the language to describe this connectivity, the responsibility of the people who kill through paper and ink.

*

In a similar vein, how much do we really know, or understand, about the financial underpinnings of Nazism? How familiar are we with the businessmen and the white-collar backers of fascism? History teaches us about the rise of the Nazis, about the Munich putsch, Hitler's imprisonment in Landsberg, the writing of *Mein Kampf* and a hundred other matters, taking us up to his coming to power in January 1933. But who paid for the party in the early years? Who rescued it from potential bankruptcy? Who funded the 1932 and 1933 election campaigns? Who funded the national advertising campaign? How were offices of the NSDAP established? How were the secretaries and telephones paid for?

In 1927 the party had been on the verge of bankruptcy when the right-wing publisher Hugo Bruckmann, and his wife Elsa, introduced Hitler to the industrialist Emil Kirdorf at their Munich home on 4 July, and, after a four-hour discussion, Kirdorf agreed to pay off the majority of the party's debts. But, more significantly, he also introduced Hitler to many leading industrialists and financiers, who would support the party through the challenging economic years of the Great Depression. Hitler always remembered the crucial role played by German business in funding the nascent National Socialist movement, but it seems that history has been more forgetful.

On 20 February 1933, just two weeks before the March elections which infamously consolidated Hitler's power (in the wake of the Reichstag Fire), a meeting took place at the Berlin villa of Hermann Goering, the newly appointed president of the Reichstag. That evening at six o'clock, twenty-five of Germany's leading industrialists and businessmen assembled – among them Hjalmar Schacht, president of the Reichsbank, Gustav Krupp (armaments and heavy industry), Georg von Schnitzler and three other directors of IG Farben (chemicals and pharmaceuticals), Günther Quandt (armaments and metals), Albert Vögler (steel), Ludwig von Winterfeld of Siemens (electrical engineering), and Kurt Schmitt of Allianz (insurance). Hitler and Goering both made speeches – Hitler's lasting more than an hour. They explained quite openly that their objective was the destruction of the parliamentary system and the end of the organised left in Germany, Goering stating bluntly that the forthcoming election would 'surely be the last one for the next ten years, probably even for the next hundred years'. On hearing this, the twenty-five industrialists, the elite of German business, pledged over 2 million Reichsmarks towards the Nazis' fighting fund for the election. This, it should be noted, at a time when the party was desperately short of funds.

Two weeks later, in the 5 March elections, the Nazis increased their share of the vote by 10.82 per cent, to 43.91 per cent, adding 5.5 million votes in the four months since the previous election. Just as Goering had predicted, there wasn't another democratic election in Germany for sixteen years, during which time over 60 million people had been killed in the deadliest war in history. So why do these businessmen and industrialists, so critical to the survival of the Nazi Party, not share at least some of the historical vilification that's been attached to the Hitlers, the Himmlers and the Heydrichs? Without the funding from big business and industry, Nazism would never have got off the drawing board.

*

Even less visible to us today, the Dutchman who led the world's largest oil company in the 1930s. In 1936, on his retirement from Shell, when so many were trying to flee Germany, Henri Deterding, shockingly, made the reverse journey. He took his family from Buckhurst Park, just outside Windsor – to Berlin – to a villa in the leafy lakeside suburb of Wannsee, where their neighbours now included Albert Speer and Josef Goebbels. He also bought an enormous estate in Mecklenburg, north of Berlin, where he went hunting frequently with another Nazi friend, Hermann Goering. He even bought Goering his own hunting lodge at Rominten, and in return received a portrait of the *Reichsmarschall*, signed 'To my dear Deterding, in gratitude for your noble gift of the Rominten Hunting Lodge'. He had a similar portrait of Hitler in his new residence, thanking him 'in the name of the German people, for your noble donation of a million Reichsmarks'. In his retirement, as we've seen, Deterding continued to actively support the Nazis, and when he died in 1939, he was given a state funeral by the party in Mecklenburg and Hitler sent this personal message, consciously or unconsciously Germanifying his name: 'I greet thee, Heinrich Deterding, the great friend of the Germans.'

But if you look for this part of Shell's past in another of its official histories, what do you find? Just a few lines regretting Deterding's late eccentricities, written in a kind of headmasterly 'more in sorrow than in anger' tone:

> Tainted by his late and brief association with the Nazis, Deterding left the saddest possible memory for his former colleagues . . . but the man they all liked and admired had, in truth, died several years before.

And on the substantive issue of Shell's role in fuelling Nazism? Nothing whatsoever – apart from these two shameful sentences:

> Before the outbreak of World War II, Germany, Italy and Japan were ominous and unpleasant as customers, but still just possible to deal with in business. However, in the same years Mexico shifted politically very much to the left, and made itself an impossible business partner.*

*

20 September 2004, a farmhouse not far from Reigate, Surrey

Through the strangest sequence of events I find myself sitting in an unfamiliar house on this soft autumn afternoon, patting an elderly black Labrador, and waiting for the story of a life, several lives, to begin. Opposite me, sunk into a jade-green armchair, a woman I've never met before starts talking to me in a voice huskied by years of smoking – around eighty, eyes still flirtatious, carefully made-up, with vigorous, darting hand movements that belie her age. Henri Deterding's daughter, Ella, is taking me back seventy years into her past.

'I often try to re-create the garden in my mind. It was a paradise. That's the only way of describing it. There's a lot of rubbish talked about old age, but that is absolutely true – that thing about child-hood memories becoming so vivid with age . . . The garden at Buckhurst Park was simply vast – even after years we were still dis-covering new places. I can now, as I'm talking, see so clearly the avenue of cherry trees, I can feel the blossom on my face, then we turn to the right, and we're into the French garden and I'm sitting by the sundial showing my sister Olga how to make daisy chains. We had no idea of its perfection then. Or our privilege. It was just the world we grew up in.

---

* Both quotations from *A Century In Oil: The Shell Transport and Trading Company, 1897–1997*, by Stephen Howarth, 1997.

'In the spring and the summer we would play until the dusk came. Just the two of us, no, I don't think we ever minded being on our own so much. I had Davy, our Border collie, and the horses, and Thomas, the head gardener's son, was often round. And if we ever got bored, a car could be sent for one of our friends from Windsor. It's only as you get older that loss can be understood. In a way I realise now that for most of my adult life I've been seeking a return to that garden. And as a child you have no comprehension of privilege really. You take as you find. It just is. We could ride for an hour and still not come to the edge of the estate. We were always finding new corners – the chestnut glade by the stream where we made dams, the dilapidated walled garden with the Victorian greenhouses, the door to the ice house that had completely mossed over, the plum trees that we discovered just behind there one summer, and gorged ourselves on. Thrilling. And just to be left to our own devices! Of course there were mealtimes. They would seem very formal by today's standards – the maids all in black and white, and the butler (from Hungary, with a name which sounded very exotic to us). The long table. Grace always. If Mama wasn't there our nanny would say it. But it's the freedom I really remember, so different from nowadays – when children are so fussed over and so . . . '

Ella's voice trails off. I notice a delicate ruby ring on her left hand, long, elegant fingers and nails still manicured, somehow at odds with the liver spots on her arms. The hand circles the air of the drawing room trying to find the word.

'. . . Supervised! that's it. Supervised, so that no risk is permitted at all. They're not even allowed to fall over! All the paranoia today about children, it just seems mad to me. What kind of adults will that create? All that suspicion and sheltered upbringing? Bloody little monsters, that's what they'll turn into!'

I didn't expect to like her, but I'm warming to Ella now. There is something no-nonsense, unsentimental about her. A desire to speak directly. Maybe this outspokenness increases with age? And the fact she's a smoker helps as well – as she reaches for another Silk Cut, I ponder why I have such a soft spot for smokers. They generally seem so much, well, just so much warmer than non-smokers. Maybe it's an awareness of their own fallibilities which makes them more tolerant of others, or maybe it's the calmness that comes with the rhythmic quality of smoking? . . .

I'm momentarily distracted. Ella is now describing the intricacies of the family tree, children from Deterding's earlier marriage, Henry and Roland, his first wife, Dutch, a house called Kelling Hall in Norfolk. I try to get her back on track, steer her gently to her own experience, and her relationship with her father. That's why I'm here: to try to see what exists behind the two-dimensionality of the Deterding legend.

We go into the kitchen, followed by the drooping Labrador. Ella puts the kettle on and goes off to find a book of photographs. I'm beginning to feel a little uneasy now. The dog looks up at me and his trusting look gives me a little stab of guilt. When you get older, how many people are interested in listening to your stories? Am I just using this? I take the boiling kettle off the Aga as Ella returns holding a large leather album in one hand and a book in the other. We start to leaf through the old photographs. They show a lost world. Of chauffeurs, of orangeries, of empire.

'That's Dunbar – he was my favourite horse when we moved – a gorgeous chestnut . . . you can't get the colour from this picture of course. My sister's on Fordy, a present from the car chap.'

'And who's this you're with? Is that the gardener's son?'

'No, he was taller . . .' She examines the picture, bringing it closer. 'No, I don't know. It could be one of the drivers' children, I don't remember.'

'And this must be your mother?' A woman all in white with a fine hat, laughing and leaning back against an open-topped car.

'Yes, that's her – Lydia. Actually that's rather a flattering picture.'

I detect a resentment, just a scent of hurt.

'What was she like?'

'Oh, she was . . . well, very flirtatious, very quick-witted, good fun. Before Pa she was married to an Armenian general, General Bagatoumi. At least that's what she said – you could never be quite sure with her stories, they were half true, half embroidered. Yes, lively and glamorous was Lydia – everything we weren't. Don't think she ever really wanted children. Far too busy with parties and travelling. Of course I worshipped her, but she never really had time for me. Thought I was rather plain, I think. She preferred my sister. She used to greet her with outstretched arms and sweep her up off the ground. And she'd sometimes look at me with a puzzled expression: "I don't know who Ella looks like." People say you shouldn't have favourites but that's absurd. Just the way it is. I ended up closer to Pa, Olga was closer to Mama.'

'And what about your father? You haven't really talked about him.'

A pause. Ella reaches for another cigarette. Momentarily I'm disconcerted, perhaps I've been too direct. She must be defensive about her father, surely. She looks up at me, almost challenging:

'What do you want to know?'

'What's your first memory of him?'

She puffs out her cheeks and breathes out, slowly, trying to retrieve memory:

He was – I mean I can't remember the first – but I suppose my main recollection is this ball of energy. He was short and fiery, could be very impatient. Of course, he wasn't around very much when we were small. We'd hear the car coming back late in the evening if we were still awake, crunching on the drive. Mama would tell us about his meetings with Churchill and Lord This and Lord That, but it doesn't mean anything when you're a child, does it? He had all these phrases he'd repeat. I remember once he was teaching us to dive – it must have been the summer – anyway, it was very hot and we were by the pool at the back of the house. And we're trying our best, trying to please Pa, but at one point Olga wants to give up, and says "I can't do it!" And

I remember he then got very angry, quite red in the face, and barked at us, as if we were soldiers on parade: "*Can't*?! No such thing as can't! Got to have guts!" and he made Olga carry on until she managed a dive that wasn't a belly flop. That's probably why he was so bloody good in business, I suppose. He had that stubborn streak, always felt himself a loner, going against the grain. Even when he was at the top. He also had this thing about not lying. Not because of anything to do with religion – he just thought it was "silly, because to get out of it you have to tell another twenty". That's good advice, actually . . .

It is that time on an autumn afternoon when the last of the light has emptied from the sky. And only silhouettes of skeletal trees can be seen in the garden. Ella switches on a lamp with a yellowing shade. Part of me wants to challenge her about her father, but another part of me is pleasantly surprised at her openness, so I feel it's better not to interrupt her flow; let's go where the river takes us.

'You know Pa never went to university? His two brothers did, but not Henri. But he was brilliant at maths, got a job in an Amsterdam bank, and after a while was sent to the Dutch East Indies. He sorted out a serious financial crisis they were having there, but the bank didn't even promote him. His first connection with Shell, well, I'm not sure about the date but it was with a man called Kessler. And in those days Royal Dutch mainly produced kerosene for lamps. And when Kessler was going through real problems Pa took kerosene as security, you know, credit against his loan. Soon after, Kessler asked him to join the company. Then came the boom years and it really changed from a kerosene-producing company to an oil company. Round about that time Pa persuaded the King of Holland to buy a lot of shares in Royal Dutch (he could persuade people to do almost anything!) and became good friends with Queen Wilhelmina. Of course the British navy switching from coal to oil, that was also hugely important, and that's when Pa became friends with Churchill. He let them have the oil at a very cheap price. Churchill offered him British citizenship soon after, but he said "I'm staying a Dutchman!" so they made him a KBE instead.'

Hardly pausing for breath, she takes another cigarette from the packet, lights it in an elegant movement, and sinks back into her chair with a sigh: 'When Pa took over Shell it had been going through a bad patch – the end of the Samuel years [Marcus Samuel – the founder of Shell]. Anyway, a lot was sorted out, and soon things were flowing smoothly, but there was one problem. Pa had always had this obsession about all the oil near Armenia and the Caspian, then what happens in 1919, or 1920? Yes, the Bolsheviks confiscate the lot. He was very anti-Bolshy his whole life – in fact that was one of the reasons he married Lydia, they shared this very strong anti-Bolshevik thing. He wasn't too fond of Jews either – "thieves" he called them, "They're going to ruin the world." I suppose that sounds bad nowadays, but a lot of people shared these kind of views then ... Anyway, all before my time really. I was born in '25, then Olga in '27, and well, my first memories were all of Buckhurst Park, as I've told you, and that wonderful garden. Late 20s, early 30s. And then everything changed.'

The house is quite still. Only the sound of the Labrador's deep breathing.

'When did that world end for you?'

'With the divorce. I was eleven. 1936. Buckhurst Park went to Lydia as part of the settlement, and then we were just told we were going to Germany with Pa. It was around this time that he stood down from Shell. And those last years spoilt everything that he had achieved. If that hadn't happened he'd probably still be remembered today as the greatest Dutchman ever. He had a huge estate, Dobina, near the Polish border – he was crazy about hunting. And he admired what Hitler was doing. I don't know when the first contact was, but I know he went to Berlin to meet him, and they made some kind of deal. Yes, when he was still at Royal Dutch, and then later he lent him a lot of money as well. But there had been other deals as well, I think in the early 1930s when he first started supplying oil to Germany on a kind of credit arrangement.'

'What did you feel about moving to Germany?'

'Well, we weren't thrilled about it. But of course we didn't have any choice, just had to get on with it. Nanny came with us, that made it easier, and she liked me. We lived just outside Berlin, in Wannsee, and the house seemed very small after Buckhurst Park. We were sent to a grammar school in Golzow – all German-speaking, so we had to learn it pretty quickly. We were driven in the car every day, and I remember at first, when we really didn't know any German, I was desperate to pee but we couldn't ask the chauffeur to stop. So I had to use some kind of dish and then throw it out of the window! Not how young ladies were supposed to behave! And that's when we first came across Lotte as well – Pa's new wife. She'd been Pa's secretary, so of course we blamed her for the divorce. She was a very controlling woman, very cold to us. And after a few weeks at Wannsee, Nanny had a huge row with her, and she was out immediately. That was very hard for us because we'd been together for so long – Nanny, Olga and me. We didn't even see her to say goodbye. Later Lotte tore up the photos of Buckhurst Park in front of us – that was a horrid thing to do. And it really affected Olga, she wasn't a survivor like me. She went into her shell more and more. That's probably where her depressions started. After a few months we were sent away to a boarding school in Dresden. And we hardly saw Pa after that. You'll laugh at this, but we didn't even know how to dress ourselves; you see, everything had always been done for us.

'We were away at the school in Dresden when we heard about Pa. It was very frightening. We were called to the governess's room, and on the first day told, "Your father is very ill," and then the next day, "Your father has died." That was it. We were told to pack, but no coloured clothes. Feelings of pure fright. We were then taken to Berlin by people we didn't know, to a shop in the Kurfürstendamm, where we were both kitted out all in black, and finally we were taken back to Dobina. When we arrived Lotte was still in St Moritz with Pa's body – that's where he'd died – at Chalet Olga. February 1939. Never had a day's illness in his life, and suddenly gone. Something strange about that. And there was no autopsy either – I only learnt about that later.

'We just waited for the body to be flown back to Dobina. A kind of limbo. And in those days everyone dressed in black, and all I remember was Olga and I in this huge barn catching mice. In our black dresses! It's curious that was one of the only times we were there without Lotte. Dobina was very wild – vast pine woods, flattish, a little like Breckland. In the summer the best trout streams. And we could go on our bikes for mile after mile. Left completely to our own devices. Just come back for meals, which were served by Pa's butler in a green jacket, and even then sometimes we'd eat the second course first, and then just put the other food in napkins and run back to the woods. Running barefoot. I can still feel the pine needles tickling as we ran.

'The funeral was at Dobina. In the old riding school. I remember they cut hundreds of Christmas tree branches so that the whole place was padded with green. And Pa's coffin was there. Lotte appeared and told us, "You must say goodbye to your beloved father," but we just ran outside into the woods. The next day a procession of black cars, flags, uniforms, all the bigwigs from Shell and Royal Dutch were there. And lots of senior Nazis, of course. But as children we didn't know who they were. Except Hitler, and he didn't come, I think he just sent a wreath. Our stepbrothers Henry and Ronald, from Pa's first marriage, they flew over in a small plane. They were wonderful, much older than us and very reassuring. Later on, just before Germany invaded Holland, Henry went over to Amsterdam, stuffed the plane with Pa's share certificates and came back! He was quite a character. Loved hunting and fishing too. A few weeks later we were sent back to England but Lydia didn't want much to do with us. I remember going to Buckhurst Park for the last time and her telling us (she'd remarried and had more children by this time): "Henry and I feel that as we have four children of our own we can't take you as well, so we're going to send you to our sister's." So that was it – we were sent to Baddow, and then later to board again at St Felix's.

'Lotte inherited Dobina, and Chalet Olga as well. She spent most of the war in Montevideo, helping Germans get to Argentina, I think. She ended up retreating to a high-walled house in Geneva, completely paranoid, batty. I can't say I was very sympathetic, after the way we'd been treated. After she died some people told us that we should claim back our rights on Dobina, but so much time had passed, and anyway Olga and I, our memories of it were so bound up with Pa's death and those unhappy years in Germany . . .

'Olga did her higher cert. and nearly got into Oxford, I got my O levels. Lydia didn't want to see us in the war years. Buckhurst Park was taken over by the Ministry of Shipping. After the war I married, wanted to have kids. Made a pretty decent go of it all. Olga had a very difficult time, I don't think she ever really recovered from the divorce, Germany, all the disruption. Though she did work with Albert Schweitzer in Africa for a time. She died twenty years ago. It was sad when Olga was older, because whenever I started to talk about Buckhurst Park she'd stop me. As if she just wanted to blot out everything to do with childhood – the positive as well as the traumatic. Lydia had other children after she remarried, but I think her selfishness destroyed all of them in different ways. She moved to Monte Carlo eventually. She died there in 1980. We saw each other from time to time. I've never been able to explain in a rational way the power she had over me. Mother and child, I suppose, as simple as that. Even after all the pain she'd caused I still felt so drawn to her. I always longed for her to appreciate me. I just would have liked her to say, "You've done really well, better than all of us." But she never did.'

Dark now, in the warmth of the taxi threading down Surrey lanes back to the town, trying to make sense of the last hours. Not only learning more about the collaboration of Deterding and Shell with Nazism, and wondering if we will ever truly understand the implications of this relationship, but also finding out about the details of all of these lives, Henri Deterding and his family. Behind the grand edifices of history and the official records and the pompous self-justifications of businessmen and politicians, this is what exists. This is the reality. The fragility of life. A child desperate to be loved. A sister who never recovered. The grief that is carried with us.

PART FOUR

Fire and Water

11

A Hillside in Grosseto; A Dream of My Father

Today I reached the end of a book I hadn't read for many years –
Moments of Reprieve by Primo Levi – and, as I turned the final page,
the past leapt into the present. The synapses of memory rapidly firing. On the back inside cover was a drawing – not in my hand –
a rapid doodle in black ink. It was a portrait of a young woman's
face. I instantly recognised it as Erin's, and was transported back
twenty-five years to when we lived together in Italy. Suddenly I saw
the sitting room of our small apartment by the canal and the cherry
tree by the front door, I was walking into the centre down San
Antonio, through Piazza delle Erbe, to meet friends in Zanneletto's
. . . I could smell the sweet chestnuts being roasted in the autumn,
see the braziers flaming in the squares, I could touch the almond
blossom that frothed in profusion in the Colli Euganei before
spring arrived. All from this single image.

*

In all the travelling we did that year, there is a time that remains
vivid in my memory. Perhaps because this recollection is so

sensory, I return there whenever this particular scent reaches my nostrils as the weather turns colder.

As late autumn fuses with early winter, and the darkness comes, it's the sweet smell of woodsmoke. And I always associate it with that little village clinging to the hillside. The time when Erin and I stayed with a friend who lived in one of the ancient Etruscan settlements of Grosseto. It felt like we'd slipped away from the twentieth century altogether, and, buried in the chestnut forests there, Italy and all its manic energy was suddenly impossibly far away. The previous two months had been exhausting, jangling – moving from London, then having to leave Perugia suddenly, and then, via a short stay in Bologna, we'd ended up finding work in Padova. But we were still living in a hotel room, not easy, living and working out of a single shared room. So this place was balm to our spirits.

Erin's friend Lorenzo, a lithe and mercurial Italian-American artist, had moved there a few years ago. Erin had always had an intense curiosity about people who didn't conform, and places off the beaten track – things I loved about her. But I thought she'd exaggerated the remoteness of this corner of Grosseto. It turned out she hadn't. There was a single telephone in the village, up in the tiny trattoria above, so when you wanted to contact Lorenzo you had to call the trattoria. A woman answered, always sounding surprised, and a little suspicious. And then you heard footsteps, a door opening, and the woman's voice shouting over the village rooftops, '*LOR-EN-ZO!! LOR-EN-ZO!! TEL-EF-O-NO!!!*' And then, a couple of minutes later, the sound of running, and Lorenzo, out of breath, grabbing the phone, '*Pronto? Hi!*'

*

The first days of calm after months of rushing. Coming into that little stone house at night, out of the sharp wind, a sense of sanctuary. The low beams, the fire, a wooden table, three sturdy chairs, a bed, candles, hearth. Closing my eyes, that earthy, sweetest smell of home, logs burning. The promise of days here, and hoping we can rekindle our spirits. Soon, watching the flames leap, red wine and laughter, feeling suddenly that all is possible again. Astonished how rapidly things can shift, lifting with fire and hope . . . We go to sleep that night cocooned in a carved wooden bed that Lorenzo tells us came with the house, so it's probably centuries old. His neighbours are away, he'll stay at their place tonight, and soon leaves us, solicitiously making sure we have enough blankets. We go into our dreams watching the flickering embers of the fire, thinking of all the inhabitants of this place who've done the same over all the winters of the last thousand years.

Before fully waking, the blurred warmth of the other, mingling of feet, fingers unfurling. Winter outside, but here we're cosy as the womb and soon reaching for each other. Brush of skin against skin, eyelash on cheek, toes reaching down, following curve of legs, so gently, teasing, hairs tingling, responding. And soon all the coiled tension of the last weeks dissolving . . . Later, hungry for the day, we pull the shutters back, and are amazed by what we can see in the daylight – far below us, and almost vertigo-steeply, a deep, wooded valley, a curving stream, two stone bridges, and beyond, a rocky mountain that reminds us of Mont Sainte-Victoire and Cézanne – but in outline only, because not the reddish ochre of Provence but a grey-whiteness of the volcanic rock here. Winding tracks through the trees beckon down the valley. The wind of the morning shaking the bone-white branches, like fine brushes, sun firing the treetops.

Over the next days we walk these Etruscan paths, marvelling at how hundreds of years of peasants' feet and donkeys' hooves have created these distinctive, sunken ways in the rock, sometimes ten or twelve feet deep, carved, scraped, hollowed out through use. Beyond our valley we find other settlements, equally ancient, clustered together on hillsides, amidst the forest. Terracotta pools of angled roofs encircled by trees. So easy to imagine a lone rider on horseback coming out of the woods, and having the same view 300, 400 years ago. When the sun dips beyond the ridge the temperature drops, and we walk back to the village briskly. As we get closer we can see a figure working on a rooftop bordering the wall of the village, with the cliff falling eighty feet below.

The figure pauses, and then waves to us, and only then do we realise it's Lorenzo, working on the house he's attempting to renovate for a studio. He beckons us up to have a closer look. He's done a lot of the structural work, and virtually finished the new roof, but it will still be a year or so till it's properly habitable. He shows us the sixteenth-century tiles he's using, given by another neighbour, his boyish enthusiasm bubbling over at the fact they're still in such remarkable condition. He turns over a tile to show us something he found, after scraping away the moss – an inscription '*Wivere Pace*' ('Long live peace' – with the old Latin spelling of '*vivere*'). On other tiles he's discovered the paw prints of cats and dogs. The liveness of the animals, frozen in the clay 400 years ago, and now giving a kind of literal and allegorical shelter for another age.

As we walk to the top of the village, where the trattoria is, we go through an arch dividing the oldest part of the village from the rest. Under the arch there are hundreds of rusted nails, each one denoting a villager who has died. The black-and-white notices are long gone, but the nails remain, pockmarking the surface, the older ones rusting into the stone like dried blood. Each nail a life spent here. A little further on we bump into Mario, a friend of Lorenzo's – a man in his seventies, a crumpled face, lopsided smile, wearing a curious green, triangular hat. Lorenzo begs him to bring another load of wood down to the house. Mario protests, he can't do it this evening, he begins to walk away. Lorenzo makes a face, does the 'praying hands' gesture, and explains he has guests, what will they think if the village can't even provide wood for them? Where is the hospitality in that?! Mario smiles sardonically, realising he's trapped, telling him, with playful taps on his chest, 'Lorenzo! You will put me in my grave! OK, OK, I give up, but one load, OK? I give in! *Stasera, sí!*' He walks away, down the cobbled path, waving his right hand in the air behind him.

As we get to the trattoria we ask Lorenzo about his relations with the villagers. Well, of course some of them think he's mad, but others respect what he's done, and the fact he's restoring two houses. He doesn't have the 'deep and meaningful' conversations with people here, which he used to have in the city, but that's OK. 'It's so light here. It suits me. "*Allegro*", if you get my drift.' And there's a kind of code of behaviour, completely unspoken, but understood by all who live here. People help each other, they have to, it's the only way of surviving. Soon after he arrived a couple of years back, the old woman whose house he was renting at first, while renovating his own, asked if he knew anything about cars. She took him to a large shed on the edge of the village and revealed, to his amazement, a fine silver 1949 Lancia. It had been her husband's pride and joy, and now she wanted to give it to her nephew, but, she shrugged her shoulders – it hasn't started for years. Lorenzo, with a little help from a friend, managed to get it working, much to the woman's delight. The next day, returning from a walk, he found five magnificent roof beams propped against his house. No note or anything. He asked around; nobody knew where the beams had come from. A week later the old woman died suddenly, and at her funeral the daughter asked Lorenzo if he'd received the wood. Her mother had wanted him to have it.

I'm happy to be sociable for a day, even two, at a push, but soon I'm feeling an overwhelming need to have time to myself, to write and think. The next day Erin heads off with her camera, and as Lorenzo's still working on the roof of his studio, I borrow his neighbours' house to do some writing. First I light a fire. The instinct of this action, learnt as a child growing up in the country – always the joy of just using a match and some newspaper, and then feeding the smallest, driest twigs into the fire, and seeing the flame take hold, then gradually adding thicker kindling, and, after a few minutes more, knowing the intense glow will now be able to deal with a small log. I know intimately how English oak, ash, elm and apple burn, but I'm unsure about these Italian logs – different types of wood, some chestnut, and some with a curious sheen on the bark which reminds me of cherry. But soon the flames are lapping round the kindling, and I reach for the thinner logs. The fire hisses and fusses around them at first, but within ten minutes the flames are established, and soon I'm able to feed on the heavy piece of old roof beam that Lorenzo has discarded from the studio. It will burn until dusk, maybe even through the evening, my companion today, giving out its stored energy from the sun of centuries ago.

And here I sit in my coat and scarf, at the beaten-up old wooden table, in the irregularly shaped, bare room, fire blazing, looking out through the rectangle of window to the other side of the valley. From time to time I can hear Lorenzo hammering on the roof, a dozen houses away, and occasionally the crackle of voices, exclamations, laughter. But the hissing of the fire is more constant. In the corner of the room I see a dusty cassette recorder, and out of curiosity, press the 'play' button. A single cello, Bach surely. It sounds like the quintessence of wood itself this afternoon echoing in this room of wood and stone.

I look into the fire, mesmerised as always. I think about how rare such moments are. The struggle for time. This is what most of our lives consist of, in our supposedly rich world. The 'luckier' ones talk of five or six weeks' holiday a year. Many people batter themselves into submission in cities doing soul-destroying work, and then feel pathetically grateful for a few weeks' remission. And for what? 'Time off.' It doesn't begin to make sense. And I find myself wondering just how much writing I'll *really* be able to do in the coming months, trying to juggle the demands of teaching, a relationship. I see my twenty-four-year-old self in a way I haven't before, with an almost ironic detachment, as if observing myself from a distance. I turn the music off, and take out my battered typewriter from its blue case.

*

The sound of the fire was sound enough, needing no recorded music. The light of the room was light enough, needing no artificial bulb. The warmth of the fire was warmth enough. He stretched his feet, sensing the prickling of cold bones, the beginning of thawing from the heat, the blood coursing, warmer, through his veins.

And suddenly he was with his father. Some years before, on an icy evening, above the old house. Returning from the fields and wood cutting. Walking steadily down the hill, in the tractor's ruts, the barn silhouetted against the last silver of the dusk. Walking just in front of him, almost home now, he stops. They pause together, for only a matter of seconds. They look down to the house below. Curtains not yet drawn, the light from the two windows spills out. Promise of warmth, the fire inside, the dark beams, supper, family. Nothing said between them, just a silent appreciation of that moment, shared.

My father loved fire. After dark I would sometimes find him still outside, tending the shuddering remains of a bonfire. Hypnotised and drawn by its elemental simplicity – the neat rings of charred wood circling at the edge of white-hotness – he, with his back against a tree, smoking. Or gathering the stray twigs that had avoided the fire and feeding them back into this sun. Or bringing down larger, springier boughs, with some force, on the core of the fire, sending a skyful of sparks into the black above.

To live by fire.

And inside, seeing him so many times in his chair by the fire, reading, then putting down a book just to immerse himself in the flames. I see him stroking the side of his nose in that gentle and reflective way, and losing thoughts of Lucretius or Rilke in the hissing of a cherry branch or the imminent collapsing of an elm log – matter into ash and particles lifted relentlessly skywards. The patterns of black lines, webbing across the pulsing red. Collapsing of time.

To die by fire.

The twenty third of September nineteen eighty five – Monday 23 September 1985. The last time I saw my father alive. How a date can grow so vast in one's consciousness. Not vaster than 25 December for a child, but much more constant. A companion that digs you in the ribs on the most gentle of summer mornings, who whispers in your ear in the middle of a February night. The meaning of grief.

He walked up the front path with me, helping to carry my bag to the car. I was moving into my first flat in London later that day. A

Monday morning, like so many others. Of course neither of us knew we would never see each other again. I've tried, many times, to return to that short walk, only forty paces or so, from the front door of the house to the barn. Trying to recall the details, as if, by doing this, the passage of time, and what happened later that afternoon, could somehow be altered.

I vividly remember the energy of those moments. The sense that here was a rite of passage – my first day of complete independence as an adult. Moving to London, the city I'd always loved with a hunger. And the irony that, on this very same day, he was also experiencing a rite of passage, though in the opposite direction, quite literally so – his first day of early retirement from University College London. So, for different reasons, both of us were in the highest of spirits, gently teasing each other, aware that we would never be son and father in quite the same way again. We put my bag in the boot of the car and then we hugged. That strange awareness that your father, once a giant to you, is now an inch or two shorter. The tricks that time plays. As the car reversed I wound the window down and said something about our phone line being connected later in the week, I'd call with the new number. The utter ordinariness of those words. The last I would ever say to my father. We drove away. As the car turned out of the drive I looked back – as I still do – to see a figure waving, and then walking back down the path to the house.

I've completely lost track of time. Lost in the fire and memories. But I'm returned to reality with knocking at the heavy door – Erin asking if I realise what time it is. Supper's almost ready, the gas is running low, come and eat. I leave the fire for a while . . .

*

July 2006, Suffolk coast

I'm back at the same window by the Suffolk coast but everything has changed. The shingle that separates me from the sea and seemed so relentlessly stony has sprouted hundreds of bushes crowned with white flowers that I do not know the name of. The path to the cottage has almost disappeared between crowds of neck-high cow parsley, which releases its curiously acrid smell as you push through. And the Arctic winds that battered so restlessly in January have been replaced by a balming summer breeze which carries the scent of clover and a continuous ululating of skylarks. The shaggy black cat who has become my companion here met me as I started to unpack the car last night, two amber eyes emerging from the darkness. He follows me inside and moves straight to the corner of the small kitchen where I put down his milk. Considering I haven't been here for almost a month this behaviour raises certain questions about the memory of animals.

This time a week ago I was in China. An experience of extreme urbanisation that is as far as you could get from this place. Curiosity led me to accept the invitation – from the Royal Society of Arts, to be part of an Anglo-Chinese delegation of artists and educationalists looking at responses to climate change – but the trip has disturbed me, as it did my fellow travellers. Seeing cities that are growing by 3 million a year, witnessing what must be the most extensive building programme anywhere in history, these experiences concentrate the mind, provoke it. Back in London, putting out my recycling box, I found myself smiling ruefully at the absurdity of such an action in the face of vast global forces. 'How with this rage shall beauty hold a plea, / Whose action is no stronger than a flower?'

My sleep patterns have been all over the place since returning. Thirteen hours at first. Then, over the next days, despite deep tiredness I wake after four or five hours and can't go back to sleep. Part of me feels it serves me right – there is considerable violence in flying 12,000 miles for a week's discussion of climate change. And the environmental and political purpose of the trip does not take away this cost, only deepens the paradox. But sometimes it is in precisely these states, of discombobulation and disturbance, that new awarenessnes can break through, when your exhausted body can be ambushed by an idea coming out of the long grass.

The fox cubs in my garden in London are now tumbling into their adolescence – their mother holds them down with her front paws to clean them, but they're half as big as she is now. And almost fearless. I can open the kitchen window and they're not disturbed. One comes right up and looks in, two, three feet away. It senses another animal but my silent stillness intrigues. We spend a minute, perhaps longer, eyes locked together. When the cub blinks I blink too. As if wanting to reassure, in some primal way. At such a moment I feel myself released from the rational world. I want these moments to lengthen. I want to let go utterly of the informational and factual hum that persistently dulls our senses. This stare of the young fox encompasses an entire universe. And one that has nothing to do with newspapers or the Internet. One that will be here when all our chatter and vanities are long buried under landfill and waste. What voice will make the last human sound ever heard on earth?

Two dreams have disturbed me recently. The events in each dream have nearly evaporated on waking but leave traces of the accompanying emotion. In the first, Johann, a friend and writer, has died. Physically he may be an old man now but he has kept the vigour and rigour of the passionate young activist and critic he once was. His death seems quite impossible and I'm shaking as I wake. I'm only partly reassured to realise it was a dream. I never use that demeaning adverb 'just' in conjunction with dreams. Fighting my instinct to ring Johann immediately, I reflect that we haven't spoken for several months, though his spirit has been with me, a patient and constant companion through these first months of writing. I wait until the evening, but I'm disconcerted all day, I can't settle. I hear the long bleep and imagine the phone ringing in that kitchen in the mountains far away. The deep voice of Brigitte, Johann's partner, answers. We exchange thoughts about the late arrival of the summer but I'm impatient to know about Johann and say that he has been in my subconscious. Is he alright? 'He's fine,' she drawls, 'that is, as far as I know. But your subconscious is a little off target. He's not here, he's in Paris.' I ring the other number. Another woman's deep voice, Natalia, Johann's friend and collaborator. Husky, expressive and strongly accented by her native Russian still:

'Dan! That's in-cred-ible! We have been talking of you, just now! About how you and Johann met for the first time . . .' And now I can hear her calling to Johann. 'Jo-hann – you won't believe it! It's Dan!'

I can make out several voices, laughter in the background. A table of friends. And Johann's familiar 'No?!', that sudden and simultaneous explosion of surprise and questioning. And relief eases through my body. I feel myself untensing. I sense his bearlike warmth making his way towards the phone, cigarette in hand.

'Hello, Dan? Yes, literally just as you rang we were speaking your name! A synchronicity, wonderful, no? Does that ever happen to you?'

'Once or twice, yes. But there must be something in the air today, Johann, our subconsciousnesses must be speaking to each other because I had a strange dream about you last night.'

(I hesitate. On grounds of superstition alone I can't bring myself to tell Johann about the fatal content of my dream. And anyway, what is the etiquette of telling friends they've died in your dreams?) I decide to be vague:

'. . . It was quite disturbing, well actually, very disturbing, so I'm very relieved to hear your voice. And nothing's been wrong?'

'Well, my knee's still a bit stiff, but no, apart from that, nothing. I've been in good spirits. And you? How's the writing going?'

I tell him about the sense of deep concentration that the cottage by the sea has given me. And, conversely, how I've found it extremely difficult to focus being back in London. The proximity to means of communication. Even if they're not used – the knowledge that the phone in the other room could ring at any moment, or that emails are piling up unread. And the simplicity of that room by the sea with nothing to distract you. The beauty of uninterruptibility. As Michel Tournier recognises in *Vendredi*:

> the transformation which solitude was affecting in his own
> personality . . . he discovered that for all of us the presence

of other people is a powerful element of distraction, not only because they constantly break into our activities and interrupt our train of thought, but because the mere possibility of them doing so illumines a world of concerns situated at the edge of our consciousness but capable at any moment of becoming its centre.

I also tell him about the fox cubs in the garden. Another exclamation of delighted surprise and then Johann says, rather elliptically, 'The foxes are your paragraphs', a reference perhaps to the unpredictability of what comes next. How the book that emerges is never the same as the book that's planned, new ideas leaping into the pages like the young foxes. I refer back to the curious workings of the subconscious, and learning to trust this more, but Johann's not having this: 'But isn't all this talk about "subconscious" just Freudian bullshit? Because what you're actually describing is a way of seeing, at the very edge of what is possible, no?'

'It's like that passage in *Austerlitz* about the way we've been looking at history in the wrong way . . .'

'Exactly! Yes!'

I hear him draw on his cigarette.

'Let me tell you something which happened to me recently. I was in Spain, coming back by train, and we'd reached Barcelona station, where we were waiting for a few minutes. The train was very crowded, I was reading, but I must have been aware, at the very edge of my vision, of a certain agitation. There was a group of Chinese, or they may have been Koreans, I don't know, but anyway, they seemed unsure about whether they should get off the train here. There was coming and going and some confusion, and maybe because of this (it's very unlike me, I never normally would do this), I checked to see if my suitcase was still in the place behind me, between the backs of seats. It had sketchbooks in and the manuscript of something I'm working on. Anyway, it wasn't there! The train was about to leave, I rushed off, very agitated by now, and there on the platform was my case, thank God. I got back on the train and it left almost immediately. Now, you could say this was my subconscious at work.'

'But really it was your peripheral vision.'

'Right! Yes, peripheral vision. Exactly!'

*

The other dream was three days ago. In fact, the trace of this dream was so indistinct that all I had on waking was the sense of a momentary imprint, the brush of a hand on the face. But, in that blurred state between waking and full consciousness – that inchoate drifting – as I had my tea, looking out over the garden, I knew my father had visited me in the night. And we had travelled somewhere together. But the more I tried to grasp the detail, the further away the dream slipped.

Then, out of this morning haze, with the suddenness of a radio tuning in, my mind jolts me back twenty-one years. Everything in violent clarity, half a life away. 23 September 1985. That night journey from the fringes of north London to Colchester. Details that can never be wiped from my memory – all vividly here again. Paralysed by shock. The uncontrollable falling of grief. In the upstairs room in Ayesha's house, on what was going to be our first day of real independence – moving into that flat up the hill from Tufnell Park. And the moment *before*. That is what is hardest to think of now. The normality of that time. We had been waiting for Ayesha's mum to give us a lift, piling stuff up in the hall downstairs, and we were lying on the floor upstairs with, of all strange things, *Wogan* coming from the television in the corner. And wired permanently in my memory, absurdly so, at the exact moment when the phone rang, we were watching Théâtre de Complicité do some routine involving a man being wrapped in vast lengths of Sellotape.

Ayesha is handing me the phone. It's my brother. Strange, how would he have this number? I take the phone. He sounds out of breath.

But I cannot be sure what happens next. Or exactly what he says. I remember he doesn't tell me immediately but instantly, from his broken voice, I know something devastating has happened. And then I'm throwing the phone across the floor. An instinctive reaction, a revulsion against what was coming, as if this action could stop what was happening. And in this pause, maybe only two or three seconds, I'm hyperventilating and swearing continuously. Ayesha is in the room looking on horrified. Somebody in the family is dead. My brother is about to tell me. My mind rapidly flashes the three possibilities past, over and over in a frenzied Russian roulette – mother, father, sister, Corinne, Mark, Meg, mother, father, sister. One is dead. Impossible. But real. This is happening. Maybe more than one dead? An accident? I retrieve the phone, kneeling on the floor. I somehow ask the question. Do I ask about Corinne first? I think so. No – it's not her. Not possible to describe this moment, no words for it. Death passes to my father – it's him, Mark. My brother is saying something about a fire in the fields, they found him in the top field, burnt. Insanely I hear myself urgently whisper down the phone: 'But he'll be OK, yes? He's burnt but there's still a chance, yes?' I know this is impossible but I need to hear it. And if, by a miracle, there was just a breath, a misting of the mirror, then there is a way back. We will nurse him back, over months. Just a breath. And all is possible again. 'No, it's too late, he's dead. He was dead when they found him.'

The next hours have the furtive quality of a nightmare. Separated from those you love, desperate to get home, across a city and beyond. And these are the details that have lain dormant for all these years, and, with the inexplicable workings of the mind and memory, have decided to reappear on this summer's morning twenty-one years later. I'm in the back seat of a car, on the right-hand side, eyes next to the window. Ayesha's mum is driving; Ayesha is next to me on the back seat, holding my hand. The North Circular, moving eastwards, drizzle now falling. Images of Mark fill my mind, his bearded face, his low chuckle, meeting him for lunch at University College, the way he stroked the side of his nose as he read, his gentle wisdom, his love of Socrates. But nothing that can be said now, here in the car, beyond giving directions. Head for the A12 Chelmsford, Colchester. I'm numbed. Close my eyes. This will go away. Blinking through the glass smeared by the rain, I can't understand how the red buses still make their way through the streets, cars still accelerate away from traffic lights. The insane normality of appearances when my world has been destroyed. London suburbs melt back into the night with the last black cab, catseyes now lead us curving north-eastwards. Just the hum of engine, every undulation of the road. At one point I come out of my trance and thank Ayesha and her mum for doing this, and they say of course it's OK. I'm more exhausted than I can ever remember. We're now heading down the slip road for Colchester. The familiar roundabout, I guide us along the Avenue of Remembrance to the second roundabout. Left towards the station. The familiar meeting point, tonight turned into something terrible. The young priest Father Michael is here, on the platform, with my sister. We hug and sob for I don't know how long. The tragedy that always happened elsewhere, to other less fortunate people, has come home. We have now become the people who others pity, the subject of hushed glances and shivered relief, enabling others to feel that perhaps their daunting problem that evening was not quite so impossible to face after all.

Down dipping lanes, curiously I can even remember Father Michael's car – a dark blue estate. He takes us a different way home, not through Stoke-by-Nayland, but down the lane past the Copella farm, to the Boxford bypass. At the house, a police car, an ambulance still there. Oddly, I cannot remember the moment of meeting my mother. Was she even there when we got back or had she gone to formally identify the body? Later that night I walk with my brother, up the middle path together through the little wood, vowing that, whatever our differences in the past, this will make us closer. Up to the place where it happened. Needing to know details. Needing to be told. We stand on the gentle slope of the field. You can still smell the burnt stubble. The burnt earth. He'd been burning the little piles of wild oats that he'd made in the summer at the side of the field. The field he was working in when J. and I embarked on our first walk together six weeks before, my father stopping to wave. A breeze must have spread one of these small fires to the stubble, and then as he tried to put it out, being overcome by the smoke. Corinne and Meg had found him – they'd been black-berrying along the top hedge. There are details that I never want to know, have never asked about, and this moment is one of them. Walking back, near to the house, I overhear a policewoman talking into her crackling walkie-talkie, and I catch the words '*victim was an elderly gentleman*'. These words shouldn't matter and yet they do, I find myself furious with the WPC. You know nothing about him so how can you speak about him? Gentle? Yes, he was a gentle man. Elderly? Absolutely not. Fifty-three years old. His first day of early retirement from UCL.

By the way, grief never leaves you. It just changes its shape.

*

Why now, why on this June morning do these images surface? The dream, of course. Yes, but why that dream in the first place? That cannot be called peripheral vision, surely. And today, for the first time, really, I think about Ayesha and her mum on that journey. What must those hours have been like for them? Knowing that nothing could be said, nothing could help the distraught person in the back of the car. Ayesha was never very emotionally expressive at the best of times, so this must have been torture for her. What did they talk about on the way back to north London? Did the house feel different to them when they walked in? Did that phone call hang like a spectre in that upstairs room?

But there is something else here. That night journey down the A12. Without being conscious of it until now, I've been repeat-ing that same journey, again and again, over the last months. The decision to write at this place by the sea means returning to my past, every two weeks. And the night drives down from London, I've told myself there's less traffic, fewer lorries, but surely there's another, deeper reason. As if part of me has never accepted what happened that evening, as if I'm still trying to find an answer in that night road, in the speed and the blackness. Some things can only be released through the rapidity of thought that comes with movement. For most of my life, not needing a car in London, I've taken the train from Liverpool Street, that's the journey I've known every detail of. Only in the last months have I got to know each curve and rise of this road. And how to explain the mystery of a journey, a landscape? Even along the dullest motorway, at moments, you can be ambushed by something, a force field of energy. Just past Colchester the road begins to dip down and down, a sign to Stratford St Mary, a long curve round to the left, under a bridge. The point where Essex becomes Suffolk. There is no rational explanation, but driving down this hill at night, at this precise point, I feel my future, present and past all colliding. My body begins to shudder involuntarily. There is so much we cannot know. Or maybe our bodies know before our minds.

*

A month ago I drove down late, after a long talk with a friend whose father was dying in a hospital in Australia. Although I've never met the friend's father, I felt as if I knew him well, through my friend's vivid accounts of his life – of his passion for literature (reading Turgenev and Gogol aloud to his son as a bemused eleven-year-old), and his energy (in his eighties he was still obsessed by mountain walking, doing thirty-mile hikes, complaining that his son couldn't keep up). A force of nature. So I'm shocked by my friend's resignation. He seemed upset that the doctors hadn't 'let him go'. His father had been extremely ill for months, and now has no knowledge of what's going on around him, or who anybody is, and has just lost his sight. I asked if he's going to go out there, to be with him when he dies, but he said no, that they'd already said goodbye to each other last year. 'We knew it was the last time, and I felt we'd said all that could be said.'

I pack the car, gulp some extremely strong coffee to stay awake, and head out of Hackney at just after eleven. A need for very loud music – the Clash gets me out of London and onto the A12, then a frustratingly dull programme on the radio about poetry in Cuba. A squall of rain, then heavier. Past Chelmsford and it's now torrential, visibility very limited, cars slowed to 40, 35 mph. I pull into a petrol station to let it pass. Inside the shop I get a sandwich and talk to the guy working there. He says it reminds him of monsoon rains, he hasn't seen anything like this since he was a child in Kerala. As I eat my sandwich in the car, the rain still unrelenting, battering the roof of the petrol station, I look back at the man in his illuminated bubble and consider the strangeness of the world we now inhabit. The distance between the noise of the Indian village of his childhood and working the night shift in this petrol station on the A12. Was this the England he dreamed of as a boy?

One a.m. now, and I reach the ring road around the town that wants to be a city. I pull into the twenty-four-hour supermarket but I've forgotten that it's Sunday, so I'll have to make do with the odds and ends I've brought with me from London. Only fifteen minutes to go. I put on a Nick Cave CD I've never listened to before. It was given to me two years ago by a friend, but I found the title – *The Secret Life of the Love Song/The Flesh Made Word* – and the concept of two lectures read by Nick Cave rather offputting. But everything is about timing. I'm past the last town now, at the bend where the railway crosses. A dozen men in fluorescent yellow coats, emergency work, 'Road Closed Ahead'. So, how the hell do I get to the coast road from here if I can't go this way? The rain's still coming down hard; one of the men breaks off, and bends down to my window. I take in his dark, curly hair swept by the rain and a rough jawline of stubble as he explains that I'll have to go back, take the lane on the right, and then connect up with the main road further ahead. He shrugs apologetically and smiles, apparently it's quite a long way round.

I reverse, take the road he suggested, but ten minutes later I'm completely lost, down a side road, no signposts. But I'm absorbed by Nick Cave now – his sonorous, rambling voice strangely reassuring on this wild night. He's quoting Auden, the moment of trauma – the way that we all need to be shocked into another state, released.

And then, to my amazement, he's talking of his father, and his sudden death. Onto smaller lanes now. Navigating more by instinct than anything else. Water in streams pouring down each side, and red earth washed into the middle of the lane. Looking more like Africa than Suffolk. Potholes, more of a track now. The words continue, interspersed with songs of yearning, where the love is very intertwined with death. Cave's now talking about Lorca's writing on 'duende' – the inexplicable sadness that is found in so much great writing and music. This quality that is instantly recognisable but impossible to imitate. 'Dylan has always had it, Leonard Cohen deals specifically with it. Tom Waits and Neil Young can summon it.' The road dips down towards a bridge, and in the pools of the headlights the black glassiness of flood water ahead. Can't turn round so reverse the car back up the hill, round corners, exhilarated by now, I don't care how long this takes. The deep Australian voice is now describing a new love, and the curious choice of recording or living at such moments. He writes a new song, one verse each month, as the relationship blossoms. I want to scream at him – 'As soon as you write it down you're killing it! Don't make it so conscious!' But it's too late – the relationship is over. And the song now moves to magnificent anger, Cave spits out about his brave-hearted lover, running back to his mother, with a venom that has me taking my hands off the wheel whooping in solidarity, remembering my own experience with a lover running back to Spain just at the moment we were beginning to open up to each other.

I'm back on the right road now, but I'm subtly disappointed. It feels like an extremity has retreated. The straight road through the forest is deserted tonight. Too wet even for the deer and the rabbits. It's almost 3 a.m. when I arrive at the end of that final track – only the sea ahead of me. And, unbelievably, within a minute, my companion the shaggy black cat appears, looking more bedraggled than I would ever have thought possible for a cat to be.

How People in Organisations Can Kill: The First Factor

Listening some years ago to an interview with Dr Gwen Adshead, a consultant forensic psychotherapist based at Broadmoor Hospital, I was struck by a phrase she used in relation to the 250 or so men she helped to treat in the unit, some of the most dangerous and disturbed patients in the country – she said they were 'like survivors of a disaster'. Later, in the same interview, she talked of how becoming a parent had made the work sadder for her, because she began to 'see all these men as the small boys they were . . . how they might have been – with all the promise that children have'. And how the catastrophic nature of what happened to a majority of these boys in their formative years, the extremes of abuse and neglect they experienced, then extinguished all of those possibilities. With these reflections, emerging from years of work at Broadmoor, people who had been labelled 'criminals' and 'patients' became human beings again. I began to think about the imagination and patience needed to work in such a place, the desire to enter the minds of intensely damaged people, to try to understand how they reached the point of violence, the point of killing. And then to spend years, trying to help repair the minds of people who are chronically psychologically disabled.

I was also fascinated that Dr Adshead referenced the work of Gitta Sereny – specifically her account of the life of Franz Stangl, the commandant of Treblinka, *Into This Darkness* – as this is a book which has haunted me for the last twenty years, and contributed directly to the focus of my work on the psychology of perpetrators. To attempt to understand the mind of a man who ran a camp which exterminated almost a million people takes us into territory which is terrifying. The immediate human instinct is to be repulsed; but until we comprehend the complex interaction of individual psychologies and societal forces that lead to such extremities, we will never be able to progress. Like Dr Adshead, I have often questioned the casual usage of the word 'evil' – especially when it's used about a person, as in 'He/she is just plain evil' – which has always seemed to me simply an excuse for lazy thinking, or rather no thinking at all. I also don't feel that the religious origins and associations of the word are very helpful in getting us to understand in more depth how people's states of mind can lead to appalling crimes or events.

*

Yet there is one obvious difference between the men whom Dr Adshead works with, and the men I've researched for the last twenty years, all the men whose minds I've tried to get inside.* Those I've investigated killed hundreds, thousands, even millions of people – yet none ever killed directly, with their own hands. From their desks, from their computers, from their mouths came words, memoranda, orders, reports which meant that numerous people were killed. These people would argue that there may not have been an intent to kill. Yes, people died, yes, it was extremely regrettable, but they were not responsible. Or rather they were only responsible in as much as they were part of a system, a large organisation that was involved in war or politics or trade all in extremely challenging circumstances.

It is shocking to me that our societies spend hundreds of millions of pounds researching definitions of 'psychopath' and 'sociopath', creating institutions to house such inmates, to protect the public from these violent offenders, yet almost nothing on investigating the psychology that leads to organisational killing. An individual psychopath, if free, and if factors combine to trigger attacks, might kill five or six times in their life; a government or an oil company can carpet-bomb cities, killing thousands, or wipe out the ecology of an entire region. And then do it again. And again. Seemingly with impunity.

Perhaps this is a reflection of our media's obsession with 'psychopaths', and the fact that there exists a mass readership for such material. A cynical voice in my head knows how marketing works, and

---

* I explore the disproportionate gender balance in desk killers, and what the clinical psychologist Simon Baron-Cohen terms the 'extreme male brain', in the second volume of *I You We Them*.

understands that simply adding the magic words 'psychopath' or 'evil' to the title of a book or film can trigger hundreds of thousands of additional sales. Another factor in the inability to take organisational killing seriously is perhaps the way it is far easier for us to focus on a single, aberrant human being than to look at how complex cultures and agencies within an organisation can enable killing to take place. Just as it so much easier in psychotherapy to focus on the individual's problems and 'neuroses' than to suggest that the kind of society we live in might contribute directly to unhappiness and depression.

The challenge we are left with is that few of the desk killers we've already met could be called 'psychopaths'. It is the challenge that Primo Levi and Hannah Arendt also left us with – the relative normality of many of the perpetrators. Not surprisingly, this is a difficult reality for us to accept, because it means we cannot distance ourselves from such people. We have to understand that in many ways they are closer to you and me than we would like to acknowledge.

Over twenty years of thinking about these questions, I've begun to wonder if it might be possible to identify certain factors, certain criteria that are often found in desk killers, people who kill from their organisations. There has been remarkably little academic research on this specific area, so I have had to create my own approach – not an abstract or academic one, but one based on two decades of thinking and reading about these issues. I've found it helpful to root my analysis in looking at individual lives and specific historical and contemporary examples. In the process of doing this, I have identified certain factors which enable people to kill without feeling a direct sense of personal responsibility. I describe these factors in the course of the pages which follow, and the books which follow too; but I don't want these to be seen in any way as a definitive list, more like the opening up of a conversation which takes place over a long time. Not all of these factors will be found in any one case of organisational killing, but they often inter-link, and sometimes overlap:

- Incrementalism
- 'Normalisation' and peer conformity
- Language and dehumanisation
- Abstractifying victims: from individuals to anonymous masses
- Distancing yourself from the act of violence
- Transferring personal responsibility to authority's responsibility
- Compartmentalisation of thought
- Workaholism and the 'narcissism of frenzy'
- Prioritisation of abstract systems over the human being
- Looking away or wilful ignorance

Incrementalism

The hundreds of – often extremely small – steps taken throughout a life; but each one significant, each one leading to the next stage, each leading to desensitisation of the individual.

Perhaps the most vivid illustration of incrementalism can be seen in the lives and careers of those who worked in the concentration and extermination camps in Nazi Germany and occupied Poland. The writer Tom Segev has described the way in which there was a kind of dual linear progression in their training – virtually all of those who eventually became concentration-camp commandants began at Dachau, under the tutelage of 'Papa' Eicke, while many of those who ultimately became extermination-camp commandants were employed earlier in the *Aktion T4* 'euthanasia' programme under Christian Wirth. I was also very struck by Segev's observation that

> They adjusted to their tasks at the camps from year to year, from camp to camp. Each stage prepared them for the next. They hardened . . . the brutality itself increased by stages, and the commandants accompanied that development. At the same time they rose in rank and acquired more responsibility.

217

Joseph Kramer, the commandant of Belsen, put it more succinctly, before his execution: 'We came a long way from Dachau to Bergen-Belsen.' But perhaps the most instructive example of how the process of incrementalism works can be seen in the life and career of Franz Stangl, the commandant of Treblinka. It is estimated that during the year that Stangl was in charge, 23 July 1942 to 19 August 1943, around 900,000 Jews were murdered at Treblinka. He escaped to Brazil after the war but was extradited to West Germany in 1968, was tried in 1970 in Düsseldorf and sentenced to life imprisonment. There, in April 1971, Gitta Sereny spent weeks interviewing him (the raw material that went into making *Into That Darkness* the landmark it became). I'd like to try to focus on the many possible steps, some of them very small, by which Stangl gradually becomes familiar with violence and horror, so that he became able to do his genocidal work:

Step 1. He's born in Altmünster, Austria, in 1908 – the young boy is close to his mother, his father is brutally violent to his son. The father dies when Franz is eight, his mother remarries.

Step 2. He leaves school at fifteen, becomes an apprentice weaver, learns to play the zither and starts to give lessons. At eighteen he does his exams and becomes the youngest master weaver in Austria. Later he called this 'my happiest time'. However, in the economically depressed mid-1920s, nobody can afford to take on a young weaver, however talented. So he has to look for other work.

Step 3. He attends the Vienna School Police institution, where sadistic training methods are used. Violence becomes normalised, and Stangl sees much older adults, figures of authority and respect, using violence as a central aspect of training.

Step 4. After general police training he undertakes an intensive course in surveillance and detective work, which he shows a strong aptitude for. (Later Stangl called this 'the first step to catastrophe', though I would say he was already on the way.)

Step 5. In autumn 1935 he's transferred to the political division of the *Kriminalpolizei* in a town near Linz, where his duties involved 'ferreting out anti-government activities' (primarily investigating social democrats and communists).

Step 6. In 1938, following Germany's annexation of Austria – the Anschluss – Stangl, as a Catholic, is strongly affected by Cardinal Innitzer's call for Catholics to co-operate fully with the Nazis.

Step 7. In November 1940, following a series of police promotions, Stangl is directed in a letter from Himmler to report to Tiergartenstrasse 4 ('T4' – the administrative centre of the 'euthanasia' programme that's just beginning). He's informed that he's been given an important and demanding position of police superintendent at a 'special institution' run by T4. He is flattered and excited by this new opportunity and career promotion.

Step 8. He talks further to the administrators at T4 and learns more of the work going on at this 'special institute'. He's told it involves 'mercy-killing' but only for those severely handicapped, i.e. incurables. He's also told his role will be to head the security at the facility and that there has to be total secrecy. He accepts these conditions.

Step 9. He arrives at Schloss Hartheim and is introduced to the doctors and the man responsible for all of the 'euthanasia' centres in the Reich, and the man later designated as the inspector of the extermination camps – Christian Wirth.

Step 10. Stangl reads a treatise on the Church's attitude to euthanasia by Professor Meyer, a Catholic theologian, and is reassured by the verdict that in certain circumstances it is 'defensible'. In this way Stangl deflects responsibility from himself to a more senior figure of authority (in a strikingly similar way to Adolf Eichmann after the Wannsee Conference).

Step 11. Later Stangl visits a convent for severely handicapped children, many of whom are to be killed. Again he describes being reassured: 'Here was a Catholic nun, a Mother Superior and a priest. And they thought it was right. Who was I then to doubt what was being done?'

Step 12. In February 1942, the 'euthanasia' programme at Hartheim is halted and Stangl is given a choice – he can return to Linz or move to a new post near Lublin in Poland. Because he didn't get on well with his former boss in Linz, he opts for the latter.

Step 13. Stangl visits Lublin for the first time in spring 1942 and meets Odilo Globočnik, the SS and police leader responsible for the extermination camps. Globočnik talks about a new 'supply camp' currently being built at Sobibor – would Stangl consider a posting there?

Step 14. He accepts the Sobibor position. On arrival, he recognises a new brick building exactly like the gas chamber at Hartheim. Doubts about the post he's accepted begin in Stangl's mind, but it's too late.

Step 15. Stangl visits Wirth again, this time at Bełżec – he comes across him standing over pits of hundreds, perhaps thousands of bodies. Now, seeing the reality of these 'supply camps', he tells Wirth he cannot do this job, but Wirth simply sends him back to Sobibor.

Step 16. Although he now realises that what is happening is clearly a crime and discusses it with a colleague, there seems to be no way out – he's afraid of what would happen to his family if he simply resigns from his post.

Step 17. Wirth comes to Sobibor to complete the building work. When it is finished he gasses twenty-five Jews in front of Stangl's eyes. Stangl tells himself he'll try to get a transfer as soon as possible.

Step 18. But as the first transports arrive, in May 1942, Stangl is still at Sobibor. He buys a 'nice linen, off-white' suit with a matching white riding jacket to mark the first train's arrival.

Step 19. In June 1942 his wife and two girls come to visit, staying only 5 km away. His wife has heard the dreadful rumours and confronts him – Stangl evades responsibility by denying being the commandant, his task is only related to construction.

Step 20. Just after this, Globočnik informs Stangl he's being transferred to the newly built camp at Treblinka.

Step 21. At 9.30 a.m. on 23 July 1942 the first transport of around 5,000 Jews arrives at Trebilinka. Later in the summer Stangl arrives – by this stage there are 10,000–15,000 Jews being killed every day. He calls it like witnessing 'the end of the world' and goes straight back to Globočnik, saying he cannot do this, but again he is sent back to Treblinka.

Step 22. By the end of 1942, Stangl is promoted to commandant. One of his first actions is the creation of a special garden, an aviary and a small zoo. He also builds a bakery; in his words, 'we had a wonderful Viennese baker, he made delicious cakes, very good bread'. At the same time, the camp is now operating at full capacity, with up to six transports arriving each day – each train containing more than 3,000 Jews (Treblinka at its peak was killing almost 20,000 Jews every day).

Twenty-two possible steps, each involving numerous smaller decisions. At each stage moral resistance fades, at each stage the level of violence witnessed increases. Each step leading further, incrementally, towards genocide. As Segev says of Stangl: 'All the assignments he performed prepared him psychologically for what came next.'

Stangl is certainly an extreme example – but in the way that each stage becomes normalised, and then leads to the next, it is probably little different from many career paths. The journey over twenty-five years from idealistic geology student to pragmatic oil industry executive. Or from the school chemistry lab to working on trigger mechanisms for nuclear weapons. Or the career that begins with fascination about Mendel's experiments and genetics, and ends up in biotech research, genetically engineering a tobacco seed that doubles the addictive nicotine content of tobacco plants.

12

A Pool in East London

I return to that drawing of a face on the back cover of the book. Like opening memory itself. I look more closely and I now see that the face appears to have a trace of a tear on the left cheek. As if Erin, by drawing this in a book of mine, was wanting to communicate something about herself she found hard to express. The photos from that year show two young lovers smiling, looking into the camera – on trains, in cafés – all the usual things. But I'm struck now by a difference between drawing and photography: however 'good' or 'bad' the drawing is, it is *itself*. A drawing cannot pose. So this small sketch, probably done in no more than a couple of minutes, seems to express more than all the photographs that were taken that year. We were in our early twenties, Erin escaping the constrictions of the Ireland she'd grown up in, me escaping a decade of extreme Conservatism in Britain. Italy seemed like an answer at the time, and we did explore a lot in that year – learning about another culture that seemed a world away from that we'd experienced before, learning about ourselves, and what it meant to be together. Intense, funny, insecure, passionate, hedonistic, melancholic, turbulent. Sometimes all of those in the same week. Often, looking back on your younger self, you can feel an impatience, even a kind of harshness, at the black-and-whiteness of judgement, the arrogance of youth, the delusions. But today all I feel is a tenderness for two young people, unsure about so much, trying to make sense of a journey that was just beginning.

On the facing page at the back of the book, she's jotted down, in her sloping handwriting:

> *Public swimming hours.*
> *Mon–Sat. – 12.40–18.30*
> *Sundays & Holidays – 9.00–18.30*

Erin was a passionate swimmer, so these times probably relate to the pool at Abano, which we'd get a bus to on Friday afternoons, when we'd finished teaching. In fact, it was she who really got me into swimming, something that lasted even when our relationship was over. She did it rather cleverly: knowing my weakness for 'people's palaces', whether the Festival Hall or the Moscow metro or the New York Public Library, she took me to the pool at Marshall Street in Soho. I was entranced by the green marble and gold edging; the swimming seemed almost incidental, just to be in that temple made you feel better. And, slowly but surely, swimming became a central part of my life.

*

My local pool in Hackney can't be compared to Marshall Street in any way. About the only thing they have in common is their Victorian origin. Where Marshall Street is all marble and brass, my pool is pale beige tiling and a functional steel roof. You have no chance of seeing anyone well known popping in here for a dip, whereas in Soho, you couldn't do a breaststroke without striking actors or TV presenters. They wouldn't be seen dead in Bethnal Green. It's about as far from 'aspirational' as it's possible to get. The pool's edges are worn and cracked, and a kind of green algae sometimes appears on the changing-room walls, because of the damp, presumably. When I was younger such things would have bothered me, but now it just seems 'lived-in' – in the way that a lined face shows the humanity of the person. I think I subconsciously identify with the pool as I get older – both of us accepting our imperfections, both of us a little rough around the edges now, showing our age.

Every few years the management make ridiculous attempts to 'rebrand' the pool as a 'twenty-first-century fitness experience' or something equally absurd, but these are always doomed to fail. The pool is resolute in its scruffiness. Short of being pulled down and rebuilt, it's completely unreformable. Occasionally the company that owns it puts up posters and signs saying things like: 'Aqua Leisure: Excellence is the Only Option', or other preposterous mantras. The regular swimmers just smile at these with ironic detachment, and continue their lengths. And the lengths are one of the reasons we come, because unlike most pools in inner-city London, which are usually twenty-five metres, this one is longer, eccentrically so – possibly the only pool in the city to be 33.33 metres. When I first asked one of the staff I thought they were winding me up, but since then I've paced it out, and it does indeed seem to be 33.33 metres. For people interested in length swimming (which seems to be most of us here), this is helpful because it means more time swimming and less time turning at the ends.

You might think the pool would be relatively quiet, considering its worn state, but you'd be wrong. At times, particularly school holidays, it becomes very busy. I've also learnt to avoid lunchtimes, when you get a particularly frantic type of swimmer, presumably connected to having limited time off work. My preferred time is Monday and Thursday evenings – when the pool stays open later, and the few people using it seem far more relaxed; that sense of leaving behind the stresses of the day.

After many years of going at these particular times you'd think that I'd recognise other regulars, but there are only a couple of faces I nod at. Strangely enough, you recognise people more by their (sometimes strikingly individual) ways of swimming. This is a diplomatic way of putting it. There's an elderly man who has a habit of smacking the surface of the water with his hand, as he does his slow crawl, as if determined to displace as much of the pool as possible. If you're swimming in the same lane this becomes infuriating, especially if you're doing breaststroke, because every time you pass each other, you get a face full of spray. Yet, curiously, when he rests at the shallow end after a few lengths, he emanates a benevolence and calm quite at odds with his style of swimming. The pool is usually set up in four wide lanes – so that in each lane people can swim up one way, and back down the the other side of the lane. The lanes are designated 'fast', 'medium', 'slow' and there's an unspecified one (generally off-limits to the public because being used for swimming lessons). Generally the fast lane is dominated by younger women and men propelling themselves, with metronomic rhythm, up and down with their crawl. There's a more diverse demographic mix in the medium lane, mainly doing breaststroke. And then the tentative swimmers – parents with children, the elderly, people with infirmities, the over-weight, the underweight – occupy the slow lane, some of them barely swimming at all, spending more time just chatting in the water. I've also come to recognise a group I call 'Buddhist swimmers', who don't like to be hurried in any way. Though confident in the water – long, meditative strokes – they nearly always stay in the slow lane as well, swimming in their own bubble of calm. Signs by each lane, with arrows, instruct the users to swim either clockwise or anticlockwise.

I've always remembered reading something that an American psychologist and writer wrote, in a playful article titled '101 Solutions to All Your Problems', or something like that. He said, 'Drive for space and not speed.' So for years I've adopted this approach for driving, especially on motorways, and it works – you can nearly always find a place that's less crowded. This seems so simple, yet if more people actually drove like this the accident rate would proba-bly be halved overnight. When I started swimming I also began to use this method. And so, when entering the pool, I never head for a specific lane, but start by looking at the traffic in all of them. Occa-sionally, and wonderfully, you'll come out of the changing room and realise the whole pool is blissfully empty, only one or two swimmers in each lane. But usually you'll need to do quite a bit of counting and lane comparison before choosing. Sometimes I'm amazed at how fixed people are about swimming in a particular lane, oblivious to the fact that a neighbouring one is far less busy. If there are six or seven swimmers in the middle lane, but only two in the fast lane, it seems obvious to me to swim in the fast lane. Or the slow lane. It doesn't really matter, just find the place with the most space.

Swimmers divide into two categories which essentially define their swimming, and probably their attitude to life as well. There are what I call 'free' swimmers and 'length counters'. It would be tempting (but wrong, I think) to divide these on gender grounds alone, i.e. men as counters, and women as freer – in my experience there are just as many the other way round. I cannot stress enough the depth of the philosophical divide between these two types. 'Free' swimmers perhaps sounds too positive – we could also call them 'aimless' swimmers. Time and distance are unimportant for these people. One day they might come for forty-five minutes, another day twenty. There's no reason to push themselves, no point. The action of swimming is the main thing. A space for the body that essentially frees the mind. These swimmers often talk about being able to 'lose themselves' when they're swimming, being able to 'process things' as they swim. It's essentially the therapeutic approach to the swimming pool. Erin was very much in this category.

Though I may sound a little critical of free swimmers, this is probably because I could never be one, and perhaps am a little envious. I'm genuinely curious about what it would feel like not to care about the time or the distance you've swum. I suppose it could be an extraordinary liberation. The only time I've experienced this in any way is swimming in the sea with friends on holiday, which is lovely, but bears so little relation to 'swimming', as I think of it, that it seems a different activity altogether. Holiday swimming, by its very nature, is something out of the ordinary, and so any normal rules do not apply.

Sometimes (but whisper this carefully!) I wonder whether free swimmers might actually be happier people. I occasionally have fantasies about crossing over to the other side, but ever since I started swimming I have always been a 'length counter', and no doubt always will be. For me it's all about time and distance, it's about pushing yourself as hard as you can, about shaving seconds, parts of seconds, off times. I'm intensely competitive with myself. I make myself swim when it's zero degrees outside, or in the middle of a heatwave. I swim when I'm sad or happy. Feeling a little ill is no excuse – in fact I've often found that a vigorous 1,200 metres is an effective way of chasing off a burgeoning cold. And the reason for all of this? Some say it's just chemicals being released, but I think it's more than that. It would be hard to explain to a non-swimmer, but there is an extraordinary energy that can come when your rhythm is established, and when your breathing, your arms and legs are all working in total synergy. At these moments, you seem to go into a kind of trance, it's not about concentration any more, but letting go. (Though still remembering to count the lengths of course!) And afterwards, the sense of your *whole* body singing, a kind of zinging energy field around you as you emerge into the outside world again. And I know it does miraculous things for the mind as well. For people involved in any work that's sedentary – writing being an extreme example – there are so many dangers inherent in spending most of your days seated in front of a screen. And swimming is the perfect antidote.

I should explain at this point that I'm not a very skilful swimmer, nor very fast, but I am assiduous. Like most 'length counters', I have developed an extremely detailed routine, which I've followed for almost thirty years now, and which I stick to – rigidly. I come into the pool thirty-five to forty minutes before closing time, which gives me a few minutes to do my stretches before beginning the swim. With exactly thirty-two minutes to go, as the second hand of the clock at the end of the pool completes its minute, I launch myself. The aim is to do precisely thirty-two lengths (just over 1,066 metres) in thirty-two minutes. If I'm swimming in a twenty-five-metre pool, I adjust the target to forty-two lengths (1,050 metres) in the same time. I start in two-length bursts, then halfway through move to three lengths, and finish with four-length sections. Every second length, as I'm coming back down to the shallow end, I glance up at the clock expectantly, checking my time, and then trying to increase my pace, however fractionally. The majority of these lengths are breaststroke, but I do incorporate backstroke (in the two-length bursts) and sidestroke (in the three-length bursts). As the pool attendant blows the whistle to signal the end of the session, I'm usually turning for my final length. One final push. I finish with half a length of backstroke, then rapidly turn over to check the clock, and see if I've achieved my target time. Very, very occasionally – maybe once every two years – I'll lose concentration and forget how many lengths I've done. This, needless to say, is extremely aggravating, and erases the value of that swimming session entirely.

There is a real poignancy in doing the same physical activity over many years. And that is you become aware of the very gradual changes in your body. You may disguise these to yourself, by running for shorter times, or swimming slightly fewer lengths, but you know your body's capacity is reducing, however slowly, year by year. In my twenties and thirties I would do fifty lengths (around 2 km) without even thinking about it, and sometimes sixty. For a few years in my late thirties, forty-two lengths became the norm, in my early forties thirty-eight seemed pretty good, and now in my late forties, I'm down to thirty-two. At the moment going below thirty seems unthinkable, but who knows, in five or ten years . . . You're probably beginning to understand why swimming is not primarily a relaxing activity for me. You might be amused, or horrified, at the numerical detail of what I've outlined above, but I doubt if it's wildly different from many who run or swim or go to the gym regularly.

Set against all these numbers and counting and extertion, I should also say that the mind seems to go into some very curious corners when you're swimming. The thoughts that come can be so lateral. As inexplicable as dreams, or as darkly comic as Woody Allen films. Perhaps this is not so surprising if we step back and consider what's actually happening here – you're almost naked, surrounded by strangers, all suspended in water. You might expect thoughts about birth or sex, but I find I spend a disproportionate amount of time thinking about mortality. The fact that none of us know the time of our death before it happens. Every year we live through the day on which we'll die, with no notion of this shadow at all – the exact opposite of the birthday. Nearly all of our lives consist of deferred actions, everlasting lists, whether written down or not. All that we die with unfinished, incomplete, all the epiphanic conversations we thought there would be time for, but as the moment lumbers inexorably closer, we then understand that there is no more time. That life (if only we'd known it) was always provisional. We never reached where we thought we might reach. The summit of the mountain was always illusory.

Other people's deaths are somehow encompassable. Our own has a ring of impossibility around it. It plays tricks with how we think of time. We can say, 'How strange, that was the last time she ever saw her brother, two days later she was dead.' Yet we rarely consider the last time we will see the people who are most important in our lives. The last time our skin will touch the Mediterranean Sea. The last time we will eat a perfectly ripe peach. Maybe those times have already passed . . . We may feel, even when we get older, that life still stretches out in a kind of infinity. We could not be more wrong. To really know, to understand that our days are ticking by, that they are limited, and that we have no idea of when everything will stop. To live like this, all the time, would be unbearable – I'm not sure the human brain is wired this way. In the final scene of the film version of Paul Bowles' novel *The Sheltering Sky*, the author appears as himself in a Tangier café, face wizened with age, but blue eyes still dancing mischievously – the apotheosis of life facing death. He says this looking directly into the camera:

> We get to think of life as an inexhaustible well, yet everything happens only a certain number of times – and a very small number really. How many more times will you remember a certain afternoon of your childhood? Some afternoon that's so deeply a part of your being that you can't even conceive of your life without it. Perhaps a few times more? Perhaps not even that? How many more times will you watch the full moon rise? Perhaps twenty? And yet it all seems limitless.

*

But the reason I need to describe this swimming pool, and my relationship with it, is not primarily to do with death – rather the opposite, in fact. Over the last few years, I've begun to think about the people who use this place in a different way. When I started coming here the only thing that mattered to me was the water, that this was a place where I could swim up and down for forty-five minutes. The other people using this space were simply challenges I had to navigate around. To a certain extent this is still true. London is a heavily populated city, all of us, from time to time, become aggravated by the sheer press of bodies. It is a difficult experience to have to force yourself onto a Tube train at rush hour, to have to stand with your head bowed to fit inside the door. And then imagining the panic and suffocation if anything serious happened and the train stopped between stations for half an hour, an hour . . .

Because of such cramped existences I sometimes feel that most Londoners hold themselves on an extremely tight rein, and that it can take very little to set us off. That, paradoxically, living and working in such close proximity to others has not meant that we now find this easier, just that we have developed coping mechanisms. You can see this every day in the swimming pool. People trying to find a kind of freedom in the water, in the elemental escape. And then, when others impact upon this small moment of release, the anger can become even greater, people lash out – a kind of 'swim rage', a distant cousin of 'road rage'. Nearly everything comes down to selfish behaviour – the sense that people do not really believe they are using a space which is shared with others, or completely fail to see the impact their actions will have on other swimmers. I have become fascinated by observing the behaviour of people using the pool and the way that some have curious concepts of sharing public space.

- A Sunday afternoon, the pool is full. A young guy decides he's going to do his butterfly anyway, in the medium lane. He does one length, creating havoc. After the second length, two older women start to remonstrate with him. At first he

231

ignores them, and then he begins to get aggressive, saying, 'You don't control me! I can swim how I want!' Eventually the attendant intervenes, and the young guy leaves the pool with a volley of swearing.

- A Thursday evening, the three lanes are oddly busy, but I notice the unnamed lane is relatively quiet, there are three Turkish girls playing at the shallow end. Because the unnamed lane never uses the 'clockwise' or 'anticlockwise' signs, swimmers have to negotiate where they do their lengths. In this situation I always prefer swimming up and down as close as possible to the lane divider (meaning I have to negotiate around other swimmers only on one side).

I'm really pleased that my favourite position is free and so I start doing my breaststroke up and down, next to the lane divider. After a dozen lengths I notice a young couple getting into the pool at the deep end, and positioning themselves dangerously close to 'my' line. So I keep my line, and when I reach the other end, they have to move slightly as I touch the edge of the pool and start my return length. I've made my point, they will now understand that this small area of water (no more than a yard across) is not available and will move to another, unoccupied, part of the wide lane. But no. When I turn at the shallow end I see that the girl is doing her crawl in *exactly* the line I've just swum! This breaks all the unspoken etiquette of the pool – the fact that when you join a lane you respect the swimmers who were there before you. I'm not going to let them get away with this, so I keep swimming along the precise line that I have been for the last few minutes. We're on collision course. I can see her white swimming cap getting closer and closer, she's doing her crawl, pretending not to notice. Neither of us are going to give in. We collide. Words are exchanged, but I continue my line. Eventually the couple realise they've bitten off more than they can chew and move further over into freer water. A small victory for pool protocol, but an important one.

232

Such examples, especially when written down, might seem petty or even comical, but such behaviour led to loss of temper and aggravation. I find myself thinking about the nature of the society we live in, and asking what this kind of behaviour says about us as a people. I'm sure we can all think of many other examples of people's inabilities to share public space, and perhaps this is not only a modern phenomenon. But I have a strong feeling that we are all much more in our own 'bubbles' now than we've ever been before. An image from Jonathan Franzen's novel *The Corrections*, published around the turn of the century, made a lasting impression on me. It was a depiction of an American suburban house, viewed from the outside, with five different windows illuminated. A family, admittedly rather a dysfunctional one – parents and three children – were in five separate rooms, staring into their five individual TVs and computers, all in their bubbles of techno-glow. It struck me as a powerful metaphor for the anomie of modern life, yet at the time I also thought Franzen was exaggerating somewhat.

But today, the reality of such atomised existences is all around us, every day. An enormous amount of this is attributable to the way new technology is being used, which means that people may be on a bus or a Tube but literally will not know what's going on around them, because they have headphones on so they can't hear anything (except what they're listening to). People walk in the street, but they're not looking at their surroundings or other people, because they're staring at their little screens, or texting as they walk. What concerns me in all of this is the unspoken, but growing, belief that the only really important thing is that your own needs are satisfied. That you have your techno-toys wherever you go, and if somebody tries to 'invade your space' you lose your temper. It's almost as if our entire societies are now becoming stuck at the developmental level of a self-absorbed four-year-old child having a tantrum.

So, if common understandings about behaviour in shared public space are breaking down, then what are the implications? And is there a relationship between our ability to share public space and

233

our ability to behave democratically? On the second point, the connection is clear, and it rests on whether or not people *really* believe they have equal rights. And, if you do, your own behaviour must reflect this. This is, of course, easier said than done, because it also goes against so much of our society's obsessions with unrestricted notions of individualism and the free market. But really believing in equality, as far as I can see, means starting to realise that one of the most significant acts of resistance we can make is to change our own behaviour. Gradually trying to reduce the *I* and the *me*, and thinking far more about the *you* and the *they*. Reducing the volume when we speak, wanting others to have more voice. Perhaps most of all, we would have to learn how to really listen. Not the listening that we habitually think we're doing – the nodding, the 'a-huh'ing (when we're actually already thinking about what we're going to say next) – but a real desire to know what the other is saying, thinking or feeling. What the philosopher Simone Weil describes as the quintessence of love – the real belief in the existence of another human being.

And this connects to my fascination with observing behaviour in my local swimming pool in Hackney, because, at a microcosmic level, it is a representation of society in all its challenging and messy reality. It's where people come together. The swimming pool as the archetypal democratic space. I've seen ninety-year-olds swimming there, I've seen nine-month-old babies with armbands there. I've seen Buddhists and bankers rubbing shoulders with each other. I've seen people from every race and background imaginable using this place – it's probably one of the most ethnically diverse spaces in the whole of the country. And although I have written about examples of selfish behaviour, considering I've been coming to swim here for fifteen years, on reflection, it's pretty remarkable how few such incidents there are.

And if sometimes there are ructions in the pool, if there are occasionally cross words shouted between the lanes, then is that really so serious? Or isn't this simply the reality of any truly democratic space? Not the idealised Athenian model, but a grittier exchange.

234

The cultural theorist Stuart Hall, interviewed a few years before he died, spoke about his conception of democracy and its relationship to what he termed 'the multicultural question':

How can we recognise the true, real, complicated diversity of the planet? . . . Different histories, different cultures, over long periods of time, have produced a variegated world, but the barriers are now breaking down. People find themselves obliged to make a common life or at least find some common ground of negotiation . . . The 'multicultural question' has now arrived right into the middle of the societies that have lived the last 200 years pretending that they could draw a boundary between themselves and the others . . . or that they could regulate the lives and the economies of other people because they were, or looked, different, and this provided a legitimate basis for their exploitation. I am interested in the impact on these European societies in particular . . . of having to live with difference, with people who dress differently, speak differently, have different memories in their heads, know a different way of life, follow a different religion – how are they going to live in greater equality but also with *difference*? How are these often conflicting objectives – equality and difference – to be reconciled?

. . . That trade-off is going to be an untidy row. Don't think it is going to be what is called, these days, 'social cohesion' – which is a polite form of assimilation of 'the other', and represents in effect the abandonment of the multicultural principle. There is going to be nothing cohesive about it at all. It's going to be a bloody great row. Any form of democratic life . . . is a big, staged, continuous row. Because there are real differences, and people are deeply invested in them and so they have to find ways – difficult ways – of negotiating difference, because it's not going to go away.[*]

---

[*] In conversation with Bill Schwarz at Queen Elizabeth Hall, London, February 2007.

So what would it mean to 'swim democratically'? To start with, you'd have to examine your own swimming more critically, and the effect it has on other people. The first thing would be to acknowledge that, just as I have been annoyed or aggravated by others' ways of swimming, so my swimming must have, at times, wound others up. For example, my swimming 'for space and not speed' means that often, although technically I'm a 'medium-paced' swimmer, I'm actually swimming in the 'slow' lane or the 'fast' lane because there are fewer people there. So, for the genuinely slower swimmers, they get overtaken by this serious-looking man doing vigorous breaststroke and causing little waves. And for the faster crawlers, 'Why is that man doing breaststroke in our "fast" lane?' We all have a tendency to consider our own actions as 'normal'; I think it's exactly the same when we swim. I consider my pace of breaststroke to be appropriate; I get impatient when there's a slower person doing breaststroke ahead of me, because it means having to alter my position to overtake. I also get crabby if there's a faster breaststroke swimmer coming up behind me – what's their problem?! What's wrong with swimming at a relaxed pace?

Sometimes I wonder if the problems really are 'out there' as much as 'in here'. My father, in his many years of commuting by train (another overcrowded, contested public space) between Manningtree and London, would say that he could realise his mood by noting his attitude to his fellow commuters on any given day. If he was fed up or tired for some reason, he'd survey 'them' with a jaundiced, generalised eye, only seeing a mass of avaricious businessmen. If he was in a good mood, he'd get chatting to somebody in the buffet car, and recognise that behind the suit and tie, there was an interesting, complex human being, fascinated by rock climbing or the Greek Orthodox Church or Miles Davis or whatever it might be.

I would like to be able to swim in a similar spirit, and be able to go beyond seeing simply a mass of other swimmers, to really appreciate everybody's uniqueness. More than this, one day it would be extraordinary to be able to feel another swimmer's love for what they were doing, as vividly as my own. And to know that their love was equally important, a representation of the rights that we share in this society. And if this might be possible in a London swimming pool, then go beyond the walls of the pool, and the boundaries of the city and consider how transformative such imaginative empathy could be. If we could feel the rights of citizens in Nigeria or Iraq or Afghanistan as keenly as we feel our own. If we could really believe that they love their land and their rivers and their forests no less than we do. The political implications of such a shift in our structures of thinking and feeling – 'senti-pensando', as the writer Eduardo Galeano puts it – would be incalculable.

Occasionally I get a tantalising taste of such a future in my local pool. On a good day, when my spirit is alive to the world, I glimpse what living democracy means, and am moved intensely by what we share in that faded municipal building in my city – seeing grandparents, who've probably been swimming here for seventy years, now bringing their grandchildren; watching a teenage Bangladeshi girl turning at the deep end, with astonishing dolphinesque acceleration; noticing a tattooed East End geezer doing the most elegant backstroke you've ever seen. The vast multiplicity of humanity, all making our own different ways through the waters of life.

How People in Organisations Can Kill: The Second Factor

'Normalisation' and Peer Conformity

The way that something that shocks or appals at first can later become acceptable if we see those around us going along with it.

Tolstoy makes this statement at the beginning of Chapter Thirteen of *Anna Karenina*: 'There are no conditions of life to which a man cannot get accustomed, especially if he sees them accepted by everyone around him.' Watching *Shoah* again recently, I was struck to hear the following words spoken by the Polish farmers who worked the fields right next to Treblinka throughout the war – bearing out, precisely, the accuracy of Tolstoy's assertion:

> Farmer 1: It was terrible, you used to hear them crying out.
> Farmer 2: Yes, at first it's hard . . . then you get used to it.

And this testimony from Richard Baer, one of Auschwitz's commandants. On leave in Hamburg, he described on one occasion witnessing a little girl 'flaming like a torch. She had been hit by a phosphorus bomb dropped by British planes. She burned to death in front of my eyes. That happened before I came to Auschwitz. You can get used to everything.'

But the people I would like to concentrate on in this section are the doctors who worked at Auschwitz; the following quotations are drawn from interviews conducted by Robert Jay Lifton for his seminal work *The Nazi Doctors*, and concentrate on the experiences of two doctors – Ernst B* and Hans Delmotte. First, the testimony of Ernst B:

> In discussing patterns of diminished feeling, Ernst B told me that it was the 'key' to understanding what happened

---

* Later revealed to be Dr Hans Münch, interviewed by Gitta Sereny, 'The Man Who Said No', in *The German Trauma*.

in Auschwitz. In also pointing out that 'one could react like a normal human being in Auschwitz only for the first few hours' he was talking about how anyone entering the place was almost immediately enveloped in a blanket of numbing. Under increasing pressure to select, most SS doctors underwent what he viewed as an extraordinary individual-psychological shift from revulsion to acceptance: 'In the beginning it was almost impossible. Afterward it became almost routine. That's the only way to put it.'

This shift involved a socialization to Auschwitz, including the important transition from outsider to insider. Alcohol was crucial to this transition. Drinking together, often quite heavily, on evenings in the officers' club, doctors 'spoke very freely' and 'expressed the most intimate objections.' Some would 'condemn the whole thing' and insist that 'this is a filthy business [*Schweinerei*]!' Dr B described these outbursts as so insistent as to be 'like a mania [*Sucht*], . . . a sickness . . . over Auschwitz and . . . the gassings.' Such inebriated protest brought about no repercussion – indeed, may even have been encouraged – and was unrelated to commitment or action. Consequently, 'whether one condemned it or not was not really so much the issue.' The issue, as Ernst B defined it, was that 'Auschwitz was an existing fact. One couldn't . . . really be against it, you see, one had to go along with it whether it was good or bad.' Mass killing was the unyielding fact to which everyone was expected to adapt.

Whenever an SS doctor arrived at Auschwitz, the process was repeated as questions raised by the newcomer were answered by his more experienced drinking companions: He would ask, 'How can these things be done here?' Then there was something like a general answer . . . which clarified everything. What is better for him [the prisoner] – whether he croaks [*verreckt*] in shit or goes to heaven in [a cloud of] gas? And that settled the whole matter for the initiates.

This is Dr B, now describing the selection process the new doctors had to witness:

> When you see a selection for the first time – I'm not talking only about myself, I'm talking about even the most hardened SS people . . . you see . . . how children and women are selected. Then you are so shocked . . . that it just cannot be described. And after a few weeks one can be accustomed to it . . . And that [process] cannot be explained to anybody . . . And one can . . . only experience [it to know it]. The expert can record it, but he cannot enter into it – 'know it from the inside.' But I think I can give you a kind of impression of it. When you have gone into a slaughterhouse where animals are being slaughtered . . . the smell is also a part of it . . . not just the fact that they [the cattle] fall over [dead] and so forth. A steak will probably not taste good to us afterward. And when you do that [stay in the situation] every day for two weeks, then your steak again tastes as good as before.

In the case of Dr Delmotte, we can see the strategies that the Auschwitz authorities used to habituate him to his work, aiding the extermination process:

> At the first selection he was taken to, Delmotte became nauseated and returned to his room quite drunk; what was unusual, however, was that he did not leave his room the next morning. Dr B heard that Weber [Dr Bruno Weber, chief of the 'Hygienic Institute' at Auschwitz], upon visiting Delmotte, found him 'catatonic . . . completely blocked'; Weber thought at first that the young doctor had been stricken with a severe illness but concluded that he had simply had too much to drink. When he finally emerged in an agitated state, he was heard to say that he 'didn't want to be in a slaughterhouse' and preferred to go to the front, and that 'as a doctor his task was to help people and not to kill them.' It was an argument, Dr B said, that 'we never used' in Auschwitz: 'It would have been totally point-

less' . . . B also stressed that Delmotte approached the medical profession 'with high ideals and great enthusiasm,' that he had 'grown up in an SS cadet camp' and was 'determined not to betray his SS ideals,' and that he had declared (though this only when drunk) that he would never have joined the SS if he had 'known that there was such a thing as Auschwitz.'

Lifton then describes the remarkable lengths that the Auschwitz authorities went to in order to assuage Delmotte's distress at what he was now being expected to do. Dr B found out that the new commandant, Arthur Liebenschel (Rudolf Höss's temporary successor), took a 'therapeutic' approach, and had been sympathetic to Delmotte, telling him, 'I can certainly understand this. One must first get used to a new environment.' Liebenschel then organised, in collaboration with Dr Weber and Dr Eduard Wirths, the chief SS doctor at Auschwitz, a three-part 'therapeutic programme' for Delmotte.

First, Delmotte was given Mengele as a kind of mentor figure, Mengele was able to appeal to Delmotte's shared 'SS idealism', and persuade him to change his viewpoint by arguing that even if one thinks that extermination of the Jewish people is wrong, or is being done in the wrong way (Delmotte, according to Dr B, believed that 'Jewish influence' had to be combatted but disapproved of the Auschwitz method) . . . since prisoners became sick and died terrible deaths, it was 'more humane to select them.' Also he used the 'combined patriotic, nationalistic, racial, and biomedical argument that, during this wartime emergency, one should do nothing to interfere with the great goal being sought: 'the triumph of the Germanic race.' Within two weeks Mengele's persuasion had done the trick and Delmotte began to take part in the selections again.

Secondly, Liebenschel agreed with Weber's suggestion, as a 'good psychologist,' that Delmotte's wife, very unusually for an SS doctor at Auschwitz, should be allowed to live at the camp. We know from Dr B that she possessed great beauty and great amorality, as he put it – 'no heart, no soul, no nothing' . . . But it seems that Delmotte's regular sexual access to her made him calmer, more 'quiet.'

Finally, Delmotte was given another intellectual mentor (for the research and writing involved in his dissertation) – an eminent, elderly Jewish prisoner physician, a former professor and widely acclaimed scientist who became a 'father figure' to Delmotte, according to other doctors at Auschwitz. The two men became very close, and Dr B felt that the professor 'contributed the most toward helping Delmotte out of his [difficulties]'. Lifton tells us that Delmotte then selected without further incident until selections were discontinued in Auschwitz in the autumn of 1944.[*]

Again, there might be a temptation to consider such examples as extreme. Yet anyone who has experienced military training or war situations would recognise significant parallels with the examples given above – the survivalist need to adapt rapidly or else go under, the continuous comparison of oneself with one's fellow soldiers and the strong appeals to patriotism. There is also the extensive use of alcohol or drugs – as can be seen in the recent wars in Iraq and Afghanistan – to anaesthetise against the most disturbing aspects of war, and finally, the selective use of respected elders in pastoral care when a soldier is experiencing exceptional difficulties.

---

[*] Delmotte committed suicide in 1945.

PART FIVE

Walking into the World of the Desk Killer – Four Journeys

'History walks on two feet.'

Karl Marx

13

The Doctors of Wannsee Meet in a Villa by the Lake

1. Night Train to Berlin: Fifty Paces from T4 to the Philharmonic

27/8 December 2003, Brussels Midi

Past midnight. Icy wind. Drifts of rain sweep across the platform. Two hours here waiting for the Berlin train. Bit dazed from last night still, only two hours' sleep, watching Shoah *again in preparation for this journey, only finishing at 6.30 this morning. Struck by the drabness of this station, especially compared with the modernity of the Eurostar terminal. Peeling concrete, fag ends everywhere, accentuated by continuous dripping and harsh glare of sodium lights. Desolate. Tarkovsky territory.*

Train pulls in, forty minutes late, my seat is occupied by a Turkish family but decide not to do the uptight English thing about it, soon find another half-empty compartment, slide down next to the window. Into a kind of trance. A fug of warmth and darkness. I fall into sleep listening to a middle-aged South American man chatting to two Chinese girls. Come round to a train nightscape through the glass – Belgian towns, rushing delivery vans, wettened, blackened streets, beads of Christmas lights. And, as so often before, thinking of the eyes of the deported, through the cracks of the wagons, travelling

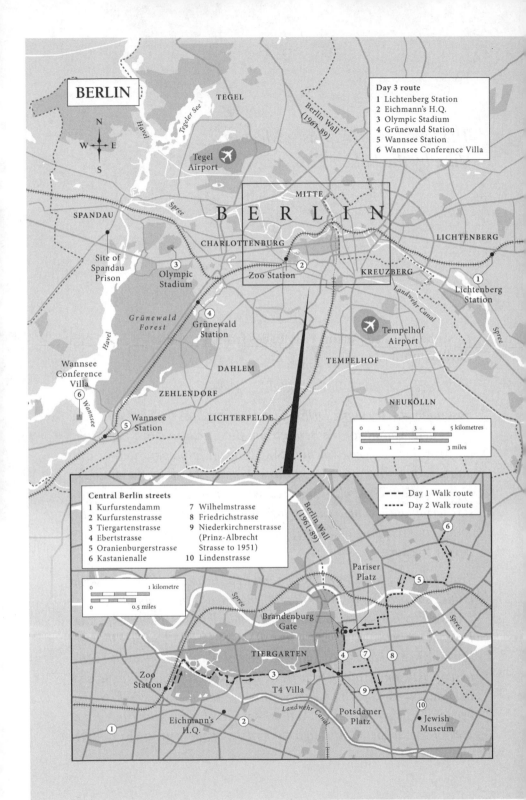

BERLIN

N
W ← → E
S

TEGEL

Havel

Tegel See

Berlin Wall (1961-89)

Tegel Airport

SPANDAU

Spree

MITTE

B E R L I N

LICHTENBERG

Site of Spandau Prison

CHARLOTTENBURG

Olympic Stadium ③

Zoo Station ②

KREUZBERG

Landwehr Canal

① Lichtenberg Station

Grünewald Forest

Grünewald Station ④

Tempelhof Airport

Spree

DAHLEM

TEMPELHOF

Wannsee Conference Villa ⑥

Havel

ZEHLENDORF

LICHTERFELDE

NEUKÖLLN

Wannsee ⑤ Station

Wannsee

Day 3 route
1 Lichtenberg Station
2 Eichmann's H.Q.
3 Olympic Stadium
4 Grünewald Station
5 Wannsee Station
6 Wannsee Conference Villa

0   1   2   3   4   5 kilometres
0   1   2   3 miles

Central Berlin streets
1 Kurfurstendamm
2 Kurfurstenstrasse
3 Tiergartenstrasse
4 Ebertstrasse
5 Oranienburgerstrasse
6 Kastanienalle
7 Wilhelmstrasse
8 Friedrichstrasse
9 Niederkirchnerstrasse (Prinz-Albrecht Strasse to 1951)
10 Lindenstrasse

- - - Day 1 Walk route
······ Day 2 Walk route

Berlin Wall (1961-89)

0   1 kilometre
0   0.5 miles

Spree

⑥

Pariser Platz

⑤

Brandenburg Gate

Spree

TIERGARTEN

④ ⑦ ⑧

Zoo Station

③

T4 Villa

⑨

①

Eichmann's H.Q.

②

Potsdamer Platz

Landwehr Canal

⑩ • Jewish Museum

these same tracks sixty years ago, the glinting rails leading ever further eastwards and away from safety.

Coming into Berlin, Sunday morning. Surprised by the rawness of my emotion, confronted by the fact of the passage of time. Last time here, August 1984, with Ayesha. Twenty years old! That very nerve-wracking hitching, having to bribe the East German border guard in the middle of the night because my passport was about to expire. Only getting out of that due to Ayesha's excellent German. The bizarre sunken road that led to West Berlin, fenced off on both sides. The wall. Another century now. Old friends dispersed, lost with the passage of time.

*

Ten days. A journey long in the planning. Days to travel through Berlin, physically and conceptually – to try to understand the forces that culminated in the meeting at Wannsee which has so dominated my thoughts these last years. Days in which we'll see Auschwitz and Monowitz for the first time. The exact place that Primo Levi analysed with his chemist's precision. And by travelling in the depth of winter, perhaps we will avoid the mass tourism aspect that I've always found so disturbing. Then finally to Lodz and Chelmno – and a full circle will have been completed, from the town in Switzerland which manufactured the *gaswagen* to the remote area of Poland where they were used. The place where Simon Srebnik was forced to sing, as he relates in the opening sequence of *Shoah*.

J. and I have talked for years about these places, these sites of catastrophe, and now, finally, we will be seeing them together. I don't think I could do this alone. And J. has been my companion from the earliest years of this quest, so it is entirely right that we'll be meeting, in a few minutes, at the Berlin station this train is now pulling into. We have a guide on this journey too, in the form of an invaluable book by Martin Gilbert, which J. gave me five years ago – *Holocaust Journey*. I open the book, and see that J.

has inscribed it in his elegant writing, 'For Dan, In hope of a future journey together . . .' It is also almost exactly twenty years since we met, since Platform was born, so these ten days are also a way of marking this milestone.

Stepping down onto the platform with my heavy rucksack – J. there immediately, taking off his black hat and bowing in exaggeratedly formal greeting. Wonderful to see him. Both of us a bit shot away from our overnight journeys so we find a café just out of the station, at the top of the Kurfürstendamm. J. also feeling a bit funny about Berlin – bad associations with a girl here in the late 1980s. Then, following Gilbert, we walk up the Landswehr canal, past the place where Rosa Luxemburg was murdered, then along a tree-lined street to see the Spanish Embassy, a rather pompous neoclassical edifice. Eagles over the door with Franco's slogan '*Una, grande, libre*' ('One, great,

free'). Surprised by that detail of Gilbert's that Franco refused to deport any Spanish Jews. Round the corner, the former Danish Legation, built by Albert Speer. Shocked by its blandness, total lack of anything distinctive. In Rauchstrasse, two more Speer buildings, the former embassies of Yugoslavia and Norway. We reflect on the laziness of many historians who repeat the cliché that 'all that remains of Speer today is a few lamp posts in Berlin'.

We walk eastwards along Tiergartenstrasse. How much this street has occupied my mind over the last years. Or rather, what was planned from a villa on this street, at Tiergartenstrasse 4 – 'T4', as the Nazi 'euthanasia' programme became known – which killed over 70,000 people in its first phase between September 1939 and August 1941, including children, the elderly and mentally and physically disabled patients. It feels like the Kensington of Berlin

249

– a wooded park to the left, embassy buildings to the right. And the former Krupp villa. Imagining all the meetings of industrialists and Nazi leaders here. Now, we see it's a Jesuit college. We continue, past the site of the former British passport control office, picturing thousands of Jewish Germans queuing up here in the 1930s as the situation became more and more desperate.

A couple of hundred yards further on and we've arrived at the site of the T4 villa. There is a small plaque here but nothing else to mark the place. We are confused by Gilbert's account: he describes a piece of wasteland where it is still possible to see 'the occasional brick or broken stone' of the building that was once here. But there is nothing at all here now. Although the view from the villa over the park opposite would doubtless have been the same. As the bureaucrat killers looked up from their desks. Or left for their lunches.

Today, perhaps fifty yards behind where the T4 villa stood, thousands gather every week at one of the global shrines of classical music – the Berliner Philharmonie, home to the Berlin Philharmonic (overseen when we were there by the conductor Simon Rattle).

*

The 'euthanasia' killings were organised from this place – which was given the title the 'Charitable Foundation for Institutional Care'. Hitler had appointed his own doctor, Professor Karl Brandt, and Reichsleiter Philipp Bouhler of the Chancellery to oversee the programme of supposed 'mercy deaths'. But the details of the operations were organised by SS Oberführer Viktor Brack, based here at Tiergartenstrasse. The killings were carried out at six sites across Germany, all psychiatric hospitals – Grafeneck, Brandenburg, Bernburg, Hartheim, Sonnenstein and Hadamar, between January 1940 and August 1941. At these hospitals, small, improvised gas chambers, often disguised as 'shower rooms', were created. Carbon monoxide gas, supplied by BASF (then part of the IG Farben corporation), was used in the gas chambers, and afterwards some of the victims' bodies were dissected for supposed 'medical science', gold teeth were extracted, and then the bodies were burned in crematoria. All techniques that were later used, on a far larger scale, in the extermination programme. Many of the key personnel in *Aktion T4* such as Viktor Brack, Christian Wirth, Philipp Bouhler, August Becker and Albert Widmann, and others working on the security side, such as Franz Stangl (then a security police superintendent at Hartheim), were subsequently transferred to the *Aktion* Reinhard extermination programme in Poland, where they used the experience of mass murder they had first gained in *Aktion T4*.

As the news of the 'euthanasia' programme became more publicly known in 1940 and 1941, there was growing disquiet and even protest from relatives of disabled citizens, and also from some within the Lutheran and Catholic Churches. This protest culminated in Bishop Galen of Munster publicly criticising the 'euthanasia' programme in sermons in July and August 1941, and sending a direct appeal to Hitler to stop the Gestapo killings – the victims were 'our compatriots, our brothers and sisters. Poor unproductive people if you wish, but does this mean that they have lost their right to live?' Although reports of Galen's sermons were not printed in the German press, leaflets were soon widely circulated in what the historian Richard Evans has described as 'the strongest, most explicit and most widespread protest movement against any policy since the beginning of the Third Reich'. Shortly afterwards, on 24 August 1941, Hitler ordered the T4 programme to be suspended.*

Apart from the killing of almost 300,000 human beings, the most shocking aspect of the T4 operation was the collusion of many senior doctors in organising mass murder – doctors who all would have signed the Hippocratic Oath vowing to save lives, not to end them. As we walk down towards Potsdamer Platz, the new towers of commerce and skyscrapers looming ahead of us, J. and I remember the shattering impact of first encountering Lifton's book on the doctors of Auschwitz. I tell J. about another remarkable work which examines the systematic corruption of the medical profession under Nazism – *Cleansing the Fatherland* by Götz Aly, Peter Chroust and Christian Pross. It's now known that 38,000 doctors had joined the Nazi party by 1942 (more than half of all doctors in Germany at the time) and that 7 per cent of doctors were members of the SS (compared to 1 per cent of the general population). The authors describe the 'collective amnesia' of the German medical establishment in the post-war years, and their inability to face the reality of their profession's direct complicity with the worst horrors of Nazism.

*

We walk on, the roar of traffic at Potsdamer Platz making it impossible to talk. This part doesn't seem like Berlin at all, the bland modernity of this financial quarter, the shimmering glass-and-steel towers could be any city. Extraordinary to think that only twenty years ago this was a wasteland – the place where Wenders filmed the elderly Berliner sitting surrounded by dereliction, lost in his memories of

---

* See chapter notes for further details on the T4 programme, and the subsequent *Aktion 14f13*.

his pre-war city, in *Wings of Desire*. We decide to head north, up Ebertstrasse, relieved to be away from the noise, with the winter trees of Tiergarten now on our left, waving to us in the afternoon light, and the sense of dusk not far away.

2. Thoughts on Perpetrators: A Single Piece of Paper in a Washington Museum

The reason we've come to Berlin can be traced back to an afternoon I'd spent in Washington five years before, at the United States Holocaust Memorial Museum. I had already begun my research then, but what I discovered in Washington that day gave it an extra impetus. Before I take you into the museum, I want to share a challenge the historian Daniel Goldhagen laid down at the beginning of his powerful work, *Hitler's Willing Executioners*, published in 1995:

> Until now the perpetrators, the most important group of people responsible for the slaughter of European Jewry, excepting the Nazi leadership itself, have received little concerted attention in the literature that describes the events and purports to explain them. Surprisingly, the vast literature on the Holocaust contains little on the people who were its executors . . . Certain institutions of killing, and the people who manned them, have been hardly treated or not at all . . . We must therefore refocus our attention, our intellectual energy . . . onto the perpetrators . . . What exactly did they do when they were killing? What did they do . . . while they were not undertaking killing operations? Until a great deal is known about the details of their actions and lives, neither they, nor the perpetration of their crimes can be understood. The unearthing of the perpetrators' lives, the presentation of a 'thick', rather than the customary paper-thin, description of their actions . . . lays the foundation for the main task – namely to explain their actions.

The main thrust of what Goldhagen is saying here is surely right, even though he underestimates the complexity of the task of creating the three-dimensional portraits of perpetrators he alludes to here. Although he goes on to analyse, in compelling detail, the actions, the killings of many ordinary German police, soldiers and volunteers, one of the few weaknesses of the work for me is that the vast majority of his subjects remain two-dimensional 'perpetrators', and to this extent I feel he fails the task he sets himself. On a wider philosophical level, I am also sceptical about whether such actions can ever be truly 'explained' – regardless of the amount of information available.

But Goldhagen is certainly right about identifying a vast lacuna at the heart of Holocaust historiography, what might be summarised as 'perpetrator psychology' – detailed investigations of both those who killed directly and those who planned and organised the genocide. With the exception of key work by Raul Hilberg, Robert Jay Lifton, Hannah Arendt, Gitta Sereny, Christopher Browning, Yaacov Lozowick and Götz Aly, up to now remarkably little has been written on this subject, though there have been recent indications that this might be beginning to change. There are extremely complex societal and political forces at play here that have an impact on changing emphases in historical study, what aspects of research are prioritised, and why certain books or films receive widespread cultural coverage and others sink without trace – how to explain the initial ignoring of Primo Levi's work yet the enormous response to Anne Frank's diary, both published in the immediate post-war years? Why did Raul Hilberg's monumental work *The Destruction of the European Jews* have to wait so many years to find a publisher? What can explain the extraordinary global level of media interest in the trial of Eichmann in 1961 when in the late 1940s and 50s many of his former colleagues had melted back into German civil society, some even into government positions? Why did it take fifty years for survivor testimony to start to be gathered together systematically? The initiative that developed into Steven Spielberg's project to record interviews with those still alive – Survivors of the Shoah Visual History Foundation.

254

This challenge to begin thinking about the perpetrators in a different way first struck me forcibly when, in November 1998, I visited the Holocaust Memorial Museum in Washington. In one corner of a large room, people are crowding around a particular exhibit that has received much media attention – a rolling film of the *Einsatzgruppen* (the mobile execution squads) in action on the Eastern Front. This is how the American author Philip Gourevitch describes what he saw:

> Peep show format. Snuff films. Naked women led to execution. People are being shot. Into the ditch, shot, spasms, collapse, dirt thrown in over. Crowds of naked people. Naked people standing about to be killed, naked people lying down dead. Close-up of a woman's face and throat as a knife is plunged into her breast – blood all over. Someone holds a severed head in his hand. Mass graves of thousands. Naked. Naked corpses. Street beatings. The gun, the smoke, a figure crumbles. Naked corpses. Naked women dragged to death. Shooting. Screaming. Blackout. The film begins again.

There is minimal information next to this exhibit about either the victims or the perpetrators. Now I want to take you to the other side of this room, where nobody seems very interested in a traditional glass case of documents. I'm reflecting on the hypnotic power of the moving image over the static, disturbed by the voyeurism and conformism of the crowds in front of the TV monitors, drawn to this corner of the room, some because they've heard about the controversy, others simply because the large group of people must mean something, so why not see what they're looking at? Feeling almost a sympathy for the plainness of the paper exhibits, I start to study each one in compensatory detail. My eyes are drawn to one of the documents – a simple list of names. I'm rooted to the spot by this single sheet of paper:

Dr Josef Bühler	*State Secretary, Generalgouvernement for Occupied Territories of Poland*
Adolf Eichmann	*SS Lt Colonel, Reich Security Main Office, Section IV B4 (Evacuations)*
Dr Roland Freisler	*State Secretary, Reich Justice Ministry*
Otto Hofmann	*SS General, Race and Settlement Main Office*
Reinhard Heydrich	*Head of Security Police and Security Service (SD); Head of RSHA*
Gerhard Klopfer	*SS Brigadier General, NSDAP Party Chancellery*
Fredrich Wilhelm Kritzinger	*Ministerial Director, Reich Chancellery*
Dr Rudolf Lange	*Commander of Security Police, Latvia*
Dr Georg Leibbrandt	*Reich Bureau Chief, Reich Ministry for Occupied Eastern Territories*
Martin Luther	*Assistant State Secretary, Foreign Office*
Dr Alfred Meyer	*NSDAP District Leader, Reich Ministry for Occupied Territories*
Heinrich Müller	*SS Lt General, Head of Secret State Police (Gestapo)*
Erich Neumann	*State Secretary, Office of the Four Year Plan*
Dr Karl Eberhard Schöngarth	*SS Brigadier General, Commander-in-Chief, Security Police, Generalgouvernement for Occupied Territories*
Dr Wilhelm Stuckart	*State Secretary, Reich Interior*

These are the names of the fifteen individuals who attended what has become known as the Wannsee Conference, held in a villa in the leafy west Berlin suburb of Wannsee on 20 January 1942. The gathering was initiated by Heydrich to pull together as many agencies of the German state as possible to discuss the implementation of '*die Endlösung der Judenfrage*' ('the Final Solution of the Jewish question'). Actually there were sixteen people present, but, tantalisingly, we do not know the name of Eichmann's female secretary, the stenographer, who took shorthand notes on the meeting, without whom there would be no Wannsee Conference minutes in the first place. I have often thought of this young woman, sitting at the side table, touch-typing, while the fifteen men around her talked of extermination. How Eichmann would have prepared her for this meeting, how he would have emphasised the need for total secrecy, total discretion. And the discussion she witnessed – about how an entire race was going to be erased from history – yet this woman herself has vanished without a trace. And I reflect on the lack of curiosity about her shown by all the historians, predominantly men, who have ever written about Wannsee. The minutes which Eichmann later created from her synchronous record are what has survived – but this was only a summary document, a substantially edited account of the meeting, because much of what had been discussed could never have been written down, due to the nature of the 'over-plain talk' about methods of killing the Jews which took up the last part of the meeting. Eichmann later explained that he had to clean up the language used, when he created the official version of the minutes.

I'd known about the conference for some time – the minutes have been referred to as 'perhaps the most shameful document of modern history' – but I had never seen this list of attendees before. I was struck by how few of the names were familiar – I only recognised Heydrich, Eichmann, Müller and Freisler. But the aspect of the list that astonished me was the repetition of those two little letters – 'Dr'. Seven men with doctorates there! What I had previously assumed to be primarily a meeting of representatives of the security services, the military and the police – the SS, *Einsatzgruppen* and Gestapo – was actually also a meeting of German civil society, with senior representatives from the Interior Ministry, the Foreign Ministry and the judiciary. All of them highly educated men, not just graduates but lawyers, judges, ministers. Some of the attendees like Bühler, Freisler, Neumann and Stuckart carrying the title of *Staatssekretär*, equivalent to the rank of permanent secretary in the British Civil Service.

Returning to London, I resolved to find out as much as I could about these seven individuals – the doctors of Wannsee. I started at the British Library, with little luck. Nothing substantive seemed to have been written about these doctors. One of the most infamous meetings in history yet these planners and bureaucrats had been deemed not significant enough as subjects for study. Thousands of books exist on Hitler, Himmler and Goering, every conceivable aspect of the Holocaust, yet nothing on these men who actually met and co-ordinated the agencies which enabled the 'Final Solution' to happen.[*]

3. London, the Wiener Library: Copy Number 16/30

Sometime in the winter of 1998–9, I first set foot in the Wiener Library. All that follows here is tinged by a slight sadness because, by the time these words will be read, the Wiener Library as I knew it will be history – literally – because the library is about to move to a new space and will soon be housed at new premises, in Russell Square, in a former Birkbeck College building. But when I first encountered the library it was in Devonshire Place (just around the corner from Great Portland Street Tube). To gain access you had to press a large, white bell on the outside of a handsome, whitish-grey house. A voice would then buzz you in, and you entered a tiled hallway with dark wood panelling and a curving staircase that took

---

[*] It took until 2017 for the first detailed work on the men of the Wannsee Conference to be published: *Die Teilnehmer* ('The Participants'), edited by the German historians Hans-Christian Jasch and Christoph Kreutzmüller, seventy-two years after the minutes of the meeting were first discovered.

you up to the first floor. Pushing a heavy wooden door, you stepped into the main library – a single room perhaps fifteen yards long, high ceilings, with dark wood bookcases, floor to ceiling, carrying an unparalleled collection of books and documents on modern German history, and the Holocaust in particular. Although I felt quite shy initially, on subsequent visits I began to exchange nods with other regular users of the library, glances of recognition. Some were elderly, bespectacled, but seemed tenacious in their research, some were students, clearly baffled by the fact the library's main resource for finding anything was still (at that time) a series of little wooden drawers with thousands of handwritten entries on small, rectangular cards. But there was historical treasure buried there, if you persevered . . .

It was in this room, at the end where the windows looked out over Devonshire Place, that the librarian (an owlish man in early middle age) first handed down to me – from a shelf so high that he needed a small stepladder to reach it – an exceedingly large file of green leather, which contained a facsmile copy of the original minutes of the Wannsee Conference and other correspondence. Over the next hours I then discovered the extraordinary story behind this document's survival. Eichmann, a comparitively junior figure at the meeting, had been charged with the drafting, organising and distribution of the minutes. After his initial draft, Heydrich then checked it carefully, to ensure that all the agencies represented were shown to have committed themselves collectively to the actions agreed. Eichmann then had thirty copies made, understandably stamped '*Geheime Reichsacche!*' ('State secret!').

The combination of the obsession not to leave any paper trail for 'the unwritten order'[*] (the term sometimes used to denote Hitler's verbal instructions for the 'Final Solution' to be carried out) and the fact that during the last weeks of the war mass destruction of documents became routine – both of these factors meant that twenty-nine out of the thirty copies were destroyed. But a single copy had been deposited in a Foreign Office file marked '*Endlösung der Judenfrage*' by a

---

[*] *The Unwritten Order* is also the title of a book by the historian Peter Longerich, in which he examines Hitler's central role in the 'Final Solution'.

conscientious clerk in Department D III, the *Judenreferat* (the Foreign Office departmental section for Jewish matters). It was marked copy number sixteen and had been sent to Martin Luther (assistant state secretary at the Foreign Office, and one of the attendees). The Wannsee Conference minutes and correspondence were at the centre of two folders documenting nearly five years of material on the 'Jewish question', from 25 January 1939 to 20 November 1943. Many of the Foreign Office records including these files were moved out of Berlin in late 1943 following Allied bombing of the city. First they were taken to Krummhübel near the Czechoslovakian border, and then in 1944 they were moved again to castles in the Lower Harz mountains. And it was here that the Foreign Office records were discovered by Allied troops on 27 April 1945.

However, the full significance of the Wannsee Conference minutes was only understood two years later, in March 1947, when a member of the US prosecuting counsel for the later Nuremberg Trials was combing through these Foreign Office files for evidence. In the weeks and months that followed, the real import of this document emerged. But it is a remarkable fact that at the first Nuremberg Trial (1945–6) the conference was hardly mentioned; indeed many of the details of how the Nazis had organised the 'Final Solution' were not yet understood. This is exemplified by the fact that Francis Biddle, one of the American judges at the first Nuremberg Trial, had not even heard of Adolf Eichmann as the trial was about to begin in November 1945 – writing in the margin of one of the trial documents, next to Eichmann's name, 'Who is he?' The Wannsee Conference only became infamous two years after the war had ended, and the minutes were only published in 1951. By such miraculously unlikely acts of documentary survival is history made possible – to later emerge into the light and be pieced together, word by word, page by page.

*

Eichmann was responsible for organising the distribution of the minutes (his office IV B 4 – Jewish Affairs – we can see marked at the top left in the letter below). We can also see from this letter that they were sent out by Heydrich's office on 26 February 1942, a month after the Wannsee Conference.

In the second sentence, Heydrich emphasises that 'Since the basic position regarding the practical execution of the final solution of the Jewish question has fortunately been established by now, and since there is full agreement on the part of all agencies involved', there is a need now for a further meeting of specialist officials 'for the necessary discussion of details' regarding what has been discussed at Wannsee. This will take place at Kurfürstenstrasse 116, and Heydrich asks that people 'contact my functionary in charge there, SS-Obersturmbannführer Eichmann'. The 'details' Heydrich refers to here are the establishment of three designated extermination camps in Poland in spring 1942 – at Belzec (operational from April 1942), Sobibor (fully operational from mid-May), and Treblinka (operational from late July), and also the construction of four vast gas chambers and crematoria at Birkenau – just to the north-west of the existing Auschwitz concentration camp – which began in July 1942 (fully operational by March 1943).

Luther himself has scribbled over the top: 'Pg[*] Rademacher please [send] written notification that you are the specialist official and that you will participate.' And after this he has initialled and dated the letter 28/II, indicating that the minutes and letter were sent by courier directly to Luther. Rademacher was head of Department D III, the *Judenreferat* section at the Foreign Office. The follow-up meeting took place on 6 March 1942, at Eichmann's office in Berlin.

*

In spring 1999 I return to the Wiener Library, hoping to find further details on the doctors of Wannsee. I'm more and more surprised that nothing substantive seems to have been published on these men, and this event. And then, one day, I come across a booklet published by the House of the Wannsee Conference – a memorial and museum institute based at the villa – and I start to piece together more biographical information about each of the participants. Over time I've been able to gain a clearer picture of why each of these men would have been invited to the meeting in Wannsee in January 1942 – what their particular expertise was in the field of solving the 'Jewish question'.

---

* 'Pg' is an abbreviation of '*Parteigenosse*', i.e. fellow party member.

This is Dr Georg Leibbrandt. He was born into a German émigré family near Odessa in 1899, and became skilled in several languages. In 1919, in the wake of the Russian Revolution, he fled to Germany, and this experience, together with later Stalinist purges which claimed several relatives still in Ukraine, contributed to his extreme anti-communist views. From 1920 he studied theology, philosophy, history and national economy in Tübingen and Leipzig. He gained his doctorate in 1927 (on the history of Swabian emigration to Russia), and then travelled widely to the USA, Canada, Switzerland, Britain and France on research trips. He began to publish work on how ethnic Germans had successfully settled in Russia and America, praising their colonising skills.

In 1933 he was introduced to the leading Nazi ideologue Alfred Rosenberg, who appointed him head of the Eastern Division of the newly formed Office of Foreign Affairs, and Leibbrandt joined the Nazi Party. In this role he worked on the issue of Russian Germans, and how they could play a greater role in the Reich, creating the VDR (the 'League of Germans from Russia'). He also began to co-ordinate a series of propaganda publications on Bolshevism, and the supposed linkage between Bolsheviks and the Jews. In 1941 he was promoted to become director of the political department for the Reich Ministry of Occupied Eastern Territories (RMO), serving under Rosenberg. In this position Leibbrandt was fully informed about the murderous activities of the *Einsatzgruppen*, and the beginnings of the Jewish genocide on the Eastern Front throughout autumn 1941. We also know that he and his more senior colleague, Alfred Meyer, met with Heydrich in October 1941, and Leibbrandt and Rosenberg travelled to meet Himmler the following month – both meetings to discuss how to maximise the numbers of Jews in the Eastern Territories who could be included in the 'Final Solution' – all this happening just weeks before the Wannsee Conference.

Dr Wilhelm Stuckart, born in 1902 in Wiesbaden, into a Protestant family. He joined the youth wing of the Nazi Party when he was still at school, and from 1922 he began to study law in Munich, where he participated in Hitler's putsch the following year. He gained his doctorate (in commercial law) in 1928, and became a junior trial judge, but soon left to work full-time for the Nazi Party. When Hitler came to power in 1933 Stuckart was promoted to ministerial director at the Prussian Ministry of Education, and promoted again the following year to become state secretary at the Reich Ministry of Science, Education and Culture. In 1935 he moved to head the office for constitutional affairs at the Reich Interior Ministry, becoming state secretary, and it was in this role that he helped to draw up the infamous Nuremberg Race Laws, which created the supposed 'legal' framework for stripping German Jews of their rights, and defined how 'purity' of the Aryan race was to be measured. The following year he became chairman of the Reich Committee for the Protection of German Blood.

He would have known most of those who participated in the Wannsee Conference – he and Gerhard Klopfer were both involved in the publication of the journal *Reich, Volksordnung, Lebensraum* ('Reich, Population Control, Living Space'), in autumn 1941; and Stuckart had also met Roland Freisler, Erich Neumann, Heydrich, Müller and Eichmann at an important meeting Goering instigated on 12 November 1938 at the Ministry of Aviation to discuss Hitler's order that the 'Jewish question' be 'resolved one way or another'. He was also one of a select group briefed by Hitler in October 1939 on extreme measures to deal with the Polish population following the invasion. His seniority in the Reich can be gauged by his activities in the immediate run-up to the Wannsee Conference – on 24 November 1941, we know that he had lunch with Himmler to discuss Jewish policy; the next day, a decree that had been drawn up by Stuckart became law – which stripped Jews who had fled or been deported of their German citizenship and assets; and on 1 December, we know that Stuckart also met with Heydrich to discuss the 'Final Solution'. At Wannsee, with his legal expertise, he represented the most powerful link between the German state and the Nazi Party.

Dr Josef Bühler, born in Württemberg in 1904, came from a large Catholic family. In 1922 he went to Munich to study law (like Stuckart, participating in Hitler's putsch of 1923), and gaining his doctorate in 1930 – the year he joined the law practice of Hans Frank. In 1933 he joined the Nazi Party, and when Frank was appointed Bavaria's minister of justice, Bühler followed his boss, practising as a lawyer in the Civil Service of the justice department. In 1935, on Frank's recommendation, he was promoted to senior prosecutor at the Munich Regional Court, also becoming a key member of Frank's staff. This relationship continued when Frank was made governor general of occupied Poland towards the end of 1939, Bühler becoming his chief of staff in Krakow, and eventually deputy governor. In 1940 he was given the most senior rank of State Secretary of the Administration of the General Government that ran occupied Poland.

Here in Krakow, from their headquarters at Wawel Castle, these two lawyers began an almost unparalleled reign of terror over Poles and Jews alike. Bühler pushed for the enforced removal of Poles to Germany for slave labour, and helped to organise a 'special pacification operation' in May and June 1940 which resulted in the massacre of 3,500 Polish intellectuals. Governor Frank and Bühler also played key roles in the establishment of Jewish ghettoes in Polish cities and the subsequent implementation of the genocide. Frank described Bühler as one of his two 'closest collaborators' in Poland, and both would have been kept informed of all the details of the exterminations in their territory as the 'Final Solution' gathered momentum. Bühler had a close working relationship with Himmler (who had already made him an honorary SS *Brigadeführer*) – indeed Bühler met the Reichsführer on 13 January 1942, only a week before Wannsee, and declared himself 'delighted' at their discussion about division of responsibilities regarding the solution of the 'Jewish question'. So, he was the obvious representative of the General Government to be invited to the pivotal meeting in Berlin.

Dr Karl Eberhard Schöngarth, born in Leipzig in 1903, joined the Nazi Party in 1922. He too studied law (and political science) in Leipzig, being awarded his doctorate in 1929 (on 'The Refusal of Notices of Termination of Employment Contracts'), before becoming an assistant judge for the Prussian judicial service. He joined the SS in 1933, and two years later the Gestapo office (initially in the press section but eventually becoming head of its church affairs department). In 1936 he joined the SD (the intelligence services of the SS), and was promoted to be head of the Gestapo in Dortmund and Münster. In November 1940 he was promoted again, becoming commander of the Gestapo in the General Government. In this capacity he had two prime responsibilities – firstly, monitoring and fighting Polish resistance figures (like Bühler, he played a key role in the 'special pacification operation' of May 1940 which murdered thousands of Polish intellectuals), and secondly, co-operating with the SS on anti-Jewish measures.

Not content with being a 'desk man', commanding from his grand Gestapo headquarters on Magdeburger Strasse in Krakow, as the Einsatzgruppen began to move across eastern Europe in July 1941 Schöngarth requested a special assignment from the head of the Reich Gestapo, Arthur Nebe. This he was granted, and shortly afterwards Schöngarth arrived in Lemberg (Lviv today) with his own mobile killing squad – Einsatzkommando zbV. For the next two months he personally oversaw the massacres of thousands of men, women and children. In a single ten-day killing spree, between 21 and 31 July 1941, he reports to the RSHA HQ that 3,947 people had been eliminated in Lemberg and surrounding villages in east Galicia.

On his return to Krakow in autumn 1941, Schöngarth became a central figure in the SD Training School at Bad Rabka (a spa town halfway between Zakopane and Krakow). Here Schöngarth and other senior figures in the SS and SD would give lectures and seminars on torture and killing methodology to potential SS leaders and concentration-camp personnel, mainly Germans and Ukrainians. Most of the courses ran for three to six months, and in the woods behind the school, the students were able to practise their new skills on live targets – hundreds of local Jews were tortured and murdered here. Local Jewish children were also regularly used for live target practice, so that the SS students could improve their machine-gun and rifle technique.

We know that Schöngarth had a briefing with Himmler a week before the Wannsee Conference, and that he attended a dinner with Himmler and Heydrich on 14 January 1942. As he was one of Heydrich's most senior representatives in the General Government, and highly experienced in the realities of mass murder, he was seen as a useful addition to the meeting at Wannsee, able to give the more desk-bound civil servants a more 'practical' understanding of the nature of their shared mission.

This man is Dr Alfred Meyer. He was born in Göttingen in 1891, so was one of the older attendees of Wannsee. During the First World War, he served as a young officer on the Western Front, was wounded and spent two years in a French POW camp at the end of the war. Returning to Germany, he continued his law degree at the University of Bonn, eventually switching to political science, gaining his doctorate (an extremely nationalist account of 'The Belgian People's War') in 1923. He then worked for a mining firm in the Ruhr as a business clerk (later he claimed to have been a 'legal advisor'), before joining the Nazi Party in 1928, when his career finally began to take off. In 1929 he became head of his local Nazi Party branch, and a year later he was elected, unexpectedly, to the Reichstag when the Nazis did far better than predicted in the 1930 elections. Here he met the influential Alfred Rosenberg, who became an important friend and ally. The following year he was promoted to be gauleiter (regional governor) of northern Westphalia, and two years later, when the Nazis have taken power, Hitler appoints him Reich governor of Lippe. In 1938 he was promoted again, to become senior president of Westphalia.

In July 1941, with the invasion of the Soviet Union under way, the Reich Ministry for the Occupied Eastern Territories (RMO) is created, and Rosenberg was chosen to head this ministry, and Meyer is appointed his deputy, becoming state secretary to the RMO. In this role, he had extensive power over the administration and economy of the occupied Eastern Territories; together with Rosenberg, he developed new strategies on both the exploitation of captured Soviet territory and the extermination of the inhabitants, in particular the Jewish population. Eichmann later maintained that the initiative to 'industrialise mass murder' had come from the RMO rather than Heydrich's RSHA. We know that Meyer, as well as meeting Heydrich in October 1941, had also attended a briefing for gauleiters in Hitler's apartment only six weeks before the Wannsee conference, on 12 December 1941 – the meeting when Hitler called for 'the destruction of Jewry', explaining that 'the world war is upon us; the extermination of the Jews is the necessary consequence'. It is significant that the RMO was the only ministry to have two representatives invited to Wannsee (Meyer and Leibbrandt); Rosenberg must have been confident that his deputy and political director would do his department justice at this prestigious gathering of Reich personnel.

Dr Rudolf Lange, born in Weisswasser in 1910, was the youngest man, and most junior in rank, at Wannsee. He studied law at the University of Jena, and began his doctorate in 1932 (on 'The Right of Instruction of the Employer'). He also joined 'Germania' here – a far-right, anti-Semitic fraternity grouping which revolved around fencing. Still studying when Hitler took power in 1933, he joined the SA (the Nazi storm troopers), and volunteered for the party. He was awarded his doctorate in 1936, and began to work for the Gestapo in Berlin, where he soon realised he'd found his real 'vocation'. In 1937 he joined the SS and also became a full member of the Nazi Party. The following year he was promoted to the Gestapo in Vienna, where his responsibilities included 'fighting the enemy' (particularly Jews and the Church) – he would have been especially busy in November 1938, organising terror during the days of Kristallnacht, along with another ambitious young SS officer, Adolf Eichmann. In June 1939 Lange was appointed deputy head of the Gestapo in Stuttgart, then had spells running the Gestapo in Weimar and Kassel.

He was promoted again in 1940, to become deputy head of the Gestapo in Berlin, at just thirty years old. But, like Schöngarth, he preferred more active duties than office work in Berlin, so in spring 1941, newly promoted to SS *Sturmbannführer*, he joined his former Vienna boss, Dr Walter Stahlecker, who was then preparing to lead Einsatzgruppe A into action for the first time. In July 1941, in the wake of the German invasion of the Soviet Union, they arrived in Latvia, and began one of the most systematic of all the exterminations in Riga and the surrounding areas. As well as his Gestapo responsibilities, Lange was put in charge of Einsatzkommando 2. By the end of the year, Stahlecker proudly reported to Berlin that his Einsatzgruppe had eliminated 249,420 Jews. Lange's view on the work they had accomplished was simple – 'the goal of EK2 was that radical solution of the Jewish problem by killing all Jews'. For the next two years Lange would be based at his headquarters on Reimersa Street in Riga; from here, in his new role as commander of the Security Police, he coordinated much of the 'Final Solution' in Latvia – as well as personally overseeing mass executions, he was also a key figure in the deportation of German, Austrian and Czech Jews to Latvia. Only six weeks before Wannsee, Lange had overseen the murder of 24,000 Latvian Jews of the Riga ghetto in a matter of days. Heydrich was impressed with his work, and invited Lange to Wannsee because, like Schöngarth, he could speak from his direct experience.

270

And finally, the last doctor of Wannsee on the list from the Holocaust Memorial Museum in Washington – Roland Freisler. Freisler was born in Celle in 1893, and after school in Kassel, he studied law at the University of Jena (like Lange). For most of the First World War he was a Russian prisoner of war, but on his release he continued his law studies at Jena, being awarded his doctorate (on 'The Basics of Company Organisation') in 1922. Two years later he set up a legal practice in Kassel with his brother, soon establishing a reputation for defending extreme right-wing clients (especially new Nazi and SA activists). He also became a city councillor there in 1924, joined the Nazi Party and began his rapid rise in the movement, becoming deputy gauleiter of Hessen-Nassau-Nord.

By 1930 he'd established a national reputation as the Nazi leader in Kassel and 'an incorrigible enemy of the Jews'. He became a member of the Prussian Parliament in 1932, and the Reichstag a year later. On Hitler's coming to power he was appointed state secretary in the Prussian Ministry of Justice, and in 1934 he was promoted again, to state secretary in the Reich Ministry of Justice, moving with his family to Berlin. As well as his legal responsibilities – for policy on penal legislation and execution of sentences – he lectured and published widely, advocating that 'German criminal law should serve the preservation of the German people and the safeguarding of the National Socialist state'. He also became a prominent proponent of race laws, heading a legal delegation to Italy in 1938, and meeting Mussolini, congratulating the Italian leader on passing such laws. On his return from Rome in November 1938, just three days after

Kristallnacht, he participated in Goering's meeting to discuss the resolution of the 'Jewish question', along with Stuckart, Neumann, Heydrich, Müller and Eichmann.

In the first years of the war, Freisler became more and more pre-occupied with developing ever harsher laws against Jews and Poles, arguing that the death penalty was the appropriate punishment for even minor offences. Only days before the Wannsee meeting he'd written that he expected judges and attorneys in Poland to 'feel like soldiers in the political troop of German ethnicity'. Heydrich regarded him and Stuckart as the two most senior juridical authorities, who would lend a spurious veneer of 'legality' to the discussions on the 'final solution' of the 'Jewish question'.

My continued digging into the backgrounds of these men produced only limited information, although I did discover that there was in fact another attendee of Wannsee who had a doctorate (missing from the original list at the Holocaust Memorial Museum in Washington).

This man was Dr Gerhard Klopfer. Born into a farming family in Silesia in 1905, he studied law in Breslau and Jena (like Stuckart and Freisler before him), and completed his doctorate in 1929 (on 'The True Duty of the Employee in the Employment Relationship'). He became a junior judge in Düsseldorf in 1931, joining the Nazi Party two years later. After a short period on the planning staff of the Prussian Gestapo, in 1935 he joined the staff of Deputy

Führer Rudolf Hess, where his career really took off. His immediate boss here was Martin Bormann, then Hess's chief of staff, who thought highly of the young lawyer and soon appointed him as his personal aide. Here Klopfer worked on issues of co-ordination between the Nazi Party and the state. In 1938, promoted now to ministerial secretary, he developed policies on the expropriation of Jewish businesses.

In May 1941, following Hess's flight to Scotland and capture, the office was renamed the Party Chancellery, and Bormann was appointed its head, with Klopfer his deputy. Klopfer became a highly important liaison figure between the party Chancellery and the Reich Chancellery, where he had weekly meetings, ensuring Hitler's decrees were smoothly enacted. His wide brief also included issues of constitutional law and he headed the unit on 'Race and National Character' as well. In this capacity he was a leading voice in debates over the definition of how 'Jewishness' should be measured. His view was that the Nuremberg Race Laws of 1935 did not go far enough, and that laws on the issue of the *'Mischlinge'* (Jews of mixed race – i.e. of combined Jewish and Aryan ancestry) needed to be tightened. He was also one of the editors, together with Stuckart and others, of the journal *Reich, Volksordnung, Lebensraum* in autumn 1941. As well as being one of the most senior bureaucrats in the Reich, Klopfer also had a parallel rank in the SS, eventually rising to become *Gruppenführer*. Although ideologically a 'pure' Nazi, and highly qualified to speak on issues of race and the Jews, Klopfer's invitation to the Wannsee Conference, as Bormann's deputy, would not have been a simple matter for Heydrich – because of his own rivalry and difficult relationship with Bormann, and questions of territorial claim over which agency would be given the power to organise the 'Final Solution'.

*

Perhaps the single most striking feature of these eight men's biographies, these eight men who sat down to discuss how genocide could be co-ordinated, is that seven of them had trained as lawyers. With the exception of Lange and Schöngarth, these men never killed directly, and never witnessed killing with their own eyes. Indeed most of them rarely left their offices in Wilhelmstrasse, where the majority of the ministries were based, yet, from their desks, they made a critical contribution to the extermination of 6 million human beings. The fact that all of these men spent so many of their formative years at universities unsettles me to a degree that I find hard to express.

My disquiet may be connected to the fact that my grandfather and father were both academics, and I grew up with a feeling of great affection for all that universities represented – not just in the narrow sense of the gaining of qualifications but rather the process of opening yourself to the world that real learning and enquiry involves – the meeting of minds, the spirit of scepticism. So, discovering that these men – presumably like numerous other intelligent, young people growing up in Germany in the 1920s – had gone through the experience of university, and emerged with extreme authoritarian, nationalist and racist views was shocking to me. I would not have been so surprised had they been studying in the mid-1930s, when Nazism had already taken control of all the institutions of Germany, but the fact that they were at university in a decade when the progressive Weimar Republic and international movements such as the Bauhaus were in the ascendancy, when feminism was making great advances, more than anywhere else in Europe (equal education rights for men and women, equal pay in professions) – this seems to defy easy explanation.

Yet the further I've researched, the more examples I've found of links between the intelligentsia and genocidal institutions of the Third Reich – highly educated graduates, doctors and professors figure in senior positions in many of the agencies which participated in mass murder. To give just a single example, many of the leaders of the *Einsatzgruppen* were drawn from academia. Einsatzgruppe A (responsible for more than 360,000 killings in total) was headed by Dr Walter Stahlecker (doctorate in law from the University of Tübingen). Einsatzgruppe C (responsible for almost 120,000 killings) was commanded by Dr Otto Rasch (holder of two doctorates – one in law, the other political economy), and later by Ernst Biberstein (a former Protestant pastor who had studied theology); also working at high levels in Einsatzgruppe C were Dr Erwin Weinmann (medical degree from the University of Tübingen) and Dr Max Thomas (who had a medical degree and specialised in psychiatry). A commander in Einsatzgruppe D, responsible for the killing of 14,300 Jews in three days at Simferopol in Crimea, was Dr Werner Braune (who held a doctorate in civil law from the University of Jena). And the head of Einsatzgruppe D (responsible overall for more than 90,000 killings) was Dr Otto Ohlendorf. He, before the war, had studied economics and law and had held the post of research director of the Kiel Institute for the World Economy – a life of academia behind him.

*

There were three other 'white collar' attendees of the Wannsee Conference (i.e. the non-SS/Gestapo men): Friedrich Kritzinger, Erich Neumann and Martin Luther – all three high-ranking civil servants, though none of them held doctorates.[*]

Kritzinger, after serving in the First World War, passed his bar examinations in 1921 and went straight to work in the Reich Ministry of Justice. In 1931 he was promoted to *Unterstaatssekretär* (assistant secretary of state), and became a highly regarded legal expert. In 1938 he moved to the Reich Chancellery, joining the Nazi Party relatively late (though he had always been a supporter of far-right, nationalist politics). He eventually rose to become state secretary, heading Division B, where his areas of expertise were on matters concerned with 'Jews and Persons of Mixed Blood' and dealing with other 'Jewish problems', such as helping to form policy on deprival of property and limiting Jewish rights of appeal. He worked closely with Stuckart in November 1941 on a brutal new decree, which played a key role in preparing the ground for the Holocaust – the eleventh decree of the Reich Citizens Act which deprived German Jews of their citizenship and stripped them of their assets after deportation. After the war, he claimed that he'd felt uneasy at Wannsee, that he'd done what he could to mitigate the worst anti-Jewish measures, and that he hadn't been fully aware of the 'atrocities perpetrated . . . against the Jews'. But the historical record, and particularly the recent research by Stefan Paul-Jacobs and Lore Kleiber,[*] do not support the post-war attempts, by himself and his family, to justify his actions and portray him as little more than a conscientious Prussian civil servant of the old school.

Neumann was also a trained lawyer and a career civil servant who, like Kritzinger, had fought in the First World War and been wounded. After a short spell at the Prussian Ministry of the Interior, in 1923 he joined the Prussian Ministry of Commerce. In 1932 he was promoted to *Ministerialdirektor* (permanent secretary) in the Prussian Ministry of State, having developed a reputation in the field of debt management and currency reform. A year later, having joined the Nazi Party, he became a member of the powerful Prussian State Council, where his work came to the attention of Goering, and where he also would have met Freisler and Stuckart.

---

[*] See their chapter on Kritzinger in *The Participants: The Men of the Wannsee Conference* (ed. Jasch and Kreuzmüller).

In 1936, when Goering formed his Office of the Four Year Plan (essentially using the Prussian State Ministry as the core of this new department), Neumann was given increased responsibilities and made a member of the general council. Two years later, after accompanying Goering on a visit to Italy, he was promoted further, and eventually became state secretary at the Office of the Four Year Plan, and one of Goering's most trusted staff. He attended two important meetings on the resolution of the 'Jewish question' in autumn 1938, and became a key figure in the 'Aryanisation' of the economy – not just in Germany, but in the occupied Eastern Territories in the early years of the war. He encouraged German banks to work with the company he'd helped to set up, Kontinental Oil, in the exploitation of oil reserves in the recently conquered new territory in the east. At Wannsee, as well as representing his boss Goering, he also acted for several ministries connected to the German economy – Labour, Finances, Food, Transport, and Armaments and Munitions.

Luther's career was the most unorthodox of all of the Wannsee attendees. He'd left school with no qualifications and joined the army to fight in the First World War. He then started several businesses in haulage, interior design and furniture removals, eventually becoming financially independent. He joined the Nazi Party in 1932, becoming an activist in south-west Berlin, where he became friends with the Ribbentrops, doing building work and interior decoration for the future ambassador to Britain. In 1936 he was given the job of creating a Party Liaison Office by Ribbentrop, and, when his boss was made Foreign Secretary two years later, Luther moved with him to the Foreign Office, and was soon heading the new Abteilung Deutschland (Germany Department), handling the Foreign Office's liaison with SS and police, Jewish policy and ambassadorial appointments, among other matters.

His rapid rise was further confirmed when he was promoted to *Unterstaatssekretär* in July 1941. As well as now liaising with Himmler and the Reich Security Main Office, he was overall head of Section D III – which included the *Judenreferat* section dealing with Jewish matters. In this capacity, together with his deputy Franz Rademacher, he developed the idea of deporting Europe's Jews to Madagascar (an idea which Heydrich later took over). In autumn 1941 Luther and Rademacher had been directly involved with the decision to 'liquidate' the Jews of Belgrade, resulting in the shooting of 8,000 men. They were also informed of all the *Einsatzgruppen* reports from the Eastern Front throughout this period, so Luther would not have been surprised by either the strategy for the 'Final Solution' presented at Wannsee, or the methods discussed. Luther's knowledge of diplomatic procedure, and how different occupied countries might react to Jewish deportations, was a factor in his invitation to the conference, but Heydrich was also keen to ensure that the SS and Eichmann's department would get full co-operation from the Foreign Office when they began to organise the mass deportations.

*

We can learn a certain amount from such biographical information – facts relating to careers, party affiliations, areas of expertise – but I'm also struck by the limitations of such an 'externalised' approach to people's lives. At several points while reading the recently published, extremely detailed book on *The Participants: The Men of the Wannsee Conference*, I felt exactly this disquiet. And it seems that my unease was shared by at least some of the contributors to this work as well. You can research all the facts of a career, you can find out where someone worked, what they wrote in a memorandum to their boss, but when we're trying to understand how people came to their beliefs, or justified genocide to themselves, we're still left with gaping holes. Two of the contributors acknowledge these lacunae at the end of their chapters on Dr Lange and 'Gestapo Müller' – writing of Lange, 'It is not clear if he was born into an antisemitic family or whether his views were formed by his social life at university', and of Müller, 'his motives – especially his ideological convictions – remain largely in the dark still today'.

Perhaps this is the reason why often it has been the non-historians who have had the greatest insights into history, because they come at their subjects from multiple and varied perspectives. Professor Mark Roseman is humble enough to acknowledge this reality in the first chapter of *The Participants*; he reflects in the following way about the authors of key books about Nazi perpetrators: 'the salient works that left their mark on scholarship and continue to be worth reading, despite their flaws [are] Arendt's account of Eichmann, Haffner's short but still telling biography of Hitler, or Sereny's encounter with Franz Stangl . . . [all] penned by non-historians.'

I want to get beyond the desiccated facts of a career, the external actions of a bureaucrat, beyond the ranks and titles, and try to find the human beings underneath. Before our 'doctors of Wannsee' become fossilised in history, can we allow them to breathe? Or is it too late to ask such questions?

- How might we get to know Georg, Wilhelm, Josef, Karl Eberhard, Alfred, Rudolf, Roland, Gerhard, Friedrich Wilhelm, Erich and Martin?
- What were these men taught as boys in primary school? Were they brought up to be 'seen and not heard'?
- What stories did they read growing up? Were they thrilled by the tales of Karl May of German settlers in America battling against the savages? Or did they enjoy *Peter Moor's Adventures in South-West Africa* and the narrator's account of how African tribes had been necessarily exterminated?
- Did some of them have Jewish friends and neighbours growing up? What were the games they played together?
- Who were their professors at university? Were they ever taught academic scepticism?
- How important was friendship to them?
- Who did they love? Did they all marry? Did they all have children?
- What were they like as fathers?
- How much did they confide in their partners?

- Where did they live? What did they see out of their windows?
- When they weren't working, how did they relax? Did they holiday in the mountains or by the sea?
- And after the war, what did they tell their children? Or did they never speak about what happened?

On that frosty January day, in their cars on the way to Wannsee, what went through their minds before the meeting?

And, two hours later, leaving the villa by the lake that afternoon?

*

4. Hannah in Berlin; Christian Behind a Door in the Ruhr

28 December 2003, Berlin

We continue our walk in Berlin. We walk further up Ebertstrasse, and, to our right, suddenly visible on a gently sloping hill, is the '*Denkmal für die ermordeten Juden Europas*' – the Memorial to the Murdered Jews of Europe. We're astonished at the scale of the site – perhaps the size of two Trafalgar Squares – on what must be some of the most expensive land in the world. A field of stone slabs is taking shape. Even though the memorial is not yet finished, it carries a disorientating power as we walk through the rows, seeing the city in a fractured new light.

The Reichstag on the left, the Brandenburg Gate on our right, very struck by the fact that the last time we were here the Gate was behind the wall in the East, and only the top of the horses could be glimpsed. Now we walk through to Pariser Platz and get a taxi to our friend Hannah Hurtzig's place. Through Alexanderplatz, thoughts of Döblin and Fassbinder, reading and seeing their epic works for the first time. The ugliness of the buildings here is noticeable. Past the Volksbühne to Hannah's quiet street.

Her flat is at the top, with a little terrace. It's airy. Primary colours. With a beautifully organised wall of books from the floor to the ceiling, all in one place. Hannah seems tired, an end-of-the year weariness. Her intense fire seems to be burning lower. She's always defied the ageing process and looked ten, fifteen years younger, but today, yes, she could be in her fifties. But still that striking mop of wild, wiry, silver hair. And those darting blue eyes. She tells us she's had a terrible year, but she doesn't really want to talk about it. We open the wine we've brought and soon we're off. A long talk about my focus on perpetrator psychology these last years. Yes, she can understand it, and she thinks it's absolutely right. But she is also concerned about the obsessive nature of such work, and the danger of burnout. It's happened to her twice in her life, and both times related to work on the Holocaust as well. Nothing else seemed important. Especially helping with the Akko Theatre work – the extraordinary collaboration between Israeli and Arab writers and performers that created a series of performance events between 1991 and 1998. We talk at length about the children of the perpetrators, the sense of responsibility that many of them have and the remarkable work that some of them have done – especially Hilde Speer (on anti-racism and peace campaigning), and Martin Bormann Junior's work as a pastor.

I tell her of a meeting I'd had with a German artist some years before. We will call him Christian. He is a successful sculptor in his mid-sixties. Tall, an open face, dark, soulful eyes, and carrying a kind of shyness with him. He doesn't live in Germany any more, though he occasionally works there. We met at a conference in Newcastle, where we were both speaking about art and ecology. It was the evening of the final day and we found ourselves in the corner of a not very cosy bar on the university campus. Christian was asking more about the work on the subject of the *Schreibtischtaeter*, which I'd spoken of in the conference, so I talked more about this. We eventually got onto the controversy that was then raging about Goldhagen's book, and the role of 'ordinary Germans' in the Holocaust. But he expressed impatience with the way this book had been deemed 'controversial'. He wondered whether I might be interested in his own story . . .

I was born in 1941 and grew up on my parents' farm, just outside Gelsenkirchen in the Ruhr. My father, very much the Prussian officer class, was a major in the Wehrmacht and away on the Russian front for most of my first years. I only have vague memories of him on leave, this unknown man in a uniform bending down to stroke my hair. So the farm, a large, imposing place with a moat all around the farmhouse, was run by my mother. She used Polish forced labour, as was common throughout Germany in the war years, and used to call them 'my workers'. No, there didn't seem anything strange about this, you just accept what is around you as a child. OK, my father was away, but that was the same for most of my friends.

It's curious thinking back now, I can remember the sky burning at night and the sound, like a kind of thudding, of distant bombing, but my most vivid memory of those war years was that sweet smell of melting tar. There was one of those temporary bridges they'd put up over the river, and my sister and I would play there. It must have been an incredibly hot summer, 1944, or maybe it was 1945? We'd just watch the bubbles swell and then prick them. Tar doesn't seem to do that any more, does it? They've probably improved it. Either that or the summers aren't as hot . . .

At the very end of the war the Americans finally arrived. We were all sheltering in the cellar, terrified. We could hear voices, boots stamping, and then the cellar door was opened, and I was astonished to see a black soldier, the first black person I had ever seen! The only word I recognised in the mysterious sounds that came out of his mouth was 'schokalade', but we were too afraid and just shook our heads. Of course, a few weeks later when we'd got used to the soldiers we took the chocolate they offered. Father returned some months after the end of the war. It was hard because I'd got used to being the only male, I was probably quite spoilt in a way, just me, Mother and my two sisters. And Father wasn't the smiling man on leave any more. He had a fierce temper. We all tried to keep out of his way when he was like this. And the devastation around was – well, it's hard to describe. All the local towns had been bombed, the roads had huge potholes, there were twisted wrecks all over the place, nearly all the bridges had been blown up. So travelling around was very difficult.

Anyway, in the year or so after the war I started to go to school. And then I realised that, compared to my classmates, I was very lucky. There was real hunger at that time. Desperate poverty. People standing at the side of the roads pathetically trying to sell a pair of battered shoes, a single tin of meat. Food was so short in those months, so to live on a farm was a great advantage. I found I was surprisingly popular. It was around that time that it happened, a couple of years after the end of the war. You have to understand that we children who were born in the war were not old enough to have been brainwashed by the Hitler myth. If anything it was the other way round, our first memories were of defeat, bombings, knowing our country had lost the war. So, although we couldn't have articulated it like this, looking back now I think all of us were very angry with the world we'd been brought into.

Some evenings Mother and Father would disappear to see friends. I must have been six or seven. But I remember it seemed quite exciting. I had to look after my sisters, and we were given biscuits on these evenings, a kind of gingerbread. It made me feel very grown up – giving out the biscuits, telling my sisters when they had to go to bed, and then trying to wait up until I heard that my parents had returned safely. But mostly I drifted off to sleep before this. And then one evening Mother told us that we all had to go to bed earlier than usual as some friends were coming to the house. This hardly ever happened and I was curious. I wanted to know more, to see who these friends were. So a couple of hours after we were supposed to have gone to bed I tiptoed down the back stairs. As I got closer to the kitchen I could hear singing, many voices. The singing faded away and I could hear my father's voice, deep and deliberate, talking in the way he'd sometimes talk when he'd been drinking. I could feel my heart pounding away, on the threshold of another world. I edged closer to the door. It was an old wooden door which never closed *properly, and through the crack I could see Father standing up at the far end of the table, with a glass raised in his hand. My childhood ended at that moment. There were half a dozen men and women, only one couple I recognised, from the neighbouring farm. But all the men were in Wehrmacht uniforms, including my father. And on the wall, behind them all, a huge red flag with the swastika in the middle. Photographs were spread over the table. Everyone was now raising their glasses, a toast, names I didn't recognise, and then a thunder of laughter, another toast. I edged back into darkness, feeling everything falling away. And from that moment I never trusted my parents again.*

I withdrew into myself more. I couldn't speak about what I'd seen – my sisters were too young, they wouldn't have understood. And it was dangerous to talk to friends about such things. As soon as I could I left home, went to Hamburg, started working as a commercial draughtsman, because I'd always been good at drawing. Later on I moved to Vienna, studied at the art school there – that's where I met my wife. She came from a prosperous, Viennese Jewish family, very politically engaged. Many of her relatives had been murdered in the war. Her father had survived though, and had become quite a well-known journalist and a communist. Immediately after the war they'd lived in Moscow for a time. Her mother was from Russia, from the Caucasus.

I've only been back to the farm three times in fifty years. Father died in 1961 when I was twenty; I went back for the funeral. Two years later, when Anna and I were engaged, we went there, to see my mother. I suppose as some kind of a test. She was polite to Anna over dinner, asking questions about her family, though I did wonder at the time whether she would have been interested in her if she'd been from a working-class background. After dinner, I couldn't believe what she did – of course we'd got onto politics. Mother was so proud of the German economic revival, we felt it was shocking that so many of the Nazi-era people had now been rehabilitated – bankers, lawyers, judges, even government ministers who'd supported Hitler totally. Now back in positions of power. You can't understand anything that happened in Germany in 1968 and the 1970s, the Red Army Faction, all of that, without understanding the fury with which my generation, the war babies, the children of the ruins, looked at their parents and grandparents. Anyway, later on, inevitably, we got onto the war. And that's when she did it – Mother got out the albums of photographs that my father had taken on the Eastern Front. Knowing that Anna's grandparents, her uncle, aunt and two cousins had all been killed at Auschwitz. As if it was a crowning argument she showed us pictures of Ukrainians in the streets, welcoming the German troops.

'You see! They were happy we were there! How can people talk about "invasion"?'

We couldn't stay there. We drove through the night, reaching the border at dawn, hardly able to speak. We've never been back to Germany together. All our children were born in Spain – that's where we settled in 1965. I still do some commissions in Germany, in fact much of my work has been about the disaster of those years, the wounds that continue long after war finishes, but I've never wanted to live there. The last time I went back? That was about five years ago. I'd been working on a project just outside Bochum, so it seemed churlish not to . . . well, you know. Mother wasn't very well. She'd been in hospital. She was seventy-three then, no, seventy-four. My sister and her husband had taken over the running of the farm by then, she only had her chickens to look after. And I thought, well, with the passage of time. Maybe I'd been too hard on her? People do change. After all, she'd come out to Spain to see the children a couple of times, and that was fine. And when we talked on the phone, we didn't argue any more.

But it was still difficult for me driving back, past Gelsenkirchen, seeing the familiar rows of poplars, over the bridge, and then the farmhouse, with an unfamilar new building next to it (which my sister and brother-in-law had built for their family). She'd always been very fit and healthy, looked younger than her years, but now, the woman who came out to greet me as I got out of the car was an old woman. I was shaken seeing her, she shuffled rather than walked. I suppose I felt many conflicting things. Guilt *inevitably was part of it. But more a sense of pervading sadness that we'd never been able to get over the past. We sat down to lunch, which my sister had made. Awkward conversation followed, going through the motions, asking about each other's families, the grandchildren. Afterwards, we went through to the sitting room to have coffee. Mother still insisted on making that. I was glancing over the bookshelves and yes, they were still there, next to the dictionaries, in pride of place –* Mein Kampf *and* The Protocols of the Elders of Zion. *I felt as if I'd been kicked in the stomach. The silver-haired woman appeared with the coffee on a tray and a plate of ginger biscuits, and I turned to her and said: 'Mother, things can never be healed between us until you put those two books in the garbage where they belong.'*

That was the last time I saw her. She never changed. There was no happy ending.

The winter dusk had now come. I was entirely oblivious to the bar around us, the students hunched over their beer. I had no idea how much time had passed since Christian had begun his story. But I felt there was a kind of fate in our meeting and the sharing of this particular experience from his childhood. We sat in the gloaming in silence. Christian finally turned to me and said: 'That's why I didn't have to read *Hitler's Willing Executioners*. I knew his thesis was right, because I had lived with it from the age of seven.'

I'm staring at a black-and-white image from the book '*The Good Old Days*': *The Holocaust as Seen by Its Perpetrators and Bystanders.* I've looked at this picture over many years, but I still find the meaning hard to take in. The image is a handwritten card, with pictures and small photographs – a card sent from an *Oberwachtmeister* of the *Schutzpolizei* (sergeant major of the security police) on the Eastern Front back to his family in Germany. There are drawings of a violin, a drum, a top hat and an accordian, and flowers below. There are also two photographs – of piles of dead bodies – murdered Jews. The message, in ornate handwriting, reads:

Der Kreig selbst	[The war has not
uns Frohlinn und Laune	taken away our cheer
noch liess	and good spirits
Hier sagt alles	This says it all
Dies 'Paradies'	This 'Paradise']

*

Perpetrators. Victims. Bystanders. These three words that attempt to categorise responsibility.

In Christian's story some of the positions seem clear. His father was a perpetrator, clearly proud of killing for his country. Anna's family were victims. But after that, distinctions are harder. Where can Christian and his sisters be placed? He was a bystander, certainly, but so young that all three were also surely victims. His mother, a fascist all her life, anti-Semitic, but she never killed anyone. But what would it mean to call her a 'bystander'? How can we calculate the impact of the tens of millions of ordinary Germans who never did more than put a cross beside Hitler's name at the ballot box? The majority who never lifted a gun in their lives? The ones who bought the newspapers, baked the bread, worked in the factories? Yet through their approval (whether expressed or not), through the billions upon billions of words and small actions carried out (or, equally important, small actions not done) by this majority, genocide became possible in this most civilised of European countries.

*

At the end of the evening we walk round the corner, find a hotel on Kastanienalle, Hannah telling us of her fury about how immigrants are being treated in Germany now, how the government have now said that it's not enough to be born here to get German citizenship. She and some friends are considering setting up an informal agency to do marriages of convenience for supposedly 'illegal' immigrants.

We end up in the Prater Garten, and I get a sense that the old Berlin is still alive. It's not been entirely erased by the thrusting modernity of Potsdamer Platz and skyscrapers of glass. Here it's all dark wood, bustling tables, a small red stage at one end with a piano. I go to the bar to ask if they are still serving food. A wonderful mixture of groups of old women drinking on one side, and shaven-headed students on the other, men with dogs sitting by the bar, lesbian lovers canoodling in a corner. And overseeing everything, an extremely camp waiter in his fifties who could have stepped straight out of an Isherwood story, directing the mayhem with aplomb and raised eyebrows.

As I return to our table Hannah is disagreeing passionately with something J. has just said about his reasons for still not having a mobile phone: 'No! Come on, that's just lazy bullshit! Just be honest, you like control!' I love this Berlin directness! Or maybe it's more Hannah than Berlin. A couple of hours with her and you feel totally reinvigorated. Later, when J. and I are back in the hotel, we try to put our finger on what it is about her. A kind of fierce curiosity about the world that most people lose as they get older. And a childlike, but quite unselfconscious, way of asking questions or giving her opinion. Of course, that kind of intensity can't be easy to live with. So the turbulence of her relationships is hardly surprising. But this leaves her the energy to engage with art and activism and her academies and a thousand other things.

5. Walking from Morning till Night

29 December 2003, Berlin

As we walk south from our hotel, we're reflecting on the remarkable, peaceful transition that Germany has made since Reunification, and how challenging it is when you've lived through years like we have to fully understand their historical significance. J. reminds me of Hans Magnus Enzensberger's famous reflection on the political genius of Mikhail Gorbachev in peacefully dismantling a totalitarian regime: 'Any cretin can throw a bomb. It is 1,000 times more difficult to defuse one.'

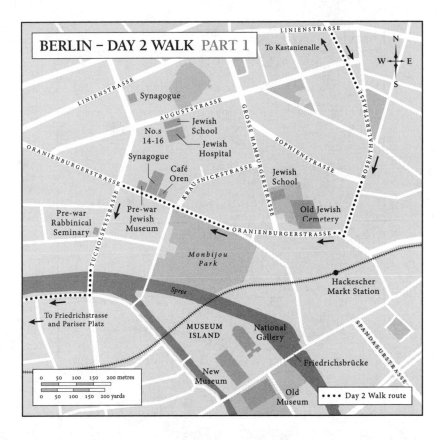

Into Oranienburger Strasse, with J. telling me about the scandals that only emerged later of the corporations that were involved directly in the negotiations about Reunification in 1991. Yes, but we agree it's still quite an achievement to have carried out that transition with no bloodshed. Dominating Oranienburger Strasse is the restored golden dome of the synagogue. We learn from Gilbert that this was the centre of Jewish life in Berlin in the 1920s and 30s. There were rabbinical colleges in the neighbouring streets where Kafka and Leo Baeck (who later contributed so much to the Wiener Library) studied, there were Jewish hospitals, schools and cafés, Einstein gave a violin concert here. I think of my friend Peter; his grandparents would have known this place intimately as they were pillars of this vibrant community and owned many of the cinemas in the city, and when they became successful moved out to a villa in (of all places!)

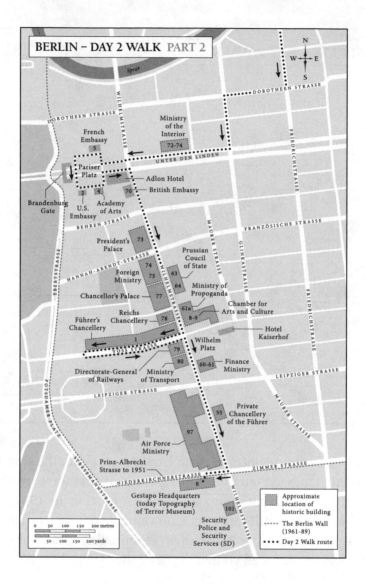

Wannsee. They would come here, to Café Oren, to meet friends, to see and be seen. We also discover that, with the cruellest timing, just six days before Hitler came to power, on 24 January 1933 the Berlin Jewish Museum was opened in the building next to the synagogue.

Over the river, past an island of museums. Friedrichstrasse. Memories of the mysterious U-Bahn that absorbed my imagination

and senses when I was last here in 1984. It took you through
this part of East Berlin without stopping. Three or four ghost
stations hardly lit at all, including Friedrichstrasse, where – it
seems impossible now but I saw them with my own eyes – East
German guards were standing, watching over this subterranean
nothingness as our train looped from the West back to the West.
Perhaps once every few years they actually had something to
do . . . Now at Pariser Platz, no need to ask which building is the
US Embassy. Vast concrete blocks and dozens of armed soldiers
outside to thwart suicide bombers. The paradox of the 'super-
power' – the intense sense of vulnerability created by intolerance. It cannot feel pleasant to work here. Just along from the
embassy is the Academy of Arts building, where Albert Speer
was based between 1937 and 1942 in his role as Hitler's architect
(*Generalbauinspektor fur die Reichshauptstadt*), designing megalomaniacal schemes for the future capital of the Reich.

We turn into Wilhelmstrasse, passing the modern British Embassy
on our right. Wilhelmstrasse is a dullish, mainly residential street
– lots of 1970s and 80s cheaply built blocks of flats. It's hard to
imagine that sixty years ago this street was the hub of totalitarianism, from where dozens of ministries oversaw the occupation of
most of Europe. Very few of the old buildings survive.

This was the Foreign Ministry in the 1930s and 40s. It would have hummed with communications between Ribbentrop and Molotov about the non-aggression pact. But it's also where, in early December 1941, Assistant State Secretary Luther received his first invitation to a meeting to discuss '*eine Gesamtlösung der Judenfrage in Europa*' ('a total solution of the Jewish question in Europe'), originally to have taken place at the International Criminal Police Commission, Am Grossen Wannsee 56–58, on 9 December 1941. Due to the 'exceptional importance' of the meeting, as Heydrich put it, the invitation was delivered personally by courier, who would not have had far to travel – a matter of only 500 yards or so up Wilhelmstrasse from Heydrich's head office of the *Sicherheitspolizei* and SD (Security Service) based in the Gestapo headquarters at Prinz-Albrecht-Strasse. The original meeting had to be cancelled at the last minute because of 'events that were suddenly announced' (the bombing of Pearl Harbor and the US's entry into the war), but on 8 January 1942 Heydrich wrote to Luther and the other invitees again to reschedule the meeting that has gone into history as the Wannsee Conference. Only known about because copy number sixteen of the minutes was originally sent to this building in Wilhelmstrasse to the civil servant Martin Luther.

A little further down from the Foreign Ministry, past where Freisler worked at the Ministry of Justice (opposite Goebbels'

Ministry of Propaganda), also on the right-hand side of the street was Albert Speer's vast Reich Chancellery and the Führer Chancellery, Hitler's headquarters (where Kritzinger and Klopfer had their offices).

We learn from a sign here that the Chancellery stretched 400 metres down Vossstrasse, so we pace this distance and are astonished at the scale of the original building. It stretches most of the way from Wilhelmstrasse to Ebertstrasse (where we walked yesterday). The sheer size of the Chancellery is the apogee of megalomania. And we're again aware that it's only by walking on the ground that you can really understand history. Gilbert's map and assertion that the site of the courtyard where Hitler's body was burned is now a children's playground must surely be wrong. If the Chancellery was 400 metres long then the courtyard behind it couldn't possibly be where the playground is today.

Instead we end up just before dusk in a banal car park at the back of Vossstrasse talking about the insanity of those final days in the bunker, Speer's farewell visit with the Russians less than a mile away, the macabre description of the final concert of the Berlin Philarmonic with surviving Hitler Youth as ushers distributing cyanide capsules to the audience. It's very strange to think of the bunker complex still there, a hundred feet or so beneath us. The

Russians blew some of it up but presumably there are still some remains here. Of course we can respect the desire of the authorities not to create anything that could be used as a neo-Nazi place of pilgrimage, but for anybody intrigued by history there is something frustrating about what remains hidden, just out of view. And the power of place. The knowledge that these things happened here below our feet.

But away from one of the most written-about sites of modern history, I catch sight of another building – on the south side of Vossstrasse – one that is completely derelict now. There are no signs here but it's certainly a building that predated the war. Could this be the former Directorate General of the German Railways? We're confused again by Gilbert – he refers to 'the building that stood on this site', but surely this must be the original building? This also is a site of mass murder, the place where the deportation of millions of human beings was organised, but because this was a place of planners, of train timetablers, you will not find it on any historical tour of Berlin. Nobody glances at the former German Railways HQ here, while a few hundred yards further on down Wilhelmstrasse, past the vast surviving Air Ministry (ironically, one of the few central Berlin buildings to survive mass bombing), many people walk through the ruins of the ex-Gestapo headquarters at Prinz-Albrecht-Strasse 8 – where Müller once worked obsessively, 'hardly ever [coming] out of his office' – now a museum, The Topography of Terror. And just around the corner, Heydrich's Berlin base at the Reich Main Security Office at Wilhelmstrasse 101 – where Lange and Schöngarth would report, when returning from Riga and Krakow. A little further back, at Leipziger Strasse, was Goering's Four Year Plan headquarters, where Neumann worked.

It's getting much colder now; J. is tired, he says he'll meet me back at the hotel later. I decide to go to the Jewish Museum, designed by Daniel Libeskind, which is open for another hour. The museum is astonishing. Not so much the content but the experience that the building itself carries. It's so powerful in its own right I feel it should not have been filled with information. We have too much information in the world but too few places that can move us. The windows throughout are violent slashes, razor wounds pointing towards all the areas of Berlin where deported Jewish families came from. Underneath, sloping down and then up, the three disorientating Axes of Continuity, of Exile, of Holocaust. This last one leading up to the Tower of the Holocaust. An attendant opens the heavy door and I'm suddenly in what seems to be a vast darkened space. Extremely cold and impossible to make out where the walls start or end. And nobody else here. Surrounded by this nothingness, my eyes look upwards, the instinctive habit of the frightened child, and eventually I make out the smallest source of light – a thin cone coming from high up. But this only intensifies the sense of isolation. Outside is Berlin, a night in late December 2003, but here it seems beyond time and space. I sink down to the floor, my back against the coldness of the stone, my eyes finally able to see a little further. I stay here transfixed for I don't know how long.

From time to time the door is opened and light spills into the dark, momentarily giving edges to the space. But the few who come in leave again almost immediately. How to deal with emptiness? An erasure of such proportions.

*

Still shaken, I go back into the museum. I read that when the Nazis came to power there were 560,000 Jews in Germany. Of these,

276,000 emigrated before the war, 200,000 were deported and murdered, 4,000 committed suicide and just over 25,000 survived (9,000 in concentration camps, 15,000 through mixed marriages and 1,500 by going underground). But I'm perplexed by these figures, as they don't add up to 560,000 – the only explanation I can think of is that the total number includes Jews who subsequently died 'natural' deaths as well. Another information panel says that today there are around 100,000 Jews living in Germany, 20,000 of whom are the children of survivors and former German citizens, and 80,000 being more recent immigrants from Russia, a figure that's apparently increasing by around 10,000 each year. There's also a map showing the geographical breakdown of the Holocaust, with the number of Jews killed from each country, by these figures totalling 5,578,329:

> Poland – 3,000,000
> USSR – 1,100,000
> Hungary – 569,000
> Czechoslovakia – 149,150
> Lithuania – 143,000
> Germany – 141,500
> Netherlands – 100,000
> France – 77,320
> Latvia – 76,500
> Greece – 67,000
> Yugoslavia – 63,300
> Austria – 50,000
> Belguim – 28,900
> Italy – 7,680
> Estonia – 2,000
> Luxembourg – 1,950
> Norway – 762
> Albania – 200
> Denmark – 60
> Finland – 7
> Bulgaria – 0

There is, of course, something inherently problematic about such a stark presentation of such decontextualised data, as listing this way alters our reception of this information almost imperceptively – Germany's role is diminished and the countries it occupied appear to bear greater responsibility for the killings. It is also surprising to see Romania and Britain (specifically the Channel Islands) omitted from this list. And I also don't understand the figure shown here for numbers of German Jews killed – 141,500 – when the panel of information I've just read has described 200,000 being deported and murdered.

I go to collect my coat and bag from the cloakroom. On a wall in the entrance I'm disturbed to see this list of some of the museum's sponsors – I can't help but feel that it's a kind of money-laundering-through-sponsorship exercise, as though such transactions could wash away the criminal responsibility of these corporations, all so closely allied to fascism in the past:

BASF
DaimlerChrysler
Dresdner Bank
Deutsche Bank
Deutsche Bahn
Siemens

BASF – one of the four main subsidiary corporations of IG Farben, the builders of Auschwitz III (Buna-Monowitz); DaimlerChrysler – as Daimler-Benz, users of mass slave labour; Dresdner Bank – the bank that led the Aryanisation of assets process; Deutsche Bank – whose loans built Auschwitz and who were bankers to the SS and IG Farben; Deutsche Bahn – who, together with the Directorate General headquarters we saw earlier today, organised the trains to Treblinka, Belzec and Auschwitz; Siemens, also users of wartime slave labour on an industrial scale.

6. The Grey Zone and Grunewald

30 December 2003, Berlin

Our last day in Berlin. We leave our hotel in Kastanienalle and head to the station at Lichtenberg, from where we're going to catch our train tonight. After we've sorted out our tickets we find a left-luggage place and leave our heavy packs here. We then head for Kurfürstenstrasse, and get off the bus halfway down the wide street. We're looking for 115–16, but again we're struck by the selectivity of history's gaze. In a city which probably now has more monuments, museums and documentation about the Holocaust than any other in the world, there seems little memorialisation here. Eventually, a hundred yards or so from the Hotel Sylter Hof, we do find a small marker of the importance of this site – a bus shelter for the No. 20 line, with information panels and large photographs of Adolf Eichmann. For this was close to the site of the former Office for Jewish Affairs, where Eichmann worked for years, with his relatively small team, patiently building the most detailed picture of the Jewish community in Germany and beyond. Developing the bizarre scheme for mass Jewish emigration to Madagascar. And later, from here, co-ordinating the logistics of the Holocaust, the round-ups of Jews, the deportations, the trains.

Although the actual building was demolished in 1961 (the same year as Eichmann's trial in Jerusalem), and although the street is now full of blocks of flats built in the 1970s and 80s, there are one or two mature trees on the opposite side of the road that may have been here sixty years ago as saplings. And as we think about Eichmann here, pausing at his desk, looking out of his window across Kurfürstenstrasse as the leaves on the trees reflected the changing seasons, Primo Levi's words, in the Afterword to *If This Is a Man*, come back to me – he's describing what he later would call 'the grey zone' – a place disturbingly beyond our normative conception of 'good' or 'evil', a zone epitomised by the middle managers of genocide:

> We must remember that these faithful followers, among them the diligent executors of inhuman orders, were not born torturers, were not (with a few exceptions) monsters: they were ordinary men. Monsters exist, but they are too few in number to be truly dangerous. More dangerous are the common men, the functionaries ready to believe and to act without asking questions, like Eichmann, like Höss, the commandant of Auschwitz, like Stangl, commandant of Treblinka, like the French military of twenty years later, slaughterers in Algeria; like the Khmer Rouge of the late seventies, slaughterers in Cambodia.

In one of the last pieces he ever wrote, at the very end of *The Drowned and the Saved*, Levi went even further, explicitly connecting perpetrators in the SS with ourselves:

> The term torturers alludes to our ex-guardians, the SS, and is in my opinion inappropriate: it brings to mind twisted individuals, ill-born, sadists, afflicted by an original flaw. Instead, they were made of our same cloth, they were average human beings, averagely intelligent, averagely wicked: save for exceptions, they were not monsters, they had our faces.

This view was strikingly shared by Hannah Arendt, who, having witnessed Eichmann's testimony during his trial, and having spent much of her life investigating the psychology of totalitarianism, wrote this in *Eichmann in Jerusalem*:

> The trouble with Eichmann was precisely that so many were like him, and that the many were neither perverted nor sadistic, that they were, and still are, terribly and terrifyingly normal. From the viewpoint of our legal institutions and of our moral standards of judgement, this normality was much more terrifying than all of the atrocities put together.

J. and I catch another bus, hoping to connect with a station that will take us to Wannsee. As ever, we're fighting against the clock. And, as so often, trying to save time, you end up losing more. Our bus swings round into some crazed one-way system, taking us far away from where we want to go. We get off at the first opportunity, but we're now in the middle of a nightmarish concrete jungle, part offices, part building site, and a dual carriageway going through the middle of it. We look at the map again but it's hard to tell exactly where we are. We try to get onto another road, but our way is blocked by more construction works. We backtrack to the bus stop and head in the other direction, now infuriated by the chaos surrounding us. An enormous stadium appears around a bend – the Olympic one from the infamous 1936 games? Finally we reach a U-Bahn station, but there's a sign saying that because of engineering works there are no trains between Christmas and New Year. I flag down a taxi and we ask to go to the closest (functioning) station. Dusk is not far away and I'd wanted to get to Wannsee in the light.

We drive for ten minutes; there's now woodland on our right, a sense of the edge of the city, the houses are detached with gardens. The taxi pulls up outside a curious station building, rather grand with a parade of shops outside. It reminds me of the station at Kew Gardens. The same sense of being on the very edge of a vast city,

but away from the hurly-burly. Flower shops. Estate agents. Deli-
catessens. The next train to Wannsee is not for twenty minutes
so we wander along the platform, and it's only then I see the sign:
'Grunewald'.

A bizarre coincidence – by getting lost in Berlin, we've ended
up at the station where the deportations of Berlin's Jews started
from. Over 50,000 people between 1941 and 1945. Many had
lost their homes through Speer's massive rebuilding programme,
though, as always, he denied knowledge of that. I wonder how
many would have come from the bustling streets where we were
yesterday morning around Oranienburger Strasse? And how
would they have been transported here? For my friend Peter's
grandparents, it would have been a much shorter journey, just
a few stops from the even wealthier suburb of Wannsee. The
woodedness of the area also has a curious link to Speer – apparently it was his initiative that led to the reforesting of Grunewald
in the late 1930s.

We find a memorial here, as powerful in its simplicity as anything
I've seen. The platform and railway track that was used for the
deportations is now disused, but etched into each sleeper is the precise detail of every train that left here: the date, the number of people
it carried, the destination. We learn about the first train:

18.10.41, 1,251 Jews, Berlin to Lodz

and then we walk all the way along the sleepers until we get to the marker for the final deportation train.

27.3.45, 18 Jews, Berlin to Theresienstadt

With the war lost, with massive shortages of transport, these trains were still leaving almost daily. We've never been more struck by the obsessive and insane nature of this extermination. After our frenetic criss-crossings of the city these last days and all that we have learnt, somehow this knowledge stuns us at a different level.

All we can do is walk along, very slowly, and try to take in the meaning of every single piece of rusting track, and all the lives extinguished.

At one end of the tracks, a wooden building, perhaps a waiting room, has been left to the elements. The other end disappears into a little copse, gradually the hardness of the rails being overgrown by saplings and bushes. A bespectacled old man walks his dog, but there's nobody else here.

I look up and suddenly I'm struck by something else. Immediately overlooking the railway is a row of substantial villas with gables, they look late nineteenth century, probably dating from the early days of this suburb. The solid houses of doctors and civil servants. One of them is now converted into a hotel, but the others are no doubt still homes to the Berlin professional classes. A desirable address, with the beech forests to one side and a fast train link to the centre. And a comfortable sense of slightly fading gentility, without the thrusting ugliness of new money and modernity. The Berlin equivalent of Hampstead, maybe.

And now an image comes into my mind with a strange vividness. I suddenly see this place sixty years ago. It's a bright winter's afternoon like this one, with interspersed flurries of snow, and a piano lesson is about to begin in that middle villa, just there. The daughter notices, with disdain, as her teacher walks into the drawing room, that the sole of one of his shoes is beginning to peel away. As her parents have repeated so often, there may be a war on but that is no excuse. The lesson begins, but there are shouts from outside, and now dogs barking. The same as last week. The teacher strides to the tall windows, sees the familiar crowd of Jews on the platform below surrounded by dogs, a huddled mass of gesticulation and luggage. Why can't they do this at night? He draws the thick curtains and the lesson resumes. The girl hasn't practised the Schumann (the seventh movement of 'Kinderszenen' – not even one of his harder pieces), and the middle section is still very poor. The teacher watches her fingers plumply pound the keys, casually butchering every nuance of the piece, and he winces inwardly. He tries to find words to help her, which do not betray his impatience. After all, he needs the girl more than she needs him. He glances up at the ornate clock on the mantelpiece, only another twenty-five minutes and it's over for another week. He begins to consider what he'll do with the marks he's earned. Supper at the Kaiserhof tomorrow, or he could buy the brooch that his girlfriend saw last week? Finally the hour is up, the practice (which the girl will not do) is set, pleasantries with the mother exchanged. The curtains are drawn back. The platform now is almost deserted, two young policemen are sitting on a bench smoking, and not even the presence of the odd discarded hat or suitcase might hint that 1,100 people had just begun their journey to extinction.

*

7. Discussing Genocide in Ninety Minutes: the Wannsee Conference, 20 January 1942

It was a Tuesday morning. Berlin was still in the grip of a deep frost, but the conditions did not delay the meeting by more than a few minutes. Heydrich flew in from Prague in his own plane, JU-52, landing at an airstrip on the western edge of the city. For the last four months, as well as his role as head of the RHSA and Himmler's right-hand man, he had been appointed as acting *Reichsprotektor* of the western part of occupied Czechoslovakia, retitled the 'Protektorat' of Bohemia and Moravia by the Nazis. Due to his ruthless suppression of Czech dissent – over 400 summary death sentences, and 5,000 arrests within his first two months – he has already become known as 'the Butcher of Prague'. But over the last days and weeks his mind has been preoccupied with a greater challenge than the establishment of a police state in the Protektorat. Because on 31 July 1941 Goering had written to him, instructing him 'to carry out all necessary preparations in regard to organisational, practical and material matters for a total solution of the Jewish question [*Gesamtlosung der Judenfrage*] in the German spheres of influence within Europe'. So, for the last weeks, as he's shuttled between his new residence, the elegant chateau and estate at Panenské Břežany, just north of Prague, to his headquarters at Hradčany Castle in the city, he has been focussed on preparations for the meeting today in Wannsee. He works with the habitual, ferocious energy that has won the admiration of both Hitler and Himmler, but still finds space for evenings of chamber music (he plays the violin in the string quartets), and time with his family – his wife Lina and their three young children, Heider, Klaus and Silke.

Eichmann, who had been inspecting the ghetto at Theresienstadt (in the north of occupied Czechoslovakia), only arrived back in Berlin late the previous evening after a difficult journey. Those who had travelled the furthest – Schöngarth, who had come from Krakow, and Lange, who had journeyed from Riga – would have been put up overnight in the guest accommodation upstairs in the Wannsee villa (a Security Police newsletter spoke highly of the facilities here). The other participants were driven in ministry cars from across Berlin. We know that Klopfer and Kritzinger travelled together, as they were old friends who both worked at the Chancellery. And it's very likely that Meyer and Leibbrandt, departmental colleagues, shared a car too, coming from the RMO ministry building near Tiergarten.

As the conference invitees drove through the prosperous suburbs of south-west Berlin that morning, the streets getting broader and leafier, doubtless they reflected on the prestigiousness of the invitation, and the other senior figures of the Reich who would be there. As they sped through Zehlendorf towards Wannsee, Stuckart would have passed close to his imposing villa, wondering whether a further promotion would mean he might soon be able to move his family into the most prized area of Wannsee itself – the place where Reich luminaries such as Goebbels, Speer, Funk (the finance minister) and Hitler's physician, Dr Morell, all had their grand houses. What none of the men may have known, as their ministry cars drove along the pine-fringed avenues of Wannsee, was that this borough had been one of the most mixed parts of Berlin, where prosperous Christians and Jews (such as Peter's grandparents) had lived together for more than a hundred years. They were even buried side by side in the local Friedhof cemetery, where Christian crosses and Jewish Stars of David were both seen together. As they arrived, their cars crunching the gravel of the drive, some of the attendees might have recalled hearing about the financial scandal surrounding the former owner of the villa, Friedrich Minoux (the wealthy, right-wing industrialist), which had led to him handing the property over to the Gestapo in May 1941, who had turned it into a guest house for senior Security Police and SD personnel. The publicity leaflet boasted 'a music room and games room (billiards), a large meeting room and conservatory, a terrace looking on to the Wannsee, central heating, hot and cold running water and all comforts'.

So the 'board of directors' are finally ready to meet, bringing together nine different agencies of the Reich.

Before the meeting begins, as our fifteen men arrive, stamping the ice from their boots in the elegant circular entrance hall and chatting over coffee, let us remember the power dynamic today. Heydrich, both because he has initiated the meeting and due to his position as head of the Security Police and the RSHA, is the dominant figure. Even Müller (chief of the Gestapo) is answerable to him. And Heydrich has, not surprisingly, packed this meeting with his own people – apart from Müller, we have Schöngarth (the chief of the Security Police in occupied Poland), Lange (chief of the Security Police in Latvia) and Eichmann (Section IV B4, Evacuations). We can expect these four men to work as a block, supporting their boss Heydrich on every matter that is discussed. Although Eichmann is certainly the most junior figure in rank at the meeting, he has already built a reputation as an expert on Jewish issues, so his name is known to some of those attending today – indeed he's already met Stuckart, Neumann and Freisler at Goering's meeting in 1938, and he knows Lange from their shared time in Vienna. When it comes to details of Jewish populations in different countries, Heydrich will be deferring to the statistical and documentary work that his young specialist at the Office for Jewish Affairs has prepared for this meeting.

So who is Heydrich most concerned about today? Who will he be keen not to offend? Remember, it's tempting to view such a gathering as an ideologically driven and coherent group coming together for a specific purpose, but, as in all governments or all large corporations, there are always territorial battles and power struggles going on. Neumann will be a powerful player today as he represents the Four Year Plan office, which effectively drives the economy, and he will be reporting back directly to Goering after the meeting. The co-operation of the powers on the ground

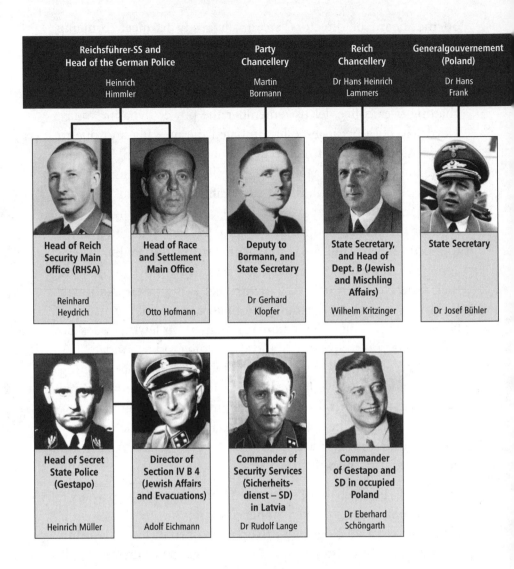

Reichsführer-SS and Head of the German Police	Party Chancellery	Reich Chancellery	Generalgouvernement (Poland)
Heinrich Himmler	Martin Bormann	Dr Hans Heinrich Lammers	Dr Hans Frank

Head of Reich Security Main Office (RHSA)	Head of Race and Settlement Main Office	Deputy to Bormann, and State Secretary	State Secretary, and Head of Dept. B (Jewish and Mischling Affairs)	State Secretary
Reinhard Heydrich	Otto Hofmann	Dr Gerhard Klopfer	Wilhelm Kritzinger	Dr Josef Bühler

Head of Secret State Police (Gestapo)	Director of Section IV B 4 (Jewish Affairs and Evacuations)	Commander of Security Services (Sicherheits-dienst – SD) in Latvia	Commander of Gestapo and SD in occupied Poland
Heinrich Müller	Adolf Eichmann	Dr Rudolf Lange	Dr Eberhard Schöngarth

in occupied Poland (represented by Bühler), and the occupied Eastern Territories (represented by Meyer and Leibbrandt) will be critical if Heydrich's plan is to go forward smoothly, so he will need to be careful here. Bormann is always a potential threat, and has the direct ear of Hitler, so he'll also have to show his representative Klopfer respect. Finally he needs to be careful with the

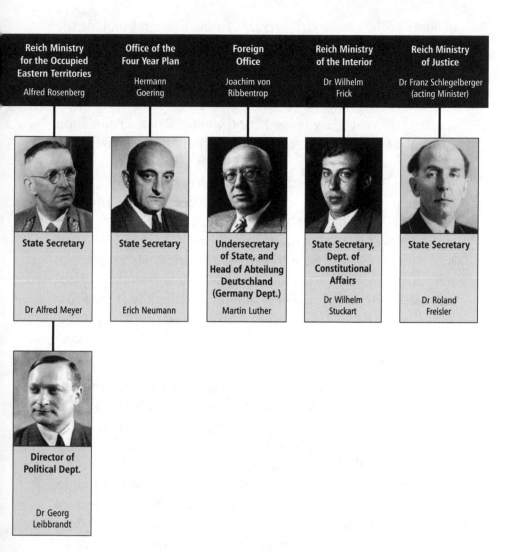

Reich Ministry for the Occupied Eastern Territories	Office of the Four Year Plan	Foreign Office	Reich Ministry of the Interior	Reich Ministry of Justice
Alfred Rosenberg	Hermann Goering	Joachim von Ribbentrop	Dr Wilhelm Frick	Dr Franz Schlegelberger (acting Minister)
State Secretary	State Secretary	Undersecretary of State, and Head of Abteilung Deutschland (Germany Dept.)	State Secretary, Dept. of Constitutional Affairs	State Secretary
Dr Alfred Meyer	Erich Neumann	Martin Luther	Dr Wilhelm Stuckart	Dr Roland Freisler

Director of Political Dept.
Dr Georg Leibbrandt

tone of what is said, because some of the other gentlemen coming from the ministries and more 'civil' backgrounds may not be accustomed to the more direct, even 'muscular' language used by the SS and the Security Police.

We know from Hannah Arendt that Eichmann and Heydrich also 'expected the greatest difficulties' in getting the agreement of some of the senior civil servants to the new proposal for the 'Final Solution'. There are wide differences in the ideological backgrounds of the permanent secretaries and undersecretaries. While Heydrich felt that some – such as Klopfer and Stuckart, who only a few months before Wannsee had founded the new journal, *Reich-Volksordnung-Lebensraum* ('Reich, Population Control, Living Space') – could be relied upon, others were less trustworthy. He feels concerned that the general culture of the ministries is still not sufficiently ideologically committed to Nazism; it is known that some of the undersecretaries and legal experts had joined the party relatively late – after Hitler's accession to power in 1933. Kritzinger had only joined in 1938. This fact would certainly have disturbed Heydrich. He senses that both Kritzinger and Neumann will need watching today – both still seem to be too close to the old, impartial ethos of the Prussian Civil Service. Two lawyers who may be overly 'legalistic' and possibly inflexible about the methods needed in expediting the 'Final Solution'.

We're now heading into the conference room overlooking the Wannsee lake. Through the tall windows you can see the gentle slope with pine trees and benches going down to the water. Quite a place to watch the sun go down on a summer's evening, though today all is whited out by the frost. Our participants are now ready, sitting round the long, rectangular wooden table. In the corner, just behind Heydrich, sits Eichmann (deemed too junior a figure to sit at the main table), and next to him is the only woman in the room, the secretary who, directed by Eichmann, will record an almost verbatim account of the meeting today on her stenography machine – 'almost' because some things can never be written down. That's why Eichmann sits beside her, within whispering distance. He and Heydrich will subsequently use this account to create their own paraphrased version of the minutes of the meeting – the *Besprechungsprotokoll*.

*

Proceedings begin just after midday. Unusually, there is no formal agenda, but this suits our organisers' purposes. Having been briefed in detail by Eichmann over the preceding weeks, Heydrich makes his lengthy opening presentation (which takes up the first half of the meeting): an extensive overview of the past history of the 'Jewish question' in the Reich and a proposal for moving towards an *Endlosing* ('final solution'). As he speaks, we can picture him, hear him – this most feared figure among the Nazi leadership, this man with the 'ever watchful instincts of a predatory animal . . . a tall, impressive figure with a broad, unusually high forehead, small, restless eyes as crafty as an animal's and of uncanny power, and a wide, full-lipped mouth. His hands were slender and rather too long – they made one think of the legs of a spider . . . His voice was much too high for so large a man and his speech was nervous and staccato.'*

He establishes his authority and explains that the Reichsmarschall himself, Goering, has appointed him, as head of the Security Police and the SD, to lead 'preparations for the Final Solution of the Jewish question in Europe'. He goes on to emphasise the need for all central agencies directly involved in this matter to co-ordinate their actions, hence this meeting today.

What he doesn't explain here is that the 'preparations' are already far more than that – for forty-four days now, since 8 December 1941, the Saurer trucks have been in operation at Chelmno, and up to 40,000 Jews and Gypsies have already been gassed. Nor does he mention here the *Einsatzgruppen* operations which have been under way for more than six months on the Eastern Front, and which have already killed hundreds of thousands of Jews – as Lange and Schöngarth can testify from their direct experience. Müller, as head of the Gestapo, knows in detail about all of this – since July 1941, he

---

* Comments made by Heydrich's protégé, Walter Schellenberg, quoted in the opening chapter of *The Killing of SS Obergruppenführer Reinhard Heydrich* by Callum Macdonald.

has been receiving reports at his desk at 9.30 each morning of '*Ereignismeldungen UdSSR*' (USSR Event Notifications). On occasions he asks for more detail, for instance requesting 'particularly interesting illustrative material' as Hitler wishes to be 'presented with ongoing reports of the work of the *Einsatzgruppen* in the east'. And, over the preceding few months, Eichmann has already witnessed the beginnings of the mass-murder programme. In the preceding August, he'd been briefed by Heydrich that 'The Führer has ordered the physical extermination of the Jews', and over the autumn of 1941 and early winter of 1941–2, Eichmann began a tour of the killing fields – seeing *Einsatzgruppen* mass shootings in Minsk, the *gaswagen* operation at Chelmno, and, later on, several visits to Auschwitz and Birkenau.[*]

Heydrich then – and this is aimed particularly at Bühler (Poland) and Meyer and Leibbrandt (Eastern Territories) – points out that the Reichsführer (Himmler) and himself will be directing this matter centrally 'without regard for geographic boundaries'. We know that Himmler and Heydrich had had a series of meetings in mid-November 1941 to co-ordinate policy on 'eliminating the Jews'. On the rest of this page he's reminding his colleagues of how measures taken against the Jews over the last years have evolved, particularly the need for increased emigration away from the *Lebensraum* of the German people, which necessitated the establishment of a special Reich Central Office for Jewish Emigration (Eichmann's department) in January 1939. The last sentence on this page is fascinating both for the light it sheds on Heydrich's psychology and also his need to reassure some of the more traditional Civil Service men here today – he talks about the aim of these policies as being 'to clear the German living space *by legal means* [my emphasis]'.

---

[*] I will return to Eichmann's tour of the sites of mass murder in Book Four – 'Arendt in Jerusalem'.

NG - 2586

Die Federführung bei der Bearbeitung der
Endlösung der Judenfrage liege ohne Rücksicht auf
geographische Grenzen zentral beim Reichsführer-SS
und Chef der Deutschen Polizei (Chef der Sicherheitspolizei und des SD).

Der Chef der Sicherheitspolizei und des
SD gab sodann einen kurzen Rückblick über den bisher geführten Kampf gegen diesen Gegner. Die we-
sentlichsten Momente bilden

a/ die Zurückdrängung der Juden aus den
    einzelnen Lebensgebieten des deut-
    schen Volkes,

b/ die Zurückdrängung der Juden aus dem
    Lebensraum des deutschen Volkes.

Im Vollzug dieser Bestrebungen wurde als
einzige vorläufige Lösungsmöglichkeit die Beschleu-
nigung der Auswanderung der Juden aus dem Reichsgebiet verstärkt und planmäßig in Angriff genommen.

Auf Anordnung des Reichsmarschalls wurde
im Januar 1939 eine Reichszentrale für jüdische Auswanderung errichtet, mit deren Leitung der Chef der
Sicherheitspolizei und des SD betraut wurde. Sie
hatte insbesondere die Aufgabe

a/ alle Maßnahmen zur Vorbereitung einer
    verstärkten Auswanderung der Juden zu
    treffen

b/ den Auswanderungsstrom zu lenken.

c/ die Durchführung der Auswanderung im
    Einzelfall zu beschleunigen.

Das Aufgabenziel war, auf legale Weise
den deutschen Lebensraum von Juden zu säubern.

Now he goes on to detail both the challenges and the successes of the accelerated emigration programme so far. Despite the organisational difficulties, 537,000 Jews have been compelled to emigrate between 1933 and October 1941, 360,000 from Germany itself, 147,000 from Austria and 30,000 from Bohemia and Moravia. He is pleased to report that the costs of emigration were financed by the Jews themselves and Jewish political organisations. (At the mention of this detail, Eichmann, who had been responsible for the success of Austrian Jewish emigration, doubtless feels flushed with pride, listening to his boss's appreciation in front of this audience of senior Reich figures.)

But now, Heydrich says, the war situation means that Jewish emigration is impossible, indeed it has been prohibited by Himmler (since 30 October 1941). And we arrive at the centrally important sentence of this meeting, which, as you can see here, has been underlined – whether by Luther or a colleague in the foreign office we don't know:

'As a further possible solution, and with the appropriate prior authorisation by the Führer, emigration has now been replaced by evacuation to the east.'

This is the only time in the whole meeting when Hitler is invoked directly, and it is the first recorded mention we have of the move away from expelling the Jews to 'evacuation to the east', which was to become a common, and chilling, euphemism for the establishment of the extermination camps in Poland and the setting up of the extensive transport and personnel infrastructures necessary for mass killing.

Next Heydrich gives the detailed breakdown of the figures Eichmann had prepared for the meeting concerning the total number of Jews to be taken into consideration in this 'Final Solution' – some 11 million.

We know from Edwin Black's work *IBM and the Holocaust* that the Nazis had used the most advanced information-gathering techniques on their opponents since coming to power in 1933. This included

NG - 2586

Neben dem Reichsmark-Aufkommen sind De-
visen für Vorzeige- und Landungsgelder erforderlich gewesen. Um den deutschen Devisenschatz zu
schonen, wurden die jüdischen Finanzinstitutionen
des Auslandes durch die jüdischen Organisationen
des Inlandes verhalten, für die Beitreibung entsprechender Devisenaufkommen Sorge zu tragen.
Hier wurden durch diese ausländischen Juden im
Schenkungswege bis zum 30.10.1941 insgesamt rund
9.500.000 Dollar zur Verfügung gestellt.

Inzwischen hat der Reichsführer-ᛋᛋ und
Chef der Deutschen Polizei im Hinblick auf die
Gefahren einer Auswanderung im Kriege und im Hinblick auf die Möglichkeiten des Ostens die Auswanderung von Juden verboten.

III.   Anstelle der Auswanderung ist nunmehr
als weitere Lösungsmöglichkeit nach entsprechender vorheriger Genehmigung durch den Führer die
Evakuierung der Juden nach dem Osten getreten.

Diese Aktionen sind jedoch lediglich
als Ausweichmöglichkeiten anzusprechen, doch
werden hier bereits jene praktischen Erfahrungen gesammelt, die im Hinblick auf die kommende
Endlösung der Judenfrage von wichtiger Bedeutung
sind.

Im Zuge dieser Endlösung der europäischen Judenfrage kommen rund 11 Millionen Juden in Betracht, die sich wie folgt auf die einzelnen Länder verteilen:

372923

the now infamous Hollerith tabulating machine (an early kind of quasi-computer that used punch-card technology), which had been pioneered by IBM in the 1920s. IBM's German subsidiary was called Dehomag (*Deutsche Hollerith-Maschinen Gesellschaft*), and Dehomag provided, and maintained, the Hollerith machines which were used extensively by the Nazi government and the Gestapo from 1933 onwards, for official census data but also for detailed information gathering on Jews and political opponents. Until December 1941, Dehomag's general manager in Germany reported directly to IBM president Thomas Watson in New York. After America's entry into the war (which meant that it was no longer legal to trade directly with Germany), IBM in New York established a subsidiary in Poland, Watson Business Machines, which played a significant role in facilitating the logistical operations necessary to implement the Holocaust.

The statistics relating to Jewish populations across Europe which Eichmann had provided for Heydrich's presentation at Wannsee, were not Eichmann's work alone. He'd collaborated closely with Dr Richard Korherr (Himmler's hand-picked Inspector of Statistics at the SS) and Roderich Plate, Korherr's assistant, a racial census expert. Based at their office at Friedrichstrasse 129, and working with Dehomag experts skilled in data supplied by IBM's Hollerith machines, Korherr and Plate provided Eichmann with the detailed figures on the numbers of Jews left in Germany and occupied Europe in early 1942 – which we see Heydrich referring to here at the Wannsee Conference. The figures for Germany, and much of the occupied territories, based on precise data, were extremely accurate. However, other estimates – especially for unconquered lands such as the USSR – were grossly inflated, as can be seen in the table on page 317.

You'll see that this page is divided into two sections – at the top, the Greater Reich, including all the occupied territories, then below, a rather strange combined grouping of German allies, enemies and neutral countries. Some of these figures are extremely up to date – for example, 34,000 for Lithuania – which a year before had a population of almost 250,000 Jews, so over 200,000 had been killed

L a n d	Zahl
A. Altreich	131.800
Ostmark	43.700
Ostgebiete	420.000
Generalgouvernement	2.284.000
Bialystok	400.000
Protektorat Böhmen und Mähren	74.200
Estland - judenfrei -	
Lettland	3.500
Litauen	34.000
Belgien	43.000
Dünemark	5.600
Frankreich / Besetztes Gebiet	165.000
Unbesetztes Gebiet	700.000
Griechenland	69.600
Niederlande	160.800
Norwegen	1.300
B. Bulgarien	48.000
England	330.000
Finnland	2.300
Irland	4.000
Italien einschl. Sardinien	58.000
Albanien	200
Kroatien	40.000
Portugal	3.000
Rumänien einschl. Bessarabien	342.000
Schweden	8.000
Schweiz	18.000
Serbien	10.000
Slowakei	88.000
Spanien	6.000
Türkei (europ. Teil)	55.500
Ungarn	742.800
UdSSR	5.000.000
Ukraine 2.994.684	
Weißrußland ausschl. Bialystok 446.484	
Zusammen: über	11.000.000

in the six-month period preceding this meeting. But, of course, these other figures, of the Jews already murdered, appear nowhere in this document. The Nazis were always careful to avoid documentary reference of 'the unwritten order' and so a plethora of euphemisms was employed instead – 'Jewish question', 'Final Solution', 'evacuation to the east'.

Dr Lange in particular would have examined this list with professional pride, noting the low figure of only 3,500 Jews left in Latvia. As head of Einsatzkommando 2 there, he had directly overseen the killing of 60,000 Latvian Jews in the period up to December 1941. Dr Schöngarth's hands were also dripping in blood, having commanded his Einsatzkommando zbV (in eastern Galicia), which had murdered almost 4,000 Jews in little more than a week in July 1941. Maybe one, or both, of them would have described their service to the Reich at this point? But such direct language ('very blunt words', as Eichmann later put it) would never have made it into these minutes.

Notice also here, next to Estonia, a ghostly white space and the word '*judenfrei*' ('free of Jews'). This was true – half of the population of 2,000 Jews in June 1941 had been massacred and half had fled eastwards to the USSR. In fact, this is another feature of this page – the obsessional recording of even the smallest Jewish populations – 4,000 in Ireland, 3,000 in Portugal, 200 in Albania. Because of the outcome of the war (and a minority of countries where there was courageous opposition to antisemitism, notably Denmark and Bulgaria), some of the communities listed here were only minimally affected.

But how can our eyes, flicking down this list of figures today, transmit the real meaning to the brain? What do we do with such information? Faced with the most monstrous mass death sentence in history, the human mind cannot cope. Part of us might be tempted to mock the megalomania of this document – the targeting of 11 million human beings – but then we have to realise that half of that 'target' *was* reached. The scale is far beyond our capacity to imagine. Three million Polish Jews. Five hundred and sixty nine thousand

NG - 2586

Bei den angegebenen Judenzahlen der verschiedenen ausländischen Staaten handelt es sich
jedoch nur um Glaubensjuden, da die Begriffsbe-
stimmungen der Juden nach rassischen Grundsätzen
teilweise dort noch fehlen. Die Behandlung des
Problems in den einzelnen Ländern wird im Hinblick
auf die allgemeine Haltung und Auffassung auf gewisse Schwierigkeiten stoßen, besonders in Ungarn
und Rumänien. So kann sich z.B. heute noch in Rumänien der Jude gegen Geld entsprechende Dokumen-
te, die ihm eine fremde Staatsangehörigkeit amt-
lich bescheinigen, beschaffen.

Der Einfluß der Juden auf alle Gebiete
in der UdSSR ist bekannt. Im europäischen Gebiet
leben etwa 5 Millionen, im asiatischen Raum knapp
1/4 Million Juden.

Die berufsständische Aufgliederung der
in europäischen Gebiet der UdSSR ansässigen Juden
war etwa folgende:

In der Landwirtschaft	9,1 %
als städtische Arbeiter	14,8 %
im Handel	20,0 %
als Staatsarbeiter angestellt	23,4 %
in den privaten Berufen - Heilkunde, Presse, Theater, usw.	32,7 %.

Unter entsprechender Leitung sollen
im Zuge der Endlösung die Juden in geeigneter Weise im Osten zum Arbeitseinsatz kommen. In großen
Arbeitskolonnen, unter Trennung der Geschlechter,
werden die arbeitsfähigen Juden straßenbauend in
diese Gebiete geführt, wobei zweifellos ein Groß
teil durch natürliche Verminderung ausfallen wir.

Hungarian Jews. Many of whom Eichmann was later instrumental in deporting to Auschwitz with the end of the war only a matter of months away – knowing the war would be lost yet still his compulsion to do the most 'conscientious' job possible. More than three and a half million human beings murdered – the entire population of Berlin today – from just two countries.

Heydrich then goes on to highlight – in the top paragraph here – some of the challenges that will be faced. For instance, 'a Jew in Romania, even today, can still buy for cash the appropriate documents that certify officially that he is of foreign nationality' (and so not Jewish). Despite the editing of this document, the extreme cynicism does appear clearly at times. At the bottom of the page, Heydrich describes how 'the Jews are to be utilised for work in the east in a suitable manner. In large labour columns, separated by sex, Jews capable of working will be dispatched to these regions to build roads, and, in the process, *a majority of them will undoubtedly be eliminated by natural causes* [my emphasis]'. 'Those who ultimately survive will have to be given *suitable treatment* [my emphasis] because they undoubtedly represent the toughest strain and therefore constitute a natural elite that, if allowed to go free, would turn into a germ cell of renewed Jewish revival (witness the experience of history)'. So, whether they survive the forced labour or not, the outcome is the same: death.

He then details how the process of implementation of this 'Final Solution' will move from west to east. First the Jews will be moved to 'so-called transit ghettoes', then they will be transported further to the east. There will be a small number of exceptions – Jews over the age of sixty five, those with war injuries and those with war decorations (Iron Cross, first class). Theresienstadt has already been earmarked to receive these groups.

Finally Heydrich explains that the precise timing of each major evacuation will depend largely on military developments and will need the detailed collaboration between specialists in the Foreign Office, the Security Police and the Security Service. He then

NG - 2586

Der allfällig endlich verbleibende Rest-
bestand wird, da es sich bei diesem zweifellos um
den widerstandsfähigsten Teil handelt, entsprechend
behandelt werden müssen, da dieser, eine natürliche
Auslese darstellend, bei Freilassung als Keimzelle
eines neuen jüdischen Aufbaues anzusprechen ist.
(Siehe die Erfahrung der Geschichte.)

Im Zuge der praktischen Durchführung der
Endlösung wird Europa vom Westen nach Osten durch-
gekämmt. Das Reichsgebiet einschließlich Protektorat Böhmen und Mähren wird, allein schon aus Grün-
den der Wohnungsfrage und sonstigen sozial-politi-
schen Notwendigkeiten, vorweggenommen werden müssen.

Die evakuierten Juden werden zunächst Zug
um Zug in sogenannte Durchgangsghettos verbracht,
um von dort aus weiter nach dem Osten transportiert
zu werden.

Wichtige Voraussetzung, so führte ⚡-Ober-
gruppenführer H e y d r i c h weiter aus, für die
Durchführung der Evakuierung überhaupt, ist die ge-
naue Festlegung des in Betracht kommenden Personen-
kreises.

Es ist beabsichtigt, Juden im Alter von
über 65 Jahren nicht zu evakuieren, sondern sie einem Altersghetto - vorgesehen ist Theresienstadt -
zu überstellen.

Neben diesen Altersklassen - von den am
31.10.1941 sich im Altreich und der Ostmark befind-
lichen etwa 280.000 Juden sind etwa 30 % über 65 Jahre alt - finden in den jüdischen Altersghettos weiterhin die schwerkriegsbeschädigten Juden und Juden
mit Kriegsauszeichnungen (EK I) Aufnahme. Mit dieser

discusses specific, local factors in Slovakia, Croatia, Romania, Hungary, Italy and France.

At this point, when Heydrich has been expounding for almost forty-five minutes, we have our first minuted contribution from another participant – it is recorded that Luther (of the Foreign Office) points out that 'dealing with these problems thoroughly will cause difficulties in some countries, particularly the Scandinavian states, and therefore he suggests deferring the settlement of this matter in these countries for the time being. Given the very small numbers of Jews there such a postponement would not amount to a serious restriction.' But, he emphasises, the Foreign Office sees no major difficulties in south-eastern and western Europe. Hofmann then states that he 'intends to send a specialist, from the Race and Settlement Main Office, to Hungary as soon as Heydrich is ready to tackle the matter there'.

Halfway through the conference there is a short break for refreshments, and we learn from Eichmann that alcohol is served and after this the participants relax more and the discussion becomes more of a 'free-for-all' with people responding to the issues Heydrich has raised.

The next section of the meeting is dominated by a bafflingly detailed discussion over exactly how Jewishness is to be defined – four pages of the minutes (not reproduced here) – with particular reference to 'the problem of mixed marriages [*Mischenen*] and mixed parentage [*Mischlinge*]'.

Very few will be exempted from evacuation, and even those who are 'will be sterilised in order to prevent the *Mischlinge* problem once and for all' And then another characteristically cynical remark from Heydrich: 'Sterilisation will be voluntary, but it is the precondition for remaining in the Reich.'

Towards the end of the debate about the treatment of *Mischlinge*, Hofmann observes that the sterilisation will have to be carried out on a wide scale because 'once the *Mischling* faces the choice

zweckmäßigen Lösung werden mit einem Schlag die
vielen Interventionen ausgeschaltet.

Der Beginn der einzelnen größeren Evakuierungsaktionen wird weitgehend von der militäri-
schen Entwicklung abhängig sein. Bezüglich der Behandlung der Endlösung in den von uns besetzten und
beeinflußten europäischen Gebieten wurde vorgeschla-
gen, daß die in Betracht kommenden Sachbearbeiter
des Auswärtigen Amtes sich mit dem zuständigen Re-
ferenten der Sicherheitspolizei und des SD bespre-
chen.

In der Slowakei und Kroatien ist die Ange-
legenheit nicht mehr allzu schwer, da die wesentlich
sten Kernfragen in dieser Hinsicht dort bereits einer Lösung zugeführt wurden. In Rumänien hat die Regierung inzwischen ebenfalls einen Judenbeauftragten
eingesetzt. Zur Regelung der Frage in Ungarn ist
erforderlich, in Zeitkürze einen Berater für Juden-
fragen der Ungarischen Regierung aufzuoktroyieren.

Hinsichtlich der Aufnahme der Vorbereitun-
gen zur Regelung des Problems in Italien hält Obergruppenführer H e y d r i c h eine Verbindung
Polizei-Chef in diesen Belangen für angebracht.

In besetzten und unbesetzten Frankreich
wird die Erfassung der Juden zur Evakuierung aller
Wahrscheinlichkeit nach ohne große Schwierigkeiten
vor sich gehen können.

Unterstaatssekretär L u t h e r teilt
hierzu mit, daß bei tiefgehender Behandlung dieses
Problems in einigen Ländern, so in den nordischen
Staaten, Schwierigkeiten auftauchen werden, und es
sich daher empfiehlt, diese Länder vorerst noch

between evacuation and sterilisation, he will prefer to be sterilised'. This a clear recognition that 'evacuation' will be seen for
what it is – extermination. Stuckart then expresses his concern that implementing the detailed differential treatments and
exemptions just discussed could cause 'endless administrative
work'. Why not simply move to a policy of forced sterilisation
(*Zwangssterilisierung*) for all?

This is one of the major surprises of the conference, what Eichmann
later referred to as the 'conversion' of Stuckart away from the Interior
Ministry's previous policy regarding the *Mischlinge* and *Mischenen*.

After this the discussion moves on to the question of the war economy. Neumann warns that 'Jews now working in essential war
industries cannot be evacuated as long as there are no replacements
for them'. Heydrich reassures him that these Jews 'would not be
evacuated anyway'.

Dr Bühler now raises the key issue of how the 'Final Solution'
should proceed. He declares that the General Government (occupied Poland) 'would welcome it *if the Final Solution of this question
would begin in the General Government first because the transportation problem was no overriding factor there* [my emphasis]'.

This must make reference to the fact that the expansion of extermination camps in Poland meant that the Polish Jews would have
very little distance to travel. We know that Himmler had met
Globočnik (the SS and police leader in Lublin) on 13 October
1941 to discuss how Lublin's Jews would be dealt with, and four
days later Globočnik and Governor Frank (Bühler's boss) further
discussed these proposals. By November 1941 the extermination
camp at Belzec had been started to be built and personnel formerly
deployed on the T4 'euthanasia' programme were already on site.
We also know that the *gaswagen* at Chelmno had been in operation since December 1941. Bühler would have been aware of both
of these initiatives. However, his remarks here imply that he also
had learned of expansion plans for Auschwitz and the proposed

NG-2586

ling, vor die Wahl gestellt, ob er evakuiert oder
sterilisiert werden soll, sich lieber der Steri-
lisierung unterziehen würde.

Staatssekretär Dr. S t u c k a r t
stellt fest, daß die praktische Durchführung der
eben mitgeteilten Lösungsmöglichkeiten zur Berei-
nigung der Mischehen- und Mischlingsfragen in dieser Form eine unendliche Verwaltungsarbeit mit
sich bringen würde. Um zum anderen auf alle Fälle
auch den biologischen Tatsachen Rechnung zu tragen,
schlug Staatssekretär Dr. S t u c k a r t vor,
zur Zwangssterilisierung zu schreiten.

Zur Vereinfachung des Mischehenproblems
müßten ferner Möglichkeiten überlegt werden mit
dem Ziel, daß der Gesetzgeber etwa sagt: "Diese
Ehen sind geschieden".

Bezüglich der Frage der Auswirkung der
Judenevakuierung auf das Wirtschaftsleben erklär-
te Staatssekretär N e u m a n n , daß die in
kriegswichtigen Betrieben im Arbeitseinsatz stehen-
den Juden derzeit, solange noch kein Ersatz zur
Verfügung steht, nicht evakuiert werden könnten.

SS-Obergruppenführer H e y d r i c h
wies darauf hin, daß diese Juden nach den von ihm
genehmigten Richtlinien zur Durchführung der derzeit laufenden Evakuierungsaktionen ohnedies nicht
evakuiert würden.

Staatssekretär Dr. B ü h l e r stellte
fest, daß das Generalgouvernement es begrüßen würde, wenn mit der Endlösung dieser Frage im Generalgouvernement begonnen würde, weil einmal hier das
Transportproblem keine übergeordnete Rolle spielt

setting up of other extermination centres, that would be able to deal with a dramatically increased level of killing – most probably from a meeting he himself had with Himmler just a week before Wannsee, on 13 January 1942.

In a further reference here, Bühler remarks that, moreover, 'the majority of the two and a half million Jews in question were anyhow unfit for work [*arbeitsunfahig*], and therefore the sooner they are dealt with the better. Finally, it's recorded (and here again we can see the hand of Heydrich and Eichmann in the editing of these minutes) that Bühler understands that Heydrich is 'in charge of the final solution of the Jewish question in the General Government' and that all agencies there would assist him in this work.

As the end of the meeting nears, there is 'a discussion about the various types of possible solutions' (the term *Lösungsmöglichkeiten* is deployed here).

Eichmann testified later that the minutes concealed the fact that there had been open discussion about methods of killing at Wannsee and that 'certain over-plain talk and jargon expressions had to be rendered into office language by me' (i.e. euphemised). More specifically, Eichmann admitted under cross-examination in Jerusalem that the meeting then discussed 'the business with the engine' (an oblique reference to the *gaswagen*), and shooting – Dr Lange and Dr Schöngarth would both no doubt have contributed their experiences in the *Einsatzgruppen* here – but there was no mention of poison gas. Experiments with Zyklon B had already occurred at Auschwitz but were at too early a stage of development to be discussed.

Eichmann was particularly surprised at the language some of the civil servants used:

> these gentlemen . . . sat together, and in very blunt words they referred to the matter . . . at that time I said to myself: look at that – Stuckart, who was always considered to be a very precise and very particular stickler for the law, and here the whole tone and all the manner of speech were totally out of keeping with legal language.

NG - 2586

und arbeitseinsatzmäßige Gründe den Lauf dieser
Aktion nicht behindern würden. Juden müßten so
schnell wie möglich aus dem Gebiet des Generalgouvernements entfernt werden, weil gerade hier
der Jude als Seuchenträger eine eminente Gefahr
bedeutet und er zum anderen durch fortgesetzten
Schleichhandel die wirtschaftliche Struktur des
Landes dauernd in Unordnung bringt. Von den in
Frage kommenden etwa 2 1/2 Millionen Juden sei
überdies die Mehrzahl der Fälle arbeitsunfähig.

Staatssekretär Dr. B ü h l e r stellt
weiterhin fest, daß die Lösung der Judenfrage im
Generalgouvernement federführend beim Chef der
Sicherheitspolizei und des SD liegt und seine Arbeiten durch die Behörden des Generalgouvernements
unterstützt würden. Er hätte nur eine Bitte, die
Judenfrage in diesem Gebiet so schnell wie möglich
zu lösen.

Abschließend wurden die verschiedenen Ar-
ten der Lösungsmöglichkeiten besprochen, wobei so-
wohl seitens des Gauleiters Dr. M e y e r als auch
seitens des Staatssekretärs Dr. B ü h l e r der
Standpunkt vertreten wurde, gewisse vorbereitende
Arbeiten im Zuge der Endlösung gleich in den be-
treffenden Gebieten selbst durchzuführen, wobei
jedoch eine Beunruhigung der Bevölkerung vermieden
werden müsse.

Mit der Bitte des Chefs der Sicherheitspolizei und des SD an die Besprechungsteilnehmer,
ihm bei der Durchführung der Lösungsarbeiten entsprechende Unterstützung zu gewähren, wurde die
Besprechung geschlossen.

With the caution and cynicism befitting two Nazi lawyers, the Wannsee Conference ends, as we can see in the penultimate paragraph of the minutes, with Dr Meyer and Dr Bühler saying that 'in connection with the final solution certain preparatory measures [should] be carried out in the occupied territories at once, but in such a way as *to avoid alarming the local population* [my emphasis]'.

The 'preparatory measures' Meyer and Bühler reference here are the various constructions which have already begun or have been planned – the extermination camps at Belzec, Sobibor and Treblinka, the ongoing *gaswagen* at Chelmno – all of these in the occupied territories.

The meeting had lasted approximately an hour and a half.

*

We learn from Hannah Arendt that afterwards:

> Drinks were served and everyone had lunch – 'a cosy little social gathering' designed to strengthen the necessary personal contacts. It was a very important occasion for Eichmann who had never before mingled socially with so many 'high personages'; he was by far the lowest in rank and social position of those present . . . he acted as secretary of the meeting [but] he was permitted, after the dignitaries had left, to sit down near the fireplace with his chief Müller and Heydrich.

And Eichmann later recalled, with breathless excitement, this memorable moment of being able to socialise with his bosses for the first time – you get the sense of the little man from the provinces so desperate to impress his Berlin superiors, the stars of the Reich, and to be accepted:

For the first time I saw Heydrich smoke a cigar or a cigarette, and I was thinking: today Heydrich is smoking, something I have not seen before. And he drinks cognac – since I had not seen Heydrich take any alcoholic drink in years. After this Wannsee conference we were sitting together peacefully, and not in order to talk shop, but in order to relax after the long hours of strain.

Presumably this last sentence is a reference to the weeks of preparation leading up to Wannsee, not the ninety minutes of this murderous meeting.

8. The Villa and the Lake Today

30 December 2003, Berlin

J. and I are still in Grunewald station waiting for our train. It arrives with 'Wannsee' on the front. Even today train and metro destinations in Berlin can make you shudder – 'Oranienburg'* in one direction, 'Wannsee' in another. There's only about half an hour of light left today. Streams of traffic run alongside us trying to beat the rush hour, between the train tracks and the beech woods. The lake of Wannsee comes into view. Bobbing boats and wooden jetties. At Wannsee station we get a taxi and within minutes are following the southern shore of the lake, dipping down a tree-lined street, with large detached houses on each side. For the last five years this place has been intensively in my thoughts, ever since seeing that single sheet of paper in Washington. We're at the gates now. They're locked. Momentary worry, but then I see a bell and we're buzzed in. And now the villa is in front of us – that infamous view. As so often with buildings, it seems smaller in reality than in photographs.

---

* A Nazi concentration camp situated just north-east of Berlin which opened in 1933, primarily to hold political opponents of the regime, including many communists.

The dusk is almost here so we skirt the villa, taking a path between rhododendron bushes, and go down towards the lake to try and take pictures before it's too dark. Cedar trees, wooden benches. The clinking of masts from the boats on the lake. An extraordinarily peaceful scene. Even during the war years it would have been an oasis of calm here. I can almost hear the laughter of officers on leave, the richochet of balls from the billiard table. And on that bench, two comrades gazing out over the water and talking of what they will do when the war is over.

Inside the villa, the whole of the downstairs has been turned into a museum, the fourteen rooms each concentrating on a different aspect of the Holocaust. A relief to see such a clear, almost stark, exhibition. Just black-and-white photographs, informative texts and diagrams. No interactive distractions here. But after the intensity of the last days, J. and I only have the energy to take in limited amounts of this. After a while we come into the grandest room, the place where the conference took place. High windows on one side looking down to the lake, a glass-topped table in the middle of the room with the minutes of the meeting, a diagram and photographs showing the fifteen participants on the wall behind.

But I sense here the limitation of information. This room should be quite different from the others. This room should not be about texts and diagrams and the transferral of information. It needs a different level of imagination. J. and I talk about this – it is a room designed to fit conventionally into a museum, when here you need an utterly different experience. We wonder what it would be like if there were names by each place around the table, with headphones, and you could listen in to the process of the meeting. You could hear Dr Stuckart proposing forced sterilisation or Dr Bühler requesting that the 'final solution' begin in Poland. And for the silent voices of the conference you could have the participants describing their backgrounds, how they came to be involved and what happened to them after the war.

We've learnt from Gilbert that there is an educational centre and archive here as well. We ask whether it's possible to visit this, and are soon invited upstairs. There's a large library where we're greeted by two very energetic young historians, a man and a woman, who immediately make us feel welcome and ask about our interest. We discuss the term '*Schreibtischtaeter*' (desk killer) and they confirm that this term first became widely used in Germany after the Eichmann trial in 1961. We wonder why the concept, which surely is not limited to Nazi Germany, has never become an established phrase in English. Then I ask about material on the doctors of Wannsee and I'm extremely surprised that, even in German, there is very little information available. We talk about Mark Roseman's book which was published the previous year – very useful in many ways, but again limited on the backgrounds of the bureaucrats. After a while they find a book which has more detailed biographies but they are still only summaries.

While these pages are being photocopied for us, we discuss the educational work that's organised here. The man explains that in addition to the hundreds of guided tours each year, they organise around

500 seminars for groups in three categories – vocationally orientated for adults, for teachers and teacher trainees, and for young people. The focus of the first of these is to explore 'why nearly all professional groups and institutions . . . and professional associations participated in the systematic segregation, discrimination, deprivation of rights of the Jews' and to investigate the psychology and behaviour which enabled this to come about. The groups that participate in these seminars come from branches of the Civil Service, the judiciary, accountancy, health and social services, psychology, trade unionism, the military and the police. So, by being confronted about the structures and ways of thinking and behaving which resulted in genocide, all these groups in contemporary German society can learn and carry the lessons into their work today. We're then shown pictures of soldiers from the German army participating in such a

session in the room of the Wannsee Conference. We're fascinated by this and extremely impressed. It is an outstanding example of how history should be used actively to shape the present, and over the next days we continue to think about the implications of this for our society. How remarkable it would be if all those working at the Tate galleries in Britain, those working at Lloyd's insurance, at Barclays, Royal Bank of Scotland and HSBC, were invited to seminars on Britain's pivotal role in the slave trade and the opium wars, and how all of their institutions were founded upon such barbarism.

We're the last to leave. Our discussions have carried us well past closing time. We thank the historians and soon we're walking out of the gates and back towards Wannsee station, inspired by what we've just learnt. It's past six o'clock now and we realise we haven't had any lunch so we go into the little bar outside the station. Another world completely. A group of men are gambling with dice at the bar. An elderly couple take minutes to shuffle across the bar to their table, where they then drink in silence. We order bratwurst and beer; the man behind the counter is seriously unfriendly, but in such situations I take a perverse pleasure in being even more amiable, so I order another couple of beers with a grin.

9. Judging the Desk Killers

So what became of our eight doctors of Wannsee?

> One – Dr Freisler – was killed in a Berlin air raid (3 February 1945).
> Two committed suicide – Dr Lange (February 1945); Dr Meyer (May 1945).
> Two were executed – Dr Schöngarth (March 1946); Dr Bühler (August 1948).
> Three were interned, and then released – Dr Leibbrandt, Dr Stuckart and Dr Klopfer.

For the five who survived the war, their differential treatment and sentencing reveals a profoundly disturbing imbalance between judgement about the criminal responsibility involved in 'direct' killing and judgement regarding 'desk' killing. Schöngarth was clearly a mass murderer, a 'direct' killer (though, bizarrely, he was convicted and executed not for being the commander of Einsatzkommando zbV, responsible for the murder of thousands in eastern Galicia, nor for his senior role in the barbarities of Bad Rabka, but for his order to shoot a single Allied pilot, a POW who had crashed in the Netherlands in 1941).

But the desk killers were treated very differently. Dr Stuckart – co-author of some the most antisemitic laws in modern European history, and a key figure in designing the 'legal' framework for the deportation and extermination of the Jews (and who you'll also remember proposed compulsory sterilisation of the *Mischlinge* Jews at Wannsee) – at his trial in 1949, was sentenced to only three years ten months' imprisonment, and then immediately released because of 'time already served'. Even allowing for his poor health, this seems a staggeringly lenient sentence, especially given the fact that the judges specified in their verdict that

> Without a doubt, the laws and decrees drafted or approved by Stuckart himself were a cornerstone of the plan to almost completely exterminate Jews . . . [he was one of the men] who participated from the peace and quiet of their ministry offices [but] are just as criminal.

Even after the full import of the Wannsee Conference had emerged, in 1950 a denazification court in Hanover merely declared him a *Mitläufer* (fellow traveller) and fined him 50,000 DM. Afterwards, he worked in local government, becoming treasurer for the town of Helmstedt, and then took a position in an institute to develop the Lower Saxony economy. He died in a car accident in 1953, and received a glowing obituary in the *Frankfurter Zeitung*, written by former colleagues from the Reich Interior Ministry: 'The deceased was an upstanding and selfless man of exceptional talent who worked tirelessly . . .'

Dr Leibbrandt – Rosenberg's deputy, who in October and November 1941 had met Heydrich and Himmler to discuss how more Jews could be included in the extermination programme and who, immediately after Wannsee, hosted a meeting to widen the definition of *Mischlinge* Jews in the occupied Eastern Territories – was interned at the end of the war. When interrogated, he initially claimed that he 'could not remember the Wannsee Conference'. Charges against him were eventually dropped in 1950 and he was released from internment. A year later a denazification court in Kiel declared him 'not incriminated' and he returned to civilian life, working as a lobbyist for the city of Wilhelmshaven. Later in life he also was a representative for the steel company Salzgitter (set up by Goering in 1937, still going strong today, with sales of £7 billion in 2016), and, in his spare time, he also became an active member of the American Cultural Institute in Munich. He died peacefully in Bonn in June 1982, having lived to the ripe old age of eighty-two.

And the extreme antisemite Dr Klopfer, one of the most influential of all Nazi bureaucrats and Martin Bormann's deputy, what became of him? He was arrested in 1946, having changed his identity to 'Otto Kunz', and was then interned in various camps for four years. When interrogated about his participation at Wannsee, he claimed that Heydrich had only talked about the 'emigration of the Jews', to which his investigator tartly replied, 'Then you must have slept through the meeting.' But again, in the growing Cold War of the post-war period, no war-crimes charges were brought against him by the US prosecutors, and his case was handed over to a denazification court in Nuremberg. Again, the verdict of this court was shockingly lenient, finding Klopfer to be a *Minderbelastete* (lesser offender), fining him 2,000 DM and giving him a probation period of three years. He was released in 1950, two years later he was working as a tax advisor and, by 1956, he'd resumed his career in law – opening a practice on Zinglerstrasse in Ulm.[*] He continued to practise until his retirement, prospering and buying a farm in Langenburg. He was eighty-one when he died in January 1987, peacefully at home. A notice in the local Ulm newspaper marked the passing of the last participant of the Wannsee Conference with this sentence: 'In memory of Dr Gerhard Klopfer, who passed away after a fulfilled life in the service of all those in his sphere of influence.'

The fact that two of these men – who had sat around the table with Heydrich and Eichmann discussing how genocide could be more efficiently organised – were able to live out their post-war lives, not in prison cells but in freedom, without any real sanction, is an insult towards any notion of justice. It demonstrates, in the most vivid possible terms, the way that desk killers, those who kill by decree and orders, who never see the eyes of their victims, have often been able to evade all responsibility – just as they continue to do today.

*

By a curious coincidence, in March 1987, only a few weeks after Dr Klopfer had been buried in Ulm, J. and I were hitch-hiking past that city. I looked at my journal from that trip and was intrigued to read that we'd got a lift outside Ulm that day with two US servicemen, working at a nearby American army base, both of them ambitious young officers, already fast-tracked for promotion. Although grateful for the lift, we were not impressed by their hawkish jingoism, or by the Voice of America that they listened to uncritically. I noted at the end that I'd written that these two men seemed 'both perfectly banal and perfectly dangerous'.

Banal and dangerous. Not dissimilar to our men of Wannsee. The lawyer of Ulm being buried. And for a moment I wonder whether

---

* When I met Claude Lanzmann, in March 2000, we talked about my early research into the 'desk killers,' and specifically the Wannsee Conference. I asked whether he had tried to contact any of the surviving participants when he was making *Shoah*. He pointed to a picture of Klopfer – 'I almost managed to interview him.' 'In Ulm?' 'Yes, I was there. I tried to film him on the street but he escaped me.' For further details see chapter notes.

this seeming banality isn't partly responsible for their historical invisibility. Books on Hitler, Himmler and Mengele still sell in vast quantities. Perhaps it's simply more engaging to read about perpetrators who are seen to be 'evil'. Or is it because learning that lawyers and civil servants, educated graduates, have played central roles in genocide is too disturbing, too close to our own societies? Those words of C. S. Lewis come back again – 'the greatest evil is ... done ... in clean, carpeted, warmed and well-lighted offices, by quiet men with white collars ... who do not need to raise their voices.' The offices of Kurfürstenstrasse 116, the offices of Wilhelmstrasse, the offices of Prinz-Albrecht-Strasse 8, the offices of IG Farben, the offices of Bayer, the offices of Shell, the offices of Halliburton, the offices of the Pentagon, the offices of Whitehall. And the terror, the destruction which has been set in motion from these buildings. Why have we, as yet, not been able to understand this phenomenon?

In *Cleansing the Fatherland*, the authors Götz Aly, Peter Chroust and Christian Pross investigate some of the medical personnel who ran the 'euthanasia' programme from Tiergartenstrasse, where we walked two days ago. They look at the way that many of the men who worked there later transferred their skills to administrating aspects of the Holocaust. They also reflect upon the limitations of the legal judgement of these bureaucratic perpetrators after the war, and make the following observation:

> Much of what is known about the Nazi period has been uncovered not by historians but by police commissioners and prosecutors ... But the prosecutors' interest is limited. They are concerned with finding *individual proof of violent crimes* [my emphasis]. Thus, they did not know how to handle someone like Ludwig Trieb; they did not accept the planning files he almost forced on them. At first they did not even look for Herbert Becker, head of the T-4 Planning Department ...
>
> The judiciary pushed the bloody side of the Nazi regime into the foreground, thus obscuring the structures and goals at the root of the mass murders. The crimes became

338

individual aberrations . . . The distorted image obtained from legal documents is preferred in the literature . . . The cost, however, is the historical truth. Paradoxically, this image diminishes the real horror of the National Socialist state.

We can see exactly the same process at work with the sentencing of the Wannsee doctors. Because Stuckart, Leibbrandt and Klopfer had not either killed directly, or directly ordered killings, they were found to be 'minimally incriminated' or 'lesser offenders'. And yet numerous concentration-camp guards, with vastly less criminal responsibility but who had killed prisoners directly, were executed immediately after the war.

Tom Bower, in *Blind Eye to Murder*, widens this examination and finds that whole sections of German society (such as industry and finance) that had colluded critically in Nazism went virtually unpunished after the war:

> Schacht's acquittal, Speer's lenient sentence and the failure to prosecute Krupp made nonsense of the original intention of condemning the industrial and financial section of the German Establishment. Murder in occupied Europe and in the gas chambers had been exposed and condemned, but murder in the factories and mines had gone unpunished.

And indeed, of thirty-two senior Nazi industrialists and financiers initially indicted after the war, only six ever came to trial. Eleven out of IG Farben's twenty-three directors escaped conviction altogether. Hermann Abs was one of those directors, and as a banker had also been one of those most responsible for Deutsche Bank's financial support of the Nazi Party. Abs spent just three months in an internment camp and later resumed his work at Deutsche Bank. He was chairman until 1995. An even more extreme case concerns Dr Hans Globke, another doctor of law, like so many of the men of Wannsee. He was the civil servant at the Ministry of the Interior who was responsible for drafting the Nuremberg Race Laws, together with Dr Stuckart. Not only was he released from intern-ment in 1946 and never prosecuted, but, even more shockingly, he became chief of staff to Adenauer's government from 1953 to 1963. The outrageous post-war whitewashing of Nazi *Schreibtischtaeter* is perhaps best summed up in the words of the British lawyer Sir Percy Mills, defending the steel and arms manufacturer Krupp and other industrialists in post-war trials – senior management who had been enthusiastic proponents of wartime slave labour (often referred to as 'extermination through work'). Mills said this, quite shamelessly, in defence of his clients: 'They were not Nazis – they were businessmen.'

To understand such realities is to understand the 'rage against the fathers', as it has sometimes been described, the post-war whitewashing of history which went on in Germany, and which incensed those like Gudrun Ensslin who argued: 'They'll kill us all – you know what pigs we are up against – that is the generation of Auschwitz we've got against us – you can't argue with the people who made Auschwitz.'

I would suggest that we as a society still suffer from a myopic view of how to assess organisational killing – we still, for the most part, share the narrow police approach to dealing with murders (i.e. looking for 'individual proof of violent crimes'). We have not really moved on to be able to judge bureaucratic killing or corporate kill-ing in a clear way – or those who plan and finance such killing – witness the immense difficulties that have arisen over recent years with the proposals for even limited 'corporate manslaughter' laws (in my view ridiculously narrow in their focus). Or look at the fail-ure, even in the clearest possible case of corporate killing – Bhopal, where up to 16,000 people were estimated to have been killed through Union Carbide's negligence in 1984 – to hold any of the American executives to account.

Even activists can fall into this trap of fetishising the *act* of violence, rather than the causation of that act. I heard a report of a conference that took place in the Netherlands not long ago, focussing on the abuses of oil corporations. The star turn was an American lawyer who had brought human rights cases against corporations, and at one point he apparently started to warm to his theme, shouting at the delegates: 'We need rapes, we need torture, we need killings! that's the kind of ammunition we need to nail these people'. By focussing too much on the act of direct violence we fail to understand the psychology and structures which have caused the violence in the first place. Our historical focus on 'direct' killing has actually worked to disguise a more disturbing reality – that of bureaucratic and corporate killing. To show this reality, we need to find a new kind of language:

- How are we to show the violence of a spreadsheet?
- How are we to show the violence of a set of minutes?
- How are we to show the violence of an idea?

Often the violence of capitalism is rendered invisible. Often the violence of the desk killer goes unseen. We have few records of the meetings of those gentlemen in the Netherlands, Portugal and England who pioneered the organisation of mass slavery. The most tenacious work in archives will not give us accounts of how the directors of the East India Company reacted to the starvation of 11 million Bengalis. I cannot show you the minutes that detail the 'damage limitation' discussions of the directors of Shell on the afternoon of 10 November 1995, when news of the execution of Ken Saro-Wiwa and his eight fellow Ogoni activists came through. But it's very hard to believe that such meetings did not take place.

*

That is the extraordinary aspect of the Wannsee minutes – not only did they survive (thanks to that scrupulous filing clerk in the Foreign Office), but this is a document where the violence, for once, bleeds from the paper. And from this meeting, from this simple document, and the thirty copies subsequently sent to ministries across Berlin and occupied Europe, flows an immediate unleashing of vast organisational resources at the height of war – trains, guards, lorries, wire, dogs, searchlights, guns, barracks – stretching out from Berlin in an insane starburst of lines. With the words of the Führer, just ten days after Wannsee, echoing through the continent, 'the result of this war will be the annihilation of Jewry' . . .

Within seven weeks of this conference the first transport of 1,001 Jews from Theresienstadt leaves for the newly constructed Belzec death camp on 11 March. And preparations for the extermination centres at Treblinka and Sobibor are fully under way, creating in their wake vast amounts of administrative work on construction, transport of guards, police and materials, and the need for hundreds of trains and thousands of personnel to be deployed, all across Europe. Telephones ring from Drancy on the outskirts of Paris to the smallest town by the Black Sea. Thousands of telegrams and messages flit back and forth between Tallinn in the north and the Greek islands to the south. An army of officials are checking census forms, preparing lists, meeting with Jewish authorities. Another battery of bank staff are organising forms for the transfer of assets. Other clerks are desperately trying to find warehouses big enough to store millions of clothes. Two hundred and thirty miles to the east of Berlin, along an unmetalled country road, every day now the Saurer lorries continue to shuttle between the tiny village of Chelmno and the forests of Rzeszów with their deathly loads of 'merchandise'. And three hundred miles away, towards Krakow, a substantial increase in road and rail traffic can now be seen around the Polish town of Oświęcim. IG Farben's huge Buna chemical works is getting more slave labourers every day and the builders are busy delivering bricks, wood and cement in enormous quantities to the little hamlet named after the birch woods surrounding it – Birkenau.

And, far removed from all this sound and fury, in his Berlin office Adolf Eichmann is calm. From his desk he looks out over the linden trees that line the Kurfürstenstrasse. After Wannsee, as Cesarani recounts, he feels a weight of responsibility lifted from his shoulders. As he put it:

I felt something of the satisfaction of Pilate, because I felt entirely innocent of any guilt. The leading figures of the Reich at the time had spoken at the Wannsee Conference, the 'Popes' had given their orders; it was up to me to obey.

This view was certainly not shared by the court that tried him in Jerusalem nineteen years later and sentenced him to death. The prosecutor Gideon Hausner, as we know, had opened the trial with this analysis of the challenge that faced the court – of the need to look at murder in a different way:

> In this trial we shall encounter a new kind of killer, the kind that exercises his bloody craft behind a desk, and only occasionally does the deed with his own hands . . . But it was his word that put gas chambers into action . . . Eichmann was the one who planned, initiated and organised, who instructed others to spill this ocean of blood. He is responsible, therefore, as though he with his own hands had knotted the hangman's noose, lashed the victims into the gas chambers, shot and thrust into the open pits every single one of the millions who were murdered.

And the judgement that came at the end of Eichmann's trial was absolutely groundbreaking in at last understanding the culpability of the desk killer – the person who rarely sees their victim but has causative responsibility for the death. It remains a radical statement on the nature of criminal responsibility, and one that continues to influence jurisprudence today – for instance in the establishment of the International Criminal Court in The Hague:

> In such an enormous and complicated crime as the one we are now considering, wherein many people participated, on various levels and in various modes of activity – the planners, the organisers, and those executing the deeds, according to their various ranks – there is not much point in using the ordinary concepts of counselling and solicit-

ing to commit a crime . . . the extent to which any one of the many criminals was close to or remote from the actual killer of the victim means nothing, as far as the measure of his responsibility is concerned. On the contrary, in general the degree of responsibility increases as we draw further away from the man who uses the fatal instrument with his own hands.

10. Lichtenberg: Eastwards

30 December 2003, Berlin

Heading back north-east across the city now on the S-Bahn, exhausted, just staring out of the window in a kind of vacancy. The raised nature of these trains, fifty feet above the city, gives Berlin a theatricality that is absorbing. And this is only intensified at night. Remembering Wings of Desire *– the illuminated angel above the trees of Tiergarten. Back across Friedrichstrasse – wondering exactly which building the SS statisticians worked in with their IBM Hollerith machines – over the River Spree, and soon we're at Lichtenberg station. We could be in a different city altogether – a world away from the glass skyscrapers of Potsdamer Platz, the streets outside have a run-down feel, accentuated by dim lighting. We still have an hour before our night train to Poland leaves so we find a bar and ask whether they do any food because we doubt there'll be anything on the train. They obviously don't get many tourists in here as the bar owner, a woman in her fifties, is very solicitous, bringing over a tablecloth and even lighting a candle for us. This provokes a few ribald comments from the locals at the bar; I ask J. what they're saying but he couldn't catch it, though we can guess the meaning.*

We mull over the last days. We discuss again the seriousness of intent of this society to try to come to terms with what was done here between 1933 and 1945 – the huge Memorial to the Murdered Jews of Europe at the absolute heart of the city, the Jewish Museum, the rebuilt synagogue on Oranienburger Strasse and the quietly inspiring educational programme at Wannsee that we heard about this afternoon. And yet it's taken sixty years for this to happen – two whole generations since the end of the war. J. asks about the denazification process in the late 1940s – why was it so limited? I think the Allies concentrated, understandably, on the Nuremberg Trials. But there was a serious problem with these – however scrupulous the process of these trials were, they were always going to be seen by some as 'victors' justice'. We wonder what might have happened had the Allies handed Goering and company over to be tried by German judges. It has often been said that there were so few judges that retained any integrity through the Nazi years, but, if this obstacle could have been surmounted, it would have been remarkable to have witnessed German courts passing judgement on the Nazi leadership after the war.

Reading the accounts of those post-war years, two aspects become very clear. Firstly, there is a simple sense of exhaustion; particularly after 1947 and the first wave of trials, it's as if the will to hold many accountable just fades away – not so much from the lawyers but particularly from the Allied politicians. Secondly, the start of the Cold War had a major impact, and pragmatism then replaced the need for justice. When the Allies became aware of the extent to which whole professions (like the judiciary, the police, academia) had been Nazified they were then faced with a dilemma – not so far from the situation in post-war Iraq – whether to go for root-and-branch reform (i.e. get rid of almost everyone and start again), or whether to remove only the most incriminated. Not surprisingly, the latter, the path of least resistance, won the day. It wasn't until the 1960s – and the trial of Eichmann in 1961 marked the beginning of this shift – that the enormity of the Holocaust began to register with many Germans. And then, in 1964 came the Auschwitz trials in Frankfurt, and a renewed desire for justice. And, of course, the significance of this was that now it was German courts sitting in judgement on German perpetrators. But it's still astonishing that it took twenty years for this to happen. And it's still shocking, inexcusable, that so many senior Nazis, such as Abs and Globke, actually retained powerful positions in government and finance, and were even promoted. Not to forget our doctors of Wannsee.

Realising we only have fifteen minutes before our train leaves, we wolf down our food and get back to the station just in time to see the train arrive. We find our couchette and are relieved, as we pull out, drizzle now coming down across east Berlin, that we seem to have the cabin to ourselves. The lack of sleep over the last days has finally caught up with us. I hardly have time to register that the beds seem smaller than they used to be, that my feet now rest on the wall of the compartment, or that we're now heading into Poland – new territory for me – before the rocking motion has lulled me to a deep sleep. The train gathers speed, rattling relentlessly eastwards . . .

14

Carpathian Days

31 December 2003, Krakow to Sanok

Gently rolling hills now as the afternoon light begins to fade. Over New Year we're heading for the mountains in south-west Poland to pause for a couple of days before heading on to Auschwitz and Chelmno. Patches of snow visible on the higher ground now, dusting the forest. We change trains at a kind of halt outside a village, not a proper station, just a single platform, as we're deeper into the countryside now. Onto a smaller two-carriage train that will take us on to the south-eastern corner of Poland. Another hour, another change of train; we get coffees from a little kiosk on the platform. Finally we reach the small industrial town of Sanok. This is as far as we can go before the year ends, no more local trains heading further south-east towards the mountains, which we were hoping to reach tonight.

They can't get many tourists here, not even in the summer, and tonight there's only one other guest at the Hotel Three Roses. J. and I dump our rucksacks and then set out to find something to eat. The drizzle of the afternoon has now become determined rain. We walk through the town square but there are no restaurants, just a parked lorry, a generator, and a few bedraggled people trying to set up a stage – for which there seems to be no audience whatsoever. A closed town. A single, solemn pizza bar. We see an elderly couple going into a restaurant next to the town hall, we follow them, can hear music from above, and visualise Polish stews, a log fire. But a moustached man bars our way before another door, and says something we do not understand. His meaning is clear, however, gesturing us out the way we came, with a shrug and a pursed movement of his whiskers.

Defeated by the deadness of the place, we head back to our hotel. We attempt to communicate the urgency of eating to our hosts. After considerable discussion between the blond girl at reception and the manager, the lights of the restaurant are switched on, revealing sickly paintings of waterfalls and forests in synthetic blues and greens. The menus include such offerings as 'Five Testes Meat' and 'Stewed Fat Dogs'. We opt for a safer choice. Cotlet? *No. Not available.* Any other kind of meat? Another shake of that teenage head. Ah well, never mind. Fish? '*Rybia*' is carp, I think. *No. Not possible.* Defeated by now, we gesture for her to tell us what is available. *Tortellini in brodo.* Not very Polish, but this seems to be all that there is, so we nod.

As we eat, we plan our journey, wondering how far up that valley towards the Ukrainian border we'll be able to get tomorrow. I try to see us through the eyes of the girl, now sitting at a table in the corner – two travellers deep in conversation, with maps and notebooks spread out on the table in front of them. They talk like students, their unshaven faces even look like students, but older surely . . . We ask for two more beers – *Zwiec* ('Jshuh-viets', at least we know this important pronunciation). Half past eleven, and there are now signs of growing animation, a group of young people come into the hotel, flecks of snow on their coats, then a couple, another group, all making their way downstairs to some basement bar. J. is now telling me about his first contact with Poland in the late 1980s, through a trip that the Scottish arts impresario Ricky Demarco organised, and the electrifying effect of first coming across Kantor's theatre. That ability to create an

348

entire dramatic language seemingly without reference to anything else going on in the world of theatre at the time – wild-eyed men carrying wooden crosses, women crying lamentations, and Kantor directing everything himself, moving his actors around the stage – a combination of conductor and Old Testament prophet.

A few minutes before midnight, we decide to go back to the town square and see if anything is stirring in this strange town. As we leave the hotel we're astonished by what we see. Not only a white drift of snow coming down, with impeccable timing in the minutes before the new year's arrival, but a river of young people now flowing before us. A magical transformation. Hundreds now from every street and alley in a torrent towards the town square. Sparklers, bangers cracking, excited glances, throbbing bass coming from the lorry stage ahead of us. And the square is now full, two or three thousand bodies packed together, like moths drawn to a giant flame. Bottles smashing, couples tonguing, the music pulsing louder. We're a different generation to most of those here, gatecrashers from another world, but it doesn't matter. A momentary sense of a kind of time vertigo, of disbelief that we've been working together for almost twenty years now. Chaos gathering pace, the noise level rises to a kind of frenzy, fireworks are being let off at all angles in the square. Bottles now being thrown. Fire-brigade crews look on with detached amusement. 'Not much "health and safety" going on here!' I shout to J. The snow is settling thickly.

We retreat from the square, sliding down the narrow streets, and wind our way back to the hotel. From our room's little balcony (that tilts rather alarmingly when both of us stand on it), we watch as a middle-aged couple next door light a solitary Catherine wheel in their garden. A few slugs of slivovitz. *Happy New Year, dear friend! Here's to the next twenty years!* The following hour or so is a bit hazy, but I do recall that the evening ended with us switching on a vast, ancient TV in the corner (which might actually have been holding the ceiling up) and becoming strangely absorbed in a film about Moses, dubbed into Polish.

New Year's Day 2004, Sanok to Ustrzyki Górne

We wake to a white-out, which seems to have stilled the whole town. As if to say to all of us – '*New Year, begin again, everything is possible.*' After breakfast we return to the town square, where last night's wild youth have been replaced by a sedate stream of the elderly flowing into Mass in the church on the corner. Soon we're walking gingerly on the ice, heading back down the hill to the station with our heavy packs. We're rather frustrated at the bus station when it emerges we have to wait three and a half hours for the next bus to Ustrzyki Górne, the little village in the mountains where we're staying for the next couple of days, so we walk back to a hotel we passed at the bottom of the hill and have an early lunch. Very few customers here either, the room hung with dark velvet drapes and gloomy oil paintings of landscapes. J. wants to start talking about recent emotional turbulence in our lives, but I'm not in the mood for such a conversation; not yet, wait until we've got to the mountains. Then we'll have the space that is needed for such subjects.

Sitting at the back of the bus, cocooned in the warmth, as we turn south out of Sanok, onto a much smaller road that soon begins to rise. No snow clearance here, so we're driving into the white and soon it's hard to see where the edge of the road begins and ends. I move into a kind of trance-like state that sometimes comes with journeying. Higher and higher we climb, the engine labouring now. Dusk comes early and soon it's night. The bus, full as we left Sanok, has gradually emptied most of its passengers, only half a dozen of us left as we thunder on, surely too fast in these conditions, but I guess the driver must be used to them. I return to my reveries, willing to put my fate in the hands of this stranger. Despite the darkness, J. is still trying to read the map by the light of his torch, and tells me the massive outline of a ridge to our left is the border with Ukraine.

Finally (it's only 6 p.m. but feels like midnight), we arrive. Literally the end of the road. The bus turns round and we emerge from it into a one-street village, the Carpathians and thick forest on three sides and a river rushing below. We notice two bars and a little shop as we make our way back down the road towards our hotel, the Gorski. It's snowing heavily again, and as we walk, a young Polish guy starts talking to us in German. He's from Warsaw but loves coming here to camp in the mountains, yes, even in winter. He recommends a little bar further up the street, and heads off into the dark. Knots of children pass us on toboggans, as we slip and slide towards our hotel – a curious one-storey building, which seems more like a health spa than anything else. But there's a decent-looking restaurant and our room, though small, is perfectly comfortable. Our base for the next days – a pause between the intensities of Berlin and the prospect of Auschwitz and Chelmno next week.

Soon into a deep sleep, not disturbed for a moment by the familiar sound of J.'s pencil scribbling notes in his green notebook. An hour later we're donning our thick fur hats and venturing up to the top of the village to Andrej's Bar. Down some steps, we push the wooden door open, music swelling out, to reveal a tiny space packed with people clustered round a fine open fire at the centre of the room, roaring away. But not as much as the revellers here, who all appear to be in varying states of benign drunkenness. A woman in her fifties wearing a cowboy hat is dancing with, or rather is slumped against, a much younger guy, who looks delightfully sheepish. Occasionally, the woman raises her head, and then goes back to fondling the man's arse, to the great amusement of the drinkers looking on. We soon realise that being polite foreigners will not get us very far here, so I push to the bar and hold up two fingers pointing to a beer bottle to the landlord (Andrej, presumably), short and dark, his forehead gnarled like a tree trunk, with a thick moustache. Two bottles are rapidly produced, and he waves away my banknote with an impatient gesture. I soon realise that the rate of drinking in his bar means that there's no point paying for each beer as you go along. You just settle up at the end. (God, what the Poles could teach the rest of the world about how to run a bar. . .) It's not really possible to talk in here, but that doesn't matter, the intoxication is infectious and we're soon laughing along with everyone else, and occasionally shouting something to each other.

Then, from the other end of the bar, the sudden sound of glass smashing, Andrej leaps over the wooden counter with remarkably youthful vigour for a man of his age, and starts hurling swearwords at the cause of this disruption. The object of his rage – a man, significantly sozzled – appears to wilt under the rain of abuse and slinks out of the bar, only to re-emerge a minute later at the door to attempt to regain his honour by throwing a stream of insults at Andrej, who volleys back an even louder river of swearing, accompanied by a glass propelled from the bar, which smashes behind the unfortunate man. He can see Andrej is not backing down, and reluctantly retreats back up the stairs and out into the icy night. We're captivated by this spectacle, as is the whole bar, but a young couple sharing our table, who look like students, appear mortified, and the girl leans over and in halting English says:

'Please, excuse! This people behave very bad. Please excuse my countrymen.'

'No, not at all!' We smile back. 'No problem! We're not shocked. London is just like this too, on some nights.'

We have a couple more beers here, and some Polish sausage and chips, and then head back to the hotel bar, a fantastically kitsch 1970s affair in yellows and browns. The bar here seems to be open as long as anyone wants to drink, so we order some whiskies and settle down at a table in the corner. Partly stimulated by the drink, I decide to be direct with J. We've been moving constantly for several days, so this is the first time we can really catch up with each other properly. I don't feel we've really talked frankly for quite a while, but this feels like the right time. He mentioned on the train to Sanok something about 'feeling lost' over the last couple of years. Does he think this might be connected to a loss of nerve in his work in this period? Maybe, or perhaps it's more just a sense of exhaustion; he feels pretty burnt out, and this could have contributed to his loss of focus.

We reflect on J.'s habitual need to compromise and that desire to keep everyone happy – surely there's a tension between this way of working and the absolute focus that's sometimes needed to create something remarkable? That sense of mission. Think about those he really admires – Beuys, for example, or William Morris. Completely obsessed, totally driven, and extremely selfish for much of their working lives. Nightmares to live with, totally inconsiderate to those around them, but, my God, what they brought into the world! The challenge for both of us is that we've grown up so strongly influenced by feminism, and therefore, naturally, we're intensely suspicious of this idea of the 'artist genius' as some egotistical male who puts everything into their work – traditionally supported by a battery of long-suffering women who create a domestic environment that can enable His Important Work to continue unimpeded and undisturbed. I remind J. of that quote of Rilke's about the fundamental choice that artists have to make: 'Either happiness or art . . . All the great men have let their lives become overgrown like an old path and have carried everything into their art. Their life is stunted like an organ they no longer need.'

But just because we reject this model as outdated, doesn't mean that we shouldn't think seriously about artistic focus and how it can be achieved. I tell him about something Germaine Greer said in an interview once:

> It's not the academic life that's attractive, it's the life of the mind rather than the struggle with relationships. Relationships survive, I think, because you don't question them too much – you're not a perfectionist about them – whereas the life of the mind, you just keep on going. You can be as demanding as you want to be of yourself and your material.

We decide that that's enough for one night, wave goodnight to the barman and head to our room.

353

2 January 2004, Hotel Gorski

Waking with hangovers. Snow still falling. The little river behind the hotel completely iced over now. On top of the hangover I seem to be developing a cold, so after breakfast, as J. sets out to explore the valley, I head back to the room and settle in next to our radiator to do some more reading. Because the only book of Primo Levi's that J. has read is *The Periodic Table*, I've promised to give him an overview of Levi's work before we reach Auschwitz in three days, and so I've been rereading *If This Is a Man, The Truce* and *The Drowned and the Saved*.

There's often an initial doubt when you return to books that have meant so much, but not in this case. Levi writes with staggering precision and power, and I'm moved more than ever by the moral rigour with which he examines himself and others – and, above all, by his unrelentingness. I very much like what the author and critic Paul Bailey says of him, that he's 'one of that select band of writers with whom it is possible to sustain a lasting friendship . . . [who] offers us "explicit recipes for being human".' I start to jot down notes from the opening section of *If This Is a Man*. Today I'm strongly affected by a line that I didn't remember from the book. It comes when he's describing the dawn arriving at the Fossoli camp[*] near Modena, the day he's due to be deported from Italy with his friends and colleagues and many others. He writes of dawn coming 'like a betrayer' and the ensuing despair and panic among everyone, and then this single line that is so calmly devastating: 'Many things were then said and done among us; but of these it is better that there remain no memory.'

And then we begin the journey, with Levi and his 649 fellow human beings.[*] The roll call of names at the camp, the SS corporal

---

[*] Later on, reading Ian Thomson's biography of Levi, I learn about the reason for the Fossoli camp's growth from 200 to 700 Jews in early 1944 – which was mainly attributable to the organisational zeal of a former lawyer from Wuppertal, Friedrich Bosshammer, then SS chief of Jewish operations in Italy. It was he who ensured that there was an 'economically viable' number of Jews in the Fossoli camp to make a transport to Poland possible. His deputies did the paperwork that enabled the necessary co-operation between the SS and the Italian State Railways. Based at his grand headquarters in Verona, the lawyer Bosshammer was the quintessence of the *Schreibtischtaeter* – murdering thousands without moving from his desk.

announcing there were '*sechshundert und fünfzig Stück*' (650 pieces) – immediately the human beings have become objects. Then loaded on buses and taken from the Fossoli camp to the train at Carpi, and, at the station there, Levi describes receiving the first blows, so new and senseless that he only feels 'profound amazement: how can one hit a man without anger?' Five days and five nights of vicious cold and thirst follow. Packed together, forty-five people in Levi's wagon. And looking out through the slits, the pain of seeing the other world continuing, the world they are leaving behind. A woman friend remembers, 'We were already, at this point, outside life. Normal existence – cars, fields, farms – seemed another country to us. It was very galling . . . to see those free people going about their ordinary lives. On the plains near Padova we saw girls on bicycles. The world outside was there – but it was not for us.'

And then the lesson that Steinlauf, the former sergeant in the Austro-Hungarian army, gives Levi a week after his arrival at Buna-Monowitz. His anger that Levi thinks it's a waste of energy to try to wash and keep clean. We're all about to die, what is the point? The ex-army man replies:

> Precisely because the *Lager* [camp] was a great machine to reduce us to beasts, we must not become beasts . . . to survive we must force ourselves to save at least the skeleton, the scaffolding, the form of civilisation. We are slaves, deprived of every right, exposed to every insult, condemned to certain death, but we still possess one power, and we must defend it with all our strength for it is the last – the power to refuse our consent.

If This Is a Man must be one of the most brutally sensory books ever written. Today, in the warmth of the hotel, I'm repeatedly assaulted by Levi's merciless detail of the impact of the changing temperature, and how this means life or death for the prisoners. The coming of the Polish winter, in October,

355

means that in the course of these months, from October till April, seven out of ten of us will die. Whoever does not die will suffer minute by minute, all day, every day: from the morning before dawn until the distribution of the evening soup we will have to keep our muscles continually tensed, dance from foot to foot, beat our arms under our shoulders against the cold. We will have to spend bread to acquire gloves, and lose hours of sleep to repair them when they become unstitched . . . Wounds will open on everyone's hands, and to be given a bandage will mean waiting every evening for hours on one's feet in the snow and wind.

Just as our hunger is not that feeling of missing a meal, so our way of being cold has need of a new word. We say 'hunger', we say 'tiredness', 'fear', 'pain', we say 'winter' and they are different things. They are free words, created and used by free men who live in comfort and suffering in their homes. If the *Lagers* had lasted longer a new, harsh language would have been born: and only this language could express what it means to toil the whole day in the wind, with the temperature below freezing, wearing only a shirt, underpants, cloth jacket and trousers, and in one's body nothing but weakness, hunger and knowledge of the end drawing nearer.

In the same way in which one sees a hope end, winter arrived this morning. We realised it when we left the hut to go and wash: there were no stars, the dark cold air had the smell of snow. In roll-call square, in the grey of dawn, when we assembled for work, no one spoke. When we saw the first flakes of snow, we thought that if at the same time last year they had told us that we would have seen another winter in the *Lager*, we would have gone and touched the electric wire fence . . .

Something else that strikes me today is the way that for much of the book Levi locks us into an unbearable present tense ('I feel', 'he lifts', 'I try', 'they watch', 'we fall'). The cumulative effect of reading this is that we experience the time in the book as almost endless, which is terrifying. Such a simple technique, yet devastating – for example, see how he uses it in the short chapter 'The Work'. By keeping in this tense relentlessly, Levi makes us walk the ground with him, lift the steel, feel it cut into his shoulder, fall into the mud. He wants us to be with him in that place. He will not let us go. He wants us to understand that human beings are responsible for this. And that such behaviour continues as we read his words from our positions of comfort. The numerous places of suffering that are still in our world, and that, by averting our eyes, we allow to continue.

I put aside the book. It is afternoon now and J. is still out in the mountains. How necessary, having this space, as if suspended in time, in some place of recovery or sanitorium. *The Magic Mountain* indeed. I reflect on our shared project – the twenty years of Platform. I sense we're now moving into new territory when both of us will need more space, to write, to explore our own creativity away from the collective pressures of management and the headspace that administration colonises. This excites me greatly, the idea of evolving a new shape for the organisation, allowing new forms of creativity to blossom. But I see J.'s nervousness about this, doubts about his role. I pick up two letters that he sent before Christmas and reread them, accompanied by the gentle ticking of the radiator and the white hillside beyond. The heat of the room is gently soporific, and as dusk approaches I doze, waking as J. returns from his explorations. And then we swap positions, as I venture outside for a short walk, and J. does some writing. Lower energy today, but that's fine. In the evening we eat in the hotel, and end up playing pool in the bar with some local Polish guys who, rather to our surprise, are even worse than us.

3 January 2004, Hotel Gorski

Feeling a lot better today, yesterday's rest seems to have headed off my oncoming cold. Between breakfast and lunch J. and I do a very curious, yet very necessary, thing. I sit in our room and finish a letter to him, which I'd started writing on his fortieth birthday, eight months before. And J. finds another room, on the other

357

side of the hotel, and writes to me. Sometimes it is not because of lack of importance that things do not get finished. In fact, quite the opposite. In this whited-out landscape I reread my unfinished pages, written on a spring day, in my garden in east London last year – thoughts about how we've been able to work together so powerfully, how much our intense friendship has been the foundation on which Platform has flourished.

I try to pick up the threads of the letter and start writing again. I reflect on the manic pace of our work over the previous couple of years, the challenges of this but also its exhilarations. I wonder if this journey may be too much for both of us, too disturbing. I write another dozen pages or so – some of which are about men, vulnerability and intimacy: how although there has been a great shift in our lifetimes, I still feel there are challenges in what we express to each other, limits which sometimes frustrate me. And sometimes I wonder if we will ever get back the totality of trust we shared in the early days. I think back to the year or so when we shared the house in Brixton – when our bedrooms and even our journals and diaries were open to the other. But how much of this is simply nostalgia? For surely there can be no return. I sense we're on the threshold of something amazing – that after years of labouring, a harvest is coming. And perhaps part of this process is trusting our own voices more. Allowing these to have greater freedom, not always having to filter everything through the lens of collectivity. And this prospect shouldn't seem threatening, but actually liberating.

I write the last sentences as a further flurry of snow whitens the window.

So, my friend, I come to the end of this, my longest letter to you. I hope we can talk more about all these things in the next days, as we walk through snow and mountains, through cities and camps and killing grounds. There is much I cannot express here – to do with optimism and endurance, to do with ageing, to do with feeling blocked and having breakthroughs. But I hope, through walking with you, to find the words. Thank you for a remarkable twenty years. Our journey is only just beginning . . .

We deliver our letters to each other, smiling and acknowledging the odd, Victorian formality of such an exchange, sending it up by bowing to each other, and then we return to our rooms to read them. Just the hum of the radiators. And the rustling of the paper being turned over. What is it in our society that means we can talk of war, of sexuality, of climate change, of pornography, of crime, of violence, yet the difficulty that exists is in trying to find words for the love between men?

After lunch we wrap up very warmly, and walk to the last village in Poland, Wołosate. Up to the top of the road and then heading left-wards near Andrej's Bar, and making towards the ridge, an ice land-scape, sub-zero. Only trees breaking the whiteness. The Carpathians above us curving between Poland and Ukraine. Hardly a sound in the forest but we can see bird tracks through the snow.

Near to Wołosate, we sit down in a snowy field and have what has to be the coldest picnic of our lives – eating herrings from a tin and then chocolate in minus ten, minus fifteen. On the way back down, dusk with us now and the temperature dropping quickly, I tell him about the Levi I've been rereading, and suggest starting with *If This Is a Man* and *The Truce*. J. seems receptive to this, even enthusiastic. His mood seems to have really lifted in the last day or so, and this in turn has given me renewed energy for the days ahead.

In the evening, back at the hotel, in a quiet corner of the bar, I read excerpts of Levi, and we talk about the life of the quiet chemist from Turin who had never planned to be a writer, but found writing an urgent necessity after the war, to try to make sense of what he had lived through.

4 January 2004, Ustrzyki Górne to Krakow

In the bus, coming down the valley, the windows encrusted in ice. The bus filling at every stop with surprising numbers of hikers. I'm fascinated by the young Poles who surround us, by their courtesy towards each other. Teenagers with none of the aggression that's habitual in London. I've seen that kind of gentleness in young people only once before – in rural Ireland. Could it, in some way, be related to Catholicism, or is it more to do with living in the countryside? The trees and occasional farm buildings outside are now visible again as the ice melts on the windows.

Through Sanok again, on to Rzeszów, and then reaching Tarnów in the early evening. On the train to Krakow, we continue our talk about Levi, and read excerpts of Martin Gilbert which relate to some of the towns we're passing on the train. After some hesitation, I decide to show J. the passage in Gilbert that has haunted me since I first read it five years ago – perhaps the single most disturbing piece of writing ever committed to paper by a direct witness of the Holocaust: Jan Karski's description of what he experienced at the railway siding of Izbica*, a transit camp for the Belzec extermination camp, twenty kilometres north of Zamość in south-eastern Poland, only an hour north-east of where we are travelling this evening.

Karski was an important figure in the Polish underground, and had been asked by Jewish leaders to witness the extermination of the Jews in the Warsaw Ghetto and at Izbica, so that the Allies could learn the reality of the genocide that was taking place in Poland. So, in September 1942, risking his life, Karski travels with a member of the Jewish underground from Warsaw to a village near Izbica. And there he's taken to a village shop, run by a member of the Polish resistance who's helping the Jewish underground, where he changes into an Estonian militia uniform – Ukrainians were the principal nationality working alongside the SS at Izbica, Belzec and other extermination camps, but there were also small numbers of guards from the Baltic states. Shortly afterwards, an Estonian guard working at Izbica (but also co-operating with the Jewish underground – for his own, very mixed, reasons) arrives to collect Karski and take him to the camp. Karski then describes, in extraordinary (at times almost hallucinatory) detail, what he witnesses on this early-autumn afternoon at Izbica.

I do not have religious belief any more, so it is strange to find myself reaching for the word 'sacred' to describe this writing of Karski's. Yet this is the word I return to. It is because he is writing at, and

---

* See chapter notes for more details on Izbica.

then beyond, the limits of human understanding and endurance. It is not only that he risked his own life, repeatedly, in order to witness first-hand the extermination of the Jews in Poland, it is that he then attempted, with supreme effort, to communicate to the wider world what was happening. And in these actions, and the words that followed, quite beyond our conception of human limits, there is a quality that can only be called sacred. In the face of such terror, to still insist on the act of witness.

These things happened. This is what Karski comes back to, over and over again. Human beings did these things to other human beings. And they happened on this earth, not very far away from where I am writing these words. I also need to know what happened; perhaps it's impossible to know why it happened, but I feel it's my responsibility to know what was done, to know what human beings are capable of. If Primo Levi or Jan Karski have the courage to try to find words for what they experienced, I will find a way of listening to them. And while they were seeing these barbarities, many other human beings looked away. Many of us now would describe that looking away as having a criminal aspect, or, at the very least, an aspect of culpability. But what does looking away mean today? And what to do with knowledge of such things, should you choose to know?

On the almost empty train, I pass the book over to J. so he can read this passage:

> The camp was about a mile and a half from the shop . . . It took about twenty minutes to get to the camp but we became aware of its presence in less than half that time. About a mile away . . . we began to hear shouts, shots and screams. The noise increased steadily as we approached.
>
> 'What's happening?' I asked. 'What's the meaning of all that noise? What could it be?'
>
> He shrugged. 'They're bringing in a "batch" today.'
>
> I knew what he meant and did not enquire further. We walked on while the noise increased alarmingly. From time to

time a series of long screams or a particularly inhuman groan would set the hair on my scalp bristling.

'What are the chances of anyone escaping?' I asked my companion, hoping to hear an optimistic answer.

'None at all sir,' he answered, dashing my hopes to the ground. 'Once they get this far, their goose is cooked.'

. . . As we approached to within a few hundred yards of the camp, the shouts, cries, and shots cut off further conversation. I again noticed, or thought I noticed, an unpleasant stench that seemed to come from decomposing bodies mixed with horse manure. This may have been an illusion. The Estonian was, in any case, completely impervious to it. He even began to hum some sort of folk tune to himself. We passed through a small grove of decrepit-looking trees and emerged directly in front of the loud, sobbing, reeking camp of death.

It was on a large, flat plain and occupied about a square mile. It was surrounded on all sides by a formidable barbed-wire fence, nearly two yards in height and in good repair. Inside the fence, at intervals of about fifteen yards, guards were standing, holding rifles with fixed bayonets ready for use. Around the outside of the fence militiamen circulated on constant patrol. The camp itself contained a few small sheds or barracks. The rest of the area was completely covered by a dense, pulsating, throbbing, noisy human mass. Starved, stinking, gesticulating, insane human beings in constant, agitated motion. Through them, forcing paths if necessary with their rifle butts, walked the German police and the militiamen. They walked in silence, their faces bored and indifferent. They looked like shepherds bringing a flock to the market or pig-dealers among their pigs. They had the tired, vaguely disgusted appearance of men doing a routine, tedious job.

. . . To my left I noticed the rail tracks which passed about a hundred yards from the camp . . . On the track a dusty freight train waited, motionless. It had at least thirty carriages, all filthy. The Estonian followed my gaze . . .

'That's the train they'll load them on. You'll see it all.'

We came to a gate. Two German non-coms were standing there talking . . . I hung back a bit. The Estonian seemed to think I was losing my nerve.

'Go ahead,' he whispered impatiently into my ear. 'Don't be afraid. They won't even inspect your papers. They don't care about the likes of you.'

We walked up to the gate and saluted the non-coms vigorously. They returned the salute indifferently and we passed through, entering the camp, and mingled unnoticed with the crowd.

'Follow me,' he said quite loudly, 'I'll take you to a good spot.'

We passed an old Jew, a man of about sixty, sitting on the ground without a stitch of clothing on him. I was not sure whether his clothes had been torn off or whether he, himself, had thrown them away in a fit of madness. Silent, motionless, he sat on the ground, no one paying him the slightest attention. Not a muscle or fibre in his whole body moved. He might have been dead or petrified except for his preternaturally animated eyes, which blinked rapidly and incessantly. Not far from him a small child, clad in a few rags, was lying on the ground. He was all alone and crouched quivering on the ground, staring up with the large, frightened eyes of a rabbit. No one paid any attention to him either.

The Jewish mass vibrated, trembled, and moved to and fro as if united in a single, insane, rhythmic trance. They waved their hands, shouted, quarrelled, cursed and spat at each other. Hunger, thirst, fear and exhaustion had driven them all insane. I had been told that they were usually left in the camp for three or four days without a drop of water or food. They were all former inhabitants of the Warsaw Ghetto. When they had been rounded up they were given permission to take about ten pounds of baggage. Most of them took food, clothes, bedding, and, if they had any, money and jewellery. On the train, the Germans who accompanied them stripped them of everything that had the slightest value, even snatching away any article of clothing to which they took a fancy. They were left a few rags for apparel, bedding, and a few scraps of food. Those who left the train without any food starved continuously from the moment they set foot in the camp.

There was no organisation of any kind. None of them could possibly help or share with each other and they soon lost any self-control or any sense except the basest instinct of self-preservation. They had become, at this stage, completely dehumanised. It was moreover, typical autumn weather, cold, raw and rainy. The sheds could not accommodate more than two or three thousand people and every 'batch' included more than five thousand. This meant that there were always two to three thousand men, women and children scattered about in the open, suffering exposure as well as everything else.

The chaos, the squalor, the hideousness of it all was simply indescribable. There was a suffocating stench of sweat, filth, decay, damp straw and excrement . . . We had to squeeze our way through this mob. It was a ghastly ordeal. I had to push foot by foot through the crowd and step over the limbs of those who were lying prone. It was like forcing my way through a mass of sheer death and decomposition made even more horrible by its agonised pulsations. My companion had the skill of long practice, evading the bodies on the ground and winding his way through the mass with the ease of a contortionist. Distracted and clumsy I would brush against people or step on a figure that reacted like an animal, quickly, often with a moan or a yelp. Each time this occurred I would be seized by a fit of nausea and come to a stop. But my guide kept urging and hustling me along.

In this way we crossed the entire camp and finally stopped about twenty yards from the gate which opened on the passage leading to the train. It was a comparatively uncrowded spot. I felt immeasurably relieved at having finished my stumbling, sweating journey. The guide was standing at my side, saying something, giving me advice. I hardly heard him, my thoughts were elsewhere. He tapped me on the shoulder. I turned toward him mechanically, seeing him with difficulty. He raised his voice.

'Look here. You are going to stay here. I'll walk on a little further. You know what you are supposed to do. Remember to keep away from Estonians. Don't forget, if there's any trouble, you don't know me and I don't know you.'

I nodded vaguely at him. He shook his head and walked off. I remained there perhaps half an hour, watching this spectacle of human misery. At each moment I felt the impulse to run and flee. I had to force myself to remain indifferent, practise stratagems on myself to convince myself that I was not one of the condemned, throbbing multitude, forcing myself to relax as my body seemed to tie itself into knots, or turning away at intervals to gaze into the distance at a line of trees near the horizon. I had to remain on the alert too for an Estonian uniform, ducking toward the crowd or behind a nearby shed every time one approached me. The crowd continued to writhe in agony, the guards circulated about, bored and indifferent, occasionally distracting themselves by firing a shot or dealing out a blow. Finally I noticed a change in the motion of the guards. They walked less and they all seemed to be glancing in the same direction – at the passage to the track which was quite close to me.

I turned toward it myself. Two German policemen came to the gate with a tall, bulky, SS man. He barked out an order and they began to open the gate with some difficulty. It was very heavy. He shouted at them impatiently. They worked it frantically and finally whipped it open . . . The whole system had been worked out with crude effectiveness. The outlet of the passage was blocked by two carriages of the freight train, so that any attempt on the part of one of the Jews to break out of the mob, or to escape if they had so much presence of mind left, would have been completely impossible. Moreover, it facilitated the job of loading them onto the train.

The SS man turned to the crowd, planted himself with his feet wide apart and his hands on his hips and loosed a roar that must have actually hurt his ribs. It could be heard far above the hellish babble that came from the crowd.

'*Ruhe, ruhe!* Quiet, quiet! All Jews will board this train to be taken to a place where work awaits them. Keep order. Do not push. Anyone who attempts to resist or create a panic will be shot.'

He stopped speaking and looked challengingly at the helpless mob that hardly seemed to know what was happening. Suddenly, accompanying the movement with a loud, hearty laugh, he yanked out his gun and fired three random shots into the crowd. A single stricken groan answered him. He replaced the gun in his holster, smiled, and set himself for another roar: '*Alle Juden, raus – raus!*' For a moment the crowd was silent. Those nearest the SS man recoiled from the shots and tried to dodge, panic-stricken, toward the rear. But this was resisted by the mob as a volley of shots from the rear sent the whole surging mass forward madly, screaming in pain and fear. The shots continued without let-up from the rear and now from the sides too, narrowing the mob down and driving it on a savage scramble into the passageway. In utter panic, groaning in despair and agony, they rushed down the passageway . . . Here new shots were fired. The two policemen at the entrance to the train were now firing into the oncoming throng corralled in the passageway, in order to slow them down . . . The SS man now added his roar to the deafening bedlam.

'*Ordnung, Ordnung!*' he bellowed like a madman.

'Order, order!' The two policemen echoed him hoarsely, firing straight into the faces of the Jews running to the trains.

Impelled and controlled by this ring of fire, they filled the two carriages quickly.

And now came the most horrible episode of them all. The Bund leader* warned me that if I lived to be a hundred I would never forget some of the things I saw. He did not exaggerate. The military rule stipulates that a freight carriage may carry eight horses or forty soldiers. Without any baggage at all, a maximum of a hundred passengers standing close together and pressing against each other could be crowded into a carriage. The Germans had simply issued orders to the effect that 120 to 130 Jews had to enter each carriage. These orders were now being carried out. Alternately swinging and firing with their rifles, the policemen were forcing still more people into the two carriages which were already over-full. The shots continued to ring out in the rear and the driven mob surged forward, exerting an irresistible pressure against those nearest to the train. These unfortunates, crazed by what they had been through, scourged by the policemen, and shoved forward by the milling mob, then began to climb on the heads and shoulders of those in the trains.

These were helpless since they had the weight of the entire advancing throng against them and responded only with howls of anguish to those who, clutching at their hair and clothes for support, trampling on necks, faces and shoulders, breaking bones and shouting with insensate fury, attempted to clamber over them. More than another score of human beings, men, women and children gained admittance in this fashion. Then the policemen slammed the doors across the hastily withdrawn limbs that still protruded and pushed the iron bars in place. The two carriages were now crammed to bursting with tightly packed human flesh, completely hermetically filled. All this while the entire camp had reverberated with a tremendous volume of sound in which the hideous groans

---

* Leon Feiner, the leader of the Jewish Socialist Alliance (known as the Bund), whom Karski had met earlier. For more on this meeting see Book two, Chapter two: 'The Use and Abuse of Words: Jan Karski and Albert Speer'.

and screams mingled weirdly with shots, curses, and bellowed commands.

Nor was this all. I know that many people will not believe me, will not be able to believe me, will think I exaggerate or invent. But I saw it and it is not exaggerated or invented. I have no other proofs, no photographs. All I can say is that I saw it and that it is the truth. The floors of the carriage had been covered with a thick, white powder. It was quicklime. Quicklime is simply unslaked lime or calcium oxide that has been dehydrated. Anyone who has seen cement being mixed knows what occurs when water is poured on lime. The mixture bubbles and steams as the powder combines with the water, generating a large amount of heat. Here the lime served a double purpose in the Nazi economy of brutality. The moist flesh coming into contact with the lime is rapidly dehydrated and burned. The occupants of the carriages would be literally burned to death before long, the flesh eaten from their bones. Thus the Jews would 'die in agony', fulfilling the promise Himmler had issued 'in accord with the will of the Führer' in Warsaw, in 1942. Secondly, the lime would prevent decomposing bodies from spreading disease. It was efficient and inexpensive – a perfectly chosen agent for their purposes.

It took three hours to fill up the entire train by repetitions of this procedure. It was twilight when the forty-six (I counted them) carriages were packed. From one end to the other, the train, with its quivering cargo of flesh, seemed to throb, vibrate, rock and jump as if bewitched. There would be a strangely uniform momentary lull and then, again, the train would begin to moan and sob, wail and howl. Inside the camp a few score dead bodies remained and a few in the final throes of death. German policemen walked around at leisure with smoking guns, pumping bullets into anything, that by a moan or motion betrayed an excess of vitality. Soon, not a single one was left alive. In the now quiet camp the only sounds were the inhuman screams that were echoes from the moving train.

Then these, too, ceased. All that was now left was a stench of excrement and rotting straw and a queer, sickening, acidulous odour which, I thought, may have come from the quantities of blood that had been shed, and with which the ground was stained.

As I listened to the dwindling outcries from the train, I thought of the destination toward which it was speeding. My informants had minutely described the entire journey. The train would travel about eighty miles and finally come to a halt in an empty, barren field. Then nothing at all would happen. The train would stand stock-still, patiently waiting while death penetrated into every corner of its interior. This would take from two to four days. When quicklime, asphyxiation, and injuries had silenced every outcry, a group of men would appear. They would be young, strong Jews, assigned to the task of cleaning out these carriages until their own turn to be in them should arrive. Under a strong guard they would unseal the carriages and expel the heaps of decomposing bodies. The mounds of flesh that they piled up would then be burned and the remnants buried in a single huge hole. The cleaning, burning and burial would consume one or two full days.

The entire process of disposal would take, then, from three to six days. During this period the camp would have recruited new victims. The train would return and the whole cycle would be repeated from the beginning.

I was still standing near the gate, gazing after the no longer visible train when I felt a rough hand on my shoulder. The Estonian was back again. He was frantically trying to rouse my attention and to keep his voice lowered at the same time.

'Wake up, wake up,' he was scolding me hoarsely. 'Don't stand there with your mouth open. Come on, hurry, or we'll both get caught. Follow me and be quick about it.'

I followed him at a distance, feeling completely benumbed. When we reached the gate he reported to a German officer and pointed at me. I heard the officer say, '*Sehr gut, gehen*

Sie,' and then we passed through the gate. The Estonian and I walked awhile together and then separated.

Karski returns to the village shop, and then collapses, physically and mentally. For the next two days and nights he has a violent fever, vomits uncontrollably, both food and blood. Only on the third day, with the help of the shopkeeper, does he have enough strength to return on the train to Warsaw.

*

J. reads by the dim light of the train carriage. He's not scribbling notes in pencil as he usually does. He doesn't say anything. Fifteen minutes, maybe more. He finishes and looks out of the window, as if defeated. When I try to talk to him, he waves me away in a gesture I don't think I've ever seen him use before. I question whether giving this passage to J. was the right thing to do. Words can create physical changes, sometimes changes that are too subtle for us to comprehend. As the train now edges through Płaszów, floodlit factories on a site of yet more butchery, I try to remember those lines of Viktor Klemperer: 'Words can be like tiny doses of arsenic: they are swallowed unnoticed, appear to have no effect, and then after a little time the toxic reaction sets in after all.'

We're back in Krakow, coated in white now, sparkling at night. We find our hotel just off the square. All faded 1930s grandeur, pale greens and white, fine ironwork around the lift. J. is silent. I hear myself becoming jollier to counteract this unusual situation. We go out to try and find somewhere to eat. The waistcoated man at reception in his sixties, with limited but elegantly accented English, isn't sure about restaurants at this time, but picks up a brochure: '*To-morr-ow tours? Ausch-witz? Salt mines?*'

He recites this with a kind of sing-song intonation. A much-repeated offer, made to every guest. And obscenely jarring. It is precisely why, despite all my research over the last decade, I have never been to Auschwitz. To have been made into just another tick on a tourism itinerary seems a blasphemy. Day 3: Prague, Kafka's old town, the Charles Bridge, Mozart; Day 4: Krakow, breakfast in the Market Square, trip to Auschwitz, back in time for a concert in the cathedral . . . It's late now, Sunday and out of season, most of the restaurants are already closed. We end up in an almost deserted fast-food place, picking at unappetising kebabs. The wildness of the mountains and Andrej's Bar seems a world away.

15

Walking into Whiteness

5 January 2004, Krakow

Patchy sleep. Breakfast in the hotel. J. seems to have recovered and we talk through the plan for today. To our surprise there are no direct trains to Auschwitz this morning but I spot one going to Trzebinia, halfway to our destination. I have an idea, and we board this train. The snow has got thicker, the train creaks along slowly, and after half an hour or so stops altogether at a small station – this must be Trzebinia. We sit on a bench, swaddled

in scarves and hats, and I start to read to J. Fifty-nine years ago
Primo Levi was here – in fact just over those tracks, there by the
station building. Some weeks after the liberation of the camp,
in February 1945, travelling from Krakow to Katowice, he tries
to transmit to other people what had happened to him, he tries to
find the words:

> I climbed down on the platform to stretch my legs, rigid
> from the cold. Perhaps I was among the first dressed in 'zebra'
> clothes to appear in that place called Trzebinia; I immediately
> found myself the centre of a dense group of curious people,
> who interrogated me volubly in Polish. I replied as best as I
> could in German; and in the middle of the group of workers
> and peasants a bourgeois appeared, with a felt hat, glasses and
> a leather briefcase in his hand – a lawyer.
>
> He was Polish, he spoke French and German well, he was an
> extremely courteous and benevolent person; in short he pos-
> sessed all the requisites enabling me, finally, after the long year
> of slavery and silence, to recognise in him the messenger, the
> spokesman of the civilised world, the first that I had met. I had
> a torrent of urgent things to tell the civilised world: my things,
> but everyone's, things of blood, things which (it seemed to me)
> ought to shake every conscience to its very foundations . . . he
> questioned me, and I spoke at dizzy speed of those so recent
> experiences of mine, of Auschwitz nearby (yet, it seemed,
> unknown to all), of the hecatomb from which I alone had
> escaped, of everything. The lawyer translated into Polish for
> the public. Now I do not know Polish, but I know how one
> says 'Jew' and how one says 'political'; and I soon realised that
> the translation of my account, although sympathetic, was not
> faithful to it. The lawyer described me to the public not as an
> Italian Jew, but as an Italian political prisoner. I asked him
> why, amazed and almost offended. He replied, embarrassed:
> 'C'est mieux pour vous. La guerre n'est pas finie.' . . .
>
> I felt my sense of freedom, my sense of being a man among
> men, of being alive, like a warm tide ebb from me. I found

myself suddenly old, lifeless, tired beyond human measure . . . My listeners began to steal away; they must have understood. I had dreamed, we had always dreamed, of something like this, in the nights at Auschwitz: of speaking and not being listened to, of finding liberty and remaining alone. After a while I remained alone with the lawyer; a few minutes later he also left me, urbanely excusing himself. He warned me against speaking German; when I asked for an explanation, he replied vaguely: 'Poland is a sad country'. He wished me good luck, he offered me money which I refused; he seemed to me deeply moved.

We stare across the tracks at the builders repairing the waiting room opposite. Levi alone on that platform. And an aloneness only accentuated by the crowd around him. And all the voices in his head, all the faces of dead friends. What part of the human spirit, at such a moment, would want to go on? The catastrophe of Auschwitz. Coming through, somehow surviving. Slowly regaining strength and the will to go on. And then this second annihilation. What does 'survival' mean if your words cannot be heard? Then Levi returns to Italy and writes *If This Is a Man*. From summer 1945 to early 1946 he is possessed by the necessity to communicate his experience. He writes in an urgency of pain and finishes the book in a matter of months. Only by writing does he feel he can start to live again.

But I'm baffled by our society's inability to hear Levi for fourteen years. This book, of immense power and awesome restraint, sinks virtually without trace on its appearance in Italy. Rejected by all the major publishers, it comes out under the imprint of a small Turin publishing house, Francesco de Silva, in October 1947. No more than 1,500 copies are sold. And then – in a remarkable historical echo of the fate of Melville's *Moby-Dick* (also almost totally ignored on publication, the surviving books later incinerated in a warehouse fire), the remaining 1,000 books are subsequently destroyed by a flood in a warehouse. It receives only modest reviews, and Levi returns to his work as an industrial chemist on the outskirts of Turin. What was it in 1947 that meant the world could not hear Levi? A societal inability to hear, which shifts imperceptibly over the years?

Eleven years later, in 1958, the respected Italian publishers Einaudi finally agree to bring out a new edition of *If This Is a Man*; in 1959 Orion publish the first English translation, but even these editions do not make a dramatic impact at first. It is only with the publication of the German edition in February 1961, which sells 20,000 copies immediately, that the book finally gains the acclaim it deserves – fourteen years after it came into the world.[*] Jorge Semprún, another survivor, and writer of exceptional insight, reflects on the eighteen-year delay between his writing about the experience of deportation and suffering at Buchenwald (*Le Grand Voyage*), and its publication – similar to Levi's own experience of the delay between his ignored first writing and the global audience he'd gained on the publication of his second book, *La Tregua* (*The Truce*). It was

> as though an ability to listen had developed on its own, beyond all the petty circumstances of our own lives, within the almost unfathomable progress of history. A development all the more remarkable and fascinating in that it coincides with the first accounts of the Soviet Gulag that managed to surmount the West's traditional barrier of distrust and misunderstanding: Alexsander Solzhenitsyn's *One Day in the Life of Ivan Denisovich* appeared in that same spring of 1963.

What are the voices today that we as a society cannot hear?

*

There are no trains to Oświęcim for an hour and a half. And the buses are going everywhere except there. So in the end we get a taxi the last twenty kilometres. We enter a nondescript town. Light industrial buildings on the outskirts. A gleaming new BP garage.

---

[*] Most remarkably, even after the success of the English and German editions of *If This Is a Man*, the first Hebrew edition was only published in 1988 – a year after Levi's death. On the wider question of several key works of the Holocaust only finding publication in 1960–1, see chapter notes.

Having read and thought so much over the last twenty years about Auschwitz, this arrival is something of an anticlimax. We leave our rucksacks in the left luggage at the station, conscious of the irony of such a place in this town, and then buy a map of the town at a kiosk opposite. We have a very clear plan of what we want to do today – we will try to link the original Auschwitz camp (known as Auschwitz I) with the Buna-Monowitz complex (referred to as Auschwitz III). We walk south for a few minutes, parallel to the train tracks, past some ugly, three-storey brick houses, then turn left down S. Leszczyńskiej, a long, straight road with cherry trees on each side. On our right, ruined factories. I immediately wonder when these were built. Of every building in this town, like every elderly person here, the question will be – *before* or *after*? And imagine being a child growing up here – the albatross of history round your neck. How would you reply when people asked you where you came from?

After fifteen minutes or so we reach the museum complex where the main camp was, on our left. Most of the snow in the expansive car park is undisturbed today, just a single coach with a bored-looking driver smoking his cigarette and waiting. Perhaps a dozen other cars. Off season. We head towards the entrance to the museum, though we are not going to go in. We have another map in our heads, an entirely different focus and set of questions. Instead, we enter the bookshop outside the museum. A middle-aged woman with glasses stands up and puts down her reading as we come in. In my halting Polish I ask if she speaks English:

'*Czy pani mowi po angielsku?*'

'Little yes.'

The bookshop, though small, seems extremely well stocked, with several hundred publications ranging from leaflets to extensive academic works.

'Could you tell me what you have on Buna, or Monowitz, or IG Farben?'

She looks rather taken aback; this is obviously not a familiar enquiry. 'Ah, there is not . . . we do not have – ah yes, maybe there is little in this book, a chapter, but in German only. One moment please.'

She goes to the back of the shop and rummages among some lower shelves. She comes back looking relieved:

'There is in this book something – one part.'

She hands me *Auschwitz Prisoner Labor* and yes, there is indeed a four-page chapter titled 'The Role of IG Farbenindustrie in the Economy of the Third Reich, and the Origins of the Firm's Use of Prisoner Labor' and ten references to 'Monowitz (Buna)' in the index. Four pages out of the hundreds of books in this shop.

'So, nothing else? Just about Buna or Monowitz?'

'Sorry, no.'

'And is this the only bookshop? Is there another inside the museum?'

'Yes, you may try, but . . .' She shrugs her shoulders and looks doubt-ful. I buy the book and also the official Auschwitz-Birkenau guide. Just as we're leaving she remembers something:

'Moment please. Do you have a map?'

We lay the town plan over the counter.

'I think there is monument at the Buna-werke. I haven't been there, but I believe there is monument. Yes, there.' She points to a minus-cule black column on the map with no writing to identify it. We thank her and leave.

I try the little bookshop just inside the museum entrance – the young man just smiles and shakes his head, 'Nothing, sorry.'

Outside again in the thin January sun, J. is looking at an enlarged aerial photograph taken at the end of the war. On this map three places are outlined in red – Auschwitz I (where we are), Auschwitz II (Birkenau) and Auschwitz III (Monowitz). I'm perplexed by the inverse relationship between the geographical extent of the three sites and their cultural and historical visibility. The Auschwitz that the million visitors a year pour into* is the one we're standing outside. This is where the gate bearing the words '*Arbeit Macht Frei*' can be seen. Though culturally this camp occupies a central place in our received imagery of the Holocaust, the historical reality is significantly different – Auschwitz I was primarily a camp for Polish prisoners and political opponents of the Nazis. And geographically it is surprisingly small, less than one square kilometre. Auschwitz-Birkenau, more than ten times larger, where the vast majority of the 1.2 million human beings were murdered, is visited by only a small proportion of those who arrive in their tour buses at the Auschwitz I museum complex. And Auschwitz III, which in geographical and economic terms was both far larger and strategically more important than either of the other camps, barely exists today in terms of memorialisation. It is hardly visited at all. And the official Auschwitz guide book of twenty-four pages contains only half a sentence on Auschwitz III/Monowitz:

> and in 1942 the camp in Monowitz near Oświęcim – KL Auschwitz III – was established on the territory of the German chemical plant IG-Farbenindustrie.

We begin our walk from Auschwitz I to Auschwitz III, and as we walk we reflect on why this erasure has occured. Primo Levi will be our guide on this walk today. By the perimeter fence of Auschwitz I, looking into the grounds now dominated by snow-laden trees, I read his account of the train journey from Italy to Auschwitz, the train edging out of the Adige valley, how 'we passed the Brenner at midday of the second day, and everyone stood up, but no one said a word . . . Among the forty-five people in my wagon only four saw their homes again; and it was by far the most fortunate wagon.' Then the arrival in the town we were now standing in, the selection: 'of

---

* In 2003, when we made this journey, the visitor numbers to Auschwitz were just under a million people a year. Since then, numbers have increased significantly, with 2,053,000 visitors to the museum and memorial site in 2016.

our convoy no more than ninety-six men and twenty-nine women entered the respective camps of Monowitz-Buna and Birkenau . . . of all the others, more than five hundred in number, not one was living two days later.' Levi arrives in Auschwitz in late February 1944, almost sixty years ago, and the number 174517 is immediately tattooed on his arm as recorded in the camp's chronicles[*]: 'February 26th 1944: 650 Jewish men, women and children from the Fossoli camp arrive in an RSHA transport from Italy. After the selection, 95 men, given Nos. 174471–174565 and 29 women, given Nos. 75669–75697, are admitted to the camp. The remaining 526 people are killed in the gas chambers.'

It's getting colder now, dipping well below freezing, and stopping to read, even for a few minutes, is difficult, we're stamping our feet in the snow. We walk on, turning the corner of the perimeter fence, and starting to walk eastwards, surprised at what looks like an incongruous orchard inside the camp, but as fruit trees grow quickly we soon realise that probably none of these were there sixty years ago.

We arrive at the back entrance of the camp, and, without knowing why, I feel drawn in. Just in front of us is a kind of bunker with a grass roof, sloping down at each side. And then the stabbing realisation. This is the only complete gas chamber and crematorium which survives. Not purpose-built as the later four at Birkenau were, but an improvised killing centre, formerly a vegetable store from the days when the camp was a barracks for the Polish army. I'm astonished at its proximity to the road that we've walked along and other buildings – barely thirty yards away is an imposing block that I later discover was the SS hospital. The four other gas chambers and crematoria at Birkenau were situated at much greater distance away from other buildings in the camp. Weren't the authorities concerned at all about this proximity? About the screams that surely would have penetrated into the camp from here?

As we look up at the flat-roofed, grey concrete bunker with a tall brick chimney at the back, I remember that Filip Müller – a

---

[*] From *Auschwitz Chronicle 1939–1945*, ed. Danuta Czech.

Czechoslovakian Jew, one of the few survivors of the Auschwitz *Sonderkommando* – describes what happened here, at this exact place, sixty-two years ago. He'd arrived at Auschwitz on 13 April 1942, on one of the earliest Holocaust transports from Slovakia with 1,076 fellow Jews.[*] He is then forced to work with the other members of the *Sonderkommando*, undressing the bodies of the corpses in this, the first gas chamber used at Auschwitz, and then incinerating them in the crematorium's two ovens next door. He witnesses with his own eyes how the techniques of the SS officers evolve to make the process of mass murder run ever more smoothly. Instead of using extreme violence to force people into the gas chamber, they realise that subtler methods are far more effective. He describes watching a group of several hundred Polish Jews being brought into the yard where we're standing; they have no idea that they are only a few feet from the gas chamber where they will die in a matter of minutes. The psychological manipulation by the SS is devastating:

All at once the crowd fell silent. The gaze of several hundred pairs of eyes turned upwards to the flat roof of the crematorium. Up there, immediately above the entrance . . . stood Aumeier, flanked by Grabner and by Hossler . . . Aumeier spoke first . . . he talked persuasively to these frightened, alarmed and doubt-racked people. 'You have come here', he began, 'to work in the same way as our soldiers who are fighting at the front. Anyone who is able and willing to work will be all right'. After Aumeier it was Grabner's turn. He asked the people to get undressed because, in their own interest, they had to be disinfected. 'First and foremost we shall have to see that you are healthy', he said. 'Therefore everyone will have to take a shower. Now when you've had your showers, there'll be a bowl of soup waiting for you all'.

Life flooded back into the upturned faces of the men and women listening eagerly to every word. The desired

---

[*] '634 Jewish men and 443 Jewish women, sent from Slovakia by the RHSA, receive Nos. 28903–29536 and 4761–5203' (also from *Auschwitz Chronicle 1939–1945*). Müller's number was 29236.

effect had been achieved: initial suspicion gave way to hope, perhaps even to the belief that everything might still end happily. Hossler, sensing the change of mood, quickly began to speak. In order to invest this large-scale deception with the semblance of complete honesty, he put on a perfect act to delude these unsuspecting people. 'You over there in the corner', he cried, pointing at a little man, 'what's your trade?' 'I'm a tailor', came the prompt reply. 'Ladies or gents?' inquired Hossler. 'Both', the little man replied confidently. 'Excellent!' Hossler was delighted. 'That's precisely the sort of people we need in our workrooms. When you've had your shower, report to me at once. And you over there, what can you do?' He turned to a good-looking middle-aged woman who was standing right in front. 'I am a trained nurse, sir', she replied. 'Good for you, we urgently need nurses in our hospital, and if there are any more trained nurses among you, please report to me immediately after your shower' . . .

All the people's fears and anxieties had vanished as if by magic. Quiet as lambs they undressed without having to be shouted at or beaten. Each tried his or her best to hurry up with their undressing so that they might be the first to get under the shower. After a very short time the yard was empty but for shoes, clothing, underwear, suitcases and boxes which were strewn all over the ground. Cozened and deceived, hundreds of men, women and children had walked, innocently, and without a struggle, into the large windowless chamber of the crematorium. When the last one had crossed the threshold, two SS men slammed shut the heavy iron-studded door which was fitted with a rubber seal, and bolted it.'

Müller then describes other SS men with gas masks climbing onto the crematorium roof, and pouring crystals into the six openings. At this moment all the trucks in the yard turned on their engines, to prevent anyone in the nearby camp buildings hearing the sounds of the dying, shouting from inside. Aumeier and the others checked their watches to see how long it took for the sounds to cease, and then proudly boasted to the junior officers who'd been observing the process: 'Well, you two, have you got it now? That's the way to do it!'

Later in summer 1942, the four purpose-built gas chambers and crematoria at Birkenau become operational, and the focus of the mass killings moves from Auschwitz I to Birkenau – two kilometres north-west of where we are standing.

*

The temperature falls perceptibly as we go inside the chamber. Nobody else here. A blackened oblong of stone and concrete, streaked walls, dimly lit by naked bulbs.

No words here.

Nothing.

Nothingness.

We walk into the adjoining room – the prototype crematorium. Two ovens survive, with the proud logo of their manufacturers, Topf & Söhne, of Erfurt – so proud of having supplied ovens to the Reich that they retained their brand name after the war.[*]

At the back of the ovens is a kind of storeroom, and inside we can make out dozens of rusting metal implements, used for dealing with the remnants of charred bodies. Some are like twisted rakes, some like pitchforks, some not like any known object, improvised for barbarism. Seeing these, in an instant, the work of Joseph Beuys is illuminated. The rusted scream that all his work returns to. Knowledge stained irrevocably.

---

[*] In 1961 Levi discovered that Topf & Söhne were advertising a 'new and improved' cremation method for civilian use. Levi was outraged. He asked his friend Alessandro Garrone, a Turin magistrate and human rights campaigner, to write an article for *La Stampa* on this subject. Garrone did so, but Topf did not respond (see Ian Thomson's biography, *Primo Levi*). Levi also notes in the preface to *The Drowned and the Saved*, published in 1986, that 'Topf . . . was still in operation in 1975 building crematoria for civilian use, and had not considered the advisability of changing its name.' Topf was eventually declared bankrupt in 1996.

We leave, shaken and without words. We're walking eastwards again, just outside the perimeter fence, past little houses, wondering who would want to live here. Then along a busy main road, up to a roundabout, and we cross the River Soła, where Commandant Höss and his children used to enjoy swimming.

Through a little park, following what seems to be a kind of ring road around the town, fields on our right. I take photographs every 500 yards. Up a slight incline towards blocks of flats, ten, twelve storeys tall, following the road swinging to the right, and into older buildings now, what seems like another town. Marked on our map as 'Osiedle Chemików' (chemists' estate) – surely related to the vast chemical works that IG Farben built at Monowitz? After another mile or so these houses peter out, another avenue of trees, every branch etched in ice. And just beyond, we arrive at the south-western corner of the Buna complex. We've come three, maybe four kilometres across the town.

We start to walk northwards, next to a main road. Behind red-and-white barriers to our right, we see a sign with the words *Firma Chemiczna Dwory*' on it, and lorries carrying liquid nitrogen waiting to go in. It astonishes us that this part of Buna at least is still functioning as a chemicals plant. That a corporation can simply take over a site of mass murder and continue to do business here. A little further on the right and we see what must be the monument – an abstract barbed-wire motif, but it's thickly covered with snow and ice and there doesn't appear to be any inscription, nothing to explain to people passing by the nature of this place, its origins. We dig for some time, scraping off the ice, trying to find any words, trying to unbury history, but there seems to be nothing there.

We are losing the light now and flurries of snow are beginning. We return to the south-western corner and start to walk along the southern perimeter of the complex, next to constant traffic on the road to Zator.

But we've misjudged the sheer scale of this complex. It's vast. A straight line continuing for kilometre after kilometre. I'm concerned now that we will not even be able to reach Monowitz, the site of the camp where Primo Levi was imprisoned for that unimaginable year. The traffic roars along the icy main road. But still, to our left, behind concrete posts and rusting barbed wire, the chemical works sprawls on. Industrial sheds, tangled pipelines, chimneys, towers of brick. A repeated question in my head: which of these buildings were there in the 1940s? This strange yet insistent notion of bricks and windows as witnesses, as if they bore the traces of the people who once brushed against them. On one of the sheds a number in white paint – 739; any detail could be significant, so wiping the flakes of snow from the lens, I take another picture. It amazes me to see some of these buildings still functioning – some that would have been here during the war, buildings which Levi and his slave-labourer colleagues helped to build, their chimneys still spewing smoke into the sky. On some of the buildings, more painted figures – 761, 922. I take more photographs, wanting to document everything. Twenty minutes, twenty-five minutes walking this straight line, under metal bridges and more pipelines. Almost dusk now, the temperature has dipped viciously. After half an hour walking this perimeter, a sign on our right – 'Niwa Monowicka'. We have arrived.

*

Monowitz. We are here. The little rectangle on the map, just at the south-eastern corner of the Buna complex. I have had a visual image of this place for over twenty years, since first reading *If This Is a Man*. For some reason, this small patch of land has inhabited me, hasn't let go. I return to the thousands of people who lived and suffered and died here and the minority, Primo Levi among them, who survived. On reflection, three of these four verbs seem quite inadequate: 'died' is factual, the others we cannot know. What would living or suffering or surviving mean in such a place? How to reach the reality of these words? When, of the people, we have only traces.

388

Somogyi, the Hungarian chemist, who died on 26 January 1945, the day before the Russians arrived

Lakmaker, the seventeen-year-old Jewish boy from the Netherlands

Maxime, the Parisian tailor

Sertelet, the peasant from the Vosges

Alcalai, the Jewish glazier from Toulouse

Schenck, the Jewish businessman from Slovakia

Alberto, the twenty-two-year-old Italian and Levi's inseparable companion and sharer of food

Towarowski, the Franco-Polish Jew, twenty-three years old

Cagnolati, the young peasant from the Vosges

Kosman, the Reuters correspondent from Alsace

Askenazi, the Greek barber from Salonika

Arthur, the thin peasant from the Vosges

Charles, the thirty-two-year-old schoolteacher from Lorraine

Brackier and Kandel, the two other chemists chosen to work in the laboratory

Levi and Levi, the two other Levis working in the chemical *Kommando*

Kraus Pali, the Hungarian from Budapest – tall, thin, glasses, a clumsy worker

Beppo the Greek, twenty years old

Kuhn, the old man who thanks God for not being selected, provoking Levi to write 'If I was God I would spit at Kuhn's prayer'

Sattler, the huge Transylvanian peasant

Rene, young and robust, but selected for death

Wertheimer, sixty, with varicose veins

Monsieur Pinkert, the diplomat who'd worked in Warsaw at the Belgian Embassy

Jean, the student from Alsace, twenty-four years old, for whom Levi tries to translate Dante

Limentani, from Rome

Frenkl, the spy

Stern, the squinting Transylvanian

Alex, the kapo, so dismissive of the doctors, the intelligentsia

Mendi, the rabbi and militant Zionist from Russia

Balla

Chajim, the Polish watchmaker, a religious Jew, Levi's bunk companion

Ziegler

Iss Clausner

Piero Sonnino, Levi's friend from Rome

Henri, the polyglot Frenchman, the manipulator, survivor

Elias Lindzin, the muscled dwarf of Warsaw, always moving, always working

Alfred L, the cold engineer

Schepschel, the Galician

Moischl

Lorenzo, the civilian worker who, by reminding Levi that there could be 'a just world outside', connected him to his humanity again and gave him the strength to go on

Templer, the *Kommando* organiser and exceptional soup eater

Fischer, the Hungarian who doesn't eat all his bread immediately

David

Sigi, the seventeen-year-old from Vienna

Bela, the Hungarian farmer

Felicio, the Greek

Resnyk, the Pole who lived twenty years in Paris, thirty years old, shares Levi's bunk

Waschmann, the rabbi from Galicia, who discusses Talmudic questions in Yiddish with Mendi

Finder

Kardos, the engineer, who tends to wounded feet and corns in the evening

Walter Bonn, the civilised Dutchman, and fellow patient of Levi's in the Ka-Be ('infirmary')

Schmulek, the Polish Jew, albino, a blacksmith, selected for death from the Ka-Be

Steinlauf, the former sergeant in the Austro-Hungarian army, a man of good will who scolds Levi for not trying to keep clean

Schlome, the sixteen-year-old Polish Jew, who is amazed that there are Jews in Italy

Diena, Levi's first bunk companion

Mischa

Flesch, the interpreter, a German Jew, fifty years old, a former soldier

Mr Bergmann, the elderly man

Mr Levi, who asks about where their women have been taken

Freddie Knoller, the cellist from Vienna

Rudy Kennedy, the Jewish boy from Rosenberg, who works in the electrical *Kommando*

And all the others we do not have names for:

> Null Achtzehn – the boy who cannot remember his name and so has become a number
>
> the Galician
>
> the gigantic French Häftling
>
> the pale Dutch boy in the chemical *Kommando*
>
> the two Hungarian boys who died on the final march out of Monowitz
>
> the rascal from Trieste
>
> the tall, red-haired Frenchman from the Drancy transports
>
> the Hungarian doctor who studied in Italy, the camp dentist
>
> the Yiddish storyteller
>
> the young companion of Schlome
>
> the brother of Henri, who died in Buna

And:

> The young man hanged in November 1944 for helping the *Sonderkommando* revolt in Birkenau, in front of all the prisoners here, who shouts out, with his last breath, 'Comrades, I am the last one!' Nobody responds, the band plays and Levi feels 'oppressed with shame':

> the SS watch us pass with indifferent eyes: their work is finished . . . the Russians can come now: there are no longer any strong men among us, the last one is hanging above our heads . . . The Russians can come now: they will only find us, the slaves . . . To destroy a man is difficult, almost as difficult as to create one: it has not been easy, nor quick, but you Germans have succeeded.

And those, the vast majority, who are not recorded at all.

*

We turn down Niwa Monowicka, under trees laden with snow. In my mind is something which Daniel Goldhagen says at the opening of *Hitler's Willing Executioners*. It remains for me a defining statement of this paradox – the total impossibility of understanding the real meaning of genocide yet also the ongoing human obligation to try. And, inherent in the trying, the necessity to not allow ourselves to become numbed – to return again and again to the fact that these are *individual* deaths, multiplied unthinkable numbers of times:

> Explaining this genocidal slaughter necessitates . . . that we keep two things always in mind. When writing or reading about killing operations, it is too easy to become insensitive to the numbers on the page. Ten thousand dead in one place, four hundred in another, fifteen in a third. Each of us should pause and consider that ten thousand deaths meant that Germans killed ten thousand individuals – unarmed men, women and children, the old, the young, the healthy, and the sick – that Germans took a human life ten thousand times . . . the Jewish victims were not the 'statistics' that they appear to us on paper. To the killers whom they faced, the Jews were people who were breathing one moment and lying lifeless, often before them, the next.

We reach the end of Niwa Monowicka, expecting to find some buildings connected to the Monowitz camp, some remnants at least.

But there is nothing here.

Or rather there is no trace of the concentration camp where the slave labourers for the Buna plant were imprisoned. A hamlet has taken its place, perhaps twenty, twenty-five houses, no shops, not even a church, round a grid of little lanes. Dusk now, we walk on, exhausted and appalled at the extinction of history represented here. We look in vain for a monument, for even a single panel of historical information, but there's nothing.

It feels necessary to speak Primo Levi's words here, in the face of this erasure. In the shelter of an apple tree, shaking now, both with the cold and a growing anger, I read to J. – Levi's first hours in this place with his ninety-five fellow prisoners, his total shock. Clothes taken. Stripped of all possessions. Hair shaved off. Disinfected. Given rags to wear. Tattooed on left arms. Tormented by thirst:

> Then the door opens and a boy in a striped suit comes in, with a fairly civilised air, small, thin and blond. He speaks French and we throng around him with a flood of questions which till now we had asked each other in vain.
>
> But he does not speak willingly; no one here speaks willingly. We are new, we have nothing and we know nothing; why waste time on us? . . . I asked him (with an ingenuousness that only a few days later already seemed incredible to me) if at least they would give us back our toothbrushes. He did not laugh, but with his face animated by fierce contempt, he threw at me 'Vous n'êtes pas à la maison.' And it is this refrain that we hear repeated by everyone: you are not at home, this is not a sanitorium, the only exit is by way of the chimney. (What did he mean? Soon we were all to learn what it meant.)
>
> And it was in fact so. Driven by thirst, I eyed a fine icicle outside the window, within hand's reach. I opened the window and broke off the icicle but at once a large, heavy guard prowling outside brutally snatched it away from me. 'Warum?' I asked him in my poor German. 'Hier ist kein warum,' (there is no why here) he replied, pushing me inside with a shove.

I also read of the importance of shoes in this place:

> Death begins with the shoes; for most of us, they show them-
> selves to be instruments of torture, which after a few hours of
> marching cause painful sores which become fatally infected.
> Whoever has them is forced to walk as if he was dragging a
> convict's chain . . . he arrives last everywhere, and everywhere
> he receives blows. He cannot escape if they run after him; his
> feet swell and the more they swell, the more the friction with
> the wood and the cloth of the shoes becomes insupportable.
> Then only the 'hospital' is left: but to enter the 'hospital' with
> a diagnosis of '*dicke Füsse*' (swollen feet) is extremely danger-
> ous, because it is well known to all, and especially to the SS,
> that here there is no cure for that complaint . . .

Levi then details the 200 different work squads (*Kommandos*)
which the prisoners are divided into – electricians, carpenters,
mechanics, etc. – and the German and Polish civilians who oversee
the slave labour. In such a place it is absurd to think about a future.
All energy is put into somehow getting through the day. To think is
a form of torture. It is an endless nowness, in which human beings
rapidly become slaves:

> Here I am, then, on the bottom. One learns quickly enough to
> wipe out the past and the future when one is forced to. A fort-
> night after my arrival I already had the prescribed hunger,
> that chronic hunger unknown to free men, which makes one
> dream at night, and settles in all the limbs of one's body. I have
> already learnt not to let myself be robbed, and in fact if I find
> a spoon lying around, a piece of string, a button which I can
> acquire without danger of punishment, I pocket them and
> consider them mine by full right. On the back of my feet I
> already have the numb sores that will not heal. I push wag-
> ons, I work with a shovel, I turn rotten in the rain, I shiver in
> the wind; already my own body is no longer mine: my belly
> is swollen, my limbs emaciated, my face is thick in the morn-

ing, hollow in the evening; some of us have yellow skin, others grey. When we do not meet for a few days we hardly recognise each other.

We Italians had decided to meet every Sunday evening in a corner of the *Lager*, but we stopped it at once, because it was too sad to count our numbers and find fewer each time, and to see each other ever more deformed and more squalid. And it was so tiring to walk those few steps and then, meeting each other, to remember and to think. It was better not to think.

These words, speaking of the barbarity of what happened here, exactly here, sixty years ago – the terror, the physical exhaustion, the losing of humanity, these words spill into the winter dusk. Being here, in January, it is impossible to imagine that through a winter like this, the prisoners only had clogs on their feet, ragged trousers and not even the coats that we have (which we are shivering through) – just thin jackets. And that day after day after day they were worked to death.

A mother goes past, wheeling her bicycle, her daughter looks back at us, these two visitors from elsewhere, strange hats, shivering under the tree, reading aloud. We walk on. I begin to see houses, some of them small farms, which have incorporated what were long, brick buildings, and made them into barns, outbuildings. Surely the remnants of the blocks where the exhausted prisoners tried to sleep. I take more photographs, coming to the end of another roll of film. I read again, we walk on, another photograph, another flurry of snow. The light meter falls lower and lower; I'm having to go down to a sixteenth, an eighth of a second. I must try and be still, but my hand is shaky. I rest it on signposts and tree branches, desperate to capture this moment, to try and wrest some visibility back from this place. We turn a corner, heading back to the beginning of the hamlet. I try to wind the film spool on but there is no resistance. A sinking feeling of panic. The film has snapped, probably the freezing temperature. So even the camera now has joined the dusk and the snow and history in conspiring to erase this site.

There is one final reading I want to do. At the corner of a low farm building I read Primo Levi's account of his interview with Dr Pannwitz, a senior German chemist working at Buna, examining Levi to see if his chemical knowledge might be useful to the Reich, useful to IG Farben.* I have always found this the most shocking moment in the book – the meeting of two men who, in civil society, in peacetime, would have treated each other as colleagues, as equals, yet here, during the war, Pannwitz looks at Levi as a scientist might look at a monkey – how can this animal be used?

> Pannwitz is tall, thin, blond; he has eyes, hair and nose as all Germans ought to have them, and sits formidably behind a complicated writing table. I, *Häftling* [prisoner] 174517, stand in his office, which is a real office, shining, clean and ordered, and I feel that I would leave a dirty stain whatever I touched. When he finished writing, he raised his eyes and looked at me. From that day I have thought about Doctor Pannwitz many times and in many ways. I have asked myself how he really functioned as a man; how he filled his time, outside of the Polymerisation and the Indo-German conscience; above all when I was once more a free man, I wanted to meet him again, not from a spirit of revenge, but merely from a curiosity about the human soul. Because that look was not one between two men; and if I had known how completely to explain the nature of that look, which came as if across the glass window of an aquarium between two beings who live in different worlds, I would also have explained the essence of the great insanity of the third Germany.

---

* The interview took place in the office of the Polymerisation Laboratory, Bau 939. Reading this account recently, I suddenly remembered the curious painted triple numbers on the buildings in the chemical complex we walked past.

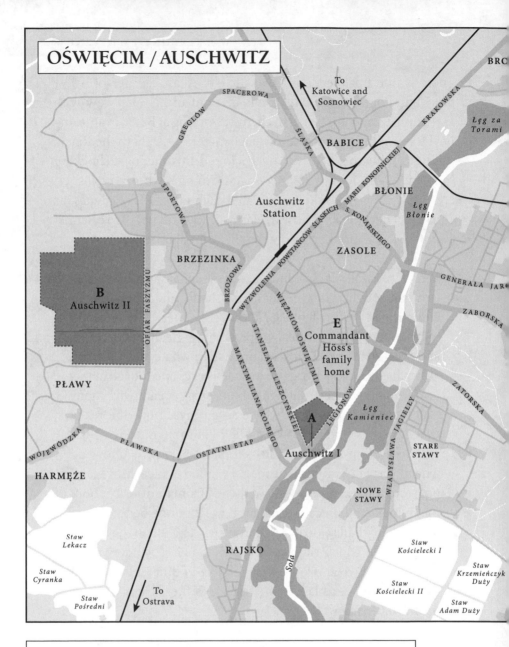

OŚWIĘCIM / AUSCHWITZ

To Katowice and Sosnowiec

BRO

Łęg za Torami

SPACEROWA

GREGLOW

SPORTOWA

ŚLĄSKA

BABICE

KRAKOWSKA

BŁONIE

Łęg Błonie

Auschwitz Station

WYZWOLENIA POWSTAŃCÓW ŚLĄSKICH MARII KONOPNICKIEJ

S. KONARSKIEGO

ZASOLE

GENERAŁA JAR

BRZEZINKA

BRZOZOWA

WIĘŹNIÓW OŚWIĘCIMIA

ZABORSKA

B
Auschwitz II

OFIAR FASZYZMU

STANISŁAWY LESZCZYŃSKIEJ

E
Commandant Höss's family home

LEGIONÓW

ZATORSKA

PŁAWY

MAKSYMILIANA KOLBEGO

Łęg Kamieniec

WŁADYSŁAWA JAGIEŁŁY

STARE STAWY

WOJEWÓDZKA

PŁAWSKA

OSTATNI ETAP

A

Auschwitz I

NOWE STAWY

HARMĘŻE

Staw Lekacz

Sola

RAJSKO

Staw Kościelecki I

Staw Krzemieńczyk Duży

Staw Cyranka

Staw Pośredni

To Ostrava

Staw Kościelecki II

Staw Adam Duży

A Auschwitz I (main camp)

B Auschwitz II (Birkenau)

C Auschwitz III (Monowitz) – (run by the SS & IG Farben)

D The Buna Complex – IG Farben's chemical plant, built by Monowitz slave labourers in 1942 – today still run as a chemicals plant by Firma Chemiczna Dwory

E Commandant Höss's family home

F Chemical workers' estate – (for IG Farben civilian employees)

G Monument to the Buna slave labourers

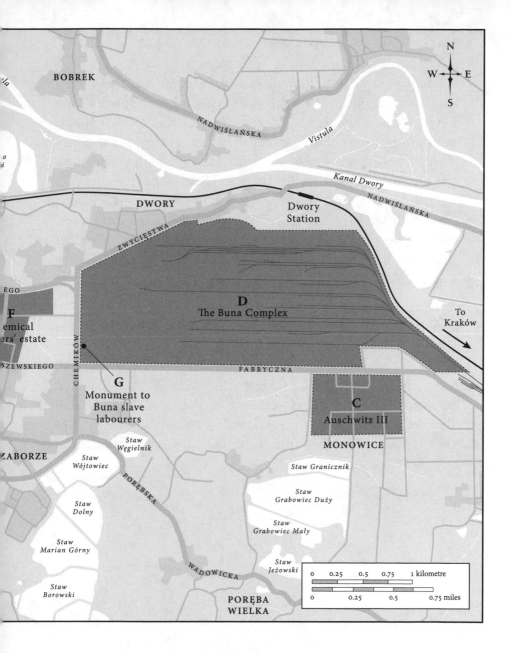

BOBREK

NADWIŚLAŃSKA

Vistula

Kanal Dwory

NADWIŚLAŃSKA

DWORY

Dwory
Station

ZWYCIĘSTWA

EGO

F
emical
rs' estate

SZEWSKIEGO

CHEMIKÓW

D
The Buna Complex

To
Kraków

FABRYCZNA

G
Monument to
Buna slave
labourers

C
Auschwitz III

MONOWICE

ZABORZE

Staw
Węgielnik

Staw
Wójtowiec

PORĘBSKA

Staw
Dolny

Staw
Marian Górny

Staw Granicznik

Staw
Grabowiec Duży

Staw
Grabowiec Mały

WADOWICKA

Staw
Jeżowski

Staw
Borowski

PORĘBA
WIELKA

| 0 | 0.25 | 0.5 | 0.75 | 1 kilometre |

| 0 | 0.25 | 0.5 | 0.75 miles |

N
W — E
S

It is dark now, we begin to walk back towards the main road. I am suddenly overwhelmed – if this is all that is left of the place Primo Levi and tens of thousands suffered, the place of *If This Is a Man*, a book central to our understanding of the last century, where one of the defining experiences of humanity and inhumanity happened, then what hope is there for others? Those whose agonies will never be filmed, those whose words will never be heard, let alone published? We have only traces of fragments of lived experience. The fragility of everything is stupefying, overwhelming. We sit at the side of the road, in the snow, with no more words, appalled by this place.

We get back to the main road, shivering, shocked by the drop in temperature that has come with the dark, it must now be minus fifteen, maybe colder. Miraculously, after a few minutes, a bus appears. We flag it down and soon are heading back into Oświęcim. I take my gloves off, fumble for our water bottle, but the liquid has turned to ice. If Primo Levi were here, he would be able to explain the precise nature of the chemical process which has occurred over the last hours. Warmth returns to our fingers. The bus thunders on into the night.

16

The Patience of a Hand and a Pencil

Oświęcim–Lodz–Koło–Chelmno–Rzuchów

5 January 2004, Oświęcim to Lodz

Back at the station in Oświęcim, J. and I retrieve our packs from the left luggage and then are disturbed to find that our connecting train to Sosnowiec does not seem to be on the departures board. This is where we pick up our connection to Lodz, and the next two days we have an extremely tight schedule so we must reach Lodz tonight. We check with the woman behind the misted-up information window, but, in response to us pointing to our printout with the Sosnowiec train time shown, she simply shakes her head rather pityingly. The train does not exist, or at least it isn't running this evening. We decide to get a taxi these thirty kilometres or so. Getting into the warmth of the car, exhaustion suddenly hits us. We've pushed ourselves to the limits today, we don't even have the energy to talk. Just the comforting sound of the windscreen wipers against the snow, and beyond the glow of collieries and the heavy industry of Silesia.

Our driver has taken to his task of getting us to Sosnowiec on time with relish – overtaking everything in our path using a technique of flashing his headlights in warning as we go. With the freezing conditions this is almost certainly dangerous, but, in our deep tiredness, we're in that zone beyond worry where fatalism takes over.

We make our connection and sleep the couple of hours to Lodz. As we edge into the city at night I try to remember fragments from *The Chronicle of the Lodz Ghetto* that made such an impression on me as a student twenty years ago, but can only recall the image of the crazed, tyrannical figure of Chaim Rumkowski, the Nazi-appointed chairman of the ghetto's Jewish Council, who commanded a 600-strong personal police force, demanded that stamps were created in his image and was insistent on being transported around his tiny, doomed kingdom in a carriage drawn by a skeletal horse.

There's deeper snow here, further north. We edge along icy pavements from the station towards the main street and find a hotel, faded art deco touches, paint peeling. Our room is decorated in the kind of thick 1960s oranges and purples with swirling lampshades and wallpaper that has gone so far out of fashion that it once again has a kind of aesthetic appeal. A hot shower, then I'm keen to find a restaurant but J. says he's 'too tired to eat'. Not a combination of words I've ever heard from him before. He's gone into a strange, withdrawn mood, where I cannot reach him, which troubles me. Maybe I've underestimated the effect of these days, not just the physical demands but the emotional impact too.

But, in the end, we do go out. The city of Lodz seems to centre on Ulica Piotrkowska, a single, extremely long and straight street – the longest in Europe, we learn later. Just round the corner we come across a series of large stars and names marked on the pavement outside a cinema. Lodz has always been the centre of the outstanding Polish film industry. There's one for Wajda, and here's one for Kieslowski. I kneel down and kiss the star to try and make J. laugh. This is supposed to be a lively, student city but it's almost totally dead tonight, out of term-time, presumably. We ask about eating in the few bars that are still open but it's 11 p.m. now and we just collect shakes of heads wherever we go. We end up in a subterranean Irish bar, adorned with photographs of visiting world leaders who have, rather improbably, made it here – Gerhard Schröder, Madeleine Albright and François Mitterrand. But there's only J. and I tonight and we're drinking extortionately expensive Guinness and trying to understand what we've experienced today. J.'s withdrawn-ness wears off as the Guinness begins to do its job.

Both of us are still amazed by the fact that the vast chemicals plant which IG Farben built in the war, at least a large section of it, is not only still there at Oświęcim, but is still operating. And we wonder at how such a reality seems to have gone unnoticed. IG Farben, at that time the second-largest transnational corporation in the world, and Auschwitz their greatest single investment of the 1940s. And the continuity of IG Farben – this is what has not been looked at in detail yet – the continuity of the capital and, in many cases, the personnel. Flowing out of that single corporation – BASF, Bayer, Agfa, Hoechst and Interhandel (later taken over by UBS as we've already seen). Hadn't Rudy Kennedy dug up information in the late 1990s that BASF were still paying out pensions to employees who had worked at IG Farben in the war years? Some of whom had even worked at Buna, organising the slave labour, overseeing Rudy Kennedy, Freddie Knoller, Primo Levi and the other thousands of prisoners there.

*

6 January 2004 (Epiphany), Lodz to Koło

Wake with a hacking cough and a temperature, I don't know how much sleep I got, but it seemed like a long, feverish night. The effects of the last days are really catching up now. Not good timing, but I will not let my physical state interfere with what needs to be done over the next day and a half.

J. is worried about whether we can reach Chelmno and still connect with our Berlin train tomorrow lunchtime, and is making sceptical comments about our plans. 'But we *have* to do this,' I say. 'Whatever it takes.' I don't like his doubt, and my Taurean stubbornness takes over, drawing on extra reserves of adrenaline and sheer determination. But I am aware that this can-do spirit that I'm giving off this morning is at odds with my weakened physical state. And, perhaps unfairly, I'm frustrated with J. I feel I'm having to generate this energy for both of us, when, if I was at home I would have dosed myself with medicine by now and gone to bed for a couple of days. I'd appreciate some encouragement, some reassurance, but I don't think it's going to happen today. I feel I've probably overestimated his capacity to take in what we've seen, read and experienced over the last days.

A breakfast of powdered coffee and chicory and yellowing rolls. An elderly priest sits in a corner of the very brown, high-ceilinged room, lugubriously reading the paper. Piped piano music does not lighten the mood. Then out in search of information about Lodz and how we can get to Chelmno. The main street is much more impressive today, wider than it seemed last night and crowded, bustling. In one direction you can see it continue straight for a mile or more, the other way there's a slight incline so it dips over the horizon. Very ornate wrought-iron shop frontages and art deco designs, expressions of the former wealth of the city, all based on its textiles industry. The 'Manchester of Poland' as it was once called, and as populous and productive as its English cousin at its peak in the 1930s. In 1939 Lodz had 750,000 inhabitants and the engine of this thriving city was a community of 200,000 Jews. Almost entirely eradicated. Of this original population (the second largest after Warsaw), Gilbert tells us that only a hundred Jews survive today.

We walk along these streets and try to imagine the emptiness here on the day after the ghetto was established – the first in Poland, created in February 1940. And then the even greater emptiness after the clearance of the ghetto in autumn 1944. The heart of the city simply gone. We do not really have the ability to understand such a thing. Or to imagine the twelve-year-old Simon Srebnik here surrounded by death: 'All I'd seen was corpses . . . in the Lodz Ghetto I saw people take a step and fall dead. I thought that's how things were, it was normal. I'd walk the streets of Lodz and in a hundred metres I'd see two hundred bodies.'

In a small bookshop just off the main street, we buy maps and books on the Lodz Ghetto (there's nothing on Chelmno), and the proprietor draws a map of where to find the tourist office.

There an extremely enthusiastic young couple try to help us. We explain the nature of our historical research. Not many travellers come to this city, certainly not in January, and fewer still visit Chelmno by public transport. Maps are examined, phone directories consulted. There isn't anywhere to stay in Chelmno itself and there are no official hotels even in Koło, the nearest town, but after a while they manage to find a room above a restaurant there. And there's a bus that leaves in an hour. We talk to this couple about their background, both are history graduates, and ask them how much Lodz commemorates its Jewish past. Only in the last few years has an effort really been made. There is a ghetto archive office and a small museum now that can be visited – if we were here for longer they could arrange for it to be opened for us. There will also be commemorations in summer 2005 for the sixtieth anniversary of the end of the war. On the way back to our hotel to pick up our bags we notice that in the pedestrianised section in the centre of the main street there are tens of thousands of small paving stones, all with names on them. Presumably commemorating the war dead, but it would be interesting to know how many of the stones record those 200,000 Jewish citizens of Lodz.

As we leave the city, the deranged figure of Rumkowski, 'King Chaim' as many Jews in the ghetto sarcastically referred to him, still echoes in our minds, together with the mocking ghost memory of hooves on the Lodz cobbles – Rumkowski in his rickety wooden carriage pulled by a skeletal horse, surrounded by his 'police'. This image of his collusion with Nazism – simultaneously absurd and horrifying. Yet, once again, the urge to simply condemn seems shallow. We are still unable to fully understand the moral morass that the Nazi occupying powers dragged the Jewish authorities into – using a corrupted concept of 'ghetto autonomy' which began by stressing survival through employment and ended up with getting the Jewish authorities to organise the transports of their own people to the extermination camps. I remember how Primo Levi ends his reflection on 'The Grey Zone', with those haunting words about Rumkowski, warning us not to think we would behave so very differently:

> We are all mirrored in Rumkowski, his ambiguity is ours, it is our second nature . . . as . . . described by Isabella in *Measure for Measure*, the Man who, 'dressed in a little brief authority, most ignorant of what he's most assured . . . plays such fantastic tricks before high heaven as make the angels weep.' Like Rumkowski, we too are so dazzled by power and prestige as to forget our essential fragility: willingly or not we come to terms with power, forgetting that we are all in the ghetto, that the ghetto is walled in, that outside the ghetto reign the lords of death and that close by the train is waiting.

*

Soon we're sitting at the back of a bus heading out of Lodz to the north-west, and reading Martin Gilbert again, our companion on this long journey. Flat lands fringed by lines of willows. Here and there a barn, a farm. All the towns and villages we pass through over the next hour were once primarily Jewish communities – Zgierz (5,000 Jews killed in the first months of the war), Orzoków (more than 2,500 Jews gassed at Chelmno), Łęczyca (all 1,700 Jews gassed at Chelmno in April 1942), Dąbie (all 975 Jews of this village were driven to Chelmno and gassed in the Saurer trucks on 14 December 1941, a week after the first killings there). Looking at the map, an image of a vast inverted funnel of killing comes into our minds – with Lodz at the widest point, to the south-east, and then all the intermediate towns and villages further north and west being channelled towards the narrow point of the settlement of Chelmno.

As the bus stops in the little square of Grabow I have a strange feeling that I've seen this place before. Later I remember that it was here that Lanzmann recorded his interview with an elderly Polish couple:

> 'Barbara, tell this couple they live in a lovely house. Do they agree? Do they think it's a lovely house?'

'Yes.'

'Tell me about the decoration of this house, the doors. What does it mean?'

'People used to do carvings like that.'

'Did they decorate it that way?'

'No, it was the Jews again. The door's a good century old.'

'Did Jews own this house?'

'Yes, all these houses.'

Dusk approaches and so too does the village of Chelmno, seventeen years after first seeing it in *Shoah*. On our left the bulbous spire of the church comes into view, a dip, and then, that must be the place, just there. The site of the old castle, where the people were put into the *gaswagen*. It's gone in a couple of seconds as we drive by – it looks quite unremarkable, like a disused car park, with some gates and a prefab building at the front. There doesn't appear to be any memorial at all here. We'll return tomorrow. The bus drives on, through the forest of Rzuchów and finally we arrive in Koło. Some ten-storey blocks of flats on the edge of town, but the centre is older. And obviously completely off any tourist route. As we get out of the bus gaggles of teenagers giggle and point at the two backpackers, amazed that anyone would visit their parochial town.

We eventually find our restaurant, run by a neat, middle-aged woman, slightly nervous, and her teenage son, who shows us to a room on the floor above. It's a semi-official place, there are several rooms up here, and a single shower at the end of the corridor. But the room's more like somebody's apartment than a hotel room; at one end there's a long dining table, there are heavy glass cabinets on two sides and twin beds. The boy, who speaks more English, confirms that we can eat there later on and also books us a taxi for 6.45 tomorrow morning. We've realised the only way we can visit Chelmno properly, walk to the Rzuchów forest and still make it to Konin by midday to catch our Berlin train, is by using taxis.

Again a sense of running against the clock, making use of every hour we have left. I'm still feeling pretty lousy but the adrenaline is taking over now. Why don't we try to walk to Powiercie this evening before supper? This was the original arrival point for Jews and Roma during the first phase of Chelmno's existence as a centre of extermination from 1941 to 1942, before the railway link, which today no longer exists, was built from Koło to Chelmno village. It's only about two kilometres out of town to the south-east.

*

Of all the sites of the Holocaust, Chelmno is the one that poses the greatest challenge to our understanding. The fact that the most detailed publication available on Chelmno, by Manfred Struck, is called *Chelmno/Kulmhof: Ein vergessener Ort des Holocaust?* (*Chelmno: A Forgotten Site of the Holocaust?*) is itself revealing. As is the fact that there is still no English translation of this work twenty years after its publication. So, over the next hours, J. and I try to piece together what we can about how this *Vernichtungslager* actually worked. The complex reality is that what is called 'Chelmno extermination camp' did not exist only at that geographical location, Chelmno village – but rather operated over three distinct sites, nine kilometres apart, as can be seen in the map opposite.

The complexity of operations at Chelmno has defeated many historians – perhaps because it's only by coming to this place, by walking between the sites, that you can understand how all the aspects fit together. Our guide for so much of this trip has been somebody with an almost encyclopedic knowledge of the Holocaust – Professor Martin Gilbert, yet even he seems to stumble when he reaches Chelmno. He writes the following in *Holocaust Journey*, which J. and I are confused about: 'Chelmno. This is the village from which the camp got its name, though the camp itself is just over six kilometers to the north-west. At a later point in the history of the camp, when it was re-opened for one month in 1944, the deportees were held here in Chelmno, in the local and somewhat dilapidated castle.'

408

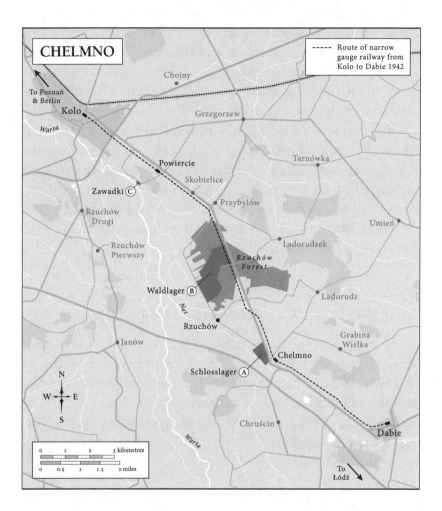

A: the '*Schlosslager*' (the Castle camp) in Chelmno village (where the SS *kommando* and the *gaswagen* were based);

B: the '*Waldlager*' (the Forest camp) in Rzuchów forest (where the bodies were taken in the *gaswagen* and dumped in mass graves, and later incinerated);

C: the large brick mill at Zawadki (just south of Powiercie), which was used as a holding facility for up to 1,000 deportees at a time.

The *Schlosslager* in Chelmno village was the centre of operations – this was where the SS officers and *kommando* were based, this was where the *Sonderkommando* was housed, this was the place where the *gaswagen* queued up to collect their loads of deportees, who had been transported to the *Schloss*. In 1944, the deportees were indeed held in Chelmno village, but not at the *Schloss* (which had been destroyed in 1943), but in the Catholic church next door. One of the most devastating realities of what happened at Chelmno is the knowledge that in July 1944 thousands of deported Jews spent their final nights in the Chelmno church, and then the *gaswagen* backed up to the church doors to take them to their deaths.

There were two distinct phases in Chelmno's operational existence as an extermination centre – the first was from 7 December 1941 to 7 April 1943; the second ran from 23 June 1944 to 18 January 1945.

At the beginning of the first phase, in December 1941, most of the victims were Jews from the towns and villages closest to Chelmno (like the places we'd driven through earlier today). The majority of them were simply transported on trucks directly to the *Schloss* at Chelmno, but if there were too many for the *gaswagen* to deal with immediately, the deportees would be taken to the mill at Zawadki, just outside Koło, and imprisoned there overnight, without food or water. When larger numbers started to be transported in early 1942 – for example, 5,000 Roma from the '*Zigeunerlager*' (the Gypsy camp) in Lodz in January 1942, and 10,000 foreign Jews who had been housed in the Lodz Ghetto in January and February 1942 – they would then be sent by train to Koło, and afterwards on to a smaller, single-gauge railway to Powiercie, two kilometres from Koło. From here they would subsequently either be transported straight to the *Schloss* to be killed, or on to Zawadki, to be held overnight. Eventually, in July 1942, the single-gauge railway was extended from Powiercie to Chelmno village, and so most of the deportees arrived at the *Schloss* by train.

By late summer 1942, with well over 100,000 Jews and Roma already murdered and buried in mass graves, the SS realised that the combination of decomposing bodies and the hot summer meant a major possibility of epidemics breaking out, and so the decision was made to build open-air crematoria pits in the *Waldlager* in Rzuchów forest, and from this time on, all the bodies from the *gaswagen* were burnt. Meanwhile, the Jewish *Sonderkommando* were forced to dig up the decomposing bodies so that they too could be incinerated.

By early 1943, with the other (more efficient) extermination camps such as Treblinka and Birkenau now working at full capacity, and the vast majority of the local Jewish population already exterminated, the orders came to close down the Chelmno operation. All signs of both camps were to be eradicated, because the SS didn't want to leave any traces of their crimes behind. The *Schloss* in Chelmno was blown up on 7 April 1943, and the crematoria in the *Waldlager* were also destroyed; the remaining bodies were burnt, and then the bones and ashes dumped in the River Warta. When this process took too long, the authorities purchased a *Knochenmuhle* (a bone-crushing machine) from Schriever and Company in Hamburg.* The local *gauleiter*, Arthur Greiser, and the SS camp commandant, Bothmann, organised a special dinner at the Hotel Riga in Koło to thank the SS officers in the *kommando* 'on behalf of the Führer for the work . . . done in Kulmhof' (the German name for Chelmno). All SS men in the *kommando* and the police guards received four weeks' special leave, and an invitation to stay at Greiser's country estate.

However, this was not the end of Chelmno/Kulmhof as a killing centre – there was to be a second phase. Bothmann's *kommando* returned from the Balkans a year later, in May 1944, to reopen a

---

* Information about the purchase of the *Knochenmuhle* from Germany, and an earlier attempt to get Rumkowski to supply one from the Lodz Ghetto, comes from Raul Hilberg, *The Destruction of the European Jews*, in the chapter 'Erasure'.

smaller extermination operation to deal with the last of the Jews from the Lodz Ghetto – the last ghetto which had been producing war supplies for Germany. Because the *Schloss* had been destroyed, the church in Chelmno was now used as the main 'reception centre' for deportees. And in the forest new buildings and crematoria pits were constructed. The Jews were then either put in *gaswagen* at the church, or transported to the forest camp, made to undress and give up their valuables there, before being forced into the *gaswagen* and killed. Their bodies were burnt immediately afterwards. Between 23 June and 14 July, 7,196 Jews from the Lodz Ghetto were murdered in this second phase of Chelmno's operations.

After mid-July 1944 the SS deported the remaining Jews from Lodz directly to Auschwitz-Birkenau, so operations at Chelmno were shut down for the second time, and the *gaswagen* were sent back to Berlin. In September the SS began another attempt to remove evidence of the exterminations, and when the *Sonderkommando* had completed this task, forty of them were executed. The forty-seven remaining Jewish members of the last Chelmno *Sonderkommando* were executed by the SS on the night of 17 January 1945, as the Soviet army was approaching. Miraculously, a fifteen-year-old boy, shot in the head, managed to survive. This was Simon Srebnik, whose unforgettable testimony opens Lanzmann's film *Shoah*.

*

We set off alongside the main road we had come in on earlier this evening, but it's pitch-black now and extremely cold again. We wrap scarves around our faces, only leaving slits for the eyes. Slipping on the ice, passed by thundering lorries, after about half an hour we reach a turn-off to the right. This must be where the first railway terminated at the village of Powiercie, and then the deportees would have been taken from the trains and forced down the lane we're now walking, towards the river, and the large brick mill at the hamlet of Zawadki where up to 1,000 people could be held overnight. The following day they would have been transported in trucks to the *Schlosslager* in Chelmno village, where they were told they were going to have baths, and be deloused, before being sent on to a work camp. Moments later, they were forced into the *gaswagen*, and murdered during the five-kilometre journey to Rzuchów forest. In the middle of the forest, teams of *Sonderkommandos* then worked clearing the trucks, extracting gold teeth and then burying the dead in mass graves, in later years burning them on vast pyres.

Beyond any houses now, the lane leads through a pine wood. Our talking thins to a trickle. There's no way I'd walk here alone. It feels heavily sinister. I register the age of the trees; some of the more massive pines would have been saplings in the 1940s. Eventually we're through the trees and arrive at a bend in the road. There are a couple of weak street lights here that cast a cold glow and we can make out a very ugly square building that was formerly the Gestapo headquarters; now, as Gilbert tells us, a peasant family lives there. Quite unimaginable to live in such a place. A little further, there's another bend in the road, where the River Warta comes to meet it, and four or five more houses. We're reading Gilbert by torchlight and we realise this lumpy patch of rubble and rough ground between the lane and the river must be where the mill once stood – there are only foundations now and outcrops of brick here and there, which we can see by scraping the snow away with our feet. We scramble over to the river and look back. The desolation of this place seems more total even than Auschwitz, even than Monowitz, if that's possible. There, some buildings have survived; here there is not even a wall. No record, no trace of what was suffered here, where, each day, up to a thousand human beings were crowded together in their last hours on earth. Some on nights like this, with the temperature well below freezing; some in the summer when thirst would have been desperate. Would the guards have walked the few yards from the river to the mill to stop these cries or would they have regarded it as a waste of time, considering the families packed together in the mill only had hours left to live?

I try to document this place, though doubting any of the photographs will come out. The flash comes on, a dog starts barking, but nobody comes out of their houses. Eighty-two children from the

Czech village of Lidice were here in June 1942, having already been separated from their parents following the reprisal massacre of their village that occured after Heydrich's assassination in Prague. Simon Srebnik was here too as a child. Having seen his father shot in front of him in the Lodz Ghetto, his mother having been gassed on arrival in Chelmno, he was only saved by his singing voice. And there, before us in the moonlight, is the river where he sang. Where the young Srebnik would row along with his SS guard, singing Polish folk songs, the guard teaching him Prussian marching songs in reply.

We walk back into Koło along a track that more or less follows the course of the river. The houses begin again, many of them brand-new villas with balconies and festooned with chains of Christmas lights. We're the only people eating in our restaurant when we get back. We sit by a grand fireplace but there's no fire, just neat stacks of logs that look like they've been there for years. Just for decoration. But perhaps it's just as well as the heating is on full blast and is making us sweat. We devour soup and some kind of beef stew and look at maps for tomorrow. Slivovitz upstairs, an almost hot shower, then bed. Food, drink, warmth, cleanliness, shelter, rest. The diurnal assumptions of our lives. Until they're not there any more.

*

7 January 2004, Koło to Chelmno, Chelmno to Rzuchów

Terrible night, hardly any sleep at all, sweating profusely, impossible to get comfortable. Whenever I lay my head down it triggered a rasping cough, which seemed totally unaffected by the almost continuous consumption of Polish lozenges I'd bought yesterday. Also worried that all this would be disturbing J.'s sleep, so trying to smother the sound of coughing in the pillow. A relief when the morning came. Packed up, coffees downstairs and our taxi turns up a few minutes before 7 a.m. The driver, greying hair and a long moustache, introduces himself as Krystof, shakes our hands formally. We make sure our host translates very clearly that we need to go to Chelmno, and then we'll need to be picked up from the memorial site in the forest at exactly 11 a.m. to get to Konin in time for our train. Lots of nodding, smiles, yes, it's all clear.

As we're driving out of Koło, I wonder whether it's possible to fit in going back to Zawadki where we were last night so I can get better photographs. We manage to communicate this to Krystof, who agrees with a nod, *'Kein problem, kein problem.'* As we drive down the lane, he looks in the mirror, with anxious eyes, and asks us: *'Vater? Mutter? Grossvater? Hier tod? Schmerz.'*

I am touched by Krystof's concern that we might have lost relatives here. Perhaps more so because of the antisemitism that may have surrounded him growing up. We shake our heads, and try to explain *'Historia'*, and mime the action of writing. This primitive method of communication must work because he nods and says, *'Ah, bucher, ja?'* We get out for a few minutes and I take some photographs at the site of the old brick mill:

When we get back to the taxi Krystof is on his mobile. He seems to be arranging something, he keeps looking up at us. When he finishes, he explains in his halting German that he knows a man who can help with our research. We gather that this man has a small museum at Chelmno, and will be there in thirty minutes to open it up, especially for us! We thank him warmly, and try to imagine a London taxi driver taking this kind of trouble with two foreigners. We drive on, south-eastwards, along this arrow-straight road through the whitened fields, fringed by the willows following the River Ner – which joins the Warta close to the site of the mill at Zawadki.

Through the forest, Krystof slows down to point out the place (the large car park by the main memorial site) where we need to be picked up in three hours. He nods and points reassuringly to eleven on his watch. Out of the forest and on towards Chelmno village. I'm absorbed by the landscape, as I was when I first saw images of it in *Shoah*. The same view the drivers of the trucks would have had returning from having delivered their loads, on their way to collect the next. That first short journey on 7 December 1941, what would have gone through the drivers' minds? As they were shown, once the people were inside the back of the Saurer, how to connect the exhaust to the hole in the bottom of the truck? As they drove away from the *Schloss*, what sounds would have penetrated to the driver and his passenger in the front of the truck? How long did it take for such work to become routine? And then would they have started to look at this surrounding landscape more closely? As the seasons changed and the trees exchanged their leaves for frost. Or would they have thought more about their bonuses (generous), holiday leave (lengthy) and the local girls in Koło they'd met the evening before?

We park just inside the gates of the former castle, in front of the prefab building we saw yesterday as we drove through the village. Krystof's friend hasn't arrived yet so we walk over to the church. The same church that appears in *Shoah* when Simon Srebnik is reunited with the villagers from the war years who remember his singing. The shocking moment when some of these local people begin to say that, well, of course it was sad what happened, but after all, the Jews were the richest and they did kill Jesus. And then a Polish man relates a tale of a rabbi addressing his community of Jews near Warsaw, and, supposedly, telling them that because they had condemned Jesus to death, perhaps it is right that 'the blood should fall on our heads.' And throughout all of this Srebnik stares straight ahead, a strange and haunting smile on that face that has suffered beyond any human limit. It was here as well, in summer 1944, when the *Schloss* had been destroyed, that the church was used to imprison Jews, and that the *gaswagen* backed up to the church doors – exactly where we are standing – and the SS guards forced the people into the vans. A despicable union of corrupted Catholicism and fascism – united in the shared faith of antisemitism.

Krystof is now waving to us, the man has arrived. We're introduced – this is Zdzisław Lorek, fifty years old, maybe a little more, bearded, long grey hair in a pony tail, and darting blue eyes of intense seriousness. He radiates an urgency, an extraordinary presence. He has no English, and even less German than Krystof, but despite the lack of a shared language, the next hour or so is quite remarkable. He unlocks the prefab hut, and waves us inside as Krystof drives off. The main room is a rectangle approximately six yards long and four yards across, but almost every square inch of the walls is covered with maps, photographs and objects he's painstakingly collected over many years. It seems like his life's work, this excavation, and it's clear that it's all been done on minimal resources without much funding from government or any other source. All the objects and photographs are labelled, meticulously, in sloping, handwritten capital letters. On the first wall he shows us on a map that there was a single-gauge railway that was extended from Koło and Powiercie to Chelmno in summer 1942. He shows us an aerial photograph from this time and points out where the track used to run close to Chelmno village.

In the middle of the room there are glass cabinets with objects found on this site – bent spoons, passport photographs, children's toys, glass bottles. On the facing wall he points to a diagram of a lorry and a list of companies that manufactured the trucks used for the *gaswagen* – Saurer is there, but also Opel and Magirus (both German companies, the latter based in Ulm). I'm rapidly noting down other details, a 'Muzeum Motoryzacji i Techniki' in Warsaw which seems to be Zdzisław's source. And books which need to be followed up too. Then he's showing us photographs of some of the SS personnel involved and I recognise Walter Rauff. I suddenly remember all the material I've brought along from my research at the Wiener Library and soon pull it out and give it to Zdzisław. I can easily get more copies. He's delighted to have this material, shaking my hand repeatedly and looking through the pages hungrily. We communicate in single words, in a kind of pidgin hinterland between German and English, but we understand each other – '*Rauff Obituarie?*' '*Ja* The Times, *Zeitung angliski* – *Rauff tod in Chile, Santiago*,' and then I point to the date – 1984.

Zdzisław then gestures for us to come into his tiny office in the next room. A single chair, a single table, a single-bar electric fire. And everywhere, folders full of material, papers, photographs he's been researching on Chelmno for the last years. On the perpetrators, on the victims, on the (very few) survivors. He starts to show us a folder containing the names and known data on the SS guards and drivers stationed here – most of them from the Prinz Eugen Waffen SS unit – all written out carefully, in pencil, in his neat capital letters:

BURMEISTER, Walter (driver)
GIELOW, Hermann Friedrich Oskar (driver)
LAABS, Gustav (driver)
HERING, Oskar (driver)
HÄFELE, Alois (guard)
MÖBIUS, Kurt (guard)
HEINL, Karl (guard)
MEIER, Martin (assistant driver)
BOCK, Walter (guard)
BURSTINGER, Erwin (*gaswagen* supervisor)
KÖNIG, Bruno
PILLER, Walter (deputy commandant)

There's also Srebnik's evidence here from one of the trials (session 66/document T/1299). There's a newspaper article from 31 March 1963, reporting the outcome of a Chelmno Trial in Bonn, where Laabs and Häfele were given fifteen-year sentences (with hard labour), and Burmeister, Möbius and Heinl were given shorter sentences. It seems there had been another, earlier, trial in Poland, in Lodz, in 1945, after which Piller and Gielow were executed. There's also information about a survivor I hadn't heard of – Mordechai Zurawski. Lanzmann states at the opening of *Shoah* that 'of the 400,000 men, women and children [sent to Chelmno] only two came out alive: Mordechai Podchlebnik and Simon Srebnik', but this appears to challenge that statement.* And Gilbert also relates the testimony of another Chelmno survivor – Yakov Grojanowski, whose story I'll relate in a moment. Zdzisław is now pressing the book we'd heard about into my hands: *Chelmno/Kulmhof, Ein vergessener Ort des Holocaust?* (*Chelmno: A Forgotten Site of the Holocaust?*).

---

* See chapter notes for further information about the survivors of Chelmno.

No computers, no scanning, not even a photocopier here. Just a staggering sense of this man's single intent, this man's singular determination that memory shall survive in this place. And at this moment I think back to Dr Kastelmann at Saurer's office in the Swiss lakeside town, 'We've got a history, but we don't live on this history . . . it's a completely different company than it used to be. We don't live in the past'. I think about all the corporate executives across the world wanting difficult histories to go away, wanting the past to be buried under a blanket of continual nowness, continual promise of future growth. As John Gray puts it in *False Dawn*, 'Free markets are the most potent solvents of tradition at work in the world today. They set a premium on novelty and a discount on the past. They make of the future an infinite re-run of the present'.

Zdzisław's life and work, these two small rooms, are the utter antithesis to almost everything that our current world tells us to value. In place of forgetting and 'moving on', a tender excavation of the past; instead of speed and software, the patience of a hand and a pencil; in place of promise and PR and profit, the relentless seeking of facts. Because it is the only thing that can now be done for the hundreds of thousands of people who died here. And in his humanity and his understanding that memory and justice are inseparable, I find a hope that moves me so much I have to turn away.

*

Now he's beckoning us outside. We walk maybe fifty yards behind the hut and Zdzisław is scraping the snow away with his hands to show us the foundations of 'Schloss Kulmhof', as the SS called it – the small castle that was the centre of killing operations between December 1941 and April 1943. During this period the cellars were used to house the 'gravedigger squad', the *Sonderkommando* of Jews, including Mordechai Podchlebnick and the young Yakov Grojanowski from the nearby village of Izbica Kujawska, one of the very few men ever to escape this *Sonderkommando*, who then provided only the second direct eyewitness account of the exterminations. When he eventually reached the Warsaw Ghetto at the end of March 1942 and communicated what he'd witnessed, the historian Dr Emanuel Ringelblum urged him to write down every detail.

For fourteen days in Chelmno and Rzuchów forest, Grojanowski was forced to see and do things that are beyond human understanding. His 'job' and the work of those in the *Sonderkommando* was to empty the *gaswagen* of the dead when they arrived at the *Waldlager* in the forest, remove the valuables and then bury the Jews and Roma in mass graves, packing them in tightly to save space. Often the men would come across relatives or friends amongst the corpses they were burying. On the eighth day, Grojanowski heard his parents and his brother had been buried. Of the thirty or so members of this squad, at the end of each day, the eight who had buried the corpses had to lie face down on them, where they would then be shot in the head. Grojanowski arrived here on 6 January 1942 and escaped on 19 January. These words are his words:

> When we came into the second courtyard we were pushed out of the lorry. From here onwards we were in the hands of black-uniformed SS men, all of them high-ranking Reich Germans. We were ordered to hand over all our money and valuables. After this fifteen men were selected, I among them, and taken down to the cellar rooms of the *Schloss*. We fifteen were confined in one room, the remaining fourteen in another. It was still bright daylight outside but down in the cellar it was pitch dark. Some ethnic Germans on the

421

domestic staff provided us with straw. Later a lantern was also brought. At around eight in the evening we received unsweetened black coffee and nothing else. We were all in a depressed mood. One could only think the worst, some were close to tears. We kissed each other and took leave. It was unimaginably cold and we lay down close together. In this manner we spent the whole of the night without shutting our eyes. We only talked about the deporatation of Jews, particularly from Koło and Dabie. The way it looked we had no prospect of ever getting out again.

During the second phase, when Chelmno was reactivated as an extermination centre in summer 1944, the *Schloss* became the main gathering point for deportees, the collecting point for the *gaswagen*. Throughout its existence as a death camp this relatively small site (the *Schloss* and some outbuildings, perhaps a square of no more than 100 yards across by 200 yards long) was surrounded by high wooden fences and heavily armed groups of SS. Franz Schalling was one of these guards:

Our guard post was in front of the castle. The Jews arrived, half dead already, from the ghetto. An SS man stood at the top of the steps . . . Then the Jews were taken down to two big rooms where they undressed, gave up their rings. Then they had to run down more steps, along an underground corridor into the *gaswagen*. They were beaten and screamed. It was frightful, frightful. The trucks were like removal vans, pretty big trucks with double doors at the back . . . the driver fed the pipe into the bottom of the van via a hose . . . there were two trucks, a big one and a small one. From the gate we could hear the revving of the engine. The truck was starting and then it began to move. We opened the gate and they drove off towards the woods. You couldn't hear anything as they drove by.

Some details that Schalling omits to mention are extremely telling because they indicate the level of thought and acute cynicism that went into the psychology of mass murder. Grojanowski tells of the testimony of another prisoner, Mahmens Goldmann, the only person who ever experienced what happened inside the *Schloss* and survived. He'd arrived with his community of Jews from Kłodawa on 11 January 1942, and later related this account to a member of the *Sonderkommando*:

When they arrived at the Schloss they [the Jews of Kłodawa] were at first treated most politely. An elderly German, around sixty, with a long pipe in his mouth, helped the mothers to lift the children down from the lorry. He carried babies so that the mothers could alight more easily and helped dotards [the senile] to reach the *Schloss*. The unfortunate ones were deeply moved by his gentle and mild manner. They were led into a warm room which was heated by two stoves . . . The elderly German and the SS officer spoke to them in this room. They assured them they would be taken to the Lodz Ghetto. There they were expected to work and be productive. The women would look after the household, the children would go to school and so on. In order to get there, however, they had to undergo delousing. For that purpose they needed to undress down to their underwear. Their clothes would be passed through hot steam. Valuables and documents should be tied up in a bundle, and handed over for safekeeping. Whoever had kept banknotes, or had sewn them into their clothes, should take them out without fail, otherwise they would get damaged in the steam oven. Moreover they would all have to take a bath. The elderly German politely requested those present [do so] and opened a door from which 15–20 steps led down. It was terribly cold there. Asked about the cold, the German said gently they should walk a bit further: it would get warmer. They walked along a lengthy corridor to some steps leading to a ramp. The gas van had driven up to the ramp. The polite behaviour ended abruptly and they were all driven into the van with malicious screams.

Zdzisław shows us the exact place where the underground corridor ran, and the steps which ended at the open doors of the
gaswagen. Here terrified human beings were chased, funnelled
into the Saurer lorries waiting, back doors open. It happened
here, in this place. He gestures to signify the truck leaving
towards the front gate. He has been trying to get all of this excavated; the site resembles an archaeological dig. It is bizarre that
despite unprecedented historical focus on the Holocaust there is
not any official memorial at this place where hundreds of thousands were murdered. It appears that the preservation of this site

is down to Zdzisław and a small group of committed volunteers. He walks us over to open pits and trenches a short distance away that he's currently trying to excavate, trying to persuade the Polish government to support this work.

Rusting enamel bowls and twisted metal spoons lie next to piles of earth, pathetic remnants of what happened here. The only traces left. Items now seeing the daylight after sixty years. We walk back towards the front gates and ask him how many thousands of people altogether does he think died at Chelmno. He takes a stick and writes a number in the snow very precisely:

We have to leave now. We thank Zdzisław for everything and we do so with our eyes as well as our words. For an hour, without a common language, we've been able to understand each other. We write down our addresses, promising to send each other further research. More handshakes and then we're walking away. I turn round, as if to check the reality of what we've just experienced, and see Zdzisław climbing back into his hut. We walk away through the front gates and then pause. These are the moments that fate gives when you allow it the chance. The inspiration of this man and his absolute determination for the past to be unburied. It reminds me of something Rebecca West writes in *Black Lamb and Grey Falcon*:

> If during the next million generations there is but one human being born in every generation who will not cease to inquire into the nature of his fate, even while it strips and bludgeons him, some day we shall read the riddle of our universe.

*

We turn left out of the village and walk in silence the four kilometres or so to the edge of Rzuchów forest. The route the *gaswagen* took sixty years ago. The counting of steps through a peaceful winter landscape with a watery sun now emerging. The absoluteness of the darkness then, the press of bodies, the coughing and screaming as the carbon monoxide started to enter the space. What could only have seemed like a nightmare, but no waking up.

This is what the drivers saw through the windscreen as the sounds from the back of the truck began to fade:

After half an hour's walking we've reached the edge of Rzuchów forest. Most of the children, women and men would by now have died. We walk this straight road deeper into the trees, and after another kilometre, turn off to the left, as the *gaswagen* did. We've counted 4,881 yards from the gates of the *Schloss* in Chelmno to this point. Along a forest track now, tall pines and firs on each

side. Mr Falborski (a Polish forestry official working near to the *Waldlager*) remembers seeing the *gaswagen* quite regularly; the local people knew what was going on:

They [the pits] were between 500 and 700 metres from the road, but even if you looked you couldn't see them. [The lorries] went at moderate speed, even slowly. It was a calculated speed, because they had to kill the people inside. If they went too fast, the people weren't quite dead when they arrived [in the forest]. Once one of them skidded on a bend. I arrived half an hour later to see a forest warden named Sendjak. He said 'Too bad you were late, you could have seen an overturned wagon'. The doors had opened and the Jews fell onto the road. They were still alive. A Gestapo man, seeing the Jews crawling, shot them with his revolver. He finished them off. Then they brought the Jews who were working in the woods and they righted the wagon and put the bodies back in.

429

Eventually we come to the clearing in the forest where the *gaswagen* delivered their loads, and the *Sonderkommando* buried them in enormous pits. Later, to eradicate the evidence, orders were given for the decomposing bodies to be dug up and burned in vast pyres and ovens. This sloping field in front of us looks smaller than I'd remembered from the opening of *Shoah*. Perhaps the trees have encroached over the last twenty years. But Simon Srebnik walking here as a forty-seven-year-old man, yet looking much older, is still totally vivid for me, him stopping, bending down to pick up the earth, his eyes trying to go back more than thirty years: 'It's hard to recognise but it was here. They burned people here . . . Yes, this is the place . . . No one can describe it . . . And no one can understand it.'

We walk down the slope and past a strange, almost haphazard assortment of official and unofficial memorials – walls with names and photographs, the occasional gravestone, and here and there a panel of information. A concrete monument to the 4,953 Jews of Bełchatów (a town twenty-five miles south of Lodz) who were killed here in August 1942. Other plaques to particular families murdered here. The children of Lidice. There's not a single other visitor here today. We sit on a bench under the pine trees, and read silently the words of Grojanowski, describing what he experienced here, on the first day of his fourteen days in the *Sonderkommando*:

Wednesday 7 January 1942

We drove in the direction of Kolo . . . till turning left into the forest; after half a kilometre we halted at a clear path. We were ordered to get down and line up in double file. An SS man ordered us to fall in with our shovels, dressed, despite the frost, only in shoes, underwear, trousers and shirts. Our coats, hats, gloves etc. had to remain in a pile on the ground . . . Already on our way in to the forest we saw about fourteen men, enforced gravediggers from Klodawa, who had arrived before us and were at work in their shirtsleeves . . . All in all we were guarded by thirty gendarmes. As we approached the ditches the men from Klodawa asked us in whispers, 'Where are you from?' We answered, 'From Izbica.' They asked how many of us there were and we replied twenty-nine. This exchange took place while we worked . . .

We didn't have long to wait before the next lorry arrived with fresh victims. It was specially constructed. It looked like a normal large lorry, in grey paint with two hermetically closed rear doors. The inner walls were of sheet metal. There weren't any seats. The floor was covered by a wooden grating, as in public baths, with straw mats on top. Between the driver's cab and the rear part were two peepholes. With a torch one could observe through these peepholes if the victims were already dead. Under the wooden grating were two tubes about fifteen centimetres thick which came out of the cab. The tubes had small openings from which gas poured out. The gas generator was in the cab, where the same driver sat all the time. He wore a uniform of the SS death's head units and was about forty years old. There were two such vans.

When the lorries approached we had to stand at a distance of five metres from the ditch. The leader of the guard detail was a high-ranking SS man, an absolute sadist and murderer. He ordered that eight men were to open the doors of the lorry. The smell of the gas that met us was overpowering, The victims were Gypsies from Lodz. Strewn about the van were all their belongings: accordions, violins, bedding, watches and other valuables.

After the doors had been open for five minutes orders were screamed at us, 'Here! You Jews! Get in there and turn everything out!' The Jews scurried into the van and dragged the corpses away. The work didn't progress quickly enough. The SS leader fetched his whip and screamed, 'The devil, I'll give you a hand straight away!' He hit out in all directions on people's heads, ears and so on, till they collapsed. Three of the eight who couldn't get up again were shot on the spot. When the others saw this they clambered back on their feet and continued the work with their last reserves of energy. The corpses were thrown one on top of another, like rubbish on a heap. We got hold of them by the feet and the hair. At the edge of the ditch stood two men who threw in the bodies. In the ditch stood two additional men who packed them in head to feet, facing downwards.

The orders were issued by an SS man who must have occupied a special rank. If any space was left, a child was pushed in. Everything was done very brutally. From up above the SS man indicated to us with a pine twig how to stack the bodies. He ordered where the head and the feet, where the children and the belongings were to be placed. All this was accompanied by malicious screams, blows and curses. Every batch comprised 180–200 corpses. For every three vanloads twenty men were used to cover up the corpses. At first this had to be done twice, later up to three times, because nine vans arrived (that is nine times sixty corpses).

At exactly twelve o'clock the SS leader with the whip ordered: 'Put your shovels down!' We had to line up in double file to be counted again. Then we had to climb out of the ditch. We were surrounded by guards the whole time. We even had to excrete on the spot. We went to the spot where our belongings were. We had to sit on them close together. The guards continued to surround us. We were given cold bitter coffee and a frozen piece of bread. That was our lunch. That's how we sat for half an hour. Afterwards we had to line up, were counted and led back to work.

What did the dead look like? They weren't burnt or black: their faces were unchanged. Nearly all the dead were soiled with excrement. At about five o'clock we stopped work. The eight men who had worked with the corpses had to lie on top of them face downwards. An SS man with a machine gun shot at their heads. The man with the whip screamed: 'The devil, get dressed quickly!'

J. and I stop reading, trying to comprehend that all this occurred, and only a few yards away from where we're sitting. By coincidence, on precisely the same date as today – 7 January – sixty-two years ago. Perhaps some of the older trees were here then, almost certainly the temperature would have been similar. We're swaddled in layers of coats and scarves and hats, so trying to imagine doing what Grojanowski and his fellow prisoners in the *Sonderkommando* did simply defies belief. J. asks about Grojanowski's escape, and I then relate how he manages to get out of a lorry window on 19 January 1942, the first morning that no SS escort follows the lorry to work. Terrified of being recaptured, he makes his way across fields and through woods, is given food and shelter by Polish villagers (who all seem to know that 'they are gassing Jews and Gypsies at Chelmno'). Eventually he reaches the still dominantly Jewish town of Grabow (where we were yesterday just before dusk):

I asked where the rabbi lived.
'Who are you?' he asked.
'Rabbi, I am a Jew from the netherworld!'
He looked at me as if I was mad. I told him: 'Rabbi, don't think I am crazed and have lost my reason. I am a Jew from the netherworld. They are killing the whole nation Israel. I myself have buried a whole town of Jews, my parents, brothers, and the entire family. I have remained as lonely as a piece of stone.'
I cried during this conversation. The rabbi asked: 'Where are they being killed?'
I said: 'Rabbi, in Chelmno. They are gassed in the forest, and buried in mass graves.'
His domestic (the rabbi was a widower) brought me a bowl of water for my swollen eyes. I washed my hands. The injury

on my right hand began to hurt. When my story made the rounds many Jews came, to whom I told the details. They all wept. We ate bread and butter; I was given tea to drink and said the blessing.

The rabbi's name was Jakub Szulman, and he later wrote to relatives in Lodz, ending his letter:

> Do not think that a madman's writing. It is the cruel and tragic truth (Good God!). O Man, throw off your rags, sprinkle your head with ashes, or run through the streets and dance in madness. I am so wearied of the sufferings of Israel, my pen can write no more. My heart is breaking. But perhaps the Almighty will take pity and save the 'last remnants of our People'. Help us, O Creator of the World!

*

The day after the distraught Grojanowski was telling Rabbi Szulman of what was happening at Chelmno, the desk killers of Wannsee met in Berlin to decide how to co-ordinate the 'final solution' more efficiently. Only weeks later, in March 1942, Eichmann came to Chelmno to see for himself what 'the business with the gas engine' looked like in practice. For a man used to murdering by paper and telegrams it was clearly a step too far, as he related to the court in Jerusalem that sentenced him to death nineteen years later:

> There was a room – if I remember correctly – perhaps five times as large as this one. Perhaps it was only four times as big as the one I am sitting in now. And Jews were inside. They were to strip and then a truck arrived where the doors open, and the van pulled up at a hut. The naked Jews were to enter. Then the doors were hermetically sealed . . .
>
> I couldn't even look at it [the van]. All the time I was trying to avert my sight from what was going on. It was quite enough for me what I saw. The screaming and the shrieking – I was too excited to have a look at the van. I told Müller that in my report.

He didn't derive much profit from my report and afterwards I followed the van. Some of them knew the way, of course. And then I saw the most breathtaking sight I have ever seen in my life.

The van was making for an open pit. The doors were flung open and corpses were cast out as if they were some animals – some beasts. They were hurled into the ditch. I also saw how the teeth were being extracted. And then I disappeared; I entered my car and I didn't want to look at this heinous act of turpitude . . . for hours I was sitting at the side of the driver without exchanging a word with him. Then I knew I was washed up. It was quite enough for me. I had to leave because it was too much, as much as I could stand.

*

It's nearly 11 a.m., the time we're due to meet Krystof back at the road. He's there, pacing up and down, smoking a cigarette. He greets us warmly. We're greatly relieved to see him, now being certain of making our connection back to Berlin. He gestures to the official museum here, a small, dark wooden building by the road, '*Ja, kein Problem!*' He points to his watch. '*Zehn Minuten, OK?*' So we make a rapid tour of the little museum. Photographs of Roma families. Photographs of some of the eighty-two children of the village of Lidice in Czechoslovakia:

These boys and girls were murdered here in June 1942 in reprisal for the assassination of Heydrich in Prague. He took eight days to die – perhaps there is a God after all. Heydrich, of course, was the dominant force at Wannsee, as we've seen, and co-ordinator-in-chief of the extermination process. We buy two publications about Chelmno, take some leaflets and soon we're in the taxi, speeding towards Konin and the train that will take us back westwards to Berlin (and then on to London). We leave Krystof at the station with warm handshakes and smiles and all our remaining Polish money. Our train, which started in Moscow, is only a few minutes late, and on the platform we reflect on how far we've travelled since we left Berlin ten days ago.

On the train, reading one of the Chelmno books, I stare at a photograph of a primary school class from the village of Lidice. And then at another, a small black and white picture of a brother and sister from the same village. Four, maybe five years old in 1942. With no inkling of what was about to happen a few months later. The random moving of a hand over a map in an office in Prague or Berlin. The selection of their small village for total extermination. I count back, these two would have been born in 1937 or 1938. They would have been sixty-five or sixty-six years old today.

And as our train picks up speed, and the forests flicker past, I'm remembering something told to me long ago. It's the memory of a girl who also would have been four, maybe five years old, at the time. And I've found it disturbing and inexplicable in equal measure, and it's troubled me for many years.

The girl was an only child then, born in London in 1937, so she was only two when the war broke out. Her father, Sid, was blind (from the First World War); he was also a proud socialist who, with any excuse, would wear in his lapel the largest red rose he could find. She was less close to Dolly, her mother, who seemed to worry for all three of them. And when war broke out seriously (after months of the so-called 'phoney war'), and the bombing started, there was even more than usual to worry about. She remembered (this perhaps her earliest memory) the drama of the bomb alarms wailing and being carried downstairs, through the garden in her 'siren suit', grey on the outside with a beautiful, bright red lining, which she loved, to the Anderson shelter. There the three of them would wait, hearing the thuds of the bombs on the docks a couple of miles away, and the shattering of glass being blown out. The skies blood red over Petherton Road; she not scared at all. For her the amazement of new sounds, a child's excitement in midnight interruptions of sleep; for her parents a debilitating fear.

When the bombing intensified the family was evacuated to the small village of Newton Longville, now a suburb of Bletchley, but then a mile outside, to the south. They were housed on a farm at the edge of the village, and her mother became the housekeeper. The farm's owner, Lesley, was from a religious family; his parents had bought the farm for him at the outbreak of war, because they were pacifists and farmers were exempt from military service, because farming was regarded as an essential occupation. The girl and her parents were happy here, despite Dolly's complaints about the state of the place and how hard it was to clean. Later, a cousin and an aunt joined them, and they lived in the other end of the farmhouse. For the daughter it was an adventure. She was fascinated by everything – the farm, the animals, a sheepdog that became a loved pet for her, and the wild flowers that she first came across on walks, guiding her father, and which she'd then bring back for the neighbour Mrs Lovell to identify, who would then teach her the names. And her garden was simply miraculous for the girl. What were those ones, the pink and white lovelies? 'Japanese *hon-ey-moons*' is what she heard, only realising years later that Mrs Lovell had been pronouncing 'an-e-moans' – her phonetic reading of 'anemones'. They would pick baskets of cowslips together to make wine, and after the harvest they would go gleaning, as country people had done for centuries. It was the right of all villagers to gather any ears of wheat or corn that were left after the farmer had cut the fields, and Mrs Lovell would then feed whatever they found to her chickens. Mr Lovell kept ferrets in a sack, which terrified the young girl, but he also showed her a magical trick with a pumpkin: if you wrote your name, quite small, with pin pricks when the pumpkin was just beginning to grow, within weeks it would swell and your name would swell with it! All of these experiences sowed seeds in the young girl, which germinated a life-long passion for the natural world, and flowers in particular. One of the numerous and strange by-products of war.

But the shadow of the war reached the village; how could it not? The three of them would listen to the Home Service around the radio in the kitchen, Sid keeping up a commentary on the need for 'opening up a second front' to help our Russian allies who seemed to be fighting fascism alone in the middle of the war. And there was terrible news of the death of 'Little Bert', killed serving in the Far East – the nephew who had been more of a son to Dolly, who she'd raised after her sister-in-law had died young. The shock of the news was so severe that she lost the child she'd been carrying. From London there was more grim news – Dolly's brother's house in Queensbury Street was heavily bombed, killing Uncle Bert and the lodger upstairs.

Then one day her parents took her down to the village green, where, next to the church, a large lorry was parked. They explained that there was going to be a test of the gas masks, and there was nothing to worry about. Other parents and children were there as well. The children were given gas masks decorated with cartoon animals; she was handed a black and white one with a smiling Mickey Mouse on, and it was soon fastened tightly with the rubber straps on the back of her head. The girl started to panic, as parents and children began to walk up the planks that led into the back of the van. Her father tried to reassure her: 'Don't be silly! If something's wrong it will just make your eyes a bit sore.' His grip was tight on her hand. Against her will she was pulled up the ramp and into the back of the lorry. An ascending terror. Going into that darkness and the gas. An instinctive, overwhelming No. But now she was inside. The doors were then closed, and she was crying, gulping frantically under the mask. Minutes that lengthened with the relentlessness of nightmare. Shaking and traumatised. A five-year-old girl. My mother.

*

Postscript, Pembrokeshire

This chapter, which I finished today, looking out over the bay where I've been writing, was hard to complete. Partly due to the fact that it was half written when I broke off from the first draft some years ago, and so going back to the exact place where I'd left the writing felt strange, considering the complexities of life that have intervened in the last years; I don't feel I'm quite the same person who started the chapter.

But the greater reason was the testimony of Grojanowski. I know that it is among the most important of all accounts of the Holocaust, the Holocaust which exterminated Roma as well as Jews, as Grojanowski details here. And that what he describes is the end product (quite literally, as the SS would have seen it) of the industrialised killing carried out in the vans manufactured by Saurer in the lakeside town of Arbon where we began this last part of our journey. It would have been perverse not to include Grojanowski's account. The full testimony, which I first came across in Martin Gilbert's *The Holocaust* many years ago, runs to twenty-six pages and is, even for people who expose themselves to such material, gruelling to read. I'm not sure I can read such things any longer.

Yesterday, in a gap from writing, and knowing I was about to embark on the last part of this chapter, I took the book with me on a walk to the west side of the peninsula, to reread the section and to try and catch the last of the afternoon's sun. I found a sheltered spot and propped myself up on a rock, between the incoming tide making its calming repetitions on a deserted beach below me, and a dozen or so sheep grazing above me. I start the chapter (all of what I quote above is from the first two days of Grojanowski's ordeal), and I notice something in the language: on the third day he starts to use the phrase 'when we drove to work', by the fourth day he's talking about 'our place of work' and 'we consumed our lunch' and 'after the evening meal'; interspersed with the barbarism he's describing are these words of every day banality – the routine of work – which shock deeply in the context. But maybe this speaks strongly of the human need to adapt, even in the most terrifying circumstances, to attempt to find approximations of normality amidst the nightmare?

I realise reading it that I want rage and despair and madness as a response, but Grojanowski writes with a level-headed factualness that is pushed to such extremes of blunt statement (often without any detectable emotion) that it borders on mirroring the psychotic behaviour of his guards. On the eighth day he relates: 'a small baby wrapped in a pillow was thrown out of the lorry. It began to cry. The SS men laughed. They machine-gunned the baby and tossed it into the ditch.' That's it. Nothing else said. So we have the obscenity of the act, and then the obscenity of silence in the face of the act. Two days later he records: 'At midday I received the sad news that my brother and parents had just been buried. At one o'clock we were already back at work. I tried to get closer to the corpses to take a last look at my nearest and dearest.' That's all. The experience of reading such things is to make you rage, to make you almost as savage as the SS – you just want one of the men to attack a guard wildly, to kill one of them even though they'll be shot instantly. That unforgettable passage from Nadezhda Mandelstam's *Hope Against Hope* comes into my mind:

> When a bull is being led to the slaughter, it still hopes to break loose and trample its butchers. Other bulls have not been able to pass on the knowledge that this never happens and that from the slaughterhouse there is no way back to the herd. But in human society there is a continuous exchange of experience. I have never heard of a man who broke away and fled while being led to his execution. It is even thought to be a special form of courage if a man about to be executed refuses to be blindfolded and dies with his eyes open. But I would rather have the bull with his blind rage, the stubborn beast who doesn't weigh his chances of survival with the prudent dull-wittedness of man, and doesn't know the despicable feeling of despair.
>
> Later I often wondered whether it is right to scream when you are being beaten and trampled underfoot. Isn't it better to face one's tormentors in a stance of satanic pride, answer-

ing them with contemptuous silence? I decided that it is better to scream. This pitiful sound, which sometimes, goodness knows how, reaches into the remotest prison cell, is a concentrated expression of the last vestige of human dignity. It is a man's way of leaving a trace, of telling people how he lived and died. By his screams he asserts his right to live, sends a message to the outside world demanding help and calling for resistance. If nothing else is left, one must scream. Silence is the real crime against humanity.

Perhaps this is what Mandelstam *thought* she would do *in extremis*. It is part of our human condition to express rage and despair. But, it slowly dawned on me reading yesterday, that what Grojanowski is describing is a kind of paralysing numbness which can only shut down the body's normal responses when confronted with the unimaginable. And, in this context, to make a judgement of the human being going through this inhuman experience is simply impossible. We have no right.

But, however you navigate around the subject, these pages are shattering to the human spirit. As I close the book I suddenly realise four sheep have come so close to me I can put out my hand to touch them. They've been as absorbed by their grazing as I've been by my reading. But it's chilly now, I get up with a shiver, and climb back up to the cliff path. As I get there, a single, madly enthusiastic skylark hovers above me, singing wildly into the blue of the evening. For ten minutes or so he alternates between this position and riding the top of a bushy stem about three yards away, undulating in the wind and continuing to sound his burbling glory. I have never been more in need of that song.

BOOK TWO

SILENCE AND SPEAKING

Preface

To the West

St David's Day, 1 March 2012, Hackney to Pembrokeshire

Suddenly the valley opens before me. The last sun on a spring day, glimpse of the River Wye snaking silver through trees, the green of the fields luminescently green, almost glowing in this early-evening light. And my spirits racing as I sense the border, just beyond the next hill, the country I've loved from childhood. My foot easing off the pedal, the road emptying as I move westwards, no rush now. Past the hill, the way sweeps down to the valley below, the red dragon approaches on its green background – '*CROESO I GYMRU*', 'Welcome to Wales' – which I always hear with an exclamation mark even if it isn't there on the sign. I sing the words, just as we did as kids, crossing the border in the back of our old Renault 4 – the moment of no return, leaving the flatlands behind. Summer, the wild promise of weeks by the water and the trees and the mountains, days of Cnicht and Cadair Idris and the Island and Llyn Hywel and the Pennant valley and the Llanfrothen rockslide . . . an ocean of time before we'd have to think about school again. And today, crossing the border, a similar sense of exhilaration – not holidays now, but the prospect of a full week's writing ahead.

Over the last year or so I've discovered a rhythm, a way of working, which has been intensely liberating. Every three or four weeks, I load up my little car in Hackney and head to the west, to a house balancing on the very edge of Wales, by the sea. I've found that I can do seven or eight days' writing before the isolation starts to unnerve me. An immersion of intensity, a kind of temporary hermit state, before I feel the pull of the city again. Almost a year lived like this. Hit-and-run raids on chapters. Seven days, 11,000, 12,000 words. Each time another twenty-five pages, another chapter, completed. Then back to London. And finding an inexplicable power in these darting journeys to the west. It was just an instinct, as primal as a migrating bird, that I needed to go in that direction, that I needed a different energy, far away from the North Sea and the east-coast shingle where I began this writing six years ago. Now the rhythms of the tides in Wales, together with the rapidly changing skies and light, the coastal paths and marshes, the estuaries and inlets, the curlews and peregrines, the mossed oak woods and rivers, have become my companions, and I look forward to seeing them again with an urgency that amazes me, because, up to now, I've always thought of myself as a city boy, the word 'Londoner' imprinted on my DNA.

Through the borderlands, Pencraig, Llangarron signed to the right, Crocker's Ash, Symond's Yat off to the left, no language in control now. Through the last of the Forest of Dean, twisting down through the trees, thinking of Dennis Potter, his childhood here which rooted his whole life, and his beautiful anger at the end. Down to the plain at Monmouth and that most theatrical of junctions, the four roads meeting at the bridge over the Wye, points of a compass, suggesting all directions are possible. Lights turn to green, straight on, through the tunnel leading west, and, finally, all traces of England are left behind. The traffic empties out even further as dusk approaches, off at Raglan, then the magnificent sweep of the road towards Abergavenny, demanding a surge of speed, at one with the car, a single entity moving through space and time. All the associations with this place over the years. Walking the Black Mountains with J., sleeping in the ruins of Llanthony Priory under the stars. The Brecon Beacons that cloudless October with another old friend, now living in America. The Walnut Tree weekend for our mother in 1997, only days after Labour's victory. In the cottage seeing images of Robin Cook as the new Foreign Secretary speaking about a British government having an ethical foreign policy for the first time. Bitter now to think of such a memory post-Iraq and all that's followed from that . . .

Always the choice that comes at the end of this road – if it's summer or still light, and I'm in the mood for twists and turns, I go right, through Abergavenny and take the road to Brecon. One of the loveliest anywhere – between the Black Mountains massing above Crickhowell on one side and the Beacons answering on the other. Up to Bwlch, hairpin bend. Just beyond, the lake at Llangorse and Llangasty, places of sanctuary, recovery. Beyond Brecon, bends winding down to Llandovery and Carmarthen. But, in other seasons, or in the dark like tonight, I go left, taking the Heads of the Valleys road.

As I cross the River Usk, I reflect on my curious, and very recent, love of driving. For most of my adult life, more than twenty-five years, I never had a car. Living and working in London, it was quite unnecessary, and on top of that, the more I worked with my organisation, looking at the global impacts of oil, the more critical I became of car culture. In many respects I still feel that our society needs to revolutionise its transport policies, its whole approach to renewable energy – the entire system needs radical change. But, when I started writing this work, I faced a more immediate challenge. Knowing that I could only work in places far from the distractions of the city, how would it be possible to transport half a dozen boxes of books and papers and research materials, by public transport, to a remote place in the countryside? A paradox soon became apparent: for lovers of wildness and solitude – the places that most lend themselves to reflection and writing – cars become essential.

But this, alone, is to give too simple an explanation; to suggest an instrumentalist solution to a specific problem, the car as a necessary evil. Yet over the last year I've begun to realise the intense creativity that driving can release. That these repeated journeys, the very process of rapidly moving through landscape, does something. And so the means has become just as creative as the end. The six- or six-and-a-half-hour journey between Hackney and West Pembrokeshire as created a liminal space, a suspended state of being. Literally so – a couple of feet above the tarmac in a little metal box – but also a time for all the jumbled thoughts in my head about the next chapter to be thrown up into the air, to be gathered when they fall – in a different order, on the other side of this small island. So, as I drive westwards, although I'm following the tarmac with my eyes, my mind is already beginning to write the chapter I will be starting the following morning. And also it's a space to relinquish all the London lists in my head, all the obligations, the 'oughteries' of the city. And escaping too the temptations of sociability, leaving behind the phone, email and also all the piles of papers and bills on various tables and kitchen surfaces. The hundred diurnal distractions that are the greatest inhibitor of any real creativity. Switch off all those tasks in your head, watch the lights marked 'urgent' fade and die one by one, and for the next seven, eight days, drift only in a sea of thought and words.

I've also come to understand that the rhythms of driving, though obviously quite different from walking, are no less mesmerising. Especially if you avoid motorways as far as possible – which in my experience encourage a zombie-like state of continual, suffused aggression – and use the old main roads where you're able to feel more connected to the landscape. The experience of rapid movement over several hours, seeing the day fade to dusk and darkness, glimpses of trees at night, foxes darting into the hedge, names of unknown villages flashing by, radio programmes whispered into your ear, music vibrating on a powerful sound system – all these can work together to create a flowing, dynamic state of intensity, which I can only compare to a kind of timeless meditation, on the rare occasions I've achieved such a state. It's about being sensorily taken to another place – and, by the end of these hours, when I'm on the narrow Pembrokeshire lanes and can smell the sea, it's always very late, no other cars are on the road, so like some lone rider from the past, galloping through the night with a message, I feel I'm on a solitary mission; nobody else is moving through the darkness. Then it's time for the final piece of music – always the same piece – and, as the last notes fade, then only the sound of the tyres on the road and the wind coming in from the sea.

Over the Usk, across the other rivers – Ebbw Fach, Afon Ebbw, Sirhowy, Rhymney, Cynon. Valleys plundered by empire but at least these rivers still run free. The lights of Nantyglo and Tredegar, far down to the left. Tredegar, the birthplace of Aneurin Bevan, and also of the Tredegar Workmen's Medical Aid Society. By the 1920s virtually all of the 24,000 people of the town were covered by this health service, established by miners for their families – the prototype for what later became our National Health Service, a beacon of social justice in the world – all from this single valley, this town. And just beyond, Blackwood – home of the Manic Street Preachers – Nicky, James, Sean and Richey – yes, wearing their hearts on their sleeves, but these boys, what hearts, what sleeves! Unparalleled poignancy and sweet melancholia of their valley music – the 'hiraeth' they always return to.

Long ascent to Hirwaun. Once the last deep mine in Wales. Our Platform initiative 'Homeland' and talking to Tyrone O'Sullivan of the Hirwaun NUM about Orwell's writing, and understanding that electricity doesn't come into our cities by magic, but by the labour of thousands of people. The road now all the way down from Pontneddfechan following the River Neath to Swansea. Late now. Few cars on the road, so Manics or Dylan or Arcade Fire turned up to glory pounding noise, and then releasing the car on the downward hill, to significantly over the limit. Feeling the engine given free rein. Just like the horses galloping down the hillside here, for centuries before. Speed as pure speed. Beyond all daily compromises, under the shelter of the night. Not risking anything to anyone else. Answering the instinct inside.

449

Dry-mouthed, ecstatic, pushing further, always. Something recovered in this moment, from wild, unchained pasts. Then easing off the accelerator as the roundabouts begin, back into the realm of street lights, Aberdulais, Neath.

Meeting the M4 at the Jersey Marine junction, waving a hello in the direction of my Swansea friend who loves his Gower with an evangelical intensity. Fifteen miles in ten minutes, the end of the motorway, down the hill to Pont Abraham, sometimes stopping for petrol and a chat with the friendly woman who works here through the night. The final hour now, and the finest road of them all, darting into Pembrokeshire with the intent of a quivering arrow – Cwygwili, Llanddarog, Gelli-Uchaf. Crossing the Towy at Carmarthen, then left. Sarnau, Bancyfelin, St Clears, Zabulon, Whitland, Llandewi Velfrey (momentarily slowed by the 40 mph limit through this sleeping village), Narberth, Robeston Wathen, crossing the Eastern Cleddau, Slebech and soon coming down into Haverfordwest. I used to follow the signs that took you round the town in an unnecessary loop past Merlin's Bridge (quite a name!) – but sadly no signs of mystics today, just a burger chain by a roundabout. These days I go straight up the hill, up through the town's handsome main street. Still some taxis here, if a weekend night, some straggling teens making their way home. Just beyond the town I pull over for the final ritual. Twenty minutes to go. Everything now slowing down.

Very late now. I always pause at this lay-by, open the window to get the scent of the earth and the wind. Branches waving above, and the glow of distant refineries far off. The final music. The same piece now which has travelled with me for the last year, but each time I hear something new. So late coming to Beethoven (my absurd snobbery of avoiding so 'popular' a composer for years). Even more ridiculous thinking that this had never bothered me with Shakespeare. Number Seven. Bernstein, New York Philharmonic. I slide the disc in and then drive off, very, very slowly. The opening chord, urgent, sense of crisis. Concentrating on each breath. Tentative clarinets, then soothing. Utterly linked to the winding road, dipping now through tree tunnels and bends. Slowing to 25 mph at most here, down to 15 for the corners. Music rising again. The flutes playing off each other. Now they play that single, repeated note, gathering pace, then answered by the orchestra's swelling response. The theme comes in, hesitantly at first, then repeated with more confidence. Suddenly a badger scuttles out from the hedge. I dip my lights, slow to a crawl, watching him scurry ahead, looking for a gap. The road clear again, rising, jabbing horns and strings, gathering pace now towards the end of the first movement, powerfully at first, and then even more wildly. Stabbing, urgent, vibrating crescendo turning your whole body into an instrument.

The second before the slow movement begins. Waiting. Surely it cannot be as astounding again. That single note fades. The strings so slow, barely able to move. As if all the suffering of the world has come together in one place, at one time. I slow down again, listening now with my heart. Exhausted music, pregnant pain, blocked, leaden. Deathly march, defeated souls. Repeated now, but even quieter, as if breath is leaving the body. At a higher pitch strings come in offering compassion, at this lowest point, utterly unexpected. Rising now, more and more instruments joining in. And two minutes, thirty-eight seconds in, the lifting that defies understanding. The most miraculous single moment in music.

Tonight, I'm thinking of the poet Yannis Ritsos, whom I've been reading recently, and about what it means to come through, despite everything. Bereaved, exiled, imprisoned, tortured. Suffering that didn't take his humanity away but released it into the world. When he's twelve years old, his older brother dies of tuberculosis, his mother dies five years later, his father goes mad and dies in an asylum, his sister breaks down and is on the verge of death as well. He writes this for her, at that moment:

> I am a maimed ant that has lost its way in boundless night.
> Whatever I loved death and madness took from me. I remained
> alone beneath the ruins of the sky to count the dead. I have no
> more tears. I have no fear. I have nothing else for them to take

451

from me. Poor, naked, and all alone – here are my riches that no one can take from me. I will not knock on any door. I will not beg. Without bread without a sack without a bond I take the road west with long and steady strides, naked and entire, worthy to touch God.

*

The year before, a moment I will never forget, speaking these words with a class of students in a college with peeling paint in Soho.

They were an advanced class, and we had been together for several months, so a level of trust had been established. People felt able to take more risks, reveal more of themselves, perhaps. Some of the students were refugees, several were politically active, and they had suggested a week where we looked at the question of resistance – how we are able to fight, how those who have gone before us have fought, with whatever they have, and sometimes using art, writing, music, films, poetry.

A young Somalian woman spoke passionately about the work of the educationalist Paulo Freire and his belief that language is the greatest weapon of change – that 'to speak the true word is to transform the world.' She told us that coming across Freire's ideas had changed the direction of her life. Sparked by this, a Peruvian student read a piece he'd written – about how his parents had left school before they could learn to read or write, and so he and his sister had had to become the 'interpreters' between them and the world. Because of this their parents always revered the written word and would give them books whenever they could afford to – he said that books were like maps of a foreign country for his mother and father – a country that he and his sister could travel to, but they could only see from across the border. We then talked about how poetry and music have an unparalleled power to communicate emotion directly. We read the poem by Yannis Ritsos. I was suddenly aware of the stillness in the room, the heating ticking in the pipes. The silence was broken by a Russian student, a woman in

452

her early forties who said she wanted to tell us about the poet Osip Mandelstam – like Ritsos, he'd had an indescribably difficult life, which ended in one of Stalin's Gulags. His last poem from Siberia was short, only four lines – perhaps we could learn it together? So we stand in a circle, shoulder to shoulder, as she gives us the words, and we give them back, line by line, and then the whole poem. Spoken back in all the accents of the room until everyone has it in their hearts. Mandelstam living on beyond the Gulag. And when the last voice has spoken the last words – 'You left me my lips, and they shape words, even in silence' – the same Beethoven slow movement started to play. I look around the circle and see some brows furrowed in concentration, some smiles of recognition. Beyond language to our shared humanity.

*

The darkened road, moonless tonight. Not meeting a single car. The turn off to the village, precisely at the moment of the music's lifting. As if never heard before, as if ambushed, I'm driving blinded by tears. Astonished again by how this can happen, the ability of these vibrated sounds to unlock something inside, and not become dulled by repetition. Extraordinarily rare, even with the most loved music. And then I realise that the music – these vibrations from sound waves in my inner ear – is only a part of this. That of course it is the accretion of memory and association that becomes indistinguishable from the music itself. Remembering the faces in that classroom, remembering Ritsos and Mandelstam, remembering what they endured and how they resisted. And feeling instinctively that Beethoven wanted his music to be with people in this way. To be connected to our struggles. Often failing, often deaf and numbed and despairing. But the astonishment of human solidarity too, of feeling an arm on your shoulder, of being lifted up. And sensing that he wanted his music to be more than music – he wanted it to be a living force.

Down a hill, the sharp left-hander at the end, these last minutes, each twist and bend so familiar now. The lane off to the islands.

453

The farmhouse selling wood. The little bump of the bridge. I put the window down, the wind's buffeting now replacing the music. The water suddenly there, on the left, in its inky loveliness. Climbing the narrow road, through the tree tunnel, the final ascent. Turning at the brow of the hill. The white house in front, sweeping right, and the entire bay laid out below. Still there in every detail. The houses deeply slumbering. Third gear, second, not wanting to make a noise, slipping past the pub and then up the narrow track behind the house, turning in, cutting the engine. Six hours, thirty-four minutes from Hackney. Five hours, four minutes driving time. Opening the car door, an owl calling. The sound of the incoming sea. Trilling of a distinct curlew. Strange to hear that sound in the dead of night. Down the dark steps, opening up the house. So chill at this time of year after the winter, despite the neighbours having put the heaters on last night. Takes two or three days to warm up. Back up to the car, with my last energy, unloading bags, food, books, papers, printer in five or six sorties. Then, in coat and scarf, back outside with a beer and a chair. Feet up on the sea wall, feeling the rhythms of the driving fading and the pulsing rhythms of this place taking over. Tides and sky and birds and trees. My companions for the next seven days and nights. And words already beginning to form, not yet recognisable, but somewhere on the very periphery of my consciousness.

*

Two days later.

Several pages into the chapter now, I write until most of the day's light has gone. Then scan my map for somewhere new to walk. As I leave the house, it's almost beyond dusk. From the inside looking out, it would now be dark. But eyes – even our not very sharp human ones – can adjust and make things visible on the darkest of nights. The path along the clifftop unfurls in a whitish thread before me. Gusts from the sea batter with increasing frenzy, one blast almost has me over. Eyes try to make out the dark purplish soil but it's not visible. My pace slows. I allow my boots to feel ahead, giving them fractionally more time than they'd have in the daylight. Keeping to the pale line of the path. But it's narrow and thousands of other boots have deepened it into a rut which makes it difficult to walk. The entire body utterly focussed on the feet, responsive to each step. A little deeper there, the tiniest muscles reacting. Uphill. Something in the path, a protruding rock. Go round it. Tipping forward, muscles between the balls of my feet and the toes stretched, answering the call. The slope now flattening out, the path widening, I'm able to walk almost normally, not quite striding but with a regular rhythm again. And a guide has joined me, white rump of a wheatear, just back from its Africa wintering, flitting ahead ten feet, waiting companionably, then, when I've caught up, taking off again, flashing its tiny rear (its original name 'white-arse' toned down for Victorian sensibilities to 'wheatear'). Together we walk and fly for several minutes. To the left, hundreds of feet below, the continuous roar of the sea. Only the whiteness of the surf visible, hitting the cliffs then melting. Another mile and we dip down towards the bay. The hardest thing at night, downhill. The misjudgements that can tip you forwards. The path curves round to the right. A gate, joining the other path coming up from the bay.

Walking inland. Stone wall on my left. A gap. Two sleeping sheep startled by my presence worry off with that characteristic fussiness, which in turn disturbs other sheep across the hillside in a snowstorm of movement. Ten minutes more and I've finally got to the road. The rubber of my boots making a slightly more audible sound. Only two miles or so back. Wildly westwards, at this most westerly point of the country. Walking into the stars. The Plough high to my right. Straight ahead the last traces of silver-grey over the island. Not yet folded into the night completely. The sun, gone for an hour and a half, still staining this last patch with its light. Then my turn to be startled – so absorbed in the night sky, almost under my feet, the sound of an animal approaching. A dog? No, fox! Even in this dim light I can see his outline a few yards away, his back arched, tensed, utterly still, watching me. I freeze, not wanting to scare him. Seconds pass, both of us holding our breath, and then he retreats, back the way he came, pausing at one moment, to glance back and check that I'm not following. From nowhere Speer suddenly in my mind again. Walking in the Spandau garden. Walking round the world in his mind. For a man fatally lacking in imagination an inexplicable thing, something like that. Escaping from a shipwrecked life. Survivor of a disaster. A single farm building. One light on downstairs. Box files on the windowsill. Cavernous blackness of the barn next door. A few months ago I saw them harvesting here in the last of the late-summer light. In fact the combine followed me back, but on the other side of the hedge, its lights illuminating the same road I'm walking now, but in the opposite direction.

Thoughts come at times like these. And memories. They come in multitudes, leaping through the mind like young deer. The yearning not to go to bed as a child, when there was still light in the sky. Day not over. Hearing voices from outside, coming up to our bedroom, deeper my father, laughter my mother. Not yet. Day not over yet. Thinking of that now, it seems like an instinctive, child's pre-sentiment of death. Putting off death. There's still some silver-grey in the sky. Not yet. Day not over. This road too. Walking westwards into the night, the last gasp of light. Urge to keep walking, postponing the going back to the inside world, the static staleness of a house at night. Here movement still unfolding, no end. The road now cresting the ridge, the place, always breathtaking, where both seas can be seen.

Wilder to the south, only the lighthouse on the distant island. A curious red glow, I count the seven-and-a-half-second interval between the flashes – *one-and two-and three-and four-and five-and six-and seven* – and the red comes again. To the north, momentarily I cannot distinguish between the distant lights of the villages fifteen, twenty miles across the bay and the lights of the ships in the sea. Then it becomes clearer: the villages are tiny beads of whitest light; the ships have yellower lights, warmer. This island people. Defended. Yet also the astounding violence of the British through the centuries. Empire violence, now violence of a different kind. More refined, by laptop and algorithm. The impacts felt far away from here. The wind has dropped. My feet are in a trance, carrying me along now. If the sea wasn't there I'd just keep walking into the west. *Shooting star!* At the very edge of my vision, but still absurdly miraculous. Not as flamboyant as the August ones, but lovelier in its March loneliness. Behind me now as I turn around, a stream of moon on the black road picking out puddles as silver plates. Pause to look back. The faintest sodium glow of the only town anywhere near here, twenty miles or so to the east. London impossibly far away. My other life away. *What was it just then? Something on the very periphery of thought. An idea that connects with . . . ?* No. It's gone. Maybe it will return with walking. This stretch of road, it was here, that moment listening to Patti Smith in the car. Utterly transported by 'Wing' – deep and celestial in the same voice. Feathers and lead together. How Blake would have connected with that. Almost back now. One more curve. Hedge carved so patiently by the work of the wind there. Life's work. *Oh yes, that's it, I remember now. Books get finished when their authors grow tired of talking about them.* Something like that . . .

*

Remembering back to that Suffolk shingle in winter. Everything moving so slowly. And now, as the days quicken towards spring, this second book begins. A different energy. A publisher on board. The difference between writing into a vacuum, hoping these words would be read, and now knowing they will be. These days I'm moving continually between east and west. A friend is letting me use this house by the sea in Wales. Her mother got too frail to climb the stairs last year and had to move out, so, in the limbo of indecision about what to do with the place, I can be here to write.

When I'm down here I walk every day, regardless of the weather – this movement an indispensable part of my daily rhythm. Most of the time I sit at my table in the downstairs window overlooking the bay. But in those two or three hours of walking – even when I try to fool myself I'm not thinking about the chapter I'm working on – my feet and mind will conspire to subtly process what I've written – to digest, to spark new ideas. And so, on a windswept headland, or down a mossy lane, I'll sometimes find myself scrabbling around for paper and pen to capture these fugitive pieces of thought before they blow away. But often the landscape here absorbs me almost entirely, taking over my senses. Finding a new path through oak woods, or following a lane down to an estuary inlet at dusk, with the tide racing in across mudflats. Watching the behaviour of oystercatchers and gannets and seals. The sight of the dark purplish earth, the scent of wild garlic, the sound of the marker buoys in the Haven, calling through the night.

*

Spring is beginning now. Tiny shoots of bracken are starting to unfurl like babies' fingers opening. On both sides of the deep lanes the grass is that burstingly fresh green you only see in early spring. Soon to be speckled with yellows and blues and pinks of buttercups and bluebells and campion. The birds are going wild with activity, waking from their winter sulks, skulking in hedges and bushes, now they're on the tops of branches singing to the skies and to each other. Each day I stop work a little bit later, to walk somewhere new. Depending on the weather – on the cliffs or inland, on footpaths or little lanes. I always try to be walking half an hour before dusk; and I usually end up returning in the dark. This means my writing days are partly determined by the seasons: in the height of summer I can work till nine, even half past nine, and still do my walk. But now, in early spring, I finish at three or four, walk till sixish, then come back to the house, make a fire, have a short rest, watching the flames reflect on the beams and the ceiling, and then return to my window to work for another two or three hours or more, often late into the night. The house is at the very edge of the village, so as I look out over to the other side of the bay, I can see the single road that threads all the cottages together. At night a dozen street lights here keep me company with their soft yellow glow, long after the last light in the village houses has been switched off. And then the only sound is the dark water, lapping fifteen feet away, on the other side of the sea wall. Into the early hours, tapping away, sometimes so absorbed that the tide comes up stealthily, in the time it's taken to write half a page, and now the street lights dance in blurred zigzags of light, reflected in the water.

*

The journeys in this book, are, with two exceptions, not physical journeys but explorations into history, psychology and morality. Questions I've been perplexed by for more than twenty years. What is the precise relationship between perpetrators, victims and bystanders? What are the different aspects of responsibility that flow from these words – the responsibility on us to understand the actions of perpetrators, the responsibility of witnesses to speak, and, perhaps the hardest to grasp, the responsibility of societies to hear?

How can we explain the voices that are heard, and the voices we cannot hear? The experience of human suffering, and then the sometimes extraordinarily difficult attempts to transmit the meaning of that suffering through language? Or, at times, the way that suffering defies language altogether. In these pages we will encounter women and men who have gone through some of the most traumatic experiences it is possible to imagine. Some did not survive, some survived but could not speak, some attempted to find words for what they had lived through. Jan Karski at Izbica and in the Warsaw Ghetto. Primo Levi at Monowitz. Jorge Semprún at Buchenwald. Some we have only names for, fragments of their last hours. Koita Yaguine, Tounkara Fade, Aisha Duhulow. The French philosopher Simone Weil, living in London in 1943, in wartime exile, tried to look at the meaning of human suffering in a way that had never been attempted before. In one of the last essays she wrote, 'La Personnalité Humaine, le juste et l'injuste', she says this:

At the bottom of the heart of every human being, from earliest infancy until the tomb, there is something that goes on indomitably expecting, in the teeth of all experience and crimes committed, suffered, and witnessed, that good and not evil will be done to him. It is this, above all, that is scarred in every human being . . . Every time that there arises from the depths of a human heart the childish cry which Christ himself could not restrain, 'Why am I being hurt?', then there is certainly injustice.

But who is listening? And what are the conditions in which we can really hear the suffering of others – as Weil puts it, the 'attentive silence in which this faint and inept cry can make itself heard', 'the tender and sensitive attention which is needed to understand its meaning'?

Connected to this question of suffering is a question about the nature of silences. Silences not just of traumatised individuals, but of whole societies. Silences of survivors, as well as silences of perpetrators. I grew up with such silences. The silence of my father about what he had experienced in the Korean War in the early 1950s. A silence even more shocking because of his love of language and philosophy and life. Even as a child, I realised instinctively that something was wrong. And as I became a young man, the same age my father was when drafted to Korea, I found his silence even more baffling. I met a blank wall when I tried to talk to him about it. Today I've come to think that much of my enquiring, over the course of my adult life, into genocide and war and suffering, must stem from this original and implacable silence. I also wonder at the way love deepens after death, and how dialogues with my father continue to grow. He died many years ago – half a lifetime away now – yet he is entirely alive to me still, a completely vivid presence.

There were other silences too growing up in Britain in the 1970s and early 1980s – whole societal silences in a country which I was told prized freedom of speech, and which had pioneered the concept of the free press. Some of these silences are now being broken, for instance the silence surrounding the systematic phys-

460

ical and sexual abuse of many children, within all kinds of institutions, and outside of them too. But some of the silences we haven't begun to come to terms with yet as a society – particularly that which concerns the violence inflicted on multitudes of human beings across the world, over many centuries, through the practices of British colonialism. Again, a systematic, supposedly legitimised violence – often using 'free trade' as a smokescreen – which claimed millions upon millions of victims. The selectivity of British historical memory is staggering. At the same time, the Second World War has become our defining national event of the last century – the 'Good War' – taking on almost mythic proportions, seemingly growing with every year of commemorations and memorials. I wonder how it is possible that children still grow up in our society with only the most cursory knowledge of Britain's central role in the slave trade, and even less understanding of genocides and atrocities carried out by our ancestors in Tasmania, Kenya, India and China. How do different societies come to terms (or not) with their pasts, and how does this then contribute to national psyches, and ongoing patterns of behaviour today?

On an even more fundamental level, how can the relationship between concepts of 'civilisation' and 'barbarism' be explored? What is the meaning of Walter Benjamin's famous provocation that 'there is no document of civilisation which is not at the same time a document of barbarism'?[*] Rather than tackling such a vast question with abstract philosophical propositions, I have attempted to root this exploration in a physical place – a walk between two sites – one associated closely with 'civilisation' and the Enlightenment, the other a place of fascism and mass murder – a walk between Goethe's house in Weimar and the gates of Buchenwald concentration camp. During the course of this walk, we eavesdrop on writers and thinkers who have been strongly in my mind over the last years, people who have spent much of their lives struggling with this interrelationship – George Steiner, Jorge Semprún, Primo

---

[*] *Über den Begriff der Geschichte* (Theses on the Philosophy of History), VII, 1940.

Levi and Sven Lindqvist, among others – and through listening to these voices, and creating a kind of dialogue between them, perhaps we can then travel further and see new kinds of connections. Most importantly, understanding continuities from the past to our world today, and the behaviour of those who exercise power, from an office in Washington or a boardroom in Berlin.

This leads me on to perhaps our greatest challenge – one of the threads that runs throughout this work is the attempt to travel into the minds of the perpetrators. And, to do this, we have to begin by trying to relinquish the label of 'perpetrator' and see the human beings beneath that term. To understand that men and women, of flesh and blood, create the circumstances that enable genocide and terror to happen. States do not torture, men and women do. Corporations do not kill, men and women do. And so it's critical that we try to get to know these people – not as 'them', not as a group, but as individuals. And it is only by doing this that we can then begin to see if there are any common patterns, any psychology or behaviour that connects people who have killed within organisations across different centuries. In the next chapters, we will meet people who have tortured, we will get inside the heads of those who have run extermination camps, those who have caused devastation to developing countries, but also the people who have enabled these things to happen – the planners, the bureaucrats, the businessmen and -women of today. Some of the people we'll meet are from interviews I carried out in a small university office, some are from past interviews – but having reflected on these conversations, and wider research over many years, I then try to determine if there are common aspects of psychology and behaviour which link people who kill from their desks, all who kill for their organisations.

Among these, and a key figure in my enquiry, the quiet man at the heart of Nazi Germany – the very civilised and educated Albert Speer, the epitome of the desk killer. Very much a figure of our times, startlingly modern, a corporate man to his fingertips, who almost never saw his victims and believed that the gods of technocracy would solve all our problems. A man who, as the saying goes, would never harm a fly. A man who considered himself entirely apolitical, yet through his organisational expertise, from his desk in Berlin, he was responsible for more destruction than anyone apart from Hitler or Himmler. After the war, helped by a remarkable priest in Spandau prison, Georges Casalis, he tried to understand his own responsibility. For some years he attempted to become a different man. Regardless of whether or not he ultimately succeeded, what I am most fascinated by is his attempt to change. Is it possible to be both appalled by the crimes that somebody has committed, yet also moved at their attempts to understand what they have done?

There is another strand that runs through this book, perhaps a more surprising one – love. The love of the women in the Atacama Desert, the love of my father, the love of Jan Karski, the love of Georges Casalis, and, finally, we return to Simone Weil, a woman who had an impossible love for the world, a love which killed her in the end; she understood both the transformatory power of love, and also the annihilation that comes when it is no longer there. We love, we lose love, we try to love again. Perhaps, in the kind of world that I am exploring here, love is the greatest form of resistance to power.

PART ONE

Survival and Speaking

1

A Hand in the Desert

There are figures silhouetted against a desert, perhaps half a dozen. Spread out in the vastness of that place. Dusk is approaching. Moving slowly, they are not walking with the intentionality that walking usually involves. They're moving as if in a kind of meditation or trance. Stopping at times, kneeling in the sand. Touching the desert, occasionally picking up a handful of dust. The Atacama Desert, a name first heard as a child; the driest place on earth.

I'm watching them today, but they are here on many days, and some of them will be here, walking like this, until they die. One day perhaps you may watch them too. They are women – relatives of some of the thousands of people murdered by the Pinochet regime in Chile between 1973 and 1990 and then dumped in unmarked graves in the desert or the mountains or the sea. And they are looking for the traces of these husbands, these brothers and sisters, these sons and daughters. Fragments of bone in the desert. Watching this, at first you are incredulous. And then, astonishingly, you see a woman's palm outstretched, and a finger gently pointing to five small pieces of phosphate of calcium found here, and, as the voice describes these fragments, the calcium becomes bone, the bone becomes a human being. Another woman describes being given the foot of her brother, with some of the sock still attached. The only part of him left. That night she cannot sleep, she comes downstairs, and describes, in a voice that seems distant to her, as if telling of another person's experience, how she strokes his foot again and again and again.

They are in a film by Patricio Guzmán, *Nostalgia for the Light*, that I saw for the first time today. It's the kind of film that makes you weep – for what it shows, but also for what it is. A meditation on the interrelationship between memory, suffering and justice. Because the film doesn't fit any established category, the distributors initially did not know what to do with it – they didn't understand how such a philosophical film could be sold to an audience. And, not for the first time, I find myself thinking about what is surfaced in our world. What is put before our eyes? We now have cultural, technological and scientific capabilities that would have sent Leonardo and Blake and Einstein spinning into raptures of ecstasy – and yet, what is created from these unprecedented possibilities? A demented digital chatter of consumerist narcissism. Human beings who spend far more time staring at screens than at the faces of their loved ones. Societies obsessed by the daily stupidities of celebrities, with millions employed in media to fawn and ogle over every last restaurant or shopping trip. Billions are spent every day on creating and distributing such images of mind-numbing banality. An industry of asininity. And – at the same time – we are told that there is not enough money to keep libraries open, not enough resources to support independent cinemas, or even to distribute nationally a miraculous film like *Nostalgia for the Light*.

But, looking further at this question of how and why certain ideas find audiences in our societies and others don't, I wonder about the limitations of our supposedly liberal, 'inclusive' cultural institutions – broadsheet newspapers, art galleries, theatres, the BBC. What ideas surface here? Who exactly is included? Beyond the bubble of the 'commentariat' in their urban echo chambers, whose voices are heard? That crucial political question always comes to mind – 'Who's *not* in the room?' And why? A literal answer to this (perhaps the kind of answer a child might give) is that some of these voices belong to people who are not in our continent, and so they would have to shout extremely loudly to make themselves heard. But surely in the globalised world of instant communication, which we're always being asked to celebrate, this shouldn't still be the case? And what of the unheard voices of those much closer to home? Sometimes it seems to me our media is more committed to demonising the poor and the vulnerable rather than giving their thoughts and feelings expression. And so a circle of being unheard, and the unarticulated rage that comes with that, spins round again, with its predictable cycle of incomprehension and violence.

What is surfaced in our world?

That is the miraculous quality of Guzmán's film. The fragments of bone, the fragments of memory, returning. The giving of space and time and attention to people who have been completely marginalised in their country. One of the women talks of how they are treated as pariahs for their insistence on finding the traces of their relatives, their insistence on justice. A world where values have been turned upside down. We meet a former architect who stayed sane in the concentration camp in the desert by drawing everything, and by looking at the stars. He paces his apartment before our eyes, counting the steps aloud, recreating the process by which he memorised the details of his imprisonment – how he'd measure every room, every distance between buildings, and then, at night, he'd draw incredibly precise plans. Once finished, he'd tear them into pieces, hide them and destroy them the following day. But the action of drawing had already meant that they were committed to memory; he had already outwitted his jailers, and on his release, was able to recreate, to the last metre, every foul detail of the concentration camp and the buildings used for torture. And when these were published, the regime was baffled at how accurate the details were. Perhaps they didn't understand the power of human memory.

I have never before witnessed a camera used with such tenderness. The space that each person is given, silences and hesitations

469

allowed. Humanity allowed. The roaring of the wind through the desert as they tell their stories. And how these testimonies seed and grow in us, long after the film has finished.

*

A few months ago I switched the radio on. A journalist was describing being in New York a decade before – the day before 11 September 2001. The volatility of the markets at the time. Another BBC correspondent told of the killing of an Afghan warlord on this same day, which, in retrospect, might have suggested that something was up . . . Yet another programme about the tenth anniversary of the Twin Towers, that terrible day. I snapped the radio off, wearied by such repetition. I was relieved to be here in the stone cottage by the sea, away from TV and the Internet and the blanket coverage of such an anniversary. I tried to locate my impatience. It was not to do with people speaking of their grief and loss. Of unbearable pain. Curiously, this is bearable, even necessary, to hear. It reminds us of love. It takes us away from abstraction and to the reality of each individual death of each individual mother, father, sister, brother, daughter and son. After all, this is exactly what the Guzmán film does, and does so poignantly. So that can't be the problem. 'What is surfaced in our world?' That's the nagging voice in my head, that's my discomfort. The vast disparity between the cultural visibility of what happened in New York with the attack on the Twin Towers and the cultural invisibility of what happened in Chile twenty-eight years before. On exactly the same day – Tuesday 11 September.

*

The first refugee I ever met was Chilean. It was winter 1983–4, the height of the Miners' Strike. Even in Cambridge the strike was all around you – every day activists from University Left would collect money for the miners in buckets throughout the city centre, the yellow badges saying 'Support the Miners' were everywhere, there were food and clothing collections, and of course many packed meetings and rallies. But the one I remember most vividly had no speakers from the NUM or the Labour Party. Ayesha, my punk friend, took me to a Miners Benefit Night of music, film and poetry, organised by the Chilean refugee community in a church hall near the Tech. I was intensely moved that these people who had suffered so much themselves were now organising for the British miners – their *compañeros*. Thirty years on, some of the details of that night are hazy – the titles of the films we watched, or the poetry we heard – but I do remember Chilean music and dancing and the intensity in that room, which was overwhelming. And one particular encounter has stayed with me.

In a gap between the music I got talking to a shortish man, perhaps in his early thirties, with a mop of dark, curly hair and eyes that darted rapidly, nervously. He spoke with a feverish need to communicate. Francisco was his name, a doctor from Santiago, who'd been at medical school at the time of the Pinochet coup. He patiently told me about what had happened in September 1973, gave me an abbreviated history lesson about Salvador Allende, his election in 1970, the remarkable socialist programme that he'd brought in, and his growing popularity with the people, despite American-sponsored strikes. He also introduced me to the name of Victor Jara, and told me of his haunting voice, his songs that were also poetry. He thrust a book with a picture of Jara into my hands. The face of a gentle man. He looked like Leonard Cohen's younger brother. He read me a translation of one of his songs – a reworking of the prayer 'Our Father' for the working man and woman. It was called 'La plegaria a un labrador' ('Prayer to a Farmer'):

Stand up, look at the mountains
Source of the wind, the sun, the water
You, who change the course of rivers,
Who, with the seed, sow the flight of your soul,
Stand up, look at your hands,
Give your hand to your brother so you can grow.
We'll go together, united by blood,
Today is the day

We can make the future.
Deliver us from the master
Who keeps us in misery.
The kingdom of justice and equality come.
Blow, like the wind blows
The wild flowers of the mountain pass . . .
Clean the barrel of my gun like fire
Stand up, look at your hands,
Give your hand to your brother so you can grow.
We'll go together, united by blood,
Now and in the hour of our death.
Amen.

And then Francisco told me of Jara's brutal murder, following days of torture after the coup. And that the soldiers had first broken his fingers – knowing the power of his music, knowing that his hands were a weapon, the soldiers had mutilated his fingers first. This detail has always stayed with me. He then described being in Santiago on that day – 11 September 1973, people looking up incredulously as military jets (supplied by the British, as he told me) dive-bombed the Moneda Palace repeatedly, where President Allende was meeting with his ministers. Plumes of smoke above the city, trucks of soldiers, people in shock, powerless to deal with this attack. And how Allende, when he realised what was happening, started to speak to the people via a radio link. And he just kept speaking, knowing he and his comrades were soon going to die.

As we finished our conversation, Francisco pressed into my hand a square piece of paper with these words written on it: the last words of Salvador Allende, to the Chilean people, as the Moneda Palace was being bombed that day:

This is the last time I shall be able to speak to you . . . I will repay with my life the loyalty of the people. I am certain that the seeds we have sown in the conscience of thousands and thousands of Chileans cannot be completely eradicated. Neither crime nor force are strong enough to hold back the process of social change. History belongs to us, because it is made by the people.

Over the last thirty years, I've copied this out many times, given the words to students, read them out at events, and still carry them with me on a battered square of red paper in a corner of my wallet. The words urgently communicate that, just as Victor Jara's voice can never be silenced, Allende's vision can never vanish, because both are built of hope, and hope is inextinguishable. It still burns today as I'm writing this, on the news I hear that young Chileans are occupying the universities to fight for their rights to free education and self-expression.

Once, in America, I took this shabby piece of paper out and showed it to a Chilean writer I had just met, a burly middle-aged man, bullish, combative. His father, an advisor in one of Allende's ministries, had been arrested after the coup, was held for days and tortured. The family were given twenty-four hours to leave Chile, but couldn't stay together – his brothers and sisters were dispersed with distant relatives across France, Germany and the United States. When I gave him the red paper with Allende's words typed out, he couldn't believe it that these words had travelled with me for so long. That the suffering of his country thousands of miles away was remembered by a stranger, and recorded ('*recordar*', from the Latin '*recordis*', to pass back through the heart).[*] He hugged me and thanked me. Solidarity. In that instant I understood the meaning of the word.

*

My mind is still in Chile tonight. Is it in the numbers killed that we judge a catastrophe? What if the bodies have never been found? The thousands of the 'disappeared'. And how do we consider the systematic use of torture by the military? And the legacy of this

---

[*] From *The Book of Embraces* by Eduardo Galeano.

horror in people still alive today; once tortured, how can you ever trust again? More than 30,000 people tortured by the Pinochet regime. Electric shocks to the genitals, rats and dogs let loose on prisoners. And Kissinger, the US Secretary of State at that time, could dare to say, in response to attacks on this regime for their multiple human rights violations: 'Please, spare us your political science lectures!' A remark which no doubt contributed to his winning of the Nobel Peace Prize – one of the greatest acts of (unintentional) satire in the twentieth century.

But perhaps the most shocking element of all: this attack on Chileans did not come out of a blue sky from an enemy living far away, it came from within the society, led by the military – though with the extensive support of the CIA and US and British intelligence. And so the perpetrators of these monstrous crimes were not vaporised, as in New York, in a moment together with their victims, but were treated as part of the 'international community' and continued to receive full diplomatic status. Reagan hosting Pinochet in Washington, Thatcher later inviting the mass killer to tea at Downing Street. Even after the return to democracy in Chile, only a tiny minority were ever held accountable for what they'd done. Most of the perpetrators still walk free. The final insult to the relatives of the dead and disappeared – to have to pass the torturers and killers of your children in the streets of Santiago.

2

The Use and Abuse of Words:
Jan Karski and Albert Speer

I don't think Albert and Augusto would have got on, if they'd ever met. Albert probably would have found Augusto *uncouth* in that military way, perhaps even *uncivilised*, a bit of a thug. Augusto would have regarded Albert as *stuck-up, superior*. Yet, curiously, Albert was responsible for a different scale of killing and suffering than Augusto ever achieved. The man in the suit was vastly more dangerous than the man in the uniform. Speer and Pinochet. An unlikely coupling. The only label they share is that unhelpful word 'perpetrator' – unhelpful because like so many quasi-scientific labels, the effect is to distance us from the human, and create a flat and unemotional world of facts, of objects, of reports. A world that both Speer, the architect and planner, and Pinochet, the military man, would recognise and feel comfortable in. And there lies the problem, or one of them. It seems to me a mistake to use the language of the perpetrators to try to understand their behaviour.

But to what extent is there a real desire to understand them? Speer was a central figure in the evolution of this work many years ago, yet now I feel an aversion, bordering on repulsion, towards him. I feel a strong disinclination to give him any further attention. Some of this is to do with Speer's vanity. That behind the supposed humility at the Nuremberg Trials and during his imprisonment at Spandau, behind the charm he displayed towards Gitta Sereny, I have an instinct of a man of almost insatiable ambition and ego. And there is something deeply offensive about the sheer volume of writing, the dozens of books, the millions of words that have been expended trying to unravel the 'mystery' of Speer. Especially in relation to the invisibility of the vast majority of his victims. Not to mention the fact that through his writing and media outings he made a significant amount of money, enabling him to live out his days in considerable comfort. It is only in the last couple of years that I have begun to realise how much he revelled in such attention, how much he needed this spotlight.

My anger towards him is accentuated at the moment because I have just finished reading Jan Karski's remarkable memoir, *Story of a Secret State*, about his experience in the Polish undergound in the Second World War. Karski and Speer were near contemporaries – Karski born in 1914, Speer born in 1905 – and shared more than their experiences of living through the war. Both came from comfortable middle-class backgrounds: Karski a family of entrepreneurs and merchants, Speer a family of architects and industrialists. Both were somewhat reserved, polite young men, groomed to be part of the ruling classes of their respective countries, Poland and Germany, with bright futures ahead of them by the mid-1930s. The young men, smartly dressed, may even have passed each other on the streets of London in 1936, where Karski was seconded to the Polish Embassy for a year, and where Speer was working on redesigns for the German Embassy in Carlton Terrace. By summer 1939, Karski, with his master's degree in law and diplomatic science, was already establishing a reputation as a young diplomat, having served in posts in Germany, Switzerland and Britain; Speer, by now Hitler's architect, was basking in the glory of having just completed the new Chancellery building in Berlin in record time. But after 1 September 1939 and the German invasion of Poland, the shape of their lives, and the moral choices they would now have to make, could not have been more different.

*

By a strange quirk of history, on the day the Germans begin their attack, Karski, a reservist in the Polish cavalry, is stationed in an army barracks in Oświęcim – the same barracks that the Germans later appropriated to become the Auschwitz I concentration camp. Karski is up early on 1 September, preparing for a day's riding in the local countryside. He is shaving at 5.05 a.m. when two huge explosions shake the barracks – part of the very first wave of bombing of the Second World War. The start of Germany's first blitzkrieg. The camp is already in chaos, the horses panicking and breaking out of the stables. The Luftwaffe then returns with wave after wave of incendiary bombs. He describes the barracks being evacuated with the German advance imminent. And he gives a remarkable detail here, which goes some way to understanding more about one of the reasons why the Germans chose this town as the centre for their regional concentration-camp system – he explains that as the Polish soldiers approach the station in Oświęcim to retreat, they are shot at from the houses nearby by German settlers living in the buildings opposite the station. As their train eventually pulls out to Krakow, Karski takes one last look at 'the treacherous windows of Oświęcim'.

After this he is arrested by the Russians, advancing from the east; later he manages to secure his release from a Soviet camp in the Ukraine, avoiding the Katyn massacre by the skin of his teeth, and returns to Poland to work underground in the resistance movement – the most organised and coherent of all such opposition to Nazi occupation in the Second World War. His intelligence, courage and phenomenal memory are soon recognised and he becomes a courier for the Polish government in exile, first taking messages (via extremely hazardous mountain routes) to France, then, after France's defeat, to Gibraltar, and from there on to Britain and the United States.

Once, in Slovakia in June 1940, he is captured, then interrogated and tortured over five days by the Gestapo, who suspect that he is a courier for the Polish underground. He has several ribs broken, and loses many teeth; he describes the pain of the beatings he endures as being 'something like the sensation produced when a dentist's drill strikes a nerve, but infinitely multiplied and spread over the entire nervous system'. On his fifth evening in captivity, he's reached a point of despair where he knows he will not be able to survive any more torture. As the thought of cracking and betraying his comrades is unbearable to him, he realises the only course of action left to him is to try to commit suicide, using a razor blade secreted in the sole of one of his boots. He feels overwhelmed by hatred and disgust for the world, which surpasses even the physical pain he is in. He describes thinking of 'my mother, my childhood, my career, my hopes. I felt a bottomless sorrow that I had to die a wretched, inglorious death, like a crushed insect, miserable and anonymous.' He realises that in all probability nobody will ever learn how he's died or even where his body lies. And then, when the guards have finished their evening rounds, he draws a cross in soot on his cell wall, and writes with his finger 'My beloved motherland . . . I love you', and then he cuts his wrists, watching the blood forming in pools around his legs. Eventually, he loses consciousness.

He wakes in a Slovakian hospital, in Prešov, with guards in the ward. He's told that he was found only moments from death, and is now to be given a blood transfusion – the Gestapo sense how important this member of the Polish underground could be. Karski

478

understands they want to save him only so that the information he has can be extracted through further torture. But, before that can happen, he spends some days in the hospital slowly recovering. A Slovakian nurse smuggles in a newspaper, and Karski reads the headline 'France Surrenders!' and is filled with renewed despair. Only Britain now stands between Nazism's domination of the whole of Europe. As a devout Catholic, all Karski can do is pray. He prays passionately that Churchill and his fighting men will be given strength and courage, that they will never admit defeat.

After eleven days, he is abruptly transferred under armed guard to another hospital in a town in southern Poland, which Karski recognises as Nowy Sącz – by coincidence, the place where Karski had stayed a month earlier, with comrades in the Polish underground, before crossing the border into Slovakia. He begins to think there might just possibly be a chance of escaping. But first he has to evade the attentions of the Gestapo guards stationed around the clock in his ward.

On the second day in hospital he starts to moan feverishly, whispering that he knows he's close to death, and needs to see a priest urgently, so that he can receive absolution before he dies. The Gestapo guard grudgingly agrees, and follows Karski, in a wheelchair, helped by a doctor and a nurse, down to the hospital chapel. Here Karski enters the confessional, while the others wait outside, sitting on the chapel pews. And then, after his confession, an extraordinary exchange unfolds with the elderly priest, all in whispers, a conversation that will save Karski's life and lead to the priest's death. Jan hesitates, trying to work up the courage to ask the priest for help. The priest tells him again, 'Go in peace,' but Jan doesn't move. Eventually he whispers, 'Father, I want you to carry a message to someone for me . . . her name is Zofia Rysiowna. She lives at 2 Matejko Street.' Eventually the priest replies, 'And what is it that you want me to tell her?' Karski gives his resistance code name, and asks the priest to tell her that he is being held at the hospital, it's a matter of life and death. The priest hesitates again, telling Karski it's an abuse of the confessional, but yes, on this occasion he will convey the message. A few days later, in one of the most remarkable operations of the Polish underground during the war, a team of resistance fighters, in co-operation with nurses, doctors and priests at the hospital, manage to spring Karski from his imprisonment.*

Over the next two years Jan, under his resistance name of Witold Kucharski, becomes an indispensable leader of the resistance in Poland, working underground in Krakow and Warsaw, helping the Polish Bureau of Information and Propaganda, establishing methods of gaining greater access to Allied radio broadcasts, and co-ordinating publications of Polish resistance books and leaflets.

In summer 1942 Karski is chosen to be the courier for one of the most vital missions of the entire war – to give the Polish government-in-exile, based in London, a complete overview of the political and military capacity of the resistance in Poland, and communicate exactly what is needed at this critical point in the conflict. This is the exact moment when the extermination of the Polish Jews is accelerating – the first waves of deportations from the Warsaw Ghetto to Treblinka begin on 22 July. Although the relationship between the Polish resistance and the Jewish underground is continually problematic – inevitably affected by historic antisemitism in Catholic Poland – Karski himself had always been strongly philosemitic. He had been influenced powerfully by growing up in Lodz (with its 40 per cent Jewish population in the 1920s and 30s), and by his mother's insistence on respect and equality for all faiths and ethnicities; indeed many of his closest childhood friends were Jewish. So when it is suggested to Karski that he should meet with Jewish leaders before leaving Poland, he agrees enthusiastically This meeting is to change Karski's life for ever. It also proves to be of great historical significance.

*

---

* For a detailed account of Karski's remarkable rescue, see *Karski: How One Man Tried to Stop the Holocaust* by E. Thomas Wood and Stanislaw Jankowski, Chapter Four: 'Sacrifice'. He only discovered towards the end of his life that thirty-two Poles, including two priests and a doctor, had been executed by the Germans in August 1940, in reprisal for this escape.

'There is nothing a man will not do to another;
nothing a man will not do for another.'

*

'Listening to an Earthquake'

One day towards the end of August 1942, Karski is in Warsaw and receives a message that he is to meet two Jewish underground leaders in a bombed-out house in the suburbs of the city. By the time he has found the rendezvous, it's close to dusk. Karski enters the building and meets the two men, senior representatives of the Jewish community in Poland. He never learns their real names (the entire underground worked on code names for reasons of security), but we now know they were Leon Feiner, the leader of the Jewish Socialist Alliance, known as the Bund, and Menachem Kirschenbaum, head of the main Zionist organisation in Poland. Karski immediately recognises the political significance of this – that these representatives, who before the war would have been bitter enemies, are now in the same room, united in the face of imminent annihilation. They converse in whispers, around a single candle, and what Karski learns appals him, as he later recounts, the memory seared in his mind for the rest of his life:

> It was an evening of nightmare, but with a painful, oppressive kind of reality that no nightmare ever had. I sat in an old, rickety armchair . . . I didn't move . . . perhaps because what I was hearing had frozen me to the spot in terror. [The two men] paced the floor violently, their shadows dancing weirdly in the dim light cast by the single candle . . . It was as though they were unable even to think of their dying people and remain seated.

Both men make it clear to Karski that the predicament of the Jews, and their own fate, is completely hopeless. They have already accepted the inevitability of death. Karski is struck by how Feiner carries himself – his stoicism, his air of refinement; he could easily have been passed 'as a Polish nobleman'. Kirschenbaum is younger, far more nervous and emotional. He explains, with passionate force, the fundamental difference between Poland's position and that of the Polish Jews:

> Many of you will die, but at least your nation goes on living. After the war Poland will be resurrected. Your cities will be rebuilt and your wounds will slowly heal. From this ocean of tears, pain, rage and humiliation your country will emerge again – but the Polish Jews will no longer exist . . . Hitler will lose his war against the human, the just and the good, but he will win his war against the Polish Jews.

He breaks down at this point, Feiner tries to calm him. Karski then talks about his mission to London and his hopes of meeting Allied leaders, possibly even Churchill and Roosevelt themselves, explaining: 'you must give me your official message to the outside world. You are the leaders of the Jewish underground. What do you want me to say?' Feiner then states that neither the Polish underground nor the Jewish resistance are able to stop the extermination of the Jews, so the main responsibility now rests with the Allied powers – 'only from outside the country can effective help for the Jews be brought'. And he added, 'Let not a single leader of the United Nations be able to say that they did not know that we were being murdered in Poland.' History will hold them responsible if they fail to act.' They inform Karski that already almost 2 million Jews in Poland have been killed. They give him extremely precise details of the deportations from the Warsaw Ghetto – how these had begun in July with 5,000 people a day being transported in sealed trains to extermination camps, but soon this figure had risen to 6,000, 7,000, and then 10,000 per day. The chairman of the Jewish Council, Adam Czerniakow, had already committed suicide, knowing there was nothing more he or anybody could do. Three hundred thousand had now been deported, and just over 100,000 were left in the ghetto. Although these figures are impossible to comprehend, Karski has a strong feeling these men are not exaggerating.

482

In the flickering, half-lit room the three men then urgently discuss what can be demanded from the Allies and the Jewish organisations in the West. Feiner and Kirschenbaum urge several actions: that the Allies should now include the prevention of the physical extermination of the Jews as one of their official war aims; that the German civilian population should be informed (through air drops of leaflets, radio and other means) of Hitler's genocide, so that they could not later claim ignorance of what was being done; that the Allies should make a public appeal to the German people to pressure the Nazi regime to stop the exterminations. They should declare that, if the genocide continues, the German people will be held collectively responsible for it; that, if none of the above manages to halt the extermination programme, then the Allies should carry out reprisals – through the bombing of sites of cultural importance in Germany, and through the execution of German POWs in Allied captivity, who still profess loyalty to Hitler after hearing of his genocidal crimes.

Karski listens intently, but at this last point tells them it's impossible, he knows the British, they wouldn't consider killing prisoners because it would be against international law, and making such a demand would only weaken the Jewish case. But Kirschenbaum hisses back: 'Of course, do you think we don't know it?! . . . We do not dream of it being fulfilled, but nevertheless we demand it. We demand it so that people will know how we feel about what is being done to us, how helpless we are, how desperate our plight is.' 'We are dying here! Say it!' the Zionist leader then adds. Karski nods, and agrees to carry these messages verbatim. He later recalls the despair of the two men at this point:

> They paused for a moment as if to let the knowledge of their true condition sink into me. I felt tired and feverish. More and more these two frantic figures pacing the floor in the shadowy room, their steps echoing in the hollow silence, seemed like apparitions, their glances filled with a burden of despair, pain and hopelessness they could never completely express.
> Their voices were pitched very low, they hissed, they whispered, and yet I continually had the illusion that they were

roaring. It seemed to me that I was listening to an earthquake, that I was hearing cracking, tearing sounds of the earth opening to swallow a portion of humanity . . . I kept quiet for fear of saying something that might be considered inappropriate, given the enormity of the problem they were sharing with me.

They also urge Karski to ask President Raczkiewicz to intercede with Pope Pius XII – to persuade him to use all powers of the Catholic Church to try to stop the exterminations. And Polish Prime Minister Sikorski should also order Poles to give all assistance possible to Jews, and make clear that any blackmailers of Jews will be executed by the Polish underground. Material assistance is also discussed – provision of money and arms to the Jewish underground, and currency and passports for escaping Jews, and the right of asylum for the small minority of those who may get to Allied countries.

But they also have an uncompromising message to Jewish leaders in the West. Feiner approaches Karski, and grips his arm so hard that it hurts. Karski looks into his eyes, moved by the unbearable pain in them, and listens:

Tell the Jewish leaders that this is no case for politics or tactics. Tell them that the earth must be shaken to its foundations, the world must be aroused. Perhaps then it will wake up, understand, perceive. Tell them that they must find the strength and courage to make sacrifices no other statesmen have ever had to make . . . This is what they do not understand. German aims and methods are without precedent in history.

He releases Karski's arm at this point, and then speaks slowly and with great deliberation as though each word were costing him an effort:

You ask me what plan of action I suggest to the Jewish leaders. Tell them to go to all the important English and American offices and agencies. Tell them not to leave until they have obtained guarantees that a way has been decided upon to save the Jews. Let them accept no food or drink, let them die a slow death while the world is looking on. Let them die. This may shake the conscience of the world.

Karski is reeling now, shivering, totally drained by the experience of having listened to these men for the last hours, knowing the responsibility of what he has to communicate – if he is able to get to London alive, that is. But Feiner hasn't finished yet: 'I know the English. When you describe to them what is happening to the Jews, they probably won't believe you.' After all, he himself had been sending telegrams and detailed written reports to London over the previous months, and these seemed to have achieved nothing. No, Karski needs to see for himself what is happening, so that he would not be relying on their word-of-mouth accounts. He needs to witness the extermination with his own eyes. This would mean his testimony cannot simply be dismissed. Feiner then explains that they can smuggle him into the Warsaw Ghetto, and possibly into one of the extermination camps, but he needs to understand something first – this will mean risking his life. Karski realises how dangerous this will be, yet also understands the critically important nature of this act of witnessing, and accepts without hesitation. They agree to make the arrangements as soon as possible and notify him. He leaves the ruined house that night, seeing the two men 'standing in the nebulous, wavering light, two dejected shadows that wished me goodnight with a feeble warmth that denoted a trust in my person rather than any confidence in our enterprise'.

*

A few days later, in the last week of August 1942, during a lull in German activity within the ghetto, Feiner meets Karski again, and they enter an apartment building at Muranowska 6, a house in central Warsaw bordering the ghetto wall. Here the building's caretaker meets them and takes them down to the cellar, where a young fighter in the Jewish Military Union, David Landau, is waiting for Feiner and the 'very important Polish man'. Landau leads the two men down to an earth passage, only four feet high, which has been excavated under the ghetto wall, emerging forty yards later in the basement of a house within the ghetto. Once they arrive in the basement, Feiner and Karski are given ragged clothes with Stars of David on, and a different escort then takes them out of the house into the ghetto itself.

Karski is astonished at the transformation Feiner undergoes at this point, moving instantly from being a tall 'nobleman' to shuffling like a bent old man, waiting for death. Karski tries to disguise himself in the same way, stooping and hiding his face under a tattered cap. We have to remember here that Feiner is by now accustomed to the terrifying reality of ghetto existence – because he, as one of the Jewish leaders, is 'privileged' to be able to move in and out of the ghetto regularly, using this secret passage. Indeed, Karski realises that Feiner and Kirschenbaum have become adept at blending in to living in Aryan Warsaw, and then transforming themselves when they visit the ghetto, like skilled actors. We can only try to imagine what is going through Karski's mind in the seconds before the three men emerge from the basement into the daylight of the ghetto.

He describes the forty yards of earth which they have crawled through as connecting 'the world of the living to the world of the dead', and, despite the vivid descriptions of what had been happening in the ghetto that he'd heard from Feiner and Kirschenbaum, Karski is totally unprepared psychologically for what he now sees:

> To pass that wall was to enter into a new world utterly unlike anything that had ever been imagined. The entire population of the ghetto seemed to be living in the street. There was hardly a square yard of empty space. As we picked our way across the mud and the rubble, the shadows of what had been men or women flitted by us in pursuit of someone or something, their eyes blazing with insane hunger . . . apart from their skin, eyes and voice there was nothing human left in these palpitating figures. Everywhere there was hunger, misery, the atrocious stench of decomposing bodies, the pitiful moans of dying

children, the desperate cries and gasps of a people struggling for life against impossible odds.

Karski sees people holding on to walls for support, barely breathing. He hears their cries offering to barter rags of clothing for morsels of food. He smells, and then sees, naked corpses left in the street. He finds out from his guide that the Germans have instituted a burial tax that nobody can afford to pay. From an upstairs window of one of the houses, he witnesses a 'game' that two teenage boys, with pistols, are 'playing' in the street below. They are members of the Hitler Youth, and they are, quite literally, hunting Jews. The pavement below has emptied now, but Karski sees one of the boys taking aim at a spot just outside his line of vision. Then a shot rings out, followed by the sound of breaking glass and the terrible cries of a man in agony. The boys walk off, towards the ghetto exit, smiling at each other, and 'chatting cheerfully as if they were returning from a sporting event'. Karski is in shock now. He cannot move or speak for several minutes. Eventually the guide takes him and Feiner out of the ghetto and back to the land of the living.

Two days later Karski makes another, longer, visit to the ghetto so that he can memorise even more of this apocalyptic desolation to take with him on his mission to London – to shake the conscience of the world. After this, Feiner asks him to do one further act of witnessing, this one even more dangerous – to go into an extermination camp and see the Nazis' 'final solution' in action. And so, in early September 1942, Karski and a guide take a train to Lublin, and then a car further east to the village of Izbica Lubelska.[*]

How is it possible for us to understand the impact of these three episodes on him? The word traumatic – if we use it in its original Greek sense of *trauma* meaning 'wound', and not today's overused synonym for disturbing or upsetting – perhaps gets us close to what Karski experienced. It's clear that he never truly recovered from

---

[*] It is here that Karski, disguised as an Estonian guard, witnesses the events that are recounted towards the end of Book One.

what he saw. I feel that his decision – to risk his life to witness these atrocities, and then to attempt to tell the world what was happening – puts him in a category of moral courage and fierce altruism almost without parallel. He knew that he probably would not come out of this alive; and, even if he survived, he knew that he would be emotionally and psychically wounded for the rest of his life.

Reading, or hearing, Karski's words will almost certainly affect your way of looking at the world too. His testimony at the end of *Shoah* is astounding. It overwhelms us, takes us into territory beyond the human capacity to process; it is also mesmerising. In the end, though, we realise that Karski's act of witnessing is perhaps the ultimate embodiment of humanity. Each word of his, however terrifying, paradoxically takes us further away from the annihilation that Nazism attempted. As Hannah Arendt later wrote, 'holes of oblivion' (which totalitarian regimes attempt to create) 'do not exist ... there are simply too many people in the world to make oblivion possible. One man will always be left alive to tell the story.' This was why Lanzmann pursued Karski for years when he was making *Shoah*, trying to persuade him to be interviewed, and it's why he gives him more time than any other witness who appears in the course of those nine and a half hours of film.

You will never be able to forget his face. The astonishing dignity of this man as he speaks. You can see the physical manifestation of complete trauma in Karski's body, as he begins to give his testimony. His body is fighting with his memory. His eyes dart as he travels back thirty-five years in his mind to that August afternoon in Warsaw. His voice attempting to be calm but trembling: 'Now ... now I go back thirty five years. No! I don't go back!' He fights the panic that comes with memory, knowing that he is about to open the wounds again, seeing the days of barbarism again in his mind. The act of remembering tortures him, and yet he then says, 'I understand this film is for historical record, so I will try to do it.' The staggering personal cost of bearing witness. The weight on his shoulders as he begins to speak. And then the vivid clarity of these words, emerging in a flow of total intensity, as if he cannot operate any of the usual filters we use when describing terrible events. He simply describes the reality of what he saw with his own eyes. Though he repeatedly emphasises the limitations of words and our human imagination when faced with such an apocalypse.

There is a passage towards the end of *Story of a Secret State* in which he attempts to describe his physical and mental state having just returned to the village of Izbica Lubelska, having seen the extermination of Jewish men, women and children at the camp. I have never heard anyone refer to this moment in Karski's life, but it demonstrates graphically the impact this act of witnessing had on him. When he gets back to the little shop where the Polish resistance man is sheltering him, he immediately strips off the uniform he's been wearing and washes himself obsessively in the kitchen behind the shop, flooding it in the process. Then he goes outside, at the back of the shop:

I wrapped my coat around me and went out into a tiny vegetable garden. I lay down under a tree and with the promptness of utter exhaustion, fell asleep. I awoke with a start, from some nightmare, I think. It was dark, except for a large, brilliant moon. I was stiff with cold and for a moment I could not remember where I was and how I had got there. When I did, I dashed inside the house and found an empty bed. My host was asleep. It was not long before I was too.

I awoke in the morning. The sunlight, though not strong, was giving me a painful headache. My host stood over me asking if I was ill. I had been talking and twisting restlessly in my sleep. As soon as I got out of bed I was seized with a violent fit of nausea. I rushed outside and began to vomit. Throughout that day and during the next day I continued to vomit at intervals. When all the food had been emptied from my stomach, I threw up a red liquid . . . I slept brokenly for the balance of the day and throughout the following night . . .

The images of what I saw in the death camp are, I am afraid, my permanent possessions. I would like nothing better than to purge my mind of these memories. For one thing, the recollection of these events invariably brings on a recurrence of the nausea. But more than that, I would like simply to be free of them, to obliterate the very thought that such things ever occurred.

*

Less than a month later, on 1 October, Karski begins his epic eight-week journey to Britain. But, before he leaves, at 5 a.m. with the dawn curfew barely over, he attends a secret Mass in Warsaw, in the rectory behind the Church of the Holy Cross, on Karkowskie Przedmiescie. Here, Father Edmund Krauze, chaplain to the Warsaw resistance, and a dozen of Karski's closest friends gather to celebrate a final Mass together, which Jan finds intensely moving. At the end, there is another ceremony, which his friends have prepared for him:

> Father Edmund asked me to approach the altar which had been improvised in his room and made me kneel down. He then bade me open my shirt and bare my chest. Surprised, and not at all aware of what was to follow, I obeyed his instructions. He took a pyx* in both of his hands, smiled gently at my confusion, and spoke solemnly:
> 'I have been authorised by those in whom the authority of the Church is vested, to present you, soldier of Poland, with Christ's Body to carry with you on your journey. Wear it throughout your journey. If danger approaches, you will be able to swallow it. It will protect you from evil and harm.'
> He hung the pyx about my neck. I bent my head and prayed. Father Edmund knelt beside me and prayed with me. There was a deep reverent silence in the room. All I could hear was the faint clicking of the beads in someone's rosary.

---

* A small, round receptacle, usually made of wood, but in this case silver, containing the Eucharist, used by priests to transport the consecrated host outside of the church, often to parishioners who are very sick or dying.

His journey takes him first to Berlin by train, with a swollen jaw (helped by a friendly dentist) so that he can avoid speaking to anybody. He has no way of knowing as the train crosses the border to Germany, but he would not see Poland again for thirty-two years. In Berlin, Karski has some hours to wait before his train to Paris, and so he decides to visit Rudolph Strauch, an old friend from his months in Berlin as an intern at the Polish Embassy in 1935. Karski tells us that the Strauch family had always been 'deeply liberal and democratic' in their values, and so he has strong expectations that they would be opposed to Nazism. He finds their house, not far from the station, but Rudolph and his family have changed greatly. Jan is appalled by the effect the last seven years of fascism have had on Rudolph as this former liberal repeats, mantra-like, 'The Führer knows what he is doing' throughout their conversation about the war.

They go to a cheap beerhouse near Unter den Linden. Jan has to disguise his real feelings throughout the meal; the talk moves to the 'problem' of the Jews and Rudolph and his sister simply repeat the Nazi line. When Jan tries to argue with them, Rudolph says that although he's fond of him, it's clear that 'all the Poles are the enemies of the Führer and the Reich' so they will have to break off their friendship. Karski leaves the beerhouse anxiously, wondering if he's perhaps being followed down Unter den Linden. At the end of the street (though Karski's unaware of this), the lights in the windows of the Arms Ministry are still burning; Albert Speer and his aides are working late into the night again, planning how to double weapons production to support the assault on the Russian front. Karski walks back to the station, reflecting bitterly on the loss of his friendship, and how the corruption of an entire society in Germany has happened in a matter of a few years.

From Berlin he makes his way to Paris, then over the next weeks, Lyons, across the Pyrenees on foot, Barcelona, Madrid and Gibraltar – from where he is finally flown to London, arriving on the evening of 25 November 1942. Given the importance of his mission, he expects to be met at the RAF base by senior Polish diplomatic officials, but British intelligence tells him that he will be kept in quarantine until his case has been 'resolved'. Karski is appalled by this further delay, and for two days he is held at the Royal Victoria Patriotic Schools building in the middle of Wandsworth Common, which is being used by MI5 during the war. All that is in his mind during these days is the critical need to transmit what he has seen, yet he is now imprisoned by MI5 in supposedly 'free' London.

Finally, on 28 November, following furious Polish diplomatic protests, Karski is transferred to Polish Interior Ministry official Paweł Siudak, who drives him to his flat, where he stays for the next two months. Karski is extremely agitated, and when the Polish interior minister, Stanisław Mikołajczyk, arrives that evening to debrief him, he cuts him off, saying that he has vital messages for several Polish figures in London, but more urgently still, there are issues of life and death concerning the Jews of Poland. It is imperative he speaks to the British government as soon as possible, 'without their help the Jews will perish. I have to see Churchill! . . . Immediately! I have important information!' Siudak and Mikołajczyk watch him pacing wildly up and down the room, describing the atrocities he's witnessed with vivid animation. They decide that he needs rest for several days, and he will only be allowed to meet certain Poles, and all of these meetings will be strictly supervised.[*]

The one outside visit he is allowed to make during this time is to a Polish church on Devonia Road in Islington, Our Lady of Częstochowa and St Casimir. Here Monsignor Władysław Staniszewski hears Jan's confession, and is shown the pyx given to him by the priest in Warsaw. Staniszewski removes the Eucharist and gives Karski Communion. Jan asks to keep the silver pyx as a memento, but the monsignor suggests it would be better if was hung on the church's portrait of the Madonna of Częstochowa, as an offering for Karski's safe passage. Jan agrees, and, apparently, to this day, in the little church, you can see the silver pyx hanging on the painting of the Madonna.

---

[*] Prime Minister Sikorski later tells Karski, 'You were crazy when you got here. We couldn't let outsiders see you in that shape.'

Within days Karski starts to meet high-ranking Polish officials, and arrangements are soon made to meet Jewish members of the Polish National Council. His eyewitness accounts of what he's seen are electrifying, and word now begins to spread of the young Polish courier. Already his confirmation of the genocide of the Jews starts to ripple out, and by 1 December the World Jewish Congress in New York have been informed by telegram: 'Have Read Today All Reports From Poland . . . Jews in Poland Almost Completely Annihilated . . . Believe The Unbelievable'. On 2 December Karski arrives at Stratton House, Piccadilly (just next to Green Park Underground station) to meet Szmul Zygielbojm, the socialist Bund representative on the Polish National Council.* Karski's role now is to use his photographic memory and celebrated powers of recall to give extraordinarily detailed accounts of what he's witnessed. He later describes this period of his life as being little more than a 'tape-recorder'. But what he was transmitting was explosive. And he recognises the impact his words have on all those he meets.

He details what he has witnessed in Poland – accounts of the Nazi occupation and the Polish underground resistance and what he has seen in the Warsaw Ghetto and at Izbica. He has personal meetings with many of the most senior politicians and agencies among the Allied powers, including General Sikorski, the Polish prime minister in exile in London, Sir Anthony Eden, British Foreign Secretary, the United Nations War Crimes Commission and many others. In early December 1942, largely based on Karski's reports, the World Jewish Congress issued their statement 'Annihilation of European Jewry: Hitler's Policy of Total Destruction'. In late spring 1943 he travels to the United States and personally briefs President Roosevelt in the White House.

Despite Karski's devastating testimony – which he hopes, in Feiner's words, will help 'to shake the conscience of the world' – and despite the pleas of several Jewish leaders in the West, no Allied

---

* For a detailed account of Karski's meeting with Zygielbojm and his mission to inform the Allies about the Holocaust see the forthcoming volume of *I You We Them* – Book Four, Chapter One, 'The Abyss Opens'.

intervention to stop, or even temporarily halt, the ongoing mass murder of the Jews is forthcoming.

*

While Karski is being tested beyond human limits, fighting with every shred of his being against fascism and for the survival of his country, Speer's career is going from strength to strength. In the same week in June 1940 that Karski is recovering in hospital following his torture by the Gestapo and attempted suicide, Speer is accompanying Hitler on a triumphal tour of Paris, being photographed in front of the Eiffel Tower as the Führer's right-hand man (quite literally so). In his huge office in the Academy of Arts he's creating the vastly bombastic masterplans for the new Berlin that Hitler has ordered, with the Kuppenhalle – 'The Great Hall of the People' – designed to dwarf St Peter's in Rome and hold 180,000 spectators. It would be hard to imagine a greater contrast between the selflessness of Karski – risking his life repeatedly for his country, giving up his links even to his own family and friends to work in the underground – and the career-driven vanity of the other, providing first the visual identity for Nazism and later the military means by which it would fight.

When Karski is meeting Feiner and Kirschenbaum in the ruined house on the edge of Warsaw, and then witnessing the appalling realities of the Warsaw Ghetto in August 1942, Speer is at the zenith of his powers in his new job as Reich minister for armaments and war production. In this month, Speer is basking in the glory of having achieved, in only six months, huge increases in output – 27 per cent in weapons production, 25 per cent in tank manufacture and 97 per cent in ammunition production. On 19 August Speer is meeting Hitler to discuss how 'a further million Russian labourers' can be supplied to the German armament industry, using 'any necessary compulsion' to achieve this end. In September, when Karski is at Izbica, we know Speer and Sauckel and others are deliberating on how to improve productivity among workers, Speer suggesting that the SS and police start taking more serious action 'and putting those known as slackers into concentration camps'.

Perhaps, though, the starkest difference between these two men can be seen after the war, in the way they spoke about their experiences. At the end of 1944 Karski published his *Story of a Secret State*, a rallying cry for Polish resistance and Allied co-operation, but also an attempt to make sense of all that he'd witnessed in the war. An attempt maybe to heal his shattered self and, by sharing some of his most appalling experiences, perhaps to try to exorcise the power of those memories. But, although the book was successful, and in many respects Karski was seen as an archetypal hero of the Polish resistance, he had a far more bitter view of himself and his war years. All he could see was the futility of his efforts to inform the West of what was happening, the total inaction of Allied governments in the face of the knowledge he brought them about the Holocaust. Now, in the post-war years he vowed he would try to forget what had happened and never speak of his experiences again: 'At that time I hated humanity, I broke with the world . . . I imposed on myself a pledge never to mention the war to anybody.'

All of this could not contrast more starkly with Speer. Or rather, the Albert Speer of his later years, following his release from Spandau prison in 1966. The Speer who had secretly written his autobiography in jail, then negotiated lucrative book deals for *Inside the Third Reich* on his release. The Speer who milked the media circus that followed him for most of the late 1960s and early 1970s. The Speer who never tired of telling his story to anyone who'd listen, to any magazine or broadcaster who'd pay. The flood of books and articles and TV appearances; a torrent of self-justification and vanity masquerading as humility. Hoping the key questions of knowledge and responsibility would get lost in the sheer volume of words. Elusiveness disguised as openness.

*

'Political Events Did Not Concern Me'

What is that famous phrase of St Augustine's? 'Hate the sin, but not the sinner'. Well, we can try. Although Speer may be a deeply troubling figure, he is also central to any enquiry into the psychology of the leadership of the Third Reich. Why is this? How to explain the fascination of Speer, the compulsion, against better instincts, to be drawn in to him, like moths to flame? At the Nuremberg Trials after the war he was virtually alone among the senior Nazis in condemning Hitler and accepting collective responsibility for what had been done, including the mass murder of the Jews, Roma and many others – even though he strenuously denied any direct knowledge of that. Whether this was a genuine position or an extremely manipulative strategy, it certainly helped to save him from execution. His release from Spandau in 1966, after twenty years in prison, coincided with a period when there was a significant increase in interest, both from historians and the wider public, in the Third Reich and the war years. It also occurred at the height of the 150 'NS Verbrechen trials' (Nazi Crimes trials) held between 1958 and 1968.[*] So he became a figure of fascination for many; an embodiment of living history – a senior Nazi on television screens in the 1970s. A person who had known Hitler more intimately than anyone else. And, most importantly, a senior Nazi who had publicly recanted, who had accepted that Hitlerism, at least by the end, had become insane. A Nazi who had, to a great extent, appeared to atone for his criminal responsibility. It seemed almost as if he had wanted to take the sins of Germany of those years onto his own shoulders, and try to expiate them.

But I think there are other important aspects to Speer which explain why so much has been written about him. The first is his undoubted intelligence. While not possessing the analytical skills or the capacity for scepticism to be a real intellectual, he was, nevertheless, capable of exceptional insight and was vastly more reflective than

---

[*] The Bergen-Belsen trial happened in 1962 in Hanover, the Treblinka trial took place in Düsseldorf in 1964, the Auschwitz trial started in Frankfurt in the same year, and the Einsatzgruppen 1005 trial occurred in Hamburg in 1968.

any of his colleagues in the leadership of the Third Reich. And certainly a world away from the gallery of Nazi monsters like Goering, Himmler and Goebbels that has been passed down to us since the war. However, this of course is double-edged; precisely because of his mental abilities, many people found it even more shocking, even more of an enigma, that someone so intelligent could become involved in such a barbaric enterprise. Indeed Georges Casalis, the minister in Spandau prison who was to play such an important part in Speer's post-war life, confronts him directly about this after his first service in the prison:

> I told him that I considered him more blameworthy than any of the others. First of all, because he was the most intelligent. But secondly, he was, to my mind, not only more responsible than the six other prisoners, but perhaps more than anyone in Germany, except for Hitler himself, for extending the war. Thanks to his efforts, I told him, this terrible war had lasted at least a year longer than it might have.

Casalis here is referring to Speer's work as Reich minister for armaments and war production, which he was appointed to by Hitler after the death of Fritz Todt in a mysterious plane crash on 8 February 1942.

As minister for war production, Speer also proved himself to be a remarkable organiser, co-ordinating both weapons and construction programmes with brilliant management skills (skills which he'd already demonstrated as head of the Baustab Speer, his organisation for building and construction). In his capacity as Hitler's chief architect, by autumn 1941 he was already directing tens of thousands of building workers across the whole of Europe. However, this position was minor in comparison to the responsibilities he inherited in his new position as Reich minister; when he took over this role he had responsibility for 2.6 million workers; by 1944 this had risen to 14 million (not including workers in occupied countries), making him one of the most powerful figures in Nazi Germany. As Casalis said, he has often been credited (if that is the right word) by historians with extending the length of the war by at least a year, because of his abilities to increase weapons and tank production dramatically, even under the most adverse circumstances.

The third aspect is the sheer modernity of Speer. How his technocracy and managerialism connects him directly to our current world. When we read his words, and listen to him speaking, we seem to hear a contemporary business executive. It is entirely plausible that he might have said:

> Had I been born twenty years later I would be a highly respected man today. Maybe the head of Daimler-Benz, chairman of the board of Hoechst, chief executive of Deutsche Bank.*

*

In all the thousands of pages I've read about this man, coming across Gitta Sereny's book *Albert Speer: His Battle with Truth* marked a watershed for me. Moments of real epiphany are rare, but I can still remember where I was – in Suffolk, sitting by the fire, the night before Christmas Eve 1996, everyone else in the family had

---

* Lines given to Speer by Esther Vilar in her play *Speer*.

gone to bed – when I came across one particular passage in this book. It was on page 184, towards the bottom. Speer is speaking about Hitler's 'fetish for secrecy' and the way that nobody should seek to know more than was required 'for the enactment of his or her duties'. And then he says this – two sentences which instantly opened up new thoughts:

> Hitler required us *not only to compartmentalise our activities but also our thinking* [my emphasis] . . . He insisted that each man should only think about his task and not be concerned with that of his neighbour.

Could compartmentalisation be the key? This was the psychological aspect that underlay so many of the events that had most disturbed me – and still disturb me today – the Saurer memorandum, the people working in the Shell Centre the day after the executions in Nigeria, in fact anybody working for a transnational corporation who cannot see those affected by their work. So to find Speer talking about this process as being central to how he and many others in Nazi Germany operated was fascinating. He explains that such compartmentalisation was formalised by General Order No. 1 (Grundsätzlicher Befehl Nr. 1) on 11 January 1940, forbidding the 'thoughtless passing on of decrees, orders of information specified as secret', and that this order was posted up on the wall of every office and building: 'Every man need only know what is going on in his own domain . . .' Subsequently, I came across this passage in *Inside the Third Reich*, in which Speer goes into greater detail about this psychological process:

> Worse still was the restriction of responsibility to one's own field. That was explicitly demanded. Everyone kept to his own group – of architects, physicians, jurists, technicians, soldiers or farmers. The professional organisations to which everyone had to belong were called chambers (Physicians Chamber, Art Chamber), and this term aptly described the way people

were immured in isolated, closed-off areas of life. The longer Hitler's system lasted, the more people's minds moved within such isolated chambers.

However, in addition to this externally imposed kind of compartmentalisation, Speer goes on to describe something even more pernicious – his own, voluntary, isolating of himself; his own psychological collusion in this way of thinking and operating. He gives the following view of himself – which is both revealing and quite bizarre considering his role as the chief architect of the Third Reich and designer of the infamous Nuremberg rallies. Speer says that, up until the end of the war, he'd always considered himself to be essentially apolitical:

> I felt myself to be Hitler's architect. Political events did not concern me . . . I felt there was no need for me to take any political positions at all . . . I was expected to confine myself to the job of building. The grotesque extent to which I clung to this illusion is indicated by a memorandum of mine to Hitler as late as 1944; 'The task I have to fulfil is an unpolitical one. I have felt at ease in my work only so long as my person and my work were evaluated solely by the standard of practical accomplishments.' But fundamentally the distinction was inconsequential. *Today it seems to me that I was trying to compartmentalise my mind* [my emphasis].

It seems clear that there is a strong continuity in the process that Speer is describing here, and the activities of numerous organisations today, numerous corporations. The specialisation that's demanded in so many fields, the way that this increases the potential problems of people only discussing issues within a 'bubble' of known and understood, coded, internal languages. And the consequent danger of decisions then being made that are based on 'groupthink' rather than rigorously interrogated ideas. Wasn't this precisely the kind of decision-making that led to the banks' absurd speculative schemes which in turn triggered the economic crisis of

2007–8? This, together with the single-minded focus on the task that needs to be done, the ruthlessness involved here – the way this brings with it a deliberate blindness to anything outside the fulfilment of the task.

But there is something else in Speer's behaviour, and his later reflections, which is equally disturbing – again, precisely because of how applicable they are to today's globalised economy. At the heart of this is Speer's worshipping of new technology, his faith that it could overcome almost all challenges, could provide virtually all of the answers, and his awareness that, in such a technocratic world, there would inevitably be casualties. And considerations of human empathy or moral implications would have to be swept aside. In a little-known and very rarely quoted passage, which I believe to be absolutely critical to understanding not just Speer but contemporary capitalism, he says this about his working relationship with specialists in the armaments industry:

> Basically, I exploited the phenomenon of the technician's often blind devotion to his task. Because of *what seems to be the moral neutrality of technology* [my emphasis], these people were without any scruples about their activities. The more technical the world imposed on us by the war, the more dangerous was this indifference of the technician to the direct consequences of his anonymous activities.

Again, it's not difficult to think of many parallels in our societies. The brilliant aeronautical engineers doing cutting-edge research into refining how unmanned planes can fly even higher – who cannot connect their work to the use of drones to kill human beings in Afghanistan and Pakistan. Or the way that talented geologists working in exploration departments of major oil companies rarely link their skilled seismic testing with the ultimate reality of the earth's catastrophic heating up caused by carbon emissions generated by the continuing use of fossil fuels. When I hear the word 'technology' being used in a kind of evangelical way, apparently without reference to the human beings who are affected or without a sense of the wider moral framework, it makes me shiver. Take this example from John Browne, who was at the time CEO of BP, regarded, curiously, as a 'progressive' voice within the oil industry, speaking in 2000 – here talking evangelically about the way technology will conquer all before it:

> Historically all the fears of shortages . . . of food, of water, of land were disproved by change, by technical breakthroughs, which substituted one thing for another, and through fundamental shifts in productivity . . . Now, to an unprecedented extent, technology has the ability to repeat that process, embracing a radical and transforming change beyond all previous experience . . . We face a revolution in the way the economy works driven by new technology. A revolution which I believe will have major beneficial consequences for the environment.[*]

I doubt that Browne would see the parallels, but in the quasi-religious zeal of this language – seemingly expressing overwhelming faith in the ability of technology and productivity to solve everything, in the way technology is viewed as somehow separate from society, from human beings – I hear echoes of Speer's detachment, his way of thinking.

The historian Hugh Trevor-Roper – writing immediately after the war, when he'd been given exceptional access to intelligence material in Berlin relating to Hitler and the Nazi leadership[†] – came to believe that 'in a political sense, Speer is the real criminal of Nazi Germany, for he, more than any other, represented that fatal philosophy which . . . made havoc of Germany and nearly shipwrecked the world. His keen intelligence diagnosed the nature and observed the mutations of Nazi government and policy . . . he heard their outrageous orders and understood their fantastic ambitions; but he did nothing.' He then goes on to say this, about Speer's fatal decoupling of technocracy from political reality:

---

[*] Reith Lectures, 'Respect for the Earth', 2000.
[†] Published in March 1947 as *The Last Days of Hitler*.

Speer was a technocrat and nourished a technocrat's philosophy. To the technocrat . . . politics are irrelevant. To him the prosperity, the future of a people depends not upon the personalities who happen to hold political office, nor upon the institutions in which their relations are formalised . . . but upon the technical instruments whereby society is maintained, on the roads and the railways, the canals and the bridges, the services and factories wherein a nation invests its labour, and whence it draws its wealth. This is a convenient but ultimately fallacious philosophy.

Trevor-Roper's assessment of Speer is confirmed later by Speer himself, describing how he felt able to separate his work life completely from all the wider aspects of Nazism. And how, driving in to his office in the centre of Berlin from his villa on Schwanenwerder, by the lake in Wannsee, he was able to focus entirely on the business that lay ahead that day, and not concern himself with anything beyond it.

Politics to me was noise and vulgarity. If I thought of it at all, it was only as an interruption to the quiet and concentration I sought . . . fanaticism of any kind simply had no place in it.

*

The most frightening aspect of Albert Speer is that he never really died. We are appalled by Hitler, Himmler, Goebbels and Goering, but – like children needing to be comforted by the deaths of the 'baddies' in films and books – we can see the images of their dead bodies, shudder and mutter 'never again'. But Speer has never left us. We can see him everywhere today. He's there in every micromanaging CEO, in every workaholic government minister, in every technocrat who turns away from the human consequences of their work, in everyone who decides not to see something that they know may cause moral discomfort. In the last months of the war, the *Observer*, presciently, wrote this:

> Speer is, in a sense, more important for Germany today than Hitler, Himmler, Goering, Goebbels or the generals. They have all, in a way, become the mere auxiliaries of an organising genius who alone leads the massive fighting machine. He is very much the successful average man, well dressed, civil, uncorruptable, very middle class in his lifestyle, with a wife and six children. Much less than any of the other German leaders does he stand for anything particularly German, or particularly Nazi. He rather symbolises a type which is becoming increasingly important in all belligerent countries: the pure technician, to whom politics is of no importance . . . Therefore not *actually* a Nazi . . . pure technical and managerial ability, and it is this lack of psychological and spiritual ballast and the ease with which they handle the terrifying technical and organisational machinery of our age that make this type go so far nowadays . . . We may get rid of the Hitlers and the Himmlers, but the Speers will be with us for ever.

PART TWO

Silences of the Fathers

3

My Father and His Silence

The photograph is not more than an inch and a half square, and yet it expresses so much of the man I remember. So much contained in that downward look and gentle smile. It's one of two images of my father which I keep with me. The picture was taken when we were on holiday in Germany in summer 1973, staying with friends just outside Bamberg. Strange to realise that he was then the same age that I am now. Such a comparison makes me feel uneasy somehow. Perhaps all comparisons with parents are like this.

There are a hundred things I could say about this second picture. But perhaps words are unnecessary. I return to my father's gaze, and the sensation of him being there, at my shoulder, which I miss most, and sometimes think I can still feel.

*

This picture I saw for the first time only recently. My mother was clearing out old boxes and came across one containing assorted remnants of Mark's past. Among these was a carrier bag full of papers and photographs to do with his two years in the Royal Anglian Regiment. It was taken in Korea, where he was unfortunate enough to do his national service, including more than a year fighting in the Korean War, between 1951 and 1952 – the first war sanctioned by the newly formed United Nations. Together with a few tiny black-and-white photographs of smudged hillsides and jeeps and clusters of comrades, there was a diagram showing drawings of 'Mortar Shell Crater Analysis' and 'Typical Ricochet Markings'. And dusty maps, browned with the years, showing the curve of the River Imjin-Gang, and two lines marked in red pencil, presumably the front-line positions of the UN forces and the North Koreans. Amongst the close contours of the hills (Mansok-tong, Kawang-son, Simgok), circles in pencil, with arrows, possibly showing lookout positions or planned reconnaissance missions. There were also a couple of small notebooks, a soldier's service and pay book, and a little army diary for 1952, blue leather, traces of Korean mud on the spine, which I'm holding in my hands today. It tells me that 9 February, in 1952, was a Saturday. I can see Mark has written, in his characteristic neat italics, '*14.30 – conference Brigade HQ am*'. Then there's a note on another page, '*Mess bill £3*' and '*10.30 – A Coy C br B Patrol*'. I scan each day, hoping for a trace of life lived, but find mainly jotted codes, impenetrable to my civilian eyes: '*16.00 – All MMG lpt at CP*', '*0500 – Coy IBW for "Swift"*', '*1000 Pr 183 w OCD*'. Occasionally there's something comprehensible – on 5 February he's written in pencil, '*am. Take Sgt CLOUGH and Cpl PUGH to their WYOMING posns*'; on 29 April, '*leave 0900 Kansas recce*'; and, among all the patrols, recces and briefings, on 13 July a rare invasion from another world – '*12.30 – Tom's birthday, booze*'. It is almost impossible to see the war in these pages; you would need a specialist to decode what much of these abbreviations must have meant. Just once, on 12 May, the meaning is clear: '*Flynn killed Sexton wounded*'.

Korea was a particularly dirty war. In some respects it was the prototype for Vietnam, with carpet-bombing, the first widespread use of napalm and many civilian deaths. I try to imagine the hell of those months, and I fail. He was a first lieutenant with command responsibility for a platoon. Unimaginable – this boy just out of school, nineteen, twenty years old (though he looks even younger in this picture), responsible for twenty men in total, many of them older than him. I find a typed list of their names – *O'Higgins, Roger, Wilson, Blewitt, Guyer, Kennedy, Brand, Corbett, Marshall, Barrett, Bunch, Collins, Emanuel, McBrien, Ormsby, Pickersgill, Roche, Ross, Hussey and Thomas.* When soldiers in his platoon were killed it was his responsibility to write to their parents. My eyes pass over that list of names again, and wonder how many of them survived this war.

Later on, Mark became an academic, lecturing at University College London for more than twenty years. He was a classicist who embodied the Socratic challenge that 'the unexamined life is not worth living', both for himself and everyone he came into contact with. Not only was he a loved teacher, but a wonderful conversationalist too – rigorous but also gently ironic, wise and humorous. A fitting intellectual companion for his loved Athenian sceptic, who he would often talk about as if he was an entirely living presence. Curiously (perhaps out of loyalty to the Socratic oral tradition), he never published anything. He was always busy in the department, and as well as his seminars and lectures he was also admissions tutor and responsible for pastoral care of the students in the faculty as well. Younger colleagues who published papers 'willy-nilly' (a phrase he often used) were objects of gentle mockery, as were some in authority who seemed to believe there was a correlation between the quality of the teaching in a faculty and the quantity of papers published.

But as I got older, especially when I reached university, I began to find his opposition to publishing rather strange. One day, when I was home, and after he had decided to take early retirement from UCL, I challenged him about this. Why didn't he write? We were in a pub in the nearby village and I said, because his passion for Socrates was so strong, and obviously there were many things that the Athenian could teach our world – why not communicate these things to a younger audience? I think he was surprised by the question. In my mind now I can see him vividly, head tilted slightly to one side, taking another cigarette out of the packet (Consulate, with the green and white trim), as if this would help with the answer.

He had a curious way of tapping the cigarette gently on the packet three times before lighting it, and then he said, 'Well, I might just do that. After all, I'll have the time now.' Within a year he was dead.

But his qualities and beliefs live on in my mind. He was highly reflective, vigorously intellectual, a left-wing Catholic who admired liberation theology greatly. And as a father a gentle inspiration, loving, funny, wise. A dream of a father. He never quite understood my obsession with football as a boy, but in the summer we'd play cricket, which was more his game, and he'd teach me how to spin the ball. Inevitably, when I hit adolescence, we had our clashes, but nothing different from most sons and fathers.

Thirty years after his death I still think of him on most days – he is simply a part of my life. At times of difficulty I talk to him and try to hear that voice I trusted more than any other, try to hear what he would do in my place. And sometimes I can still hear myself, as an angry teenager, taunting him for being 'too liberal', 'too wishy-washy', too forgiving. He was very keen about 'not writing people off just because you don't share the same political label', trying to find something good in everyone – which really tested my patience in the early 1980s, the heyday of Thatcherism. Though I used to remind him that his Christian tolerance did not extend to 'Mrs T' as he called her. I think 'loathe' would be the right word for his feelings. As a serious Catholic he was particularly incensed by her misappropriation of the words of St Francis of Assisi, on becoming prime minister, 'Where there is discord, may we bring harmony . . . where there is despair, may we bring hope.'*

When we were growing up there was little we didn't talk about in the family, often around the kitchen table that was at the heart of the house. Supper times were particularly long and lively affairs, with animated discussions buzzing, us children struggling to compete with adult voices, often using volume to compensate for the knowledge we did not yet possess. And it was fascinating to see

---

* A characteristic misquotation by Thatcher; the prayer actually opens with 'Where there is hatred, let me sow love'.

our parents arguing passionately, especially about religion – Mark Catholic, Corinne atheist, with occasional forays into agnosticism. Sometimes we felt like the umpire observing two particularly well-matched tennis players, as the arguments pinged back and forth across the table. We learnt that you could disagree strongly on quite fundamental things but still love and respect each other. And we were always encouraged to talk, to express ourselves, especially if we were worried about something. Openness was very important.

'And yet and yet' (as he would often say to introduce a dissenting view), there was one way in which Mark was a closed book: he would hardly ever speak about Korea – not to Corinne, not to us, not to any-one. And yet this had been an experience which had shaped him as a young man. Perhaps it would be more accurate to say misshaped him, because he emerged from his time in Korea with what we would rec-ognise today as post-traumatic stress disorder, though those words did not exist then, nor any medical support to deal with the devasta-tion of what he'd been through. When he returned to England to take up his scholarship at Oxford he had a severe breakdown in his first term, most of which he later said he'd spent 'staring at walls', utterly contemptuous of the supposedly bright young things all around him who he found vacuous and disconnected from the realities of the world that he'd seen. He left soon afterwards, and then spent a couple of years doing various odd jobs in London like driving delivery vans, but not settling at anything. It took him years to gradually put the pieces of his life back together, to begin to connect with people again, to learn to trust. Though perhaps Korea always remained a darkness on the edge of his consciousness, the shadow of which he could never quite escape, even in the much happier years that followed.

There were only three things about Korea that we learned from him:

1. He would describe how remarkable the experience of his faith was in that context – Catholic soldiers would be given a grid reference and a time, and at that point and moment a priest would arrive in a jeep, put a wooden cross on the bonnet and start to say Mass. He remembered the soldiers

kneeling in the mud to receive the Eucharist. He told us that in this context, when you didn't know if you would still be alive the next day, Catholicism became a vital part of his life.

2. He told us about the experience of being with his platoon one day, coming up a hill, and then being bombed by American planes, and how that had affected his attitude to the American military ever since. I remember as a child puzzling over the meaning of those words 'friendly fire'.

3. There were two tips for mountain walking, gleaned from his time in the Korean hills. During rests on Welsh walking holidays he would explain that if you lie with your boots raised, the blood circulates more and prevents the feet from getting heavy. Secondly, most accidents on mountains happen when you're coming downhill, so it's always best to do gentle zigzags when descending.

Oh yes, and then there was the phrase that he'd learnt that became a family joke because it was always used when we'd taken a wrong turning on a journey, or wasted a large amount of time on something. At these moments he'd always come out with: 'Well, remember – time spent in reconnaissance is never wasted.'

Anyway, my general feeling growing up was that, although it was a little strange, given his openness about most things, my father's silence about Korea was understandable. It was part of his protectiveness, a desire to shield us from knowledge that we didn't need to know, about a brutal war that had done him serious mental and emotional damage. Over recent years I'd been beginning to think more about the meaning of that silence, and then I read, in America, in the first week of September 2001, Susan Griffin's astonishing work about men, war and silence, *A Chorus of Stones*. A book so raw that it's taken a lot of time for me to come to terms with it. This is surely what Kafka meant when he wrote: 'I think we ought to read only the kind of books that wound and stab us . . . We need the books that affect us like a disaster, that grieve us deeply, like the death of someone we loved more than ourselves, like being banished into forests

513

far from everyone . . . A book must be the axe for the frozen sea inside us.'

The power of this book for me lay in its vertiginous layering and intertwining of historical analysis and familial memory, the personal and the political as one. A recurring theme is how suffering is passed down through families, and about the role of silence in the transmission of that suffering. Griffin explores how much of this pain results from men's experience of war and violence, and suggests that if silence is used to try and cover this up it will always re-emerge as trauma or violence in subsequent generations: 'My father suffered from the silence of his father, and I suffered from his silence in turn.' She asks an interviewee about their father's experience of World War Two – he'd fought in the Battle of the Bulge. What was it for him, this great and terrible battle? She cannot say. He never spoke of it at home.

You can perhaps imagine my experience reading this book, questions I'd long wondered about rising to the surface. What I didn't expect, however, was a growing anger towards my father, realising the multiple, subtle impacts that his silence had had on me, on all of us in the family. So much for wanting to 'protect' us from the truth . . . But my feelings also oscillated wildly, often to pity and sadness. There were times reading when I felt Griffin could have been writing directly about Mark. The following words I reacted to viscerally, because they described precisely the way that he felt contaminated by what he'd experienced:

> I remember David . . . telling me what he had witnessed in Korea. His voice was so low it could hardly be heard in the recording I made, he spoke in the way I have heard women speak of rape or abuse, as if in the very telling something monstrously ugly is brought into being. The terror and brutality seemed to brand him, making him in his own mind irredeemably inseparable from the ugliness. Yet what he saw defied description. It was told more in the difficulty of telling than in the telling itself. He could name the mutilations, intestines falling out of

the body, along with shit, blood, pus, but no one who had not been there could have any idea. It was only over time I began to grasp what he was saying to me. It was not just the physical fear he was feeling, it was the weight of something sordid.

Later, reading Primo Levi, I began to understand more about the relationship between such traumatic witnessing of brutality and the shame that takes over afterwards – even if the person in question was not directly involved with causing the horror. Levi sees this shame in the eyes of the Russian soldiers who liberate the remaining prisoners at Monowitz on 27 January 1945:

> It was that shame we knew so well, the shame that drowned us after the selections, and every time we had to . . . submit to some outrage: the shame . . . that the just man experiences at another man's crime: the feeling of guilt that such a crime should exist, that it should have been introduced irrevocably into the world of things that exist, and that his will for good should have proved too weak.

Reading *A Chorus of Stones*, I boomeranged between raw anger and waves of sympathy for Mark. I felt confused. Part of me trying to connect with the young man who had experienced the horror of Korea. No, not yet a man, more a sheltered boy of nineteen, only a year out of school. But another part of me, a growing part, wondered whether his silence about atrocities he'd witnessed in Korea had, in some way, contributed to my need to probe into horror and genocide. Or would that have happened anyway? I remember the power of seeing *Shoah* for the first time, only a year or so after Mark had died, and being overwhelmed by the sense of uncovering the past in those nine and a half hours of film. Lanzmann's dogged persistence to find what had been buried. And then, so much of our work in Platform, focussing on making visible aspects of our culture that are hidden, structures of power. None of this negative – quite the contrary – but working in such a way, especially spending decades researching genocides and perpetrators, carries a cost. Remember Lanzmann's words about having spent years 'trying to look into the black sun which is the Holocaust'.

But as we get older, we also become more understanding of our parents' limitations. The balance to be struck between telling your children about the realities of the world and terrifying them – this is probably the hardest decision of all. The desire for them to grow up, open-eyed, able to understand the capability of human beings to do terrible things, yet also the primal need to protect them for as long as possible. And maybe a lot of Mark's silence was more to do with this. It is one thing to have traumatic memories yourself – of having to kill to stay alive, of seeing your friends and fellow soldiers maimed and dying, of not being able to save them. It is another to put these realities into somebody else's head, and then to see that other person's view of yourself shaken for ever.

The gentle, loving father – now with a machine gun in his hand.

4

The Silences of Societies in the Face of Atrocity: Germany, France, America, Britain

I'm still puzzling this through – this question of silence. The silence of the individual and the silence of a society. And the different qualities of silences. The silence here by the sea mesmerises. It stills me, whatever state I've brought down from the city. From the moment of waking it calms me. Every grass bending in the breeze outside the window, the line of slate-grey sea on the horizon, even the soft whirring of the fridge only accentuates the stillness. The silence pulsates here, and, as it absorbs me into its world, I feel myself changing, allowing myself to be carried along by its rhythm, as if trying to communicate, to reassure. All shall be well and all manner of thing shall be well. There is something about not hearing a human voice for hours, or even days, which stills me, and enables other hearing to happen. So this silence feels almost wholly benevolent. There is another silence that is rare and blissful and this is the state of being with someone you love and not needing to say a word. Walking through a valley, reading by a fire, looking up from a café table.

But silence can also be extremely violent. When entire societies are silent in the face of atrocities they have committed this creates a kind of moral corrosion. Sebald describes this process vividly, reflecting on his childhood in the peaceful Bavarian village of Wertach im All-gäu, just after the war:

> I had grown up with the feeling that something was being kept from me: at home, at school, and by the German writers whose books I read hoping to glean information about the monstrous events in the background of my own life.

Sebald found the apparent calm of the village and his family deeply disturbing. It was as if the child, born at the end of the war in 1944 and having no conscious memory of it, nevertheless intuited the cataclysmic violence in every gesture of his parents and in the selective memory of the Bavarian villagers. And an anger grew from there, only finding expression many years later in his writing. He understood, because he'd grown up amongst it, the lethal potential of silence in the face of trauma. The artist Anselm Kiefer, born only ten months after Sebald in March 1945, had a strikingly similar experience of an organised societal silence in the years after the war in Germany: 'We had no information about the Third Reich when I was in school. And about Auschwitz – we were not informed about this, not in the family, not in school – nearly nothing.'

This German silence is personified in Sebald's work by the figure of the teacher Paul Bereyter, and his subsequent suicide, in *The Emigrants*. It is there in the broken figure of Jacques Austerlitz, who realises too late in his life 'how little practice I had in using my memory, and conversely, how hard I must always have tried to recollect as little as possible, avoiding everything which related in any way to my unknown past' – words that express what a generation of young Germans felt about their parents after the war, that their forgetting was an intentional act. Only when Austerlitz is an old man do scraps of memory begin to 'drift through the outlying regions of [his] mind' and he can see again the star-shaped fortress and 'a lightless landscape through which a very small railway train was hurrying, twelve earth-coloured miniature carriages and a coal-black locomotive under a plume of smoke wafting horizontally backwards, with the far end of the plume constantly blown this way and that, like the tip of a large ostrich feather'.

It was precisely because Sebald had spent most of his adult life wrestling with this issue of silence in the face of the Holocaust, and because he understood the corrosive effect of such denial, that in autumn 1997, in a series of lectures in Zurich ('Air War and Literature' – later published with other material in the collection *On the Natural History of Destruction*), he tackled another silence. This time his focus was on the silence of his compatriots regarding the firebombing of Germany by the Allies in the last years of the war – a subject which was then regarded as a taboo for the vast majority of Germans. Only the extreme right didn't share this silence, so nearly all writers and intellectuals (with the notable exceptions of Heinrich Böll and Günter Grass) ceded the territory to the far right, and avoided discussing these Allied war crimes. *On the Natural History of Destruction* is a relentless examination of both the atrocities committed by some of the Allied bombing and the deliberate 'amnesia' of post-war Germany regarding these acts of targeted civilian killing. At the beginning of the work he describes the bombing of Hamburg by the RAF, supported by the US 8th Army Air Force on 27 July 1943. It was code-named 'Operation Gomorrah' and its aim was to destroy the city completely. From the Allied perspective the operation was a success. More than 30,000 men, women and children died on that single evening:

> At 1.20 a.m. a firestorm of an intensity that no one would ever before have thought possible arose. The fire now rising 2,000 metres into the sky, snatched oxygen to itself so violently that the air currents reached hurricane force, resonating like mighty organs with all their stops pulled out at once . . . the flames shot up as high as houses, rolled like a tidal wave through the streets at a speed of over 150 kilometres per hour . . . The water in some of the canals was ablaze. The glass in the tramcar windows melted . . . When day broke . . . horribly disfigured corpses lay everywhere. Bluish little phosphorus flames still flickered around many of them; others had been

roasted brown or purple and reduced to a third of their normal size. They lay doubled up in pools of their own melted fat . . . Other victims had been so badly charred and reduced to ashes by the heat, which had risen to 1,000 degrees or more, that the remains of families consisting of several people could be carried away in a single laundry basket.

Sebald is most disturbed by the fact that such events had never really been spoken of. He observes that post-war German society had 'developed an almost perfectly functioning mechanism of repression'. He wonders whether this lack of verbal expression links to wider questions, whether there is 'some connection between the German catastrophe ushered in under Hitler's regime and the regulation of intimate feelings within the German family'.

I can still remember where I was when I first read the above description of the Hamburg firebombing; I remember putting the book down on the park bench and feeling physically sick. And then waves of anger. Part of this is an entirely understandable human response, but I reflected later that much of this anger was connected to reading this as a British man – not exactly a sense of shame or responsibility, but more the fact that I had lived for many years with only the vaguest knowledge of such events. That I, who had made myself consciously aware of so much in terms of war and modern history, had not felt the need to look at this. It shocked me that such knowledge was simply not part of our British consciousness, and that it had taken a German writer to bring this to the surface. It also troubles me deeply that in the heart of London, a city I love greatly, there stands a statue to the pioneer of this devastating policy of area bombing, the man who ordered this mass killing of civilians, as well as the firebombing of several other cities. There, on the Strand, outside St Clement Dane's Church, you can read this inscription, which is supposed to represent the views of our society:

MARSHAL OF THE ROYAL AIR FORCE
SIR ARTHUR HARRIS BT GCB OBE AFC

IN MEMORY OF A GREAT COMMANDER AND
OF THE BRAVE CREWS OF BOMBER COMMAND
MORE THAN 55,000 OF WHOM LOST THEIR
LIVES IN THE CAUSE OF FREEDOM

THE NATION OWES THEM ALL AN
IMMENSE DEBT

I am not a pacifist. The Second World War was one of the – very few – justifiable wars of the last hundred years, but area bombing of civilians is indefensible, whether it happens in London or Hamburg or Hiroshima or Aleppo. Our ongoing silence about the atrocities of Hamburg, Dresden and Cologne is deafening. It weakened the war against fascism because the method was fascist, making the destruction of Guernica pale in comparison. In fact, three years before the area bombing of Hamburg took place, Albert Speer recalls Hitler planning a very similar kind of firebombing for London:

> Have you ever seen a map of London? It is so densely built that one fire alone would be enough to destroy the whole city, just as it did two hundred years ago.* Goering will start fires all over London, fires everywhere, with countless incendiary bombs of an entirely new type. Thousands of fires. They will unite in one huge blaze over the whole area. Goering has the right idea: high explosives don't work, but we can do it with incendiaries; we can destroy London completely.

Today many consider Harris a war criminal for his indiscriminate killing of tens of thousands of civilians. And it is highly likely, had Britain lost the war, that he would have been executed by the Germans. But I feel more conflicted about the men who served in Bomber Command, those 55,000 who died, representing the highest proportion of deaths of any branch of the armed services during the war. Almost half of those who flew never returned. If it's possible to

---

* Presumably a reference to the Great Fire of London in 1666, nearly 400 years before Hitler was speaking, not 200 – indicative of his rather shaky grasp of history.

set aside for a moment the question of the moral legitimacy of these bombing raids, it must have taken a great degree of courage to have flown on those missions, knowing that half of your comrades would never return. The majority of the targets in the first part of the war were military and industrial installations. For those in the bomber crews these missions would have created few moral dilemmas. However, when the policy changed and the area bombings of whole cities began in 1943, those airmen would have known that tens of thousands of civilians would be killed. And to have been able to release bombs with such knowledge must then have demanded an extreme, and morally dubious, form of moral compartmentalisation.* What then is the responsibility of the individual airman in such a situation? Consider the enormous amount of attention given, rightly, to Hitler's notorious *Kommissarbefehl* – issued in March 1941, sanctioning the killing of non-military, political personnel in the imminent invasion of the Soviet Union. Why have British airmen who were 'only obeying orders' not been subject to the same degree of scrutiny as the Wehrmacht who obeyed the *Kommissarbefehl*?

Yes, 55,000 men from Bomber Command lost their lives in the war; but 42,500 civilians were killed in the firebombing of Hamburg in the week of 'Operation Gomorrah'. Fifty-five thousand air crew in the 2,193 days of the war; 42,500 children, women and men in *a single week*. And then how many of us have any knowledge at all of what happened in Tokyo on 9–10 March 1945? An event even more invisible to us than the firebombings of Hamburg and Dresden, yet, in a single evening's raid, 105,000 men, women and children in that city were incinerated. At least the officer responsible for ordering this raid, General Curtis LeMay, had the honesty to admit afterwards that if the Allies had lost the war, he would have been tried for war crimes.

There is also a dramatic disparity between the extent of these atrocities, and our understanding of the bombings of British cities in the Second World War. The attacks on Coventry and London form one

---

* I look at this specific example of moral compartmentalisation in more detail in the subsequent section 'How People in Organisations Can Kill'.

part of a kind of national folk memory – the 'Blitz spirit' has entered the language as testament to the indefatigability of the British people in the face of fascist assault. Yet we cannot see the fascism inherent in the firebombing of the Japanese capital city and its civilians. We rightly remember the dead of Coventry and the London Blitz, but – to put these bombings into some kind of historical context – 1,236 people were killed in raids on Coventry between August 1940 and August 1942, and 28,556 people were killed in the attacks on London between September 1940 and May 1941. A total casualty figure of just under 30,000 civilians killed by bombing over a two-year period – the same number killed in Hamburg on a single night.

And, five months later, how can we begin to describe Hiroshima and Nagasaki?

Annihilation.

Japanese children, women and men, hundreds of thousands of them, vaporised by our side – supposedly fighting 'the Good War' against fascism. Still the most obscene act of terrorism ever committed – quite literally the creation of a state of terror for the people of those cities – dwarfing all that al-Qaeda and the 'Islamic State' have ever done. No warnings, no dropping of atomic bombs in remote areas as a demonstration of what could be done – but exploding two nuclear weapons on cities full of children, women and men, the vast majority of whom had little or no responsibility for the war the Japanese state was fighting; 140,000 human beings killed at Hiroshima, 80,000 killed at Nagasaki, and thousands more dying in subsequent years from injuries, radiation and birth defects caused by the two bombs.* Ever since I first found out, as a child, about these crimes of state terrorism on an unimaginable scale, 6 and 9 August became oppressive shadows for me with every summer that passed. I don't believe we as a society have begun to come to terms with the evil that was unleashed, in our names, on those two days in 1945.

---

* Ninety thousand died immediately at Hiroshima on 6 August 1945, with a further 50,000 dying of injuries by the end of December 1945; 40,000 died on 9 August 1945 at Nagasaki, with a further 40,000 dead by the end of the year.

*

Years before he became an artist, Joseph Beuys was a pilot in the Luft-waffe in the Second World War, flying many missions on the Eastern Front as a rear-gunner, and being shot down once, following which event (depending on who you believe) he was either saved by Tatar tribesmen who wrapped his body in fat and felt for twelve days, or retrieved by a German search party and taken to a military hospital. But, either way, the war left him wounded, both physically and emo-tionally. For the rest of his life he was driven by the need to address the violence of silence, especially relating to the permanent scar of the Holocaust, and Germany's cultural death during Nazism, which had allowed all else to follow. Seeing Anselm Kiefer's work recently at an exhibition in London I was struck once again by all he shares with his mentor Beuys – far beyond the remarkable textural qualities in both artists (the felt, fat and rusted metal in Beuys, the straw, ash and wire in Kiefer). They also shared a belief that Germany had had to create a new language and culture for itself, after the absolute dead end represented by Nazism – this sense of a culture which had com-pletely self-destructed. He puts it like this in a 2011 interview:

> The Germans have cut themselves off from half of their culture; they have disabled themselves. One thing is the Holocaust, the other is the amputation of oneself. All of the culture of the 1920s and 30s, in all its fields – theatre, philosophy, cin-ema, science, etc – disappeared.

Beuys, like Sebald and Kiefer, had enjoyed a seemingly peaceful childhood – growing up in the valley of the Rhine in Cleves, near the Dutch border. But, being a generation before Sebald, he had the mis-fortune to be old enough to participate in the war. Afterwards he suf-fered a series of breakdowns throughout the 1950s, the years of the German 'economic miracle', recuperating only slowly on a farm not far from his childhood home. He came to art as a way of dealing with his own wounds and fragility, but soon he realised the connection between his war-shattered self and Germany's traumatised identity.

He never bought the myth of renewal because he felt all was being built on foundations of amnesia. Many of the people who built the camps and ran the institutes of the Reich were still in power.

The first public art commission he put in for, in March 1958, was an international competition for a memorial at Auschwitz. I vividly recall seeing this piece, now arranged as a vitrine, in a museum in Darmstadt. In its conjunction of images – melted wax, a mummified rat, a tangle of rusted wire, electric rings, medicine phials – an essence of the insane terror of Auschwitz is transmitted. It remained, for him, the dark backing of the mirror in which all his subsequent work was reflected. In 1975 he created a piece – *Show Your Wound* – installed in a bleak concrete subway in Munich, consisting of mortuary trolleys and sinister-looking tools and medical equipment. It is not possible to look at these trolleys and implements without thinking of the Holocaust, the shadow that Beuys continually returned to. He knew this wound could never heal as long as people treated it as a finished episode in history, safely distanced from the present. He was haunted by the continuity of the Holocaust, in patterns of thought and behaviour:

> The human condition is Auschwitz, and the principle of Auschwitz finds its perpetuation in our understanding of science and political systems, in the delegation of responsibility to groups of specialists and in the silence of intellectuals and artists. I have found myself in permanent struggle with this condition and its roots. I find that we are now experiencing Auschwitz in its contemporary character . . . Ability and creativity are burnt out, a form of spiritual execution takes place, a climate of fear is created – perhaps even more dangerous because it is so refined.

*

Some years ago I was watching TV in the early hours, aimlessly flicking from channel to channel, when I came across black-and-white images of what seemed to be some kind of massacre. There were shots of police attacking demonstrators, bloodied heads. I started listening to the men and women interviewed, speaking in French, and immediately started recording the programme (this was in the days of VHS, when I'd always have a blank tape on standby). I pieced together what they were saying. This event had happened on 17 October 1961, following a peaceful demonstration for Algerian independence, and, most shockingly, it had happened in the centre of Paris. I was disturbed that I'd never heard about it before. I was even more disturbed by what I learnt subsequently. The witnesses were describing being rounded up in the police headquarters on the Île de la Cité, close to Notre Dame Cathedral – the Paris police chief at this time was Maurice Papon, the former senior Vichy official and Nazi collaborator. These are the words of two of these witnesses, Idir Belkacem and Cherhabi Hachemi:

The courtyard was full of Algerians. We heard they were going to finish us off. The police told us: 'It's your last day on earth. Pray, because you won't ever be seeing your family again. We brought you here to be eliminated pure and simple. Every single one of you.' We were petrified. To protect ourselves we all huddled in the centre of the courtyard but the Algerians in the front rows fell like dead leaves.

They beat us with truncheons of a kind I'd never seen before. They had cords attached to the ends. They put the cords around people's necks. They did it to me, but by reflex I had lowered my chin, and it stayed there [at this point Hachemi gestures to between his lower lip and chin]. Then they began to garrot people. I saw people losing consciousness. Their eyes bulged out and they lost consciousness.[*]

Dozens of human beings were butchered in the picturesque heart of 'the City of Love'. Their bodies were being washed up along the banks of the Seine for weeks afterwards. To this day it is not known

---

[*] From *Drowning by Bullets*, directed by Philip Brooks and Alan Hayling, first broadcast in 1992.

exactly how many were killed – estimates by historians suggest between one hundred and two hundred people were murdered by the police that night. I had never heard about this state massacre; my French friends had never mentioned it to me. At the end of the documentary the reason for this became clearer, as the narrator explained how France had attempted to eradicate all traces of the murders by imposing a news blackout and making sure that no images made it into the media. And this state of 'organised forgetting' continued for the next thirty years.

But it would be a mistake to think of this determination to forget as wholly a product of government or establishment forces. To their eternal shame, the left in France – including the then influential Communist Party – colluded in this act of collective amnesia by not organising a single strike or demonstration against this appalling crime. They feared being associated with 'the enemy'. But four months later, in February 1962, when nine French Communist Party supporters were killed by police at a demonstration in Charonne, Paris subsequently ground to a halt as the organised left called out more than half a million mourners to the funerals, led by the familiar figures of Jean-Paul Sartre and Simone de Beauvoir. Yet nothing just a few months before for the possibly hundreds of murdered French Algerians. France seemed to be saying: 'This did not happen.'

A mantra that the country also used with regard to its pre-war engagement with fascism and then its wartime marriage with Nazi Germany. I have always been suspicious about a certain French national narrative with regard to the Second World War – particularly the enormous amount of weight given to the activities of the French Resistance. This doesn't mean I don't believe in the exceptional courage of the women and men who did take part in anti-Nazi actions – just that they were not only a minority of the population, but, in most areas of France, a tiny minority. And yet, to hear many post-war French politicians and intellectuals talk, you would imagine that half the country had been active in the Resistance. (I've often wondered, wryly, if this was the case, how it had ever been possible for the Germans to occupy France for four and a half days, let alone four and a half years.)

But my suspicion had always been an instinctive one – that is, until recently, when I discovered more about the reality of France's co-operation with fascism. No, 'co-operation' is not quite accurate, because it suggests that the fascism was not home-grown, when in fact it was. In the wake of the Dreyfus case, in the first decades of the twentieth century fascist and viciously antisemitic publications thrived. Catholic newspapers with huge circulations like *La Croix* and *Le Pèlerin* prided themselves on being in the vanguard of the fight against 'the perfidious Jew'. Edouard Drumont and Alphonse Daudet had published their bestseller *La France Juive* in 1886, but Charles Maurras, a philosopher and propagandist, took matters to a new level of fanaticism in 1908 with the publication of *Action Française* – a national daily newspaper named after the influential political movement of the same title which had been founded nine years before. Maurras and his associate Maurice Pujo composed this piece of popular doggerel as its anthem:

The Jew having taken all,
Having robbed Paris of all she owns,
Now says to France:
'You belong to us alone:
Obey! Down on your knees, all of you!'
Insolent Jew, hold your tongue ...
Back to where you belong, Jew.*

And its influence continued to grow, just as antisemitism grew after the First World War, and throughout the 1920s and 30s. By 1920, even supposed intellectuals such as Proust, Gide, Rodin and T. S. Eliot were regular readers. Other ultra-conservative movements followed in its wake: Croix-de-Feu, a black-leather-jacketed paramilitary organisation, founded in 1928 (which by 1937 had more members

---

* I am indebted to Carmen Callil's exceptional work *Bad Faith* on the French fascist leader, Louis Darquier, commissioner for Jewish affairs under the wartime Vichy government, for this quotation and for other material in this section.

than the combined Communist and Socialist parties – 750,000 – including a young François Mitterrand); Pierre-Charles Taittinger, later to establish the champagne dynasty, founded Jeunesses Patriotes in 1924, an extremely xenophobic league of Catholic youth. Hardly surprising when the founding father admired Hitler and Mussolini so much, praising the former for 'the constant development of racism in all classes of Germans . . . [He] makes their heart beat under their brown shirts'. There was also extensive financial backing for these fascist movements from the businessmen of the day, including not only Taittinger, but also Jean Hennessy (of the cognac dynasty) and Eugène Schueller (founder of L'Oréal).

So threatening had this plethora of leagues and movements become – sixteen of them consolidating in 1934 to form the Front National (sadly, still thriving today) – that in 1936 the government dissolved the paramilitary leagues. But they simply renamed themselves and formed new parties.* In 1936 Jacques Doriot founded the fascist Parti Populaire Français, and styled himself the 'French Führer'. In 1937, the Rassemblement Anti-Juif de France (the Anti-Jewish Rally) was established, together with its weekly newspaper, *L'Antijuif*, with Louis Darquier as its president, soon openly funded by the Nazi government in Germany. By now all of these organisations, and others such as Propagande Nationale, and the Mouvement Anti-Juif Continentale, had large and well-funded headquarters in Paris, and were becoming more and more powerful with each month that passed.

As successive governments fell, the shift to the far right now moved to parliament and the national assembly. Hatred of 'the foreigner' and Jews in particular gathered pace at a terrifying rate. In the wake of Hitler's invasion of Austria in March 1938 came one of the most shocking moments in modern French history – the French government, two years *before* Nazi occupation, in April and May 1938, passed a series of decrees against 'aliens' (code for Jewish refugees), which, in their effect, replicated aspects of the infamous Nuremberg Laws established by the Nazis in 1935. These new laws in France banned

---

* The Jeunesses Patriotes becoming the Parti National Populaire; Croix-de-Feu becoming the Parti Social Français.

'aliens' from opening businesses and working in particular trades and professions. The laws also demanded the immediate repatriation of unregistered 'aliens' and those without valid work permits (i.e. thousands of Jewish refugees); 20,000 Jews in France were affected by these decrees, many were jailed, and a significant number chose suicide rather than forced expulsion back to Nazi Germany. Many, such as Walter Benjamin and the young Hannah Arendt (already living in exile in Paris having fled from Nazi Germany), began to see the writing on the wall – particularly when even Jewish organisations themselves didn't want to oppose such developments, fearing this would only create a backlash and increase antisemitism further.

So, given all of this, it really should come as no surprise that, three years later, Darquier's office at the Commisariat Général aux Questions Juives was issuing certificates to prove pure, Aryan blood. Or that the CGQJ had a whole department of archetypal desk killers – an entire office of accountants, insurance clerks, lawyers, brokers, bank clerks, currency dealers – to organise the supposedly 'legal' plundering of Jewish property and assets. Or that Darquier and company met Heydrich in Paris in spring 1942 to discuss how the deportations of the Jews in France should begin. Or that it was the French police, not the SS, who would co-ordinate the round-ups and make sure the trains that left for Auschwitz were as full as possible. Or that, between 27 March 1942 and 11 August 1944, at least 75,721 Jewish men, women and children were deported by the Vichy government to Auschwitz and Sobibor, on trains provided by the French state railways and staffed by French guards.[*]

Or, to return to my shock that evening seeing those black-and-white images of massacre – perhaps we shouldn't be surprised that Maurice Papon, chief of the Gironde prefecture, who had organised the deportation of two convoys of Jews from Bordeaux in 1942, should in 1961 be the chief of police in Paris, responsible for the mass murder of the Algerian demonstrators.

---

[*] In seventy-eight train transports, mainly from Drancy station in north-east Paris. Only 2,560 of the 75,721 people deported survived. It is also important to record that the Vichy government imprisoned over 30,000 Sinti and Roma in internment camps, many of whom were later deported to Dachau, Ravensbrück, Buchenwald and other concentration camps.

I tried to imagine how a child whose mother or father had been killed that night would feel in the light of such a response from the state. Would it not be experienced as a second assault? First they have killed our parents, and now they deny it happened. I think back to Primo Levi's despair at Trzebinia, having survived but knowing the truth of his experience had not been accepted. Only the persistence of the survivors, the courage of the photographer Elie Kagan and the filmmaker Jacques Panijel, eventually broke the silence. Panijel's film *Octobre à Paris* had been seized in 1962 and banned from being shown for many years in France (being officially released only in October 2011). The work of the historian Jean-Luc Einaudi was also a crucial factor in France beginning to talk about this silence, with the publication of his book *La Bataille de Paris* in 1991.

In the weeks after I saw *Drowning by Bullets* I tried to find out as much as I could. I talked to many contacts, including activist friends, but nobody seemed to have heard about the events of 16/17 October 1961. When I next went to Paris I asked my friends there, but, again, little seemed to be known. I walked all around the Île de la Cité and the bridges, trying to find any monument to the victims of this massacre. In a city famous for its *grands projets*, surely there would be at least a statue, a memorial commemorating this episode? After hours of searching this is all I found, the only trace of that night's terror – a single, rectangular plaque perhaps eighteen inches across, down some steps, on one side of the Pont Saint-Michel:

A LA MEMOIRE
DES NOMBREUX ALGERIENS
TUES LORS LA SANGLANTE
REPRESSION
DE LA MANIFESTATION PACIFIQUE
DU 17 OCTOBRE 1961[*]

My original shock was now replaced by anger. The language used, the cynical evasiveness of the state not telling us that the French police had murdered almost 200 peacefully demonstrating citizens – but using the passive construction 'killed' instead. And the terrible vagueness of that word 'numerous' – the fact that the French government has never bothered to have a full investigation into the massacre, the greatest post-war loss of life in the city of Paris. Even today, despite President Hollande's belated acknowledgement of responsibility in 2012, in a terse, three-sentence statement which referred to 'the bloody repression' of 17 October 1961, it will be interesting to see whether this event makes it into the French school history syllabus.

Quite rightly, there are now monuments and museums in France to the 75,721 Jewish men, women and children deported to Auschwitz and Sobibor.[†] And, finally, albeit belatedly, there seems to be a growing acceptance of French responsibility for the critical role the French state played in the deportations of its Jewish citizens. Indeed, in 2009 there was a ruling by the Council of State, France's highest judicial body, that stated: 'the Vichy government held responsibility for deportations'. The Council of State further

---

[*] 'To the memory of numerous Algerians killed during the bloody repression of the peaceful demonstration of 17 October 1961'.

[†] It took until November 2015, seventy years after the end of the war, for the French government to announce that it would pay £39 million in compensation to Holocaust survivors, in recognition of the role the state railways (SNCF) played in transporting these 75,721 victims to German concentration and extermination camps (*Guardian*, 3 November 2015).

ruled that 'Nazi officials did not force them to betray their fellow citizens, but that antisemitic persecution was carried out willingly.'*

If it took the French state sixty-seven years to admit its role in the Holocaust (from its first organised transport from Drancy to Auschwitz in 1942 to the Council of State's admission in 2009), then when can we expect a proper memorial to the murdered French Algerians?

*

Walking in the face of extinction. It's a curious feeling. Especially in a country which has been known to call itself 'the land of the free'. In October 2003 I was staying with associates in the Baltimore suburbs, together with a friend and colleague from Platform, preparing a keynote lecture we were due to give at a conference in Pittsburgh two days later. It was late afternoon, the house was quiet, my friend was working upstairs and I was writing in the back garden under a weeping willow. Surprisingly hot for October. My friend appeared at the window and asked how I was getting on. OK, but I could do with a break, how about a walk? So we decided to walk down to the shop next to the gas station, about twenty minutes away.

Suburban America. Churches, clapboard houses, some with flag-poles outside. Sycamores and maples in their autumn finery, rusted oranges and fiery crimsons. And swathes of green verges, the grass cut oddly short considering this was public land. We were the only people walking and got some curious looks from the passing cars, usually the driver the sole occupant. Station wagons, SUVs, the occasional yellow school bus. We passed a housing development, only recently completed and still advertising the few apartments not yet sold. My friend read the sign for 'Susquehannock Apartments' and then she said, 'Every time I come to America I'm confronted with the knowledge that the country was built on genocide. I just cannot get used to it. And the silence about this disturbs me more

---

* 'France "Responsible" for Holocaust Deportations, Court Rules' by Peter Allen, *Daily Telegraph*, 16 February 2009.

each time I come.' As she says this, for a split second I'm in the original forest on this slope, my ears pick up the pulsing of birdsong,
I can see a clearing ahead, woodsmoke, the sound of voices. Then
back to the rumble of traffic and this smoothly manicured grass and
the narrow path leading down to the gas station and the shop.

Later that day, reading Arundhati Roy's *The Ordinary Person's Guide
to Empire*, I come upon this passage, describing Noam Chomsky's
thoughts on the founding of America:

> During the Thanksgiving holiday a few weeks ago, I took a
> walk with some friends and family in a national park. We came
> across a gravestone, which had on it the following inscription:
> 'Here lies an Indian woman, a Wampanoag, whose family and
> tribe gave of themselves and their land that this great nation
> might be born and grow.'
>
> Of course, it is not quite accurate to say that the indigenous
> population gave of themselves and their land for that noble
> purpose. Rather, they were slaughtered, decimated, and dis-
> persed in the course of one of the greatest exercises in geno-
> cide in human history . . . which we celebrate each October
> when we honor Columbus – a notable mass murderer himself
> – on Columbus Day.
>
> Hundreds of American citizens, well-meaning and decent
> people, troop by that gravestone regularly and read it, appar-
> ently without reaction; except, perhaps, a feeling of satisfac-
> tion that at last we are giving some due recognition to the
> sacrifices of the native peoples . . . They might react differently
> if they were to visit Auschwitz or Dachau and find a grave-
> stone reading: 'Here lies a woman, a Jew, whose family and
> people gave of themselves and their possessions that this great
> nation might grow and prosper.'

Genocides which occurred before the twentieth century are inevitably more challenging to quantify, and more liable to differing estimates, according to the political and cultural bias of those making
the calculation. But the respected anthropologist Henry Dobyns

spent much of his working life looking into this question, and in his seminal work, published in 1966, *Estimating Aboriginal American Population: An Appraisal of Techniques with a New Hemispheric Estimate*, he settles on a figure of between 9,800,000 and 12,250,000 Amerindians living in the geographical area which now constitutes 'the United States' in 1500. We know that by 1900 these numbers had been reduced to 237,000–250,000. So, using the median estimated figures gives us a fall in numbers from 11,025,000 to 243,500 – a catastrophic demise of about 98 per cent of the indigenous population of North America in just 400 years.

I know that, after many years of planning, the Museum of the American Indian has now opened on the Mall in Washington. A fact that should be welcomed, like the opening of genocide museums and museums commemorating slavery, but when these primarily focus on the historical past without seeing how that past has shaped our present, I fear they become monuments of dry sterility. I also wonder if there really is an appetite among Americans today to confront the reality of their founding myths. To look far beyond the Pilgrim Fathers and Jamestown and New England to the culture, and subsequent genocide, of the peoples who were here for thousands of years before the settlers arrived. But this is just speculation about the curiosity, or lack of it, in the American people, so perhaps the attendance figures for different museums in Washington, taken from their own websites, should speak for themselves. These are the comparative figures for three museums in the nation's capital in 2015:

- The National Air and Space Museum: 6.9 million visitors.
- The National Museum of American History: 4.1 million visitors.
- The Museum of the American Indian: 1.2 million visitors.

*

What, then, is the relationship in a society between accumulated historical silences and taboos, and subsequent thought and behaviour? Nothing in history can be regarded in isolation from what has gone before. The industrial *methods* of gas chambers and mobile gas vans used to murder on a vast scale in the Holocaust may have been entirely new, but the *minds* of the people who conceived these genocidal plans were formed in the early years of the twentieth century, influenced by all that was happening at that time.

When I began this research in the late 1990s, I was powerfully affected by the work of Daniel Goldhagen, who had just published *Hitler's Willing Executioners*. The second chapter of this book examines the nature of historical antisemitism in Germany, and Goldhagen posits the development, in the late nineteenth century, of what he terms 'eliminationist antisemitism'. He makes a very persuasive case, drawing on much research which had been done at that time. For instance, he cites that between 1870 and 1900, no less than 1,200 publications were concerned with looking at 'the Jewish problem', as it was termed – despite the fact that Jews comprised barely more than 1 per cent of the population at this time. He also quotes another significant study by Klemens Felden which examined fifty-one prominent antisemitic writers and texts they had written between 1865 and 1895, and found that more than half of these proposed 'solutions' to 'the Jewish problem' – nineteen of these 'solutions' calling for the physical extermination of the Jews.

By the beginning of the twentieth century there clearly existed an extremely virulent, widespread antisemitism within Germany, but it seems a serious limitation in Goldhagen's analysis to look only within Germany's borders for the seeds of Nazism and genocidal thinking. The Swedish writer Sven Lindqvist takes a wider view, in his brilliant work on European colonialism, *Exterminate All the Brutes*:

> Europe's destruction of the 'inferior races' of four continents prepared the ground for Hitler's destruction of six million Jews in Europe . . . European world expansion, accompanied as it was by a shameless defence of extermination, created

habits of thought and political precedents that made way for new outrages, finally culminating in . . . the Holocaust.

It is these 'habits of thought' that Lindqvist returns to again and again. And such exterminist thinking was by no means confined to uneducated xenophobes – quite the opposite, it was actually at the heart of humanism and nineteenth-century ideals of 'progress'. He finds it in the liberal philosopher Herbert Spencer, who writes in 1851: 'The forces which are working out the great scheme of perfect happiness . . . exterminate such sections of mankind as stand in their way'; strikingly similar ideas can also be found in his contemporary, the German philosopher Eduard von Hartmann, who writes in *Philosophy of the Unconscious*: 'As little . . . favour is done the dog whose tail is to be cut off, when one cuts it off gradually inch by inch, so little is their humanity in artificially prolonging the death struggles of savages who are on the verge of extinction . . . The true philanthropist . . . cannot avoid desiring an acceleration of the last convulsion, and labour for that end.'

Lindqvist then makes the following argument – which I can still remember reading and being stunned by, at the beginning of my research – which challenges our societies to completely rethink the causation of nineteenth- and twentieth-century genocides:

The idea of extermination lies no farther from the heart of humanism than Buchenwald lies from the Goethehaus in Weimar. That insight has been almost completely repressed, even by the Germans, who have been made sole scapegoats for ideas of extermination that are actually a common European heritage.

He also references arguments going on in Germany in the early 1990s regarding the unique nature (or not) of the Holocaust, and he then makes this critically important observation:

But in this debate no one mentions the German extermination of the Herero people in South-West Africa during Hitler's childhood.* No one mentions the corresponding genocide by the French, the British, or the Americans. No one points out that during Hitler's childhood, a major element in the European view of mankind was the conviction that 'inferior races' were by nature condemned to extinction: the true compassion of the superior races consisted in helping them on the way.

All German historians participating in this debate seem to look in the same direction. None looks to the west. But Hitler did. What Hitler wished to create when he sought *Lebensraum* in the east was a continental equivalent of the British Empire. It was in the British and other western European peoples that he found the models, of which the extermination of the Jews is . . . 'a distorted copy'.

We are part of a European culture, for which the extinction of peoples is not a recent phenomenon, but a pattern repeated over centuries. The first documented European genocide began in 1478 – that of the advanced Berber-speaking inhabitants of the Canary Islands (then ironically called 'the Fortunate Isles') – the Guanches. Within five years of Ferdinand and Isabella sending a military force from Spain, 78,000 of the 80,000 Guanches had been killed; Las Palmas surrendered in 1494, Tenerife in 1496. Lindqvist explains that bacterial infections, the disease that the indigenous people called '*modorra*', was even deadlier than the soldiers and their guns:

> Of Tenerife's fifteen thousand inhabitants, only a handful survived. The forest was cleared, the flora and fauna Europeanized, the Guanches lost their land and thus their living. The *modorra* returned several times, and dysentery, pneumonia, and venereal disease ravaged. Those who survived the diseases instead died of actual subjugation – loss of relatives, friends,

---

* When Sven Lindqvist published *Exterminate All the Brutes* in 1992, the genocide of the Herero and Nama peoples was arguably not as widely discussed or known as it is today. However, his principal argument, regarding the inability of historians to connect this genocide to the Holocaust, still stands.

language, and lifestyle. When Girolamo Benzoni visited Las Palmas in 1541, there was one single Guanche left, eighty-one years old and permanently drunk. The Guanches had gone under.

A culture of systematic violence, exploitation and annihilation of indigenous peoples underlies so much of European thought and behaviour, in the same totally unconscious way that roots underlie a tree in blossom. We pride ourselves on our cities and culture and education, we learn about the Renaissance and the Enlightenment, we talk about the Large Hadron Collider at CERN and our latest smartphones, unable to see that all the blossom on the tree is connected to the roots. Until we have the courage to face this deeply disturbing truth, and look our shared histories in the eye, unblinkingly, we will fail to live in the present – to live fully, to be aware of what surrounds us, where we come from and why we behave as we do.

5

Vernichtung[*]

Hands digging in a desert.

Thousands of hands.
Fingernails splintering as the desperation increases.
Hands digging in a desert.

Thousands of hands.
Fingernails splintering as the desperation increases.
The primal human need for water.

Women, men, children, delirious with the heat.
No trees, no grass, no shelter, no way back to the mountains.

Only one thought:
Water.

Over days they dig.

---

[*] *Vernichtung*: German etymology, literally 'bringing to nothing' – but also used to mean extermination or annihilation.

540

In the furnace of midday they dig,
in the dusk and in the night they dig.
They dig holes as deep as high as themselves, and then dig deeper.
Still no water appears.

As their strength fades, it becomes ever more impossible to think of trying to cross the vast desert of Omaheke, and reach sanctuary on the other side.

And if they try to go back the way they came, towards their ancestral lands in the mountains, they know they will all be shot by the lines of German patrols that ring the periphery of the desert, where the water holes are. Because the 'Extermination Order' has been proclaimed, and no mercy will be shown.

So all they can do is pray for the rainy season – still weeks away – to come early. And, with the last of their strength, dig still deeper. With only their hands, some manage to dig twenty-five, thirty feet down through the sand.

But still there is no water.

Over days, and weeks, thousands and thousands of human beings die – the majority of the Herero people, in the land that today is called Namibia, but in 1904 was called Deutsch-Südwestafrika (German South-West Africa). Tens of thousands died – the vast majority of thirst and starvation – with the Germans hardly having to fire a shot.

*

The Genocide That Never Ended

I haven't been able to get these images and thoughts out of my head since I first came across an account of the 1904 extermination of the Herero people – cattle farmers who had lived peacefully for years in the rich grasslands of northern Namibia, and the mountain plateau of Waterberg. It was when I read *Exterminate All the Brutes* for the first time in the late 1990s, but I recall the physical shock as if it were yesterday. Despite having read numerous descriptions of genocides and massacres over many years, this account affected me in a different way. It seemed not to belong to this world. It seemed to be out of a nightmare. But I went over the words again to make sure I hadn't been hallucinating. No, they were all there, in black and white – it was just my head that couldn't make sense of the reality that was described:

> When the rainy season came, German patrols found skel-etons lying around dry hollows, twenty-four to fifty feet deep, dug by the Hereros in vain attempts to find water. Almost the entire people – about eighty thousand human beings – died in the deserts. Only a few thousand were left, sentenced to hard labour in German concentration camps . . .
>
> 'The month-long sealing of desert areas, carried out with iron severity, completed the work of annihilation,' the General Staff writes in the official account of the war. 'The death rattles of the dying and their insane screams of fury . . . resounded in the sublime silence of infinity'. The General Staff's account further reports that 'the sentence had been carried out' and 'the Hereros had ceased to be an independent people.'

What was done to the Herero, and also their sister people, the Nama, between 1904 and 1907 was the first genocide of the twenti-eth century. When I began researching in the late 1990s, very little had been published on the subject; it seemed to be one of the least known, one of the least understood of all genocides. I wondered whether one of the reasons for this cultural invisibility in the West, aside from our historic racism, was that imperial Germany, quite explicitly, had copied the brutal methodologies already established by the British Empire in its colonies and by the United States in its treatment of American indigenous peoples. So maybe there was a deep-rooted, and unacknowledged, shame in our cultures that did not want to see the linkage between our extermination of indigenous peoples and what Germany did to the people of South-West Africa, and later to its own Jewish population.

In the first decade of this century, at last, something began to shift; more papers and books started to be published on the Herero–Nama genocide, and documentary films began to be made. Finally this genocide was being recognised, and this process of cultural and historical visibility increased to such an extent that in 2017 the German government had to acknowledge that what happened in South-West Africa in the early 1900s indeed constituted 'genocide'. The truly shocking aspect of all of this was that it had taken Germany, and most of the world, more than a hundred years to recognise the reality of this atrocity. Shocking not only in its own terms, but also because Germany, of all countries, should have understood, long before they did, the critical linkage between the two German genocides of the twentieth century.

My own journey of understanding, which had begun with that short passage in *Exterminate All the Brutes*, continued when I read Mark Cocker's *Rivers of Blood, Rivers of Gold* in 1998, which seemed to pick up Lindqvist's broader challenge for us to understand the brutal nature of European colonial psychology. Cocker went into greater detail than Lindqvist, looking at four case studies of European exterminations of tribal peoples, including a long chapter on Germany's extermination of the Herero and Nama. By this stage I had already begun the intensive research phase of my work on the desk killer, and I had become more and more preoccupied by the question of *how* Germany's extermination of the European Jews had been possible. What had happened in the minds of an entire generation, or rather two generations, of Germans, to enable such an event to occur? Before *physical* extermination surely there had to have been a *mental and conceptual* extermination? There were certain details in Cocker's account that astonished me – for instance, the fact that Hermann Goering's father had been the first imperial commissioner in South-West Africa. The fact that a German general had issued a *Vernicht-ungsbefehl* (an 'Extermination order') in 1904, thirty-eight years before the Wannsee Conference. I had an instinct that the deeper I dug into this territory, the more disturbing the linkages between the two genocides would become.

And then, in 2010, David Olusoga and Casper Erichsen published their groundbreaking work *The Kaiser's Holocaust*. Most compellingly, they take us right into the mindset of the German colonialists, military strategists and planners at the end of the nineteenth century. For years I had wondered what the dominant ideas in German culture were when Hitler, Himmler, Goering, Goebbels and all were boys. What were they taught at school? What were the bestselling books they grew up with? What would their parents have been discussing? What were German newspapers reporting? What were the lessons learned by the governing authorities back in Berlin from the experiments carried out in South-West Africa? Now, for the first time, some of my questions were beginning to find answers.

But the more I read, the more I began to hear another voice in my head. The annihilation of the Herero and Nama should not be seen as important only because of the second genocide it prefigured; nor should it be seen as relevant only to Germany – because Germany, quite openly, followed the example of other powers, especially Britain and America. Most of all, though, I realised that this genocide needs to be read and understood on its own terms. The process of decolonisation – which some may regard as finished – has a long way to go. Decolonisation of our minds is only just beginning. To fully understand the significance of the Herero and Nama genocide we would have to see this event as part of our Western identity. We would have to acknowledge the exterminist impulses which have been at the heart of our cultures. We would have to open up this debate inside ourselves, however disturbing this process may be. We would also have to recognise that genocide can never be regarded as a finished episode. This is one of the most terrible truths of the Herero–Nama genocide – the fact that Namibia today, according to the United Nations, is the most unequal country in the world, where the top 1 per cent of the population earn more than the bottom 50 per cent, with appalling consequences for health and life expectancy.* We also should understand that this economic inequality correlates almost exactly with the race composition of the country – the top 1 per cent being almost entirely the descendants of white European settlers, the bottom 50 per cent being almost entirely the indigenous black population. It seems clear that the legacy of the genocide that the Germans began by military means in 1904 is being carried on a hundred years later by economic means – a state which could be described as 'the genocide that never ended'.

*

To look at the causation of genocide often involves going back many years – witness the enormous amount of recent research (and argument) about the way that nineteenth-century anti-semitism in Germany created (or didn't) the conditions necessary for the Holocaust to come about a hundred years later. However, the genocidal arc in the case of the Herero and Nama is far shorter, and much clearer in its historical frame – no longer than twenty-one years from the arrival of the first German settler in 1883 to the extermination in the Omaheke desert in 1904. This chapter covers a slightly longer span, taking us up to the outbreak of the First World War; I've attempted not only to show the historical stages – the *process* – by which the vast majority of the indigenous peoples of this country were exterminated, but also the way that this was not simply a military genocide: we will also meet corporations who played their roles, and key individuals from academia and science, who created the intellectual and social conditions necessary for genocide to happen – early-twentieth-century pioneers of the lethal practice of desk killing.

There are six discernible stages to Germany's colonisation of South-West Africa, so the chapter will follow chronologically, keeping focus on those with power, the prime perpetrators, at each stage:

---

* Human Development Report, UN Development Programme 2005, cited in *Colonial Genocide and Reparations Claims in the 21st Century* by Jeremy Sarkin.

- Adolf Luderitz and Heinrich Vogelsang (1883–5)
- Dr Heinrich Goering and the 'protection treaties' (1885–8)
- Captain Curt von François: 'nothing but relentless severity' (1889–93)
- Governor Theodor Leutwein: 'divide and rule', the British strategy (1894–1904)
- General Lothar von Trotha: annihilation (1904–5)
- Governor Friedrich von Lindequist: from 'extermination through work' to the 'settler paradise' (1905–14)

1. Adolf Luderitz and Heinrich Vogelsang (1883–5)

On 10 April 1883, the *Tilly*, a German sailing ship, arrived in the desolate bay of Angra Pequena, situated on what was known to European powers as the 'Skeleton Coast' of South-West Africa – a seemingly desolate stretch of coast, consisting of endless sand dunes, which runs almost 1,000 miles from the Congo basin in the north to the Orange River, bordering the Cape lands in the south. The calm of the ship's arrival on this April day belied the years of terror, gunfire and massacres that were to follow in its wake. There was a reason why this part of Africa was one of the last to be colonised – it is staggeringly dry, with a thick swathe of the Namib desert running right along the coast, and inland, the Kalahari in the south and the Omaheke further north; it seemed to be utterly inhospitable to settlement – only the British had established a single, coastal foothold at Walvis Bay. Yet what appeared to be a classic example of the '*terra nullius*' that colonialists liked to see was – fifty miles inland, where the mountains started to rise, giving way to a central plateau – a fertile country where the Herero, Nama and other tribal peoples had lived for hundreds of years.

The earliest known inhabitants of this land were the nomadic San people, who for thousands of years had hunted over a vast territory from eastern Africa down to the Cape. In the early seventeenth century, Bantu-speaking peoples arrived in waves of migration from the north. Some of these, the Ovambo, settled in what is

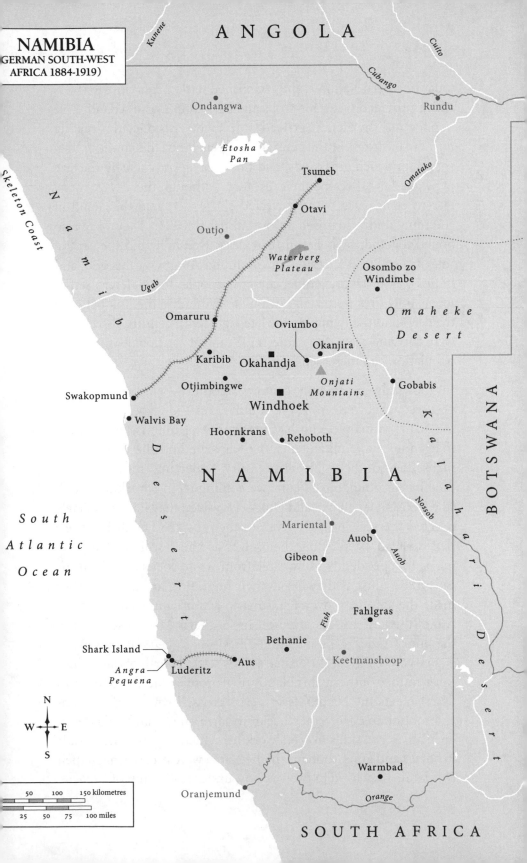

NAMIBIA
GERMAN SOUTH-WEST
AFRICA 1884-1919)

ANGOLA

Kunene

Cubango

Cuito

Ondangwa

Rundu

*Etosha
Pan*

Omatako

Tsumeb

Otavi

Outjo

*Waterberg
Plateau*

Osombo zo
Windimbe

*N
a
m
i
b*

Ugab

*O m a h e k e
D e s e r t*

Omaruru

Oviumbo

Okanjira

Karibib

Okahandja

▲ *Onjati
Mountains*

Gobabis

Swakopmund

Otjimbingwe

Windhoek

*K
a
l
a
h
a
r
i*

BOTSWANA

Walvis Bay

Hoornkrans

Rehoboth

*D
e
s
e
r
t*

N A M I B I A

Nossob

S o u t h

Mariental

Auob

A t l a n t i c

Gibeon

Auob

O c e a n

*D
e
s
e
r
t*

Fish

Fahlgras

Bethanie

Keetmanshoop

Shark Island

Aus

*Angra
Pequena*   Luderitz

N
W ✦ E
S

Warmbad

50   100   150 kilometres

25   50   75   100 miles

Oranjemund

Orange

SOUTH AFRICA

Skeleton Coast

today northern Namibia, and established settlements close to rivers which provided water for crops and agriculture. The second wave of migrants, the Herero, arrived with huge herds of cattle, looking for new pastures; in the central high plateau of the country, they soon found rich grasslands, and this area, approximately the size of Switzerland, became their territory. Although there were many Herero clans, each with an elected chief, they held their land in common, and recognised an overall tribal leader. They were also bound together by belief in their deity, Ndjambi, and the central role of their dead ancestors in communicating with this god, and in this way providing guidance to the people. In all Herero settlements holy fires were kept burning to symbolise the link between the dead and the living. By the late eighteenth century the Herero were thriving from the cattle trade, and it is thought that their population had increased to around 40,000.

In the early nineteenth century another wave of migration occurred, this time from the south, from the Cape. These were the Nama, a people who had grown out of unions between the indigenous Cape inhabitants, the Khosian, and the Dutch colonial settlers of the eighteenth century. Reflecting this mixed cultural background, most Nama were bilingual in Khoekhoegowab (the Khosian language) and Dutch. However, they had completely rejected the servant roles given to them by the Dutch Boer settlers, instead establishing themselves as small-scale farmers living as independently as possible from white society. And, in the early 1800s, just as they began their migration to the north, they made the shrewd move of starting to acquire guns and horses – two of the key sources of power in southern African societies at the time. Trade in these commodities was to become one of the engines of wealth for the Nama, as they settled north of the Orange River in the southern shrublands of Namibia, where the Kalahari desert meets the Namib desert, criss-crossed with deep canyons and mountains. Here they began to farm sheep, and also developed advanced skills in metalworking, which, together with trade in horses and guns, soon meant the Nama were prospering in their new land. They lived in twelve clans, under leadership of *kapteins*, tribal chiefs – the *Witbooi* the most powerful of these groupings ('white boys', so called because of the white bandanas they wore on their wide hats). Many of the Nama were Christian, and so in their main settlements churches were built, and European missionaries were invited to join the communities, where schools were soon established.

By the mid-nineteenth century, the Herero and the Nama, both thriving from their chosen livestock and trades, had become the dominant peoples of the land, with a combined population of around 100,000. A vivid picture of life here, with its mixture of cattle herding and trade in commodities, is given by Olusoga and Erichsen:

> At night the landscape was pinpricked by a constellation of campfires, as white traders, missionaries, Nama, Herero and San sought comfort from the cold of the desert night. The whole nation clustered around thousands of fires, telling ancient stories or dreaming of cattle, wealth or power.

*

A young man named Heinrich Vogelsang disembarked from the *Tilly* on this April day to find only a single proper building in the bay – the house of an eccentric English shark hunter named David Radford. Vogelsang was on a mission, conceived by his boss, Adolf Luderitz, a wealthy trader in tobacco and guano, based in Bremen, who wanted to establish a trading post here, eventually leading to the setting up of a German colony. Luderitz's aims could not have been clearer, as can be seen in his statement, which today appears almost a caricature of colonial evil: 'I should be pleased if it turned out that the entire colony is a colossal mineral deposit, which, once it is mined, will leave the whole area one gaping hole.'*

---

* I recently found an uncanny echo of Luderitz's comments in *Heart of Darkness* by Joseph Conrad: 'To tear treasure out of the bowels of the land was their desire, with no more moral purpose at the back of it than there is in burglars breaking into a safe.'

Vogelsang's first action was to put up a prefabricated hut in the bay at Angra Pequena, which he rather grandiloquently called 'Fort Vogelsang'. His next step was to set out for the Nama settlement of Bethanie, 120 miles inland, to meet the leader there, Joseph Fredericks, who, he'd been informed, controlled the land rights of the coastal region. With the help of a local German missionary, Johannes Bam, acting as translator, by 1 May 1883 Vogelsang had agreed a treaty with Fredericks for the land at Angra Pequena and a five-mile radius around – in exchange for £100 and 200 rifles. In August, Vogelsang returned to negotiate an even more exploitative deal – this time (in exchange for £500 and sixty more rifles) a 200-mile stretch of the coast northwards from Angra Pequena, 'twenty geographical miles' in width.[*]

Luderitz's timing was exceptional, because 1883–4 saw a sea change in German policy regarding colonisation. Reich Chancellor Bismarck had always been vehemently opposed to imperial plans, on the grounds of cost, stating unambiguously, 'as long as I am *Reichskanzler* we shall not pursue a colonial policy'. However, in the 1880s the German public, gripped by heroic reports of Saharan explorers such as Heinrich Barth and Gustav Nachtigal, became seized by 'colonial fever'. The German press and the newly formed German Colonial Society began to put increasing pressure on the government to change their approach. There was much public discussion about how the British, French and Portuguese would soon control all of Africa and force German traders out, and that Germany was about to miss the colonial boat.

From the Reich Chancellery in Berlin, Bismarck followed Luderitz's activities and German public opinion with interest. He had been persuaded that   by following the British colonial model of using companies like the East India Company, which financed their own private armies and organised the vast majority of administration themselves – the costs to the Reich of developing colonies would be limited, and the benefits could be substantial. But time was of

---

[*] With this wording Vogelsang tricked Fredericks and the Nama into actually relinquishing land rights one hundred miles in from the coast – because one 'geographical mile' supposedly equalled five standard miles.

the essence now, especially as he was hearing rumblings that Britain might make a territorial claim on the Namibian coast. On 19 April 1884 the chancellor informed Luderitz that his putative colony at Angra Pequena would receive full protection from the German state. Four months later, this was formalised as two German naval boats, under captains Schering and Herbig, arrived, flags were raised, and a proclamation read out declaring that this territory was now under the sovereignty of 'His Majesty Kaiser Wilhelm I' and was forthwith to be known as the 'Protectorate of German South-West Africa'.

In October 1884, the European powers gathered at the Berlin Conference, at Bismarck's official residence on Wilhelmstrasse in Berlin, to finalise their spheres of influence in Africa. Although Germany was a late starter, compared to Britain, France and Portugal, it emerged with freedom to establish colonies in four African countries – South-West Africa, East Africa (later Tanganika/ Tanzania), Togo and Cameroon – almost a million square miles of territory, with 14 million inhabitants.

But in South-West Africa, in early 1885 Luderitz suffered a series of disasters, died soon afterwards, and by the summer Bismarck's dream (of an informal colony run by companies, the British model) was threatened. Germany, if it was to continue its interest in South-West Africa, would now have to create a fully state-funded colonial government, including the appointment of an imperial commissioner. But who would be chosen for this important colonial role – a role that will cement Germany's 'ownership' of South-West Africa and begin the process of dispossessing the indigenous peoples of their land? Bismarck appointed a lawyer, a man whose name has an infamous ring, and provides a telling link between nineteenth-century racial supremacists and twentieth-century genocidists.

2. Dr Heinrich Goering and the 'Protection Treaties' (1885–8)

Dr Heinrich Goering – whose son Hermann, fifty-five years later, would oversee the Nazi colonisation of vast swathes of eastern

Europe and the subsequent enslavement of millions of Poles and Slavs – takes up his new post in South-West Africa in September 1885. Formerly a judge, his knowledge of law, as well as the Dutch language, are the main reasons why he is appointed by Bismarck; the colonial priority is to negotiate further treaties and alliances between the Reich and the tribal peoples, which will aid the transfer of land ownership to the new colonial power.

Goering and his retinue reach the Herero capital at Okahandja in October 1885, and eventually agree a 'protection treaty' with the tribal leader, Maharero Tjamuaha. But all his efforts to negotiate a similar deal with the Nama chief, Hendrik Witbooi, the following year are rebuffed. Witbooi, a leader of exceptional intelligence and courage, wants nothing to do with the German colonisers with their arrogance, uniforms and flags. He writes this to one of Goering's deputies: 'You . . . call yourself a "Representative". How shall I respond? You are someone else's representative and I am a free and autonomous man answering to none but God. So I have nothing further to say to you.'

Goering's tenure as commissioner ends in further ignominy, when the Herero leader Tjamuaha discovers that Goering has built an extension to his villa in Otjimbingwe over the sacred ground of a Herero graveyard. At the end of October 1888 he is summoned to explain himself, and the enraged Tjamuaha, in front of a hundred of his men, promptly nullifies the treaty they had agreed three years earlier. Goering is terrified, believes his life to be in danger, and immediately flees the country, with Germany's 'control' of South-West Africa in tatters.

We learn that Goering later told his son Hermann thrilling tales of his time in the colony; we can only speculate on such imaginative storytelling powers, and smile at his chutzpah in transforming these calamitous years into 'heroic' actions:

> Young Goering listened, his eyes sparkling with excitement, to his father's stories about his adventures in bygone days. The inquisitive and imaginative lad was . . . thrilled by his accounts of his pioneer work as a *Reichskommissar* for South-West

Africa, of his journeys through the Kalahari Desert and his fights with Maharero, the black king of Okahandja.

But although the fights with Maharero may have been fiction, the impacts of such stories on an entire generation of young Germans, such as Hermann, were real enough – in fact extremely dangerous – helping to create a potent myth of the German struggle for *Lebensraum*, a struggle that was predicated on the destruction of 'inferior races'. A concept that the children of imperial Germany at the turn of the century would have grown up with, and found entirely natural.

3. Captain Curt von François: 'nothing but relentless severity' (1889–93)

Goering's replacement arrived in June 1889 – a hardened Prussian army officer, Captain Curt von François, who had made his reputation as a mercenary contributing to King Leopold's rule of terror in the Belgian Congo in the late 1880s. François' racial fanaticism can be summed up by his view that 'the Europeans have failed to give the black man the right kind of treatment . . . nothing but relentless severity will lead to success'. He soon strengthens the German military presence in South-West Africa, and eventually establishes a new headquarters and fortress in the middle of Hereroland at Windhoek (still the capital of Namibia today).

This begins to attract the first German settlers, who start to set up farms in the vicinity, reassured by the protection of the large fort. Soon, with the beginning of Windhoek's expansion, the creation of a postal service and regular shipping links to Germany, the colonial outpost begins to take shape. He negotiates a new protection treaty with the Herero in 1890, because he has identified the key threat to German interests as the well-armed Witbooi Nama in the south, under the charismatic leadership of Hendrik Witbooi. At the beginning of 1893 François is at last sent the additional force of 250 soldiers he's been requesting from Germany; finally he can begin the military action he's contemplated for many months – but this is not to be an open battle between the army of the Germans and the warriors of the Nama.

On the night of 12 April 1893 the first German massacre in South-West Africa takes place in the valley of Hoornkrans, a hundred miles south-west of Windhoek. Hendrik Witbooi and around 1,000 of his people are sleeping in their clay huts spread across the valley. François informs his 200 soldiers that their mission that night is 'to destroy the tribe of the Witboois', but this is to be no conventional battle. The soldiers climb the steep slopes above the valley and encircle the encampment, and then, just as the sun starts to rise, with Hoornkrans still slumbering, François signals for the assault to begin. In the next half an hour, 200 rifles fire 16,000 rounds of ammunition, pounding the valley below. In the smoke and chaos and screaming, somehow Hendrik manages to order the Witbooi fighters to regroup at the far end of the valley, expecting the Germans to follow. But instead François orders his men to fix their bayonets and charge down the slopes into Hoornkrans, where they start butchering all those left behind – women, children, the sick and the elderly – and razing the place to the ground. Hendrik's twelve-year-old son is shot trying to run away, then tries to crawl towards the Witbooi fighters, but a German soldier spots him and shoots him in the head. An eyewitness describes the carnage:

> One woman was killed while her child clung to her scream-ing; a soldier shot the child through the head, blowing it to pieces . . . Houses were set on fire and burnt over the bodies of dead women and children . . . On another side of the camp all the women were killed except two, of whom one was wounded.

When the Germans finally leave, taking with them eighty Witbooi women to be used as slaves in the Windhoek garrison, the extent of the horror becomes evident – eighty women and children, and eight elderly men, all massacred.

François reports a military triumph to his superiors in Berlin, boasting that fifty Witbooi soldiers had been killed (a complete fiction), and that 'any further resistance on the part of the Witboois is out of the question'. But it soon emerges that the overwhelming majority of those killed were women and children, and vivid eyewitness accounts of the massacre now begin to appear in British newspapers, directly challenging François' account. Debate is soon raging in Berlin and London, with many muttering, shocked but somewhat hypocritically, that 'European nations do not make war in that way!'

But it is not concern about François' brutal behaviour at Hoornkrans that eventually sees him recalled to Germany, rather it is his inability to defeat Hendrik Witbooi. Remarkably, after Hoornkrans the Nama manage to regroup, and Hendrik conducts several successful raids on François and his garrison in Windhoek, at one point even cutting off the German supply routes to the coast. François and his men are confined to their fort for months. In stark contrast to François' slaughter of non-combatants, Witbooi's actions only target German soldiers, leaving settler farmers and their families unharmed. By autumn 1893 disquiet in Germany has spread, and in a Reichstag debate a speaker articulates the views of many when he states that 'François . . . must be replaced by someone else . . . Hendrik Witbooi is the real master of the country and François is no match for him.'

4. Governor Theodor Leutwein: 'divide and rule', the British strategy (1894–1904)

On New Year's Day 1894, François' replacement, Theodor Leutwein, arrives in the new port of Swakopmund and then journeys to Windhoek to take up his position as governor. His background in law and diplomacy could not have been more different to François', and he knew that the Herero and Nama should not be underestimated. Leutwein had studied Britain's global experience of colonialism in detail, and wants to enact one of their main principles – the policy of 'divide and rule' among different tribal groups. He is quite explicit about this strategy, writing that he intends to make 'the native tribes serve our cause and to play them off one against the other'. Rather than spending money and using soldiers from Germany, surely it was more intelligent 'to influence the natives to kill each other for us'.

First of all he picks off two of the smaller Nama tribes, and forces them to sign treaties accepting German sovereignty. Then he turns his attentions to Hendrik Witbooi, sending him a series of very direct letters urging him to make peace, and then, when these do not work, in August 1894, launching an attack on Witbooi and his forces in the Naukluft mountains. After thirteen days of relentless artillery bombardment, Hendrik finally accepts Leutwein's offer of a peace treaty. The terms of this deal are that the Nama are to return to the south of the country near Gibeon, where a German garrison would now be stationed. However, the Nama are to retain control over their lands and their animals, and are still to be responsible for maintaining 'peace and order in [the] territory'. These terms do not go down well, either in the settler community or back in Berlin, where many believe Leutwein's offer to the Nama to be far too 'generous'.

With the Nama now effectively neutralised, Leutwein then sets about creating as many divisions as possible among the Herero. This is made easier by the fact that there is a succession dispute following the death of Tjamuaha, with Samuel Maharero and his cousin Nikodemus competing for the role of 'paramount chief'. Samuel had been educated by missionaries and converted to Christianity, and adopted many European habits, living in a grand villa, wearing expensive, Western clothes and developing an addiction to brandy and fine wines. Nikodemus was far more traditional, a proven leader for the eastern Herero, and more popular with the people. Leutwein shrewdly considers all of this, noting privately all of Samuel's weaknesses, and then declares German support for his election, writing later to the new German chancellor, Caprivi, 'It is self-evident that a politically divided Herero nation is more easy to deal with than a united and coherent one'.

With Samuel safely elected, in December 1894 Leutwein negotiates an agreement with the Herero to limit the southern boundary of their territory to enable further German settlement – despite the fact that the nomadic, grazing livelihood of the Herero had known no definitive borders for hundreds of years. This soon creates resentment, especially with the eastern Herero, some of whose land Samuel has blithely signed away. Eventually Nikodemus's patience snaps, and in April 1896 he attacks a German patrol and then a government military post at Gobabis. Under the terms of the various protection treaties that have been signed, Samuel Maharero and Hendrik Witbooi now are forced to fight against Nikodemus and the eastern Herero. All Leutwein's cynical planning of divide and rule is beginning to bear fruit. The rebellion is crushed, Nikodemus is subsequently executed, and enormous bitterness is generated between the main Herero people and their eastern cousins.

To add insult to injury, the mid to late 1890s are disastrous for the Herero in other ways. Rinderpest (cattle plague) arrives in the country in 1896–7 and devastates the herds, some communities losing 95 per cent of their stock. The resulting malnutrition and disease leads to many Herero abandoning their way of life and seeking work and help at the German settlements and mission stations. Some Herero are forced to sell prime grazing land, giving German settlers more of a foothold in the country. There is even discussion among the colonial authorities – who had studied how American settlers had dispossessed the indigenous Indians – about establishing reservations for the Herero, to give the Germans even greater control of the land. This approach is very much the international fashion – Theodore Roosevelt (soon to be US president) had written his book *The Winning of the West* between 1889 and 1896, which spelt out the lessons of the American experience:

> The most righteous of all wars is a war with savages . . . American and Indian, Boer and Zulu, Cossack and Tartar, New Zealander and Maori – in each case the victor, horrible though many of his deeds are, has laid the foundation for the future greatness of a mighty people . . . it is of incalculable importance that America, Australia and Siberia should pass

out of the hands of their red, black and aboriginal owners, and become the heritage of the dominant world races.

*

Back in Germany in the 1890s such blatantly racist thinking is warmly accepted, colonial fever is at its height, and the 'German Western' novels and stories of Karl May are reaching a vast audience. May portrays German settlers on the American frontier, battling against the savages, and rediscovering their essential *Volkisch* roots as a colonial people. And his representation of migrant Germans escaping the cramped, industrial lives in their homeland, and finding their true spirit, is lapped up by millions of readers. Many stories are published in a magazine aimed at boys, *Der Gute Kamerad* ('The Good Comrade'), which gains a huge readership between 1887 and 1897, sales peaking at this time when Hitler is an eight-year-old boy and an avid Karl May reader. Ten years later, millions more children read Gustav Frenssen's *Peter Moor's Fahrt nacht Südwest* ('Peter Moor's Adventures in South-West Africa', published in 1908), an account of the Herero and Nama genocides from the perspective of a teenage boy.* Through his 'gripping adventures' Peter comes to realise that the indigenous peoples are barbaric and deserve the extermination that befalls them.

But more influential even than Karl May and Gustav Frenssen was the book *Volk ohne Raum* ('People without Space') by Hans Grimm, published in 1926, an epic tale of a German 'everyman' figure, Cornelius Freibott, who ends up settling in German South-West Africa in 1907 (no mention is made of the massacres that have just occurred, nor the concentration camps). He has finally found his elusive living space, room to breathe – the place where Germans can realise who they are as a people. He returns to Germany in the early 1920s to find problems, primarily the Jews, who he now real-

---

* Today we read this as a kind of Hitler Youth caricature of history, yet it was hugely popular in Germany; indeed it was one of the biggest-selling children's books in Germany in the first half of the twentieth century.

ises are not part of the 'German tribe'. This book sold hundreds of thousands of copies, and the phrase '*Volk ohne Raum*' became a Nazi rallying cry. In an age before television it is almost impossible to overstate the cultural impact of books like these; they essentially programmed the minds of entire generations of young Germans, creating the most fertile possible conditions for Nazism to then take root.

Into this cultural context steps a geographer, Friedrich Ratzel, who now creates an extraordinarily potent and dangerous academic frame to bring all these disparate colonial impulses together. Influenced by Darwin's studies of animal adaptation and evolution, Ratzel applies (or rather misapplies) Darwin's theories to human migration and 'the struggle for existence'. He believes that the colonisation of the world by the white race and the destruction of indigenous peoples is all part of this struggle, and that the drive to migration is a key factor in human evolution – based on the need for people to continually expand the amount of space they occupy.

In 1897 Ratzel publishes his book *Politische Geographie*, and his new theory of *Lebensraum* ('living space') comes into the world, a concept that would achieve genocidal force within a decade in South-West Africa, and within fifty years all across Europe. The idea rapidly gains popular currency, fuelling the push for colonisation at the end of the nineteenth century, and acting like a toxic seed germinating in the body politic of the Reich over the next decades. In all likelihood, a little boy in Linz would have come across the idea for the first time at school; certainly, twenty years later, in 1924, we know that Hitler was reading Ratzel's book in Landsberg prison, when he was writing *Mein Kampf* – and *Lebensraum* then forms a central tenet in the evolution of beliefs driving the National Socialist movement.

Ratzel is also one of the founders of the German Colonial Society in 1887, and he becomes a prominent advocate of German South-West Africa becoming an applied experiment in *Lebensraum*, with the German settlers and farmers acting as the principal agents of this colonisation. Any native peoples, or 'inferior races' as he terms them, who attempt to stop this natural development should be met with overwhelming force. And just like Leutwein, he looks to the examples of British, European and American colonisations in Tasmania, southern Brazil and North America that had been so successful in rapidly displacing indigenous peoples. As Olusoga and Erichsen note, 'these wars, that Ratzel viewed as models for future colonialism, were wars of extermination; some were genocides'.

*

As the nineteenth century ends, despite all the cattle plagues, typhus and malaria epidemics, and the continual attempted encroachments of the German colonists and settlers, South-West Africa still remains primarily in the hands of the Herero and Nama. The Germans are largely restricted to their garrison towns like Windhoek, and the surrounding areas, and even then, the vast majority of the population are soldiers – 600 out of the 780 Europeans living in the town are military personnel in 1896. Although they now had a toehold in the country, this does not satisfy the ambitions of Governor Leutwein or his superiors back in Berlin.

Having already been inspired by the example of the British Empire's 'divide and rule' strategy, Leutwein now looks towards America for ideas on the next stage of colonisation. Two factors had been critical in America's frontier settlement – the development of railways[*] and the creation of native reserves. So important does the governor believe these to be that in 1897 he travels back to Berlin and makes a direct appeal to the Reichstag for funds to help start the building of the railways. Five years later, in 1902, the first line – between Windhoek and the fast-growing port at Swakopmund   is completed, and the next year, a second line, linking the port to copper mines near Otavi, is begun, all of this also resulting in substantial losses of grazing land for the Herero. Also in 1903, Leutwein agrees

---

[*] Angelo Golinelli, the official in charge of South-West Africa in the Colonial Department in Berlin, wrote that railways in the colonies 'are built as a prelude to subjugation and pacification' (from *The Kaiser's Holocaust*, by David Olusoga and Casper Erichsen).

to a policy of native reserves, and two are established – at Otjimb-ingwe for the Herero, and Rietmont for the Nama.

By 1903, although many cattle had been sold to the settlers, only 10 per cent of farmland formerly owned by the indigenous popu-lations had been 'legally' transferred to German ownership at this point. It should be understood that Leutwein's colonial policy, how-ever harsh, was informed by his background in law and diplomacy, and so he could state, with remarkably open cynicism: 'However ruthless one's colonial policy, it is necessary to give one's actions a semblance of legality.'*

To make matters worse from the colonists' perspective, the Herero and Nama had never been wealthier. Their cattle herds were increas-ing again after the plagues, and, as prices were rising, their stock had never been more valuable. Resentment was running high, especially among the settlers around Windhoek, who saw, correctly, that the Africans still retained much of the power in the colony. The gulf between this reality, and the perception of natives as 'savages', not really humans at all, became too much to bear for many colonists. A missionary writing at this time says that 'the average German looks down upon the natives as being about on the same level as the higher primates ("baboon" being their favourite term for the natives), and treats them like animals'. In 1900, a group of German settlers wrote to the Colonial Department in Berlin expressing their views and the strategy needed in South-West Africa:

> Any white men who have lived among natives find it almost impossible to regard them as human beings at all in any Euro-pean sense. They need centuries of training as human beings, with endless patience, strictness and justice.

*

---

* A phrase which anticipates the lawyers and civil servants of the Wannsee Conference, and Heydrich's emphasis on clearing 'the German living space *by legal means*' (regardless of the wider genocidal intent).

Given this febrile atmosphere among the colonists, and growing anger among the Herero and Nama at the regular mistreatment of their people by the settlers, it didn't require much for the situation to escalate. The blue touchpaper was lit in the tiny settlement of Warmbad on the southern border of South-West Africa. It all begins in late October 1903 with a dispute between the leader of a minority tribal group (the Bondelswarts) and a Herero woman on her way to the Cape Colony (later South Africa). The local German commander, a Lieutenant Jobst, hears about this dispute, and summons the Bondelswarts leader, Jan Christian, to appear before him. Christian ignores the order as the dispute has already been resolved, and he doesn't believe Germany should have any power regarding inter-ethnic disputes anyway. Jobst, enraged at this lack of respect, as he sees it, goes round to Christian's house with two aides. Christian is dragged out of his house, resisting furiously; Jobst then orders the soldiers to shoot him, which they do. Before he dies, he whispers, 'Now the war starts.' Jobst and the two soldiers are then killed by the Bondelswarts.

As news of these deaths reach Windhoek and Berlin, the reaction is predictably hysterical. The kaiser insists on sending huge military reinforcements immediately to all of Germany's territories in Africa, 'less we lose all our colonial possessions', and Leutwein (though privately furious with Jobst for escalating such a minor dispute) is forced to issue a declaration of war against the Bondelswarts. In late November 1903, he leads a force of soldiers 500 miles south to crush the supposed rebellion, leaving the arrogant and inexperienced Lieutenant Zurn in charge of northern Hereroland, which turns out to be a catastrophic mistake. Zurn is based at the fortress of Okahandja, the Herero capital, where Samuel Maharero has his villa and headquarters. In early January 1904, with Leutwein still away in the south of the country, Zurn picks up a rumour from a local trader that hundreds of armed Herero are on their way to the town. Without attempting to establish the facts, Zurn orders all the whites to evacuate their houses and take shelter inside the fort. He then sends a telegram to Berlin reporting (quite inaccurately) that the Herero uprising had begun.

Soon afterwards, the German soldiers begin to fire from the fort into the town, and the real war begins.

Zurn's reputation with the local Herero had already been sullied by two deeply offensive actions. Firstly, he had ordered Herero skulls to be exhumed from revered ancestral graves in Okahandja in 1903, so he could then sell them to race scientists back in Germany to make him some extra income. And secondly, he had demanded in December 1903 that northern Herero leaders transfer significant amounts of land to German settlers, and that they agree to establish a second Herero reservation. When the leaders refused to sign this treaty, Zurn simply forged their signatures and announced that the changes had been agreed. Given all of this provocation, it is not surprising that Samuel Maharero wrote to Leutwein in early March 1904, stating: 'this is not my war . . . it is that of Zurn'. Maharero's conduct of the ensuing war was in stark contrast to the Germans' – he specifically commanded that there should be no violence against Europeans in general, or Boers, or Nama, and no German women or children were to be targeted either. The Germans had no such compunction: their war against the Herero was brutal and total – lynchings became commonplace, and from late January three gallows were erected in Windhoek to hang any captured Herero.

Even though they did not instigate it, the Herero are well prepared for war. By December 1903 Maharero and the tribe elders had been discussing if they could continue to put up with such provocations by Zurn and the German settlers. By early January they become aware that Leutwein and the majority of the German soldiers have travelled south, leaving Zurn and only a small force behind in Windhoek and Okahandja. So when Zurn's soldiers open fire on them, in Okahandja at the beginning of January 1904, the Herero respond with a force that overwhelms the Germans. On 12 January the town is seized, the stores looted and burned; the fortress is then besieged for several days, but eventually German soldiers from Windhoek manage to break through and bring reinforcements. From 12–18 January the Herero control the centre of the country, with the German garrisons largely confined to the towns, sheltering in their forts. In this period the Herero fighters attack dozens of remote German farms and settlements, killing more than 120 German settlers and traders. But, in the majority of cases, Maharero's order not to target non-Germans, or German women and children, is respected.

Although the Herero experience these early victories, their key strategic failure is that they do not capture the main towns and forts of Windhoek and Okahandja, which would have given them the critical guns and ammunition they were now running short of. And on 27 January, Captain Franke and his 2nd Field Company manage to lift the siege of Okahandja's fort. Maharero and his fighters retreat to the east, into the Onjati mountains; there is then a fierce six-hour battle here, which leaves a hundred Herero dead, but heavy casualties are also inflicted on the Germans, who lose a fifth of their troops. However, Franke continues on and by 4 February also manages to lift the siege of the town of Omaruru in the north.

Further skirmishes and battles take place in the rest of February, March and early April 1904, with heavy casualties on both sides – for instance, at Okaharui on 3 April, forty-nine Germans are killed or seriously wounded, and forty-two Herero die. But what is perhaps most remarkable, behind these statistics, is that on paper at least, the Germans have an overwhelming advantage, in terms of numbers of soldiers, modernity of weapons (such as the Maxim machine guns) and quantity of ammunition. Yet the Herero's intimate knowledge of the landscape, especially the mountains, enable them to carry out a strikingly effective kind of insurgent warfare, which means that for three months one of the largest military powers in Europe cannot defeat them.

Meanwhile, hundreds of soldiers are pouring into South-West Africa from Germany each week, with formidable additonal supplies of artillery and Maxim guns. Among the volunteers is a thirty-five-year-old Bavarian lieutenant, Franz von Epp, a keen believer in the *Lebensraum* project and an extreme Social Darwinist who views colonial war as a racial crusade. (Later he is to become General von Epp, and it is his right-wing militia that a young Adolf Hitler joins in Munich in 1922.*) By 1 March over 2,000 new German soldiers have arrived in South-West Africa. Leutwein has finally got back to Okahandja by this time, but the Herero, now a fighting force of 4,000 men, have, after their initial attacks, withdrawn to the mountains near Okanjira fifty miles to the east. Leutwein's instinct is to negotiate with Samuel Maharero, but he is ordered only to 'relentlessly suppress' the uprising, so, on 7 April 1904, he reluctantly leads a force of 800 soldiers out of Okahandja towards the mountains. He already realises that the powers in Berlin, and many settlers within South-West Africa, will only be satisfied with total destruction of the Herero – writing (without any effect, as it later transpired) to the Colonial Department: 'I do not concur with those fanatics who want to see the Herero destroyed altogether. Apart from the fact that a people of 60,000 or 70,000 are not so easily annihilated, I consider it a bad mistake from an economic point of view.'

After a skirmish at Okanjira on 9 April, the Herero retreat to the north, and at Oviumbo on 13 April they inflict a crushing defeat on Leutwein's forces, ambushing them from the hills above, and surrounding the Germans. The German forces are only saved from being completely wiped out by the coming of darkness, when Leutwein orders an ignominious retreat back to Okahandja. The news of this shocking defeat provokes a storm of outrage back in Germany, and Leutwein is informed on 9 May that he is to be relieved of his military duties, though he will be allowed to stay on as governor for a while.

---

* It was only through von Epp's organisation that Hitler met many of those who were later to become the core of the Nazi Party, Ernst Röhm and Heinrich Himmler among them. It was also von Epp's old colonial connections that enabled Hitler to procure thousands of surplus South-West African soldiers' uniforms, desert brown in colour – later giving the name to Hitler's infamous Nazi street fighters, the 'Brownshirts'. Perhaps most critically, it was von Epp who in 1920 organised an illegal loan of 60,000 marks which enabled Hitler and his supporters to buy a Munich newspaper, the *Völkischer Beobachter*, which was soon to become the key media mouthpiece for the Nazis.

5. General Lothar von Trotha: Annihilation (1904–5)

The new military commander, landing at Swakopmund on 11 June 1904, is General Lothar von Trotha, a name infamous in Namibia to this day. He was a veteran of ruthless colonial repression in German East Africa and China – where, in the aftermath of the Boxer Rebellion, he established his uncompromising reputation by ordering mass hangings of rebels and burnings of entire villages and their populations. He is proud of his racial-supremacist views, extreme even by the standards of the day, relishing the fight against the 'lower races' of the world, and the *Unmenschen* (non-humans), as he describes them in his journal on the voyage to South-West Africa. Just after his arrival, he also writes this, which proves to be terrifyingly prophetic:

> I know enough tribes in Africa . . . they are all alike. They only respond to force. It was and is my policy to use force with terrorism and even brutality. I shall annihilate the revolting tribes with rivers of blood and rivers of gold. Only after a complete uprooting will something emerge.

When von Trotha and Leutwein meet in Windhoek they clash straight away, with von Trotha saying that the governor has no understanding of the realities of war, and immediately declares a state of emergency, effectively sidelining Leutwein's civilian powers completely. For the next six weeks von Trotha sees his military strength grow to an army of over 5,000 soldiers, and he plans his strategy.

The Herero, 50,000 in number by now, have moved again, further north, to their spiritual home – the plateau known as Waterberg (Water Mountain). This place, where a forest of ancient fig trees grows, is a sacred site for the people; it is the place where, according to Herero creation myth, the first ancestors had come down from heaven, climbing through the branches of the fig trees. It had also become the main meeting place for Herero tribes to come together to make decisions. Under the Waterberg there are deep and plentiful underground aquifers which provide water for people and animals – the last water before the hundreds of miles of desert, known to the Herero as the Omaheke (meaning sandveld – dry sandy land), stretching out to the east and the south. Here, Samuel Maharero and the other tribal chiefs now hold their councils, and try to agree on a strategy, knowing the Germans will soon be coming. Based on their previous experience of German behaviour, many expect them to offer negotiations, and Maharero puts out diplomatic feelers to this end. But the Herero could not have been more wrong about their adversaries.

By early July, von Trotha's army assembled in Windhoek is now 6,000 strong, paid for by vast loans raised by the Colonial Department back in Germany, where an atmosphere of jingoistic aggression has encouraged thousands of young men to volunteer to fight. From the very beginning von Trotha is only interested in the total destruction of the Herero. In his own words, he now decided to 'encircle the Herero masses around Waterberg and . . . annihilate them with an instantaneous blow'. He dismisses out of hand the advice of experienced officers who suggest that Germany should enter into peace negotiations, and in the early days of August 1904, von Trotha and his six huge battalions leave Windhoek and begin to encircle the Waterberg.

At 6 a.m. on 11 August, von Trotha launches the first ferocious assault on the Herero. For nine hours artillery and shells rain down on the encampment, killing hundreds, not discriminating between fighters and civilians. When the warriors try to break through the German lines they are mown down again and again by the powerful Maxim machine guns. Only one corner of the encirclement – in the south-east – appears to be weaker than the rest, and by late afternoon the Herero finally manage to breach the German lines here. And by nightfall tens of thousands of Herero have escaped through this narrow gap.

However, what appeared to be salvation is in reality a fatal chimera. The Herero have fallen straight into von Trotha's trap – because this gap leads only to the Omaheke desert, which in the middle of summer will kill far more effectively than any number of Maxim guns or artillery. He had left the south-eastern force, under Major von der Heyde, deliberately smaller and less well armed than the other five battalions, in the hope that the Herero would break through at this point and then have only the desert in front of them. In the next days and weeks von Trotha sends units after the retreating Herero, into the furnace of the Omaheke, but when Herero are found, no prisoners are to be taken. As an officer recorded in his diary: 'We had been explicitly told . . . that what we were dealing with was the extermination of the whole tribe, nothing living was to be spared.' And so, in the next period, whenever the units come across Herero survivors, the vast majority are systematically executed – men, women and children alike.

But von Trotha knows that some Herero may try to return towards the Waterberg over the next weeks, and so on 16 and 26 August he issues orders to cut off access to any waterholes near the edge of the desert, and then deploys many troops all along the 250-kilometre western perimeter of the Omaheke in a chain, to ensure that no Herero can return and access the food and water of the Waterberg. The Herero's fate is now effectively sealed – they cannot go back, so they can only continue across hundreds of miles of desert, with summer temperatures touching well above forty degrees centigrade, in the hope of reaching the British colony of Bechuanaland (Botswana today). Of course, only a tiny minority of the people have the strength to reach this border.* The German units sent into the desert in pursuit of the Herero witness apocalyptic scenes, one soldier reporting that 'whoever took part in the chase through the sandveld lost his belief in righteousness on earth', another, 'cattle and men [lay] dead and dying and staring blankly . . . a number of babies lay helplessly languishing by mothers whose breasts hung down long and flabby. Others were lying alone, still living, with eyes and nose full of flies . . . at noon we halted by the waterholes which were filled to the brim with corpses.'

Over the next weeks, the combination of the furnace heat and the virtually waterless Omaheke claims thousands more Herero lives. The few who've managed to bring cattle with them into the desert

---

* It is estimated that out of the 50,000 Herero who were gathered at Waterberg in July 1904, fewer than 1,000 Herero (including Samuel Maharero) managed to reach Bechuanaland.

survive by drinking their cows' blood, but the vast majority die, most of them after having used their last energies digging into the desert with their hands, in despairing attempts to find water. As Cocker relates:

> The Herero . . . imprisoned in the Omaheke, dug desperately in its lifeless sands for water. In some places the Germans found a hundred separate holes, each two to three metres deep. In their craving for moisture some had drunk at the women's breasts, or slit the throats of their cattle and drunk the blood . . . but most simply succumbed to their exhaustion and lay down to die.

In the rare cases when they did find a trace of water – maybe twenty-five to thirty feet below the desert – chaos usually ensued, with thirst-crazed people crushing each other to reach the water, often being buried alive in the process as these improvised wells collapsed. The German Official History of the Battle of Waterberg ends with the chilling statement I first came across in the late 1990s: 'The month-long sealing of desert areas, carried out with iron severity, completed the work of annihilation. The death rattles of the dying and their insane screams of fury . . . resounded in the sublime silence of infinity.'

But von Trotha has not finished yet. He remains utterly unmoved by all reports of such suffering. In fact, he wants the extermination to be even more thorough. On one occasion, when he accompanies one of the pursuit patrols, they find two elderly Herero women, exhausted by an old waterhole – von Trotha promptly orders both to be shot. On another occasion he questions a young woman survivor and then orders her to be killed. There are other eyewitness accounts of German soldiers tossing a baby Herero boy on the bayonets of their rifles, of women and children packed into a thorn enclosure, doused with lamp oil and then burnt alive.

Seven weeks after the Battle of Waterberg, von Trotha is still urging the German 1st Field Regiment through the Omaheke in pursuit of the last remnants of the fleeing Herero. Almost one hundred miles south-east of the Waterberg, he and his soldiers pause at the last known waterhole, deep inside the desert, at a clearing called Osombo zo Windimbe. Just after dawn on 3 October 1904, von Trotha reads out a proclamation to all his troops, including Franz von Epp. It remains one of the most disturbing statements in the entire history of genocide. The proclamation was written down and subsequently translated into Otjiherero and distributed widely. A single copy of the original proclamation has survived, and is held today in the Botswana National Archives in Gaberone. It is titled *Vernichtungsbefehl* ('Extermination Order'):

I the great general of the German troops, send this letter to the Herero people. Hereros are no longer German subjects. They have murdered, stolen, they have cut off the noses, ears and other bodily parts of wounded soldiers and now, because of cowardice, they will fight no more. I say to the people: anyone who delivers one of the Herero captains to my station as a prisoner will receive 1,000 marks. He who brings Samuel Maharero will receive 5,000 marks. All the Hereros must leave their land. If the people do not do this I will force them to do it with the great guns. Any Herero found within the German borders with or without a gun, with or without cattle, will be shot. I shall no longer receive any women or children; I will drive them back . . . or I will shoot them, this is my decision for the Herero people.

The Great General of the Mighty Kaiser

As von Trotha finishes reading this proclamation, two captured Herero men are dragged towards an improvised gallows and hanged. The women and children captured with them are then driven back into the desert, with volleys of gunfire over their heads; around their necks each of them carries a 'necklace' containing a piece of paper – von Trotha's Extermination Order. The next day von Trotha writes to his superiors in Berlin, justifying this order, saying it is 'abundantly clear to me that the Negroes will yield only to brute force' and that he sees this revolt in a wider context: 'This uprising is and remains the beginning of a racial struggle.'

*

Everyone who has written about Germany in South-West Africa sees the central importance of von Trotha's Extermination Order. Lindqvist, Cocker, Olusoga and Erichsen all write eloquently of the importance of what is represented by these words – the idea that the Herero 'must vanish from the face of the earth' is understandably terrifying, not just in its own terms, but also in the light of what we know followed forty years later. Some also write about the effect the eventual publication of this order had on European public opinion – the German chancellor was horrified, not so much by the destruction of the Herero but by the potential of the written extermination order 'to demolish Germany's reputation among civilised nations'. Indeed, on 8 December von Trotha was finally forced to withdraw the order, specifically relating to Herero who voluntarily surrendered – not that this affected the ongoing killing operations on the ground to any great degree.

The chancellor was right to be worried – though the full impact on Germany's reputation wasn't felt until the publication of the 'Blue Book' by South Africa at the end of 1918. This was a remarkably detailed account of German atrocities against the Herero and

Nama, including photographs and many eyewitness statements, which had a dramatic impact on European opinion at the end of the First World War, especially in the period before the Versailles Conference, and which contributed significantly (together with accounts of German atrocities in Belgium) to the harshness of the Versailles peace terms. Even *The Times*, rarely known as a beacon of anti-colonialism, thundered in an editorial in September 1918: 'It had been widely supposed that in the oppression of Belgium the German capacity for wickedness had reached its limit. That was a foolish delusion. The inhuman outrages committed in Europe are insignificant compared to the savage abominations which were the foundation of German rule in Africa'.

But in all that has been written about the aftermath of the Herero and Nama genocide, the Extermination Order and its impact on European opinion, nobody, to my knowledge, has ever investigated the direct effect it must have had on Hitler's organisation of the Jewish Holocaust. An entire book by the eminent historian Peter Longerich investigates the precise nature of Hitler's relationship to the giving of orders for this genocide – his central thesis being that 'Hitler treated the murder of the Jews as a matter of extreme secrecy and was careful not to leave behind any written orders about the extermination. And in the cases where his instructions on this matter were recorded, he always used codified language.' Longerich's book is called *The Unwritten Order*, yet nowhere here does he consider whether Hitler may have been influenced by the furore over von Trotha's *Vernichtungsbefehl*, and the critically important fact that it had been written down – the intent for extermination made explicit. Not a mistake the government of the Third Reich was likely to repeat.

*

August 2018, Pen Llŷn

After this hottest summer for forty years, the weather has broken today. Rain is sweeping in from the sea, falling in Welsh diagonals outside my window. I'm waiting for the phone to ring. I've been expecting a call this afternoon – from a woman I've never spoken to before. We've been put in touch by a mutual friend.

As I wait I look online for any information about this woman. She's a barrister, well known for her work on prominent human rights cases. I'm interested to see if anything comes up if I search her name together with 'Namibia' 'Herero'. No, nothing seems to be in the public domain yet. Eventually the phone trills, I leave it for a couple of rings, then answer. She's apologetic that she's been so elusive – a big trial, more indiscriminate street violence in a summer of madness, has overrun, so much so that she's had to put the family holiday on hold. But that's just the life of litigation lawyers, she says. Soon we're talking about the case she's helping with – 114 years after von Trotha's Extermination Order was given, she's working with a team to explore bringing an action against the German government for the genocide of the Herero and Nama in South-West Africa.

There are so many questions that I want to ask, but at the outset of our conversation she warns me that – because of lawyer/client confidentiality – there may be subjects which she cannot speak about. Yes, I understand. We start by discussing the legal cases which have been brought against Germany so far over the last year or so. These have all been filed in New York and Washington under what is known as the ATS (Alien Tort Statute) – a part of civil law in America which allows foreign citizens to seek redress in US courts for human rights violations committed outside the United States. But all of these have failed. She isn't surprised; the US action was flawed, bound to founder and fail as it has. But along with a team of British lawyers, she is thinking of legal mechanisms to find a way forward. I hope she's right, as I've been tracking these other cases as well, and have been disappointed at their failures so far. Printouts of various articles are spread across my desk – 'Herero and Nama groups sue Germany over Namibian genocide' (BBC website, 6 January 2017), 'Descendents of Namibia genocide victims seek reparations in New York' (Guardian, 16 March 2017), 'Why the Herero of Namibia are suing Germany for reparations'

(NPR website, 6 May 2018). But none of these have gained any traction in the American legal system – as she predicted.

We talk about the reasons why these genocide cases haven't been successful so far. Has Germany recognised that what happened in Namibia between 1904 and 1906 was 'genocide'? She explains the overall position of the German government – yes, they agree that what happened to the Herero and Nama would be described as 'genocide' in today's language, but there is a paramount legal issue here. The term 'genocide' has only existed since 1948, so it has only had legal force from this date, when the UN General Assembly adopted the Convention on the Prevention and Punishment of the Crime of Genocide. So Germany is arguing that it cannot be held legally accountable for a crime which did not exist in international law when it was committed. Although in one way this seems a very cynical position, we agree that it does raise complex legal questions.

We move on to discussing some of the wider issues surrounding the Namibian genocide. Are there any examples of countries being pursued in law successfully for human rights violations or genocide? Yes, there are precedents, she says, particularly cases brought to the Inter-American Court of Human Rights. There have also been successful prosecutions for human rights violations against Guatemala and Paraguay, in which those countries had to pay reparations to victims' families; they also had to change their laws so that any repetition of these human rights abuses would be recognised as crimes. She starts to talk about the work of the International Criminal Court in The Hague, and tells me that one of the ICC's real limitations is that it is only able to prosecute individuals, and not national governments or corporations.

At the end of our conversation we move on to the way that the political and legal debate about reparations has developed over the last thirty years or so. We remember the Labour MP Bernie Grant, who spoke out in favour of reparations for slavery in the 1980s, and was attacked and ridiculed by many at the time. Well, as Gandhi said, 'first they ignore you, then they laugh at you, then they fight you, then you win'.

There are two purposes to the case the barrister is exploring. The first is to find a way to obtain significant legal and financial redress for the descendants of those murdered. But this is about more than money. The second purpose is to achieve a number of broader goals: the recognition of what happened, the assumption of responsibility, the apology. Particularly since part of the whole problem has been that for so long the reigning paradigm of international law – 'legal positivism' – the creation and construction of the West, failed to recognise indigenous peoples as possessing equal rights and legal status. There are new historical narratives to create – to achieve meaningful change in cultural and educational terms. And, of these two objectives, she says, perhaps the second is even more important than the first.

I wish her luck in the fight to come. Many people around the world will be watching.

*

Although the majority of the Herero were dead by October 1904, this did not stop von Trotha's obsessive quest to continue the extermination. Some Herero had not gathered with Samuel Maharero at Waterberg, perhaps as many as 20,000–25,000 lived in isolated settlements in the north and west of Hereroland, and hadn't taken part in the uprising at all. Throughout the autumn of 1904 and the whole of 1905, von Trotha ordered the German patrols to seek out all Herero, wherever they were, and shoot on sight. A soldier in one of these patrols stated that they were told to 'shoot, kill, hang. Whatever you liked. Old or young. Men, women, children.' The motto of these patrols was 'Clean out, hang up, shoot down, till they are all gone.' Eyewitnesses recall sick Herero women being burnt alive in their huts and mass shootings of villagers. At the end of October 1904, at Ombakaha nearly seventy Herero were massacred, after having been given assurances of safe surrender.

It is impossible to know exactly how many Herero were killed between 1904 and 1905, in the period of von Trotha's eighteen-month reign of terror in South-West Africa – Cocker estimates that between half and three-quarters of Herero died at this time: that is to say, between 40,000 and 60,000 men, women and children; Lindqvist suggests that almost all of the 80,000 Herero perished, but this seems to be an overestimate. But we do know that in autumn 1904 von Trotha wrote to Leutwein admitting that he hadn't succeeded in destroying the Herero completely. Leutwein, who had been strongly opposed to von Trotha's exterminist policy (not so much on grounds of humanitarianism but more, as he saw it, a waste of manpower and economic potential), was removed from his post as governor at the end of 1904, and left the colony after eleven years.

But a problem remained: what to do with any remaining Herero? By Christmas 1904, this issue was being discussed in Berlin by the Chancellor and the Kaiser, and senior officials in the Colonial Department. In January 1905 orders were sent to von Trotha to establish a number of *Konzentrationslager* (concentration camps) along the lines of those the British had established in the Boer War, just three years earlier. But in addition to these camps there should also be work camps, so that forced labour would benefit the colony. Von Trotha did not welcome this shift in policy, and for a period the German patrols continued their killing, but gradually he was forced to accept the surrender of the surviving Herero. By February and March 1905, hundreds and then thousands of Herero who had managed to survive began to give themselves up:

> They emerged like ghosts from the Omaheke and the distant corners of Hereroland. They dragged themselves into the German towns of Omaruru, Karibib, Windhoek and Okahandja. Most were women and children, and all were in an appalling state of advanced malnutrition . . . a missionary . . . described the Herero who arrived . . . as being 'mere skeletons covered by a thin film of skin'. Unsure how to deal with this influx, most settlers stood aside and watched as malnourished Herero died on their streets.

But, eventually, those who survived were transported to another fate. The first use of cattle trucks to take human beings to concentration camps occurred in South-West Africa in February 1905. Five such camps were established – sited at Windhoek, at Karibib, at Okahandja, and then two situated just outside the ports of Swakopmund and Luderitz. Surviving German records tell us that at their heights these camps held 14,769 people. Conditions were appalling. A missionary based at Swakopmund, Heinrich Vedder, reported on the camp and the condition of the prisoners: 'Their clothing had long since been torn to tatters. Men and women without went about in sacking, their only protection from the cold. Many got inflammation of the lungs and died. During the worst period an average of thirty died daily.'

Within the first four months, 40 per cent of the prisoners at Swakopmund died. On top of the non-existent clothing and totally insufficient rations, inmates were used on forced-labour projects like working on the harbour jetty and walls, laying railways, constructing buildings. Often the women were used, in teams of eight, instead of oxen or horses, to pull heavy loads on the railways. In another direct echo of what happened forty years later across the Reich, prisoners were also hired out, at daily rates of fifty pfennigs, to German companies such as the Woermann Shipping Line. All income generated went into the colonial government. To keep track of all the prisoners, they were issued with metal identification tags; von Trotha thought this system inefficient, and suggested marking the inmates permanently with their numbers, whether by branding or tattooing he never made clear. This idea was not used, but it had been conceived; it took another thirty-seven years for tattoos to be used on human beings in the Third Reich.

*

Throughout the Herero uprising, and their subsequent extermination from August 1904 onwards, the position the Nama took was extremely problematic. In line with Leutwein's 'divide and rule', strategy, Hendrik Witbooi had signed a treaty with the Germans, which meant that not only would the Nama stay neutral in the event of a German conflict with the Herero, they were actually supposed to provide armed support for the colonists. Samuel Maharero knew this, and in January 1904, at the beginning of the Herero uprising, he had written a powerful plea to Hendrik Witbooi to disregard this treaty and join their struggle:

> I appeal to you my brother, do not shy away from this upris- ing, but make your voice heard so that all Africa may take up arms against the Germans. Let us die fighting rather than die of maltreatment, imprisonment or some other tragedy. Tell the *kapteins* down there to rise up and do battle.

Tragically, this letter was intercepted, and so the possibility of a great anti-colonial alliance between the Herero and the Witbooi never got off the ground. And so, in line with their treaty agree- ment, a contingent of one hundred Witbooi men were sent to fight alongside the Germans at Waterberg in August 1904. Six weeks later nineteen survivors reached the village of Rietmont, where Hendrik Witbooi and his key leaders were staying. They heard the news of the Witbooi survivors – about the massacres of the Herero after Waterberg – with heavy hearts. They also realised that the often-spoken rumour that 'once the Government has finished with the Herero, they will come down to the people of Namaland' was now turning into a distinct possibility.

So it wasn't until early October 1904 that Hendrik Witbooi belat- edly began the Nama uprising against the Germans. It is impossible to know what might have happened had Witbooi and Maharero been able to co-ordinate their attacks against the colonists, but as it was, the Nama only started their war at the moment that the vast majority of the Herero had already been destroyed following Waterberg. In the first wave of attacks on colonial settlements and farms, forty German soldiers and settlers were killed, all men. Just like Maharero, Witbooi insisted that women and children were not to be harmed. The Nama were determined not to make the same mistakes that the Herero had made – open battles could only benefit the Germans with their vastly superior machine guns and artillery, so this war was to be a guerrilla campaign, fought in the desert, mountains and gorges – a landscape that the Nama knew intimately, including the locations of all the hidden waterholes. This knowledge, and strategy, was to give them a decisive advantage over the colonists. The first exchange of the war occurred at Auob in December 1904, and saw the Germans heavily defeated, with the loss of fifty-nine soldiers. Von Trotha took over command of the war in April 1905, warning the Nama, in another proclamation, that they would 'suffer the same fate as the Herero', but his tactics proved totally ineffective in the south, where the Nama insurgency went from strength to strength.

The Germans tried to negotiate a peace settlement in July 1905, but Hendrik Witbooi refused, writing back that 'peace will spell death for me and my nation'. He launched another series of attacks on German convoys in autumn 1905, but at Fahlgras on 29 October, Witbooi was badly wounded, and he died three days later. With his death, and the loss of their inspirational leader, the alliance of Nama tribes began to disintegrate. Witbooi's son, Isaak, and many of the younger Nama decided to continue fighting, while other elders began peace negotiations with the Germans. But all of this came too late for von Trotha, who had asked to be relieved of his duties, and departed from Luderitz on 2 November 1905. As he arrived in the port he received a telegram stating that Hendrik Witbooi was dead. Back in Germany, he was awarded the highest honours for his devoted service to the Reich, and told that he 'deserves the warmest gratitude of the fatherland'.

6. Governor Friedrich von Lindequist: from 'Extermination Through Work' to the 'Settler Paradise' (1905–14)

At the end of November 1905 South-West Africa's new governor arrives – Friedrich von Lindequist, who had been deputy governor under Leutwein from 1894 to 1898. His first priority is to deal with the ongoing war against those Nama clans who have not yet surrendered, but he does this by diplomacy rather than fighting, promising generous terms of surrender. One by one, fatally, the clans accept von Lindequist's promises, and by March 1906, the last of the Nama groupings has laid down its weapons. The Nama, 2,000 of them, are then transported to Windhoek, to the concentration camp just outside the town, already housing 4,000 Herero in terrible conditions. They realise too late that they have been tricked, and a few days after their arrival the new governor addresses them, saying that they are collectively guilty of murder, and that they 'all deserve to be executed'. They will atone for their crimes by being put to work.

And so begins the next phase of German colonisation of South-West Africa, which can, without hyperbole, be called 'extermination through work' – a continuation of the genocide of the Herero and Nama, but through forced labour rather than guns. Two railway projects (in the north, connecting Swakopmund and the mines of Otavi, and in the south, connecting Luderitz and Aus) take the majority of the slave labourers. Already almost 7,000 Herero prisoners are deployed on this work throughout the country – 'public-private partnerships' involving the colony and two German private corporations – Arthur Koppel AG* on the northern line, and Firma Lenz on the southern one. Arthur Koppel takes three years to complete the line from Swakopmund to the Tsumeb mine near Otavi – 352 miles, making it the longest narrow-gauge railway in the world. We do not have records of the profits this made for this company, nor the cost in numbers of Herero lives. But Firma Lenz, of Hamburg, did keep detailed records of its Herero slave labourers, noting carefully that 1,359 out of 2,014 prisoners had died creating the Luderitz to Aus railway between 1906 and 1907. A clerk employed back in the Hamburg head office even calculated, with bureaucratic precision, that this represented a casualty rate of 67.48 per cent.

This inhumanity, though, however appalling, cannot be compared to what happens on Shark Island, less than half a mile west of the port of Luderitz. Originally this 'island' – actually not an island,

---

* Arthur Koppel was a Berlin-based train and engineering company, originally part of Orenstein & Koppel, founded in 1876. In 1885 the company splits, with Orenstein & Koppel focussing on the German market and Arthur Koppel AG taking the overseas market.

but a narrow peninsula – has been used as a quarantine station for arriving German troops, but in early 1905 it becomes a concentration camp for Herero prisoners. From the beginning it has a dreadful reputation, with some Herero preferring to commit suicide rather than be sent there. It has an extremely harsh climate, with south Atlantic winds pummelling the island, often bringing air from the Antarctic and sub-zero temperatures; and sea fogs would add damp to the bitter cold.

On 9 September 1906, almost 2,000 Nama prisoners are marched from the town of Luderitz to the narrow causeway connecting the mainland to Shark Island. As they walk towards the camp, on the northern tip of the island, they can see 1,000 Herero prisoners behind the walls of barbed wire – they are starving, emaciated and traumatised. Within weeks, the Nama would be in a similar condition. In October a missionary records that every week 50 Herero and 15–20 Nama are dying there. By Christmas, this has risen to more than 120 deaths per week. Food provision is almost non-existent, mainly uncooked rice and flour; prisoners scavenge for anything edible on or around the island, but soon even the seaweed and limpets have been eaten. The makeshift huts and sacking for clothes can't possibly keep out the cold. All these conditions mean starvation, illness and death is virtually inevitable.

The small minority of prisoners who are selected as fit for work (the German term used was *Arbeitsfahige*) are soon worked to death. By October 1906, 300 slave labourers are charged with constructing a new quay in Luderitz harbour. These men and women are forced to haul large boulders across the island by hand, and then pull them into the freezing waters of the bay. By Christmas 1906, Richard Müller, the engineer supervising the harbour project, complains in a report to his superiors that instead of the 1,600 Nama prisoners he'd been promised for his labour force, he now has only 30–40, and that 17 prisoners have died in a single night. He has no concern for their survival, or lack of it, he simply wants to communicate that 'if measures are not actively taken to acquire (new) labourers, I fear the work will not be completed'. By February 1907 the harbour project is abandoned because 70 per cent of the Nama on Shark Island are now dead.

When I first learned about the Jewish Holocaust as a teenager I remember the shock of total disbelief that came with the knowledge that the Nazis established 'extermination camps' (*Vernichtungslager*) – four of them constructed between 1941 and 1942 – at Chelmno, Treblinka, Belzec and Sobibor.* I've grown to feel that the word 'camp' is inaccurate with regard to these four sites, as it implies some kind of temporary habitation, as in 'concentration camp', 'labour camp', 'work camp' – but, of course, almost nobody survived at these places, apart from the SS officers, guards and those working in the *Sonderkommando*. Auschwitz, Buchenwald, Majdanek, Dachau, Belsen – all of these were sites of mass murder on an unimaginable scale, but there were survivors who could be numbered in their hundreds, even thousands in the case of Auschwitz. At the extermination camps almost nobody survived. They existed only for the killing of those who arrived there.

And now I think of those 2,000 Nama men, women and children arriving at Shark Island on 9 September 1906, and the 1,000 Herero prisoners already there. I think about that autumn and winter, and the non-existent shelter and the almost total lack of food and the slave labour in the harbour, and the inevitable daily deaths, hundreds each month. And I think about the fact that the German authorities were completely aware of what they were doing, and intentionally allowed it to continue – indeed, the German garrison in Luderitz didn't call it Shark Island but 'Death Island', because death was the only function of the place. And I wonder, yet again, about the history that all of us have been taught. The way that some genocides are visible to us, and others are not. I wonder what percentage of people in our societies knows the name 'Auschwitz'. I would guess a large majority. I wonder how many people have ever

---

* Auschwitz-Birkenau and Majdanek were partly extermination camps, but they were also work camps. Not everyone who was sent there was killed immediately, and there were complexes of huts where the prisoners were housed.

heard the name 'Shark Island'. I would guess less than 0.1 per cent – no, not even that, perhaps only a few people in every million. Yet Olusoga and Erichsen, rightly, stress the historical significance of this place:

> The camp's main focus from September 1906 onwards was the extermination of Nama prisoners. Nama deaths were the 'product' of the Shark Island camp; forced labour was merely one of the means by which those deaths were brought about. Shark Island was a death camp, perhaps the world's first.

Another remarkable link between German colonialism in South-West Africa and Nazism in occupied Europe concerns the way that concentration-camp prisoners were experimented upon, their bodies used, alive and dead, as a means of furthering medical science. Dr Bofinger, the camp doctor at Shark Island and Luderitz concentration camp, conducted medical trials on prisoners, injecting them with arsenic and opium, among other substances, to see the effects of these substances on their bodies after death. Unsurprisingly, Bofinger's 'hospital' on Shark Island was feared, a missionary noting that '[not] even a single person recovered in the *Lazarett* [field hospital]'.

There was also a thriving trade in body parts of dead prisoners, which were shipped back to universities and museums in Germany. In the Swakopmund concentration camp, in 1905, women prisoners were forced to boil the severed heads of their dead relatives and friends, and then scrape the remaining flesh and sinews off the skulls, which were then packed into crates by German soldiers and despatched to Germany. There were even photographs of this, made into postcards by the Germans, to be sent home; they were proud of what they were doing. By 1906, the process had become more clinical, with the bodies of seventeen recently dead Nama prisoners at Shark Island first being decapitated by Dr Bofinger, who then removed and weighed each of the brains. The heads were placed in alcohol for preservation, then sealed in tins and finally sent to the Institute of Pathology at Berlin University. Here they were used by

583

'race scientists' to show supposed similarities between the Nama and the ape – just as, forty years later, Dr Mengele would send back body parts, including heads and eyes, from victims of his supposed 'medical' experiments at Auschwitz to the Kaiser Wilhelm Institute in Berlin to further the insane cause of racial science.

By the time Shark Island was finally closed in April 1907, a German military officer estimated that 1,900 Nama had died on the island. It is thought a similar number of Herero died there as well, before the Germans began to document their atrocities. And we know that 1,359 more died at the Luderitz concentration camp run by Firma Lenz, the base for that company's building of the Luderitz–Aus railway with slave labour. Well over 4,000 dead Nama and Herero between 1906 and 1907 at Shark Island and the concentration camps nearby, only a stone's throw from the town of Luderitz, population 1,000, where the settlers and traders went about their business seemingly quite unaffected by the barbaric happenings just beyond their settlement's walls.

In the German colonial census of 1908, it was recorded that 16,363 Herero remained in South-West Africa, out of a pre-war population of around 80,000. Almost 80 per cent of the Herero people had 'disappeared' – the vast majority killed by German guns, starvation in the desert and slave labour in the concentration camps. Only a fraction of the Herero had survived by escaping from the colony. A similar census, from 1911, found that 9,781 Nama were still living in South-West Africa – this from a pre-war figure of 20,000, meaning that just over half of the Nama had been killed in similar circumstances. Some Nama communities, however, had been virtually eliminated from the Witbooi clan almost nobody was still living, and less than a hundred of the Bethanie Nama survived.

This genocide ushered in what became known in Germany as the era of 'settler paradise' – 'our new Germany on African soil', as one settler breathlessly described it. And if any Herero or Nama survivors had thoughts about attempting to hold on to their own soil, Kaiser Wilhelm formally expropriated all Herero land in December 1905, and virtually all Nama land in May 1907. The following year saw another promising development for the colonists: in 1908 huge deposits of diamonds were found close to the surface near Luderitz, triggering an extraordinary 'diamond rush' in 1908 and 1909. Diamond companies used more slave labour to prospect for the diamonds, this time using workers of the Owambo people from the north of the colony. Again, the conditions were appalling; again, many slave labourers died. They would be chained together, and made to crawl across the desert on all fours, hands reaching in the burning sand for the elusive crystals. Outside Luderitz, where the Germans had created mass shallow graves for the dead of Shark Island and the other concentration camps, these Owambo workers must often have found skulls and bones, and other traces of the dead in the desert as they worked.

The number of German settlers and farmers trebled to a peak population of 15,000 in 1913. Windhoek was now a bustling new town boasting eight hotels and numerous bars and *Bierkellers*. It also had a grand new bronze statue, *The Rider*, built under the walls of the fortress, on the site of the concentration camp where only a few years earlier 4,000 Herero had been starved and worked to death. A perfect metaphor for the campaign of 'organised forgetting' that the German colony now embarked upon.

Postscript

The Desk Killers of Windhoek:
Dr Dove, Dr Rohrbach and Dr Fischer

Although guns and concentration camps and forced labour, and
military commanders like General von Trotha, were all critical factors in the genocide that took place in South-West Africa in the
1890s and 1900s, it is also important to recognise the role played
by a small but lethal army of academics and colonial officials and
intellectuals, most of who have now faded out of our historical
vision – men whose hands would never operate a Maxim gun, yet
they wrote the words, and compiled the reports, which enabled an
extraordinary level of violence to be unleashed. Three 'desk men'
in particular played key roles in creating the climate for genocide in
South-West Africa – Dr Karl Dove, a geographer and climatologist,
Dr Paul Rohrbach, a colonial advisor on economic development,
and Dr Eugen Fischer, an anthropologist.

Dove gained his doctorate in 1888 with a thesis titled 'The Climate
of Extratropical South Africa', later published as a book that became
the standard text on the climate and the agricultural potential of
southern Africa, a bible for future farmers and settlers. He was also
a board member of the German Colonial Society, which funded
the eighteen months he spent in South-West Africa in 1892–3, as

'Director of Land Settlement', coinciding exactly with François' establishment of Windhoek as the fortress-capital of the colony and the first wave of settlers moving from Germany to South-West Africa to farm and trade. Dove published four papers subsequently detailing which parts of the colony would be most suitable for crop cultivation, and also mineral analysis of different areas, showing the mining potential of the new colony.

Back in Germany, he berated Leutwein for his 'lenient' treatment of the Nama, writing to a German newspaper that he hoped 'that the Imperial Governor will not be prevented by the sentimental humanitarianism of certain quarters from sending all the [Nama] falling into his hands to the gallows . . . There is no place for sickly sentimentalism!' He later became professor of geography at the University of Jena, and then at Freiburg; he continued to publish many books on the economic geography of the German colonies (1902), German South-West Africa (1903), and a four-volume work on German Colonies (1909–13). But he is probably best known not for any of these academic writings but his views that violence towards native Africans was almost a moral duty – they could not be compared to Europeans in any way: 'As to the ideas of their sense of justice, these are based on false premises. It is incorrect to view justice, in regard to the natives, as if they were of the same kultur-position as ourselves.' He summed up his philosophy of supremacism like this: 'Leniency towards the natives is cruelty to the whites' – a sentiment which prefigured Hitler's chilling remark to his generals on 26 May 1944, justifying his *Ausrottung* – the rooting out, the extermination, of the Jews in Hungary: 'Kindness here, as indeed anywhere else, would be just about the greatest cruelty to our own people.'*

*

Former missionary Dr Paul Rohrbach was appointed as settlement commissioner to South-West Africa (the role Karl

---

* From *Stalin's War: Hitler and Stalin: Parallel Lives* by Alan Bullock, chapter 17.

Dove had played a decade earlier) in 1903. He was specifically tasked to analyse the potential of the colony for large-scale
settlement and farming, and to see what lessons could be learnt from
the British colonisation of South Africa, particularly the methods by
which they took over land from the indigenous peoples. Rohrbach
was given a significant budget by the Colonial Office in Berlin
(300,000 marks per year), and was effectively the second-most
powerful official in the colony after Governor Leutwein. He had
been selected because of his wide experience of colonial outposts,
but also because of his ultra-nationalist views – he was a fanatical
believer in Social Darwinism and the recently published work of
Ratzel on the need for Germany to expand its *Lebensraum*.

When he took up his posting he believed that the native population
of South-West Africa could be exploited by being used as an economic resource, but very quickly his views evolved in a far more
radical direction. Any missionary zeal he may have taken from his
experience in China and Asia, about paternalistically improving
the lives of the natives and spreading the Gospel, was soon replaced
by an obsessive focus on the supremacy of the white race – again
prefiguring, strikingly so, the language which Hitler and Himmler
were to use forty years later:

No false philanthropy or racial theory can prove to reasonable
people that the preservation of any tribe of nomadic South

African Kaffirs . . . is more important for the future of mankind than the expansion of the great European nations, or the
white race as a whole. Not until the native learns to produce
anything of value in the service of the higher race, i.e. in the
service of its and his own progress, does he gain any moral
right to exist.

Such logic made the displacement of the indigenous people inevitable. He wrote later that 'The decision to colonise in South-West
Africa could mean nothing else but this, namely that the native tribes
would have to give up their lands on which they have previously
grazed their stock in order that the white man might have the land
for the grazing of his stock.' And the only role left to the indigenous
Africans would be to facilitate this transition, and behave with 'the
greatest possible working efficency' as slaves to the colonists.

Rohrbach was working in Windhoek throughout 1904–5, during
von Trotha's genocidal reign, providing a continuous background
justification for the slaughter that was going on at the time –
historians have understandably focussed most of their attention on
what von Trotha did in the Omaheke, but I wonder if Rohrbach's
role, essentially providing the moral support for these actions
among the settlers and colonists, has ever been fully recognised.
In 1907, a year after he left his position in Windhoek and returned
to Germany, he published *Deutsche Kolonialwirtschaft* ('German
Colonial Economy'), which can be seen as a response to the growing controversy in Germany regarding reports from South-West
Africa at this time. Just before Christmas 1906, rumours of the conditions at Shark Island, based on missionary reports, began to reach
Berlin. A Reichstag social democrat deputy raised the issue formally
in December, and the subsequent controversy led to the colonial
budget being voted down, and the German government having to
face re-election in 1907 – what became known as 'the Hottentot
Election'. Rohrbach's contribution to the bitter debate that was going
on in Germany was to publish his book, which included this explicit
justification for what von Trotha had just done in South-West

Africa: 'In order to secure the peaceful White settlement against the bad, culturally inept and predatory native tribe, it is possible that actual eradication may become necessary under certain conditions.'

Rohrbach later took up a senior position at the Berlin School of Commerce, and published two even more influential books – *Der deutsche Gedanke in die Welt* ('German World Policies') in 1912, and *Der Kreig und die deutsche Politik* ('The War and German Politics') in 1914. These works built on his earlier themes – the need for wholesale displacement, and even extermination of native peoples, which he'd originally advocated in an African context, but now he began to see a greater scope and audience for his extreme nationalism.

Rohrbach's books were just one part of an entire movement in Germany happening in the first fifteen years of the century, together with the creation of the German Colonial School and the Colonial Institute in Hamburg. German corporations were at the forefront of this movement, not just the rail companies we've already seen profiting from slave labour, but Deutsche Bank and Krupp Steel started to offer scholarship programmes to students seeking careers in the new colonies. The impact that this cultural zeitgeist had on the formation of Nazi ideology in the early 1920s is incalculable. And though Hitler never saw African colonialism as central to his aims, he certainly wanted to use the lessons learned in Africa, Asia and America from colonial settlement, to create a vast new *Lebensraum* for German settlers in eastern Europe, involving the enslavement of the native populations. The British Empire was a continual inspiration for Hitler in this regard. As he put it:

> It should be possible for us to control this region to the East with two hundred and fifty thousand men plus a cadre of good administrators. Let's learn from the English, who, with two hundred and fifty thousand men in all, including fifty thousand soldiers, govern four hundred million Indians. This space in Russia must always be dominated by Germans.*

---

* Both quotations from *Hitler's Table Talk, 1941–1944*, introduced by Hugh Trevor-Roper (the first from 27 July 1941; the second from 9–11 August 1941).

What India was for England, the territories of Russia will be for us. If only I could make the German people understand what this space means for our future!

And, exactly as Rohrbach had argued, Hitler stated in 1942 that the Russians 'have but one justification for existence – to be used by us economically'. Hermann Goering, the son of the first governor of South-West Africa (then in charge of the megalomaniacal 'Resettlement Plan' involving the displacement of millions of people, and their replacement by millions more German settlers), enthusiastically predicted famine for millions of Soviet inhabitants in the same year, saying that 'it is as well that it should be so for certain nations must be decimated'. And, after all, who remembered the Herero or the Nama now? Who remembered the original indigenous populations? As Hitler had said: 'I don't see why a German who eats a piece of bread should torment himself with the idea that the soil that produces this bread has been won by the sword. When we eat wheat from Canada, we don't think about the despoiled Indians.'

*

Eugen Fischer studied medicine, gaining his first degree in 1898, and then a further degree, in anatomy and anthropology, two years

591

later at the University of Freiburg. Like many young medics at that time Fischer became mesmerised by the growing pseudo-science of eugenics, and specifically the theories of 'racial degeneration' propounded by influential figures such as Felix von Luschan, then director of the Berlin Museum of Ethnology. Fischer first became known for publishing a study on the skull width of Papuans in 1906, which won an international award. Next he wanted to find a mixed-race community somewhere in the world where he could pursue research into 'the bastardisation of the races'. In 1907 he came across a booklet written by a German officer who'd served under von Trotha in South-West Africa, called *The Nation of the Bastards* – about one of the twelve Nama tribes, the Basters, a mixed-race community of 2,000 people gathered around the town of Rehoboth, just south of Windhoek. They had lived there for over fifty years, and had a reputation for being close-knit, but if the women did marry outside their own community, it was usually to white men. Unlike the majority of the Nama tribes, the Basters spoke only Afrikaans, and had adopted many of the cultural traits of the Boers in South Africa; they were also known for their strong Christianity and for their conservative values.

Fischer travelled to Rehoboth in 1908 and spent two months conducting 'field research' – primarily carrying out anatomical measurements. The Basters were not impressed by his approach, an elder apparently telling him that they were 'not savages' and asking him why he didn't carry out similar examinations on the white residents of the town. Nevertheless, he took hundreds of photographs, recorded all the 'data' he'd gathered, and returned to Germany, where in 1913 he published his book, *Die Rehobother Bastards und das Bastardierungsproblem beim Menschen* ('The Rehoboth Bastards and the Bastardisation Problem in Man'), which claimed to show the process of 'racial degeneration' in successive generations of Basters – i.e. that racial features and characteristics of their Nama ancestors gradually became dominant over those features inherited from their white ancestry. Shockingly, not only was this work a huge success in 1913, but it continued to be in print until 1961.

Fischer's work contributed to the growing discussion in Germany before the First World War about *Rassenhygiene* (race hygiene) and the need to save 'our wonderful German nation', as Fischer put it, by preserving the Aryan heritage – ideas which were to become central to Nazism in the next generation. In 1921, Fischer, now director of the Anatomical Institute in Freiburg, published, together with Erwin Baur and Fritz Lens, *Human Heredity and Racial Hygiene*, which was not only very warmly received in Germany, but was soon translated into English too. This book argued that to stop the 'polluting' effect of racial degeneration a programme of selective breeding was needed to 'purify' the Aryan race. Just as Hitler digested Ratzel's theory of *Lebensraum* when imprisoned at Landsberg in 1924, we also know he was given a copy of *Human Heredity and Racial Hygiene* at this time, which impressed him greatly. Indeed, many of the ideas from this work were to reappear the following year, though in Hitler's words now, in *Mein Kampf*.

Throughout the 1920s, the supposed 'science' of eugenics became more and more influential, not just in Germany, but also throughout Europe and America; indeed, in some US states eugenics laws were actually passed, an advent welcomed by Hitler among others. In 1927 Fischer was promoted, together with Fritz Lens, to become a director of the Kaiser Wilhelm Institute of Anthropology, Human Genetics and Eugenics in Berlin, Germany's most important race-science institution.[*] When the Nazis took power in 1933, Fischer was given an additional position as rector of Berlin University, where he used his inaugural address to declare his support for Hitler. He also published a paper positing that racial mixing between Aryan Germans and Jews was damaging the German race, just as Nama blood had polluted the white ancestors of the Basters, and arguing that the time was now right for laws to be passed preventing such racial mixing.

---

[*] A third director was Otmar von Verschuer. One of von Verschuer's most promising students and protégés was later to establish an applied research institute of his own in 1943 at Auschwitz-Birkenau – Dr Josef Mengele. Indeed, the SS links with the Kaiser Wilhelm Institute were to become extremely significant over the next fifteen years, with many of the SS doctors attending courses there.

In 1935, Dr Wilhelm Stuckart[*] and legal colleagues, acting on Hitler's wishes and Fischer's suggestions, wrote the infamous Nuremberg Race Laws (consisting of the Reich Citizenship Law and the Law for the Protection of German Blood and German Honour). These laws forbade Jews, and all other non-Aryan racial groups such as 'Negroes' and Gypsies, from marrying or having sexual relationships with German citizens. Fischer's work on race science is specifically referred to in these laws, providing a spurious authority to pure racist ideology. The term *Mischlinge* (of mixed race) recurs throughout this legislation, and much of the Wannsee Conference was spent in discussion of exactly how the *Mischlinge* question – the mixed-race German Jews – should be resolved in the 'Final Solution'.

I had always assumed this term was a Nazi coinage, developed in the process of the Nuremberg Laws being drafted, but this is not the case – its origins go back much further, to 1906 in fact, to German South-West Africa. It was here that von Lindequist first passed laws banning intermarriage between German colonists and native peoples, it was here the term *Mischlinge* was used for the first time. This term and laws preventing mixed marriages were then adopted by other German colonies, in East Africa and German Togo in 1906 and 1908 respectively, making the subsequent work of the Nuremberg Laws much simpler for those drafting the legislation, as Olusoga and Erichsen note: 'The *Mischlinge* concept provided the lawyers and civil servants with both a conceptual framework and quasi-legal terminology, allowing them to formulate a system by which Germany's ancient Jewish community, with its deep and complex roots, could be classified, isolated and ultimately extracted.'

By the mid-1930s there was a veritable army of race scientists and eugenicists operating across the Reich – literally thousands of well-paid and well-funded doctors, lecturers, research supervisors and teachers, ultimately creating the intellectual and scientific authority for the measures Hitler and Himmler were now beginning to contemplate. But it is important to understand that this generation

---

[*] See Book One, Chapter Thirteen: 'The Doctors of Wannsee Meet in a Villa by the Lake'.

of doctors and scientists did not see their work as confined to the laboratory or the lecture theatre – they viewed themselves as idealistic pioneers, who were keen to go out into the world and apply the lessons they had learned, from their mentors such as Fischer and Verschuer, to real problems in the field.

An early example of one such 'problem' was the existence of 400 mixed-race children in the Rhineland – children who had been born between 1918 and 1921 during the French occupation of that territory, following the Versailles Treaty, the products of relationships between French soldiers (many from their African colonies) and local German women. One of Fischer's deputies at the Kaiser Wilhelm Institute, Dr Wolfgang Abel (who Fischer had got to know because of Abel's work examining the skeletons of Nama victims), had carried out a series of 'racial-biological' tests on a sample of these children and found them to be 'physically and mentally deformed'. Abel suggested that action was needed to prevent such people from reproducing in the future. In 1937 Fischer himself was consulted, and the Gestapo set up 'Special Commission No. 3', headed by Fischer and Abel. The commission's task? To identify and then sterlise the 400 Rhineland children, now all teenagers, but to do so in as secret a way as possible.

In the spring of 1937, these children were discreetly taken from their schools and homes to be given a 'medical examination'. After they had been confirmed as *Mischlinge*, all were taken to a local hospital where they were forcibly sterilised. With the vast amount of research now conducted on the Holocaust, I am surprised that this appalling episode is so little known. Many people learn about the T4 'euthanasia' programme which started in 1939, and killed more than 70,000 mentally and physically disabled patients, including many children – yet very few people seem to know that the enforced sterilisation of teenagers had begun two years earlier.

The continuities between the Herero and Nama genocides and the Holocaust forty years later are multiple and impossible to ignore. Few who have researched in these fields can fail to see the linkages between these exterminations and the 'habits of thought' (to go back to Sven Lindqvist's phrase) which enabled them to happen. With the understanding about these events now finally beginning to take root in our societies, it will soon not be possible to write or speak about the Holocaust without recognising the connection to the first German genocide in South-West Africa – the first German concentration camps, the first German death camp, the first German medical experiments on prisoners, the first German extermination order.

*

In the end what inhabits my mind is still the images of hands.

The hands of the women in Swakopmund concentration camp, scraping the flesh from the boiled skulls of their dead mothers and fathers and husbands and children, with shards of glass, so that these heads could then be sent to Germany for 'scientific research' – some of these skulls still there today, lying in the basements of museums and universities.

The hands of the Owambo workers, chained together, feeling in the hot sands of the desert outside Luderitz for diamonds, and finding shards of bones and skulls instead, the only remaining fragments of the Herero and Nama now almost completely exterminated from this land.

And the hands of the thousands of Herero children, women and men, digging frantically in the Omaheke desert, desperate for water, hands becoming blistered in the furnace heat, digging down deeper than their own bodies, hallucinating with thirst. Hundreds of these holes full of skeletons, left all over the Omaheke . . .

*

And the hands of men in rooms, men writing. The sound of pen on paper. All that is unleashed through words.

The hand of Heinrich Goering signing the first protection treaty at Okahandja – the ink on that piece of paper doing the work of guns and lead.

The hand of Gustav Frenssen writing about Peter Moor's adventures, sowing seeds of extermination in the minds of children.

The hand of Friedrich Ratzel as he combines the words '*lebens*' and '*raum*' to create a concept more lethal than any weapon.

The hand of General von Trotha in the desert clearing at Osombo zo Windimbe drafting his *Vernichtungsbefehl* – the first written extermination order in history.

The hands of Dove, Rohrbach and Fischer writing their academic papers and books, building their careers on a foundation of hatred for other races.

A Coda:
The Power of History and the Burning of Books

What had happened in South-West Africa between 1904 and 1908 only became widely known because of a curious combination of circumstances that occurred towards the end of the First World War. A joint British and South African force had landed in South-West Africa in September 1914, and by July 1915 the German governor surrendered. The colony subsequently became known as the British Protectorate of South-West Africa, but was, from that moment on, effectively governed by South Africa, from Pretoria. There was a great degree of continuity, however, with the majority of German institutions and businesses being allowed to stay on. Only the German military were interned as prisoners of war.

One of the first actions of General Botha, the South African military commander who had taken the German surrender, was to order the seizure and translation of all German documents. Significantly, and ominously for them as it turned out, the Germans had kept extremely detailed archives of their rule at the central colonial administration offices in Windhoek. And it was through the process of looking at this mountain of documents that more information about the Herero and Nama genocides began to emerge.

In 1917, with the prospect of victory over Germany in the war now looking more likely, the Allies started to discuss what might happen to the former German colonies. There was a strong belief, certainly among the South Africans and the British, that South-West Africa should never be returned to Germany. It was in this context that the South African government commissioned an official investigative report into the treatment of the Herero and Nama in South-West Africa in the early years of the twentieth century.

This could have made the *Report on the Natives of South-West Africa and their Treatment by Germany* a simple propaganda job, but it was actually strikingly factual and accurate, which gave it great power. The vast majority of the material used in the report came from Germany's own documents, and these were so shocking in themselves, there was no need for any exaggeration. The man chosen to co-ordinate the report was Major Thomas O'Reilly, a lawyer by background, who had been working as a magistrate in western Hereroland from 1916 onwards, where he had already come across extensive accounts of the Herero genocide. He spent three months working intensively on the draft report in the autumn and winter of 1917–18, going right back to the first dubious 'protection treaties' signed by Heinrich Goering, and up to the genocides and von Lindequist's governorship.

He also made extensive use of Settlement Commissioner Rohrbach's writings, as well as many photographs documenting the killings, concentration camps and punishments used by the colonists. But the most remarkable aspect of the report was the emphasis O'Reilly put on gathering legally sworn statements from as many survivors and eyewitnesses as he could find. It remains a document of exceptional importance and power for anyone who wants to know what the experience of genocide in a colonial context means – for the victims, the survivors and the perpetrators.[*]

---

[*] Accessible online at Florida University website: http://ufdc.ufl.edu/UF00072665/00001.

The publication in September 1918 of the 'Blue Book', as it became known – on account of the British Foreign Office's blue cover – caused a sensation around the world, and contributed strongly to the Allied decision to strip Germany of all its colonies, as well as the general toughness of the peace terms negotiated at Versailles. President Wilson of the US expressed the views of many, saying that one of the most distressing revelations about Germany's conduct was the 'intolerable burdens and injustices [put] upon the helpless people of some of the colonies' and that Germany's priorities had been 'their extermination rather than their development'. South-West Africa from 1919 onwards became a mandate under the control of the Union of South Africa (which proved to be another deeply unjust regime for the indigenous peoples). Namibia did not gain its independence until 1990 – the last country in Africa to become a sovereign state.

The fate of the 'Blue Book' in the twentieth century is a fascinating example of two phenomena. Firstly, the power of history to tell truths, and in the process, deeply disturb those who have committed crimes against humanity, or those who are the beneficiaries of such crimes. It also demonstrates the way that 'difficult histories' can be forgotten. And this is not only a passive process of memory fade (perhaps aided by subconscious desires to be free of disturbing knowledge) – amnesia can also be extremely organised, often by states or regimes who would prefer the past to be forgotten.

Any hopes the surviving Herero and Nama may have had that the new powers in South-West Africa might have been more sympathetic to them than their old masters were dashed in 1921, when all the land appropriated by the kaiser in 1905 and 1907 was redesignated 'Crown Lands of South-West Africa'. The policy of reservations for the natives was revived, and the Herero and Nama were given less than 2 per cent of the land. Not content with having 98 per cent of the territory, including all the best farmland, the white population of the country now demanded that its history also be 'cleaned up'. In July 1926, a German settler and diamond entrepreneur, August Stauch, proposed in the newly formed Legislative

Assembly that all copies of the 'Blue Book' should be destroyed. It had created 'stigma' for the German population, it was simply 'war propaganda'. The proposal was passed, and in 1927 all copies of the 'Blue Book' were recalled from libraries and government offices across South-West Africa and South Africa and burned. The editor of the main newspaper in Windhoek welcomed the destruction, saying that the white nations could now 'go forward together unhampered by the suspicion and rancour of the past'. In South-West Africa, Heinrich Heine's famous reflection that 'where they have burned books, they will end in burning human beings too' was reversed – most of the Herero and Nama had long been exterminated by the time they got round to burning the evidence.

On 10 May 1933, the Nazis began their notorious book-burning campaign at Opernplatz in Berlin. As Goebbels addressed the students on that night, telling them, 'You do well in this midnight hour to commit to the flames the evil spirit of the past,' I wonder whether anybody in that crowd knew that six years earlier, the Germans and South Africans had started burning books in Windhoek, destroying the history they didn't want to live with, imposing a Silence of the Fathers that wouldn't be broken for almost fifty years. The charred paper fragments of the 'Blue Book' falling back down to earth on that day in 1927, the earth where so many thousands of unmarked graves lay silently, as the settlers of Windhoek went about their business once again, unburdened by the past.

PART THREE

The Violence of My Country

'If there is anything we must change it is the past.
To look back and see another map.'

Anne Michaels

7

A Question from Günter Grass

Genocidal thinking does not come out of a clear blue sky. It is the result of many years of accreted prejudice, narratives and accepted violence. As we've seen, creating 'habits of thought' which are passed down, almost unconsciously, in the DNA from one generation to the next. Germany, France and the United States have been the main focus of this section, but how is it even possible to begin to honestly describe Britain's past, and its devastating impact on the rest of the world? How do we start to look at almost 500 years of extreme, and state-sanctioned, violence? Perhaps I am too close to this subject to be able to see it with any kind of objectivity, maybe I cannot see the wood for the proverbial trees, because I have grown up, indeed been entirely formed, within this forest.

George Steiner once wrote of the paradox that it was a younger, post-war generation who were able to create some of the most profound responses to the Holocaust in art and literature, rather than the generation who had suffered directly. Also, some of these 'young contemporary poets, novelists and playwrights' were not Jewish themselves. Yet it was these younger people, he wrote in 1967, 'who have done the most to counter the general inclination to forget the death camps'. I do take his point – that a distance from the direct experience can sometimes help to shape remarkable and clear-sighted responses; and, conversely, that you can be so close to an event that you are unable to focus clearly. As he puts it: 'Perhaps it is only those who had no part in the events who can focus on them rationally and imaginatively; to those who experienced the thing, it has lost the hard edges of possibility, it has stepped outside the real.'

In a similar way, maybe it is only people from *outside* our own cultures who can truly see the aspects of our societies that are invisible to us, because we have internalised them. I came across these words from Günter Grass some years ago, and they have been etched in my mind ever since:

> I sometimes wonder how young people grow up in Britain and know so little about the long history of crimes during the colonial period. In England it's a completely taboo subject.*

I had asked myself this question for many years, but it was very powerful to hear these thoughts expressed by Grass. I experienced more than the simple truth of the statement when I first encountered it. Rather, the words acted with a kind of moral force, because they were written by a German writer who had spent most of his adult life attempting to make sense of the insanity of Nazism that had destroyed so many in his own generation and others. That is also why Sebald's lecture on the firebombing of German cities and the Allied targeting of civilians holds so much power – these are men who spent most of their lives, with dogged persistence, looking at the responsibility of their country and their fellow citizens for what had happened between 1933 and 1945. And here are both of these writers, clearly perplexed and troubled, at how we in Britain have given so little of our energies to confronting our own, perhaps equally shameful, history. And also implicit within Grass's question is the knowledge that nowadays children cannot grow up in Germany without learning a huge amount about Hitler, the years

---

* Interview with Jonathan Steele, *Guardian*, 8 March 2003.

of the Third Reich and the Holocaust. So, how is it possible for us in Britain to grow up so ignorant of the barbarisms of our empire?

In the 1970s, when I was at school, it was simply because we were taught nothing about it. *Nothing at all.* Our history syllabus ended in 1870 and didn't touch the British Empire; I could have told you all about Bismarck and his Kulturkampf, the Ems Telegram, Garibaldi and the Risorgimento, but nothing at all about British colonisation, Cromwell in Ireland, the East India Company, the Opium Wars, let alone the slave trade and its role in the early years of the Industrial Revolution. So, like many children of my generation, I found my British history away from school, in books. I became very interested in the subject, beginning in my primary school years. This was the heyday of the Ladybird 'Adventure from History' books, and I began to collect them with a feverish passion. Small, hardback, vivid colours, about fifty pages each – the text and image alternating, giving both knowledge and space for imagination. *Kings and Queen of England, Book One.* An entire reign crystallised in a single image. King Alfred the Great standing proudly on a clifftop watching his boats sailing against the Danes, Rufus felled in the New Forest by an arrow in the back of his head, and a truly terrifying image of a shadowy figure about to murder two young princes in their bed in the Tower of London – Richard III, of course. But I preferred the longer ones, on a single subject.

There was something eternally optimistic about these stories, often emphasising the overcoming of extremely adverse circumstances. Even today, when from the perspective of adulthood it's impossible to ignore the colonial and racist nature of these books, I still retain a kind of affection for them. Especially for those brilliant and beguiling illustrations by John Kenney. Often I'd gaze for minutes at the details of those pictures – Francis Drake telling stories of his trip to America to a ten-year-old Walter Raleigh, surrounded by artefacts he'd brought back from the voyage: a spear, a decorated mask, a pipe; Captain Cook hunched over navigation charts, surrounded by burly Russian fishermen, trying to explain whether there was a route further to the north, through to the Atlantic – the fabled

'North-West Passage'. And that, possibly, remains a positive aspect of these books, that they made their young readers curious about the wider world, in a similar way to the Tintin books, which I loved as well, but now can be similarly critiqued on so many levels. Whatever I think today, I cannot deny that these pages were the first to thrill me into learning about history and the past.

For a few months, when I was around six or seven, I was entranced by Richard the Lionheart. Perhaps some of this attributable to the association with my most loved animal, but there was also something magnificent in his doomed quest. The attempt to reach Jerusalem. The obsessive pursuit of the crusades. The drama of his life. His capture in Vienna, trying to return to England, a king now disguised as a merchant on a donkey. But the picture I returned to, the one which mesmerised me, was the mythical meeting with Saladin – the coming together of the two enemies and cultures. Richard demonstrates his leonine strength by cutting a metal bar with a single blow of his sword. Saladin responds by slicing a silk scarf in half with his scimitar. In the picture, both men are smiling, momentarily their enmity is suspended. Both have proved themselves; there is more than one way of winning. But perhaps the most telling aspect of this page in the book is that the meeting never actually happened. It was completely compelling and real to me as a child, but had no factual basis in reality whatsoever – it was more about our need to believe it had happened; that is to say, the creating of a narrative, a myth.

Naturally, when revisiting these books as an adult, you are shocked at the propagandistic power that the author (L. du Garde Peach, MA, PhD, DLitt) and illustrator (John Kenney) wielded. The power, through their simplistic texts and vivid illustrations, to influence an entire generation of young minds in the English-speaking world, about the 'benevolent' role of England's kings and queens and, later, the British Empire. One of the Ladybird books I read again and again – to the extent that even today I can still see certain pages vividly in my mind – was the one on Sir Walter Raleigh. Reading this as a seven- or eight-year-old boy, of course I had almost no critical judgement, except whether I particularly liked, or disliked, a specific illustration.

Everything read at that age is taken on trust, and absorbed, just as the adventure books of Karl May and Gustav Frenssen would have been to the German children growing up a hundred years ago, who, thirty years later, occupied all the senior positions of the Third Reich. So imagine the effect of a passage like this on generations of British children – it's taken from the Raleigh book, as he's looking at maps with Queen Elizabeth I, surrounded by parchments and a golden globe, asking her for permission to explore in America. The queen grants this permission, and then L. du Garde Peach informs us: 'Of course, in those days, not many people had been to North America, and it was inhabited only by a few tribes of red indians. But Raleigh saw that it was good land, the sort of country in which Englishmen could plant [sic] farms and make a good living.'

The last page of the book shows Raleigh in the Tower of London, but our narrator reminds us that 'whenever we think of the age of Elizabeth, we think of the gallant gentleman-adventurer who founded the beginnings of the British Empire'.

A similar, entirely nationalistic, narrative is taken up in *Captain Cook*. One of the pictures, as Cook and his crew reach New Zealand, shows a boat of dark-skinned warriors brandishing spears and knives against sailors on a British ship. We are briefly informed that 'Here he was attacked by some of the natives, called Maoris, and was obliged to fire on them in self-defence. Cook always treated natives well, and it was unfortunate that he was on this occasion forced to take such action.'

The cover illustration shows Cook, dressed immaculately in white breeches and a navy blue and gold jacket, watching as a sailor hoists the Union Jack up a flagpole. This episode happened, we're informed, after Cook's ship was grounded on the Great Barrier Reef, off the north-eastern shore of Australia. The ship was eventually repaired, and they were able to sail away:

> but before leaving the northernmost cape of Australia, Captain Cook landed and hoisted the British flag. By doing this he claimed Australia for Britain, and it remains today, like Canada, a great self-governing Dominion in the British Commonwealth.

609

You land on a foreign shore, raise the Union Jack, and the land instantly becomes British.* The end of Cook's 'adventures' finds our hero in the Hawaiian islands, being treated 'like a god' by the Maui people, 'but this did not prevent the natives, who were great thieves, from trying to steal anything they could from the ship'. It is this 'unfriendly attitude of the natives' that leads to Cook's death, when he demands the return of a boat that they have stolen.

The Ladybird narrative of history continues: fearless, adventurous Englishmen claiming new lands for the British Empire; feckless, deceitful natives trying to steal from or attack our heroic travellers. It's easy to laugh at such crude representations from the vantage

---

* The raising of the flag to claim foreign lands is not only a British phenomenon here: in the book on Columbus, there's an almost identical picture of the landing on San Salvador, and Columbus with the flag: 'After giving thanks to God, he took possession of the island in the name of the King and Queen of Spain.'

point of adulthood, but I wonder how they shaped the minds of generations of young British children.

*

I assumed that the teaching of history must have changed significantly in the last thirty years, that there would surely be a far greater emphasis today on looking honestly at Britain's past. I decided to start by asking my two nieces – who were then seventeen and eighteen – about their experiences of learning about British history at school over the previous decade or so. I was not reassured by what I found out.

My younger niece described learning about three waves of 'invaders' at primary school – the Romans, the Vikings and the Normans; then a leap ahead to the Fire of London and Samuel Pepys ('bit boring') and also the Victorians (restricted to life in Britain, nothing about overseas territories). At secondary school she didn't do GCSE history but between eleven and fourteen the modules she remembered studying were: JFK, Jack the Ripper, Charles I, and Cromwell and the slave trade. My ears pricked up at this last topic, so I asked her more about it. She thought they'd spent about 'two to three weeks' doing this subject, 'Everyone in the class was shocked . . . I remember we learned that our economy had been based on slavery at that time. I'd heard about it before but I never understood the scale before that.' However, when I asked about wider studies of Britain and Empire, she explained they hadn't studied anything about colonisation, nothing about Britain in India, Africa, America, Australia or China. She agreed completely with Grass's comment, saying, 'We never learnt about the way Britain used to own a third of the world.' And, having friends in Germany, she also said she felt this lack of knowledge was 'quite disgusting, when you think about what young Germans learn about their history, the Holocaust and so on, they take it really seriously in Germany – unlike us'.

My elder niece, who at the time of writing is about to study history at university, said that she remembered doing the Anglo-Saxons at primary school ('that was really fun'), also the ancient Greeks and

611

Romans, the Tudors, the Victorians ('we did a Victorian school day') – but 'nothing on foreign policy or empire'. In the last year at primary school 'we did both world wars, and we went on a residential trip to a place in Norfolk, near Cromer. We were "evacuees" and were given ration books, it was really interesting.' At secondary school they studied King John and the feudal system, the Battle of Hastings, and then the Suffragettes. 'In Year 8 or 9 we did slavery and the British Empire – but we didn't spend a huge amount of time on it . . . maybe a couple of lessons. I can't really remember anything about it, except being made aware that we weren't the good guys.' For GCSE they had done four units – Medicine (mid-1800s to the Second World War), the Civil Rights Movement, the Roaring Twenties, and Hitler's Rise to Power (up to 1939). She'd also completed an EPQ (Extended Project Qualification) on 'Morality in the Twentieth Century' – 'I looked at the Holocaust, and the bombing of Hiroshima and Nagasaki.' She too agreed with Grass's analysis, repeating that British colonisation and empire hadn't formed a critical part of her history syllabus from GCSE through to A levels – 'We were never formally examined on slavery or any aspect of the British Empire.'

These limitations on history teaching about Britain's colonial past are certainly not just confined to my relatives' recent experience. The author Moni Mohsin wrote this about her children's education in London:

> For all the range and candour of their education, they haven't once encountered Britain's colonial past in school. My daughter is now in her second year of A levels. She has studied history from the age of nine, but the closest she has come to any mention of empire was in her GCSE syllabus that included the run-up to the Second World War. While studying the Treaty of Versailles, she learned that some countries had colonies at the time, and, as part of Germany's punishment, it was stripped of its colonial possessions. Period.[*]

---

[*] 'Empire shaped the world. There is an abyss at the heart of dishonest history textbooks', *Observer*, 30 October 2016.

In the same article she quotes Dr Mukulika Banerjee, associate professor of anthropology at the London School of Economics, on British students who

> arrive at university completely ignorant about the empire, that vital part of their history. When we talk of Syria today, they have no knowledge of Britain's role in the Middle East in the last century . . . Similarly they have no clue about the history of . . . immigration. They don't understand why people of other ethnicities came to Britain in the first place. They haven't learned any of it at school. So . . . at university, when my students discover the extent of their ignorance, they are furious.

What happens if a country is continually told that it has nothing to apologise for, no need to learn from its past mistakes? In this way, an entire nation, like a sickly child, can become permanently disabled, stuck in an illusory safety zone composed of past myths about its glory days, infantilised by a selective view of its own history, which may be comforting but also means it will be unable to develop into a questioning adult. Think about our own country and the narratives we have all grown up with. More and more these days I hear a persistent voice in my head that questions whether the ongoing British obsession with the Second World War, and its 'finest hour', isn't in fact a subconscious process of denial – a deflection away from the reality of history, which we cannot bear to face. The truth which, as Sebald says, 'lies elsewhere, away from it all, somewhere as yet undiscovered'.

*

But, to return to Günter Grass's implicit challenge, how *should* we begin trying to teach our children about the crimes and genocides committed in the name of the British Empire? Where would you start? There is an immediate challenge here – whereas the particular savagery of Nazism occured within a twelve-year span (or perhaps two generations, going back to its causation), the violence unleashed by the British Empire took place over almost 500 years – more than twenty generations. The contrast with Germany could not be greater. And this is not only a matter of the time frame. The Holocaust took place in a recognisably modern world – we can see television images of Hitler and Himmler chatting, of the senior perpetrators on trial at Nuremberg, we even have images and photographs of the extermination camps. For the vast majority of Britain's reign of terror around the world we have only documents from other centuries. This creates an immediate challenge for even the most inspirational teacher – how to make such distant history come alive? How to make a document listing the names and ages of slaves on a British sugar plantation as vivid as interviews with Holocaust survivors? To put it crudely – how to bridge the 'empathy gap' which inevitably exists when we cannot really see or hear people from the past?

Maybe we can only start from what we know. We know that in 1600 Queen Elizabeth I granted the first charter to the East India Company, the first truly transnational corporation in the world. We know that this organisation, in partnership with the British state, ended up ruling India. We also know that its policies were responsible for exacerbating the Bengal famine in 1770 in which millions of Indians starved to death. The company had taken over all taxation rights in Bengal (today covering West Bengal, Bangladesh, parts of Assam, Odisha, Bihar and Jharkhand) after the British victories at Plassey and Buxar in 1757 and 1764 respectively. Land taxes were immediately raised, from 10 per cent to 50 per cent, giving huge profits to East India Company shareholders and the British state – rising from 15 million rupees in 1765 to 30 million rupees in 1777. The company also forced many farmers to move from food production to growing opium poppies (for the export market, particularly to China). The dual impact of these two developments, combined with a severe drought in 1769, caused the devastating famine of 1770, resulting in an estimated 10 million deaths.

The East India Company were also responsible for exporting enormous quantities of opium to China from this period up until 1860 – averaging 900 tons a year in the late eighteenth century, rising to

1,400 tons a year by 1838. As China had banned imports of opium, realising the significant damage that addiction caused, the exports were routed via Calcutta and smuggled in by companies including Dent & Co., and Jardine Matheson & Co.* – the brainchild of two Edinburgh University graduates. There are no reliable statistics for the tens, hundreds of thousands, perhaps millions of Chinese lives devastated through the trade of opium, which gave this company its vastly profitable foundation. The trade led to the Opium Wars of 1839–42 and 1860, and the destruction of one of the wonders of the world – the Old Summer Palace, just outside Beijing. This entire complex, and the 300 Chinese people inside, were incinerated by British soldiers on 18 October 1860.

But perhaps we need to go back even earlier, to look at how the seeds of the slave trade were planted in the English psyche. The first documented English slave trafficker we know about was Sir John Hawkyns. In 1562 he 'acquired' at least 300 inhabitants of the Guinea coast, some bought from African merchants, some hijacked from Portuguese slavers, some simply seized. He took these 300 people to Hispaniola (now Haiti), where he sold them to the Spanish for the then phenomenal sum of £10,000 worth of pearls, hides, sugar and ginger. And once that first act was proved to be profitable, hundreds of other slavers followed in Hawkyns' wake.

Through the slave trade, England, and then Britain, became skilled at turning human beings into commodities. The men, women and children transported across the Atlantic in the 'Middle Passage' were classed as 'goods' not people. They were valued only in so far as they could bring profit to the sugar and tobacco plantations. To understand the extent of the commodification of human beings into objects, you only have to look at the mass killing of slaves which took place on the Liverpool-based slave ship *Zong* in 1781: 133 slaves, who had been insured just like any other 'asset', were thrown overboard and drowned when the ship was running low

---

* Jardine Matheson is still booming today (incorporated in Bermuda), with revenue up 19 per cent in the first six months of 2018, to $44.35 billion.

on water, so that the ship's owners could claim insurance on their dead 'assets'.

By 1670 there were already almost 50,000 African slaves used on Caribbean plantations. A century later there were more than 330,000 African slave labourers on the British colonial plantations in America. We now know that many of the investors who benefited from slavery were not only major shareholders like banks and shipping companies, but also the Church of England, and an army of smaller investors, respectable and upstanding men and women across the land – ministers and clerks, farmers and widows. The plantations, and the sugar and tobacco produced, became a central part of the British economy. It has been estimated that 11 million human beings were transported as slaves in English and British ships in the 271 years between Hawkyns' first trade in 1562 and the Abolition of the Slave Trade Act in 1833. I do not think we as a culture have even begun to grasp the meaning of these 271 years of atrocity, repeated again and again, the thousands of ships, the millions of people – and the fact that this trade in human beings resulted in vast profits – profits which helped to power the Industrial Revolution, as well as the establishment of many financial and insurance institutions that are still at the heart of our society today.

So, when the movement for abolition of the slave trade began in the 1750s, you can imagine the uproar across the country – how on earth would the plantation economy function without this supply of free labour? How could Britain survive without this income stream? But by 1800 the movement towards abolition of the slave trade had become unstoppable, and the British government could see the writing on the wall, and this situation meant the need for territorial expansion and diversification of the economy became urgent. There was another significant problem: an overflowing prison population, exacerbated by American independence in 1775. For almost 150 years England and then Britain had exported more than 1,000 convicts a year to the American colonies – essentially a form of white slavery, but with the significant difference that after completing a seven- or fourteen-year term, the convicts could become free. On gaining their independence, America piously declared that they no longer wanted to be a repository for Britain's criminals – preferring to replace this convict labour in the plantations with African slave labour. So Britain was faced with the question of what to do with a rapidly expanding prison population and how to replace the economic productivity lost through the abolition of the slave trade.

The Tory government of William Pitt the Younger attempted to solve these two problems with a single idea – why not transport the convicts to the other side of the world and establish new colonies there? In the 1780s a British parliamentary committee was established to investigate the feasibility of setting up a penal colony on the Namib coast; and in 1785, a ship, the *Nautilus*, was sent to survey the south-western coast of Africa to find the best place for such a colony. But it returned reporting that the Skeleton Coast was aptly named, and that colonists would face certain death there. At this point, the government began to look even further afield. Australia, as we've already seen, had been 'claimed' for Britain by Captain Cook in 1770 – this despite the fact that it had been the Dutch who had first mapped its northern and western shores; it was Cook who had named a harbour on the eastern coast Botany Bay, given its rich diversity of flora. The fact that there was an Aboriginal population on the island was of no concern whatsoever to Pitt and his ministers, all they could see was the potential of 8 million square kilometres of *terra nullius* (nobody's land) – a territorial area greater than all the countries of Europe put together.

It was primarily Cook's reports that encouraged the British government in 1786 to go forward with their curious plan, and in May 1787 the 'First Fleet' of eleven ships sailed from Portsmouth, carrying two years of supplies for a crew of 671 officers, sailors and their families (including the first governor of the colony and his staff) – and 798 convicts, housed in rather less comfortable conditions. In January 1788 the ships arrived in Botany Bay. It was not an auspicious beginning to this new world – Cook's glowing reports had not revealed the poverty of the soil or the lack of stone for constructing buildings, so the governor, Captain Arthur Phillip, ordered the ships further north to the more promising site of 'Sydney Cove', as he named it. Within four years Sydney had grown to a settlement of 3,000 people, and the colony had established itself as self-sufficient in food and had even begun exporting wheat to other countries.

By 1803 a new governor, Philip King, was now looking to expand British territory in Australia – particularly to find an island off the main territory, an isolated place where the unreformable criminals of the new convict colony could be held. Van Diemen's Land (renamed 'Tasmania' in 1856) had been sighted by the Dutch explorer Abel Tasman in 1640, though never settled. King thought this place would be perfect for his penal colony, and in 1803 he despatched an officer to land on the east coast of Van Diemen's Land, raise the Union Jack and claim the island for King George III. Over the next months, settlements were established at Hobart and Risdon, on either side of the 'River Derwent', which formed an inlet on the south-east coast of the island, and a further settlement at Launceston, on the northern coast. Within fifty years the indigenous population of the island was almost totally exterminated.

How many British schoolchildren ever learn of this genocide?

8

Crow-hunting in Tasmania

The genocide of the Tasmanian Aboriginals is extremely challenging to write about. Not only because of the casual barbarism with which these human beings were hunted down like wild animals, but also because the killings, over thirty years or so, were primarily carried out by convict bush-hunters, settlers and farmers. There was no 'extermination order', as in South-West Africa, no centrally organised military massacre, indeed the British authorities were extremely careful about what they ordered, what they committed to paper. In that long tradition of hypocrisy, and 'turning a blind eye' to things, perhaps the extermination of the indigenous Tasmanians could be described as 'A Very British Genocide'.

According to Mark Cocker – whose work *Rivers of Blood, Rivers of Gold* is a haunting account of Europe's extermination of tribal peoples around the world – the best estimate we have of the original Aboriginal population of the island at the beginning of the nineteenth century is between 3,000 and 4,000 people (though some more recent estimates put this figure higher, at around 6,000). They were hunter-gatherers, who over centuries had evolved a way of life where communities moved with the seasonal availability of a rich diversity of foods – fungi and ferns, kangaroos, possums and wombats, seals and marine plants, seabirds and eggs, oysters and shellfish. Larger prey such as kangaroos and seals were killed with throwing clubs or their highly effective hardwood spears, sometimes ten to fifteen feet long. Captain Cook, who had explored part of the island in 1777, was not exaggerating when he reported that it was 'a country capable of producing every necessity of life, with a climate the finest in the world' – though his opinion of the inhabitants was, predictably, lower, 'an ignorant wretched race of mortals', as he put it. A sentiment that the indigenous people who met Cook might well have shared about him and his men, though with rather greater justification.

The first documented massacre happened on the morning of 3 May 1804, just outside the settlement of Risdon on the River Derwent. Around 300 Aboriginals, including women and children, emerged from the trees in pursuit of grazing kangaroos. The officer in charge at Risdon, Lieutenant Moore, decided that the settlement was under attack and ordered his soldiers to fire into the crowd of hunters, killing many of them. Moore commented afterwards that he had wanted rifle practice and was pleased 'to see the Niggers run'. Over the next twenty-six years thousands more were killed, in what can be described as three phases of genocide: first, the eradication of the Bass Strait Aboriginals on the northern coast and the islands; secondly, the extermination of inland Aboriginals by bushrangers; and finally, the killing of the remainder of the population in the 'Black War' of 1825–31.

The northern coast of Tasmania had always been the main hunting ground of seals for the indigenous people. But by the early 1800s there were already more than 200 European sealers who had settled along the coast and on the Bass Strait islands, and the industry in sealskins was growing rapidly, with 100,000 seals killed for their skins between 1800 and 1806. This not only had a disastrous impact on traditional Aboriginal food sources, but the sealers also destroyed the familial bonds of the local people, by 'acquiring' Tasmanian women, who were the most skilled seal catchers, sometimes through barter, sometimes by kidnap. But effectively they became slaves to the European sealers, used for labour and sex, and

620

treated appallingly. And if the women attempted to return to their communities, the violence was brutal. One runaway was tied to a tree by a group of sealers, had her ear cut off, and flesh from a thigh, and was then forced to eat these. Not surprisingly, such behaviour resulted in all-out conflict between the European sealers and the northern Tasmanians, but the Europeans' guns meant that the fight was never going to be equal; the north-east coast became a killing ground, where corpses and skeletons of Aboriginals were soon everywhere. By 1830, we learn from Cocker that only seventy-five natives remained in the entire northern region, seventy-two of these being men, and not a single child to continue the line.

The second wave of extermination happened inland, and was triggered by kangaroo hunting. Kangaroo meat soon became the mainstay of the Hobart and Launceston settlers, but with the population of these settlements growing rapidly, and demand for meat increasing, within a few years kangaroos had become scarce, especially near the coastal areas. This in turn led to a push to hunt the marsupials inland – the territory that had always been the main hunting grounds for the Aboriginals. The most successful hunters were known as 'bushrangers', who used hunting dogs, and were mostly escaped convicts who survived by selling meat and skins to the settlers; they were some of the most hardened and violent men imaginable, regarded as 'the lowest of the low' in the colony. Competition over the dwindling stocks of kangaroos gave these bushrangers the perfect excuse to use limitless violence against the Aboriginals inland, and between 1808 and 1824 nearly half of all the remaining indigenous Tasmanians were killed – more than 1,000 people.

The psychopathic nature of many of these bushrangers is notable in contemporary accounts of their repellent behaviour. One boasted to a historian of the time that he 'liked to kill a black fellow better than smoke a pipe'. Mostly, they weren't even thought of as human beings but rather 'black crows' or 'black vermin'. Another bushranger compared shooting Aboriginals to 'so many sparrows', another one used them as target practice, while a third shot Tasmanians so he could feed them to his dogs. Others enjoyed torturing those who had been 'spared'; Robert Hughes recounts a bushranger called Carrot who forced a woman to watch her husband being slaughtered, then raped her, and subsequently made her carry her husband's severed head around her neck 'as a plaything'.

The British authorities officially denounced such behaviour; however, the fact that they had depended upon the bushrangers for years to provide meat for the colony rather undermined the moral righteousness of their words. The other significant reality is that the Aboriginals were clearly not treated as 'citizens', indeed many of the European settlers didn't even regard them as fully human, but rather the last living link between men and apes. So the idea that they would have had any kind of human rights was laughable, and their nomadic lives and lack of permanent dwellings also meant they could not claim any rights of land ownership. All this was well understood by the bushrangers, and indeed any other group of settlers who wanted to kill or mistreat the Aboriginals – they knew there would almost certainly be no serious consequences. Throughout the years of genocide, not a single person was ever put on trial for murdering an Aboriginal.

By 1824 the European population of Tasmania had grown to 12,643, with the majority of these people living around the towns of Hobart, on the east coast, and Launceston on the north coast. Sheep farming had now established itself as the main industry on the island, which again made great inroads into the landscape, reducing the forest, and further impacting on the hunting of the indigenous Tasmanians. By 1823 there were already 200,000 sheep on the island, and by 1830 this number had leapt to 1 million – 1,000 sheep for each Aboriginal still left alive.

The third wave of genocide took place between 1825 and 1831, years known as the 'Black War', which killed a further 700 Tasmanians, leaving fewer than 300 alive. The British authorities had now got rid of most of the bushrangers, so the majority of this wave of killings were carried out by farmers and stockmen, often in remote parts of the island, where any edicts coming from Hobart could be safely ignored. The term 'war' is something of a misnomer; there were no armies, no generals, the conflict involved hundreds of local incidents all over the island, and it is only thanks to the testimony of many witnesses at the time that we have accounts of the kind of killings and behaviour that took place. One farmer ripped open an Aboriginal's stomach while seeming to offer bread at the end of a knife; another farmer placed a gin trap in a barrel of flour and then watched with delight as an Aboriginal had his hand snapped off in the trap; another farmer played Russian roulette with an empty gun, before handing a loaded one over to an Aboriginal who then blew his brains out.

We also learn of two British settlers out hunting birds, who come across a group of Aboriginals in the forest. Most of them flee, except for a heavily pregnant woman who, terrified, climbs up a tree to hide. She is shot down by the hunters, immediately miscarries her baby, and then the men look on in amusement as she crawls to a creek to die.* It is worth pausing here to remember that at *exactly* the same time that such barbarisms are taking place in Tasmania, the spirit of humanism is taking Europe by storm, the Romantic movement is in full bloom, and Beethoven has just written his Ninth Symphony, containing Schiller's 'Ode to Joy' – '*Alle Menschen werden Brüder . . . Diesen Kuss der ganzen Welt!*' (All people become brothers . . . This kiss is for all the world!).

Not surprisingly, such brutal abuses fuelled the strongest reaction from the Aboriginals, and 176 British settlers were killed in revenge attacks during this period. This led to public meetings in Hobart where the authorities debated the possible responses with the settlers. The majority of the colonists favoured a policy of complete elimination of the Aboriginals now – at one of these meetings a Dr Turnbull made comparisons with neighbouring Australia, 'extermination has been adopted in New South Wales with the greatest success', so why couldn't this policy be enacted in Tasmania too? The government set up its own Committee for Aboriginal Affairs, who proposed a system of bounty payments for the capture of natives rather than their killing, and the increase in the use of con-

---

* These four accounts are taken from *The Aboriginal Tasmanians* by Lyndall Ryan, *The Tasmanians* by Robert Travers, *Friendly Mission* edited by N.J.B. Plomley and *The Last of the Tasmanians* by David Davies.

victs to guard remote farms. But the killings continued, colonists paying for roving groups of militias to patrol in search of Tasmanians – essentially death squads. These militias would attack any Aboriginals they found, even groups peacefully cooking round fires. They would be shot or bayoneted, including young children. 'Crow-hunting' became a popular sport, where families would combine country picnics with a spot of killing.

> It was a favourite amusement to hunt the Aboriginals; a day would be selected, and the neighbouring settlers invited, with their families, to a picnic . . . After dinner, all would be gaiety and merriment, whilst the gentlemen of the party would take their guns and dogs, and, accompanied by two or three convict servants, wander through the bush in search of black fellows. Sometimes they would return without sport; at others they would succeed in killing a woman, or if lucky, [perhaps] a man or two.*

I think of Jan Karski here, watching from that upstairs window as the two Hitler Youth joyfully 'hunted' Jews in the Warsaw Ghetto. But in Tasmania it's the British who hunted human beings.

Some settlers even kept 'trophies' – body parts cut off from Tasmanians they had killed. 'One European had a pickle tub in which he put the ears of all the blacks he shot.' I think here of the fourteen-year-old son of Martin Bormann being shown into Himmler's attic, and being traumatised for life, seeing chairs made from human legs and a copy of *Mein Kampf* covered in human skin. But here the farmer with the ear collection was a European man who had grown up in the midst of the Enlightenment and the values of the French Revolution – *liberté, egalité, fraternité.*

In November 1828, Governor George Arthur declared martial law in an attempt to appease the colonists. He also increased the bounties paid for capture of live Aboriginals – £5 for adults, £2 for

---

* Both this quote and the one that follows it are taken from *The Aboriginals of Tasmania* by H. Ling Roth.

children. 'Black catching' now became more popular, and lucrative, than 'crow-hunting'. But the killings continued, especially in the east of the island, where the Big River and Oyster Bay tribes were looking to avenge the murders of 240 of their people during the years of the Black War. They killed twenty European settlers in 1830, and Governor Arthur was under greater pressure than ever to take harsher action. He came up with the idea of a 'game drive', based on English hunting principles, in which a vast cordon of 2,000 British soldiers, police, settlers and convicts would sweep from the north of the island to the south-east, forcing all the remaining Tasmanians into the 'funnel' of the Tasman Peninsula. The 'Black Line' was the largest ever force used against Australian Aboriginals (Cocker notes it was as large a force as the conquistador Hernando Cortés had used to subdue Mexico), and cost around £50,000. Farcically, the entire operation, lasting from 7 October to the end of November, captured not a single Aboriginal, though Arthur argued that at least the eastern part of the island had now been cleared of aggressive Tasmanians.

By 1831 there were probably fewer than 400 Aboriginals left across the whole island, and half of these were women and children being used as domestic slaves by the settlers. What happened to the remaining 200 or so free indigenous Tasmanians in the next twenty years is as appalling as anything that had occurred since 1804 –

a phase that could be called 'killing with Christian kindness'. The central figure in this phase was a forty-two-year-old former builder from London called George Robinson. Like many people whose 'heart is in the right place', he ended up doing incalculable damage. He was evangelical in his Christianity, had a family of seven children, and was desperate to spread the 'Good News of Salvation'. Five years after his arrival in Hobart in 1824, Governor Arthur put him in charge of a group of twenty-five captive Aboriginals who were being held on the island of Bruny, just to the south of the town.

Robinson's dream was to bring 'the Word of the Lord' to this benighted remnant of the Tasmanian people. But to do this, he realised he first needed to learn more about them; he spent months learning their language and their customs. He soon understood that far from their image of 'demonic' aggression that most of the settlers saw, the people he got to know were peaceable and highly intelligent. And, given the brutality of their earlier treatment by his compatriots, it is striking, and affecting, to read Robinson's genuine sympathy for the suffering the Aboriginals had undergone – as he writes in his diary: 'The cruelties exercised upon them beggars all description . . . and their sufferings have been far greater than those of the Indians at the hands of the Spaniards.' But although this impulse to halt the Tasmanians' sufferings was real, sadly Robinson was also driven by egotism and an inflated sense of his own importance – as he wrote: 'It is no small honour conferred on me that I should be the individual appointed to ameliorate the conditions of this hapless race and to emancipate them from bondage.' He began to see himself as the 'saviour' of the Tasmanians, and it was this Christian delusion which now contributed so significantly to their final demise.

Governor Arthur now appoints Robinson to be the 'Conciliator' to the Aboriginals, and just as Arthur's 'Black Line' is reaching the Tasman Peninsula in October 1830, Robinson is completing his first journey across the island, to search for the last remaining free Tasmanians. He travels with a group of twelve of the Bruny Aboriginals, whose job it is to persuade these free men, women and children to give themselves up, and convert to Christianity.

Robinson and his band go through the wildest parts of the Tasmanian bush, through forests and brambles, across mountains and around the rocky coastal regions. His principal 'weapons' of persuasion are a flute, which he plays 'to soothe their troubled minds', and the Bible. Their first trip, lasting ten months, is fruitless, but his following trips are more successful. By 1831 he has persuaded fifty-four Tasmanians to give themselves up, and in the following four years he brings back another 140 Aboriginals to Hobart and the 'protection' of the British authorities. With the exception of the 230 women and children used as domestic servants, not a single indigenous Tasmanian remains free on the island by 1835. Robinson has completed, with his missionary zeal, the process begun with rifles at Risdon on 3 May 1804. As many dispossessed peoples have reflected – 'You taught us to pray, and while we looked up to heaven you stole our land.'

The years that follow are disturbing to describe. It is decided that a reserve should be created for Robinson's last Tasmanians, and this should be on Flinders Island, off the north-eastern coast of Tasmania. Here the Aboriginals are baptised and christened with European names, given lessons in scripture, arithmetic and needlework, like schoolchildren, and housed in dormitories. Robinson now terms himself 'the Commandant' and there are regular clothing and bedding inspections, as if Flinders Island was a minor English public school. But the water supplies are inadequate, the sanitation poor, and soon disease is rife and many are dying. Governor Arthur's response is a remarkably cynical example of the British colonial art of 'turning a blind eye' to evil: 'Even if the Aboriginals pine away, it is better that they meet with their deaths in that way, whilst every kindness is manifested towards them, than that they should fall a sacrifice to the inevitable consequences of their continued acts of outrage upon the white inhabitants.'

By 1839, only sixty Aboriginals remain alive. By 1847, when finally the British authorities agree to move them back to the main island at Oyster Cove, thirty miles south of Hobart, only forty-seven are now left. Four years later, this is down to just thirty, and by 1856, when Van Diemen's Land is officially renamed 'Tasmania', a government report about Oyster Cove states:

> There are five old men and nine old women living at the Oyster Cove station – uncleanly, unsober, unvirtuous, unenergetic and irreligious, with a past character for treachery, and no record of one noble action, the race is fast falling away and its utter extinction will be hardly regretted.

These official sentiments were echoed some years later, when the novelist Anthony Trollope made a Pacific Tour of Australia and New Zealand,[*] and remarked on the widespread killings of Aboriginals that were going on then: 'Their doom is to be exterminated; and the sooner that their doom be accomplished – so that there be no cruelty – the better it will be for civilisation.'

The face of Truganini, the woman often referred to as 'the Last Tasmanian'.[†] What do we know of her life? Or what those eyes had seen? Growing up on Bruny Island, the first contact with settlers, the 'Black War' – by the age of seventeen she had experienced her mother's murder by sailors, her uncle shot by a soldier, her sister

---

[*] From *Australia and New Zealand* by Anthony Trollope. The Maori population in New Zealand had fallen from 240,000 to just 40,000 at the end of the nineteenth century, and the British had ensured the Maori share of land owned on North Island was reduced from 11 million hectares to less than 3 million.

[†] For more information please see chapter notes.

abducted by sealers and her fiancé murdered by foresters, who then raped her. Having witnessed the violence against her own people, she subsequently agreed to help Robinson and joined him on his trips across the island to persuade her fellow Aboriginals to give themselves up. Later she was one of the first to live on the Flinders Island colony, then following the years of desperate decline at Oyster Cove, with her last relatives dying in 1871, she was, finally, alone.

All that has been read into this woman's face. Some have seen 'a fierce personal resistance to the fate of her people', others have spoken of 'her natural dignity'; I see rage in those eyes, and also incomprehension in the face of suffering. But her own words and thoughts are elusive. Some survive – for instance, on the choice she made to join Robinson's expedition across Tasmania, and act as a kind of go-between with the last Aboriginals, she reflected that: 'It was the best thing to do. I hoped we would save all my people who were left. Mr Robinson was a good man and could speak our language. And I said I would go with him and help him.' She also said that she did not want her corpse to be mutilated after her death, that she did not want her skull and skeleton to be displayed in a museum as others had been earlier – she wanted to be buried 'behind the mountains'. Despite the British authorities' assurance, even this last request of hers was not honoured.

She died on 8 May 1876, aged around sixty-five. Within two years of her funeral and burial, her body was exhumed and the Royal Society of Tasmania subsequently put her skeleton on display at Hobart Museum, where it remained until 1947. For the next twenty-nine years she was stored in the museum archives, and on 30 April 1976, just before the centenary of her death, her remains were finally passed to Aboriginal representatives; she was cremated, and had her ashes scattered in the D'Entrecasteaux Channel, which runs between her homeland of Bruny Island and the Tasmanian coast. In 2002, the Royal College of Surgeons returned to Tasmania the samples of Truganini's hair and skin which had found their way to England, in the colonial desire to analyse, categorise and systematise human beings who were considered to be 'primitive'. The last traces of this exceptional woman were finally laid to rest, 126 years after her death.

9

The British Famine:
'Slaughters done in Ireland by
mere official red tape'

In 1847, at the same time that the British authorities in Hobart were deciding what should be done with the last remnants of the indigenous Tasmanians on Flinders Island, the British government in London was facing an impending disaster in a colony much closer to home. For two successive years – 1845 and 1846 – the potato harvests in Ireland had been devastated by the plant disease *Phytophthora infestans*, better known as 'potato blight'. In 1845 between a third and a half of the crop was destroyed; the following year, the outbreak was even more disastrous: 'in a matter of 72 to 96 hours, the better part of the 1846 crop was obliterated . . . so swift and comprehensive was the destruction that a kind of mass disorientation seized Ireland'. An estimated three-quarters of the entire crop across the country had rotted away in a few days. In a country where the potato was the principal food for many people, this was a catastrophic situation. The first confirmed accounts of starvation in rural Ireland came in autumn 1846, and, with winter on its way, it was clear that only urgent action could avert a humanitarian disaster.

What happened next – the Famine (and the reasons for it) – has been argued about ceaselessly ever since, but one fact is not in doubt: a million men, women and children died, and an estimated 1.3 million others were forced to emigrate between 1845 and 1851 (a globally unprecedented level of migration[*] at that time), reducing the population of Ireland from more than 8 million in 1841 to 6.5 million in 1851. Today there is at least a widespread consensus on these figures, which originate from the detailed Irish census of 1841, recording a population of 8,175,124, and the subsequent census a decade later in 1851, in the immediate aftermath of the Famine, showing a population of only 6,552,385 (when, allowing for normal growth, the population figure would have been around 9 million).

To fully understand the meaning of these figures, the vast scale of death and emigration and their disastrous impact on the nation's development, it is worth reflecting that Ireland is the only country in Europe whose population was higher in the mid-nineteenth century than it is today. But perhaps the most disturbing aspect of the massive loss of life is that it happened in the colony closest to the heart of the British Empire – the richest and most powerful force in the world at the time. Nationalists and revisionists may argue over the details – for instance, the role of the landlords in exacerbating the crisis, the over-dependency on the potato as a crop – but one central reality is clear: if the British state had wanted to avert famine in Ireland, it had all the power and means to do so.

This is not only my opinion. The eminent Dutch-American economic historian Joel Mokyr, also with no nationalist or revisionist axe to grind, analysed the financial realities of the mid-nineteenth-

---

[*] I hesitate to use the word 'migration' here, because this might give an impression of a relatively orderly process of people moving to another country, when in reality, there were extremely high rates of mortality on what became known as the 'coffin ships'. To give just a single example, between 15 May and 17 June 1847, over 2,000 Irish emigrants died at the quarantine station of Grosse Île near Quebec. By the end of the year, 20,000 immigrants to Canada had died, a mortality rate of 30 per cent of the Irish who had made the journey to Canada. (Details from 'Erasures' by Colm Tóibín, *London Review of Books*, July 1998.)

century British and Irish states, and came to this devastating conclusion in his pioneering work published in 1983:

> There is no doubt that Britain could have saved Ireland. The
> British Treasury spent a total of about £9.5 million on fam-
> ine relief . . . A few years after the famine, the British govern-
> ment spent £69.3 million on an utterly futile adventure in the
> Crimea. Half that sum spent in Ireland in the critical years
> 1846–9 would have saved hundreds of thousands of lives . . .
> It is not unreasonable to surmise that had anything like the
> famine occurred in England or Wales, the British government
> would have overcome its theoretical scruples and have come
> to the rescue of the starving at a much larger scale. Ireland was
> not considered part of the British community.*

*

*[In Skibbereen] I entered some of the hovels . . . and the scenes
that presented themselves were such as no tongue or pen can convey the slightest idea of. In the first, six famished and ghastly skeletons, to all appearance dead, were huddled in a corner on some
filthy straw, their sole covering what seemed a ragged horse-cloth
and their wretched legs hanging about, naked above the knees.
I approached in horror, and found by a low moaning they were
alive – they were in fever, four children, a woman, and what once
had been a man. It is impossible to go through the detail. Suffice
it to say, that in a few minutes I was surrounded by at least 200 of
such phantoms, such frightful spectres as no words can describe.*

---

* *Why Ireland Starved: A Quantative and Analytical History of the Irish Economy, 1800–
1850* by Joel Mokyr. It should also be noted that it was Mokyr's research which first
established that a million people had died in the Famine (up to this point Irish historians had only estimated the figure at around half a million). Mokyr's work also raised
the question that there were potentially an additional 400,000 'averted births', i.e. births
that didn't happen due to hunger-induced amenorrhoea (absence of menstruation) and
other illnesses.

By far the greater number were delirious either from famine or from fever. Their demonic yells are still ringing in my ears, and their horrible images are fixed on my brain.

Nicholas Cummins, a Justice of the Peace
in Cork, December 1846

Disease and death in every quarter – the once hardy population worn away to emaciated skeletons – fever, dropsy, diarrhoea, and famine rioting in every filthy hovel, and sweeping away whole families . . . seventy-five tenants ejected here, and a whole village in the last stage of destitution there . . . dead bodies of children flung into holes hastily scratched in the earth without shroud or coffin . . . every field becoming a grave, and the land a wilderness.

Cork Examiner, *December 1846*

In a dark corner . . . a family, the father, mother and two children, lying in close compact. The father was considerably decomposed; the mother, it appeared had died last, and probably fastened the door, which was always the custom when all hope was extinguished, to get into the darkest corner and die, where passers-by could not see them.

Account of a man in Connaught, on opening the door
of a closed cabin, just outside the town, early 1847

*

One of the earliest voices to articulate Irish fury about the Famine was the nationalist activist and author John Mitchel. Trained as a lawyer, he witnessed the Famine years first-hand, became part of the 'Young Ireland Movement', establishing a weekly paper, the *United Irishman*, in February 1848. Mitchel's vituperative criticism of British rule, and particularly their disastrous handling of the Famine, so alarmed the authorities that in May 1848 he was tried on charges of sedition in Dublin. On 26 May he was convicted of treason and sentenced to fourteen years' hard labour in Van Diemen's

Land – the same year that the last few surviving Tasmanian Aboriginals were being transported back to the mainland, at Oyster Cove. It took two more years for Mitchel and other Irish political prisoners to reach Hobart (via spells in prison ships in Bermuda, and the Cape of Good Hope) – but Mitchel used this time to secretly start writing his *Jail Journal* which would be published to great acclaim subsequently. Three years later, with the aid of an American supporter, Mitchel escapes from Tasmania on a boat, eventually arriving in New York to a hero's welcome, in November 1853.

In America, Mitchel publishes his *Jail Journal* in 1854, but then – infuriated at the British state's attempts throughout the late 1840s and early 1850s to whitewash their record, and evade responsibility for the deaths of more than a million of his compatriots in the Famine (his own estimate was 1.5 million deaths) – he begins to write *The Last Conquest of Ireland (Perhaps)*. Originally a collection of articles serialised in newspapers in 1858, it is subsequently published in book form in 1860 (in Dublin) and 1861 (in London and New York) and causes a sensation on both sides of the Atlantic. Reading his words today, the rage still burns off the page; these are words used as incendiaries, perhaps more powerful than bombs. He eviscerates the arguments of the British authorities that the Famine was a 'natural process', possibly even the work of a God that sought to punish the Irish people for (to quote *The Times* newspaper from March 1847) 'being born and bred, from time immemorial, in inveterate indolence, improvidence, disorder and destitution'. Here is Mitchel's riposte:

> I have called it an artificial famine: that is to say, it was a famine which desolated a rich and fertile island, that produced every year abundance ... to sustain all her people and many more. The English, indeed, call that famine a 'dispensation of Providence' and ascribe it entirely to the blight of the potatoes. But potatoes failed in like manner all over Europe, yet there was no famine, save in Ireland. The British account of the matter, then, is first, a fraud, second, a blasphemy. The Almighty, indeed sent the potato blight, but the English created the famine.

Speaking 135 years later, the Nobel Prize-winning economist Amartya Sen, a world authority on famines and their causes, supported Mitchel's fundamental argument here, stating that 'in no other famine in the world was the proportion of people killed as large as in the Irish famines in the 1840s.'* Although successive generations of revisionist historians and others have criticised Mitchel for his inflammatory tone and exaggerations, it is important to understand the reasons for the enormous resonance his work had – which was due to the fact that he had identified two critical issues.

Firstly, he highlighted the fact that there had been food *exports* during the Famine years: 'During each of these five years of famine from '46 to '51, that famine-struck land produced more than double the needful sustenance for all her people.' Yet the government had decided to export this food, just at the time it was needed most urgently in the country where it had been produced. Even at the height of the Famine, when the British authorities tried to highlight their limited attempts at relief, Mitchel explains that 'A government ship sailing into any harbour with Indian corn was sure to meet half a dozen sailing out with Irish wheat and cattle.' Mitchel's assertions about the amount of food produced in Ireland in the Famine period, and the volume of exported produce may certainly have been exaggerated, and his rhetoric inflammatory, but his principal point – that large quantities of food were exported from Ireland during the Famine years – cannot be disputed.

His second critical intervention was to show that many of the senior figures in the British government were fanatical ideologues, and this explained the decisions they had made. Far from allowing human compassion to save lives, the extreme free marketeers had decided that the principle of non-intervention was more important than anything else. In an extraordinary passage, Mitchel identifies the destruction caused by nineteenth-century desk killers from their ministries in London. Ireland was

---

* From 'Starvation and Political Economy: Famines, Entitlement and Alienation', a paper Sen delivered at New York University's conference on Famine and World Hunger, 1995.

an ancient nation stricken down by a war more ruthless and sanguinary than any seven years war, or thirty years war, that Europe ever saw. No sack of Magdeburg, or ravage of the Palatinate, ever approached in horror and desolation to the slaughters done in Ireland by mere official red tape and stationery, and the principles of political economy.

Writing a hundred years later, the great historian A. J. P. Taylor echoed the core of truth that lay behind Mitchel's hyperbole – looking at the ideologically driven nature of the prime minister, the chancellor and the secretary to the Treasury, which blinded them to all human considerations, Taylor states: 'Russell, Wood and Trevelyan were highly conscientious men . . . [but] they were gripped by the most horrible, and perhaps the most universal of human maladies: the belief that principles and doctrines are more important than lives. They imagined that rules, invented by economists, were as "natural" as the potato blight.'

Sir Charles Trevelyan, the powerful assistant secretary to the Treasury from 1840 to 1859, was fanatical in his belief in the economic orthodoxy of the day – laissez-faire capitalism and, above all, the Manchester School's principle of non-intervention in markets, *under any circumstances*. He wrote this statement in his book *The Irish Crisis*, published in 1848 – in which human sympathy for the victims in Ireland is non-existent – attempting to justify the British government's response to the Famine: 'It has been proved . . . that local distress cannot be relieved out of national funds without great abuses and evils, tending, by a direct and rapid process, to an entire disorganisation of society.'

If we understand the extremity of this mindset, then we will realise why there were no attempts to ban the export of food from Ireland during the Famine years, nor would substantial funds from the British Treasury be forthcoming to feed the starving of the neighbouring island. Instead of sending food, 'Trevelyan sent his subordinates to Ireland equipped with Adam Smith's writings, like missionaries sent to barbarian lands armed with bibles.'

Much of the subsequent debate relating to what today could be called the 'perpetrators' of the Irish Famine circle around the question of intentionality. To what extent did the British government in London simply see the Famine in Ireland as a 'Visitation of Providence, an expression of divine displeasure' with that island, 'a direct stroke of an all-wise and all-merciful Providence' as Trevelyan had written? And such a belief in Providentialism could be seen as a justification for minimal intervention – Trevelyan believed that God had 'sent the calamity to teach the Irish a lesson . . . it must not be too much mitigated.' Or did the British government want to go even further, and realise it was an opportunity to deliberately reduce the population of a country they saw as poor, backward, Catholic and immoral? Mitchel undoubtedly believed the latter was the case – and, to use today's terminology, would have considered Britain's response to be 'genocidal' ('the intent to destroy, in whole or in part, a national, ethnical, racial or religious group'.)

Arguments have raged over this particular question over the last decades. There were certainly aspects of the British government's behaviour which appear to prove intent to cause harm – the most striking of these being the infamous Gregory clause, the 1847 amendment to the Poor Law passed in the House of Commons, which meant that any family holding more than a quarter of an acre of land could not be granted relief, either in, or outside, the workhouse, until they gave up their land. Peter Gray has described this as 'a charter for land clearance', and Canon John O'Rourke wrote, after the Famine, of the Gregory clause: 'a more complete engine for the slaughter and expatriation of a people was never designed'. It is estimated that up to 100,000 families were forcibly evicted from their land and homes as a result, often with fatal consequences. James Donnelly has described the impact of this law as being so 'serious that they give plausibility to charges (then and later) that there was genocidal intent at work'.

The effects of the land clearances were certainly devastating to the traditional rural pattern of agricultural smallholdings in Ireland – the so-called 'cottier' class. Between 1845 and 1851, owners of

THE VIOLENCE OF MY COUNTRY

smallholdings under five acres halved – from 181,950 to 88,083, and those owning over fifteen acres reduced from 276,618 to 90,401. All of this led to massive loss of population, not only in the south and west of Ireland – County Clare lost 42 per cent of its farms between 1847 and 1853 – but also in east Connaught and south Ulster. It is certainly true to say that this was all part of a wider strategy by the British government to fundamentally change the land ownership and agriculture of a colony that Whitehall regarded as backward and full of 'social evils', and to do this regardless of the human cost – but to move from this to suggesting that most figures in the British government wanted the entire elimination of the rural Irish people is to overstate the case. Having said this, I would also dispute the statement of the economic historian Cormac O'Grada that 'nobody wanted the extirpation of the Irish as a race'[*] – there were certainly some fanatical zealots within senior British positions who wanted the most extreme measures taken. For example, the prominent economist and government advisor Nassau William Senior said at the beginning of the Famine in 1845 that he 'feared that the famine . . . would not kill more than a million people, and that would scarcely be enough to do much good'.

And we know, from a letter Lord John Russell (who had been prime minister at the beginning of the Famine) wrote in 1868, that this was not an isolated opinion:

> Many years ago the Political Economy Club of London, came . . . to a resolution that the emigration of two million of the population of Ireland would be the best cure for her social evils. Famine and emigration have accomplished a task beyond the reach of legislation or government.[†]

Regardless of the rights and wrongs of the debate around the genocidal intent, or not, of senior British political figures and advisors, it is fascinating that Mitchel's original charge that Britain had

---

[*] From *Ireland Before and After the Famine* by Cormac O'Grada.

[†] From 'A Letter to Rt Hon. Chichester Fortescue MP on the State of Ireland', 1868.

intentionally let the Famine kill a million people is still current. No doubt he would have been delighted to learn that in October 1996, the New York State legislature ruled that 'The Famine Curriculum' must include a unit on the Irish Famine as an act of genocide to be taught in all schools in New York State and New Jersey. He would also have welcomed Tim Pat Coogan's recent work, *The Famine Plot: England's Role in Ireland's Greatest Tragedy*, in which Coogan explicitly calls the Famine 'genocide' and criticises many other Irish historians, over the years, for being revisionists who have attempted to sanitise this story. In the final chapter, Coogan looks compellingly at the cultural context in which the British perpetrators lived – the remarkable level of extreme racism towards the Irish, the portrayals in popular magazines such as *Punch* of the Irish as grinning monkeys, always plotting against the English. This, for instance, appeared in an essay in *Punch* in 1862, 'The Missing Link':

> A creature manifestly between the gorilla and the negro is to be met in some of the lowest districts of London and Liverpool – by adventurous explorers. It comes from Ireland, whence it has contrived to migrate. It belongs in fact to a tribe of Irish savages: the lowest species of Irish Yahoo. When conversing with its kind it talks a sort of gibberish. It is, moreover, a climbing animal, and may sometimes be seen ascending a ladder laden with a hod of bricks.

All of which contributed to a climate of dehumanisation which subsequently allowed a million people to die on a neighbouring island – because they were no longer seen as human beings. Such characterisations were by no means restricted to the popular culture of the time; the Oxford historian J. A. Froude in 1842 described the Irish as 'more like tribes of squalid apes than human beings'. And, similarly, in a telling link between the Tasmanian genocide and the Irish Famine, Trevelyan uses the word 'aboriginal' to describe the people of Ireland – a shorthand, in Victorian terms, for an animal halfway between an ape and a human being. In 1860, only a few years after the Famine, Charles Kingsley, the cleric, writer and historian, who had just been made chaplain to Queen Victoria at the time, on a visit to Ireland, wrote to his wife: 'I am haunted by the human chimpanzees I saw along that hundred miles of horrible country . . . to see white chimpanzees is dreadful, if they were black, one would not feel it so much, but their skins, except where tanned by exposure, are as white as ours.'*

Given Mitchel's explosive interventions, in the remainder of the nineteenth century and most of the twentieth century, it is remarkable how few concerted efforts there were to write serious critical histories regarding the Famine. It was as if generations of Irish historians had been scared off the subject. For much of the last century the debate polarised around only two works – both of them significantly flawed. *The Great Famine: Studies in Irish History*, a collection of essays edited by Robert Dudley Edwards and Thomas Desmond Williams, two Irish historians, was published in 1956, but was seen by many commentators as letting the British off the hook – O'Grada feels that it lacked 'coherence and fairness' and that in essence it made 'excuses for the attitudes of British bureaucrats and politicians'. It also was widely criticised for its dryness – 'dehydrated history' – for its overemphasis on the administrative aspects of the Famine, and lack of attention to the testimonies of human suffering.

Six years later, Cecil Woodham-Smith published her bestseller – the product of over a decade of detailed research, *The Great Hunger: Ireland 1845–49*, but though popular with nationalists for placing the blame for the Famine firmly at Britain's door once again, some criticised it for being too emotional and passionate. (Though Colm Tóibín sees enduring strengths in her approach: 'Her work is readable – something which later historians of the Famine have tried hard not to be. If she relies too much on the study of personalities, her command of detail, her insistence on the cruelty of those in charge and the misery of those who suffered, and her ability to structure the narrative, account for the book's extraordinary impact.')

---

* Quoted in *Postcolonial Borderlands: Orality and Irish Traveller Writing* by Christine Walsh.

But, putting these two works aside, the paucity of historical attention paid to the Famine for most of the twentieth century is striking. It is remarkable that, as the historian James Donnelly observed in 2001, in the fifty years between 1938 and 1988, the journal *Irish Historical Studies* published only five articles about the Famine. Only since the 1990s, prompted by the 150th anniversary commemorations, has there been a growing debate, and far more publications, on the Famine, its causes and legacies. Indeed, historian Christine Kinealy has stated that 'more has been written to commemorate the 150th anniversary of the Great Famine than was written in the whole period since 1850.'[*]

Cormac O'Grada, perhaps fairly, accounts for the nervousness of Irish historians to really confront the Famine until relatively recently as being due to the fact that they are generally 'a conservative bunch', and notes, with a trace of sadness, 'there are no Irish E. P. Thompsons.'[†] He has also written of the fear of being associated with terrorism, if you too strongly emphasise the crimes of the British state, saying that Robert Kee's groundbreaking series *Ireland: A Television History* broadcast in 1980, though warmly received internationally, was criticised by some in Ireland 'for lending succour to terrorism'. Kinealy made the same point herself but more explicitly, writing in 1997 that Irish historians have enforced a 'self-imposed censorship' for fear of providing 'ideological bullets to the IRA'.[‡]

But something began to shift in the 1990s that at last enabled a more honest and vigorous national debate to take place. Some of this movement is attributable to the aforementioned 150th anniversary of the Famine, some of the unblocking is no doubt connected to the years culminating in the Good Friday Agreement of April 1998. These moments in a country's development are seismic; at certain times there are windows, often relatively brief, when exceptional change becomes possible. And such change is no respecter of frontiers or

---

[*] Quoted in 'Historians and the Famine: a Beleaguered Species', *Irish Historical Studies* Vol. 30 (1997).

[†] O'Grada's comments are taken from *Ireland Before and After the Famine: Explorations in Economic History, 1800–1925*.

[‡] From *A Death-Dealing Famine: The Great Hunger in Ireland* by Christine Kinealy.

borders. It may begin in one country, but the effects of the breaking of silence soon fall like waves lapping over neighbouring countries.

At a concert in Cork (promoted with the jarring phrase 'The Great Famine Event') on 1 June 1997, part of the 150th anniversary commemoration, the British government began to publicly acknowledge its role in the Famine for the first time. To the amazement of the 15,000 people at the concert, the actor Gabriel Byrne read out a statement by the newly elected British prime minister, Tony Blair:

> I am glad to have this opportunity to join with you in commemorating all those who suffered and died during the Great Irish Famine . . . The Famine was a defining event in the history of Ireland and of Britain. It has left deep scars. That one million people should have died in what was then part of the richest and most powerful nation in the world is something that still causes pain as we reflect on it today. Those who governed in London at the time failed their people through standing by while a crop failure turned into a massive human tragedy. We must not forget such a dreadful event.

This has sometimes, wrongly, been referred to as an 'apology' – but saying the British government of the time 'failed' and recognising the 'massive human tragedy' that followed is not the same as apologising, or indeed accepting full responsibility on behalf of the country. Blair, with his barrister's background, would have understood the legal ramifications of a full apology, and also the financial and reparations claims that could, potentially, have followed, even 150 years after the event. But putting such considerations to one side, these words were still hugely significant. It is worth remembering that at this time the Good Friday Agreement was still ten months away, peace in Northern Ireland was far from assured, the IRA had not yet renewed the 1994 ceasefire. This statement played a key role in reassuring the Irish people that the British state wasn't locked in the past, that there was a real possibility of movement. Words about the past helped to create trust in the present, and this trust led to hope for a shared future – all gradually leading to a full ceasefire and the agreement which was signed between Britain and Ireland on Friday, 10 April 1998. The breaking of a historical silence contributed to a remarkable political change.

*

May in the west of Wales. The lanes here are bursting with the dark pinks of campion, rich buttercup yellows and wildly frothing bouquets of white cow parsley which reach out, falling forwards, tapping the car as it passes. And, here and there, still patches of blue-bells, creating a kind of purple haze in the dappled sunlight of early evening. Most days now, turning down a lane or walking up a track, I see hares ahead of me. And always then the same game. I pause. The hare pretends not to have noticed me, but then starts to lollop off the other way, with that curious, almost clumsy, looping move-ment. I follow on. The hare reaches a gap in the hedge or a gate, and then it's off. No awkwardness of movement now, as it stretches out over the grass. Always thrilling to witness the instant acceleration of speed, the perfect elongation of the limbs as it cuts the field in two, sometimes alarming the young calves or lambs, unused to seeing anything moving with this kind of velocity. Only the tips of its tawny ears now visible, moving in the long grass, then gone.

I return to the lane that stretches down towards the sea, though it's sunk so deep in these parts that only gates and occasional gaps in the thorn hedges give glimpses of dark jade-green water ahead. The hawthorn blossom this year stops me in my tracks – a relay of curving, chalk clouds billowing all along the hedge, so unfeas-ibly white that laughter is the only response. I bury my head in the flowers, a sweetness of vanilla, but something acidic too I can't quite place. Five-petalled flowers, the white underlain by veins of lightest green, almost imperceptible. Rings of tiny black pinprick stamens I've never noticed before.

From the high cliffs on the coast here, on rare days of extreme atmospheric clarity, you can sometimes see the coast of Ireland, and even make out the distant hills of Wicklow etched across the sea. Walking here, from time to time, my phone bleeps an incoming text which always makes me smile wryly at the incompetence of the technology we've been told is so intelligent – *'Welcome to Ireland! You're on our travel package, so don't forget to . . .'* But it's quiet on the coast path today, as usual I'm walking an hour or so before dusk, and a haze of milky cloud has covered the sun. There's a closeness in the air this evening, very distant rumbles of thunder. Almost no wind at all. I feel uneasy, as if the charged ions in the atmosphere are affecting my brain. I want the thunder to get louder, and the rain to rush in sheets of relief, after the week or so of intense late-spring heat we've had here.

Something haunts me about the Famine, and I can't quite put my finger on it. No, actually, more than one thing, but I'll begin with this – how few names there are of those who lived and died. How the vast majority of the accounts, even the eyewitness ones from the 1840s, tend to generalise and collectivise the victims. *People are not named.* Although the accounts are terrifying, sometimes traumatic, often you're unable to see the particular child or the individual woman or man who suffered. And yet, often the witnesses *are* named, so paradoxically, they live in our imaginations in a way that the people they are describing cannot. Could this perhaps explain what at times seems like the *abstract* nature of the Famine? I think about the testimony I've been able to find. I sit on a hummock of grass high above the incoming tide, and read again the sheets I've printed out, the accounts in chronological order as the starvation intensified.

William Forster, a Quaker, saw this in 1846:

> *The children were like skeletons, their features sharpened with hunger and their limbs wasted, so that there was little left but bones, their hands and arms, in particular, being much emaciated, and the happy expression of infancy gone from their faces, leaving the anxious look of premature old age.*

Major Parker, a Relief Inspector of the Board of Works, saw this, also in December 1846:

A woman with a dead child in her arms was begging in the street yesterday and the Guard of the Mail told me he saw a man and three dead children lying by the roadside . . . nothing can exceed the deplorable state of this place . . . On Saturday, notwithstanding all this distress, there was a market plentifully supplied with meat, bread, fish, in short everything.

Asenath Nicholson, an American teacher and writer who spent two years travelling through famine-stricken Ireland and published her account in 1850, saw this in Dun Laoghaire:

Reader, if you have never seen a starving being, may you never! In my childhood I had been frighted with the stories of ghosts, and had seen actual skeletons; but imagination had come short of the sight of this man . . . emaciated to the last degree; he was tall, his eyes prominent, his skin shrivelled, his manner cringing and childlike; and the impression then and there made never has nor ever can be effaced.

Later, at Arranmore in Donegal, she describes entering a cabin and seeing a family, or what was left of a family:

They stood up before us in a speechless, vacant, staring, stupid, yet most eloquent posture, mutely, graphically saying: 'Here we are, your bone and your flesh, made in God's image like you. Look at us! What brought us here?' . . . when we entered they saluted us by crawling on all fours towards us, and trying to give some token of welcome.

The *Telegraph* newspaper described this scene from Castlebar in County Mayo, in February 1847:

A few days ago I entered a miserable cabin, dug out of the bog; a poor woman sat, propped against the wall inside; the stench was intolerable, and on my complaining of it the mother pointed to a sort of square bed in one corner; it contained the putrid –

the absolutely melted away remains of her eldest son. On inquiry why she did not bury it, she assigned two reasons; first, she had not the strength to go out and acquaint the neighbours; next, she waited till her other child would die, and they might bury both together.

The *United Irishman* newspaper reported an inquest held on 13 May 1848, which investigated why a deceased man's mouth was stained green:

A poor man, whose name we could not learn . . . lay down on the roadside, where shortly after he was found dead, his face turned to the earth, and a portion of the grass and turf on which he lay masticated in his mouth.

And finally, this anonymous witness, with details so precise that they sear themselves into the mind:

Starvation had affected the children's bones, the jawbone was so fragile and thin that a very slight pressure would force the tongue into the roof of the mouth. In Skibbereen I met children with jaws so distended that they could not speak. In Mayo the starving children had lost their voices, many were in a stupor character-istic of death by starvation. Yet I never heard a single child utter a cry or moan of pain. In the very act of death still not a tear nor a cry. I have scarcely seen one try to change his or her position. Two, three or four in a bed, there they lie and die, if suffering still, ever silent, unmoved. *

As I reread these words I'm assailed by more questions and doubts. I'm unsure about the ability of language to communicate some real-ities. I wonder if we've been approaching this particular catastrophe

---

* Some of these eyewitness accounts come from the 'Ireland Program: Eyewitness Accounts of the Famine'; Nicholson's is taken from 'The Female Gaze: Asenath Nicholson's Famine Narrative' by Margaret Kelleher in *Fearful Realities*, edited by Chris Morash and Richard Hayes; the last in *Socialist Review*, September 1995.

in the wrong way. Has almost everything written about the Famine eluded the grasp of those writing? The silence of those starving, their unheard speech, is incomprehensible. As is the proximity of the starving to their well-fed fellow citizens, a few dozen miles away in Dublin and Bristol and London.

It seems to me that the focus on the historical arguments about *how* the Famine has been represented in history is actually a way of avoiding facing the terror at the heart of the event. (Though this begs the wider question of whether it is ever really possible to represent trauma.) I remember something that the historian Brendan Bradshaw wrote, which touches on this: 'the trauma of the famine reveals, perhaps more tellingly than any other episode of Irish history, the inability of practitioners of value-free history to cope with the catastrophic dimensions of the Irish past.' In the same essay he questions an entire approach to Irish history which he feels had always valued academic dryness over emotional and moral responses, and he concludes by making this exceptionally powerful argument – Mary Daly's strategy, like others who've written about the Famine, he asserts, is to distance herself and her readers from its stark reality: 'by assuming an austerely clinical tone, as befitting academic discourse, and by resort to sociological euphemism . . . thus *cerebralising, and thereby desensitising the trauma*' [my emphasis]. This approach is dangerous, Bradshaw argues, because it 'denies the historian recourse to value judgements and, therefore, access to the moral and emotional register necessary to respond to human tragedy.'[*]

But the aspect that Bradshaw touches on here surely goes far beyond the issue of historical representation. It raises the question of whether historiography is capable at all of communicating the reality of traumatic events; perhaps we need to look to other disciplines, other forms of representation, to truly understand cataclysmic events like starvation or genocide. I think here about the

---

* '*And So Began the Irish Nation*': *Nationality, Nationalism and National Conciousness in Pre-Modern Ireland* by Brendan Bradshaw.

way that Lanzmann's film *Shoah* radically affected our understanding of the Holocaust when it came out in 1985. A film which managed to achieve things that had eluded the most brilliant historians of that genocide for decades.

I climb higher on the path above the cliffs. Where the sea below is shadowed now it has changed to a slate grey-blue. I can just see the island three miles further round the coast, but beyond that now all is hazed. Another rumble of thunder far off, barely audible. A group of black birds are hunched on fence posts and rocks ahead of me just off the path. Too small for ravens, surely? I get closer, so near that I can see their curved, dark pinkish-red bills – choughs, eight of them, sitting in pairs, perfectly happy for me to share their space. Choughs that 'wing the midway air' at the end of *King Lear*, choughs the wild acrobats of the cliffs here, sometimes reminding me, as they fall vertically, thrillingly, pulling in their wings, of children, holding their knees, leaping, shrieking, into swimming pools. I walk on; the choughs slip off the cliffs as I go.

And suddenly something else comes to me – perhaps you've had the same thought – virtually all of the testimony concerning the Famine comes from eyewitnesses, from bystanders. The victims are viewed, the witness moves on and later writes down their account. This, again, creates an inevitable distancing, even in the most vivid accounts. Here, for instance, is a passage by Mitchel in *The Last Conquest of Ireland (Perhaps)*, describing what he sees from the windows of his mail-coach in 1847:

> In the depth of winter we travelled to Galway . . . and saw sights that will never wholly leave the eyes that beheld them: – cowering wretches, almost naked in the savage weather, prowling in turnip-fields, and endeavouring to grub up roots which had been left, but running to hide as the mail-coach rolled by . . . groups and families, sitting or wandering on the high-road, with failing steps and dim patient eyes, gazing hopelessly into infinite darkness . . . Sometimes I could see in front of the cot-

tages, little children leaning against the fence when the sun shone out – for they could not stand – their limbs fleshless, their bodies half naked, their faces bloated yet wrinkled, and of a pale greenish hue – children who would never, it was too plain, grow up to be men and women.

Again, even through Mitchel's sympathetic eyes, we have the collectivised groups of anonymous, suffering humanity – who, under the fleeting glance of the narrator, remain objectified, 'wretches' – unable to emerge as recognisable individuals, to be seen by us fully. In all that I have read on the Famine, I have not come across a single account *from a survivor themselves, in their own words,* whether written or transcribed.[*] This seems like a startling lacuna in Famine testimony. That there exists no equivalent of the electrifying testimony of Simon Srebnik, Abraham Bomba and Filip Müller in *Shoah* – those direct, unmediated voices. Or the words of a Primo Levi or an Otto Dov Kulka. It seems that there is no book, or lengthy account of the terror of the Famine, written from the perspective of one who survived. Curiously, this means that the Famine feels more distant from our times – not only compared to the Holocaust, but also to slavery, about which many powerful survivor accounts exist. This lack of words from the survivors' direct perspective creates huge imaginative challenges, not helped by other realities. In the 1840s, no visual or audio recording existed, and photography had barely been invented, so we have not a single photograph. Just those awful, generic pen-and-ink drawings, which you see reproduced wherever the Famine is written about.

What, then, if anything, can transmit to us today the real trauma of the Famine? Art? Theatre? Sculpture? Film? Possibly. Or perhaps we have to go to words and music; maybe they can take us closer? Poetry in particular seems to provide us with the rapid revelations of grief and pain that are beyond the reach of fiction. To read Patrick

---

[*] See chapter notes for more information on Cathal Póirtéir's work *Famine Echoes.*

Kavanagh's 'The Great Hunger' is a visceral experience. Though written in 1942, nearly a hundred years after the Famine, the event shadows the entire poem. It is as if his protagonist Patrick Maguire has internalised his ancestors' pain completely, the stony impulse to survive at all costs. We see him and his men moving like 'scare-crows' over the potato field at the opening of the poem, and at the end, many years later, after another October harvest has been brought in, we see him 'patting a potato-pit against the weather / An old man fondling a new-piled grave'. More than twenty years later, Seamus Heaney takes up Kavanagh's linkage in 'At a Potato Digging' – though now it's a mechanical digger that splits the soil, with the labourers swarming behind 'Like crows attacking crow-black fields'. Seeing the potatoes piled in pits takes Heaney straight back to 'Live skulls, blind-eyed, balanced on / wild higgledy skel-etons / scoured the land in 'forty-five / wolfed the blighted root and died'. Later, 'Mouths tightened in, eyes died hard / faces chilled to a plucked bird. / In a million wicker huts / beaks of famine snipped at guts'.

There are also remarkable poems by John Hewitt and Brendan Kennelly which more directly link to their ancestors. In 'The Scar' Hewitt transmits the memories of his great-grandmother, with an unforgettable image of an encounter during the Famine:

> There's not a chance now that I might recover
> one syllable of what that sick man said,
> tapping upon my great-grandmother's shutter,
> and begging, I was told, a piece of bread;
> for on his tainted breath there hung infection
> rank from the cabins on the stricken west,
> the spores from black potato-stalks, the spittle
> mottled with poison in his rattling chest.

In 'My Dark Fathers' Kennelly contrasts the sounds and images of music and dance with the silences that fell 'when winds of hunger howled at every door':

Skeletoned in darkness, my dark fathers lay
Unknown, and could not understand
The giant grief that trampled night and day.

In her brilliant work 'That the Science of Cartography is Limited', Eavan Boland takes us to the emptiness and erasure of the 'famine roads' (the 'public works' projects that the British attempted to create – as an insane way of paying starving labourers, so as not to give them famine relief, with nothing in return). Boland describes coming to a wood, on the edge of Connacht, and her partner speaking:

Look down you said: this was once a famine road.
I looked down at ivy and the scutch grass
rough-cast stone had
disappeared into as you told me
in the second winter of their ordeal, in
1847, when the crop had failed twice,
Relief Committees gave
The starving Irish such roads to build.
Where they died, there the road ended
And ends still.

The musician and singer Christy Moore incants in a repeated, soft, howl what happened on 'A Single Day' in Ireland – 14 September 1847, at the height of the Famine. On that day, as thousands of people lay starving, ships sailed out of Cork Harbour with

147 barrels of pork,
986 casks of ham,
27 sacks of bacon,
528 boxes of eggs,
1,397 firkins of butter,
477 sacks of oats,
720 sacks of flour,
380 sacks of barley,

187 head of cattle,
296 head of sheep,
and 4,338 barrels of miscellaneous provisions
– *on a single day.*

And on this same day, in the capital city on the other side of the island, away from the starvation and disease:

The Lady Mayoress held a ball
At the Mansion House in Dublin
In the presence of the Lord Lieutenant of Ireland.
Dancing continued until the early hours,
And refreshments of the most varied and sumptuous
Nature were supplied with inexhaustible profusion.
On a single day.

Desmond Egan, in his 1997 collection *Famine*, looks at the legacy of the Famine in Ireland today – the vital question of how such an event continues to shape the people and culture now. And he reflects on the taboos it has left, particularly that of shame, of behaviour that cannot be spoken of:

The stink of famine
hangs in the bushes still
in the sad celtic hedges

you can catch it
down the line of our landscape
get its taste on every meal

listen
there is famine in our music

famine behind our faces

it is only a field away
has made us all immigrants
guilty for having survived

has separated us from language
cut us from our culture
built blocks around belief

left us on our own

The sun has sunk into the sea, blurred by low cloud, only another half an hour or so of light. I walk to the path that leads back inland, Egan's words still in my head. That sense of erasure, being cut off from the land, from your culture. And how all Irish people alive today only exist because their ancestors somehow survived. But the multitude of different experiences that the word 'survived' encompasses . . .

*

Back at the house now, dark outside, I light the stove and return to Colm Tóibín's powerful essay on the Famine, 'Erasures', published in the *London Review of Books*. I'm intrigued this evening by what he writes about this particular question of survival, and its meaning; he seems to be striking at the heart of a taboo in nationalist portrayals of the Famine, when he says 'an entire class of Irish Catholics survived the Famine; many, indeed, improved their prospects as a result of it, and this legacy may be more difficult for us to deal with in Ireland now than the legacy of those who died or emigrated'. He then details his father's own local research in his home town, where he discovered the workhouse was buying oatmeal at £2 a ton in October 1845, by the winter that had doubled to £4 a ton, and by the end of 1846 it was £20 a ton. Some Catholic farmers and traders had made a killing out of the Famine years – literally and metaphorically. Tóibín then makes this point, which shouldn't be seen as taking away British responsibility, but rather spreading the responsibility in a way that reflects the reality of what took place:

It became increasingly important, as nationalist fervour grew in the years after the Famine, that Catholic Ireland, or simply 'Ireland' (the Catholic part went without saying), was presented as a nation, one and indivisible. The Famine, then, had to be blamed on the Great Other, the enemy across the water, and the victims of the Famine had to be this entire Irish nation, rather than a vulnerable section of the population.

And the ways that people survived were often as terrible as the ways that people died. All across the south and west and north of Ireland, parents had to make choices about which of their children might live, and which would die. Fathers and mothers chose to stop eating so that their children might have the little food left. In thousands of cottages, families who had barely enough for their own survival bolted their doors when they saw starving strangers, sometimes even their own relatives, coming up the tracks. Dying people littered the sides of roads, some crawling into graveyards so that they would at least die on consecrated land, corpses were often unburied, neighbours were found skeletal in their beds, having 'turned their faces to the wall'. These were the memories that people lived with afterwards, memories that carved themselves into the minds of survivors, but could hardly be spoken of. Your family had only survived because others had starved. This left a legacy of shame, as well as anger, in the Irish psyche which it is hard to overstate. 'The shame . . . that the just man experiences at another man's crime: the feeling of guilt that such a crime should exist.'

Another man's crime. More than a million human beings dying not because of anything they had done wrong, and supposedly part of the 'commonwealth', part of 'Great Britain'! This is the aspect my brain still cannot process, this is why an inchoate rage builds in me. Everything I've grown up with, everything I've been taught, tells me that you cannot write like this, you must be 'measured', you must be calm. No. Not this time. Not about this. In Trevelyan's account of the 'Irish Crisis', as he called it, the famine ended in August 1847.[*] In reality, the winter of 1847/8 was one of the most terrible periods for starvation and deaths, but Trevelyan had decided in autumn 1847 that the British 'relief' efforts should be wound down. The soup kitchens were closed, with

---

[*] This and the following material is from Robert Kee's *Ireland: A Television History* (1980), Episode Four, BBC in association with Radio Telefis Eireann.

millions still destitute and starving. Even in the workhouses thousands were dying – in Limerick workhouse alone 130 people were dying every week that autumn. But Trevelyan had had enough – in his chilling phrase it was time to let 'the operation of natural causes' take effect: 'It is my opinion that too much has been done for the people. Under such treatment people have grown worse instead of better.'

And then he set off for France for a fortnight's holiday with his family. He was knighted by Queen Victoria the following year, on 27 April 1848, in recognition for his 'services' during the 'Irish Crisis', and was rewarded financially as well, with the payment of a year's extra salary for services rendered to the Crown and empire. A little later, with the Famine still raging, an editorial in the *Dublin Freeman's Journal* asked these three questions:

- Is it not possible to continue some means of saving the people from this painful, lingering process of death from starvation?
- Do we live under a regular or responsible government?
- Is there justice or humanity in the world that such things could be in the middle of the nineteenth century, and within twelve hours reach of the opulence, grandeur and power of a court and capital – the first upon the earth?

*

Finally, I'd like to walk along the corridors and look inside the rooms of Trevelyan's Treasury, the Foreign Office and Downing Street during the years of the Famine. Barely 200 miles from where families were starving to death. As far from Whitehall, as the crow flies, as the city of York. Can you visualise all the letters written from those offices, and the hundreds of memoranda exchanged between Trevelyan and Peel and Russell and Wood? All the judgements made in these grand, panelled rooms with portraits staring down on these statesmen, all the decisions signed off on government paper, stamped with government seals. All the deaths authorised from those mahogany desks in Whitehall. And how to even begin to quantify the devastation caused by the Manchester School of political economy? Those whose savage belief in the non-intervention of the state is summed up in Nassau William Senior's phrase that a million deaths would 'scarcely be enough to do much good'.

I can see Trevelyan quite clearly, writing in his ornate office at the Treasury, looking over King Charles Street towards the domes of the Foreign Office, dipping his quill into the ink. It's 9 October 1846, the second year of the Famine is beginning. It's quite clear that hundreds of thousands are now threatened by starvation. He is replying to his colleague Lord Monteagle, a prominent landowner in Limerick (and a former Chancellor of the Exchequer), who had written to him raising his concerns about the extent of this second year of almost total potato blight, and asking the assistant secretary to the Treasury for greater government intervention. Trevelyan pauses to consider how to express his views on the crisis across the water, and then writes this:

> I think I see a bright light shining in the distance through the dark cloud which at present hangs over Ireland . . . The deep and inveterate root of social evil remains, [but] I hope I am not guilty of irreverence in thinking that . . . the cure has been applied by the direct stroke of an all-wise Providence in a manner as unexpected and unthought as it is likely to be effectual.*

---

* Quoted in *The Irish Famine: A Documentary History* by Noel Kissane.

This was not only his private opinion, casually written in a letter to a colleague; he expressed almost exactly the same sentiment at the opening of his work *The Irish Crisis* in 1848, proclaiming publicly that 'Supreme Wisdom has educed permanent good out of transient evil.'[*]

How is it possible for us today to explain what appears like Trevelyan's psychopathic coldness towards a starving population? His view that hundreds of thousands of dead was, to use a later politician's phrasing, 'a price worth paying'? In his mind he had already dehumanised the Irish people, like so many of his fellow Victorians, influenced by the vicious propaganda in newspapers and magazines of the time, as we've already seen. Once the mass of the population had been dehumanised, then a kind of repulsion could follow – they could be seen as 'monkeys' inhabiting disgusting 'hovels'. Clearances, evictions, destruction of cottages could then be seen as a method of pest control, a chance to sweep away the dirt and evil of such a society, to be replaced by a new order. The historian Jennifer Hart has perhaps come closer than many in getting to the core of Trevelyan's world view, his psyche:

> He regarded deaths by starvation as a 'discipline', a painful one, admittedly, but nevertheless a discipline, and he considered that they were a smaller evil than bankruptcy, for, through them, a greater good was to be obtained for Ireland and the British nation.[†]

We also need to consider the culture of racial supremacism which the British Empire inculcated in all its ruling parties – Britain, after all, had been chosen by Divine Providence to lead the world; this is why its empire was more extensive than any other power, why it held dominion over so much of the world.

---

[*] Published anonymously in the *Edinburgh Review*, Vol. 87, No. 175 (January 1848), titled 'The Irish Crisis', but subsequently published by Trevelyan as a book of the same title, later that year.

[†] 'Sir Charles Trevelyan at the Treasury' by Jennifer Hart, *English Historical Review* (1960).

Trevelyan's views, however extreme, were certainly not exceptional in Victorian culture. It would be a mistake to believe that policy towards the Irish Famine was dictated by only a coterie of ideological zealots; the reality was that the cultural framework which enabled the policy of non-intervention in Ireland to go ahead with such catastrophic consequences was established by a governing class consensus – a web of hundreds of economists, politicians, civil servants, clerics and journalists – all reinforcing each other's ideas into a lethal cocktail of race hatred, supremacism and laissez-faire capitalism. Trevelyan's view (from a letter quoted in Woodham-Smith, *The Great Hunger*), that 'the judgement of God sent the calamity to teach the Irish a lesson, that calamity should not be too much mitigated . . . the greatest evil with which we have to contend is not the physical evil of the famine but the moral evil of the selfish, perverse and turbulent character of the people' would have been shared by the vast majority of his contemporaries in the British government, Whitehall and Fleet Street. This, of course, is not to suggest that there weren't other voices, that there wasn't opposition to government policy on Ireland, just that, for the moment at least, these voices were in a minority.

*

At the height of the Famine at the end of November 1847, just as Trevelyan was writing his article for the *Edinburgh Review*, trying to defend British policy in Ireland, barely half a mile away from his Whitehall offices the recently formed Communist League was meeting for their second congress in an upstairs room at the Red Lion Hotel in Great Windmill Street, Soho. At this gathering, Karl Marx and Friedrich Engels, then twenty-nine and twenty-seven, were given the role of drawing up a programme for the league. In December 1847 and January 1848, they worked together writing *The Communist Manifesto*, which was first published in London on 21 February 1848. Marx viewed what was happening across the Irish Sea with horror, regarding 'the starving of Ireland into submission' as a key example of the European class struggle between

the bourgeoisie and the working class.[*] We also know from his later work that he continued to reflect on the Famine and its aftermath – this in a famous footnote in *Das Kapital*:

> the famine and its consequences have been deliberately made the worst of, both by the individual landlords and by the English legislature, to forcibly carry out the agricultural revolution and to thin the population of Ireland down to the proportion satisfactory to the landlords.[†]

He even references the cynicism of Nassau Senior, and goes on to quote from Senior's work *Journals, Conversations and Essays Relating to Ireland*:

> 'Well . . . we have got our Poor Law and it is a great instrument for giving the victory to the landlords. Another, and a still more powerful instrument is emigration . . . No friend to Ireland can wish the war to be prolonged [between the landlords and the small Celtic farmers] – still less, that it should end by

---

[*] From opening of 'Wage, Labour and Capital', based on lectures Marx had given in December 1847.

[†] *Das Kapital*, Chapter Twenty-five, 'The General Law of Capitalist Accumulation', n. 141.

the victory of the tenants. The sooner it is over – the sooner Ireland becomes a grazing country, with the comparatively thin population which a grazing country requires, the better for all classes.'

In fact, Marx devotes an entire section in this chapter to the exploitation of Ireland, not only providing a remarkably detailed picture of changes in land ownership and profits to landlords, but also a witheringly ironic and angry attack on how the Irish people had been treated – remarking in a Swiftian aside: 'The Irish famine of 1846 killed more than 1,000,000 people, but it killed poor devils only' – leaving the wealth intact for landlords to benefit from. His portrait of Ireland bristles with anger, describing the living conditions of agricultural labourers there in the 1840s as of a 'hideousness [which] far surpasses the worst that English agricultural labourers' experience'. He quotes an inspector in 1861 saying that the housing conditions 'are a disgrace to the Christianity and to the civilisation of this country'. After the Famine and the 'agricultural revolution' that followed, 'many labourers were compelled to seek shelter in villages and towns. There they were thrown like refuse into garrets, holes, cellars and corners, in the worst back slums.'

In a powerful passage, Marx details the relentlessness and grinding poverty of an Irish factory worker's life – seventeen-hour working days, twelve hours on Saturdays, for ten shillings sixpence a week. This to feed a family of five children – their diet is mainly oatmeal, supplemented by a few potatoes in the summer. At the end of this section he simply reflects, 'Such are Irish wages, such is Irish life!' He then contrasts this existence with the vast profits made by 'land magnates' in Ireland such as Lord Dufferin – pocketing millions of pounds in rent from 'the people's misery'. Marx came to understand that the real legacy of the Famine was the permanent destruction of an entire class of small, agricultural labourers in Ireland to the benefit of the colonial masters. The English aristocracy and bourgeoise, he wrote, had a

common interest . . . in turning Ireland into mere pasture land which provides the English market with meat and wool at the cheapest possible prices. It is likewise interested in reducing the Irish population by eviction and forcible emigration, to such a small number that English capital . . . can function there with 'security'.*

He would have been fascinated, but probably not at all surprised, if he had known what Trevelyan had previously written about British strategy in Ireland in strikingly similar terms, in a letter to Edward Twisleton, chief Poor Law commissioner there:

> I do not know how farms are to be consolidated if small farmers do not emigrate . . . we should be defaulting at our own object . . . If small farmers go, and their landlords are reduced to sell portions of their estates to persons who will invest capital we shall at last arrive at something like a satisfactory settlement of the country.†

Sir Charles Wood, at that time Chancellor of the Exchequer, shared this view, suggesting that more vigorous enforcement of rates payments should be adopted, in order that 'the pressure will lead to some emigrating . . . what we really want to obtain is a clearance of small farms'.‡

We should understand that such views were not universal among the British government and those working to deliver policy on the ground. In fact Edward Twistleton, who as Poor Law commissioner during the first years of the Famine had to witness many of the dire consequences of government policy, is a case in point. He was one of the few to emerge with some real moral integrity from these years. In March 1849, after many arguments with Trevelyan, he finally resigned, writing an explosive open letter to the assistant secretary at the Treasury and the British government as a whole, castigating them for their policy towards Ireland. He argued that the destitution

---

* From a letter to Sigfrid Meyer and August Vogt, 9 April 1870.

† Quoted in *The Great Calamity: The Irish Famine 1845–52* by Christine Kinealy.

‡ Ibid.

of the Irish people was the fault of the British government, that their policy of 'famine relief' had become a policy of extermination rather than salvation, and ended by saying he was not prepared to play the part of executioner any more – Britain's handling of Ireland was 'a deep disgrace'. As a final broadside, clearly aimed at Trevelyan, he wrote:

> here are individuals of even superior minds who now seem to me to have steeled their hearts entirely to the sufferings of the people of Ireland . . . It is said that the law of nature is that those persons should die . . . now my feeling is . . . wholly the contrary: that it is part of . . . nature that we should have feelings of compassion for those people, and that it is a most narrow-minded view of the system of nature that these people should be left to die.[*]

Even Lord Clarendon, Lord Lieutenant of Ireland, was forced to concede much of the substance of Twistleton's attack, writing to Prime Minister Lord Russell on 26 April 1849: 'I don't think there is another legislature in Europe that would disregard such suffering as now exists in the west of Ireland, or coldly persist in a policy of extermination.'[†]

*

In all that has been written about the Irish Famine and Trevelyan's role in it, too little attention has been paid to one remarkable episode. And it is an episode that goes to the heart of how desk killers are able to function and how they can continue to do their work. I had assumed that, as a senior civil servant at the Treasury, Trevelyan would have been desk-bound, needing to be in Whitehall all the time – just as Mitchel had written, as the Famine was raging, 'Lord John Russell sat safe in Chesham Place; and the grand commissioner

---

[*] Quoted in *All Standing: The Remarkable Story of the Jeanie Johnston, the Legendary Irish Famine Ship* by Kathryn Miles.

[†] From *A Death-Dealing Famine* by Christine Kinealy.

of the pauper system wove his webs of red tape around them from afar!' But I've recently discovered that Trevelyan did make a single trip to Ireland – to Dublin, at the height of the Famine in October 1847. But, tellingly, he didn't travel outside the capital, the place most sheltered from the impacts of the Famine, so he didn't see any of rural Ireland, where the starvation and disease was at its worst.

He stayed at the Salt Hill Hotel in Dublin, where he wrote to a priest acquaintance, Father Mathew, 'I have come to Dublin for a few days in the prosecution of my labours in the cause of old Ireland.'* We have to remind ourselves here that Trevelyan officially believed the Famine was 'over' by August 1847, and so had ordered the closing down of the soup kitchens across the country. So, what he then did in Dublin is even more baffling. On 7 October, he wrote a personal letter to *The Times* from his hotel, publicising to readers in Britain that there was going to be a national collection in all churches the following Sunday to help 'the unhappy people in the western districts of Ireland, who will again perish by the thousands this year if they are not relieved'. This, from the same man who apparently believed the Famine was 'over'! The man responsible for co-ordinating the government relief strategy is now begging for charitable donations! But, if you think this letter may have indicated a change of heart on Trevelyan's side, you would be wrong. Shortly afterwards he gave strict instructions that 'No assistance whatever will be given from national funds to unions who would help their own poor', and 'the collection of rates will be enforced . . . even in those distressed western unions'.

What is so striking about what Trevelyan writes in *The Times* is that we can detect an extremely rare expression of sentiment in what he says – those words 'unhappy people' and the choice of the expression 'perish by the thousands'. It is as if his almost sociopathic official persona is being challenged from within; as if, momentarily, Dr Jekyll has taken over from Mr Hyde. And suddenly, perhaps, we can guess why he realised he could not travel beyond Dublin – for if he came face to face with the consequences of his policies, if he saw the eyes

---

* Quoted in *Ireland: The Politics of Enmity 1789–2006* by Paul Bew.

of the starving, they would no longer be a collective mass of abstract Irish peasantry, they would be individual human beings who were suffering. They would move from being 'them' to 'him' or 'her'. And perhaps Trevelyan, deep down, knew he would not have been able to face that; today, we would say that his cognitive dissonance – his ability to continue holding contradictory moral positions – would no longer be able to function. Because here, fundamentally, was a man of duty, a man who strictly ordered his own feelings, regarded them with the suspicion he reserved for enemy forces. He was a man – in this particular respect – not dissimilar to Adolf Eichmann, who put all his energies into his official self, his work, most content behind his desk in Whitehall, issuing the orders in letters and memoranda which resulted in the deaths of a multitude of people he would never see. A man terrified of his own humanity. 'Remoteness from the suffering,' he once stated, 'kept his judgement more acute than that of his administrators actually working among the people affected.'*

Before we leave Ireland I have a final proposal for writers of history from now on, and it relates to the words which we use to describe the past. On 1 January 1801 the Acts of Union took effect, which united Great Britain with Ireland as a single state – the United Kingdom. The Parliament in Dublin was subsequently abolished, with 100 Irish MPs now sitting in the House of Commons. This constitutional state of affairs only ended with the creation of the Irish Free State in 1922. Therefore we must understand that when the Famine ravaged Ireland from 1845 to 1852, it happened *in* the United Kingdom. The policies which exacerbated the Famine were created in London, at the heart of the empire. The Poor Law commissioners were appointed by Whitehall. The army and police who carried out the clearances of cottages were paid out of British taxation. So, shouldn't we from now on start to use language which reflects these realties? The Famine was not Irish, it was British.† Our language needs to reflect this – we should begin to speak about 'the *British* Famine', or for those who want to be more precise, 'the British Famine – in Ireland'.

---

* See chapter notes for further thoughts on Trevelyan's behaviour.
† See notes for further reflections on the Famine's representation in British history.

PART FOUR

The Breaking of Silences

'What at one time one refuses to see never vanishes but returns again and again, in many forms.'

'Whenever a secret is kept it will make its way, like an object lighter than water and meant to float, to the surface.'

Susan Griffin

10

Moments of Seismic Shift:
7 December 1970, Warsaw;
2 June 2005, Belgrade;
14 August 2004, Okakarara;
14 July 2016, Berlin

Britain occupies a uniquely dangerous, and deluded, position in relation to its past. This is more than a question of silences at the heart of the British national narrative – the glaring gaps which I've written about in the preceding chapters are only part of the problem. Because not only do we come from a culture that has allowed genocide, slavery and mass killing to be done in its name – indeed which has benefited like no other country on the planet from systematic and extremely violent colonialism – we then have the temerity to pass moral judgements on other nations. Before we've even begun any serious process of re-examination of our own history. Look at British coverage of the Second World War and you will nearly always hear a combination of moral smugness (about ourselves) and rampant judgementalism (about others). The fact we have not been invaded for almost 1,000 years means that we have no conception at all of the moral chaos and dilemmas that such a situation brings. And so you have the familiar spectacle of British historians and writers and politicians disapproving of French collaboration, bemoaning Polish antisemitism and laughing at Italian fascism – all from a pedestal made from the most rotten materials. For do we *really* believe we would have behaved any differently?

This question seems to me the great value of Madeleine Bunting's 1995 book on the occupation of the Channel Islands, *The Model Occupation: The Channel Islands Under German Rule, 1940–1945* – which serves as a corrective to the myth that the British would have resisted more, collaborated less. That we wouldn't have allowed concentration camps in our midst. It is sobering to be reminded that over 1,000 people (primarily Russian slave labourers) died on Alderney between 1942 and 1945, 'the greatest mass murder which has ever occured on British soil', as Bunting rightly points out. And in a culture that is obsessed by two world wars and the importance of Remembrance Day, it is shocking to learn that these victims do not even have a proper memorial. This tells us a huge amount about our collective memory, and about our self-identity, the myths we want to keep intact, and the realities we want to avoid facing:

> Tangible evidence of the selectivity of the islanders' history is that there are no public memorials to the slave labourers . . . [This] leaves survivors like Otto Spehr baffled. In Germany, Spehr points out, the sites of SS camps have become carefully tended gardens of remembrance, often with well-funded museums and archives attached. But the site of the SS camp on Alderney is a wasteland covered with brambles. Spehr enlisted the help of Chancellor Willi Brandt, and the German government agreed to put up half the funding for a memorial on the site of Sylt, but Spehr claims Alderney refused to consider the idea.

She ends with these reflections on the selective memory of the islanders and how the past is seen:

> It is in their failure to remember and acknowledge those who were sacrificed . . . that the islanders must be judged. How can they belittle the suffering of the slave labourers? . . . How could Therese Steiner, Marianne Grunfeld and

Auguste Spitz[*] be forgotten for 40 years? . . . Only when there are exhibits in all the islands' museums to these people, and well-cared-for memorials and plaques in their memory, only when islanders talk as freely about the Jews as they do about how they made tea out of bramble leaves, will they have begun to tell the story of the Occupation.[†]

And, moving on to the post-war period, I have heard supposedly serious British historians argue that one of the reasons that Britain is less hated for its colonial legacy than some other countries was that after the Second World War it knew 'the game was up' and so divested itself of colonies 'with minimal violence'. Try telling that to the people of Kenya. In the early 1950s, Kenya was struggling for its independence and Britain responded with an extraordinary level of brutality, only beginning to be understood today. According to recent academic studies, more than 100,000 Kenyans were killed, some through shootings and beatings, many by slave labour – a programme of 'extermination through work' which the SS would have been proud of.[‡]

To give just a single example: the building of Nairobi's international airport at Embakasi between 1953 and 1958 cost many hundreds of lives through slave labour and exhaustion. The concentration camp for the slave labourers, next to the airport site, was dubbed 'Satan's Paradise' by the inmates. The historian Caroline Elkins relates that pressure to complete the building of the airport combined with 'the pervasive exterminationist attitude toward Mau Mau' created nightmarish conditions. 'Camp commandants . . . seemed to consider it their duty to work the convicts to death.' One eyewitness, Nyaga Ng'Endu, recounts what happened on a daily basis:

---

[*] The Jews deported to Auschwitz by the Channel Islands authorities, co-operating with the German occupation forces.

[†] Both quotations are from *The Model Occupation: The Channel Islands Under German Rule, 1940–1945* by Madeleine Bunting.

[‡] Figures from *Britain's Gulag: The Brutal End of Empire in Kenya* by Harvard historian Caroline Elkins, the fruit of a decade's research.

Every working detail had to have fifty prisoners. By noon of each working day up to six or seven prisoners had died. If a prisoner died it was the men in his group who would put his body onto the vehicle that would come round collecting the bodies.

Molly Wairimu, another witness:

The lorry would tip the bodies into a ditch and then drive off. If many people had died the lorries would come at ten in the morning and then at two in the afternoon. On days when not as many people had died only one lorry would come, but with bodies heaped to the top and with planks of wood along the sides to prevent them from falling off. They never used to bury the bodies, they were just dumped like logs until the ditch was full – higher than this house.[*]

The propaganda back in Britain in the early 1950s heavily emphasised the 'viciousness' of the Mau Mau guerrillas fighting the British settlers in Kenya, and the war against this 'evil' that Britain was fighting. It is true that around 100 British farmers and settlers were killed in this period, but the reprisals for these killings were out of all proportion – a thousand times greater. It was not just a matter of killings – the brutality of British treatment went beyond comprehension. Paul Muoka Nzili was imprisoned at Embakasi in 1957 and one day was pinned to the ground and castrated with pliers, by a certain Mr Dunman. In 2010 Nzili wrote, 'It took years for me to find any hope, but I have never really recovered from what was done to me at Embakasi on that day.'[†] And it is important to remember that this was happening only a dozen years after the Nuremberg

---

[*] Both testimonies from the BBC documentary *White Terror*, first broadcast in 2002.

[†] High Court Witness statement, *Nzili v. Foreign & Commonwealth Office*, 3 November 2010, as available on Leigh Day's website, www.leighday.co.uk. Many Kenyans are currently pursuing legal actions against the British government for torture inflicted on them during their struggle for independence. The government have already expressed their 'sincere regret' for the torture and suffering caused, but have yet to settle all the claims.

Trials, when Britain and the other Allies had prosecuted senior Nazis for what were rightly called 'crimes against humanity'.

Kenya – another void in the knowledge of our own history, centuries of colonial violence, like the Opium Wars, like Tasmania, like the British famines, in Ireland and Bengal – omissions which keep us in ignorance of our past, and so shame us in the present. And, in case you might think these questions are academic, or only about the past, consider for a moment the continuity of thought and behaviour that underlies centuries of such violence, and interventions in other countries by Britain, and how such behaviour continues today. Consider how the minds of our political leaders – in all parties – have been formed and then think about these men and women who thought that going to war in Iraq was the best way of resolving differences in the twenty-first century. Hundreds of thousands of people killed because men and women in countries far away believed that 'intervention' was justified. And such beliefs do not materialise out of thin air; they are formed from layers of accreted histories, laid down quite unconsciously, that begin to form national narratives, and are often left completely unchallenged.

*

So, how then are such silences in societies broken? How are these taboos, to return to Günter Grass's original challenge, finally voiced? In the last three chapters we have seen atrocities committed by Britain, Germany, France and the USA. These countries have each responded to their guilt primarily through silences, selective historical 'amnesias', differing according to the precise cultures of each society, yet all sharing certain features. Something strikes me strongly here, perhaps it also strikes you. The Holocaust came to be seen as shaming an entire society. It came to be viewed (except by a lunatic, racist fringe) as an unequivocally evil event that brought about near-universal condemnation of Germany by other countries around the world. Until it attempted to come to a kind of reckoning with its own history, Germany would not be welcomed in from the cold. Therefore, ultimately, there was pressure, both from within

671

the country and from outside, for the silence which descended after the war to be broken.

However, the British and American examples are starkly different because these societies have benefited enormously, and continue to do so, from the original acts of genocide, slavery and colonialism. To focus on Britain for a moment, and to look at just one of the sectors of its economy that has always been world-renowned – finance, banking and insurance, still today constituting 20 per cent of the economy and employing 3 million people in associated industries. Yet the majority of this sector, as we've already seen, gained its power from the Atlantic Triangle of trade, with slavery providing the central manpower and capital. Barclays, the Royal Bank of Scotland (both still in the world's top fifty financial institutions), Lloyd's of London, all springing directly from this trade in human cargo. HSBC (the fourteenth-largest financial institution in the world today) owes its origins to the East India Company and the massively lucrative opium trading that addicted millions in China. This unspoken policy of 'successful violence' has undeniably become part of the DNA of Britain and the USA.

And so, over centuries, patterns of thought and behaviour have been passed down, so that extreme levels of violence (usually taking place far away geographically – slavery, drug addiction, arms dealing, wars, 'free' trade) have become first tolerated and then normalised. Most significantly, the home populations of both countries have benefited economically from what we could call 'outsourced' violence. It is no coincidence that the USA and Britain have the largest weapons industries in the world, disproportionately large armies and (the USA at least) retain the ability to wage global wars. But this kind of violence is only the publicly visible tip of an iceberg. There is exceptional violence too in controlling the loaning of money from the World Bank or forcing islanders to leave their land so that airbases can be built (as in the case of the Pacific island of Diego Garcia), or extracting oil from some of the poorest countries on the planet.

It is worth considering the means by which such silences and denials are ended. For Germany the first stage in the process was military defeat in 1945. But of course the USA and Britain have not, yet, suffered such defeat. We have experienced no equivalent of the Nuremberg Trials, or denazification. Neither has there been the kind of conflict and internal reckoning within these countries that we saw after the break-up of apartheid South Africa. So there is no impetus to begin a process of truth and reconciliation. I wonder whether defeat, or some kind of complete national humiliation, is the only way for a society to truly start to look at itself. Perhaps such a sense of shared catastrophe enables an unblocking to take place, comparable to an individual coming through a breakdown. Suddenly a free space is created, momentarily unformed, inchoate (not unlike the instant immediately preceding revolutions), and into this space astonishing actions can take place.

Willy Brandt kneeling on the ground in Warsaw a generation after his country had annihilated that city and its people – an action so simple, yet it released an unprecedented wave of reflection and discussion. As his knees touched the stone before the Warsaw Ghetto Memorial on 7 December 1970, millions of Germans heard themselves speaking in a different way, their voices unlocked – an almost exact reverse of the process which Jacques Austerlitz undergoes as a refugee child: 'I could still apprehend the dying away of my native tongue, the faltering and fading sounds which I think lingered on in me at least for a while, like something shut up and scratching or knocking, something which, out of fear, stops its noise and falls silent whenever one tries to listen to it.'

The electrifying first moment of the breaking of a taboo, or the shuffling off of a shibboleth. The precise moment on 2 June 2005 when courageous television news producers in Belgrade, at RTS and B-92, took the decision to broadcast a film of Serbian paramilitaries, in July 1995, being blessed by an Orthodox priest just before they torture and shoot six young Muslim men in Srebrenica.[*] The soldiers can clearly be heard taunting the men, their hands tied behind their backs, as they take them down from a lorry to a clearing where they are shot at close range. For many ordinary Serbs this was a watershed which ended a consensus of denial – there could be nothing 'staged' about such footage. It was more significant, in terms of breaking the silence, than even Milosevic's extradition to the International Criminal Court in The Hague, which had happened four years before. President Tadić and Prime Minister Koštunica of Serbia immediately called the crimes 'monstrous' and 'brutal, callous and disgraceful' and announced that eight of the perpetrators, clearly identifiable from the film, had already been arrested. The most ardent Serbian nationalists at that moment must have detected at least the flickering of a question mark in their heads, as they saw the images from Srebrenica finally reaching into their homes. The repressed reality of this massacre now finally coming to light. 'Whenever a secret is kept it will make its way . . .'

Forty-four years after the massacre of the Algerian demonstrators in Paris, the director Michael Haneke's extraordinary film *Hidden* is released. The narrative centres around a protagonist, an Algerian

---

[*] Information about the screening of this footage taken from reports in Reuters (Beti Bilandzic) and *Telegraph* (Alex Todorovic), 3 June 2005.

man whose parents are both killed in the massacre when he's six years old. Although it is only referred to briefly, this is the pivot on which the entire film turns. Haneke documents the impact on individual lives of the devastation and violence that is unleashed through colonialism and the subsequent failure of an entire society to confront its past honestly. Ultimately the violence, like Banquo's ghost, will always return to haunt the perpetrators, and the silence will be broken. The only irony here is that this breaking of silence, this impassioned and angry film about France and its buried colonial history, did not come from the French. Often an outside eye sees far more. And Haneke's fury at societal 'amnesia' is more understandable knowing that his father was German and Haneke grew up in Austria, a country not known for its honesty in dealing with its own history.

In Ireland too over recent years there has been a remarkable breaking of silences about the Famine. In 1995 John Killen wrote in his introduction to *The Famine Decade: Contemporary Accounts, 1841–1851* that 'the trauma of the famine struck a deep blow to the psyche of the Irish people then and in ensuing generations. Anger, hatred, fear and compassion have mixed with shame to produce a reluctance, possibly an inability, to address the enormity of that . . . tragedy.' But the last two decades have seen a huge shift here, akin to the breaking of a conceptual dam of silence and trauma. Far more books and articles have been published about the Famine in the last two decades than the preceding 150 years. There has been particularly fascinating new research in the specific area of post-Famine trauma, and the impacts these million deaths had on subsequent generations. Work done by Chris Morash, Cathal Póirtéir, Peter Gray, Kendrick Oliver, Emily Mark-FitzGerald and Margaret Kelleher has all contributed to this ongoing debate about the legacy of the Famine in Ireland today.[*] I feel that all of these developments

---

[*] Some of the key works include *Writing the Irish Famine* (1995) and *Fearful Realities* (1996) by Chris Morash; Cathal Póirtéir's *Famine Echoes* (1995), a pioneering gathering together of oral histories of the Famine which was also broadcast in sixteen radio programmes by RTÉ in Ireland; *The Memory of Catastrophe* by Peter Gray and Kendrick Oliver (2004); and *Commemorating the Irish Famine: Memory and the Monument (Reappraisals in Irish History)* by Emily Mark-FitzGerald.

are indicative of a significant shift in how the Famine is now being represented in far broader cultural, psychological and philosophical terms than the narrow historical approach that dominated up until about the mid-1990s.

There are certain parallels here between the original silence surrounding the Holocaust in the immediate post-war period, and then the trickle of published testimonies, documentaries and academic studies that began to emerge in the late 1960s and early 1970s, becoming a flood by the 1980s and 90s when Norman Finkelstein wrote his intentionally provocative attack on what he saw as *The Holocaust Industry* (2000). Although in Ireland the initial period of relative silence was longer – more than a century before the first major study of the Famine was published, *The Great Famine: Studies in Irish History*, in 1956 – there has been a similar deluge of Famine-related writing and cultural representation since the mid-1990s. Although, curiously, not yet in the medium of film, but this will surely come in time.

As with the development of Holocaust memorials and museums throughout the world, there has also been a dramatic increase in public memorials and artworks commemorating the Famine in the last two decades, particularly in Ireland, the USA and Canada. The fact that some of these are of questionable aesthetic quality (just as is the case with Holocaust memorials) is far less significant than the fact that they exist at all. The best known is probably Rowan Gillespie's *Famine,* unveiled in 1997, a powerful group of six emaciated bronze figures, walking along Custom House Quay in Dublin. Also in 1997, the National Famine Memorial of a famine ship was inaugurated at Murrisk, in Mayo. There followed many other artworks and commemorations all across Ireland, and then diaspora communities commissioned further Famine memorials in Boston (1998), Sydney (1999), New York (2002), Philadelphia (2003) and Toronto (2007). And since 2008, the Irish government have organised a National Famine Commemoration Day.

*

14 July 2016, Pen Llŷn

Perhaps the most remarkable breaking of silences in my lifetime, is by an extraordinary coincidence, happening as I'm editing the words on this page. It is now almost two decades since I first read Sven Lindqvist, and learnt about the annihilation of the Herero and Nama in Namibia. As I researched further into the genocide it haunted me more and more. But I also grew angrier, because it seemed that this genocide was barely known about – even my well-educated friends, knowledgeable about history, looked nonplussed when I raised the subject. The disparity in historical and cultural representation between the vast amount published on the genocide of the Jews in Europe and the paucity of work about the genocide of the Herero and Nama in Namibia was overwhelming, and disturbing. The casual racism behind this under-representation was clear for anyone with eyes to see. And one particularly disturbing dimension to the Namibian genocide was that not only were the vast majority of the Herero and Nama exterminated, but their lands were then stolen and handed over to German settlers. A situation that still continues to this day, where 4,000 predominantly white farmers own 95 per cent of the territory.

In the late 1990s, as we've seen, something began to stir. It is hard to identify the exact moment, but gradually more and more was published in English about the Herero and Nama genocide – Mark Cocker published his powerful work *Rivers of Blood, Rivers of Gold* in 1998, and J. B. Gewald's *Herero Heroes* came out the following year.[*] There followed important new research coming to light, particularly about the post-von Trotha period, and the brutality of the concentration camps established in South-West Africa. And in Namibia itself the question of German compensation to the Herero and Nama began to be raised. When German President Roman Herzog visited Namibia in 1998, the Herero handed over a formal

---

[*] There had been several important works published by German historians from the 1960s onwards (particularly *South-West Africa under German Rule 1894–1914* by Helmut Bley, and *Let Us Die Fighting: The Struggle of the Herero and Nama against German Imperialism (1894–1915)* by Horst Drechsler), but little had been published outside Germany before the 1990s.

request, which was rejected. Soon afterwards, the Herero People's Reparations Committee was established, and in 2001 they filed two lawsuits under the Alien Tort Claims Act – the first, a $2 billion case

in June 2001 against three German corporations who had funded, and profited from, their colonial activities in South-West Africa – Deutsche Bank, the Woermann Line and the Terex Corporation. And then, in September 2001, a $2 billion case against the German government.* These cases were later rejected by the courts, but there was now a growing momentum which could not be halted.

14 August 2004 was a momentous day for the Herero people. It marked the centenary of the Battle of Waterberg, and the beginning of the principal phase of extermination of the Herero by General von Trotha and his soldiers. A large commemoration was planned, over several days on a site at Okakarara, near the Waterberg, and most significantly, the German government were invited to the cere- mony. They accepted the invitation and the minister for economic co-operation and development, Heidemarie Wieczorek-Zeul, was sent on behalf of the government.

---

* Information on these lawsuits comes from *Modern Genocide: The Definitive Resource and Document Collection*.

When she stepped up to the microphones, she, understandably, looked nervous. It later emerged that there had been strong disagreement between her and the German Foreign Ministry regarding the exact wording of her speech; she wanted to make the acknowledgement of genocide as powerful and unambiguous as possible – which explains the fact that the words she actually said differed, in certain critical aspects, from the official record of the speech later released.[*] I have underlined all of these differences in the speech below.

There was a hush, as if the vast weight of a hundred years of terror and injustice was being concentrated on that single moment; nobody in the large and expectant crowd knew what she was going to say. She spoke slowly, in English, at times her voice close to breaking – these are the exact words she used on 14 August 2004, in the first half of her speech, dealing with the Herero–Nama genocide – the first time that any German government representative had used the word 'genocide':

> Since I have been in the country I have listened. I have met yesterday the Herero representatives and the Nama representatives, and I think it is good also to listen. But I am also happy to be able to speak, to be invited to speak to you.
> Today I want to acknowledge the violence inflicted by the German colonist powers on your ancestors, particularly the Herero and the Nama. I am painfully aware of the atrocities committed a hundred years ago and in the late nineteenth century, the colonial powers drove the people from their land and when the Herero, when your ancestors, resisted, General von Trotha's troops embarked on a war of extermination against them and the Nama. In his infamous order General von Trotha commanded that every Herero be shot – with no mercy shown even to women and children. At the Battle of Waterberg in 1904, the survivors were forced into the Omaheke desert, where they were denied any access to

---

[*] Jephta Nguherimo's video recording of the first half of Wieczorek-Zeul's speech (which I have transcribed) can be viewed at: https://www.youtube.com/watch?v=nAufl1chc10.

water sources and were left to die of thirst and starvation. And following this, the surviving Herero, Nama and Damara were interned in camps and put to forced labour of such brutality that many did not survive.

We pay tribute, <u>I pay tribute in the name of the German government</u>, to those brave women and men, particularly from the Herero, the Nama, the Damara, who fought and suffered so that their children and their children's children could live in freedom. I honour with great respect your ancestors who died fighting against their German oppressors. Even at that time, back in 1904, there were also Germans who opposed and spoke out against this war of oppression. One of them, <u>and I'm proud of that</u>, was August Bebel, the chairman of the same political party of which I am a member. In the German Parliament <u>at that time</u>, Bebel condemned the oppression of the Herero in the strongest terms and honoured their uprising as a just struggle for liberation. I am proud of that today.

A century ago, the oppressors – blinded by colonial fervour – became agents of violence, discrimination, racism and annihilation in Germany's name.

The atrocities, <u>the murders, the crimes</u> committed at that time are today termed genocide – and nowadays a General von Trotha would be prosecuted and convicted, <u>and rightly so</u>.

We Germans accept our historical and moral responsibility and the guilt incurred by Germans at that time. And so, in the words of the Lord's Prayer that we share, I ask you to forgive us our trespasses <u>and our guilt</u>.

A staggering moment, as Wieczorek-Zeul's words went into the ears of her Namibian listeners, into the sky, at the precise place where, a hundred years before, her predecessor General Lothar von Trotha began the extermination of the Herero people. A moment as powerful as Willy Brandt kneeling at the monument to the Warsaw Ghetto uprising. A moment which, like that action, finally opened up the possibility of reconciliation and justice – though, of course, these processes take many, many years.

Some in the crowd, still wary of their old colonial adversary, shouted that they wanted a clear apology – Wieczorek-Zeul replied, 'Everything I have said in my speech was an apology for crimes committed under German colonial rule.' However (and it was a big however), she explained there would be no financial compensation from the German government, though economic aid would increase. Also, bizarrely, although this speech had seemed to accept German responsibility in uncompromising terms, according to the German government afterwards it did not constitute either an official German apology nor a formal recognition of genocide; her speech would not be adopted as government policy. Reaction to her words divided the Namibian government and the Herero people. Hifkepunye Pohamba, Namibia's minister of land, welcomed her remarks, saying, 'That is what we have been waiting for, for a very long time.' But the Herero representative Kuaima Riruako, said that although the apology was appreciated, 'we still have the right to take the German government to court'.

Pressure continued to build on the German government – both within Germany and in Namibia. The South African law professor Jeremy Sarkin made a significant contribution to the debate around reparations claims, working closely with Herero representatives, and publishing his work *Colonial Genocide and Reparations Claims in the 21st Century* in 2008. Demands grew for the return of bones and skulls of Herero and Nama victims kept in German museums and institutes, which began to be returned in 2011. There were repeated initiatives in the Bundestag for the genocide to be formally recognised, led by the Green Party and the Social Democratic Party, and in the Bundestag debate on 1 March 2012 Wieczorek-Zeul criticised the government strongly for its lack of action over real reconciliation in Namibia, but the motion was defeated. Cultural and historical representation continued to multiply – in October 2004 David Olusoga's BBC documentary *Genocide and the Second Reich* had been broadcast to widespread acclaim, and six years later, he and Casper Erichsen published the greatest work yet on the genocide – *The Kaiser's Holocaust: Germany's Forgotten Genocide.*

The demand for action continued to grow. In May 2015, the Social Democratic Party launched another campaign in the German Parliament, with a contribution from Dr Karamba Diaby, the first African-born elected member of the Bundestag, who quoted Elie Wiesel's warning to the German Parliament in 2000 about the dangers of those who want to move on, to 'turn the page' of the past, who want to forget difficult histories: 'by conspiring to obliterate the victims' memory, those who want to turn the page are killing them a second time.' In 2015, the German Foreign Ministry began referring to the mass murders as 'genocide' in its internal guidelines, and special envoys were appointed in November 2015 to facilitate an agreed new policy between Germany and Namibia. With the German Bundestag's recognition in June 2016 of the Armenian genocide by the Turks, calls to recognise the Namibian genocide grew even louder. A Green Party MP, Cem Özdemir, who had been one of the key players in the Bundestag vote, commented that 'it is the duty of our house quickly to recognise this genocide as well'.

And so, as I return to this chapter today – 14 July 2016 – a slightly humid, summer's afternoon on Pen Llŷn, the sea enveloped by mist – I return to this chapter, after months of working on other sections of the book, as I'm about to finish the section on how the silence surrounding the Herero and Nama genocide was eventually broken. I google 'German apology Namibia 2004' and I'm astonished by what appears on the screen in front of me:

Germany to recognise Herero genocide and apologise to Namibia.[*]

Germany is to recognise as genocide the massacre of 110,000 of the Herero and Nama people . . .

I check the link, and yes, the news came through at 1.57 p.m. today from Berlin! I avidly read the article. It's happened . . . finally.

---

[*] 'Germany to recognise Herero genocide and apologise to Namibia' by Justin Huggler, www.telegraph.co.uk, 14 July 2016.

In a landmark admission of historical guilt, Germany is to recognise the massacre of 110,000 of the Herero people of Namibia by German troops between 1904 and 1908 as genocide. A spokesman for Angela Merkel's government said Germany would formally apologise to Namibia.

I double-check the German government website, and there it is in black and white – a statement from a deputy spokesperson of the Federal Foreign Office, Mrs Sawsan Chebli, at a press conference held yesterday. In response to an enquiry as to why the government have used the word 'genocide' for the first time about the murder of the Hereros, she says, rather disingenuously, "There is no change of heart', the questioner should know that from 'very early on, we have spoken explicitly of genocide'. This is simply not true. I go back here to my notes, and find an interview with Dr Wolfgang Massing, who was the German ambassador to Namibia in 2004. He talks about 'a very dark chapter' in history, he talks about how Germany 'deeply regret' what happened, but he absolutely denies there was a genocide. In fact twice he talks about 'so-called extermination' of the Herero, and von Trotha's 'so-called extermination order'. Although thousands of Herero were killed, '[he] wouldn't talk about a systematic extermination of Hereros'. In her statement, Chebli also emphasises that although both governments seek a common policy statement about historical events, the German apology and its acceptance by Namibia, these developments will 'not have any legal consequences', i.e. the German government will continue to reject calls for reparations and compensation.

Nevertheless, the significance of this moment is impossible to dispute. Not only for the Herero and Nama people in Namibia and for Germany, but for the wider world. It demonstrates that a century-long silence can be broken. It shows that the crimes of the past can never be eradicated.

*

Grass parched to flattened straw in these weeks of summer sun. A desiccating heat, almost Mediterranean. Almost all the flowers gone now, the poppies are tired and faded, only yellow crowds of indestructible ragwort and the mauve of thistle heads in the fields. The dog days of summer will soon be here. Clouds of moths envelop the cottage at night. Despite the stifling heat I have to shut the windows to prevent them coming inside as I write. Reading and rereading over these last weeks. The Sereny book on Speer, Jean Améry, and Sebald's *On the Natural History of Destruction*. I find myself taking issue with Sebald on one matter – his tone of total bafflement at the German post-war silence. Is it really so surprising that a country finds it difficult to move on from its moment of greatest trauma?

There is always a tension at the heart of any writing about silence. In this way, towards the end of his lecture, Sebald describes the women refugees from the Hamburg firestorm arriving at Stralsund railway station 'unable to speak of what had happened, struck dumb or sobbing and weeping with despair. And several of these women . . . actually did have dead children in their luggage, children who had suffocated in the smoke or died in some other way during the air raid.' He finally understands that 'it is impossible to gauge the depths of trauma suffered by those who came away from the epicentres of catastrophe. The right to silence claimed by the majority of these people is as inviolable as that of the survivors of Hiroshima, of whom Kenzaburo Oe says . . . that even twenty years after the bomb fell many of them still could not speak of what happened that day.'

Sebald also fails to articulate the profound differences in the nature of varying types of silence, and the resulting effects on the second generation – the silence of the perpetrator, the silence of the survivor and the silence of the bystander. The first is perhaps the most comprehensible. It is the children of perpetrators who, most often, are the ones who feel the strongest need to break the silence of their parents – for example, the remarkable interviews with relatives of leading Nazi figures contained in *Hitler's Children* by Gerald

Posner. Niklas Frank attempting to live his life as a kind of ongoing atonement for his father's genocidal reign as governor of occupied Poland during the war is extraordinarily impressive, as is Martin Bormann's son. And the 2015 documentary *My Nazi Legacy* shows us this process in all its painful detail. Niklas Frank returns to sites of atrocities that his father had ordered, along with another (far less resolved) son of a perpetrator – Horst von Wächter, son of Otto von Wächter, governor of Galicia in Ukraine during the war. But Wächter, despite overwhelming evidence, remains reluctant to condemn his father's actions in the uncompromising terms Frank does.

There have been several very affecting books published in recent years which focus on this question of the child, or sometimes grandchild, finding out what lies behind the silence of their families, usually written in biographical terms. Martin Pollack's work *The Dead Man in the Bunker: Discovering My Father* explores the life of his father, Dr Gerhard Bast, formerly head of the Gestapo in Linz and a significant war criminal. In the third part of Rachel Seiffert's novel *The Dark Room* we meet Micha, a teacher in Frankfurt, who becomes more and more obsessed about what his beloved 'Opa' (grandpa) did in the war. He encounters a virtual wall of silence from his own family, but he does find out that Opa's letters home from the Eastern Front were all burnt after the war ('what did he write that he wanted to burn?') and eventually Micha travels to Belarus to find out for himself.

The survivors' silence seems, at first, the most surprising. Yet, in addition to the post-traumatic aspect and the well-known phenomenon of survivor guilt, there is often an inability to disconnect the traumatic experience itself from the survivor's own conception of themselves – as we've seen in the testimony of the Korean War veteran in *A Chorus of Stones*, 'the terror and brutality seemed to brand him, making him in his own mind irredeemably inseparable from the ugliness.' The children of survivors often find the impact of their parents' silence unbearable, sometimes becoming abusive. Brutal experiences, though rarely spoken of, are often passed on to the next generation. Anne Karpf has written movingly of this in *The War After*. The silence of the witness, the bystander, is the most complex, and the most politically explosive – it is the silence that affects us most today, and so I will return to this question in subsequent chapters.

I'm still wondering about the connection between individual silences in the face of violence and trauma and the wider silences of entire societies. Or how to understand the breaking of such silences on both an individual and a collective level. I'm not sure whether it's really possible for the people of a country to fully understand the suffering that they, collectively (in the form of their army or air force or oil corporations), have imposed on another people. Or to feel a genuine sense of shared responsibility. It is one thing to accept Ibsen's proposition that 'every man shares the responsibility and the guilt of the society to which he belongs'; it is another for people to actually *feel* this shared responsibility and guilt. Although of course, on an individual level, these understandings are what we expect of people when they are convicted of a crime. Occasionally such realisations are expected of an entire nation – for example, after the war, the German people, as well as the German state, were widely expected to recognise the devastation caused to the world by Nazism – and also to accept their collective responsibility for having allowed Hitlerism to continue for twelve years.

Yet I wonder how many of us in Britain and America feel responsible for the devastation caused by the illegal Iraq War of 2003 and its aftermath, for the deaths of hundreds of thousands of people. My memories of that time are of thousands of people, millions of us, carrying banners and wearing badges saying 'Not In My Name'. But, unfortunately, it was – it was in all of our names. Whether you went on the anti-war marches or not, it was our taxes which paid for the fighter jets and the bombs, just as surely as German taxpayers in the war paid for the SS and the extermination camps.

I know instinctively that empathy holds the key to unlocking this box. And I believe that this exceptional human quality can be developed in ways we cannot yet understand; in fact, I would say that if we do not evolve our abilities to feel empathy then we will not survive as a species. I also think it's possible for empathy to be transmitted vast distances, not only geographically, but also historically. I've never regarded the past as separable from the present; and I'm only interested in the past inasmuch as it can change our behaviour today. My hope is that a revolution in historical understanding and empathy has already begun. If the American people could, even for a moment, feel a connection to the desolation felt by the first peoples of their country as weapons and disease annihilated them, would they still be able to support regimes that govern through massive and systemic abuse of human rights? If we in Britain could, even fleetingly, experience the stench and feel the terror of the millions of human beings who endured the Middle Passage on slaving ships, would we ever be able to look at transnational trade or the crimes of the City of London in the same way again?

These are hopes. But, on my less hopeful days, I sometimes feel that we haven't even begun to frame the questions yet. When there is such controversy over the prime minister of our country expressing 'pain' about the deaths of a million people in Ireland, when any discussion over reparations for slavery is still greeted by most politicians with total bemusement, when oil companies who operate in our names and bring their profits back to our country are allowed to continue to devastate the environment and peoples of poorer parts of the world – then perhaps we've hardly begun this journey. When I look at the process that Germany has undergone since the war – the Nuremberg Trials, denazification proceedings (however flawed), and, more recently, the central positioning of the Holocaust in all German education – I do feel a sense of shame for our country. We as a culture haven't reached our Nuremberg yet – our time of judgement – let alone our Spandau, our process of reflection and desire for atonement. We may have decolonised most of the empire, but we haven't begun to decolonise our minds. I still see a continuum of empire – in our minds, our language, our behaviour, our trade, our corporations. Supposedly 'successful' violence, repeated century after century, from Hawkyns trafficking slaves in 1562 to Britain's participation in the illegal war in Iraq at the beginning of this century.

I often think about how our children and grandchildren will look at us in this regard – in our collective failure to come to terms with our past. In May 1953, Albert Speer wrote this letter, from his prison cell in Spandau, to his daughter Hilde:

> To reassure you however, of the dreadful things I knew nothing. The Americans told me later that they never thought I did. Even so, I'm not entirely content to leave it at that, for I ask myself what, given my lofty position, I could have found out had I wanted to. Even then, perhaps not everything, but certainly a great deal . . . I saw my fate, if you like as God's judgement – not for having infringed any laws (for my transgressions in that sense were comparatively minimal) but for the deeper guilt of having so readily and unthinkingly gone along.

Will our grandchildren judge us in the same way? They may well feel that we never asked the questions we should have asked about our past. That we lived in a state of cultural blindness. That we stood aside, we enjoyed all the wealth that trade and power brought us, without ever really considering the costs. That we so readily and unthinkingly went along.

11

Power and the Hurricane

February 2014, London to north-west Wales

A hiatus in writing. Seven months – where the unpredictable nature of life, and its challenges, has interrupted my progress. But now, at last, another journey to the west. Not to Pembrokeshire this time, but further north, to an estuary on the edge of Snowdonia. I'm desperate to return to the books. So, despite the dire winter weather forecasts, I'm filled with intense excitement as I begin to pack the car, and think about heading westwards once again this evening.

*

Adding to the anxieties of the last months, my mother had a serious fall and broke her hip in August. When she came out of hospital I spent a month looking after her at the house in Suffolk. An unfamiliar experience with someone as vigorous and independent as she is. A poignancy too. As she recovered we took little walks, every day, up the lane towards the bridge. Her arm in mine, pacing very slowly, trying to go a little further each time. The same lane where she'd helped us take our first steps as children more than forty years ago, where she'd held us as we learnt to ride our bikes.

And now, with the vertiginous circles that life brings, it is she who is holding on to my arm for support. For the first time in her life, walking slowly with a stick, I realise, with a shock that she might look 'elderly' to someone who has never known her. She's always been the one with energy, the one who has looked after others, who has helped her friends who are frailer, staying with them as they convalesce. Now she's learning to be a patient; trying, not very successfully, also to be patient with herself.

Being back at the farmhouse in Suffolk is always a curious experience – simultaneously familiar and disorientating. Perhaps the same for most people going home, returning to the house where they grew up. My brother's family now live in one part of the building, my sister's family in the house next door – 'the family commune', as I sometimes refer to it. Anyway, this was the first time for many years that I'd spent a month back there, and the first time ever that I've done all the shopping and cooking, trying to adapt to my mother's primarily vegetarian diet. I was surprised at my ability to put my life and work on hold; I felt a liberation in the necessity of dealing with this situation, being entirely present for somebody you love. It wasn't difficult at all. When she was sleeping I cooked or read; when she was awake I'd go through to the downstairs room, next to the garden, which we'd turned into her temporary bedroom while she wasn't able to use the stairs. I'd see if she wanted something to eat, or we'd talk or, if she had more energy, occasionally read something together – I remember we read the short story 'Un Coeur Simple' and *Pereira Maintains* in those days of convalescence, and marvelled at how Flaubert's provincial Normandy village and Tabucchi's Lisbon, from other centuries, could be so vividly evoked in this sunlit room in Suffolk.

In the evenings, after she'd gone to sleep, I'd return to the sitting room, catch up with emails, have supper with the rest of the family and chat about how 'the patient' was getting on. I'd often then read until the early hours, and sometimes, before going to bed, I'd open the front door and go out to the orchard to look at the August night sky, hoping for a glimpse of a shooting star from the Perseid

690

showers common in this month. Over the last years I've developed a night ritual when I'm down there – at least once during my stay, regardless of the season, whether there's frost underfoot or summer moonlight, I slowly walk around the sleeping houses. At the back of the buildings, when the river is high, you can hear the water flowing powerfully over the mill race a few hundred yards away, at other times maybe the call of an owl or the rustling of wind in the trees. But always, as I circle the houses, watching the sleeping windows, I think in turn of each person inside, and hope for their well-being. This simple action makes me go back in time to a period when our ancestors might have patrolled the fences at the edge of settlements against the dangers of the dark. But for me today it's a time to reflect on the happiness that we have, the difficulties we face, and the fragility of everything. A kind of prayer, I suppose.

One night, just a few days after my mother's operation, I begin my circumnavigation of the house. As I walk, in the early hours, all my energy is taken up with willing her recovery to continue, willing the pain to fade, willing her back to an active life again. I come round the end of the house by her temporary bedroom, and am surprised to see the lamp still on inside, light spilling out through the French windows over the garden. Through the glass I see she has fallen asleep with a book still open on her chest. The pages touching the fingers of her left hand. At least I *think* she's sleeping. Momentarily I freeze. I watch with an intensity for signs of her breathing. After one of the longest twenty seconds of my life I see the book, and her chest, slowly rise, and then fall, as she breathes. I wait a little longer just to make sure my mind is not playing tricks on me. The entire universe now shrunk to this single act of looking, a few inches of a hand, a book, a breathing body . . . yes, the fall and rise continues, and now I can breathe again. Overwhelming relief. I retreat from the glass and continue my walk around the house, wondering if anybody's ever calculated the number of breaths breathed in a lifetime. And, from watching my mother's breathing, suddenly I'm trying to imagine her watching all of our first breaths in the hospital. The most astonishing moment of our lives that none of us are able to remember.

And I have a sense that I've just taken another step into a different stage of life. A rehearsal for the unthinkable end. And our own ends as well. Whatever our age, we will never be prepared. Instantly we will fall back through time. A line comes into my head, but from where I cannot now remember – 'for, in the hour of his death, he . . . like all men, cried out for his mother'.

*

The shocks continued through the late autumn. There are times in life, perhaps fewer as you get older, when you have the illusion that you can control the circumstances of your life, that you have the power to make dynamic choices. And then life humbles you, and you realise that so much of existence is not controllable. Death, love, illness, grief – these are not well behaved or predictable in any way. Before Christmas a close friend of mine had another frightening and debilitating descent into depression. Periodically she has suffered from such episodes, but the last one was almost ten years ago, and all of us close to her hoped that she'd broken this cycle. It's incredibly hard to see somebody you love in this kind of pain, yet know the limitations of what you can do to help. To feel relatively powerless – beyond the ability to simply be there, be calm, give love.

And two other friends have experienced turbulent months as well – one having just lost her job and another being continually undermined and bullied by managers at his workplace. In the last months, I've tried to do a lot of listening, advising and caring, more than usual. Maybe there's a benefit in this, being entirely responsive to others' needs. At least, for a time.

*

The weather forecast for this evening is wild but I'm full of anticipation as I pack the boxes into the car, dodging heavy London showers. I've now managed to carve out eight whole days to work on revising the manuscript. I'm bringing all the books and papers I might, possibly, use this week. Then piling bedding and my other

692

bags onto the back seat. Finally I transfer the limited contents of my fridge into a green Hackney Council recycling crate, and also throw in coffee, coffee grinder, tea, milk, some onion soup and a couple of cans of Guinness. I aim to leave London at 7.30 or so, avoiding the worst of the traffic; I calculate I could be at the cottage in Wales by 2 a.m. As usual, I dose myself with a final, strong black coffee once the car is packed, today having a Lemsip chaser with it, to try and ward off the cold I sense is coming.

Some final phone calls and emails and then I'm off, easing through the dark, wet streets of east London. The worst of the rush hour is over, and there's a pause in the rain as well. I'm on the M11 in a few minutes, make good progress north, and after an hour or so I have my first stop, as usual, at Cambridge services, for petrol and more coffee. This place always appeals to me, this neon island by the dual carriageway, because it is about as far removed from 'dreaming spires' and academia as it's possible to imagine. There's a man in his sixties who works here, laconic but friendly, he often does the night shift. We have a little chat, I go outside to drink my coffee and ring the woman who looks after the cottage to say yes, I am coming, but I will be arriving very late, and don't want to disturb her. That's no problem, the key's in the usual place in the porch. Megan in the neighbouring house is still away, and nobody's been in the cottage since before Christmas, so it hasn't been cleaned for a while – she hopes it won't be too dusty . . . At this point I consider passing on Quentin Crisp's advice about living without cleaning, but decide her chapel sensibilities might be scandalised by hearing that 'after the first four years, the dirt doesn't get any worse'. My habitual desire to drive on smaller roads is offset by my reduced energies and the fact the radio's forecasting bad weather later on, so I stick to dual carriageways and motorways. I get to Birmingham in another hour, before striking west to Bridgnorth and Shrewsbury. On the way I pass my favourite road sign in Britain, not far from Much Wenlock – the magnificent pairing, on a single sign, of the settlements of Wigwig and Homer.

After Shrewsbury I decide to try a new route west, over the mountains. The wind is getting up, blowing rusted leaves along the country road that leads to Knockin. I'm listening to a discussion about a book I read many years ago and loved, *Monsignor Quixote* by Graham Greene. The way the guests are talking with such enthusiasm about the different belief systems represented by the communist mayor and the monsignor, and the friendship between them, makes me want to reread the book as soon as I get back to London. And there's another book, Norwegian I think, something about ice and shared secrets between teenage girls, which also sounds intriguing. One of the guests is describing his experience some time ago of sheltering in a basement in Montreal with a hundred other people during severe power cuts which lasted for days, and how they sensed the world of ice gathering all around them. And as the reviewers talk, these border roads, with their bare February trees, become entirely connected in my mind to this other kingdom of ice.

In the darkness I sense the hulk of the Berwyns away to my right. The houses get more scattered, the ground more undulating. Past eleven o'clock now, and I only meet one car every fifteen minutes or so. Darting over a crossroads, an illuminated house, a sudden curiosity about the lives that people lead in such places. Stone bridges, bends, having to slow down to third gear, second at times. Through Llangynog – a name that is strangely familiar, though I'm not able to work out why. A man staggers out of a pub, and for a moment threatens to fall into the road. I swerve to avoid him. Then the mountains really begin. And a first squall of serious rain. The headlights reach out and show me that I'm climbing above the treeline now, into a rockscape, only gorse bushes fringe the mountain road, twisting higher and higher. Round a blind bend I have to brake suddenly. Two sheep are sleeping in the middle of the road. They seem very huffy to be disturbed and shuffle away fussily. With superb timing Dylan is encanting one of the most wonderful openings to any song I know – 'When you're lost in the rain in Juarez and it's Easter time too . . .' I stop to pee at the top of the valley, in gusts of rain and wind, my arc twisting and silvered in the headlights. Sense of the land plunging away to my left. A single light from a farmhouse far away on the other side of the valley. Then roaring off into the night again with only Mr Zimmerman for company.

Hairpin bends, down and down, towards the comforting lights of Bala in the valley below. A single car precedes me through the closed-up town, always linked in my mind to Sebald's minister and wife, and the little Jacques Austerlitz, growing up here in the freezing rectory during the war. Then climbing again, the road through the Arenigs, the reservoir shimmering down below on my left, and underneath the waters, the village of Capel Celyn, flooded to provide water for Liverpool, destroying an entire community here in 1965, and, unintentionally, creating a new wave of passionate Welsh nationalism in the process. Now an unfamiliar version of 'Visions of Johanna', rockier, heavier. It doesn't really work, but I still appreciate Dylan's restless urge always to reinterpret, to try something different. But 'Ballad of a Thin Man' has never sounded more magnificent than in this outstandingly bleak landscape, with the rain now teeming down diagonally.

> You've been with the Professors, and they've all liked your looks.
> With great lawyers, you've discussed lepers and crooks.
> You've been through all of F. Scott Fitzgerald's books;
> you're very well read, it's well known,
> but something is happening here, and you don't know what it is,
> do you MISTER JONES?

Not a single car for half an hour now, nothing else moving in the landscape. Then, a mile or two from the junction at Trawsfynydd, I see the smudged spots of distant headlights in my mirror. And, although I'm driving at sixty or so, they seem to be getting closer. It's completely irrational but this car behind me, in this landscape, seems far from benevolent. Too many thrillers watched over the years, where bad things begin with a car sighted in the rearview mirror. I accelerate, but the lights are still getting closer and closer. If I can just make it to the junction before they catch me! The famous Free Trade Hall 'Rolling Stone' now beginning. That notorious cry of 'Judas!' from the crowd, and Dylan snarling back. I get to the turning, right towards Harlech, and with the street light here feel a bit calmer. But I still want to lose the car behind. Down the hill towards Gellilydan, nudging seventy. Turn off at the bottom, left towards Harlech. I stop, look back, and to my enormous relief, see the headlights speeding on towards Porthmadog. I shout after my pursuer, perhaps rather unnecessarily. Now, closer to my destination, and only six hours from Hackney – not bad going at all.

The forecasts on the radio are growing increasingly apocalyptic. Another 'great storm' is coming! The 'hurricane' of October 1987 is mentioned repeatedly, and the radio presenters are nearly breathless in their excitement, speaking as if they have biblical powers of terrible prophecy. But yes, here where the mountains meet the sea in north-west Wales, the winds are definitely building up to gale force, there are tree branches strewn across the road now, which I gingerly drive around. I've almost reached my destination. I turn up the track to the last gate, and as I open it, I see gusts of birds are being blown in from the sea, surely early warning signals of what's to come . . .

*

Living in a Western city – especially a megalopolis like London – you often feel cut off from the harsher impacts of the elements. It takes a considerable effort of imagination to really believe that the weather causes chaos and takes lives. In the city, snow comes perhaps once every three or four years – and, even then, it's polite snow. It arrives gently, usually at night, not wanting to disturb anyone, and melts away (often within twenty-four hours) without having caused any real problems. In fact, quite the opposite. If schools are closed, not only is this a liberation for the children, but, I've often thought, observing parents playing in snowbound London parks, how much they too – freed from their routines for a day – must see life differently with the coming of a white-out of the skies. A chance to start again. In the city you're also sheltered from rising waters. The wildest storms in London rarely seem to uproot a single tree.

In the winter you learn to listen, with the detachment the land-lubber gives to the shipping forecast, to news of remote villages in Cumbria being cut off by snowdrifts, or settlements in Somerset being inundated by floods. Very occasionally a particular incident might affect you directly if you venture outside the security of the city – the bad luck of a fallen tree, or a waterlogged road perhaps – but most of the time we barely register the human distress that comes with power cuts or floods. 'Thousands of homes are still without power this evening' becomes a kind of comforting background music in the winter, which has the unintended side effect of making city-dwellers subconsciously shiver, and sink deeper under their duvets with a shudder of relief. The familiarity of these words, reaching back to childhood – *Irish Sea, seven rising to eight, visibility poor; Rockall, eight, occasionally nine, severe, rising . . .*'

*

I'm writing these words by candlelight. Two tall candles shivering in an unfamiliar room by the estuary here. On the late news, coming from my little silver radio, a man's voice from London, deep and reassuring, tells me that '41,000 homes in Wales and the West of England remain without electricity tonight. The energy companies have said they are doing all they can to reconnect power supplies.' It is a strange sensation to feel included in the news for once. No longer the detached metropolitan listener, now I'm one of the 41,000. I catch myself thinking, rather bizarrely, of the Jehovah's Witnesses, and a garishly illustrated pamphlet I once read as a boy, which very precisely described that only 44,000 were chosen for salvation. It seemed an extremely arbitrary number, and though absurd in one way, in the context of the 1970s and the wishy-washy 'religion lite' I'd grown up with, I recall grudgingly admiring the chutzpah of actually putting a figure on the afterlife. But 41,000 is a little short of this figure – though still enough to fill a football stadium. A certain sense of being in a select group tonight. Select in our shared discomfort, in our sudden anxieties about torch batteries and candles. An abstract solidarity across the dark mountains with faces unknown.

I arrived two hours ago, the winds pounding the car as I pulled up by the cottage. My relief at having just made it, having arrived just in time to batten down the hatches before the storm strengthens. I switch on my torch and scuttle over to the house. My hand feels for the key under the heavy stone in the porch. I unlock the door, the keen, damp smell of an empty stone house in winter. Then automatically clicking the light switches in the hall. Nothing. Oh shit. I check the fuse box with my torch, no tripped circuits. Then switch everything off, and on again. Still darkness. I walk into the little kitchen, and then, with my beam of light, I see an entire socket has been blown out, charring the wall, and sending plastic shards across the floor. Maybe a lightning strike? And there's another burnt-out socket, down the steps in the sitting room. Damn. I thought the challenge today would be just getting here before the really wild weather took hold, but now, exhausted after the drive, I'm faced by another set of difficulties. A freezing house, no electricity, no hot water, not very helpful for my incubating cold. And then I suddenly recall what the woman said this evening – *Megan's still away*. Of course, why didn't I think of this before? Presumably nobody's staying in her cottage up the hill – not in February, surely? I remember she once showed me the secret way in, via the adjoining woodshed at the side of the house. The upturned old wooden boat that disguised the disused entrance to the kitchen. That must be worth a try . . .

As I shut the house up again, the winds pick up, and with them, rain coming down now in almost horizontal sheets. I hurry to the car, and drive back up the track, zigzagging the few hundred yards up to Megan's cottage, just below the brow of the hill. Pulling a coat over my head I make a dash for the woodshed, pull the door open, and head for the wall where the boat's hull appears in my torch beam. I duck behind it, and then reach for the ancient latch, and, with enormous relief, I hear the soft click as the door opens, with a little sigh of resistance. The sanctuary of the cottage. My torch now picks out the familiar features of Megan's kitchen. Refuge at last. I click the light switch. But, for the second time this evening, nothing happens. Maddening. Especially as I can now see the lights of the distant village on the other side of the estuary. I walk outside, up to the top of the hill, pushing against the winds that are increasing by the minute, and sure enough, on this side all is dark. All the way from Ffestiniog, down to Harlech, everything folded into the darkness, every village, every farmhouse. Oh well, nothing to be done tonight. And at least Megan's place has a woodburner, so I can get one room warm, I can heat food on top and boil a pan of water for coffee in the morning.

Power cut. Simply a reality of existence for perhaps the majority of people on this planet – at least those fortunate enough to have electricity at all. A daily, or weekly, occurrence to be worked around. But for those of us who live in what used to be called the 'developed world', who are so habituated to feeling in control of our environments, it comes as a visceral shock. We don't really know what to do, we have few points of reference. Our first instinct to reach for the phone, trying to keep our sense of outrage in check. *Why?! When? How long? How am I supposed to . . . ?! Impossible!* For those over forty there may be a distant memory of the miners' strikes of the early 1970s which ended Heath's government. The three-day week, flying pickets, eating by candlelight, paraffin heaters . . . But this all seems so long ago, literally another century, when organised labour was still powerful. It seems absurd in our time to be without electricity. To be powerless.

I find myself thinking back to the most poetic project we ever did in Platform, certainly the most idealistic. A work in the early 1990s called 'Homeland',* which asked Londoners to consider how light, that most intangible of substances, came into their city – attempting

---

* For further description of this project see chapter notes.

to break down the constituent elements of the coal burned for electricity, the copper wire in their electric cables, even the glass of the light bulbs they used – to trace these materials back to their points of production (the colliery at Hirwaun in south Wales, the copper mine at Neves-Corvo in Alentejo, Portugal, the light-bulb factory in Nagykanizsa, Hungary); of course, most of these now owned by vast US and UK transnational corporations such as Rio Tinto and General Electric. The philosophical jumping-off point for the project was to go beyond Adam Smith's concept of 'the Invisible Hand' – we attempted something more radical, asking the question whether it was possible to humanise vastly complex systems of international trade. To establish empathy between groups of people that capitalism had historically taught us to regard as 'producers' and 'consumers'. If people in a city like London could *see* the faces of the copper miners in Portugal or the lives of the Hungarian light-bulb makers, actually recognise their shared humanity, then many of the assumptions behind the abstract nature of international trade would have to change.

One of the most remarkable texts I came across as we prepared the project was a meditation by George Orwell on exactly this disconnection at the heart of capitalism – the separation between producers and consumers who never meet. He's living in Kentish Town, working on *The Road to Wigan Pier* and considering the way his entire society is dependent on coal and the miners (just as today we're dependent on oil and gas), and yet he sees no real connection between his life in London and the extraction process:

> We all know that we 'must have coal', but we seldom or never remember what coal getting involves. Here am I sitting writing in front of my comfortable coal fire. It is April but I still need a fire. Once a fortnight the coal cart drives up to the door and men in leather jerkins carry the coal indoors in stout sacks smelling of tar and shoot it clanking into the coal-hole under the stairs. It is only very rarely, when I make a definite mental effort, that I connect this coal with that far-off labour in the mines. It is just 'coal' – something which I have got to have;

black stuff that arrives mysteriously from nowhere in particular, like manna except that you have to pay for it. You could quite easily drive a car right across the north of England and never once remember that, hundreds of feet below the road you are on, the miners are hacking at the coal. Yet in a sense it is the miners who are driving your car forward. Their lamp-lit world down there is as necessary to the daylight world as the root is to the flower . . .

It is only because miners sweat their guts out that superior persons can remain superior. You and I and the editor of the Times Lit. Supp, and the Nancy poets and the Archbishop of Canterbury and Comrade X, author of *Marxism for Infants* – all of us really owe the comparative decency of our lives to poor drudges underground, blackened to the eyes, with their throats full of coal dust, driving their shovels forward with arms and belly muscles of steel.

In the process of our research for the 'Homeland' project, I remember talking to a miner, Tyrone O'Sullivan, who was then the branch secretary of the National Union of Miners at Hirwaun in south Wales. He told me that he was very supportive of our initiative, because 'anything that makes people realise that when they click a switch in London, or anywhere else, that it's not magic – that it's people's labour that brings electricity to the cities – that's got to be important'. Later in the project we discussed how it might be possible to stop people taking electricity for granted. We wondered about the potential of having one day a year when the supply of power would be cut off (apart from to essential services such as hospitals). Would the enforced absence on one day actually mean we never took such a resource for granted on all the other days of the year?

Well, now I'll have a chance to find out for myself. With a torch I go through the drawers in the kitchen and manage to find a couple of candles and some night lights, and soon I'm lighting the wood-burner. There's a fine stack of seasoned ash logs around the fireplace so I don't even need to bring in any wood from the shed next door. I'm impressed by the draw of the stove – within five minutes the

701

flames are leaping. Since childhood I've loved this moment – when the fire takes, and the sun's stored energy in the wood begins to be released. When you know it's caught, and the flames are hungrily licking around the larger twigs. At least I won't be cold tonight. Heat. Shelter. Food. The essentials. I root around in the kitchen and find two small, heavy pans with lids – I'll use these for hot water and to heat things up on top of the stove. The other cupboards are pretty bare, and Megan must have cleared her fridge before she went travelling because all that's left is an abandoned half-jar of black olives and some shrivelled ginger. Never mind, I've got my emergency rations in the car. I find a spare front door key hanging on a nail, and then make several rapid sorties outside to bring in my stuff.

The gale is becoming a storm. The sycamore tree next to the house is now being bent over at almost forty-five degrees. Even the rugged hawthorns, stubborn mountain survivors, are being hammered by the sheer force of these winds. I realise it's not very intelligent to have left the car under the sycamore on a night like this, so I go out one last time, and move the car a hundred yards back up the track, round a bend, near the gate. The winds are now so violent, coming off the sea, that it takes all my force just to open the car door. As I hurry back to the house, bending to keep my weight close to the ground to stop myself being blown over, an elderly fox lumbers across the track in front of me, low on his haunches, looking as miserable as only a drenched fox can look. I feel an overwhelming sense of companionship tonight with this other animal 'who bides the pelting of this pitiless storm' – both of us heading for our respective shelters.

I shiver with relief as I pull the door behind me. I check my phone, just after 3 a.m. now. The sitting room is already thawing. I pull the old sofa as close as possible to the stove. And then my thoughts turn to food. I'm ravenous. I root around in the Hackney recycling box and pull out half a loaf of bread, the lump of old cheddar, the tin of soup and a can of Guinness. Never have such limited resources given me greater anticipated joy. I take a glass down from a dresser, pull the ring on top of the can, hear the soft release of the widget, and then pour the dark liquid, slowly foaming, into the glass. The first slaking of thirst after hours of journeying. I savour every drop of the dark liquid. I feed more logs into the stove, thicker ones now. I take a candle into the kitchen's sharp chill to find a bowl, a spoon, a tin opener. Then back to my cocoon, feeling the warmth again. I watch the onion soup slowly begin to respond to the heat on top of the stove, tiny bubbles around the edge of the pan, I add a few chunks of cheddar and watch them melting stringily and cut a lump of bread. I eat with a kind of joy I haven't felt for a long time. Simplicity of the sweet onion and dark broth and salt tang of cheese. I'm absorbed in this moment utterly. To be warm. To be sheltered from the storm. To be fed. In my normal, insulated life, how hard it is to feel any of these things.

I look around this sitting room, illuminated by only a single candle now and the glow of the woodburner. On the massive, dark-wood dresser that dominates one side of the room I suddenly spot bottles, reflected in the light . . . I go over to investigate, and to my delight, find next to the whisky (which has never really appealed to me) a single bottle of armagnac! So now, as well as being warm on the outside I can heat my spirits on the inside . . . I'm sure Megan wouldn't mind. I pour a small glass of the brandy, and take a sip. The fumes reaching my nose moments before the spreading infusion of sweet heat ripples the back of my throat. I try to identify exactly how the intensity of this pleasure happens, the interplay between nostrils, tongue and throat; the difference between the tiniest sip and a more manly measure. I have to pour a second glass to enable my research to go further. At this point I turn on my little radio (luckily fully charged before coming away), and immediately the sounds of Schubert fill the room. At this point I just start giggling. Within an hour I've gone from despair to exhilaration. Blissful solitude, the promise of a week's writing to come, away from all the distraction and absurdity of the city with its vanities and anxieties. Fire, armagnac and Schubert. That'll do for me.

At the end of the concert, the announcer reveals that it was recorded earlier this evening in Bangor (only thirty miles away, as the raven flies, across the highest mountains), and that the concert hall had been battered by wild winds tonight, as we'd probably heard from the broadcast, but the show had to go on. Before I go to sleep I switch over to the late news and there's a report from Cricieth, on the other side of the water, with a correspondent saying that gusts of 108 mph have just been recorded at Aberdaron, further to the west, but that the 'hurricane-force winds' are now moving inland. I briefly wonder what the precise difference is between 'hurricane-force winds' and a 'hurricane' itself. As I'm reflecting on this, my mobile starts chirping its relentlessly upbeat call, and I'm temporarily back in my city world. But I see who's calling and my heart lifts. A close friend, more than a friend. 'It's 3.30 in the morning, why aren't you asleep?!' I ask him. He's just wanting to know that I'm OK, that I arrived safely. And when I tell him how wild it is here, I can hear the gentle teasing in his voice as he reminds me that *wild is what you like, isn't it?* And he has little sympathy about the power cut, surely that's part of the deal if you go to such places in February. Yes, I grudgingly have to admit that he's right.

Switching off the phone, I'm suddenly assailed by tiredness. I stretch my feet until they're only inches from the glass of the woodburner, curling and uncurling my toes as the warmth penetrates through the wool of the socks. I'm getting drowsy now. I begin to drift off, with a thick duvet wrapped around me, all the anxieties of the drive and arrival now receding . . . the infinitely comforting roar of wood burning and the metal of the stove ticking gently and the flickering of flame patterning the ceiling above.

*

I wake with a start, momentarily not knowing where I am. The unfamiliar sound – close to a wail of grief, a high keening note – of a storm turning into a hurricane outside. Then, shockingly, a grating, crashing roar culminating in what sounds like splintering rock. Instinctively, absurdly, I duck, as if the ceiling is about to give way. That must be slates coming off the roof, unless the chimney itself has gone . . . I get up with the duvet still around me like a cloak, gingerly open a curtain, but it's hard to see much in the dark. Nothing I can do except hope that this is the peak of the hurricane. I wonder how much stronger the force has to get before the glass of the windows will simply buckle and crack. The woodburner is almost out – just a few embers of one log left, flecks of dark, burnt orange amongst the ash – and, with it, the temperature in the room has dropped significantly. The clock on the wall tells me it's 4.30.

Before going back to sleep I go to the bedroom upstairs, the howling of the wind is even louder up here, and bring down another duvet, knowing the temperature will drop even further in the hours before light. I then set about reviving the stove, opening the heavy metal door, kneeling on the cold stone floor. I scrape the ash and gather the few remnants of embers together, then feed in some dry bark, and tear off splinters of wood, just thicker than matchsticks. Then, as gently as possible, blow on these, and within a couple of minutes, a plume of greyish-white smoke, and then the flame breaking through. Now I can put twigs and kindling in, and, when these have caught, some smaller logs and, within minutes, with the door an inch open to allow the cross-draught to do its work, it's roaring again. I then turn the air vent down to its lowest setting, and pack it with more logs, to give it the greatest chance of burning through the night. I move the sofa even closer to the stove, and disappear into my nest of duvets, feet closest to the woodburner. Even through the covers I can feel the heat doing its work. Within a few seconds the flickering ceiling recedes again as my eyes close, and soon I'm sinking into sleep.

*

A dream of anxiety. Not quite a nightmare, but I wake for the second time. I'm back in Cambridge, with a companion I can't identify. The place far more beautiful than I remember, and now dominated by a fine hill, which gives it an oddly Italian aspect. But there's a toxic atmosphere of high tension, strong differences of opinion, a group issuing threats, an impending sense of bullying . . . all the details frustratingly vague on waking. Light now edging the curtains. I reach out for my torch, the clock on the wall says it's 8.30. I must have had five hours' sleep in total. Not enough, but at least the hurricane roar has relented to what sounds like a high wind now. I make for the bathroom. There's a strong draught coming from somewhere and the candle gutters, threatens to go out. I finish and, as I flush, the yellow spirals away. At least that's not dependent on electricity. I hesitate by the kitchen door; shall I just pretend I've had a full night's sleep or is that ridiculous? Make a cup of tea now and watch the morning light, or try to sleep more? I'm still groggy with tiredness, and I head back to the sofa. At the window I peek outside, the trees still bending in the winds, but the sense of real danger has passed now. In the post-apocalyptic grey haze of morning I can see half a dozen end-slates which were lifted off the cottage in the night and smashed in the yard. One large branch of the sycamore has almost been wrenched off entirely – like an arm hanging out of its socket – but the tree's still standing. The sea below is boiling, bringing in all kinds of flotsam and jetsam to the shore. The grey whiteness of a winter morning.

Back in my cocoon on the sofa I close my eyes again, but sleep is not coming back. I go over the writing challenges that lie ahead this week. Hannah Arendt has been on my mind, having just reread *Eichmann in Jerusalem*. She and Hilberg together, so key to my understanding of these questions, yet I'm not sure they're represented as strongly as they should be in these pages. I've only recently discovered the true extent of the appalling witch-hunt she faced when the *New Yorker* first published the work, in sections, in 1963. The organised campaign of vilification and vicious misrepresentation captured so acutely by the German director Margarethe von Trotta in her recent film.* I turn over and watch the stove, trying to detect any flickers of flame, but there's nothing there. The wind seems to have dropped a little. At some point drift I off again, momentarily sensing I'm on a boat in the middle of a turbulent sea . . .

---

* *Hannah Arendt* (2012), with Barbara Sukowa in the title role.

Another couple of hours of sleep, and waking for the final time, my nose, outside the duvets, is intensely cold, the rest of me still warm-ish. The stove is out, the room is freezing once again. I know that I will have to get up to relight it, but I also know that this manoeuvre will mean losing the little heat that remains in my bed. With a sigh I clamber out of my nest and pull on a sweater, and then a coat. I light the stove again, then go to the kitchen and fill the smaller pan with water and bring it back to the stove top. When the water's hot enough I carry it through to the bathroom, taking great pleasure in letting the hot water chase out the icy dampness of my flannel, and then the morning ritual of feeling the heat on my face, but never lovelier than this morning. Another pan of water for my tea. Everything taking longer without power, but I'm not rushing, I'm actually appreciating more the act of waiting. I drink more slowly too, pulling the curtains back, moving a chair to the window to sur-vey the night's damage. The light in this room, even in the daytime, is pretty poor. But as the stove is the only source of heat I'll have to write in here. My laptop has almost no charge left so I'll have to write by hand. Everything feels awkward, I hear myself sighing, but immediately another voice tells me to 'Get on with it! Don't think that because of a few practical challenges today you can get away with less than your usual word limit'. And after the first hour or so it does become easier. I find myself adapting to my new situation.

After four hours I break for a late lunch – the remains of last night's soup, the rest of the bread and cheese. In the kitchen I watch three blue tits, oblivious to the wind still blowing, absorbed in extract-ing seeds from a bird feeder that's swinging just outside the win-dow. I'm curious at the pecking order – quite literally so – the way that other birds wait their turn on a neighbouring bush, and, as soon as one of their sisters or brothers moves away with their booty, another swoops down. I take my first, tentative steps out-side today. The ground is entirely saturated. I walk next door to the woodshed. The wheelbarrow has been blown right across the yard; I retrieve it and throw a load of logs in. After I've stacked the wood inside, I decide to go for a little walk up the track to see what's changed overnight. Just over the brow of the hill and down the other side, two mature oak trees, each two to three hundred years old, have been uprooted as if they were a pair of daisies. The dark, almost rusted earth around the roots as raw as an open wound. The roots still holding on to slabs of rock, like fingers gripping after death. Further down the valley I can see dozens of silver birch, shallower-rooted than the oaks, flattened like matchsticks. There'll be work for tree surgeons for the next year and beyond; at least somebody benefits from all of this destruction.

Shocked by what I've just seen, I walk back to the brow of the hill where sometimes there is mobile reception. I shelter from the wind in the lee of a ruined barn here and I phone the woman who looks after the cottage. She lives in a village a few miles to the south. Does she have any idea how long the power may be off for? And how wide an area is affected? She's apologetic about the power cut, saying that it only happened after we spoke last night, otherwise of course she would have warned me. But all the villages and houses on this side of the estuary are still without electricity, though she's just heard the power's back on in Harlech. She's talked to the farmer next door, they're saying it could be back on by nine o'clock this evening, but they can't promise that. They know where the problem is, apparently, and there's a whole team of guys working on it. I tell her I'm staying at Megan's temporarily, but there's another problem in the cottage below – the power sockets have been blown out, so even when the electricity is back on elsewhere I'm pretty sure it won't be on there. She says it could have been lightning from a week ago, it's happened once before at the cottage. Anyway, again she's apologetic, and then she gives me the number of a local electrician who's done work at the cottage before, and understands the old-fashioned wiring.

I return to the cottage, feeling my spirits lift a little. The human need for reassurance, I suppose. Armed with the knowledge I've just received, I decide the next priority is to get food and petrol, and if the power's back on in Harlech that will mean the shops are open again. As I walk up the track to the car the rain begins again, as if angry at having been left out of the night's entertainment. Welsh rain now, horizontal sheets from over the mountains, darkening the skies even more. As I edge down the track in the car, I see another oak tree completely uprooted, but luckily it's fallen into the field and not across the track. At the bottom gate, in the few seconds it takes me to open it and then close it behind me, I'm totally drenched. I reach the main road and turn right. Only one other car passes me in the next ten minutes. The only sound the manic flapping of the windscreen wipers, on maximum speed. Clearly everyone sensible is inside, waiting for this battering weather to pass. Finally I see the small town ahead, and with relief notice that the street lights are working, so the power is definitely back on here.

I park outside the little Spar and run in. The owner looks up as I appear bedraggled in the doorway. She tells me, not very warmly, that she's closing early today, actually in five minutes, so I'd better be quick. My inner hunter-gatherer takes over. I grab a basket and shovel in anything that could be useful. Bread, bacon, butter, beer, biscuits, batteries, milk, cheddar, carrots, soup, eggs, more candles . . . And at the till I spy a half bottle of cognac, and can't resist. The woman releases it from its high shelf, and, with a little sigh of disapproval, adds it to my bill. Faced with such puritanism I smile even more widely, take my change and tell her to keep warm and cosy tonight, to which provocation she responds with a scowl. But I've got what I need and head back out into what seems like dusk now, but it could just be the black clouds and rain still teeming down. I get petrol on the edge of the town, at what must be the most expensive garage in the whole of north Wales, but needs must. Driving back, crossing the invisible border of power to powerlessness, but now with supplies, I wonder whether I'm not actually beginning to *enjoy* the consecutive challenges that the last twelve hours have thrown at me.

Back in the cottage, stove revived again, a mood of greater realism takes over. I do what I usually do in difficult situations – plan for all scenarios, but always starting with the worst. Then you can only be pleasantly surprised when this doesn't happen – and usually it doesn't. So, if the power is off for another twenty-four, or forty-eight hours, what should I do? Or even longer? What then? How long will my sense of novelty in my powerless state last? How long can I go without a shower or a bath? Or without properly cooked food? I decide on thirty-six hours – and if the power's not on again by the second morning I'll head back to London, and put this one down to experience. I find a jar of chutney in a cupboard and head back to the warmth to eat some more bread and cheese. With the decision I've made I feel I've taken back an important element of control here. I'm no longer simply a passive recipient of whether energy is released back into cables or not. I make some coffee; no ability of course to grind the beans I've brought with me from London, but the instant coffee I've unearthed from the back of another cupboard is not as unpleasant as I remember. I return to my window and pick up my pen again.

*

After a minute or two I look up and see a lamp on the other side of the room is glowing. It takes me a moment to realise the full meaning of this. Silently, unexpectedly, the power has returned! I let out a wild whoop of delight, and rush through the cottage turning on every appliance I can find, as if not believing the evidence of the single lamp. Later I reflect that the power had returned at almost exactly the same moment that I had accepted my state of powerlessness.

But now, in the small amount of daylight left, I need to go down and check if the electricity's back on in the cottage where I usually write. Five minutes later I'm down the hill, clicking the switches again. No, still nothing. Bugger. It must be connected to the burnt-out sockets, just as I'd thought. Without much expectation of getting through, I ring the electrician's number from the top of the hill. Gwyn Davies answers on the second ring, and even though it's a Saturday, the end of the afternoon, he agrees to come out immediately. He's not far away and he's just finished a job, it's virtually on his way home. And a few minutes later a white van appears over the brow of the hill.

Gwyn is in his thirties, tall, friendly in a bluff kind of way, and has that air of confidence that comes from solving practical problems. My electric socket diagnosis is soon dismissed on the very reasonable grounds that they aren't electric sockets at all, but phone sockets – he shows me the wires and tells me that lightning often finds its way down phone cables like this. But anyway, that shouldn't have affected the electricity. He asks me to hold a torch and starts testing the supply. He makes a face. There's good news and bad news. The good news is that there *is* electricity coming in at the mains; the bad news is that it looks like the main fuse has gone, and this type is not very common, and all the shops are now closed until Monday. I pull an agonised frown, explaining that I'm desperate to start writing the next chapter of the book I'm working on, and I can only really do it in this place. This seems to have some effect because Gwyn then says: 'Hang on, I've just thought of something. Come with me, you can open the gates, it'll be quicker.' And soon we're heading up the track at a speed I wouldn't dare to drive. He asks me what I'm writing about, and I give him a summary, deciding to omit the fact I've been working on this for fifteen years – I don't think this would impress a man like Gwyn, used to solving problems in a matter of minutes and hours, rather than years.

Having closed the gate, I get back in the van, and he then stuns me with this question: 'Tell me, do you think there's a relationship between grief and poetry?' It takes me time to respond. 'Well, I . . . yes, I think there is. I think the reason might be that in the days and weeks of intense grief we feel more alive than at virtually any other time in our lives. But why do you ask? Do *you* think there's a connection?'

He then tells me about a good friend of his, now living and working in New Zealand. This man had been involved in a horrific mining disaster there a couple of years ago, in which more than twenty of his colleagues had been killed, but he'd survived. Gwyn visited him recently and was astonished when this friend, who'd never written anything in his life before, showed him a powerful poem that he'd penned immediately after the tragedy. And Gwyn had also experienced something similar. He'd grown up in the next village, he tells

711

me, and was extremely close to his aunt, who lived on a farm just 'up there' (he gestures to a wooded hillside we're driving past). After she died, quite suddenly, in those days when he was overcome with grief, he found himself writing a poem as well. He'd never been any good at languages or literature or anything like that at school. To this day he has no idea where the words came from. But he read it at the funeral, and everyone was intensely moved, and asked him for the name of the poet. When he told them that he'd written it himself nobody believed him.

After I get out to open the second gate, a few hundred yards further down the track, I tell Gwyn that his experience has just reminded me of something I once heard the playwright Dennis Potter say. He'd been describing the lives of many in the working-class community where he'd grown up in the Forest of Dean, and the paradox that it was only through illness and being in hospital that he witnessed people finding a kind of liberation:

> Many of these people never had a chance to be, to concentrate on the shape of their own lives – you know they'd been at work, they'd got mortgages, kids, marriages, toil, activity, habit – all making you think that what you are is defined by other people – whereas we're all sovereign, separate, human beings. And most of the time life is telling us that we're not ... [it's only] in war or a personal crisis that people find they're far more heroic than they ever give themselves credit for ... and they can begin to assemble something like a perception of the shape of their own lives.

The power we all have inside. We wait for others to give it to us. Sometimes we wait all our lives, and yet it's there all the time. The creativity we are all born with is mind-blowing. The fact that so many people never really see what they have, or don't feel it's valued in any way, and that so many others lose sight of this flame altogether, is deeply disturbing. This reality has always shocked me – the way that our instinctive creativity as young children is abused and trammelled and disfigured and mocked through later childhood and adolescence. The funnelling, the narrowing towards employment or university – how few of us survive this process. Perhaps only a tiny minority.

I think of one of the most painful, and important, pieces of writing that I've ever come across, given to me long ago by a friend who was training to be a volunteer for the Samaritans. It was written by a teenage boy who had committed suicide, but left this single trace of who he was behind – on a piece of paper. A boy whose spirit had been destroyed by the society he'd grown up in:

He always wanted to explain things, but no one cared.
So he drew.
Sometimes he just drew and it wasn't anything.

He wanted to carve it in stone or write it up in the sky.
He would lie out on the grass and look up in the sky and it would be only the sky and the things inside him that needed saying.
And it was after that that he drew the picture.
It was a beautiful picture. He kept it under his pillow and would let no one see it.
And he would look at it every night and think about it.
Even when it was dark and his eyes were closed he could see it still.
And it was all of him and he loved it.

When he started school he brought it with him,
Not to show anyone, but just to have it with him like a friend.
It was funny about school.
He sat at a square brown desk like all the other square brown desks,
and he thought it would be red.
And his room was a square brown room like all the other square rooms.
And it was tight and close. And stiff.
He hated to hold the pencil and chalk with his arm still and his feet flat on the floor, still, with the teacher watching and watching.

The teacher came and spoke to him,
She told him to wear a tie like all the other boys.
He said he didn't like them and she said it didn't matter.
After that they drew. And he drew all yellow and it was the way
he felt about the morning. And it was beautiful.
The teacher came and smiled at him. 'What's this?' she said.
'Why don't you draw something like Ken's drawing?'
After that his mother bought him a tie and he always drew
aeroplanes and rocket-ships like everyone else.

And he threw the old picture away.
And when he lay out alone looking at the sky, it was big and blue
and all of everything, but he wasn't anymore.
He was square and brown inside and his hands were stiff.
And he was like everyone else. And all of the things inside
him that
needed saying didn't need it anymore.

It had stopped pushing. Crushed.
Stiff.
Like everything else.

*

The rain is still falling. Just the sound of the windscreen wipers in
the van now, both of us lost in thought. In the distance the lights
of a village come into view, in the lee of a hill. Grey chapel, grey
roofs, no shop or pub that I can see. Gwyn pulls up outside his little
workshop. I wait in the van while he goes to see whether he's got
the right kind of main fuse, and I think about what Gwyn's just told
me, and also about the boy who died. And why it is in our society
that some people's voices are never heard, or are only heard too late.
And others feel they have a God-given right to speak. I've always
felt this most acutely walking the leafy squares of Bloomsbury and
Fitzrovia and seeing the preponderence of blue plaques. Initially
you might wonder at all the creativity and intellectual achievement
that has occurred in these fine houses, but, if you reflect further,

surely you have to examine the structures of class and privilege that underlie such creativity. All the unacknowledged labour, the army of cooks and nannies and servants, the cushion of wealth which enabled the Leslie Stephens and Virginia Woolfs and Duncan Grants to breathe the pure air of literature and art. Creative expression has very little to do with genius or genes, and a great deal to do with the environment surrounding you as a child.

This doesn't mean that great art or ideas cannot come from those born into privilege, but it does mean that we should look more closely at the reality of that privilege. And the corollary of this is even more important – and disturbing: what happens to creative expression, beauty, passion, music, poetry and art when it never finds the ability to breathe or to speak? The millions of lost voices who have never been heard. Casualties of class, race, misogyny, homophobia, intolerance. The incalculable loss of that creativity, for the people themselves but also for the evolution of our societies. And I'm not thinking only about formal creative expression here – the creation of books or art or music – I'm also thinking about how human beings create themselves, shape themselves, and what it means to live a fully expressed life. And then how such a life can spark other lives. That sense of risk and experimentation.

I look out on the grey stone village through the windscreen wipers still slapping rhythmically. On the other side of the road I can see three teenagers smoking and drinking in a bus shelter. In the dark it's hard to tell if they're boys or girls, all of them in hoodies, passing a bottle between them. I feel an ache of solidarity with these three figures, remembering teenage years in rural isolation, far from town or city, not yet able to drive. Not even able to go to the local pub, if there was one. And yet their dreams are as fierce and beautiful as anyone else's. And there must be compensations to growing up here as well – the proximity to mountains, forests and sea . . . maybe that explains a lot? I try to imagine a London electrician or plumber talking unselfconsciously about grief and poetry – and I can't. Not that they don't think about these subjects, but the idea of talking to a stranger about them – no, it's just inconceivable. Perhaps the rocks and the rivers of these parts of Wales, and the deep culture of song and storytelling, have some intangible effect on all who grow up here.

Gwyn returns, holding out two main fuses – 'I knew I had these somewhere. I'm sure one of these will work, let's give them a try,' and soon we're driving back to the cottage by the sea. Prompted by what we've been talking about, on the way back I tell Gwyn about the Brazilian educationalist and activist Paulo Freire – and an account which I've never forgotten from one of his last books, *Pedagogy of Hope*. He recounts how, thirty years before, he had been invited to the city of Recife in the north-east of Brazil to give a presentation at Amarela House, in a poor part of the city, about the relationship between freedom and authority in education. The hall is packed, with local people, mainly urban workers and labourers, and Freire speaks for a long time, citing the work of Piaget on the development of the child's moral code:

> When I had concluded, a man of about forty, still rather young but already worn out and exhausted, raised his hand and gave me the clearest and most bruising lesson I have ever received in my life as an educator. I do not know his name. I do not know whether he is still alive. Possibly not . . .
>
> He raised his hand and gave a talk that I have never been able to forget. It seared my soul for good and all. It has exerted an enormous influence on me . . . In almost every academic ceremony in which I am honoured, I see him standing in one of the aisles of that big auditorium of so long ago, head erect, eyes blazing, speaking in a loud, clear voice, sure of himself, speaking his lucid speech.
>
> 'We have just heard,' he began, 'some nice words from Dr Paulo Freire. Fine words in fact. Well spoken. Some of them were even simple enough for people to understand easily. Others were more complicated. But I think I understood the most important things that all the words together say. Now I'd like to ask the doctor a couple of things that I find my fellow workers agree with.'

He fixed me with a mild, but penetrating, gaze, and asked: 'Dr Paulo, sir, do you know where people live? Have you ever been in any of our houses, sir?' And he began to describe their pitiful houses. He told me of the lack of facilities, of the extremely minimal space in which all their bodies were jammed. He spoke of the lack of resources for the most basic necessities.

He spoke of physical exhaustion, and of the impossibility of dreams for a better tomorrow . . .

As I followed his discourse, I began to see where he was going to go with it. I was slouching in my chair, slouching because I was trying to sink down into it. And the chair was swivelling, in the need of my imagination and the desire of my body, which were both in flight, to find some hole to hide in. He paused a few seconds, ranging his eyes over the entire audience, fixed on me once more, and said, 'Doctor, I have never been over to your house. But I'd like to describe it for you, sir. How many children do you have? Boys or girls?'

'Five,' I said – scrunching further down into my chair. 'Three girls and two boys.'

'Well, Doctor, your house must be the only house on the lot, what they call an "*oitao livre*" house, a house with a yard. There must be a room just for you and your wife, sir. Another big room, that's for the three girls. You have another room for the two boys. A bathroom with running water. A kitchen with Arno appliances. A maid's room – much smaller than your kids' rooms – on the outside of the house. A little garden with a . . . front lawn. You must also have a room where you toss your books, sir – a "study", a library. I can tell by the way you talk that you've done a lot of reading, sir, and you've got a good memory.'

There was nothing to add or subtract. That was my house. Another world, spacious and comfortable.

'Now Doctor, look at the difference. You come home tired, sir, I know that. You may even have a headache from the work you do. Thinking, writing, reading, giving these kind of talks that you're giving now. That tires a person out too. But sir,' he continued, 'it's one thing to come home, even tired, and find the kids all bathed, dressed up, clean, well fed, not hungry – and another thing to come home and find your kids dirty, hungry, crying, and making noise. And people have to get up at four in the morning the next day and start all over again – hurting, sad, hopeless. If people hit their kids, and even "go beyond bounds" as you say, it's not because people don't love their kids. No, it's because life is so hard they don't have much choice.'

This is class knowledge, I say now . . .

That night, in the car on the way back home, I complained to [my wife] rather bitterly. Though she rarely accompanied me to meetings, when she did she made excellent observations that always helped me.

'I thought I'd been so clear', I said. 'I don't think they understood me.'

'Could it have been you Paulo, who didn't understand them? . . . I think they got the main part of your talk. The worker made that clear in what he said. They understood you, but they needed to have you understand them.'

We've reached the first gate on the track at the brow of the hill as I finish this story. Gwyn has been listening intently.

'Yes, I can see why the academic is upset. But I'm not sure I agree with the point of this story – at least as I understand it.'

'Why not?'

'Well, I was brought up in a Labour family, proper Labour – socialism – not the New Labour crap. Anyway, you know what we were always taught?' "Workers by hand *and* by brain" – we're all working class, whether you're an electrician or a teacher – we should focus on everything we share, don't you reckon?'

Back at the cottage, with a little coaxing of pliers, and the odd adjustment, Gwyn slides one of the main fuses in, we wait for half a second, and then we hear a whirring as the fan in the bathroom comes on, and we delightedly click the other switches. We've got back the power! And now I'll be able to write for the next week. I thank Gwyn from the bottom of my heart, he's saved the day. But he won't accept any money from me. It was an old fuse he had, and anyway, he's enjoyed our conversation, that's more than enough for him – 'By the way,' he asks me, 'I suppose you probably know where the word "conversation" comes from, do you? No? Well, my sister, who's the brains of our family, she told me it's from "*con*" – with – and "*versare*" – to turn. To "turn with somebody", which then became, you know, to turn something over, to talk about something. Well, that's what we've been doing, isn't it? Turning things over – *conversare!*' And with that unexpected etymological flourish, he's off with a smile and a wave, and I'm left contemplating the nature of power in our world. The power of a hurricane, of a child, of a voice, of a corporation, of a hand, of a pen.

And the power coming out of the wall three feet to my left, and travelling through the socket, through the copper of the plug, along a white cable and into the laptop with which I'm forming these curious patterns on a screen. Attempting to make sense of processes that I still don't completely understand. The pathways in the brain that power the nerve endings that make my fingers move across these keys. As mystical to me as the transnational journeys of Chinese coal or American gas to the Liverpool docks, by rail and lorry to the power stations, by cables to the substation down the valley, and then the final journey here, to the cottage by the water. The invisible faces of all the human beings involved, all those I will never meet, and who, in all probability, will never read these words. The power of the hand. The power of the mind. All that we cannot yet connect.

PART FIVE

Perpetrators, Victims, Bystanders

12

The Architect on Trial

Albert Speer in his cell at Spandau. For twenty years. Seven thousand, three hundred and five days (including the five leap years). The cell 3 metres long by 2.7 metres wide. Working in the garden behind the prison walls. But also the place where he became free. Where he started his 'Walk Around the World'. I return to him, in this situation, again and again and again. As if there's a truth here, something tantalisingly at the edge of my reach, which is always pulling me back, saying 'No, you haven't seen it yet – keep looking, look harder'. To do this, I know we need to go beyond Speer's public persona. Or maybe not beyond, maybe go *between* the lines of the words he so carefully spun, and then we might be able to see, or feel, or experience a deeper meaning. (As I'm writing this, outside my house, a tiny grey spider has just lowered itself rapidly onto the screen of my laptop, like a paratrooper landing; but already the thread he arrived on has become invisible.)

That phrase comes back to me – 'like the survivors of a disaster'. The seven Nazi leaders who were not executed after Nuremberg, stumbling around, not really understanding why they were still alive. Yet Speer was isolated from his former colleagues, even as the trial was taking place, and this isolation only increased in Spandau. But, in his aloneness, something began to grow: an attempt to look at the truth, an attempt to deal with his own responsibility for the catastrophe that had been unleashed. (The spider now threads his way towards me, from the top corner of my screen, spinning his way relentlessly towards my face. I put a finger through the invisible thread behind him and lift him back onto the table.)

Speer was alone among the survivors – partly because he was the only one of them who had fully accepted collective responsibility at Nuremberg for what had happened under Nazism – as he repeatedly put it: 'for being part of a government that committed such crimes'. This was something of an irony given that he was the least ideologically committed of all of the defendants. It could have been a high-risk defence strategy, but his acceptance of responsibility, and dignified behaviour at the trial (in contrast to many of his codefendants), saved him from the death sentence that most had expected at the opening of the Nuremberg Tribunal.

Despite the closeness of his personal relationship with Hitler, throughout the trial he managed to separate himself (in the eyes of the judges) from his fellow Nazis, with their strain of thuggish fascism and crude antisemitism – coming across as the thoughtful, reflective architect he'd been at the outset of his career. This strategy, as well as saving his life, created his isolation, for his position gave him an air of moral superiority which deeply angered his fellow defendants, several of whom considered him a traitor. Many of them, unlike Speer, did not accept the legitimacy of the court; indeed Goering had spoken contemptuously of 'victors' justice'. But Speer's polite demeanour of respect towards the tribunal, and penitence for the evils committed in the years of Nazism, could not have been more useful from the perspective of the authorities – who were trying to use the trial as a tool of re-education for the German people after the war. To have a top-ranking Nazi leader, at one stage the second-most powerful man in the Reich, accepting the legitimacy of the court and expressing remorse for what had happened, was invaluable for the organisers of the Nuremberg process.

However, it was far from sure that Speer's defence would work; it was a high-wire act. It centred on him admitting *responsibility* – as a senior member of the Nazi government – without ever admitting *guilt* (because guilt implied knowledge of atrocities, which Speer always vehemently denied). Hence Speer, like all his codefendants at the opening of the trial, pleaded 'not guilty' to all the indictments. But he was completely frank about accepting responsibility, as he reflected later in life, interviewed in English for a BBC documentary[*]:

> I stated . . . that I am responsible for all those things, for all the slave labour – I didn't avoid telling clearly to the judges what I did. And even I felt responsible when it were [*sic*] orders of Hitler. Others of the accused they always were claiming it were orders from Hitler. I didn't do that.

Indeed his definition of 'responsibility' seemed to go even further than many would have expected:

> There was another question which was occupying my mind very much – this was how much of a responsibility I have to carry from all those things which I *didn't* know . . . I also am responsible for everything which happened, and even if I didn't know it, in the time when I was a leading man of the government.

This, at first sight, appeared to be a highly principled position, a clear acceptance of responsibility, and yet (as so often with Speer) things are not quite as they appear. As Reich minister for armaments and war production he had had ultimate authority over the requisitioning of millions of workers for the factories building tanks, weapons and munitions (14 million by 1944). Many of these, an increasing number as the war situation deteriorated, were 'forced' labour from occupied countries (often a euphemism for slave labour), where people worked in appalling conditions, and

---

[*] *Albert Speer: The Nazi Who Said Sorry*, BBC2, first broadcast on 2 May 1996.

life expectancy was often only a matter of weeks or months. Speer had also authorised the use of concentration-camp inmates and prisoners of war as forced labourers, which was against the Geneva Convention.

So, faced with this extremely serious charge sheet, how would Speer now approach the question of his 'complete responsibility'? With breathtaking sleight of hand, which a master magician would have been proud of, he transferred most of the responsibility for the policy of recruitment of forced labour, and its dubious legality, onto his far less powerful deputy, Fritz Sauckel, who had been plenipotentiary for labour deployment from 1942 onwards. And, remarkably, the judges seemed to accept this defence. Even the American prosecuting counsel, Robert Jackson, appeared to have swallowed Speer's line, making a distinction between Sauckel – who he called 'the greatest and cruellest slaver since the Pharaohs of Egypt, [who had driven] foreign peoples into the land of bondage on a scale unknown even in the ancient days of tyranny in the kingdom of the Nile' – and Speer, who had simply 'joined in planning and executing the programme to dragoon prisoners of war and foreign workers into German war industries'. The distinction was not merely a matter of the rhetoric of legal argument, however – for the defendants it was a question of life or death. At the end of the trial, Sauckel was given the death penalty, Speer twenty years' imprisonment. His strategy had worked; he was still alive.

Many of those who have written about Speer believe, wrongly in my view, that he expected to be sentenced to death. Sereny, for instance, felt that after the verdicts were handed down, he was 'almost disappointed – he'd brought himself to expect this [the death penalty] in a "euphoria of guilt", as he called it, and when they said 20 years, and the others got death, it diminished him in his own eyes'. But this cannot be right, for two reasons. The first is that, with one or two exceptions, Speer was absolutely contemptuous of his fellow defendants, regarding most of them as 'criminals' and thugs – so to have been sentenced to the same fate as them he would have regarded as the final insult. But the second reason can be found in a revealing comment that Speer made three months into the trial. He was speaking to Dr Gustave Gilbert, an American psychologist and former military intelligence officer who had been appointed as the prison psychologist at the Nuremberg Tribunal, and had free access to the prisoners throughout the trial. In this capacity, he gained the trust of many of the former Nazi leaders, and Gilbert's *Nuremberg Diary*, published in 1947, contains some remarkable insights into the psychology of these men.

We learn from Gilbert that on 9 February 1946 he was with Speer in his cell reflecting on his architectural career, and friendship with Hitler. They were discussing the moment (in January 1945) when Speer knew that the war was lost, and told Hitler so. But his Führer said Germany would continue fighting anyway – this was the moment when Speer realised 'he was bent on utter destruction of the German nation'. Then Gilbert did something very ingenious – he showed Speer his own photographs of 'beautiful German countryside . . . Germany as it was before Hitler; and then by contrast some photographs of lines of German prisoners (destroyed manpower), the ruins of Munich (destroyed cities), a dynamited bridge (destroyed architecture), and murdered prisoners in Dachau . . . He grew more and more grim as he looked at the pictures.' And this then provoked Speer into an uncharacteristically emotional outburst:

> Some day I would just like to cut loose and give a good piece of my mind about the whole business without pulling any punches! I would just like to sit down and write one final blast about the whole damn Nazi mess and mention names and details and let the German people see once and for all what rotten corruption, hypocrisy, and madness the whole system was based on! I would spare nobody, including myself – we are all guilty. I ignored the bare truth too!

After this, we learn from Gilbert that he 'asked Speer whether he wouldn't care to write about all of this?' And Speer's reply reveals quite clearly that he expected to avoid the death penalty: 'He said he would feel freer to do it after the trial was over.'

*

There were three days at Nuremberg which Speer found particularly devastating – the days when documentary film footage of the concentration camps and atrocities committed on the Eastern Front were shown to the court, and when Holocaust survivors gave testimony. The first of these was on 29 November 1945, when a film, *Nazi Concentration Camps*, was projected in the courtroom, showing graphic images which Allied military photographers and cameramen had taken at the end of the war, when the camps were liberated – including twisted bodies left all over the ground or hanging from barbed-wire fences, and diggers piling up corpses. Speer later described this as an absolute turning point for him. What had been abstract up to this point suddenly had form, generalised 'victims' became breathing people who had suffered barbarically because of the Nazi regime – the regime he had served so conscientiously. One such person was Samuel Rajzman, one of the very few survivors of Treblinka, who testified on 27 February 1946.

He took the witness stand that afternoon, short, bespectacled, smartly dressed, looking exactly like the accountant he had been before the war. He spoke with measured, simple sentences, but what he said – describing the year he had spent in the *Sonderkommando* at Treblinka from August 1942 to August 1943 – silenced the courtroom:

> At first my work was to load the clothes of the murdered persons on the trains. When I had been in the camp two days, my mother, my sister, and two brothers were brought to the camp from the town of Vinagrova. I had to watch them being led away to the gas chambers. Several days later, when I was loading clothes on the freight cars, my comrades found my wife's documents and a photograph of my wife and child. That is all I have left of my family, only a photograph.

The Russian prosecutor, Smirnov, asked Rajzman at one point, 'How long did a person live after he had arrived in the Treblinka camp?'

> Rajzman: The whole process of undressing and the walk down to the gas chambers lasted, for the men eight to ten minutes, and for the women some fifteen minutes. The women took fifteen minutes because they had to have their hair shaved off before they went to the gas chambers.
>
> Smirnov: Why was their hair cut off?
>
> Rajzman: According to the idea of the masters, the hair was to be used in the manufacture of mattresses for German women.

At this point the president of the tribunal, Lord Justice Lawrence, intervened. Like many in the courtroom, he cannot take in what he is hearing. Even in the stark economy of the trial transcripts you can detect the astonishment in his voice as he asks the question:

> Lawrence: Do you mean that there was only ten minutes between the time they were taken out of the trucks [sic] and the time they were put into the gas chambers?
>
> Rajzman: As far as the men were concerned, I am sure it did not last longer than ten minutes.

Rajzman also described what he had witnessed at the 'Lazarett', the mockery of a 'hospital' (complete with Red Cross flag outside) – the place where those too young, or old, or ill, to walk to the gas chambers were shot. This killing ground was the fiefdom of Scharführer Menz:

> They brought an aged woman with her daughter to the building. The latter was in the last stage of pregnancy. She was brought to the 'Lazarett', was put on a grass plot, and several Germans came to watch the delivery. This spectacle lasted two hours. When the child was born, Menz asked the grandmother

– that is the mother of this woman – whom she preferred to see killed first. The grandmother begged to be killed. But, of course, they did the opposite; the newborn baby was killed first, then the child's mother, and finally the grandmother.

Rajzman estimated that 'an average of three transports of sixty cars each arrived every day' during 1942, when the train transports were at their peak – 'on an average, I believe they killed in Treblinka from ten to twelve thousand persons daily'. In a detail that must have made Speer shudder, Rajzman also revealed that some Jews, from the towns and villages closer to Treblinka, were brought there by truck, and the trucks were stamped 'Spedition Speer' ('Transport Speer').

On these days of the trial, at such moments of personal witness, Speer felt something shift within him:

> When one hears of a thousand or a million people murdered it is out of scale, it's unimaginable. But this . . . it was the first time I could visualise what happened, what was done. And yes, it made me feel personal guilt.

Perhaps he also understood for the first time something of the enormity of the barbarism which had been unleashed. That he had been living in a state of criminal ignorance for years. And that, for all his generalised talk of 'responsibility', he was only at the beginning of a process of tortuous reflection that would occupy him for the rest of his life.

13

Room 519: Into This Darkness

Like the imaginary film that sometimes plays in my head, I've also had an image in my mind for many years, ever since I began the research for this book, back in the 1990s. I'll try to describe it for you:

> I see a man, mid-forties, coming back from his work in the City of London. It's a soft summer's evening, so there's no need to put the car in the garage. He can hear the sound of his children's voices coming from the garden, and he feels an acute sense of well-being as he walks around the side of the house, only pausing to smell the honeysuckle he planted last year.
>
> Earlier that day, the man, high up in one of Britain's leading oil corporations, had presented the final spreadsheets in a report to the board of directors. This report's recommendations were accepted – a stretch of coast the length of Cornwall in southern Nigeria will soon be developed. He cannot connect this fragrant evening in the leafy fringes of the Home Counties with his work earlier that day. He cannot, or perhaps will not allow himself to, connect his life with the lives of those in Nigeria about to be affected by his work. The simple action of tapping figures into a computer in an office in the City.

If we could discover what happens in the mind of such men, and women, then change might be possible. Change of an unimaginable kind. I've never believed that the majority of those working in corporations or powerful organisations of any kind are evil. The simplifications of those in the activist world and beyond who like to demonise others have always seemed hollow to me – the need for a shrill distancing from 'the other', 'the enemy'. As if by recognising these people's humanity, you are in some way allowing them to escape censure for their actions. Letting them off the hook. Absolutely not. In fact, quite the opposite. While needing to be even more rigorous in analysing the often devastating impacts of corporations, while needing to understand far more profoundly how corporations function (particularly in terms of organisational psychology), while needing to examine in a far more complex way the interrelationships between corporations and the state – we also need to become much more subtle in how we look at the workings of the human mind.

So my starting point is the human being. Remove the label of 'corporate' and say that people are not defined primarily by what they do but by who they are. Accept that the woman or man who leaves their home in the morning to go to work is not a different species to you or I – they too may be worrying about a dying parent, they too could be puzzling over a friendship that seems to have cooled, they too might be wondering about the meaning of their lives. The inner voices that come to us in the early hours. What do you *really* want in your life? Is this love or is it more like companionship? Is this what you've settled for?

I have no doubt that the man or woman leaving the house in the morning is not so far away from the doubting, compassionate, puzzled, loving person sketched above. They'll also be juggling lists in their head, checking texts and emails, thinking about the shopping they need on the way back this evening, the babysitter for tomorrow night, the mobile phone that needs replacing . . . Basically, a human being we would recognise, in all their messy reality. But then something happens. And it happens between pulling the door shut at home and swinging into the lobby at work. Something shifts in the mind, something switches, something is suspended, and it's considerably more than a move between the private self and the public self. Something is closed down in the journey between home and work; something profoundly dangerous occurs. The ability to love, to suffer, to have human relationships is put away into a safe box, until the end of the day. And such emotions now do not have to impede the business of business. It's as if the people have somehow given themselves permission (at least for the next hours) to put their empathy away, put their compassion in a sealed box. And other forces come into play, too – not least the need to survive in a world that demands all your defences, all your alertness, to deal with the constant manoeuvring of others. On some days it's exhausting just to think about it . . .

*

July 2011

I'm sitting in a very bland office on the fifth floor of Birkbeck College on one of the few really hot days of this summer so far. Out of the single window to my left I can see the leaves of a plane tree moving gently in the breeze; on my right are shelves of academic journals and books on child development. I've borrowed the room from a friend of mine, a professor of psychology, who's on vacation with his family this week. In a few minutes a man in his sixties will walk in here and sit down opposite me, and we'll begin an interview that will last around an hour and a half.

I'm still amazed that this man has agreed to see me. He was one of Shell's most influential figures in the 1990s, and was part of the team which had to co-ordinate the executive response to the media storms surrounding both Brent Spar and the executions of Ken Saro-Wiwa and his eight fellow Ogoni. He later played a key role in the birth of the so-called 'Corporate Social Responsibility' movement in the late 1990s.

For more than ten years I've wondered about how to do this. It's taken a great deal of planning and thought to get to this stage, where the people I want to talk to – the senior executives – feel able to sit down in a room with me. Three years ago I had an idea. I had been introduced to the head of research at a well-known business school, and had been invited to give several presentations to students there, from various corporate backgrounds, on the ideas I was developing around how people in organisations are able to 'compartmentalise' their individual ethics and their organisation's 'values' into different mental boxes. The response to these seminars was remarkable; I realised I had touched an exposed nerve in the body of contemporary corporate life.

I began to discuss a proposal with the business school, to develop a research partnership with an organisational psychologist, to interview senior-level executives on this question of ethical compartmentalisation. After much searching, we eventually found our research partner here at Birkbeck, a senior academic who had published on related fields connected to organisational values. And so our triangular research partnership was born, which we've called 'Ethical Compartmentalisation in Business Leadership'. We decided to focus our initial research on senior executives who had all worked in the oil industry. There followed several months of approaches to potential interviewees, before we could go ahead; in one case, it has taken more than a year from our initial invitation to getting the individual to agree to meet.

Over the next three days, we will be interviewing six individuals. All of these women and men worked at the highest levels within the oil industry over the last forty years or so; all, except one, are now retired. They are aged between fifty and seventy-two, four are men, two are women. The companies they've worked for include Shell, BP, Amoco and Total. The places they've worked include (apart from London) the USA, Indonesia, France, Japan, Angola, Nigeria, Alaska and Colombia.

As I'm waiting for the first interviewee today I reflect on the importance of creating a sense of safety for these people. The fact this is a collaboration between my organisation, Platform, an academic institution and a business school must help, together with the usual rigorous ethical criteria that are required in academic research. The fact that all, bar one, of the people I'm interviewing are either retired or no longer working in the oil industry must also have been a critical factor in them agreeing to speak to me. I also wonder whether the choice of a university building as the place for the interview has helped. The perceived safeness of academia, maybe. And July, a good time for this too, summer holidays, a sense of the normal defence mechanisms being lowered a little.

*

But, even now, I sense enormous tensions in the people we're about to interview. The most senior, once part of the Shell directorate, when I first managed to talk to him, spent half an hour on the phone explaining why he wouldn't be much 'use' to my research. Then, when this didn't work, he began to probe my background and approach. He sounded extremely anxious, and only after a long time was I able to persuade him that I was not approaching this from a position of conventional, activist judgementalism – that my interest was much more to do with organisational psychology, looking at the detailed processes which occur when people are attempting to deal with tensions between their own sense of ethics and their organisations' values. After that, he telephoned to postpone our first meeting – a sudden medical issue. So, two days ago, I phoned him again, from Pembrokeshire where I was writing, explaining that the following day I would be driving back to London – a six-hour journey – solely for the purpose of interviewing him, and therefore I wanted to be sure there weren't going to be any further problems. No, he would be there, don't worry. So this morning I arrived early at Birkbeck, and set up the room.

My professor friend and I didn't have time to go through the correct, bureaucratic procedure for room bookings with the college office. He simply gave me his keys, sent me an email confirming all of this was agreed, and then said: 'If you don't want to be disturbed I

735

think it would be good to put up a sign on the door – anything with an acronym will do. People don't ask because they don't want to feel stupid. What's the title of the research? That sounds fine – just turn that into initials!' So I printed out the following sign, and put it on the door:

PLEASE DO NOT DISTURB
ECBL INTERVIEWS IN PROGRESS

And nobody's disturbed me so far, so his idea seems to be working. I go downstairs to get a coffee and some cold drinks. Then I go to the main entrance, and wait for the first interviewee to arrive. Months and months of preparation to simply get somebody into a room, to talk for an hour and a half.

The man is on time. I recognise him from photographs in *Business Today* and the *FT*. But today he's not wearing a tie, he's smart, but off-duty, pale blue linen shirt, tasteful ivory jacket and trousers, loafers. But he looks flushed, and furrow-browed as we shake hands. 'Look, I've come today, but only to tell you in person that I don't think I can do the interview after all. I'm terribly sorry, I know you've put yourself to a lot of trouble, but . . . you see, I looked at your organisation's website yesterday last night, and I realised more about the work you do. And I was shocked by the misrepresentations there, the inaccuracies, and I began to ask myself questions about how this research would be used. You see, I have to be very careful, even though I'm now retired.'

I had anticipated precisely this response, and had already thought through how I would deal with it. So I now spend twenty minutes talking to him, explaining that Platform are highly respected in terms of the research we do in our field, that we could never have survived for more than fifteen years working on issues concerning the oil industry if we were not scrupulously careful in terms of what we publish, that we double-check everything, and moreover, we have two lawyers on our board of trustees, who ensure the accuracy of all that goes out into the world. I re-emphasise that, in accordance with the research criteria I sent him, he has complete control over his material, that he can redact all or any parts afterwards, if he feels uncomfortable with anything he's said. Eventually he's a little calmer, and agrees that we can go ahead with the interview. But what this shows me is that people are acutely aware both of the political nature of discussing the trajectory of a career in the oil industry, but also, on a far more personal level, people know that such a conversation could bring up extremely painful issues, questions which go to the heart of their sense of identity – what you have spent most of your adult life putting your energy into. And they know, instinctively, that talking about these issues, and their own ethics, could start pulling down walls that they have spent most of their working lives building and keeping in place.

*

On this day I'm also thinking of a former student of mine, and a warning he gave me more than ten years ago now. Alberto was a high flyer at Arthur Andersen,* a globe-trotting consultant – I sometimes wonder what happened to him after Andersen imploded in the wake of the Enron scandal – who'd been based in London for a year; he was about to return to Madrid, and we'd gone out for a last drink. We were sitting in a pub in Lamb's Conduit Street, reflecting on the last six months. We'd got on very well, he was a very sensitive, intelligent man and I'd enjoyed our classes together enormously. It had been more like talking to a bookish colleague; some weeks I felt he'd taught me more than I'd taught him – about how the Opus Dei strengthened their position under Franco, or a story from Buñuel's autobiography or where to get the best serrano ham in London.

---

* Arthur Andersen were one of the largest accountancy and consultancy corporations in the world in the late twentieth century. After being found guilty of fraud and criminal complicity in the auditing of the American energy corporation Enron in 2001, Arthur Andersen was wound up – though its consultancy arm, which split from the main company in 2000, continues to operate as Accenture.

Anyway, now Alberto was asking me directly about my other work – what exactly did Platform do? And what was this research into corporations that I'd mentioned from time to time? It's what you could call a 'taxi moment'. The exhilaration of living completely in the present, knowing that you will probably never see the other person again, so what is to be lost by being totally open? So I laid out my position in detail, describing the work on the oil industry that we'd been developing recently, telling him about Ken Saro-Wiwa and Shell in Ogoni. I didn't pull any punches. I talked about my particular fascination in aspects of both corporate psychology and the way that people working in corporations can distance themselves from the impacts their corporation has. I sketched the desired future trajectory for the project and the wider intent of the work I was developing. Alberto listened intently, nodding here and there, encouraging me to go further. Behind those round glasses it was hard for me to gauge his response; his face was curiously impassive at the best of times. After ten or fifteen minutes I paused, Alberto was smiling now, he put down his wine. This is my recollection of what he said:

I agree with a lot of what you've said, which may surprise you considering my job, but I think you're wrong about two things. First of all, I'm surprised by the way you generalise. Would you talk about 'activists' as if they're some kind of collective entity? People working in corporations are as different as any other group of people – gay, straight and confused, intelligent and ignorant, selfish and . . . oh, what is that opposite word you taught me? . . . *altruistic*, yes, that's it. But most people are just trying to get through to the end of the month like everybody else. Secondly, these people you've just talked about – the oil executives, the accountants, the planners – I've known a lot of them over the last ten years and the shocking thing is they're more like you, in all sorts of ways, than you could ever imagine. They're all graduates, quite a lot of them read the *Guardian* or the *Independent*, they go to theatre, concerts, are really interested in culture, and you'd be surprised how many of them care about wider issues, they're members of Friends of the Earth and Amnesty International. It's a mistake to think of 'them' as if they're another species.

Although Alberto was generalising here too, of course, something in what he said has stayed with me. And the more I've read about war, genocide and racism, the more I've become sure that none of these are possible without the perpetrators first using that lethal third person plural – 'they'. Those four letters have been used to justify almost every act of terror and oppression, whether it's Goebbels railing against the Jews, Stalin against the kulaks, Radio Télévision Libre des Mille Collines against the Tutsis, Bush against his 'enemies of freedom'. Before killing comes simplification.

We're shocked today, rightly so, if anyone uses 'they' to generalise about any group – it would simply seem crass, absurd, to talk in generalisations about any large number of people or community – imagine hearing somebody say 'students are X' or 'Jewish people are Y', and you would immediately sense the prejudice, and discount what followed. It is a sign of the progress in our societies that we are now more aware than ever of the linkage between generalisation and racism, homophobia and other prejudices.* In a European context, though, there is one group of people in particular who still experience others generalising about them, often in the most vicious and racist way – and that is the Roma.

Some years ago when I was teaching this was brought home to me vividly. It was the time when the authorities in the Czech town of Usti nad Labem had ordered the building of a wall around the part of the town where many Roma lived – a kind of modern ghetto. There was a furious response, the European Union made strong representations, and the Czech president, Václav Havel, called it 'unacceptable', and within weeks the wall was taken down. I'd been discussing the issue with my evening class, a mixed group of adults

---

* See chapter notes for further consideration of the question of generalisation in prejudice.

from different African, South American and European back-grounds, some of them refugees, when an Italian – a friendly and intelligent woman, a doctor from Bari – could take no more of all the liberal condemnation:

> 'OK, this may be a bit strong, this wall, but you have to admit Gypsies are a problem. They're dirty and everywhere they go they steal and rob.'
> 'Are you being serious?'
> 'Absolutely! In my city we built them a whole new area, flats, all modern. And you know what they did? They just broke them up, sold off the metal piping. No, really, it's true, they're happy to live like pigs.'

At this point all my pedagogical principles about the need for free discussion went out of the window and I became very angry – for the only time in all my years of teaching – and asked her what her solution was. Maybe 'Gypsies', as she referred to them, should all be put in camps? Or why not just kill them, as had been done in the Holocaust sixty years ago? I began to talk about how genocide begins with the pronouns 'they' and 'them'. I was relieved when other students started to join in, and the discussion moved on to their own experiences of racism. After a while, the doctor lapsed into a sulky silence. Later I tried to analyse why this particular person had made me so furious. I'd heard anti-Roma prejudice before – sadly it seems to be one of the most omnipresent forms of racism in our societies[*] – but there was something almost bra-zen about her expression of it here. Maybe I was angry with myself, because my impression of her had been wrong, and so this was like being slapped across the face. I was particularly shocked that this was an educated woman in her thirties, a doctor, supposedly one of the 'caring' professions.

---

[*] As I revised this chapter, the new Italian interior minister, Matteo Salvini, promised to turn 'words into action' and begin the process of expelling thousands of Roma from Italy: 'Far-right Italy minister vows "action" to expel thousands of Roma', *Guardian*, 19 June 2018.

But I hadn't handled this well. I'd lost my temper and tried to ridicule her, instead of letting the other students argue with her, as I normally would have done. Maybe I was concerned that some of the others in the class, who hadn't spoken, silently agreed with her. Perhaps I'd been too anxious on behalf of the more vulnerable students in the group who'd suffered from racism, but didn't yet have the linguistic skills to be able to express their experience with the articulacy and fluency needed to combat the Italian doctor. Unsurprisingly, she didn't come back to the class, and I felt a twinge of regret that I'd used my position not to open up critique and discussion, but to close it down.

But, to return to what Alberto said – if we become irate hearing bigots saying 'the thing about Gypsies is they're all . . .', or racists generalising wildly about Muslims, then how can we generalise about people working in oil corporations? Or bankers? Or politicians? Criticise the action, not the person. Be as uncompromising as you like in condemning the act, but do not write off the human being. I think here of a remarkable passage in Bernhard Schlink's book *The Reader*, where he describes the confusion in the mind of his protagonist – a student who has just realised that Hanna, the woman he'd had his first sexual experience and relationship with some years before, had been responsible for an appalling massacre of Jews in the war:

> I wanted simultaneously to understand Hanna's crime and to condemn it . . . When I tried to understand it, I had the feeling I was failing to condemn it as it must be condemned. When I condemned it as it must be condemned, there was no room for understanding . . . I wanted to pose myself both tasks . . . but it was impossible to do.

Condemning or understanding, the dichotomy that is always in us. The spectrum that we're always on. Gitta Sereny's work comes to mind again, with Stangl, with Speer, the extraordinary patience and curiosity about these men, who had experienced years of being judged and condemned. Some would say she slid too far towards understanding, but I strongly disagree. Because she never forgets their humanity, their insecurities, their doubts (as well as their vanities and their self-delusions), she is able to get us beyond the label of 'perpetrator' to the three-dimensional person behind, closer than anyone has managed, before or since. And by doing this, we are able to learn vastly more about the psychology of these people – and, perhaps most frighteningly, their ability to maintain a positive self-narrative while being part of genocidal organisations.

I wonder also if there's not a relationship between ageing and a desire to focus more on understanding rather than condemning. As I get older I'm becoming more and more fascinated by doubt. Life seems dramatically richer, and more nuanced, than it did when I was younger. I'm far more interested in questions than answers. I now think of curiosity and love as inextricably connected. Finding the most beautiful and powerful questions seems to me just about the most useful way of spending a life. How far away my younger self appears! The evangelical student activist burning with certainty and righteousness, ablaze with fixed beliefs. I don't think I'd be able to talk to that young man any more. I'm not sure he'd be able to listen. If he could, I'd probably say to him, 'cherish the questions themselves, like closed rooms and like books written in a very strange tongue, live everything, live the questions now'.

*

Days in that little room at Birkbeck as a succession of women and men arrive, talk about their working lives and the ethical choices they've made, and then leave. I'm totally unprepared for how draining the experience is; an intensity of listening, over hours, of not wanting to miss a single word or inflection, each of which could be significant. I'd made a decision – influenced strongly by Gitta Sereny's approach to her interviewees – that (for the duration of the interviews) I would completely repress my instinct to judge or challenge what people told me. The most important thing was to engage with everyone in as empathetic a way as possible, to let people express themselves in the language they chose, to learn as much as I could about their backgrounds, their ethical values, what they had wanted to achieve when they started their working lives. Naturally, this was extremely difficult at times; I could feel myself straining at the leash on a number of occasions, but I never lost control, because I knew this would shut the interview down, and, in the process, remove all possibility of finding out what I wanted to discover.

The results of this approach surprised me, and I think also surprised my interviewees. They arrived nervous, expecting academic and activist cut and thrust, attack and defence, and instead here was a man who wanted to understand them, wanted to know about the choices they had made in their lives. Warm, polite, self-effacing, able to see many sides to a story, the complexity of dilemmas. And, as a result, all six women and men opened up in ways I found remarkable. I was quite unprepared for the emotions that such a process unlocked in most of the interviewees; it was strikingly like the process of counselling in some regards, as people attempted to find language for the ethical choices they had made, and reflected on different stages of their lives. Four of the six, at different moments, became visibly moved. Two of them actually cried. Finally, Alberto's warning was borne out – I couldn't help liking most of 'them', because they were not 'them' but six individuals. They do not (with two exceptions) give me a 'company line'. Some were witty and self-deprecating, one even repeatedly warned me, 'Anything I say has to be taken with a pinch of salt, from recollections so long ago, [because] you tend to remember, you know, positive things . . . when you did things well.'

Months later, I'm going through hundreds of pages of transcripts from these recordings, every 'erm', every 'eh', every 'you know', faithfully recorded by the transcriber. Those days at Birkbeck coming vividly back to life, as I experience again the words from our conversations. Although I hadn't judged or challenged during the actual interviews, now the analysis can really begin.

From all of these hours of conversation, six moments seem particularly significant. The words of the interviewees are quoted verbatim below, as are my responses – which of course I could not express during the interviews themselves:

Moment One

Anna (ex-Shell). We'd been talking for about fifteen minutes about the executions of Saro-Wiwa and his colleagues in 1995, the Brent Spar oil-rig dumping scandal in the same year and the impacts on the company, the Shell internal response to this. And then she says this:

> Shell felt literally under siege ... It wasn't just the boycotts in the petrol stations ... people were firebombing the petrol stations in Germany. They were shooting at people on our forecourts with shotguns from moving cars, and I'm not exaggerating this, Dan, at all ... Shell said, 'For Christ's sake, nobody should die over this!' And our first deep concern was that nobody should get hurt over this.
>
> *[Anna's comment 'Nobody should die over this'? seems extraordinary to me. Considering we'd just spent fifteen minutes discussing the hundreds of people who had died in oil-related conflict in the Niger Delta, in the 1990s, and the executions of the Ogoni Nine. I felt she was asking me to feel sympathy for Shell with these comments – as if she wanted to turn the company into the victim here.]*

Moment Two

David (ex-Shell). We'd been discussing the great controversy about Shell staying in South Africa during the apartheid years, and I'd raised the question of how affected Shell employees are by ethical questions from their own families, and people outside the company, and he described one evening, having dinner with Shell's general manager in South Africa:

Me: So you're getting all this pressure from outside. I mean it's a mistake to think there's this hermetically sealed little world, isn't it?

David: I'll never forget, one of the . . . erm . . . I think it was someone senior in Africa, where he was being portrayed – they did a show [a documentary] on him, and I happened to be having dinner with him and the director at that time in charge of that region, and erm, the phone rang, and he came back into the room, and he said, 'My son has just accused me of being a murderer!' Because, watching the television . . . And he said, 'I don't understand how I can explain to him that what is being shown is not . . .' I mean, the heartbreak in this man was just . . . was just dreadful!

[As he related this story David began to cry. Again we see this remarkable sense of inverted reality here – the people working for Shell do not seem to see it as one of the most powerful corporations in the world, but rather as a fragile victim of unfair public judgement and disapprobation.]

Moment Three

Paul (ex-BP). We'd been talking about Paul's role in a South American country of oil extraction, where there had been killings and serious human rights abuses, and journalists had published evidence of local paramilitaries being paid by the oil companies to supply security. Paul had been extremely articulate in the interview up to this point, but when I asked him to empathise with the affected communities, his ability to speak cogently broke down altogether:

Me: I mean, this is a more hypothetical question really . . . but did you . . . did you ever, in a way, imaginatively put yourself in the shoes of one of the villagers? Did you kind of think about what would it be like to be them in that situation?

Paul: <u>I mean</u>, I did go to a couple of meetings, public meetings, sat there with, <u>you know</u>, for ... <u>erm ...</u> where community leaders and, <u>you know</u>, in <u>erm ...</u> what's the capital of? ... And of course, <u>you know</u>, they ... some people would be, oh, he's a guerrilla, he's connected to the paramilitary ... It's very ... not as it all seems. But yes, <u>I mean</u>, the answer is that's the whole point, is <u>erm ... erm ... you know, erm ... you know</u>, what's on the ground, <u>I mean</u>, what we affect most on the ground affects us most on the ground, so it – <u>you know</u>, it really was ensuring that, <u>you know</u>, that the local communities felt much more comfortable.

[Fifteen hesitations in four sentences. A vivid illustration of the unease he felt trying to answer this question. Also one sentence here just doesn't make any sense at all no matter how many times you reread it – 'But yes, I mean, the answer is that's the whole point, is erm ... erm ... you know, erm ... you know, what's on the ground, I mean, what we affect most on the ground affects us most on the ground'. I was also astonished that Paul was based in this country for two years, so the fact that in his position of seniority he only felt a need to go to 'a couple of public meetings' shows how little direct contact there is with impacted communities on the ground. And, of course, he hadn't answered my question here, which focussed on the ability – or not – of the BP staff to empathise with those affected on the ground. Significantly, none of the interviewees who'd worked in developing-world contexts ever answered this question directly.]

Moment Four

Tony (ex-BP). We'd been discussing the same question – the extent of contact with villagers on the ground, and whether he could put himself in the shoes of the villagers affected.

Tony: In terms of when I got close to these sort of issues – an early [sort of] experience was being involved in a project to build a new LNG plant in N——, and it involved the relocation of a village, whose name was – this was the early 80s – F—— village. I remember the name because it was such an interesting episode. And it was amazing, at the time, it was an absolute eye-opener, sort of the demands the villagers were coming up with, eh, and what had been sort of . . . basically, a very basic farming village, turned out to be a village which had all sorts of interesting, not just farming, fishing and, you know, all sorts of exotic forms of agriculture which there was no visible evidence of, but, of course . . . and an elder chief of the village, who I seem to remember sort of . . . who lived in basically a mud hut before the arrival of the oil companies, decided that he needed to live in a two-storey, concrete-built house with deep-pile carpeting. This is in N——. So erm. And separate bathrooms for himself and his wife. And all these, all these, basically, demands were acceded to.

[The casualness of the assumptions here, and the underlying racism, is revealing; Tony's remarks illustrate what could be called a neocolonial mindset. Those seven words about the Liquefied Natural Gas project: 'it involved the relocation of a village' – could easily have come from the lips of a nineteenth-century colonial administrator in a distant part of the British Empire. I wondered how Tony thought his family in their Sussex village would react if a foreign energy company arrived one day and told them they all had to 'relocate' because there were gas deposits under their village?]

Moment Five

Later in the same interview, Tony described the apparently obsessive culture of health and safety at BP, when he returned to the head office after a posting abroad:

The thing that absolutely struck me, the most . . . the most visible when I came back was the safety culture, because, my first day back, two things happened: I went up a staircase at headquarters without holding the handrail, and a very junior person of staff remonstrated with me that I should hold the handrail – I thought, gosh [laughing] . . . ! Yeah. Try it one day – if you walk down a staircase in BP and you don't hold the handrail, someone absolutely [literally] will remonstrate with you. The second thing, I got into a taxi to go to a meeting across town, with a quite junior colleague, and got in the cab, my colleague said, 'You need to put your seat belt on.'

But this obsession with health and safety clearly did not extend to operations on the ground. We then reflected on what had caused the *Deepwater Horizon* disaster in the Gulf of Mexico in 2010:

Me: So attention on a micro level, but at a macro level . . . not!

Tony: Yeah.

Me: I mean, that's quite shocking, in a way.

Tony: It is shocking.

Me: The difference between those.

Tony: Well, it was a classic case of [the] company convincing itself that something was happening when it wasn't, and it was dealing with the symptoms, not the causes, if you like, and the basic problem that emerged, and it really was interesting to see . . . was this actually fundamental contradiction between the performance culture, which is about meeting targets – financial, operational, schedule, timing – and HSE, which means taking no risks, which means, if there's ever a trade-off between, you know, meeting a target for a budget or for a timeline, and a trade-off with safety, you know, you have a fundamental contradiction there.

Me: That's very interesting.

Tony: Which one predominates? And the best manifestation of this was the so-called performance contracts, that all managers above a certain level in BP had, and have, and at the time, I think 95 per cent of the bonus, the remuneration . . . was about performance. Five per cent was about HSE.

Moment Six

Isabelle (ex-BP). Isabelle was the only interviewee who had left the company for ethical reasons. In some respects, particularly as she'd always been a strong advocate of human rights, it was surprising she'd joined in the first place and then lasted thirteen years. We discussed the difference she perceived between herself and her colleagues:

> They had a different view. It wasn't the fact that they didn't have any morals, but they were able to . . . seemed to be able to leave them at the door, right? So . . . often, they were Christian people, you know, deeply religious, go to church and all of that, and they'd be doing this stuff at the . . . you know, 'I'm on the PTA,' doing all this stuff with kids and all of that, and yet, when they came through the door, they were able to sort of push that aside and they became . . . different people, in a way. But I've never been able to do that because I bring everything in . . . So, that was quite difficult, erm, because they couldn't quite understand it. They'd say, 'Well, that's fine, but, you know, you mustn't . . .' One person said to me, 'Leave your conscience at the door.'

By the end of her time, she's challenging this culture more and more, but also feeling more isolated:

> By the time I was leaving, [they used to] dread me coming to the meetings because I'd actually . . . have real debates with them and . . . and tell them that they were talking a load of bullshit, basically, and that they didn't know what they were doing. And, erm, you know, they . . . how could they sort of talk about things like the UN Charter of Human Rights . . .

and have this stuck up on their wall, when they were breaking all of it, you know?! . . . But I got more and more isolated. It was quite lonely. It was quite lonely, yeah.

She was one of only two interviewees to speak directly about how disturbing she found the experience of witnessing the impacts of the oil industry on the ground. And again, as with Paul, the more she spoke about what she'd actually seen on the ground, the more her language broke up, and hesitations multiplied:

Erm, you'd see pollution, you'd see <u>erm</u> . . . <u>you know</u>, for instance, in the Delta, it never used to get dark in parts because of the gas flaring. <u>I mean</u>, gas flaring is quite extraordinary, <u>I mean</u>, it is . . . it's just poverty, and the fact that there is so much wealth, and that extreme in how they lived as expats – <u>you know</u>, the sort of gated community. I found that very hard and I wanted to go out all the time, and I would actually go out, and that drove them mad. They, <u>you know</u>, they saw me as a security risk, in that sense, because they didn't want me to just wander off because I – I'd do anything to get rid of my drivers and things like that, so I could just go and walk and . . . it's very hard to do that, so . . . But poverty . . . <u>you know</u>, you'd look out of your window and you'd see kids, <u>you know</u>, or adults, going through the dustbins looking for things, <u>erm</u>, and <u>you know</u>, awful stories you'd hear as well from other colleagues – <u>you know</u>, people being shot. <u>You know</u>, they'd actually seen that outside, and bodies being carried off . . . <u>You know</u>, it was, <u>you know, you know</u>, you would see these sorts of things happen, erm, and . . . and to me, at that stage of it anyway, because I got so immersed in Africa and was seeing all of this, that I just kept thinking, <u>you know</u>, oil has just destroyed this country. So my . . . I started to blame everything on oil, which, <u>you know</u>, maybe that wasn't completely right, but I started to blame everything on oil, because, to me, it was fuelling everything, the conflict, because these are really big oil-dependent countries, like Nigeria and Angola, so you start to blame everything on the oil.

Just before she finally leaves, she speaks to a colleague who's retiring:

> He said to me, 'I'm so glad I'm going now, because,' he said, 'working in Angola has bothered me for so long, and I feel, you know, that's good – I can sleep better at night.' I found that quite extraordinary.

What had she learnt? How had her views on morality and ethics changed in this time?

> I think you just have to stand your ground, and you have to behave how . . . you have to treat others how you'd want to be treated, and I always want to put myself in other people's shoes all the time, and I'm not afraid to say that to people, wherever, you know . . . I think you . . . you have to. You have to have morals.

*

What else remains from these days of conversations? I was very struck by how strongly several of the interviewees emphasised their moral and religious principles – maybe in some way wanting to use these as a cloak to protect themselves from my (unspoken, but still detectable) scepticism about their desire to work in a business as dubious as the oil industry. But perhaps this is too cynical of me. There may also have been quite genuine religious and ethical impulses in the backgrounds of these people. Though, if this is the case, then I really cannot understand how it was possible for them to justify their actions – for instance, in staying on at Shell, helping to defend the company, even after the Saro-Wiwa and Ogoni executions.

There were other threads in common, aspects that were shared between the people we interviewed. The same argument was used to try and explain why Shell stayed in South Africa during apartheid, from two different ex-Shell employees. This made me sense that there had been a co-ordinated internal company 'line' issued to all employees. Incidentally, it's fascinating to look at the language both Anna and David used – making the oil company sound more like a provider of local social services rather than a profit-making business:

> Anna: I believe Shell was a force for good within that society, and Nelson Mandela said, after his release, that he was glad Shell stayed and that, erm, Shell had been instrumental in, erm, challenging the government on black housing, and providing black housing, which was technically illegal at the time, and they were able to get the law changed to allow Shell to provide black housing, and the standards by which Shell upheld during that period and respect for human rights and diversity, erm, I felt was a beacon in a very bleak period, where other companies were cutting and running. But Shell said, no, if we make a commitment to a country, then we're in for the long term; we're not just in for a smash and grab on what we can get and how much money and get away. And we don't make a commitment to the government of the day, we make it to the people of the country ... So, my feeling about Shell's performance in South Africa was one of pride and admiration, erm, that they were showing leadership.

> David: I think one of the things that was not appreciated is that, erm – erm ... we were actually encouraged to remain in South Africa. Erm, we also created educational foundations for many ANC members. Our general manager in South Africa used to place adverts in the newspapers constantly about anti-apartheid ... The feeling was that, erm, remaining there, and trying to, erm, actually influence the thinking, because, again, people didn't realise, it was a point, decimal point, you know, it was a 0.0-something percentage of our profits ... it's very interesting, there was this terrible, erm, dilemma, where people at the top of the organisation were really reluctant to remain, but felt that they were the only ones that had the clout to actually be able to speak out without – with most people daring not to. And, you know, our connections with the ANC were actually quite close at the time too, in a positive way ...

In fact, we let them have our building when they . . . when they came into . . . came into power.

Both Anna and David are emphasising the critical role Shell supposedly played in influencing the apartheid-era government and the process of peaceful transition in South Africa – yet both cannot see the gaping contradiction between this position and their argument that Shell could not influence the Nigerian government in the case of the executions of Ken Saro-Wiwa and his colleagues. They repeatedly said they could not be seen to be 'interfering' in Nigerian politics, and sought to minimise the power Shell have in Nigeria, saying that 'we're in a joint venture in Nigeria, we do not own the majority of the company'. Neither of these senior ex-Shell figures could see the obvious contradiction between these positions. David went further – even seeming to sympathise with the Abacha military regime:

But of course, the Nigerian government's reaction . . . was, well, you know, don't interfere with our policies. But again, with great respect, with great respect, so far as the Nigerian government was concerned, Ken Saro-Wiwa was not being tried for what he was saying about the oil industry, but there were five* people in [the] Ogoni tribe who were killed, and their view was that he and his henchmen were responsible for those five deaths and that nobody in the world seemed to be in the least bit concerned about these five Ogoni tribesmen who were not agreeing with Mr Saro-Wiwa. So there was . . . there were their stresses, and of course, I mean, the problem is, if a company like Shell tried to interfere with the UK government in as blatant a fashion, everybody would have their hands up, you know, and they would be up in arms.

But Shell were not alone in doing business with successive Nationalist governments in South Africa. Some years earlier I'd heard John

---

* The Nigerian government had alleged that *four* people, not five, as David states here, were killed by associates of Saro-Wiwa (this allegation was never supported with any factual evidence).

Browne, then CEO of BP, justifying why they too remained in the country during the apartheid years:

> BP of course stayed in South Africa during a very tough time during apartheid bringing our own employees to a different level of educational qualification, maximising the number of black people working inside our company. This was not wholly popular at the time but it sowed small seeds which in the right environment subsequently grew to enormous trees – some great people were available to populate part of the government – great people were there to populate part of industry.

I think that such language in the twenty-first century is extraordinary. Not just because of the language used, but the ideas behind the language, which seem completely rooted in colonialism. We could almost be listening to Lord Salisbury talking about bringing 'English civilisation . . . [to] the dark places of the earth'. BP goes to South Africa, they sow 'small seeds', the local population are then educated, and one fine day they might be trusted to take over their own country.

The final realisation I had through the process of these interviews concerns the interrelationship between location and moral responsibility. The greater the exposure of employees to the actual sites of oil extraction, the greater the moral scepticism; the greater the amount of time spent working in the UK, at headquarters, the greater the degree of trust in the company. This may be a reason why the higher your position in an oil company rises, the less chance there is that you will be posted to experience the activities of the company at the sites of oil extraction themselves. It's as if the companies appreciate that it will be far harder for senior management to continue to work effectively if they actually have to meet people directly impacted by their work. It's much safer to keep any such understanding distanced through the screen of a computer. In this way you do not have to experience, you do not have to look with your own eyes, into the eyes of other human beings whose lives are being devastated by your company's work.

754

How People in Organisations Can Kill: A Further Four Factors

- Incrementalism
- 'Normalisation' and peer conformity
- **Language and dehumanisation**
- **Abstractifying victims: from individuals to anonymous masses**
- **Distancing yourself from the act of violence**
- **Transferring personal responsibility to the authority's responsibility**
- Compartmentalisation of thought
- Workaholism and the 'narcissism of frenzy'
- Prioritisation of abstract systems over the human being
- Looking away or wilful ignornace

Language and Dehumanisation

If you change the language used about the 'other' – a potential victim – from that of a sentient being to that of an object it becomes easier to think of that person as an object, and then treat them as such. This aspect of organisational killing is extraordinarily widespread, and examples can be found in widely different international contexts.

We've already seen the use of the word 'load' to describe the people gassed in the Saurer trucks; and the way that entire memorandum evades using words that suggest the victims are human beings ('97,000 have been processed', etc.). But we should also understand that, throughout the concentration-camp system, the word 'person' to describe an inmate was forbidden. Instead the term '*Stuck*' ('item' or 'piece') was the correct terminology; and after death the word 'body' or 'corpse' could not be used – indeed it was a disciplinary offence to use such language – the correct alternative to indicate a dead human being was '*Figuren*' ('pieces').

Another common means of linguistic dehumanising is to turn human beings into animals, often the smallest, most despised creatures. The torturers under the Greek colonels referred to their victims as 'worms'. In the Rwandan genocide Hutus called their potential Tutsi victims '*inyenzi*' ('cockroaches'). Stangl, the former commandant at Treblinka, made explicit the linkage in his mind between animals and human beings, when he gave Gitta Sereny the following account:

> 'When I was on a trip once, years later in Brazil,' he said, his face deeply concentrated, and obviously reliving the experience, 'my train stopped next to a slaughterhouse. The cattle in the pens, hearing the noise of the train, trotted up to the fence and stared at the train. They were very close to my window, one crowding the other, looking at me through that fence. I thought then, "Look at this; this reminds me of Poland; that's just how the people looked, trustingly, just before they went into the tins . . ."'
>
> 'You said "tins",' I interrupted. 'What do you mean?' But he went on without hearing, or answering me.
>
> 'I couldn't eat tinned meat after that. Those big eyes . . . which looked at me . . . not knowing that in no time at all they'd all be dead.' He paused. His face was drawn. At this moment he looked old and worn and real.

*

In the reports that the *Einsatzgruppen* – the mobile killing squads – sent back to Berlin between 1941 and 1942 we also have an utterly dehumanised language, where people or victims are never mentioned, and instead a bizarre range of euphemisms are employed:

> 'cleansing activities'
> 'security measures'
> 'severe measures'
> 'a special liquidation'
> 'necessary liquidations'
> 'actions carried out in an exemplary manner'
> 'reprisal measures'

'retaliation measures'
'special tasks'

It is only rarely that the language in these reports becomes explicit, and that the people being killed are named – but even then only as a collective entity: 'Only ninety-six Jews were executed in Grodno and Lida during the first days. I gave orders to intensify these activites.'

*

But we shouldn't regard such language of dehumanisation as a historical phenomenon. It surrounds us in our time. Think about the widespread use of depersonalised euphemisms in war contexts, the way, for instance, that the Orwellian term 'surgical strike' (death = health) has now widely replaced 'bombing raid' or 'attack'. Or look at this breathless pitch from the military analyst Sir Timothy Garden, in the run-up to the Iraq War:

> With war seemingly inevitable weapon designers will be looking forward to another opportunity for field-testing new products . . . The cluster bomb remains in US and UK inventories. Here a shower of small munitions is released over the target area. They can be effective against dispersed groups of military vehicles.

- 'Products' supposed to sound like any other consumer item.
- 'Shower' as in rain, as in refreshing, as in 'it's probably just a shower' (i.e. ephemeral), when we're actually talking about one of the most appalling weapons ever invented that explodes in the form of thousands of small mines.
- Note the form of 'is released' – the passive construction – so the agents of this action – the killers – become invisible. And note the choice of that verb 'release' and not 'explode'.

757

- Finally the weapons are effective against 'groups of military vehicles' – i.e. inanimate objects, not driven by any human beings.

The language of technical jargon is particularly adept at removing any trace of humanity or suffering from the process of killing. Take this breathlessly excited description of the capabilities of the MQ-9 Reaper drone, from a USAF 'factsheet'. This drone, also known as the Predator B, is said to be employed

> against dynamic execution targets and secondarily as an intelligence collection asset. Given its significant loiter time, wide-range sensors, multi-mode communications suite, and precision weapons... it provides a unique capability to autonomously execute the kill chain (find, fix, track, target, execute and assess) against high-value, fleeting and time sensitive targets (TSTs).

So human beings are reduced to acronyms ('TSTs') – because it's much easier to kill an acronym than a person of flesh and blood.

*

Another way of removing a person's humanity is by removing their name, and replacing it with a number. This has been common in prison and military systems throughout the world; it is often regarded as the first step in trying to break the resistance of a person. Primo Levi describes, in *If This Is a Man*, the moment in Auschwitz when he became a number:

> *Häftling* [prisoner]: I have learnt that I am *Häftling*. My number is 174517; we have been baptised, we will carry the tattoo on our left arm until we die ... It seems that this is the real, true initiation: only by 'showing one's number' can one get bread and soup ... weeks and months were needed to learn its sound

in the German language. And for many days, while the habits of freedom still led me to look for the time on my wristwatch, my new name ironically appeared instead, a number tattooed in bluish characters under the skin.

I came across this image many years ago, taken by the photographer Jean Mohr, in *A Seventh Man*, John Berger's book about migrant labour in western Europe:

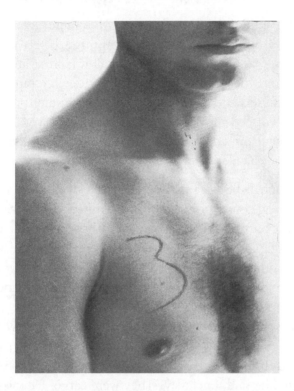

The first shock of this is to see a man reduced to a number, an object. The second shock is when we realise the man is a Turkish migrant worker and the figure has been written on him by a German doctor from a German corporation checking whether the man is fit for work. The third shock is to realise that this was happening in the 1970s, thirty years after the war – that there is a continuity in patterns of inhuman behaviour that we thought had been expunged from our world for ever.

Abstractifying Victims: From Individuals to Anonymised Masses

If you cease to see a person as an individual and only perceive them as part of an undifferentiated mass, it is much easier to kill them. This criterion overlaps significantly with the preceding concept of dehumanisation, though the linguistic aspect prefigures this; it would be hard to reach this behaviour if you hadn't already, in your language, and therefore your mind, begun the process of dehumanisation.

Towards the end of the film *The Third Man* there's a famous scene where Harry Lime (Orson Welles) is up in a Ferris wheel overlooking post-war Vienna with our narrator, Holly Martin (Joseph Cotten). Lime, the smiling, contemporary devil, tempts the good man with these words: 'Would you really feel any pity if one of those dots stopped moving for ever? If I offered you £20,000 for every dot that stopped, would you really tell me to keep my money, or would you calculate how many dots you could afford to spare?'

Again, though fictional, this example corresponds precisely to an extremely dangerous aspect of the human mind: the ability to strongly individualise ourselves and those we love – how extraordinarily complex and subtle are *our* minds and emotions! – while, at the same time, simplifying others' lives. And in extreme cases (especially with perceived 'enemies'), classifying all of 'them' as a collective, anonymised mass. Again I return to the example of Franz Stangl, interviewed by Sereny – a continuation of the previously quoted interview:

'So you didn't feel they were human beings?'

'Cargo,' he said tonelessly. 'They were cargo.' He raised and dropped his hand in a gesture of despair.

'When do you think you began to think of them as cargo? The way you spoke earlier, of the day when you first came to Treblinka, the horror you felt seeing the dead bodies everywhere – they weren't "cargo" to you then, were they?'

'It started the day I first saw the *Tötenlager* in Treblinka. I remember Wirth standing there, next to the pits full of blue-black corpses. It had nothing to do with humanity – it couldn't have; it was a mass – a mass of rotting flesh. Wirth said, "What shall we do with this garbage?" I think unconsciously that started me thinking of them as cargo . . .

'There were so many children, did they ever make you think of your children, of how you would feel in the position of those parents?'

'No,' he said slowly, 'I can't say I ever thought that way.' He paused. 'You see,' he then continued, still speaking with this extreme seriousness and obviously intent on finding a new truth within himself, 'I rarely saw them as individuals. It was always a huge mass. I sometimes stood on the wall and saw them in the tube. But – how can I explain it – they were naked, packed together, running being driven with whips like . . .' The sentence trailed off.

The word 'cargo' used here inevitably recalls the term used repeatedly by British financiers and traders involved in slavery and the transportation of slaves. To the bankers and insurers in the City of London, and other financial centres such as Edinburgh, the slaves had never been considered as human beings. That is why they were branded with hot irons (as cattle used to be branded), regarded simply as property to be traded. And on the occasions when a ship sank, deaths would not be referred to, rather cases of 'lost cargo'.

*

Without such a process of abstractifying victims, wars would be impossible. Here is a man who worked on one of the bombers involved in the destruction of Dresden describing his feelings, or lack of them:

You were on your way home, you'd done what you were supposed to do, and you never thought about what was happening on the ground. I mean if you did and you thought about it deeply, then you couldn't do the job.

However terrible conventional bombing may have been, at least the bomber crews were risking their lives every time they flew a mission. Today we have entered an era of remote killing from the skies – drone warfare, where the 'pilots' no longer have to be in the planes that are dropping missiles and bombs, or even in the same country as their victims; in fact, they are often 8,000 miles away, on the other side of the world, operating the drones from computer terminals. Twenty-first-century technology means that ever greater distances between the killers and the victims exist, and this only serves to further anonymise the people killed, and further reduce the sense of personal responsibility of the perpetrators – both factors which make the process considerably easier for the killer. In this context, the abstractification of their victims, and the emotional detachment that follows from this, only increases.

The BBC journalist Stephen Sackur interviewed several RAF pilots who were working at a joint US/UK drone mission focussing on targets in Afghanistan, based at the Creech USAF base in Nevada. Wing Commander Jules Bell explained the set-up:

> We've got something in the order of twenty to twenty-five screens that we can be looking at constantly . . . in simple terms what we're using is satellite links from Nevada, which are uplinked from the US, they are downlinked to the aircraft that is flying in the Afghanistan theatre . . . We're able, with a small time delay of perhaps two seconds, to fly the aircraft in the same way we'd fly any conventional aircraft . . . We have what we call a Ground Control Station, or GCS, [it] is perhaps caravan-sized, it typically [has] a crew of three – that's our pilot, the sensor operator and the mission co-ordinator, and we all work as a team to operate the aircraft.

The decision to fire is ultimately made by the pilot himself, but we learn that they 'would almost certainly be employing weapons at the request of the ground supported unit . . . and they are the people best able to gauge the requirement for that weapon's effect'. Andy

Bavistock, an information analyst, is interviewed. He believes he has what he calls 'bigger situational awareness' 8,000 miles away from the conflict zone, and because he's 'not got to worry about [his] own safety . . . [he] can concentrate on the mission at hand'. He also believes 'you can tell when a group of people are moving tactically, or whether it's a group of guys going to irrigate a field . . . if they're combatants they'll . . . move differently'. (I do not find his belief particularly reassuring.)

One of the most disturbing aspects of all of this is the way that the process of killing becomes so abstract that it utterly desensitises all those involved. Killing becomes completely routine, a matter of cameras and sensors and screens; no noise, no terror, no blood, no humanity – the cleanness of killing from your desk. And at the end of your shift you can just drive home, in time to read your kids a bedtime story. This is RAF officer Mark Jenkins, also then based at USAF Creech in Nevada:

> Jenkins: It is a strange situation. I have a wife and two children out here with me . . . I go and do my job, then debrief, maybe spend ten minutes on the squadron, just winding down, chatting to people about what we've been doing today, and then I've got a forty-five-minute drive home, so I just stick the radio on, listen to a podcast, whatever, just drive home – and, by the time I'm home, I'm straight into family life.

> Sackur: You can let it go? Even if it has been one of those days when you've had to use your weapons – you know you've killed people, but you can let it go at the end of the working day?

> Jenkins: You've got to. Yeah, OK, it's going to weigh on your mind. It does, I don't think you'd be human if you didn't. But I've got a family at home, and I need to be there for my family, so I deal with it. I talk to my wife about – just, general terms about what's happened, obviously I can't go into specifics . . . Yeah, I might be a little bit off . . . maybe in a bit of a strange mood for a day or so.

Yet what about the hundreds, perhaps thousands, of civilian casualties from these drone strikes, and all the families destroyed from 8,000 miles away? What about the 201 children killed in drone attacks just in the period between 2001 and 2012?[*] Presumably, not even the Pentagon could class these as 'combatants'. And although the effect on the operators of drones is disturbing, the impact on those targeted is truly terrifying – especially when those killed and maimed have nothing whatsoever to do with 'terrorism':

> Gul Nawaz, from North Waziristan, was watering his fields when he heard the explosion of drone missiles: 'I rushed to my house when I heard the blast. When I arrived I saw my house and my brother's house completely destroyed and all at home were dead.' Eleven members of Gul Nawaz's family were killed, including his wife, two sons and two daughters as well as his elder brother, his wife, and his four children ... 'I blame the government of Pakistan and the USA ... they are responsible for destroying my family. We were living a happy life and I didn't have any links with the Taliban. My family members were innocent ... I wonder, why was I victimised?'[†]

*

Finally in this section, an example, both horrific and remarkable, of what happens when out of the anonymised mass a single person suddenly appears, and can be seen as a human being. This is taken from the testimony of a Hungarian doctor, Miklós Nyiszli (from his 1946 book *Auschwitz: A Doctor's Eyewitness Account*), who worked as a pathologist, with Mengele, at Auschwitz-Birkenau. Nyiszli became completely habituated to witnessing thousands being killed in the gas chambers every day. But on one particular day something unprecedented occurred. Nyiszli was on duty near Crematorium 1, where another 3,000 people had just been gassed, when the following happened:

---

[*] Figures from the Bureau of Investigative Journalism.

[†] Report on *Civilian Harm and Conflict in Northwest Pakistan* by American NGO CIVIC, October 2010.

The chief of the gas chamber [*Sonder*]*Kommando* almost tore the hinges off the door to my room as he arrived out of breath, his eyes wide with fear or surprise.

'Doctor,' he said, 'come quickly. We just found a girl alive at the bottom of the pile of corpses.'

I grabbed my instrument case, which was always ready, and dashed to the gas chamber. Against the wall, near the entrance to the immense room, half covered with other bodies, I saw a girl in the throes of a death-rattle, her body seized with convulsions. The gas *Kommando* men around me were in a state of panic. Nothing like this had ever happened in the course of their horrible career. [*sic*]

We removed the still-living body from the corpses pressing against it. I gathered the tiny adolescent body into my arms and carried it back into the room adjoining the gas chamber, where normally the gas *Kommando* men change clothes for work. I laid the body on a bench. A frail young girl, almost a child, she could have been no more than fifteen. I took out my syringe and, taking her arm – she had not yet recovered consciousness and was breathing with difficulty – I administered three intravenous injections. My companions covered her body which was as cold as ice with a heavy overcoat. One ran to the kitchen to fetch some tea and warm broth. Everybody wanted to help, as if she were their own child.

The reaction was swift. The child was seized by a fit of coughing, which brought up a thick globule of phlegm from her lungs. She opened her eyes and looked fixedly at the ceiling. I kept a close watch for every sign of life. Her breathing became deeper and more and more regular. Her lungs, tortured by the gas, inhaled the fresh air avidly. Her pulse became perceptible, the result of the injections. I waited impatiently. The injections had not yet been completely absorbed, but I saw that within a few minutes she was going to regain consciousness: her circulation began to bring colour back to her cheeks, and her delicate face became human again.

She looked around her with astonishment, and glanced at us. She still did not realise what was happening to her, and was still incapable of distinguishing the present, of knowing whether she was dreaming or really awake . . . Her movements were becoming more and more animated; she tried to move her hands, her feet, to turn her head left and right. Her face was seized by a fit of convulsions. Suddenly she grasped my coat collar and gripped it convulsively, trying with all her might to raise herself. I laid her back down again several times, but she continued to repeat the same gesture. Little by little, however, she grew calm and remained stretched out, completely exhausted. Large tears shone in her eyes and rolled down her cheeks . . . I learned that she was sixteen years old, and that she had come with her parents in a convoy from Transylvania.

The *Kommando* gave her a bowl of hot broth, which she drank voraciously. They kept bringing her all sorts of dishes, but I could not allow them to give her anything. I covered her to her head and told her that she should try to get some sleep.

My thoughts moved at a dizzy pace. I turned towards my companions in the hope of finding a solution. We racked our brains, for we were now face to face with the most difficult problem: what to do with the girl now that she had been restored to life? We knew that she could not remain here very long.

What could I do with a young girl in the crematorium's *Sonderkommando*?

I knew the past history of the place: no one had ever come out of here alive, either from the convoys or from the *Sonderkommando*.

Little time remained for reflection. Oberscharführer Mussfeld arrived to supervise the work, as was his wont. Passing by the open door, he saw us gathered in a group. He came in and asked us what was going on. Even before we told him he had seen the girl stretched out on the bench.

I made a sign for my companions to withdraw. I was going to attempt something I knew . . . was doomed to failure. Three months in the same camp and in the same milieu had created, in spite of everything, a certain intimacy between us. Besides, the Germans generally appreciate capable people, and, as long as they need them, respect them to a certain extent, even in the KZ [concentration camp] . . . From our numerous contacts, I had been able to ascertain that Mussfeld had a high esteem for the medical expert's professional qualities . . . He often came to see me in the dissecting room, and we conversed on politics, the military situation and various other subjects. It appeared that his respect also arose from the fact that he considered the dissection of bodies and his bloody job of killing to be allied activities . . .

And this was the man I had to deal with, the man I had to talk into allowing a single life to be spared. I calmly related the terrible case we found ourselves confronted with. I described for his benefit what pains the child must have suffered in the undressing room, and the horrible scenes that preceded death in the gas chamber. When the room had been plunged into darkness, she had breathed in a few lungfuls of Zyklon gas. Only a few though, for her fragile body had given way under the pushing and shoving of the mass as they fought against death. By chance she had fallen with her head against the wet concrete floor. That bit of humidity had kept her from being asphyxiated, for Zyklon gas does not react under humid conditions.

These were my arguments, and I asked him to do something for the child. He listened to me attentively, then asked me exactly what I proposed doing. I saw by his expression that I had put him face to face with a practically impossible problem. It was obvious that the child could not remain in the crematorium. One solution would have been to put her in front of the crematorium gate. A *Kommando* of women always worked here. She could have slipped in among them and accompanied them back to the camp barracks after they had finished work. She would never relate what had happened to her. The presence of one new face among so many thousands would never have been detected, for no one on the camp knew all the other inmates.

If she had been three or four years older that might have worked. A girl of twenty would have been able to understand clearly the miraculous circumstances of her survival, and have enough foresight not to tell anyone about them. She would wait for better times, like so many other thousands were waiting, to recount what she had lived through. But Mussfeld thought that a young girl of sixteen would in all naiveté tell the first person she met where she had just come from, what she had seen and what she had lived through. The news would spread like wildfire, and we would all be forced to pay for it with our lives.

'There's no way of getting round it,' he said, 'the child will have to die.'

Half an hour later the young girl was led, or rather carried, into the furnace room hallway, and there Mussfeld sent another in his place to do the job. A bullet in the back of the neck.

Distancing Yourself from the Act of Violence

The paradoxical way in which many organisational killers strongly distance themselves from others who kill directly – with their own hands. In fact, the desk killers in such cases will often evaluate themselves favourably in contradistinction to those who kill with their own hands. In essence such organisational killers are over-focussing on the final act of violence as a way of seeking to diminish their own – equally great – responsibility for the causation of violence.

The apparent squeamishness of organisational killers in the face of physical violence, and the desire to avoid direct experience of such violence, or its immediate after-effects, at first seems surprising, but is actually relatively common, especially at higher levels of power in organisations, where there is often little necessity to take part in, or even witness, acts of violence. For example, Albert Speer describes Hitler as having such an antipathy towards witnessing violence directly that it was extremely difficult to persuade him even to visit injured soldiers, or the front line: 'As a rule he avoided not only physical, but indeed visual contact, with violence. During the later stages of the war this meant that, however important it was for morale, it was virtually impossible to get him to visit either the front or the bombed cities.'

When Adolf Eichmann was on trial in Jerusalem in 1961 he never disputed his part in co-ordinating the logistics of the Holocuast, but he became furious when accused of murdering with his own hands: 'With the killing of Jews I had nothing to do. I never killed a Jew, or a non-Jew, for that matter – I never killed any human being.' The wilful myopia here is striking – the desk killer protests 'I never killed' because they almost never see the victims killed as a result of their orders. In fact, if confronted with accounts of direct killing, they can often react with anger. For instance, Hannah Arendt observed precisely this aspect in Eichmann's behaviour as he listened to testimony:

> During the trial, he showed unmistakable signs of sincere outrage when witnesses told of cruelties and atrocities committed by SS men . . . and it was not the accusation of having sent millions of people to their death that ever caused him real agitation but only the accusation (dismissed by the court) of one witness that he had once beaten a Jewish boy to death.

Exactly the same trait can be seen in Stangl, when confronted with an accusation by a Treblinka survivor that he had been one of several SS officers shooting in the direction of an arriving transport:

> Stangl, insisiting that he had never shot into a crowd of people, appeared to be more indignant about this accusation than about anything else, and to find irrelevant the fact that, whether he shot into the group or not, these very same people died anyway, less than two hours later, through actions ultimately under his control.

Here we have three men, working at different levels within the German state, all of whom were responsible for killing on a vast, industrial scale. Three men who believed they had kept their own hands clean, that they, personally, had never killed or been violent. Psychologically, this would seem to indicate a kind of 'fetishisation' of the importance of the act of violence itself, which has the subsequent effect then of diminishing (in their own eyes) their responsibility for acts that they caused to happen – in their case the conceptualisation and implementation of genocide.

While this may be seen as evidence of extreme self-delusion on the part of these three individuals, I think we can still see aspects of such over-focussing on the act of violence itself – and under-focussing on the causation of violence – in our legal systems and wider culture today. It was there in the post-war judgement of desk killers[*] but perhaps this trait also continues in much journalism and activism today where disproportionate attention is given to detailing the violent end results of a government's or a corporation's actions (the destroyed village, the injured civilians, the dead bodies, etc.), and insufficient energy is focussed on the causation of such actions – the propaganda, the financing, the political/military/corporate co-operation – which led to the violence in the first place.

Transferring Personal Responsibility to the Authority's Responsibility

How, if you're part of a large organisation, it is always possible to diminish your own sense of responsibility and pass on the greatest share of responsibility to others, especially those at higher levels of authority.

This is perhaps the most familiar of all the categories, and links most directly with issues surrounding corporate psychology and behaviour today. I believe that the development, since the late 1990s, of the so-called CSR movement (Corporate Social Responsibility) has actually had the disturbing effect of weakening moral

---

[*] See 'Judging the Desk Killers' in Book One, Chapter Thirteen.

and ethical frameworks within companies. Creating specific departments within companies which are supposed to deal with ethical, environmental and human rights issues has allowed the majority of employees working in the corporations to defer their own sense of responsibility onto these departments, thus reducing their individual sense of moral agency, often with disastrous consequences.

This process of deferral of responsibilty is composed of two interlinked aspects. Firstly, the sense (which increases as the size of the organisation increases) that you are only 'a cog in a vast machine' – even relatively senior figures will attempt to use this excuse when confronted with malpractice or crimes. Secondly, that you are 'only carrying out orders from a higher authority' within the organisation. Both of these excuses were widely used even by senior figures such as concentration-camp commandants and their deputies after the war. We can see it vividly in a deposition Dieter Wisliceny (a deputy of Eichmann's) gave to Lieutenant Colonel Smith Brookhart on 15 November 1945 in Nuremberg. Despite his own responsibility for having already deported tens of thousands of Jews from Slovakia, he recounts the following conversation with Eichmann in Berlin in early August 1942:

Eichmann said . . . after much delay and a great deal of discussion, that there was an order of Himmler according to which all Jews were to be exterminated. When I asked him who was going to assume responsibility for this order, he said he was prepared to show me this order in writing which had been signed by Himmler. I then requested that he show me. This order was under the classification of Top Secret. This discussion took place in his study in Berlin. He was sitting at his desk, and I was in the same position opposite him, as I am now opposite the colonel. He took this order from his safe. It was a thick file. He then searched and took out this order. It was directed to the chief of the Security Police and the Security Service [Heydrich]. The contents of the order went something like this: 'The Führer has decided that the final disposition of the Jewish question is to start immediately.' By the code word [*sic*] 'final disposition' was meant the biological extermination of the Jews . . . it was an official decree. It was surrounded by a red border as a special delivery document . . . Yes, urgent document. I was very much impressed by this document which gave him [Eichmann] as much power to use as he saw fit.

We have a strikingly similar account from Otto Ohlendorf, commander of Einsatzgruppe D. Although he had personally overseen the murders of more than 90,000 Jewish people and partisans, he again defers responsibility completely to his superior officer (in his case, Himmler). We can see this process as he testified at his trial in January 1946, about a briefing he and the other *Einsatzgruppen* commanders had received from the Reichsführer on 22 June 1941:

Question: Did you have any other conversations with Himmler concerning this order?

Ohlendorf: Yes, in late summer of 1941 Himmler was in Nikolaiev. He assembled the leaders and the men of the *Einsatzkommandos*, repeated to them the liquidation order, and pointed out that the leaders and men who were taking part in the liquidation bore no responsibility for the execution of this order. The responsibility was his, alone, and the Führer's.

Question: And you yourself heard that said?

Ohlendorf: Yes.

*

At Yale University in 1961, Stanley Milgram, directly influenced by the Eichmann trial then taking place in Israel, began his famous research study 'Obedience to Authority: An Experimental View'.[*]

---

[*] See chapter notes for further reflections on the ethics of Milgram's experiment and Zimbardo's 'Stanford Prison Experiment'.

In 1963, Milgram published 'The Behavioral Study of Obedience' in the *Journal of Abnormal and Social Psychology*. This stunned the world by finding a capacity for ordinary people to obey scientific 'authority' figures by administering (what they believed to be) severe electric shocks to victims they couldn't see – in reality, actors in a neighbouring room simulating agonised screams of pain. The volunteers for this experiment were recruited from a broad range of social backgrounds, and paid for their time; they were told by the 'scientific researcher' (suitably dressed in a white coat) that they were helping in a 'learning experiment' that concerned the 'study of memory'.

They were then assigned the role of a 'teacher' who had to ask questions of a 'learner' (who was positioned in a neighbouring room, so could not be seen, but only spoken to through the wall). The teacher was then positioned in front of a large machine with the words 'Shock Generator Type ZLB' written above it, with switches ranging from 15 volts ('slight shock') to 75 volts ('moderate shock') to 255 volts ('intense shock') up to 375 volts ('danger severe shock'), finishing with 450 volts ('XXX'). The teacher was then directed by the 'scientific researcher' to ask a series of questions to the learner. If the learner got the answers wrong, the teacher was told to administer an electric shock; these increased in level of severity, until the final shock could be given at the '450 volts' level (supposedly a dangerous, possibly fatal, degree of shock). If the teacher hesitated to enforce the electric shock at any stage, they were repeatedly told by the scientific 'authority' figure that 'the experiment requires that you continue', 'it is absolutely essential that you continue'.

Before Milgram conducted the first research he asked his psychology students at Yale to predict what they thought the results of the experiment would be. The students thought only 1.2 per cent of participants would administer the maximum electric shock. The actual result, from the first round of experiments, was that 65 per cent of participants gave (what they believed to be) the maximum electric shock of 450 volts. And all of the participants gave shocks of up to 300 volts. Instead of taking personal responsibility for the decision of whether or not to give the electric shocks, the vast majority of the participants simply deferred responsibility to the authority figure next to them in the room – repeatedly asking the 'scientist' in the white coat for reassurance:

'Are you sure it's OK? That guy doesn't sound very good in there.'

'Yes, it's fine, please continue with the experiment; it's imperative for the good of science.'

'Alright Doc, if you're sure . . .'

Other common responses included comments like 'Who's going to take responsibility if anything happens to him?' – to which the scientific researcher would reply, 'The responsibility is mine – please go on, the experiment requires you to continue.'

In subsequent years, other psychologists repeated Milgram's experiment and got strikingly similar results. Milgram also conducted the experiment several more times, but with variations. It was found that the distance between the 'teacher' and 'learner' was a critical factor – i.e. when the experiment was carried out with both of them in the same room (and therefore visible to each other), the 'teacher' was far less likely to obey the order to give electric shocks. This finding links us back to what I was describing earlier (*Abstractifying Victims*), if you can see the face of a potential victim, it is vastly harder to inflict pain or death than if your violence can be delivered anonymously, for instance from a plane, or drone, or, as in the original experiment here, from another room. In other subsequent experiments it was found that if the scientific authority figure was not in the same room giving orders, the teacher was far less likely to obey. For instance, when the orders were given by telephone, the percentage giving the ultimate shock of '450 volts' dropped from 65 per cent to 21 per cent. The original experiment had used only men as participants, but in subsequent research women were found to be equally obedient as men, equally prepared to deliver severe electric shocks when asked to do so by an authority figure.

*

If we move away from the laboratory we can see how such deferral of responsibility works in real-world contexts. In an interview with the *San Francisco Examiner*, a prison guard who had worked on Death Row explained the process of having participated in many executions. His role was to strap the prisoner's legs to the chair in the gas chamber, yet he didn't appear to feel any responsibility whatsoever for his role in the deaths of the 126 men whose executions he had participated in: 'I never pulled the trigger. I wasn't the executioner . . . It never bothered me, when I was down at their legs strapping them in. But after I'd get home, I'd think about it. But then it would go away. And then, at last it was just another job.'*

But perhaps the most remarkable insight into this aspect of responsibility deferral in the psychology of the desk killer comes from the short interview Claude Lanzmann conducts with Walter Stier in *Shoah*. Stier, a member of the Nazi Party, rose to become the head of Department 33 at the Reich Ministry of Transport. His department was responsible for organising the *Sonderzug* ('special trains') in occupied Poland, including the trains used to transport people to the extermination camps of Treblinka, Belzec, Sobibor and Auschwitz-Birkenau. Yet he professed to know absolutely nothing about the nature of these camps, or who was being sent to them in such vast numbers, repeatedly emphasising that he was just a 'desk man', a harmless bureaucrat. To read these words is to understand that the Holocaust could not have happened without millions of Stiers across occupied Europe; whole armies of desk killers who never had to leave their offices.

---

* This example is taken from Albert Bandura's invaluable paper 'Moral Disengagement in the Perpetration of Inhumanities' in *Personality and Social Psychology Review* (1999).

Lanzmann: 'You never saw a train?'

Stier: No, never. We had so much work, I never left my desk. We worked day and night.

GEDOB meaning Generaldirektion . . .

Generaldirektion der Ostbahn (Head Office of Eastbound Traffic). In January 1940I was assigned to Gedob Krakow. In mid-1943 I was moved to Warsaw. I was chief traffic planner, chief of the Traffic Planning Office.

But your duties were the same before and after 1943?

Yes, the only change was that I became head of the department.

What were your specific duties at GEDOB during the war?

The work was little different from the work in Germany: preparing timetables, coordinating special train movements with ordinary train movements.

There were several departments?

Yes. Department 33 was in charge of special trains . . . and ordinary trains. Special trains were handled by Department 33.

You were always concerned with special trains?

Yes.

What's the difference between a special train and an ordinary train?

An ordinary train can be used by anyone who buys a ticket Say from Krakow to Warsaw. Or Krakow to Lemberg. A special train has to be ordered. The train is specially made up and people pay group fares . . .

Are there special trains now?

Of course, just as there were then.

A holiday train could be a special train?

Yes. For Guest Workers, for instance, workers returning home for holidays special trains are made available. Otherwise one couldn't handle the traffic . . .

You've told me that after the war you dealt with the Queen's visit?

After the war, yes . . .

If royalty visits Germany by train is that a special train?

Yes, that's a special train. But the procedure is very different from that for special trains for groups and so on. State visits are handled by the foreign office.

May I ask another question? Why were there more special trains during the war than before or after?

I see what you're getting at. You're referring to the 'Resettlement Transports'.

Yes, 'Resettlement'.

That's what these trains were called. The Reich Ministry of Transport ordered these trains – an order from the Ministry – the Reichsverkehrsministerium, Berlin.

In Berlin?

Yes. And those orders were implemented by Head Office, eastbound Traffic in Berlin. Have I made that clear?

Very clear. But who was being 'resettled' at that time?

We didn't know that. Only when we ourselves fled from Warsaw did we learn they could have been Jews, or criminals, and the like.

Jews, criminals?

Criminals. All kinds.

Special trains for criminals?

No, that was just an expression; you couldn't talk about it. Unless you were tired of life, it was best not to say anything.

But, at that time, you knew that the transports were to Treblinka or Auschwitz?

Of course we knew. These trains . . . I had destinations – mine was the last district. For instance, a train from Essen had to go through Wuppertal district, Hanover district, Magdeburg, Berlin, Frankfurt/ Oder, Posnan, Warsaw and so on.

Did you know that Treblinka meant extermination?

No, of course not!

You didn't know?

Good God no! How could we know? I never went to Treblinka. I stayed in Krakow, Warsaw, just sat at my desk.

A desk man?

I was a desk man, just a desk man.

But it's astonishing that people in the department of special trains had no inkling about the 'Final Solution'.

We were at war.

Because others working for the railways knew, people like the train guards.

Yes, they saw it. They did. But as to what happened . . .

What was Treblinka for you? Or Auschwitz?

For us Treblinka, Belzec and all that were concentration camps.

A destination.

Nothing more.

But not the end?

No. People were put there. We were told: 'A train is coming from Essen, or Cologne, or elsewhere. Room had to be made, what with the war, and the Allies advancing and these people had to be concentrated in camps.'

When did you find out?

Well, when the word got around, when it was whispered.

It was never said openly.

Good God, no! You'd have been hauled off at once. We heard things.

Rumours?

Yes, rumours.

During the war?

Towards the end.

Not in 1942?

Good God, no. Not a clue! Towards the end of 1944 perhaps.

End of 1944?

Not before. It was said that people were being sent to these concentration camps and those in poor health probably wouldn't survive.

The extermination was a big surprise to you?

A complete surprise.

You had no idea?

None at all. That camp – what was its name? In the Oppeln district . . . yes – Auschwitz.

Auschwitz was in the Oppeln district of the railway?

Yes. Auschwitz wasn't far from Krakow. We never heard a word about that.

It's sixty kilometres from Krakow.

Yes, it's not very far.

And you knew . . . ?

Nothing, not a clue.

14

The Oilman and the Broken Wing

This man's name has been in my head for a long time. A former oilman, Dutch. Now in his fifties. With that curious first name that sounds like a dance. Bopp van Dessel. For more than fifteen years I have told myself, at regular intervals: 'Why don't you try to contact him? There must surely be a way of getting hold of him.' But then, in the way that life works, other tasks that are shouting louder, with deadlines attached, get the attention, and my Dutchman gets buried again, somewhere deep in my frontal cortex, not forgotten exactly, but lost in a crowd of a million other impulses, jostled out of sight.

He trained as a marine biologist and worked in this field for some years, before becoming an environmental advisor for Shell in 1989. In this capacity he worked for three years in the Netherlands, and then in 1992 he was sent to work in Nigeria as head of environmental studies for Shell. The next two and a half years shocked him deeply, and changed the course of his life. He tried to reconcile his work with Shell with what he was experiencing on a daily basis in the Niger Delta – the vast plumes of fire of the gas flaring right next to villages, the once ecologically rich mangrove swamps now thick and blackened by oil, and also the suffering of the people of the Delta. He became furious with the Nigerian government, but also baffled that the Western oil companies could allow all this to go on in their names: 'Wherever I went I could see that Shell were not operating their facilities properly. They were not meeting their own standards, they were not meeting international standards. Any Shell site I saw was polluted. Any Shell terminal I saw was polluted. It was clear to me that Shell was devastating the area.'[*]

So in late 1994 he took the only ethical course of action available to him, and resigned from Shell. This was at the height of growing global concern about what was going on in the Niger Delta, and Ken Saro-Wiwa and the Ogoni campaign were causing massive problems for the Abacha government in Nigeria and all the oil companies operating there, particularly Shell and Chevron.

His public resignation caused national consternation in his home country. He had shattered the code of behaviour that corporations insist upon. In return for substantial financial and material benefits employees are bound by certain 'obligations' – chief among these being that any differences are dealt with internally. You *never* go public. And so a culture of silence is created, a culture of looking away, and, after a time, it hardly has to be enforced at all because the employees themselves internalise this behaviour. Self-censorship becomes vastly more effective than externally imposed rules. Even to talk with colleagues about doubts becomes unthinkable. It is in this context that the reaction to his public resignation needs to be seen. He was one of the very few Shell employees who had ever spoken out about the reality of what the oil company was doing in Nigeria, though doubtless hundreds had thought about it. How could you not? When the evidence was all around you, every day?

I've always wanted to know what precisely went on in this man's mind, in his heart, in the days and weeks before he typed that resignation letter. And then, at the moment of sending it. A wave of

---

* *World in Action*, Granada TV, 13 May 1996.

liberation? Or exhaustion? Fear? And if we could discover more about why this action was possible for him, what could then be opened up in others, in similar situations today? Beyond the bandages of PR and 'Corporate Social Responsibility', beyond the gloss of annual reports. Suddenly detectable, even from the carpeted office in the City of London, the stench of the fumes in the village, the oil blackening the waters, the mobile police starting to shoot, bullets cutting into flesh.

*

This evening, just after seven o'clock, I spoke to Bopp van Dessel. After fifteen years of having him in my mind, I'd finally managed to get his phone number via a journalist contact. With a certain amount of trepidation I press the numbers into my phone and hear the long bleeps calling across the North Sea. A man's voice answers. I explain that I've been wanting to talk to him for many years, that I'd been struck by the moral position he'd taken over Shell in Nigeria. He sounds a little cautious at first, but yes, he knows of Platform's work, he'd heard about the memorial in London we'd created to Ken Saro-Wiwa and the other members of the Ogoni Nine. I ask if he'd be prepared to take part in some new research about the relationship between an individual's ethics and the values of the corporations they work for. I explain about my research partners at the business school and Birkbeck. He says he's very interested, but emphasises that he was at Shell a long time ago now, he's not sure he can remember all the details. But yes, he'd like to do the interview, and his new work with his environmental foundation brings him over to London every now and then. So we arrange that I will send him more details of the project, and that he'll let me know when he's next going to be over and we'll do the interview then. I put the phone down, rather stunned that it had been so simple. Perhaps a wider metaphor for the things in our lives that we make so complicated in our heads, but which are actually relatively simple . . .

I turn away from my desk and reach down to stroke my grey cat, Tarka, who's just come in from the garden and is in a skittish mood. He's lying on top of an atlas I've been looking at, extending his claws, stretching out and daring me to tickle his belly, which will then trigger a playful attack of biting. But then I see he's actually got something in his mouth, a little, dark grey thing, a mouse probably. 'Tarka! That's very bad, give it to me.' But getting closer, to my horror I see it's not a mouse but a small and motionless bird. A young dunnock. He's never caught one before, he's a pretty hopeless hunter, not helped by the fact he makes an involuntary kind of cackling noise whenever he sees a bird. A feline protest against the unfairness of these winged beings coming and going as they please. I clap my hands, and rather to my surprise, Tarka slinks away, leaving the terrified bird on my floor. Absurdly, I begin to apologise to the bird: 'Oh, I'm so sorry! You poor thing!' Despite having grown up in the countryside I have a terror of wounded animals, possibly due to a traumatic memory of trying to kill a young rabbit riddled with myxomatosis that was flopping around blindly near the house, when I was nine or ten. My elder brother, with a no-nonsense approach to these sorts of things, said that the only humane thing to do was to kill it, and then invited me to do it, as a kind of test. I followed the poor rabbit around our orchard for a while and then steeled myself, picked up a large log, and struck it over the head. It fell, twitched, and then, somehow, raised itself again and flopped off, leaning slightly to one side. I hit it again. The same thing. It just wouldn't die. I then had to bring the full force of the log down repeatedly, in a mad flutter of blows, and after several minutes it did stop moving. But I knew after that experience that I could never kill an animal again.

I approach the bird nervously, but at least it's still alive. Tiny, dark eyes blinking at the unfamiliarity of its surroundings. But then I'm stabbed by concern – one of its wings is out at an angle. Shit, what do I do now? Maybe it looks worse than it is? I go to get my gardening gloves, knowing I wouldn't be able to pick up the bird in my hands. As I get closer, the bird, with its animal impulse for survival, makes a wild attempt to fly off, but can't really get off the floor – its wing is clearly broken. It ends up under my desk. I can't explain how shaken up I am by this. At the total fragility and vulnerability of this terrified bird. And the fact I can do almost nothing to help it. I go into the front room and find Tarka, looking sheepish (if a cat can look sheepish); I can't really be angry with him. Instinct and all that. But I make sure he can't do any more harm today, and shut the door.

Then I hurry back to the other room where the bird is still under my desk, now motionless. Making soothing noises, I kneel down and pick the bird up in my gloves. It's ridiculously light, not even an ounce, I should think. Yet extraordinary – an entire life working in its unimaginable complexity only a few minutes ago, now flickering, right on the boundary between living and dying, because of my cat. I carry it outside and place it on the grass, still blinking. Completely silent. Rationally I know I should kill it. I can hear my brother's voice still, after all these years. But I know I can't do that. Could there be a miracle? Could the wing be only slightly damaged? If I had more time today I'd ring my brother to ask for advice, but I have to go into town for an important meeting. I decide to leave it here, go to get a saucer of water, and then prop up the saucer so that the water is almost touching its little beak. And then, thinking about food, I dig in the earth nearby and find a worm, which I place, enticingly I hope, just next to the saucer. But no movement from the bird now. Apart from those black eyes. Still alive. Still in the world we both inhabit.

I rush into the city centre to my meeting, now feeling a new pang of remorse, not only for the injured bird, for also the unfortunate worm. I'm shocked at how casually I ranked the value of the bird's life above that of the worm. Surely a real Buddhist would be able to treat both the bird and the worm as equally worthy of life, equally part of the universe?

*

When I get back, a few hours later, I immediately go out into the garden, praying that the bird will not be there any more. Of course it is. In exactly the same position, the beak resting against the china rim of the saucer. But dead now, the eyes only half open. I carry the body to the back of the garden, find a place behind the wood stack, put the bird down with a gentleness that has no real meaning, and cover it with leaves. I go back inside and release Tarka from his front-room prison, trying to make sense of the rankings in nature – Human. Cat. Bird. Worm.

The utter fragility of the world. What does it mean to live with this? Is it even possible? If we started to consider the million things that can go wrong inside us at any moment? If we began to see the universe in a mangrove tree, or an entire galaxy in a river, how would we move through the world? To consider the multiple ramifications of every human action. This goes beyond changing our political system – it would need a kind of rewiring of our minds and the way that we think. Not just to care about cats and dogs, but to consider worms, insects, ants as worthy of our respect, worthy of life. Not just to love trees and flowers, but all things that grow, down to the smallest fern, the least noticeable grass. And I'm suddenly thinking of something that Ken Saro-Wiwa wrote about the rapaciousness of the Western oil companies, at the beginning of the fight of his life for his people and the Delta:

Oil exploration has turned Ogoni into a wasteland: lands, streams and creeks are totally and continually polluted; the atmosphere has been poisoned, charged as it is with hydro-carbon vapours, methane, carbon monoxide, carbon dioxide and soot emitted by gas which has flared twenty-four hours a day for thirty-three years in very close proximity to human habitation. Acid rain, oil spillage and oil blow-outs have devastated Ogoni territory . . .

The result of such unchecked environmental pollution and degradation include the complete destruction of the ecosystem. Mangrove forests have fallen to the toxicity of oil and are being replaced by noxious nypa palms; the rainforest has fallen to the axe of multinational oil companies, all wildlife is dead, marine life is gone, the farmlands have been rendered infertile by acid rain and the once beautiful Ogoni countryside is no longer a source of fresh air and green vegetation. All one sees and feels around is death.

And an anger comes now, realising that this is what I despise more than I can express – capitalism, at least in its current form, denies absolutely the fragility of the world. It's not even a question. The only language is financial, the only criterion is growth. Everything else is a distraction. From the perspective of the FTSE 100 or the Dow Jones or Moody's or the IMF, the world of lichens and ants and forests can be exterminated. They are just not necessary. They are not productive. When the oilmen arrive in the Nigerian estuaries or in the Siberian tundra, what are they actually seeing? I suspect that everything that exists above ground in these places – whether it's a matter of the communities affected or the forests that lie in the way – are in their minds only potential obstacles to getting the oil out of there. The black gold which must be extracted at any cost. I think of Blake's words – 'To the eyes of a miser a guinea is far more beautiful than the sun . . . the tree which moves some to tears of joy in the eyes of others is only a green thing which stands in the way.'

What connects? It all connects. If you do it to the smallest of these, you do it to me.

Worm. Bird. Cat. Human.

15

A Painting in The Hague; A Farmhouse in Suffolk;
A Stadium in Somalia

How to explain the power of this painting?

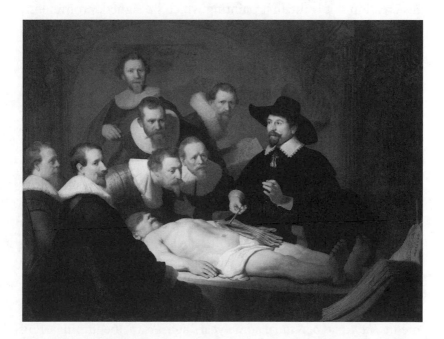

The Anatomy Lesson of Dr Tulp, painted in 1632, was the work which really consolidated the reputation of this young artist who had recently arrived in Amsterdam from Leiden.

The twenty-six-year-old Rembrandt was understandably proud of his creation – it is the first painting which he signed, prominently at the top of the canvas, with just his Christian name, Rembrandt f.[ecit] 1632 (announcing to its viewers 'Rembrandt made it'). Today *The Anatomy Lesson* can be seen in the Mauritshuis museum in The Hague, although it has been so widely reproduced that it is probably already familiar to you. I thought I knew the painting too; if you'd asked me what it was about, I would have said it was a representation of the move towards the Enlightenment – no, perhaps more than that – an embodiment in paint of the concept of 'Scientific Progress', and specifically the development of the discipline of anatomy, crucial to the growth in the study of medicine in the seventeenth century. Dr Tulp must have been a prominent surgeon of the time, and the other figures were no doubt colleagues of his, perhaps including men who commissioned this work from Rembrandt.

Yet I'd never really examined it closely until it appeared before me in *The Rings of Saturn* some years ago. At the beginning of his interpretation of this picture, Sebald, characteristically identifying with the marginalised and forgotten, draws our attention away from the famous surgeon to the figure of the dead man at the centre. This was Adriaan Adriaanszoon, also known as Aris Kindt, a thief from Amsterdam who had been executed only an hour before the anatomy lesson. In a daring visual ploy, in the whiteness of his body and its position, Rembrandt echoes the form of the pietà – the executed man becoming the dead Christ. In Sebald's simple action of naming the man, a deconstruction of power takes place – what has been an object (the body) only a few moments before, becomes a human being again, and in this moment we want to know more about Adriaan – more than Sebald, or anyone else for that matter, can tell us.

Was he really, as Sebald suggests, 'a petty thief'? Was he really hanged for stealing only a coat? Or had he been convicted of assault or armed robbery, as others believe? And then many other questions form in my mind: if 'Kindt' means 'kid', then how old was he? Was there some affection behind this nickname? Could it even have been ironic, because if you look closely at the face, this is not a young man. Was he married? Did he have children? Were the family told that his body was going to be used to further the course of scientific progress? Did they consent to this? Were they there, in the theatre of the Waaggebouw, on that January day in 1632 when he was dissected before a paying audience? After the anatomy lesson, how was Adriaan's body returned to the family? Where was he buried?

But looking at the picture again, wider questions arise. About the relationship between ourselves and this subject, specifically in terms of power and responsibility. What is the other side of the 'Enlightenment'? What does our civilisation require to move forward? Who benefits from 'Progress'? Who are the casualties? Is this what Walter Benjamin meant when he wrote, 'There is no document of civilisation which is not at the same time a document of barbarism'? And where do we stand in relation to the different classes represented in this painting? The gazes are multiple and disturbing – Dr Tulp is focussed on the paying audience, two of his colleagues in the guild of surgeons are looking at him, two others at the arm of the executed man, and the remaining three seem to be looking at us, challenging our position as the viewer. Do we align ourselves with Tulp, with Adriaan or with the other watching surgeons? Who do we most identify with? Rembrandt has placed us all as witnesses in the audience of the Waaggebouw, the temple to progress, so we might feel a certain high-minded engagement. Which would almost certainly be misplaced – after all, tickets for such events were the sell-out gig of the day. People would queue for hours to gain admission, fights would break out. So, more accurately, we're cast here simply as voyeurs, observing the whole spectacle as a kind of entertainment, a ghoulish seventeenth-century equivalent of reality TV.

The great historian of the Holocaust Raul Hilberg titled one of his last books *Perpetrators, Victims, Bystanders*. I wonder how he might have looked at this painting. Adriaan is clearly the victim here; Dr Tulp and his colleagues, though not the direct perpetrators, are certainly the beneficiaries of his execution. And the bystanders, the witnesses? Surely the audience, and, by extension, ourselves. The bystanders – those whose responsibility is the most critical, as well as the least understood.

*

If we could fully understand the psychology that underpins *The Anatomy Lesson of Dr Tulp*, we might also understand more of a mindset that still exists today. Though of course there are no longer public dissections of executed criminals, the underlying thought processes concerning the relationship between the development of societies and the casualties involved in such 'progress' survive. An enormous amount of international trade, including the vast majority of extractive industries, particularly mining and oil, are based precisely on an unspoken assumption that the world is divided into what could be called 'zones of progress' (i.e. the countries and places where these companies are based, and where their consumers and shareholders live), and 'zones of sacrifice'* (i.e. the countries and places where the minerals or oil are, essentially seen as sites of extraction, the inhabitants seen as peripheral, only necessary to deal with to aid the process of extraction and export). Companies may produce warehouses of reports and publications detailing their concern for 'community development' in their 'partner countries', hundreds of UN initiatives and NGO dialogues may be launched, but these do not even begin to impact on the fundamentally abusive psychology that has been in existence for centuries.

The psychology is so pervasive in our society that most of us do not even question it. We might notice the occasional tree but we cannot see the forest. The very idea that it's acceptable for a Western oil company to be working in a country where a civil war is raging, or where there's a military dictatorship, or where there's no independent judiciary or media – the assumption that it is acceptable for our corporations to work in such contexts is staggering. We do not seem able to understand the inevitable, catastrophic consequences that will flow when you have a corporation whose annual turnover dwarfs the GDP of the country it's operating within. Or whose international legal team and lobbyists have scoped the deal long before the official negotiations with the host government begin. Our society only appears to register concern or criticism when a company does something so blatantly wrong that it offends the powers that be (because such actions could threaten the unchallenged existence of the status quo). I'm writing this chapter in October 2011, when the following three examples of corporate abuse have come to the attention of the British media:

- ITV have reported that Arcelor Mittal, the largest steel corporation in the world, have been polluting the town of Ostrava in the Czech Republic to such an extent that on

---

* This term 'sacrifice zones' was originally coined in the Soviet Union to denote areas that would be sacrificed in the case of a nuclear war, but more recently it has been used by American environmental writers Steve Lerner and Chris Hedges to describe exploited and environmentally degraded industrial zones.

many days children and the elderly have been told to stay inside; 15 per cent of the children in the suburbs suffer from asthma, and many need to use oxygenators on a daily basis.

- The *Guardian* have revealed that Shell, according to a report by Platform and others, had paid hundreds of thousands of dollars to Nigerian government forces and militant groups in the Delta, which had resulted in the destruction of the town of Rumuekpe and the killing of sixty people and displacement of thousands more between 2005 and 2008.

- BBC's *Newsnight* have featured a report on the Scottish company Edinburgh Woollen Mill, highlighting the fact that their clothes, advertised as 'Designed in Scotland', were actually made in Mongolia, with factories staffed overwhelmingly by North Korean workers. These workers were not paid by the factory, who preferred to pay the North Korean government directly.

It is of course entirely right that all of these violations of human rights have been reported and received media scrutiny. Yet, in the same time period, what else has been happening? For instance, how much attention has been given to the role oil corporations, particularly BP, played in keeping Mubarak's dictatorship in power in Egypt for the last thirty years (including £17 billion invested in recent years); or indeed the role that the company are still playing now, working with the new regime there? I sometimes feel that we look at individual trees while not seeing the forest.

But it is not enough to focus only on the perpetrators of these abuses. The perpetrator may carry out the act of killing or plunder or trade, but the bystander will often emerge as the 'beneficiary' of such actions. Just as the residents of the seventeenth-century Netherlands no doubt benefited from the advancement of scientific knowledge achieved by dissecting the corpses of executed criminals, so we today are also the beneficiaries of 'the merry dance of death and trade', as Conrad called it. We drive and fly with hardly a thought for the oil we depend on, which flows out of countries in turmoil like blood from arteries. And usually these countries, where countless abuses have been carried out, are far away from the direct view of the bystanders, sometimes even on the other side of the world. This is psychologically more acceptable, because then there is little need for any moral reckoning with the victims involved. We do not have to look into their faces.

*

My grandmother, on my father's side, Violet ('Vidi') Hilda Waterhouse, bought this farmhouse in Suffolk and around fifty acres of land in 1939, just before the outbreak of war. My father and my aunt were brought up here (when they weren't away at schools across the country). It is the place where my brother and sister and I grew up too, and where my nephews and nieces are now children. So it's been an important part of our family's life across four generations; it seems to have become part of us. It is the stillness at the centre of my world, even if I do not go there physically for months at a time. The fact it exists means that I've felt able to lead what has sometimes felt like a risky and insecure existence in London. However problematic in terms of privilege, I know and love this place more than any other. Set in a wooded hollow, arriving and turning into the drive feels like crossing into another country, a sense of refuge, being far away from the rushing world. A slow river bends around the bottom of the garden, there are paths through the woods, ash, oak, horse chestnut. In February it is carpeted with a million snow-drops and in the summer we eat outside, under a sallow tree, in dappled shade. It is a kind of dream space, and whenever I'm there it still seems miraculous to me.

But how did my grandmother come to be buying a farmhouse and land in 1939? She was the daughter of Sir Herbert Furnivall Water-house and Lady Edith Florence, and by the time she and her sister Dody were born at the turn of the century, Sir Herbert was already established as one of London's leading surgeons, who, later in his career, operated on prime ministers (Asquith, Bonar Law) and the royal family. He had made his name, not unlike Dr Tulp, as a demonstrator in anatomy at Charing Cross Hospital, and later at the Royal College of Surgeons. During the First World War, he was a key figure in the success of the Anglo-Russian hospital in Petrograd (today St Petersburg) – a humanitarian gift from the British people to their Russian ally, then suffering major casualties on the Eastern Front, with insufficient medical resources. Waterhouse was appointed the principal surgeon, and the makeshift hospital, housed in the Belosselsky-Belozersky Palace on Nevsky Prospekt, saved thousands of lives between 1915 and 1917. For his years of work in Petrograd, and contribution to Anglo-Russian relations, he was knighted on his return to Britain in 1917.

The Waterhouses lived in a grand house at 7 Wimpole Street, and Vidi and her sister lacked for nothing as they grew up. But Vidi was a rebel from an early age. As a young woman she became politicised by hearing accounts of appalling housing conditions in the East End of London, and began to help Dame Edith Ramsay, who was then doing pioneering work on this issue, along with Philip Toynbee and others. Vidi outraged her parents by selling furniture, mirrors and jewellery from her own bedroom, and giving the proceeds, along with much of her personal allowance, to housing projects in the East End. Later she caused more consternation by declaring that she was going to become an actress. There was a stand-off with Sir Herbert, and a compromise was eventually reached – she could go to RADA but only on condition she completed a more orthodox degree first. So she went to Somerville College in Oxford and did an English degree, and then on to RADA, where she gained a Gold Medal in her final year.

The greatest scandal, however, was yet to come. She had established herself as an actress, with a certain amount of success, both on stage and radio, when she met, and fell headlong in love with, Richard Gretton, an Oxford historian. Richard had written a successful three-volume series, *A Modern History of the English People*, which had made his reputation. But he also became one of the pioneering early writers of local history, having written an innovative work, *The Burford Records.** One of the unusual features of the romance was that Richard was in his fifties and Vidi was thirty years younger. But an even greater challenge was that Richard was already married – to Mary, another Oxford historian – and living a settled life in Burford. When it became clear that this was no passing affair, Richard eloped to Paris with Vidi in 1929, leaving chaos in his wake. Oxford barred him from ever holding a post in the university again, and Mary was devastated. The couple stayed in France, but the only work Richard could secure in Paris was as an occasional correspondent for the relatively liberal *Manchester Guardian*. Most of their living costs were met through Vidi's familial wealth. My father and aunt were both born in Paris soon afterwards, and the affluent environs of their house near the Bois de Boulogne could not disguise the reality of being born 'out of wedlock' – then a serious social stigma.

A few years later Richard became seriously ill, and realising the best medical treatment was to be had in London not Paris, they returned to England in 1934, finding a house in Chalfont St Giles in Buckinghamshire, hoping this was far enough away from Oxford for the scandal not to follow them. Richard, by this stage, had developed stomach cancer and died in 1936, leaving Vidi effectively as a single mother, though one of independent means. The little family continued living at Hill House for three more years, but Vidi

---

* 'The records of no small town in England, we suppose, have been treated with more patient and scholarly care than Mr Gretton has shown in this book. His work deserves the fair and ample form in type and production which has been given to it by the Oxford University Press.' (Review in the *Spectator*, 5 February 1921.)

now felt very uncomfortable in the heart of conservative England. Any sympathy for the young widow was soon overtaken by vicious gossip when the story of her and Richard finally emerged, and life there became impossible.

Vidi started looking for somewhere more remote where they could live, far away from wagging tongues. Dody, her sister, lived in Aldeburgh (with her 'companion' Teresa – as such an arrangement was coyly termed in those days), and so had got to know Suffolk a little. In those days, years before the electrification of the railway and the subsequent commuterisation of Suffolk, it was still regarded as rather a dark county, untamed by the reach of the city, with over-grown hedgerows and many twisting lanes to explore. A world away from the suburban white fences of Surrey and Buckinghamshire. So, apparently, when Vidi saw a small photograph of the farmhouse for sale on the back of *The Times*, it was love at first sight. The price, for the Elizabethan farmhouse, barns and fifty acres of land, was just under £1,000. The 1930s was a period of extreme agricultural depression, and land prices were at historic lows. Vidi knew a bar-gain when she saw one, and snapped it up. My father loved the place the first time he set eyes on it; my aunt was completely hor-rified. She saw it as 'uncivilised, wild and as far from London as it's possible to be!' – all aspects that delighted my father.

In time the place became a refuge for more than this small family. Vidi, appalled at how she had been treated as an unmarried mother herself, set up her own haven for 'ladies in distress'. She encouraged unmarried young women who'd become pregnant, and had sub-sequently been thrown out by their own families, to come to the farmhouse as a sanctuary, for a few weeks or even months, some staying on long after the children were born. Later on, as well as supporting the rebuilding of the Catholic church in Hadleigh, she took up the cause of prison reform, and became a prison visitor. She'd been influenced by a book by a Catholic priest, *The Company We Keep*, which raised many questions about poor prison condi-tions in the 1940s. She wrote to the author, asking what she could do to help; the priest suggested she visit a young man in Chelmsford prison, who was in a bad state. His name was Gerald Caine, London Irish, Catholic. He'd been the getaway driver for an armed gang in London and had been sentenced to a long term. Vidi visited him, and they soon discovered a shared love of chess, among other things. On his eventual release a few years later, they got married, and Gerald came to live with her at the house in Suffolk. Another person seeking a fresh start, away from gossiping tongues. It is only as I've got older that I've begun to appreciate the magnificently unorthodox trajectory of my grandmother's life – from the royal surgeon's Wimpole Street residence to a cell in Chelmsford prison.

The Vidi I got to know as a child was already white-haired, bird-like, remote, and, though it wasn't properly diagnosed until later, she already had Alzheimer's. Gerald had left her some years before, and so she now lived in the house alone. She spoke in what sounded to us like an impossibly posh accent from another age, and treated us with what seemed like Victorian formality. One day when our parents had (rather worryingly) left her to look after us for the afternoon, she insisted on cooking us sausages for lunch, even though she'd made us this meal an hour before. When my older brother explained we'd already eaten, her reply was imperious and sharp, an echo of Miss Havisham, as she snapped back: 'I'm the lady of the house! And *I* decide when we're having lunch, young man, do I make myself quite clear?'

Later my parents tried to explain to us that she'd 'lost her memory', a concept that was impossible to grasp for a child. When we lost things they could be found again, so there was always the sense that this loss of memory might just be a temporary state. It must have been much harder for my father, who was always very close to her. Years later he described playing chess with her – Vidi had always been an exceptionally skilful player, and curiously, long after other faculties had gone, she still was able to play chess with concentration. But on this day, towards the end of their game, Vidi had apparently told him: 'You really must meet my son Mark, I think the two of you would get on terribly well.'

Although by this time – the early 1970s – she was clearly struggling, she had a fierce independence, and stubbornly refused to move out of the farmhouse. We would come over every Sunday to collect her for Mass. The house smelt musty and damp to us, and the pale green walls somehow were part of this too. In my mind the colour of the walls connected to an old Penguin edition of Graham Greene's *The Heart of the Matter*, which remained unfinished for years, on the small table by her chair in the sitting room. One Sunday, when my father was getting her ready to leave the house, I went through to the study with my brother, up the step past the ice skates and tennis racquets, relics from another era, and we found that the ceiling had collapsed. We ran back to tell Mark, and he thought we were just messing around, until we finally persuaded him to come and look. But the final straw was coming over one weekend and not finding her anywhere in the house. Eventually she was discovered sitting very calmly in the river at the end of the garden, completely unaware of how she'd got there, and suffering from hypothermia. At that point my parents knew that she couldn't continue to live on her own any longer.

So she came to live with us for a year or so, and when, finally, that too became impossible, my parents made the difficult, but inevitable, decision to find a home for her. Or rather, several homes – because she would repeatedly escape and, like a wounded animal, try to find her way back to the farmhouse, which she loved with a primal passion. My parents would receive calls from the police all over Essex and Suffolk, saying that my grandmother had been found, having walked twenty or thirty miles. That was one thing I could identity with, even as a young boy, the escaping and the walking – yes, that merited serious respect. She ended up in Severalls, a secure hospital on the edge of Colchester; by this time the Alzheimer's had reached an advanced stage and when we visited she had little awareness of who any of us were. The last time I saw her, the poised, proud lady had been reduced to a shadow, more interested in the box of chocolates we'd brought than anything else. And as we left, I remember shuddering, watching the other inmates gathering around her to get the chocolates, like crows attacking a carcass.

In 1973 we moved into the farmhouse, which had to be virtually rebuilt. A happy, not very eventful nine years followed and I went to university. Only by leaving home did I really begin to develop a new relationship with this place. Perhaps by seeing it, as if for the first time, through others' eyes – friends from university who couldn't believe the beauty there. A kind of idyll that was only shattered by my father's death, in the fields, in the fire of 1985. Since then my mother, with help from us, has planted over 5,000 trees in the fields, my sister and brother have established their own families here, and now a new generation of children play under the trees – my nieces and nephews. The cycle has come full circle for the third time.

*

But what does this foray into the details of my family history have to do with perpetrators, victims or bystanders?

Some years ago I was helping my mother clear out an old sideboard and we came across a box of papers I had never seen before. Among them, I found this document:

The will of my grandmother's mother – Lady Edith Florence Waterhouse, widow of Sir Herbert Waterhouse, dated 14 April 1931, which also listed all the stocks and shares held at the time of Sir Herbert's death. I was amazed to see that she had left over £84,000 (equivalent to over £4 million today). What had happened to all of that money? Presumably a lot had gone on Vidi's philanthropy – towards the rebuilding of the Catholic church in Hadleigh, perhaps. But some of that money had gone towards buying the farmhouse in Suffolk, not to mention our first house in Essex, that Vidi had also contributed towards.

But where had all this money originated? And where had it been invested? Very helpfully, together with the will, were lists of all the shareholdings of my great-grandparents, and, as I looked through them, I felt a sudden chill:

Anglo-Persian Oil Company
Buenos Aires & Pacific Railway
City of Bahia
Consolidated Goldfields of South Africa
Durban Roodepoort Deep Ltd
Indian Copper Corporation
Imperial Chemical Industries
Panama Corporation Ltd . . .

It was like reading an inventory of the British Empire and its associated partners. A roll call of the kind of globalised criminality that masqueraded as 'free trade' for hundreds of years. My hands started to shake as I turned the paper over, realising that our family had benefited from some of the vilest corporate activities imaginable. That our 'progressive' home had been built on the most rotten and compromised of foundations.

Later I started to research some of these companies. I found out that Durban Roodepoort Deep Ltd was a massive gold mine, still operating today as DRD Gold just outside Johannesburg. I discovered that it opened in 1897 and that 'it thrived in an environment of repression and extreme human rights violations'. In the hundred years up to 1993 it produced 21 million ounces of gold, and billions in terms of profits for shareholders around the world, including my great-grandparents. The precise amount of gold mined from this land is known, but the numbers of deaths and casualties of miners over this period are not documented. The Indian Copper Corporation had been established as a British company in 1930, at Ghatsila in Jharkhand, north-eastern India, consolidating a number of different mines and plants in the Singhbhum copper belt. In 1972 the Indian government nationalised the company and it became part of Hindustan Copper Ltd, under which name some of the original mines still operate. I found out from their website that the mines at Rakha, Kendadih and Chapri have combined copper reserves of 123.54 million tons. But it's hard to discover any information on the labour conditions or the history of the mining; I just find a reference that 'mining in India is . . . infamous for human rights violations and environmental pollution'; so if that's true today, I can only imagine what the situation would have been like in the early 1930s.

Years later, I'm still thinking about the relationship between my liberal, humanist family and this other story languishing unread for years on yellowing paper in a cupboard. The tranquillity of this corner of Suffolk, and the exploitation, the blood and the terror of the people who had worked in these mines, in these oilfields, eighty years ago. It's like suddenly being able to see the skull beneath the skin.

Yet perhaps my family's story in this regard is not so different from other upper-middle-class families. Any family that has wealth passed down from their ancestors would almost certainly have similar patterns of shareholding and investment, which provided the financial backbone for the British Empire. And if we were to cast the net more widely, almost everybody becomes complicit, albeit in less dramatic ways. Anyone who has a mortgage or a pension, anyone with anything invested, anyone on benefits – almost everyone, to some degree, is connected through international finance to such a story of profit and exploitation which underpins the smooth functioning of our societies. Two examples I came across when I was beginning this research show the realites of such interrelationships: I was looking through a report detailing the pension scheme of my impeccably liberal mother, the Universities Superannuation Scheme, and I discovered that the USS was heavily invested in two oil companies: British Petroleum (£373 million) and Shell Transport & Trading (£322 million). I wonder what retired academics think of a significant proportion of their pensions coming out of the ethically dubious oil industry.

*

I'm sure many of us must have puzzled through these issues, feeling the questions nagging away, sometimes buried deep, but then returning periodically, with a clarity and persistence that disturbs. What is our comfort built upon? Didn't Balzac once say that 'The secret of great wealth is a forgotten crime'? We all now seem to be beneficiaries of a system of international finance, which often shades into criminality. And who are the casualties of this? The people who get destroyed when the zones of progress and the zones of sacrifice meet. They seem virtually invisible to us . . . And the greater our supposed 'development', the more these inner voices seem to build. As the current century dawned, the historian Eric Hobsbawm eloquently described the vast challenge involved in connecting to others in our world – and the paradox that lies behind that glib label of 'globalisation':

> In a world filled with such inequalities, to live in the 'favoured' regions is to be virtually cut off from the experience, let alone the reactions, of people outside those regions. It takes an enormous effort of the imagination, as well as a great deal of knowledge, to break out of our comfortable, protected and self-absorbed enclaves and enter an uncomfortable and unprotected larger world inhabited by the majority of the human species. We are cut off from this world even if the sum

total of amassed information is everywhere accessible at the click of a mouse, even if images of the remotest part of the world reach us at all times of day and night, even if more of us travel between civilisations than ever before. This is the paradox of a globalised twenty-first century.

I sometimes wonder whether we shouldn't trust our instinctive, inner voices on some of these fundamental questions. The same voices that asked why the emperor was not wearing any clothes:

> The voice of the child says:
> 'What is profit? How is it made?
> 'But where does the money really come from?'

> The voice of the child knows
> that paper cannot create value,
> that labour is at the beginning and end of everything.

> And all the teams of treasury economists,
> the whole of the World Bank,
> all the pink pages of the financial papers
> cannot shift that voice in my head.
> A voice as clear as justice.

And perhaps the most important questions of all – how then can we connect to the lives of others? How can we open ourselves to the experiences of the majority of people on our planet who do not have access to clean water or electricity or health services? To try and connect, even on an imaginative level, or a level of knowledge, is disturbing, even painful – yet the impulse is also at the heart of what makes us human beings. It is the impulse which lies behind Primo Levi's terrible warning – describing a transmission between two worlds that are, in reality, one.

> You who live safe
> In your warm houses
> You who find, returning in the evening,

Hot food and friendly faces:
Consider if this is a man
Who works in the mud
Who does not know peace
Who fights for a scrap of bread
Who dies because of a yes or a no.
Consider if this is a woman,
Without hair and without name
With no more strength to remember,
Her eyes empty and her womb cold
Like a frog in winter.
Meditate that this came about:
I commend these words to you.
Carve them in your hearts
At home, in the street,
Going to bed, rising;
Repeat them to your children,
Or may your house fall apart,
May illness impede you,
May your children turn their faces from you.

*

The challenge of breaking out of our bubbles doesn't relate only to crossing vast geographical territories between the developed world and poorer regions. Within the same society there can exist shocking divides, which people become incapable of seeing. Recently I was listening to a radio interview with the actor Antony Sher, and he began talking about his experience of growing up in South Africa in the 1960s:

Interviewer: How politically conscious were you growing up in the years of the apartheid system?

Sher: Not at all, and it's quite a shocking, disturbing thing for me. If I look back on my youth and think of how comfortable my family were, what a joyous childhood it was, a childhood made up of beaches and brais, and so there we were living a very happy life – and we were in the middle of what was one of the atrocities of the last century – apartheid. And I didn't really learn anything about apartheid till I came here to drama school and saw South Africa through British eyes . . . When I tell people that, I can hear people thinking that I'm trying to make an excuse, or an apology. I'm not. I'm stating quite a shocking truth about human beings – *that we can live in the middle of an atrocity and not notice it if we don't want to* [my emphasis].

Interviewer: So how challenging was that for you to have to reappraise your childhood?

Sher: It was difficult, also because my grandparents had all fled persecution as Jews from eastern Europe, mostly Lithuania, at the turn of the century, and gone to South Africa – so they knew what it was like to be persecuted. And yet, as soon as they did well in South Africa, they supported the apartheid government – not in an active way, just in that middle-of-the-road way, they voted for the nationalist government. And they didn't make . . . what you would have thought were the obvious comparisons of what it had been like to be second-class citizens as they had been in eastern Europe, and that the black people in South Africa were that now. How could they not make that comparison? But again, it's very human, isn't it?[*]

And if you think this is a rather extreme example of the walls that human beings can erect to block out what is going on all around them, just reflect for a moment about the staggering levels of inequalities in our societies at the moment. That in contemporary Britain we have become used to having 'food banks' because a million of our fellow citizens do not have enough to eat. What a

---

[*] The interviewer was Sarah Walker (BBC Radio 3, *Essential Classics*, 12 January 2016).

shameful indictment of one of the richest countries in the world. Many of us would blame government policy here, vindictive official attitudes. Yes, this is certainly part of the problem. But also think for a moment about how hard we try *not to see* these million people. You may have impeccable liberal-left views, but the walls you create to separate yourself from others can be as impenetrable as steel.

The philosopher Emmanuel Levinas was fascinated in what happens when we really look into the face of another human being and all that can be triggered by such a seemingly simple action:

> The moral 'authority' of the face of the other is felt in my 'infinite responsibility' for the other . . . The face of the other comes toward me with its infinite moral demands.

These ideas were also referred to by Justin Welby, now Archbishop of Canterbury, in a *Guardian* interview with Giles Fraser on 21 July 2012 – Welby expressed strong agreement with Levinas that 'the face of the other is the true site of human obligation'. If this is true, then the converse must also be true – if you cannot see the face of the other, it is hard to feel human obligation. I was surprised to learn that Welby had spent eleven years in the oil industry, at Elf in France, and subsequently as group treasurer for Enterprise Oil, based in the City of London. Even more remarkably, it emerged that his principal area of knowledge was West Africa, and he had spent time working in the Niger Delta. I'm intrigued by how he, clearly a man of strong religious and ethical convictions, could have spent time working in such a compromised and exploitative environment. Did he find himself at times having to turn away from things he couldn't bear to face?

Welby said something which struck me powerfully in this interview. He was discussing financial and banking corruption, and the move away from face-to-face trading in the City of London to electronic trading after the 'Big Bang': 'there's something different about looking someone in the eyes and doing something dishonest, to doing it over the phone or screen'. This connects to another example, regarding what happens when we look into another's face, when we look directly into their eyes: in a 1974 lecture in New York, Hannah Arendt remarked that it is easier to kill a dog than a man, easier yet to kill a rat or a frog, and no problem at all to kill insects – 'It is in the glance, in the eyes.'

Both of these quotations link to what Hobsbawm and Levi are saying. All are fundamentally about the critical need for empathy, the vast imaginative challenge that exists to connect people in our world today, and how direct, face-to-face contact can be crucial in facilitating such a connection. I return in my mind to the men and women from the oil industry I talked to at Birkbeck. I'm not sure that any number of books or documentaries will ever convince some of them that their companies have behaved wrongly, in many countries, over many years. But, taking Levinas as inspiration, I wonder what would happen if I could introduce David from Shell to a villager from Rumuekpe, who'd seen her family killed by security forces? If they could spend some hours together, perhaps going for a walk or sharing a meal? I think about inviting Anna from Shell to meet Maria Saro-Wiwa, Ken's widow. They could sit together in a garden on a summer's evening, and they would discover they were almost exactly the same age. They might also talk about their shared religious faith, and slowly, almost imperceptibly, they could look at each other, eye to eye, and begin to express what cannot be expressed over a screen or a phone. I would like to attempt this one day . . .

But still there remains Hobsbawm's challenge of how to *transmit* between different worlds. I'm keenly aware that we live in a time when we are becoming increasingly immunised against the suffering of others – those outside our immediate circle of family and friends. So what does it take to get through the invisible barriers we've put up around ourselves, the screens and the filters we protect ourselves with? How do we start to break through the normalisation of extreme suffering in our world – the hundreds of bodies of human beings that wash up on Mediterranean beaches every year, the thousands mutilated by British weapons used in Yemen, the hundreds of thousands killed in the war in Syria that has now lasted longer than the Second World War? This condition that nearly all of us live with, summed up by that obscene phrase – 'compassion fatigue'.

*

Koita, Tounkara, Aisha and Mordechai

In the last ten or fifteen years I can think of few examples of such transmission, certainly via the written word – perhaps film and news coverage carry a greater immediate power to communicate. I puzzle over the reason why certain written accounts nevertheless do manage to 'get through'. You will be able to think of your own examples of being suddenly overwhelmed by something you've seen or read. Here are three accounts which shook me to my core. Even today, I find it difficult to read them again. To acknowledge that these events happened in the world that we inhabit. This is from a short article Stephen Bates wrote for the *Guardian*, 5 August 1999:

Dead stowaways left plea for Africa

Two young African stowaways who were found dead on Monday in the landing gear of a plane in Brussels left a handwritten letter explaining the hardships that caused them to pursue such a dangerous plan, the Brussels public prosecutor's office said yesterday. The bodies of Koita Yaguine, 15, and Tounkara Fode, 16, both from Guinea, west Africa, were found in the landing gear of a Sabena plane on Monday while it was being refuelled. The plane came from Conakry, Guinea, and had stopped in Bamako, Mali.

A spokeswoman for the prosecutions office said a postmortem examination would be made to find out whether they had died from lack of oxygen or exposure to the cold. It was not known how long they had been dead when their bodies were found, she said. The two had prepared carefully for their trip, each donning several pairs of trousers, pullovers and jackets. But that and their plastic sandals were woefully inadequate to save them in high-altitude temperatures of -55C.

It is not the boys' death which has shocked Belguim, however, so much as the letter found wrapped in their clothing, showing that they quite expected to die in their attempt to escape and making a plea for Europe to help the young people of Africa . . . The letter, addressed in shaky French to the 'Excellencies, gentlemen-members and those responsible in Europe', is a cry for help. Apparently written last Thursday, it says:

'It is to your solidarity and generosity that we appeal for your help in Africa. If you see that we have sacrificed ourselves and lost our lives, it is because we suffer too much in Africa and need your help to struggle against poverty and war . . . Please excuse us very much for daring to write this letter.'

Perhaps the only way to really understand the impact of globalisation and migration today would be to have a film, in real time, shot from the wheels of such a plane, recording the memories and thoughts of such children, with their dreams of a foreign city fading as they die.

I think of these words from *Fugitive Pieces* by Anne Michaels: 'History is amoral; events occurred. But memory is moral; what we consciously remember is what our conscience remembers.'

*

Another short article from the *Guardian*, by Chris McGreal, Africa correspondent, 3 November 2008:

Somalian rape victim, 13, stoned to death

An Islamist rebel administration in Somalia has had a 13-year-old girl stoned to death for adultery after the child's father reported that she was raped by three men.

Amnesty International said al-Shabab militia, which controls the southern city of Kismayo, arranged for 50 men to stone Aisha Ibrahim Duhulow in front of about 1,000 spectators. A lorry load of stones was brought to the stadium for the killing.

Amnesty said Duhulow struggled with her captors and had to be forcibly carried into the stadium.

'At one point during the stoning, Amnesty International has been told by numerous eyewitnesses that nurses were instructed to check whether Aisha . . . was still alive when buried in the ground. They removed her from the ground, declared that she was, and she was replaced in the hole where she had been buried for the stoning to continue,' the human rights group said. It continued: 'Inside the stadium, militia members opened fire when some of the witnesses to the killing attempted to save her life, and shot dead a boy who was a bystander.'

Amnesty said Duhulow was originally reported by witnesses as being 23 years old, based on her appearance, but established from her father that she was a child. He told Amnesty that when they tried to report her rape to the militia, the child was accused of adultery and detained. None of the men accused was arrested.

This piece I still find impossible to comprehend. It brings me to despair, and what lies even beyond that. To read it, each time, is to be assaulted again. The only words there that do not damn beyond redemption the sickness of what humans are capable of doing to other humans is that brief reference to some people attempting to save Aisha's life. And the boy without a name who also died, perhaps trying to save her.

*

And then there is the transmission of suffering which, occasionally and in some respects miraculously, can come through writing. In a short book by George Steiner – *The Portage to San Cristóbal of A.H.* – there is a single sentence that extends over three pages in a roar of pain that sears itself into your mind. An attempt at empathetic imagination unparalleled in all the writing I've ever read about the Holocaust. Steiner brings back to life, momentarily, an exterminated world:

> The garden in Salonika, where Mordechai Zathsmar, the cantor's youngest child, ate excrement; the Hoofstraat in Arnhem where they took Leah Burstein and made her watch while her father; the two lime trees where the road to Montrouge turns south, 8th November 1942, on which they hung the meathooks; the pantry on the third floor, Nowy Swiat xi, where Jakov Kaplan, author of the *History of Algebraic Thought in Eastern Europe 1280–1655*, had to dance over the body of; in White Springs, Ohio, Rahel Nadelmann who wakes each night, sweat in her mouth because thirty-one years earlier in the Mauerallee in Hanover three louts drifting home from an SS recruitment spree had tied her legs and with a truncheon; the latrine in the police station in Worgel which Doktor Ruth Levin and her niece had to clean with their hair; the fire raid on Engstaad and the Jakobsons made to kneel outside the shelter until the incendiaries; Sternowitz caught in the woods near Sibor talking to Ludmilla, an Aryan woman, and filled with water and a piano wire wound tight around his; Branka seeing them burn the dolls near the ramp and when she sought to hide hers being taken to the fire and; Elias Kornfeld, Sarah Ellbogen, Robert Heimann in front of the biology class, Neuwald Gymnasium lower Saxony, stripped to the waist, mouths wide open so that Professor Horst Küntzer could demonstrate to his pupils the obvious racial, an hour of school which Heimann remembered when at Matthausen naked again; Lilian Gourevitch given two work passes, yellow-coloured, serial numbers BJ7732781 and 2, for her three children in Tver Street and ordered to choose which of the children was to go on the next transport; the marsh six kilometres from Noverra where the dogs found Aldo Mattei and his family in hiding, only a week before the Waffen-SS

retreated northward, thus completing the register of fugitives; five Jews, one Gypsy, one hydrocephalic, drawn up at the *prefettura* in Rovigo; the last Purim in Vilna and the man who played Haman cutting his throat, remember him, Moritz the caretaker whose beard they had torn out almost hair by hair, pasting on a false beard and after the play taking the razor in the boiler room; Dorfmann, collector of prints of the late seventeenth century, doctor and player on the viola, lying, no kneeling, no squatting in the punishment cell at Buchenwald, six feet by four and one half, the concrete cracked with ice, watching the pus break from his torn nails and whispering the catalogue numbers of the Hobbemas in the Albertina, so far as he could remember them in the raw pain of his shaven skull, until the guard took a whip; Ann Casanova, 21 rue du Chapon, Liège, called to the door, asking the two men to wait outside so that her mother would not know and the old woman falling on to the bonnet of the starting car, from the fourth-floor window, her dentures scattered in the road; Hannah, the silken-haired bitch dying of hunger in the locked apartment after the Kullmans had been taken, sinking her teeth into the master's house shoes, custom-made to the measure of his handsome foot by Samuel Rossbach, Hagadio, who in the shoe factory at Treblinka was caught splitting leather, sabotage, and made to crawl alive into the quicklime while at the edge Reuben Cohen, aged eleven, had to proclaim 'so shall all saboteurs and subverters of the united front', Hagadio, Hagadio, until the neighbours, Ebert and Ilse Schmidt, today Ebert Schmidt City Engineer, broke down the door, found the dog almost dead, dropped it in the garbage pit and rifled Kullman's closets, his wife's dressing table, the children's attic with its rocking horse, jack-in-the-box and chemistry set, while on the railway siding near Dornbach, Hagadio, the child, thrown from the train by its parents, with money sewn to its jacket and a note begging for water and help was found by two men coming home from seeding and laid on the tracks, a hundred yards from the north switch, gagged, feet tied, till the next train, which it heard a long way off in the still of the summer evening, the two men watching and eating and then voiding their bowels, Hagadio; the Kullmans knowing that the smell of gas was the smell of gas but thinking the child safe, which, as the thundering air blew nearer spoke into its gag, twice, the name of the silken-haired bitch Hannah, and then could not close its eyes against the rushing shadow; at Maidanek ten thousand a day; I am not mad, Ajalon calling, can you hear me; unimaginable because innumerable: in one corner of Treblinka seven hundred thousand bodies, I will count them now, Aaron, Aaronowitch, Aaronson, Abilech, Abraham, I will count seven hundred thousand names and you must listen, and watch Asher, I do not know him as well as I do you Simeon, and Eli Barach and the boy, I will say Kaddish to the end of time and when time ceases shall not have reached the millionth name; at Belzec three hundred thousand, Friedberg, Friedman, Friedmann, Friedstein, the names gone in fire and gas, ash in the wind at Chelmno, the long black wind at Chelmno, Israel Meyer, Ida Meyer, the four children in the pit at Sobibor; four hundred and eleven thousand three hundred and eighty-one in section three at Belsen, the one being Salomon Rheinfeld who left on his desk in Mainz the uncorrected proofs of the grammar of Hittite which Egon Scleicher, his assistant newly promoted Ordinarius, claimed for his own but cannot complete, the one being Belin the tanner whose face they sprinkled with acid from the vat and who was dragged through the streets of Kershon behind a dung cart but sang, the one being Georges Walter who when they called him from supper in the rue Marot, from the *blanquette de veau* finely seasoned, could not understand and spoke to his family of an administrative error and refused to pack more than one shirt and asked still why through his smashed teeth when the shower doors closed and the whisper started in the ceiling, the one being David Pollachek whose fingers they broke in the quarry at Leutach when they heard he had been first violin and who in the loud burning of each blow could think only of the elder bush in his yard at Slanic, each leaf of which he had tried to touch once more on the last evening in his house after the summons came, the one not being Nathaniel Steiner who was taken to America in time but goes maimed nevertheless for not having been at the roll call, the one being all because unnumbered hence unrememberable, because buried alive at Bialistok like Nathansohn, nine hours fourteen minutes under the whip (timed by Wachtmeister Ottmar Prantl now hotelier in Steyerbrück), the blood, Prantl reporting, splashing out of his hair and mouth like new wine; two million at, unspeakable because beyond imagaining, two million suffocated at, outside Cracow of the gracious towers, the signpost on the airport road pointing to it still, Oszwiecim in sight of the low hills, because we can imagine the cry of one, the hunger of two, the burning of ten, but past a hundred there is no clear imagining, he understood that, take a million and belief will not follow nor the mind contain, and if each and every one of us, Ajalon calling, were to rise before morning and speak out ten names that day, ten from the ninety-six thousand graven on the wall in Prague, ten from the thirty-one thousand in the crypt at Rome, ten from those at Matthausen Drancy Birkenau Buchenwald Theresienstadt or Babi Yar, ten out of six million, we should never finish the task, not if we spoke the night through, not till the close of time, nor bring back a single breath, not that of Isaac Lowy, Berlin, Isaac Lowy, Danzig (with the birthmark on his left shoulder), Isaac Lowy, Zagreb, Isaac Lowy, Vilna, the baker who cried of yeast when the door closed, Isaac Lowy, Toulouse, almost safe, the visa almost granted, I am not mad but the Kaddish which is like a shadow of lilac after the dust of the day is withered now, empty of remembrance, he has made ash of prayer, AND UNTIL EACH NAME is recalled and spoken again, EACH, the names of the nameless in the orphans' house at Szeged, the name of the mute in the sewer at Katowic, the names of the unborn in the women ripped at Matthausen, the name of the girl with the yellow star seen hammering on the door of the shelter at

Hamburg and of whom there is no record but a brown shadow burnt into the pavement, until each name is remembered and spoken to the LAST SYLLABLE, man will have no peace on earth, do you hear me Simeon, no place, no liberation from hatred, not until every name, for when spoken each after the other, with not a single letter omitted, do you hear me, the syllables will make up the hidden name of GOD.

PART SIX

Civilisation / Barbarism

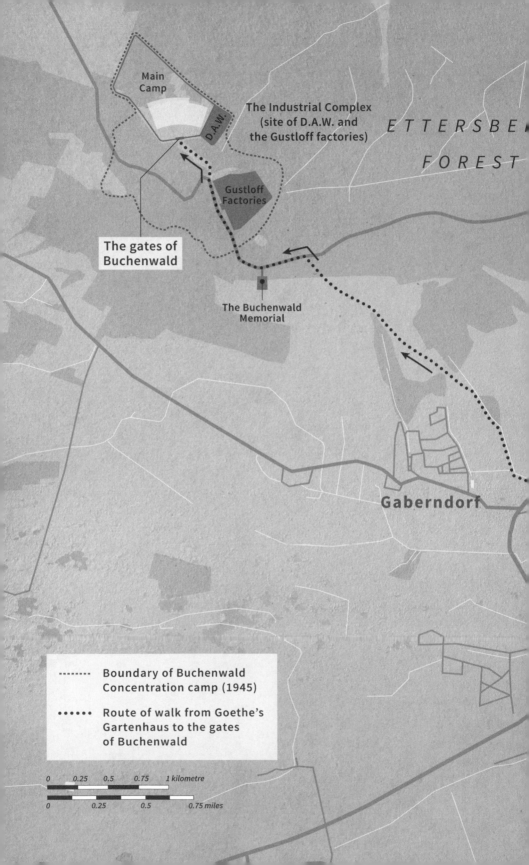

Main
Camp

D.A.W.

The Industrial Complex
(site of D.A.W. and
the Gustloff factories)

E T T E R S B E...

F O R E S T

Gustloff
Factories

**The gates of
Buchenwald**

The Buchenwald
Memorial

Gaberndorf

┄┄┄┄ Boundary of Buchenwald
Concentration camp (1945)

•••••• Route of walk from Goethe's
Gartenhaus to the gates
of Buchenwald

| 0 | 0.25 | 0.5 | 0.75 | 1 kilometre |

| 0 | 0.25 | 0.5 | 0.75 miles |

N

Ilm River

WEIMAR

Goethe's
Gartenhaus

A Walk from Goethe's Gartenhaus to the Gates of Buchenwald: 10,166 Steps

Words are seeds. Sometimes, blown from we know not where, they can lie dormant inside us for years, waiting for the conditions to grow. Sun and rain and sometimes a little help from gardeners. Nothing can grow on its own. The ecology of the mind is as interdependent as the ecology of the earth, and we need writers and thinkers and ideas just as much as any plant needs oxygen and nitrates and water. These next pages bring together several of these gardeners of the mind.

I return to five writers' words again and again. They do what even the most brilliant historians cannot do: they all have compelling things to say about the interrelationship of civilisation and barbarism in the atrocities of the twentieth century. This question which returns over and over again, like an unanswered riddle, like an image that haunts you. But these are the voices who have got closer than anyone else – George Steiner, Primo Levi, Sven Lindqvist, Jorge Semprún and Jean Améry.

At university, in my final year, I came across these words, from the preface to Steiner's *Language and Silence*:

I realise that historians are right when they say that barbarism and political savagery are endemic in human affairs, that no age has been innocent of disaster. I know that the colonial massacres of the nineteenth and twentieth centuries, and the cynical destruction of natural and animal resources which accompany them . . . are realties of profound evil. But I think there is hypocrisy in the imagination that would claim universal immediacy . . . my own consciousness is possessed by the eruption of barbarism in modern Europe; by the mass murder of the Jews and by the destruction under Nazism and Stalinism of what I try to define . . . as the particular genius of 'Central European humanism'. I do not claim for this hideousness any singular privilege; but this is the crisis of rational, humane expectation which has shaped my own life and with which I am most directly concerned.

The blackness of it did not spring up in the Gobi desert or the rainforests of the Amazon. It rose from within, and from the core of European civilisation. The cry of the murdered sounded in earshot of the universities; the sadism went on a street away from the theatres and museums. In the later eighteenth century Voltaire had looked confidently to the end of torture; ideological massacre was to be a banished shadow. In our own day the high places of literacy, of philosophy, of artistic expression became the setting for Belsen.

I cannot accept the facile comfort that this catastrophe was a purely German phenomenon or some calamitous mishap rooted in the persona of one or another totalitarian ruler. Ten years after the Gestapo quit Paris, the countrymen of Voltaire were torturing Algerians . . . in some of the same police cellars . . . It is not only the case that the established media of civilisation – the universities, the arts, the book world – failed to offer adequate resistance to political bestiality, they often rose to welcome it . . . Why? What are the links, as yet scarcely understood, between the mental, psychological habits of high literacy and the temptations of the inhuman?

Later, with his work *In Bluebeard's Castle*, Steiner makes the intellectual challenge even more explicit:

> there have been few attempts to relate the dominant phenomenon of twentieth-century barbarism to a more general theory of culture. Not many have asked, or pressed home the question, as to the internal relations between the structures of the inhuman and the surrounding, contemporary matrix of high civilisation. Yet the barbarism which we have undergone reflects, at numerous and precise points, the culture which it sprang from and set out to desecrate. Art, intellectual pursuits, the development of the natural sciences, many branches of scholarship flourished in close spatial, temporal proximity to massacre and the death camps. It is the structure and meaning of that proximity which must be looked at. Why did humanistic traditions and models of conduct prove so fragile a barrier against political bestiality? In fact, were they a barrier, or is it more realistic to perceive in humanistic culture express solicitations of authoritarian rule and cruelty?

In the middle of so much turgid, academic writing (and I was at Cambridge in the heyday of post-structuralist theory), it was electrifying to come across words of such clarity and passion. And to feel, instinctively, that Steiner was right in identifying these questions. Not that I could even attempt to find answers at that point, but it was enough to have logged the questions in my mind, waiting for a time when these could be brought out into the light again. Many years later, reading Sven Lindqvist's *Exterminate All the Brutes*, this sentence leapt off the page and reminded me forcefully of those original questions:

> 'The idea of extermination lies no farther from the heart of humanism than Buchenwald lies from the Goethehaus in Weimar.'

Triggered by this, and remembering Steiner's earlier words, an idea began to take shape in my mind – a walk that could become a meditation on the relationship between civilisation and barbarism.

By chance, in July 1999 Platform had been invited to teach in Germany, in Bochum, at Hannah Hurtzig's* Summer Academy for young artists, writers, theatre directors, film-makers and dramatists. Later in the summer we were scheduled to run a two-week seminar at the New University of Sofia, in Bulgaria. Looking at a map of Europe I realised that our train journey from the Ruhr to Sofia would take us within a few miles of Weimar. My colleagues on the trip, J. and Kay, agreed we would spend a couple of days in Weimar, and I decided to conceptualise a walk from Goethe's summer house (one of his favourite writing places) to the gates of the Buchenwald concentration camp, just to the west of the town.

*

Buchenwald had been vividly in my mind at that time because I'd just read Jorge Semprún's remarkable memoir *Literature or Life*, his account of surviving the camp. Semprún was twenty years old when he arrived at Buchenwald on 29 January 1944, a brilliant former philosophy student at the Sorbonne, and, despite his youth, already a communist activist and a veteran of the French Resistance. His year or so in Buchenwald, from January 1944 to April 1945, paralleled almost exactly Primo Levi's and Jean Améry's enslavement at Auschwitz-Monowitz. Yet the texture of Semprún's writing and his preoccupations are quite distinct from Levi's or Améry's. His engagement with literature, philosophy and activism permeates the book, he relates animated conversations with fellow inmates about the intellectual figures and debates of the time. At times Semprún's Buchenwald comes across as a kind of displaced university for partisans and Marxist philosophers.

Jean Améry writes about the vastly different experiences of these places in *At the Mind's Limits*. How amazed he is, after the war, reading *Goethe in Dachau* by a Dutch friend of his and a survivor of that camp, Nico Rost. The book relates how despite being in a concentration camp, some prisoners were able to lead a rich intellectual life,

---

* Whom we met in Book One, Chapter Thirteen.

reading and studying 'still more, and more intensively. In every free moment! Classical literature as a substitute for Red Cross packages'. Améry describes how impossible such activities were in Auschwitz. In Dachau, as in Buchenwald, political prisoners were in the majority – and this group included many intellectuals. 'In Dachau there was a camp library; for the ordinary inmate at Auschwitz a book was something hardly still imaginable'. Every trace of energy was put into surviving the brutally hard labour, the next day, and, if you did meet another thinker or writer, soon any attempt at intellectual conversation withered and died: 'The philosopher from the Sorbonne gave monosyllabic, mechanical answers and finally grew silent entirely . . . He simply no longer believed in the reality of the world of the mind'.

But Buchenwald was hellish too, despite Semprún's comment that Levi's 'experience had been so much more terrible than mine'. Between its opening in July 1937 and its liberation by American forces in April 1945, over 55,000 people lost their lives there – political prisoners, homosexuals and the disabled, Jews, Slavs, Poles, Roma, Sinti, Jehovah's Witnesses, and many others of no creed or faith. Buchenwald and Auschwitz shared something else: in both places the crematorium ovens burned twenty-four hours a day, manufactured by the same company, Topf & Söhne (from the town of Erfurt, close to Weimar) – who were very helpful in all their dealings with the SS and their requirements for more efficient ovens for burning human beings.

What moves me most in Semprún's writing, and comes across so powerfully, is the sense that in Buchnenwald a spirit of solidarity among many of the prisoners somehow survived, even in phenomenally difficult circumstances – a fraternal tenderness certainly in Semprún's case, emerging from shared political commitment and philosophical values which even Nazism, at its most extreme, could not totally extinguish.

The book opens with Semprún's account of the liberation of the camp in April 1945, and how he comes across three Allied officers (two British, one French) who, looking at him, seem to be in shock. Semprún explains that the woods are so quiet because the smoke from the crematorium drove the birds away, 'the smell of burned flesh, that's what did it'. The officers wince in evident repulsion. Semprún then reflects on how difficult it will be to communicate the experience he's managed to survive. He's very impatient with the idea of the 'ineffable', so fashionable among the literati in the post-war years:

> In short, you can always say everything. The 'ineffable' you hear so much about is only an alibi. Or a sign of laziness . . . language contains everything. You can speak of evil, its poisonous pleasures, its poppy flavour. You can speak of God, and that's saying a lot. You can speak of the rose, the dewdrop, the span of a morning. You can speak of tenderness, and the infinite succour of goodness. You can speak of the future, where poets venture with closed eyes and wagging tongues . . .
>
> But can people hear everything, imagine everything? Will they be able to understand? . . . I begin to doubt it, in that first moment, that first meeting with men from before, from the outside, emissaries from life – when I see the stunned, almost hostile, and certainly suspicious look in the eyes of the three officers. They're speechless, unable to face me.

Reading this passage again, think about the parallels with Primo Levi – the embarrassed gaze of the young Russian soldiers on horseback who liberate Monowitz; the experience on the station platform at Trezbinia. The knowledge that you have survived an unspeakable experience, but people from the 'living world' will not be able to hear what you've gone through. Although Semprún doesn't mention Levi's experience at Trezbinia, there is, towards the end of *Literature or Life*, an extended reflection on what is shared between their experiences, sparked by Semprún's shock at hearing on the radio of Primo Levi's suicide in 1987:

> On April 11th 1987 death had caught up with Primo Levi. In October 1945, though, after the long odyssey of his return from Auschwitz subsequently described in *La Tregua* (*The*

Truce) he had begun writing his first book, *Se questo è un uomo* (*If This Is a Man*). He'd written it in haste, feverishly, with a kind of happiness. 'The things I had suffered, lived through, were searing my insides,' he wrote later. 'I felt closer to the dead than to the living, I felt guilty for being a man, because men had built Auschwitz and Auschwitz had swallowed up millions of human beings, many of my friends, and a woman close to my heart. I felt as though I was cleansing myself by telling my story. I felt like Coleridge's Ancient Mariner.'

Indeed, a quotation from Coleridge's poem serves as an epigraph to Levi's last book, *I sommersi e i salvati* (*The Drowned and the Saved*) . . .

Since then, at an uncertain hour,
The agony returns:
And till my ghastly tale is told
This heart within me burns.

'I wrote,' continued Levi, 'concise poems tinged with blood, I told my story with a kind of dizzying compulsion, aloud or in writing, so often and so thoroughly that a book gradually came of this: through writing I recovered scraps of peace and became a man again.' . . .

Primo Levi spoke on several occasions about his feelings during this period, about the austere joys of writing. It was through writing that he felt himself returning, literally, to life.

Yet when it was finished – a masterpiece of restraint, an account of incredible honesty, lucidity and compassion – this incomparable book found no takers. Every major publishing house turned it down. It was finally brought out by a small press and passed completely unnoticed. Primo Levi then abandoned all literary aspirations and concentrated on his career as a chemical engineer.

And so a dream he had described, a deportee's nightmare, seemed to come true: you go home and tell everyone in your family, passionately and in great detail, about what you have gone through. But no one believes you. In the end, your stories create a kind of uneasiness, provoking a deepening silence. Those around you – even the woman you love, in the most agonising variations of the nightmare – finally rise and turn their backs on you, leaving the room.

History, therefore, appeared to be proving him right: his dream had become reality. It was only long years later that his book, *Se questo è un uomo*, abruptly obtained an audience, won a huge public, began to be translated throughout the world...

The time span between Levi's first book – a masterful piece of writing; a complete flop in reaching its audience – and his second, *La tregua*, is in fact the same as that separating the failure in 1945 of my attempts to write and *Le grand voyage*. These last two books were written in the same period, published almost simultaneously: Levi's in April 1963, mine in May.

Semprún returns again and again to the inability of the deportee and the survivor to communicate their experiences. And the way then that this leads to a sense of unreality, that perhaps your real experiences are dreams – or dreams within dreams, as he puts it. And the way these 'dreams', or rather nightmares, can invade the rest of life, and cut you off from those closest to you. Again he returns to Levi:

A dream that can awaken you anywhere: in the serenity of a green countryside, at a table with friends ... sometimes with a lover, at the very moment of love. Anywhere, in short, with anyone: a diffuse and deep despair, the anguished certainty of the end of the world – of its unreality, at any rate ... Nothing can stop the course of this dream says Levi: nothing can relieve the secret agony it causes. Even if you turn to a loved one, even if a friendly – or a loving – hand is held out to you ... Even if they guess what's happening to you, overwhelming you, annihilating you. Nothing will ever deflect the course of that dream ...

'Tutto è ora volto in caos: sono solo al centro di una nulla grigio e torbido, ed ecco, io so che cosa questo significa, ed anche di averlo sempre saputo: sono di nuovo in Lager, e nulla era vero all'infuori del Lager. Il resto era breve vacanza, o inganno dei sensi, sogno: la famiglia, la natura in fiore, la casa.'*

How to transmit the lived experience of suffering is one of the recurring urgencies of the book. Semprún describes a discussion among several camp survivors, just after the war, mostly academics – the discussion focusses on how it might be possible to communicate the 'radical evil' of what they've experienced. Documentary film is impossible, because nearly all of the most significant events were never recorded, so what is left is literature – but this will have to be more than reportage, more than mere description of horror, it will need to explore the human soul in relation to evil: Semprún says, 'We'll need a Dostoevsky!'

This transmission, however, is not only *from* Semprún and his comrades to the world, but also *to* Semprún and his fellow prisoners. Early in the book he relates an experience that haunted him for the rest of his life. Sunday afternoons were the one time in the week where prisoners had control over their time. The underground communists in Buchenwald (Semprún's grouping) used this time for secret meetings. They chose the basement ward for contagious illnesses in the infirmary complex for this purpose – for the intelligent reason that the SS's horror of contagion meant they almost never set foot in there. On a snowy day in winter 1944, a German communist leader, Kaminski, calls a meeting in the infirmary:

> I crossed the camp through flurries of snow that Sunday and entered the infirmary compound. At the door to the isolation

---

* 'Now all has changed to chaos: I am alone in the centre of a grey and turbid nothing, and now, I know what this dream means, and I also know that I have always known it: I am once more in the *Lager*, and nothing was true outside the *Lager*. The rest was a brief pause, or a deception of the senses, a dream: family, nature in bloom, home.'

hut, I tapped the soles of my boots against the iron bar provided for this purpose on the right side of the doorstep . . . Kaminski had brought us together to listen to a survivor of Auschwitz, a Polish Jew who had arrived on one of that winter's evacuation convoys. We settled ourselves in the little room . . . at the end of the basement reserved for infectious cases . . . At Auschwitz, Kaminski explained, the man had worked in a *Sonderkommando*. We didn't know what that was . . .

Semprún then relates how this man spoke to them, and the devastating impact of his words:

I no longer remember the name of that Polish Jew . . . I do remember his eyes. They were an icy blue, like the cutting edge of a broken pane of glass. I do remember his posture. He sat on a chair, absolutely straight, absolutely rigid, his hands on his knees, motionless. He never once moved his hands during the whole story of his experience on the *Sonderkommando*.

I do remember his voice. He spoke in German, fluently, in a rasping, meticulous, insistent voice . . . It was only in his voice that his overwhelming emotion broke through, like a ground-swell violently stirring the surface of seemingly calm waters. Fear that no one would believe him probably . . . Because throughout history, there have been survivors of massacres . . . but there hadn't been, and there never would be, any survivors of the Nazi gas chambers. No one would ever be able to say: I was there. You were around, or before, or beside, like those in the *Sonderkommando* . . .

He spoke for a long while; we listened to him in silence, frozen in the pallid anguish of his story. Suddenly when Ludwig G. lighted a lamp, we realised that wintry night had fallen, that we had been shrouded in darkness for some time already. We had sunk body and soul into the night of that story, suffocating, without any sense of time.

'That's it', said Kaminski . . . 'Never forget . . . Germany! My country is the guilty one – let's never forget that!' There was silence. The survivor of the *Sonderkommando* at Auschwitz, this Polish Jew . . . remained motionless, his hands spread out flat on his knees: a pillar of salt and despairing memory.

We remained motionless too.

Semprún, for all the tenderness of his writing, can also be unforgiving. He describes being inspired by Levinas's essays during his last year at school, and, on Levinas's recommendation, buying Heidegger's vast treatise *Sein und Zeit* ('Being and Nothingness') – which he's not overly impressed by. He later learns of Heidegger's abhorrent connection with Nazism, and how this bemused his friend, the Jewish poet and Holocaust survivor Paul Celan – that the rigorous, supposedly humanist philosopher had never distanced himself from the inhumanity of Nazism. After the war Celan was staying with Heidegger at his log cabin in the Black Forest, and Semprún relates what happened, or, in this case, didn't happen:

What Paul Celan wanted from Martin Heidegger, you may recall, was a clear statement on his position on Nazism. And on the extermination of the Jewish people in Hitler's camps, specifically. As you doubtless also recall, Celan was unsuccessful. He found only that silence some have tried to fill with empty chatter, or to erase from memory: Heidegger's definitive silence on the question of German culpability. A silence Karl Jaspers speaks of with devastating philosophical rigour in some of his letters.

Semprún then translates some lines from Celan's poem 'Todtnauberg' – a meditation on what name might have been written before his own in Heidegger's guest book. He hopes for a heartfelt word from the philosopher, about what had remained unsaid in their conversation. A word that never came. Semprún continues:

I think about the destiny of the German language: language of barked SS commands . . . and language of Kafka, of Husserl, Freud, Benjamin, Canetti, of Paul Celan himself – of so many other Jewish intellectuals who created the grandeur and richness of German culture during the 1930s. Language of subversion, therefore: language of the universal affirmation of critical reason . . . The hope inscribed that day in the guest book of Martin Heidegger was not fulfilled. No heartfelt word had come from the philosopher to fill this silence. Shortly afterward, Paul Celan drowned himself in the Seine.

There is a striking connection here to the corruption of an entire culture and language, with the life and experience of Jean Améry (born Hanns Mayer, in Vienna in 1912). Primo Levi relates that Mayer grew up in a Jewish family so assimilated that he hardly considered himself Jewish at all, had no knowledge of Hebrew or Zionism. He studies German literature and philosophy at university, and this was the language he loved and which he wrote in, as he begins his career as a critic. But when the Nazis annex Austria in 1938, he realises he has no future in his homeland, and emigrates to Belgium. He even feels exiled from his mother tongue. He changes his name to Jean Améry (an anagram of his original name); and he, the cultivated Germanophile humanist, now tried to write in French. He also feels it's important, at this time, as a matter of human dignity, to accept his Jewish identity more fully. Subsequently he joins the Resistance in Belgium, is captured by the Gestapo in 1943, and is tortured in Breendonk fort[*] – an experience he writes of unforgettably in *At the Mind's Limit*. After this, he is sent to Auschwitz, to Monowitz, where he, like Levi, becomes a slave labourer on the vast IG Farben Buna works.

In *The Drowned and the Saved*, Levi writes a vivid description of the different ways the German language was brutalised in Auschwitz. He and his fellow Italians learned to understand a primitive form – only inasmuch as their survival depended upon it. But Levi recognises the horror with which a German-speaking prisoner, like Améry, would have experienced the corruption of his native language:

---

[*] Sebald describes Améry's experience in Breendonk at the beginning of *Austerlitz*.

He suffered from it . . . in a way . . . that was spiritual rather than material. He suffered from it because German was his language, because he was a philologist who loved the language: just as a sculptor would suffer at seeing one of his statues befouled or mutilated.

Levi describes Améry's total dislocation at Auschwitz, his sense of being a complete outsider, though surrounded by people who were, apparently, speaking his own language. But the German of the camp was 'a barbaric jargon that he did understand but that scorched his mouth when he tried to speak it'. Like other supposed 'survivors' of the Holocaust – like Celan, like Levi – Jean Améry never recovered from his experience; he also committed suicide, in 1978. The words on his gravestone in the Zentralfriedhof cemetery in Vienna are stark in the extreme:

JEAN AMÉRY
1912–1978
AUSCHWITZ NO. 172364

*

8 July 1999, Weimar

We arrive in Weimar on a sticky summer's evening. A huge banner outside the station reminds us that it is 'European City of Culture' this year. We find our *gasthaus*, and then walk back to the centre. We pause by the Nationaltheater, where the Weimar National Assembly hosted the German Parliament briefly after the First World War, from February to August 1919, after the January 1919 election – the first time women had been able to vote in Germany, and also the first election carried out under a system of proportional representation. This was also the place where the Weimar Constitution fully established Germany as a parliamentary democracy.

In front of the theatre there's the famous double statue of friendship – Johann Wolfgang von Goethe and Johann Friedrich von Schiller, the two spiritual giants of this place. A young guy with a ponytail, a music student, is playing classical requests on a piano in the main square. How is it really possible to grasp the meaning of Weimar in German culture? It's best known as the home of those twin pillars of German thought, Goethe and Schiller, the place where Goethe lived for most of his life – arriving in 1775 at the age of twenty-six, and staying here until his death nearly sixty years later in 1832. He and Schiller met in Weimar in 1794, and then followed a rich collaborative friendship here until Schiller's early death in 1805. Our *Rough Guide* puts it thus, with admirable brevity: 'At Weimar, with Herder, Schiller and others, Goethe evolved the classical German ideal of culture as a process of personal spiritual development.' There's no directly comparable place in Britain – I suppose you'd have to fuse together Shakespeare's Stratford, Britten's Aldeburgh and Wordsworth and Coleridge's Lake District to get close to the sense of artistic centre that Weimar possesses.

And not just in literature either – it was a mecca for the greatest musicians and artists too. Bach lived and worked in Weimar for nine years as a young man (1708–17), as director of music at the ducal court. He had married his wife, Maria Barbara, a year before the move to Weimar, and this was where his first four children were born. It was the place where he created many remarkable works for organ and harpsichord and where he began writing his cantatas on a regular basis. In the nineteenth century Liszt spent almost twenty years there between 1842 and 1861, composing his finest choral and orchestral works. And in the visual arts, in 1919 Walter Gropius founded the revolutionary Bauhaus movement there with Klee and Kandinsky. It became a destination for literary and musical pilgrimage, with grand figures like Tolstoy and Wagner visiting and staying at the Elephant Hotel on the central square. It also lent its name, as we've already seen, to the short-lived Weimar Republic and that Parliament – those fourteen years that are forever associated with the twelve years of Nazism which followed. All this vibrant cultural and political activity that a large city would envy, yet one of the things that strikes us on our arrival is just how small it is – a town of only around 60,000 inhabitants.

We walk north, through Goetheplatz, and after a few minutes reach Weimarplatz, where I've heard about an exhibition, 'Rise and Fall of the Modern', currently on as part of Weimar's year as European City of Culture. The exhibition is closed, but we see the rather grim building, the Gauforum, that it's housed in – a Nazi-era edifice by one of Hitler's favoured architects, Hermann Giesler. The exhibition has managed to cause great controversy this summer by pairing Hitler's private collection of art (remarkably kitsch, by all accounts – lots of bland nudes and giant eagles flying to distant mountains) with the art of former communist East Germany. This has touched a nerve in Weimar, partly because this city was previously within East Germany, and the curator of this exhibition is West German, and the implied equivalence between Nazism and communism has not gone down well either in many quarters.

There are some photographs exhibited outside, and very inform-ative panels about Weimar and its complex history – one picture shows thousands of people saluting at a Nazi rally just by the Goethe and Schiller statue we saw a few minutes ago. A panel tells us that in December 1929, the Nazis gained 11 per cent in local elections in Thuringia, enough to gain the party its first representation in Parliament and government. Paul Schultze-Naumburg, author of *Art and Race*, was made head of culture, and appointed director of the United Art Schools of Weimar, with the specific remit of cleaning out the remnants of the 'cultural bolshevism' of the Bau-haus era. One of his first acts was to remove all the art of Kandinsky, Klee, Kokoschka, Dix and others from Weimar's museums, and in 1930 he ordered the destruction of Oskar Schlemmer's beautiful mural on the main staircase of the Bauhaus. It was the first Nazi declaration of war against what they called *Entartete Kunst* ('degen-erate art'). Seven years later, in Munich, the Nazis put on the infa-mous exhibition under the same title, which apparently broke all attendance records, with over 2 million Germans coming to laugh at the 'decadence' of Dada and Picasso's cubism.

We continue walking, down towards the river now, past the for-mer Gestapo headquarters on Kegelplatz, and find an attractive bar and restaurant with tables outside under lime trees. Over supper we look at maps, and I talk about the walk tomorrow, with the readings that I've prepared. We will be walking north-west out of the town, over the Ettersberg hill, and then through the *Buchenwald* ('beech wood') at the summit of the hill, to the camp. If J. and Kay are happy to trust in my plan, we will walk the distance between Weimar and Buchenwald in silence. Our only companion will be the voice of Semprún – the readings I've chosen from the book. We will stop every 800 yards (wherever we happen to find ourselves) to listen to his words. I will also take two photographs at these points – showing the direction we're walking in, and the direction we've come from. So, according to the arbitrary nature of where the paces take us, we may be hearing these words next to pounding traffic, in the shade of a hedge or under the gaze of curious villagers . . .

J. and Kay are happy with this plan; we order coffees and brandies, and talk of past summers and many journeys made together. I notice a group of young people at the next table. Something in their behaviour, a kind of ease with each other, and relaxation in this place, makes me realise they must be from here. I love the way that every few minutes, another couple of friends joins this group, pulling up extra chairs, to laughter, cigarettes offered, stories shared. We head back, past the house where Gropius once lived, and a little further on, Rudolf Steiner's former home, through the tree-lined streets of Weimar, to our little *gasthaus*.

9 July 1999, Weimar to Buchenwald

We walk into the centre and find a café on Schillerstrasse for a late breakfast. I go off to get more film for the camera, and then we make our way to a meadow, just to the east of the town centre. Here Goethe's famous Gartenhaus still stands, close to the River Ilm – the place where he loved to write in the summer months, given to him by the Duke of Saxe-Weimar in 1776, and which he used right up until his death in 1832. Large parts of *Wilhelm Meister's Apprenticeship* and *Faust* were written here in this tranquil place.

Outside the timbered building, in the meadow, sitting on a bench, I read these lines:

> In living nature nothing happens that is not in connection with the whole. When experiences appear to us in isolation or when we look at experiments as presenting only isolated facts, that is not to say that the facts are indeed isolated. The question is: how do we find the connections between phenomena?

And then we begin our walk, at 12.45 p.m. For the next hours the only words we will hear will be from Semprún. Only the words of a survivor will be spoken in this place.

We imagine Jorge Semprún here, at exactly this spot, on that fine April afternoon, only days after the camp was liberated, when he accompanies Lieutenant Walter Rosenfeld[*] of the American army and they begin to discuss the towering contribution of other German exiles – Adorno, Brecht, Horkheimer, Marcuse, Broch and Hannah Arendt – here by the Gartenhaus, which on that day

---

[*] Rosenfeld's family were Jewish, originally from Berlin, but emigrated to America after the Nazis came to power in the 1930s.

in 1945 is padlocked. Rosenfeld then recites the following, from Brecht:

> *Oh Deutschland, bleiche Mutter!*
> *Wie haben deine Söhne dich zugerichtet*
> *Dass du unter den Völkern sitzest*
> *Ein Gespött oder eine Furcht!*
>
> *Oh Germany, pallid mother!*
> *How have your sons mistreated you*
> *That you sit among other peoples*
> *A scarecrow or a laughing stock!*

We walk westwards into the town centre again, but this time I'm counting the paces – transferring coins from my right pocket to my left pocket every hundred yards so as not to lose count. When we stop after 800 yards, very conveniently we happen to be close to Goethe's town house on the Frauenplan:

Semprún: Trip to Weimar with Lieutenant Rosenfeld

> *The streets of the small city were almost empty when we arrived.*
> *I'd been amazed at how close it was: only a few kilometres*

separated Buchenwald from the first houses of Weimar. Of course the city wasn't visible from the camp, which had been built on the opposite side of the Ettersberg, overlooking a verdant plain with peaceful villages. But Weimar was very near, and practically deserted in the April sunshine when we arrived. Lieutenant Rosenfeld drove the jeep slowly through the streets and squares. We saw that the entire north side of the marketplace in the centre of town had been damaged by Allied bombs. Then Rosenfeld parked the jeep on the Frauenplan, in front of Goethe's town house.

The old man who finally opened the door to us was not at all friendly. At first he wanted to deny us admission. Under the circumstances, he told us, we had to have special permission from the authorities. Lieutenant Rosenfeld informed him that actually, under the circumstances, it was he, Lieutenant Rosenfeld, who represented the authorities – indeed Authority itself, with a capital A, in its extreme singularity: all the authority imaginable. This fact clearly vexed the old German, the zealous guardian of Goethe's museum-home, but he could not prevent Lieutenant Rosenfeld from entering this shrine of Germanic culture. So [he] entered . . . with me on his heels. While the old man closed the front door (I'd had time to decipher the Latin inscription above it stating that the house had been built in 1709, for the glory of God and the embellishment of the town, by one Georg Caspar Helmershausen), he shot a look of pure hatred at Lieutenant Rosenfeld, who was already going off to explore the house – and at the automatic pistol hanging from his shoulder. Then that black, mistrustful eye, brimming with desperate anger, had looked me up and down. Rather, it was my outfit he looked at. I must say it was somewhat unusual, and not very respectable. He had doubtless figured out where I'd come from, which wasn't very likely to reassure him.

In reality, we didn't need a guide to visit the house . . . Rosenfeld talked about it quite knowledgeably, providing a wealth of pertinent information. The old guardian had followed us anyway. Sometimes we heard him muttering behind us. He was itching

*to make us understand how much we were intruders, unworthy
of profaning such a place. He reeled off the names of the writers
and artists from all over Europe whom he had personally ushered through the rooms of this noble house in recent years. Lieutenant Rosenfeld ignored his mumbling, however, continuing to
tell me all he knew – and he knew a lot – about Goethe's long
life in Weimar. Finally, probably frustrated at not having provoked a reaction, the old Nazi spoke more loudly, describing –
to our backs – Hitler's last visit, when he stayed at the Elephant
Hotel in Weimar. The voice swelled with admiration in praise
of that remarkable man, the Führer. Suddenly unable to stand
any more of this, Lieutenant Rosenfeld turned around, grabbed
the old man by the collar, dragged him over to a cupboard, and
thrust him inside, locking the doors. We were able to complete
our visit in peace, out of range of his despairing and malevolent
voice.*

We walk out of the town square, the old houses give way to a bustling
street of shops and cafés, with tubs of saplings growing, as if trying
to offset the commercialism of what's on offer all around. Knots of
students browsing in a cavernous bookshop, well-dressed retirees
having their *Kaffee* and *Kuchen*. An ordinary summer's afternoon,

fast-moving clouds overhead. I check the map again, pausing at a corner; J. and Kay are a few yards behind. We cross a busy road, and now seem to be heading towards the outskirts of the town. Eight hundred yards has brought us to a stop outside a chemist's; a young woman is just locking her bike in the rack outside.

Semprún: The citizens of Weimar pay a visit to their neighbours, April 1945

A few days earlier, some of the inhabitants of Weimar had gathered in the courtyard of the crematory [at Buchenwald]: women, adolescents, old men. No men of an age to bear arms, quite obviously – those who could were doing so still, carrying on the war. These civilians had arrived in buses, escorted by a detachment of black American soldiers . . .

On that day, some of them stood at the entrance to the crematory courtyard, leaning against the high fence that usually prevented access to the area. Their faces were stiff, impassive masks of bronze as they gazed with stern attention on the small crowd of German civilians. I wondered what they could possibly be thinking and what they might have to say about this war against Fascism, these black Americans so numerous among the storm troops of the Third Army. In a way, it was the war that had made them full-fledged citizens . . . whatever their social background, no matter how humble their origins, in spite of the overt or veiled humiliation to which they were exposed by the colour of their skin, the draft had potentially made them citizens with equal rights. As though the right to kill had finally given them the right to be free . . .

In the crematory yard that day, at any rate, an American lieutenant addressed (in German) the several dozen women, adolescents of both sexes, and elderly men from the city of Weimar. The women were wearing spring dresses in bright colours. The officer spoke in a neutral, implacable voice. He explained how the crematory oven worked, gave the mortality figures for Buchenwald. He reminded the civilians of Weimar that for more than seven years, they had lived, indifferent or complicitous, beneath the smoke of the crematory.

'Your pretty town,' he told them, 'so clean, so neat, brimming with cultural memories, the heart of classical and enlightened Germany, seems not to have had the slightest qualm about living in the smoke of Nazi crematoria!'

The women (a good number of them at least) were unable to restrain their tears and begged for forgiveness with theatrical gestures. Some of them obligingly went so far as to feel quite faint. The adolescents took refuge in despairing silence. The old men looked away, clearly unwilling to listen to any of this.

The heat of mid-afternoon. Almost out of Weimar. We walk through a light industrial estate on the north-western fringe of the town.

Soon we're out in the countryside, on a dusty track heading towards the green curve of the Ettersberg. An occasional line of poplars, a dozen or so, the odd house, neatly tiled roofs, dogs come out sleepily to investigate us as we pass their gates. In all probability this is the path that Goethe and his close friend Eckermann would have taken on their regular walks 200 years ago. Their favourite ramble took them out of the hurly-burly of Weimar and onto the Ettersberg,

where they would have earnest discussions about the meaning of existence, the origins of language and the nature of religious belief. We skirt a village just below us, and pause by a small stream a little further on, in the shade of some willows to eat. Just the sound of the water, and a distant tractor from the farm on the hillside beyond.

Semprún: With his former professor, as he dies in Block 56, the invalids' block

> *Week after week, I'd watched the black light of death dawning in their eyes. We shared it, that certainty, like a morsel of bread. Death was approaching, veiling their eyes, and we shared it like . . . a sign of brotherhood. The way one shares what remains of one's life . . . The only difference among us was the time we still had left, the distance yet to cover.*
>
> *I placed a hand (lightly, gently) on the emaciated shoulder of Maurice Halbwachs: the bone was almost crumbly, on the verge of breaking. I talked to him about the classes he used to teach at the Sorbonne. In the past, elsewhere, outside, in another life . . . Dying, he would smile, fixing his eyes on me like a brother. I would have long talks with him about his books.*
>
> *Those first Sundays, Maurice Halbwachs could still speak. He was anxious to hear how things were going, to have news of the*

war. He asked me – the last pedagogical concern of the professor whose student I'd been at the Sorbonne – if I was already on the right track, if I'd found my vocation. I replied that history interested me. He nodded; why not? . . .

Soon, however, he no longer had the strength to utter a single word. He could only listen to me, and only at the cost of superhuman effort.

He listened; I spoke of spring drawing to a close, and passed on good news from the battlefields, and reminded him of what he had written in his books, the lessons of his teaching.

Dying, he would smile, gazing at me like a brother.

On the last Sunday, Maurice Halbwachs did not even have the strength to listen. Barely enough to open his eyes . . .

I took the hand of the dying man . . . In answer, I felt only the lightest pressure from his fingers, an almost imperceptible message . . . Professor Maurice Halbwachs had arrived at the limit of human resistance . . .

Then, seized with panic, not knowing whether I might call upon some god to accompany Maurice Halbwachs, yet aware of the need for a prayer, trying to control my voice . . . I recited a few lines by Baudelaire. It was the only thing I could think of.

'O mort, vieux capitaine, il est temps! levons l'ancre . . .'*

His eyes brightened slightly, as though with astonishment. I continued to recite. When I reached the line 'nos coeurs que tu connais sont remplis des rayons! . . .'† a delicate tremor passed over the lips of Maurice Halbwachs. Dying, he smiled, gazing at me like a brother . . .

We walk on. We turn to the north and start up the gentle hill that is the Ettersberg, climbing towards the thick fringe of dark green trees at the top, into the *Buchenwald.* Looking back to the east we can see Weimar in the distance, and to the south the plains of Thuringia. Reaching the forest, we take a track westwards which

---

* 'Oh Death, old captain, it's time! let's weigh anchor . . .'

† 'Our hearts, which you know are filled with light! . . .'

follows the contour of the top of the hill, our eyes now searching for the first signs of the camp, through the trees. Mainly beech, but also oak, they're so thick it's hard to see very far ahead. Eventually the track descends to a long, straight road that must have been made when the camp was constructed in 1934, the second concentration camp to be built in Germany, after Dachau in 1933. We're on the other side of the Ettersberg now, here and there the odd stump of concrete (is this all that remains of what Semprún describes as 'the Avenue of the Eagles'?). Finally, at the end of this deserted road, just beyond a ruined petrol station, the fence of the camp, and the main gate emerging before us. Flanked by a guardhouse, the gate itself seems strangely small (at variance with Semprún's memory of passing through 'the huge gate'), with the mocking message above, which greeted all new prisoners – '*Jedem Das Seine*'.* Semprún and his fellow prisoners had arrived at night, exhausted after days of transportation, greeted by a cacophony of violence: 'uproar, the dogs, the blows from rifle butts, going through the mud on the double, beneath the harsh glare of searchlights, the entire length of the Avenue of the Eagles.'

Under the gate, and those terrible words still inscribed above us, we pause. The counting is over: 10,166 yards from Goethe's Gartenhaus

---

* Literally, 'To Each His Own'; figuratively, 'Everyone Gets What They Deserve.'

to the gates of Buchenwald. A little under six miles separates these two realities – Goethe writing in his Gartenhaus and Semprún arriving at these gates in terror.

*

It is early evening now, and we're surprised to see that the camp is still open to visitors. But the car park is virtually empty, all the coaches have gone back to the city. We walk through the gate and are astonished by the vast extent of the place, stretching downwards across the hillside. Perhaps the size of half a dozen Trafalgar Squares, yet totally surrounded by the forest, visible only from the air, or the villages dotted on the plains below to the north. In this whole expanse we count only four figures – a mother and two children, and an elderly man walking alone.

Semprún: With his friend Albert – the view from the camp

> *We froze on the threshold of the hut, just as we were stepping back into the fresh air, Albert and I. Standing stock-still at the*

boundary between the stinking murkiness inside and the April sunlight outdoors. In front of us, blue sky, faintly streaked with fleecy clouds. Around us, the mostly green mass of the forest, beyond the huts and tents of the Little Camp. Off in the distance, the mountains of Thuringia. In short, the timeless landscape Goethe and Eckermann must have contemplated during their walks on the Ettersberg.

For the first time in my life the natural world, the beauty of trees, seems a mockery. In this place of such brutality, wouldn't the fact the trees just carried on coming into leaf in the spring have seemed like a savage kind of indifference? The birds, at least, had the decency to disappear from this unnatural place, where smoke from the crematorium ovens choked the air. Today, though, about twenty little finches are chattering away above us. We walk across the camp, pausing here and there, to look at a sign telling us what once existed here. With the exception of the gatehouse, the crematorium and a storage depot, virtually all the former buildings within the camp have been levelled to the ground. But, with precision, the prior position of each hut and building is marked in rectangles of gravel, and named. The power of creating sense from absence.

We find the outline of the infirmary block, no buildings remain, but it's totally vivid in my mind's eye – the place where Semprún and his comrades listened to the *Sonderkommando* survivor on that wintry Sunday, bringing a message from Auschwitz which they could not comprehend. I walk down some steps, surprised to see some of the original floor tiles and stones of the infirmary, wondering where the isolation compound would have been. And then I look down, suddenly assaulted by an object I cannot believe I'm seeing. To the right of where the doorway would have been, on the ground, there's a heavily rusted metal boot-scraper, almost horseshoe-shaped – and I realise it's the same iron scraper which Sempruún used to get the snow off his boots on that day. The smallest thing, and yet the force of transmission over fifty-five years halts me in my tracks. As if, in the middle of this emptiness, Semprún is suddenly there, at my shoulder, gesturing. At a moment like this the past and present become a single, fused reality.

Semprún: His return to Buchenwald in 1992 – a discovery

Semprún only went back to Buchenwald once, in March 1992, as part of a German television documentary on the camp made by Peter Merseburger. Semprún was accompanied by his two grandsons, Thomas and Mathieu Landman. They meet a guide at the camp, a 'taciturn and bearded' forty-year-old man. Semprún is describing his arrival at the camp and the moment when his profession is registered – a moment of critical importance, which the young Semprún doesn't realise at the time. The German prisoner who registers him (a communist like himself, Semprún guessed) doesn't want to put him down as a 'student'. Semprún continues with his story, explaining to his grandsons and the guide:

> *'Then, probably fed up with my stubbornness, he waved me aside, to make way for the next in line . . . And he wrote "student" on my card, rather angrily I think.'*
>
> *That was when the guide spoke up, calmly, evenly, but firmly.*
>
> *'No,' he said, 'that's not what he wrote!'*
>
> *We turned toward him, transfixed.*
>
> *'He didn't write down "student" but something completely different!'*
>
> *The man reached into his inside jacket pocket and pulled out a piece of paper.*
>
> *'I've read your books,' he told me . . . 'So, knowing that you were coming today, I went looking for your registration card in the Buchenwald files.'*
>
> *He smiled briefly.*
>
> *'You know how Germans love order! So I found your card, just as it was filled out on the night you arrived.'*
>
> *He held the piece of paper out to me.*
>
> *'Here's a photocopy of it! You can see for yourself that the German comrade did not write down "student"!'*

I took the paper with trembling hands. No, he hadn't written
Student, the unknown German comrade. No doubt guided by
some phonetic association, he'd written Stukkateur. I looked at
my card, my hands were shaking.

44904
Semprún, George Polit.
10.12.23 Madrid Span.
Stukkateur
29th Jan. 1944

That's what was on my registration card, filled out the night
I arrived in Buchenwald . . . The simple fact of having been reg-
istered as a stucco worker probably saved me from the massive
transports being sent at that time to Dora, the construction site
of an underground factory where the V-1 and V-2 rockets were
to be assembled. A hellish place . . . I held my registration form
in my hand, a half-century later. I was shaking. The Merseburg-
ers, Thomas and Mathieu Landman, they'd all come over to me.
Dumbfounded by this unexpected final twist to my story, they
stared at that absurd and magical word, Stukkateur, which had
quite possibly saved my life. I remembered the look in the German
Communist's eyes – a look from the far side of death – as he'd tried
to explain why it was better to be a skilled worker in Buchenwald.

Semprún's memory is reliable. In January and February 1944 the
Dora plant (only forty miles north-west of Buchenwald in the
Thuringian mountains) was working at the height of its capacity,
and with a staggeringly high level of deaths. Albert Speer, by this
time the minister for armaments and weapons production, had
visited the underground site only seven weeks before Semprún's
arrival, and had found the conditions 'barbarous' for the prisoners
working there and that the 'mortality among them was extraordinarily high'. It was one of the only moments in Speer's life when
he, momentarily, seems to have understood the human cost of the
abstract and technocratic world he ran from his office in Berlin. It
triggered a physical and emotional breakdown that put him in hos-

pital in January 1944 – the same month that Semprún's anonymous registrar saved him from transportation to Dora.

It's time for us to leave. We find the site where 'Goethe's Oak' once stood, where he supposedly not only walked with Eckermann but also met his lover Carlotta von Stein. We read that Himmler deliberately sited the camp here because of these associations, as if to taunt the intellectual descendants of Goethe, who would inhabit this place of madness – 'You see where your Enlightenment got you! All your brilliant international ideas, your philosophers, how will they help you now?' I later find out that less than a mile away, hidden by the forest to the east, is the grand hunting lodge Schloss Ettersburg (today a hotel), built for Duke Wilhelm Ernst in the early 1700s, and a place where Bach would regularly organise concerts for his patron. On the way back to the main gate, we skirt the dark grey crematorium building with its towering chimney still there. Incomprehension, still. We may know in our minds what happened, but it is another thing to see the chimney here on this summer's day, starkly etched against the blue sky – another level of knowing. We take a last look over the distant plains of Thuringia on this summer's evening, and I read a final passage from Semprún.

Semprún: Coming home

> *The same wind, the everlasting wind, was blowing across the eternity of the Ettersberg.*
> *We had arrived by car, with Sabine and Peter Merseburger, to find the televison crew waiting for us. We walked down the Avenue of the Eagles that leads to the entrance of Buchenwald. But there were no more Hitlerian eagles, no more tall columns lofting them into the sky once darkened by smoke from the crematory. There was the road, and a few barracks remained in the SS quarters. The massive entrance stood still, surmounted by the watchtower. We walked through the gate, accompanied by the bearded guide who has awaited us there. I brushed my hand across the*

*letters of the wrought-iron inscription on the gate, JEDEM DAS
SEINE: to each his due.*

*I cannot say that I was moved; that word is not strong enough.
I realised I was coming home. It was not hope I had to abandon,
at the gate to that hell; on the contrary. I was abandoning my
old age, my disappointments, the mistakes and failures of life. I
was coming home. What I mean is, home to my world when I
was twenty: its angers, passions, laughter, curiosity. Above all, its
hope. I was abandoning all the deadly despair that accumulates
in the soul, throughout a lifetime, to rediscover the hopefulness I
knew at twenty, surrounded by death.*

*We had stepped through the gate; the wind on the Etters-
berg hit me full in the face. Unable to speak I felt like running
madly at full tilt across the square, rushing down to the Little
Camp, to the site of Block 56, where Maurice Halbwachs had
died, to the infirmary hut where I'd closed the eyes of Diego
Morales. I couldn't say a word, I stood motionless, struck by
the dramatic beauty of the open space spread out before me. I
placed a hand on the shoulder of Thomas Landman, who was
by my side. I had dedicated 'Quel beau dimanche!' to him so
that later, after my death, he might remember my memories
of Buchenwald. It would be easier for him now. Harder, too,
probably, because less abstract.*

*I placed a hand on Thomas's shoulder, as though calling him
to witness in his turn. A day would come, relatively soon, when
there would no longer be a single survivor of Buchenwald left.
There would be no more immediate memory of Buchenwald.
No longer would anyone be able to say, with words springing
from physical recollection and not some theoretical reconstruction, what it was like: the hunger, the exhaustion, the anguish,
the blinding presence of absolute Evil – precisely insofar as it lies
hidden in all of us, as the condition of our freedom. No longer
would anyone be indelibly marked, body and soul, by the smell of
burning flesh from the crematory ovens . . .*

*I reflected that my most personal memory, the one kept most
to myself . . . the one that makes me what I am . . . that distin-*

guishes me from other people, at least, from everyone else . . . that cuts me off from the human race – with a few hundred exceptions – even as it establishes my identity . . . that burns in my memory with a flame of abject horror . . . and pride too . . . is the undying, stifling memory of the smell from the crematory: stale, nauseating . . . the odour of burned flesh on the Ettersberg hill.

A day is coming, though, when no one will actually remember this smell: it will be nothing more than a phrase, a literary reference, an idea of an odour. Odourless therefore.

*

As we're heading out of the main gate – we're the last to leave and a security guard is waiting, ironically, to lock us *out* of this prison camp – J. calls us over to the gatehouse. It's past 8 p.m. now, and we agree, through a series of signals, to end our silence – it's been over seven hours now. Kay has found the place where the SS had their little zoo, just outside the perimeter fence, and J. has discovered something else, inside the gatehouse, but just visible. We peer through a window to a model of the camp that J. has spotted, and soon realise another reality of Buchenwald – the industrial section of the camp was originally massive, as large as the whole of this barracks zone. Yet, as we walk to where this area was marked on the model, all we can find is one small notice showing where the DAW factory once stood – Deutsche Ausrustungswerke, where prisoners worked as slave labourers making equipment for the German war machine. Three hundred yards further south was the Gustloff armaments plant where even more Buchenwald prisoners were forced to work. Again, just as at Auschwitz-Buna, the SS saw the prisoners at the adjacent camps as expendable objects to be used in war production – whether armaments and equipment here (joint ventures in collaboration with DAW and Gustloff), or synthetic fuel and rubber at Buna-Monowitz (a joint venture with IG Farben). In both cases the genocidal and the corporate working hand in hand.

Yet, this key component of what Buchenwald was – the corporate/industrial side – is not memorialised at all. The vast majority of the factories have disappeared under the forest, without so much as a sign. Again, as at Auschwitz, it's as if this central part of the Holocaust – the collusion of the SS and corporations – is not part of the desired narrative. The camps where prisoners slept are remembered; the places where they worked, often until death, are forgotten. The fact that these 'workplaces' were funded, constructed, run and insured by companies that are still part of our economies and societies – Bayer, Agfa, BASF, Hoechst, Siemens, Allianz, Deutsche Bank – probably tells us all we need to know about the political convenience of selective remembering, and selective forgetting. Was this why, I wonder, Primo Levi, that most morally indefatigable of men, was working on precisely this subject at the time of his death? The sequel to *The Drowned and the Saved* was going to 'investigate the German industries (BASF, Siemens, Bayer) involved in the Nazi camps'.

Levi followed IG Farben's post-war developments closely, and was shocked by the supposed 'rehabilitation' of many of the senior figures in the company. In 1953 he and 10,000 other former slave labourers started a claim for damages from the company (in liquidation). In 1959 the German courts awarded damages – the princely sum of 122.70 Deutschmarks to each survivor. We also learn that in his post-war role as head of varnish production and a buyer at Siva, his chemical company, Levi, from time to time, met former representatives of IG Farben and other German companies who had operated at Auschwitz. He had dealings with Hoechst and Siemens, and in July 1954 he met managers from Bayer (also formerly part of IG Farben) at their headquarters in Leverkusen near Cologne. On this first occasion he deliberately confronted these men with the past of their company – this longed-for encounter he later called 'the hour of colloquy':

> Levi went out of his way to ruffle sensitivities at Bayer by introducing himself to former IG Farben industrialists, 'Levi, how do you do', articulating the words carefully, the Jewish surname first . . . When a Bayer director observed that it was 'most unusual' for an Italian to speak German, Levi countered:

'My name is Levi. I am a Jew, and I learned your language at Auschwitz'. A stuttering apology was followed by a silence.[*]

The heat of the day is still with us as we retrace our steps out of the forest to the brow of the Ettersberg. We decide to make a short detour here, down to the looming grey tower of a memorial we'd seen on the way up – when we get closer we see a huge bronze sculpture of figures representing the liberated prisoners of Buchenwald. It's done in full socialist-realist mode, with raised fists and flags, completed, we later discover, in 1958 by the then East German government to celebrate resistance against fascism. It is impossible to look at this monument now without a bitter taste of irony, because the 'liberation' of the Nazi camp in 1945 was not the end of Buchenwald. After the war, when Germany was split into the four military occupation zones – Britain in the north-west, France in the south-west, the United States in the south, and the Soviet Union in the east – the Soviet NKVD established 'Special Camp No. 2' at Buchenwald for their political prisoners, using much of the surviving camp infrastructure. According to Soviet records, over 7,000 prisoners died here between 1945 and 1950 when the camp was closed, but the likely death toll is much higher. There can be no more graphic example in Europe of the commonalities between Nazism and Stalinism than the continuation of the concentration camp at Buchenwald between 1937 and 1950.

We walk down the hill to the little village of Gaberndorf, which we'd skirted on the way here. J. says how powerful the coincidental conjunctions of readings and places were today – for instance, watching shoppers in the suburbs as we heard about the inhabitants of Weimar being taken to Buchenwald at the end of the war. As we get to the village we can hear the muffled sound of a brass band coming down from the church. We find a little bar and soon are downing large beers and pickled herring rolls. The brass band

---

[*] Quotation from Primo Levi by Ian Thomson, Chapter Sixteen, 'Journeys Into Germany 1954-61'.

gets louder, villagers come out of their houses to applaud, there's a jovial, but also slightly strange, atmosphere, and of course, we stick out like sore thumbs here. A teenager approaches us and asks us where we're from – '*Englanders, ja?!*' – and then mimes shooting a gun at us. We laugh, rather nervously, pay for our beers and head back towards Weimar.

Weimar looks somehow different when we get back. After all we have experienced today it would be surprising if it didn't. We're exhausted, not so much by the walking – it's only been eleven miles or so – but by the intensity of hearing what we've heard, and seeing what we've seen. We rest at the *gasthaus*, then have a late supper at another restaurant, sitting outside again, in a little square. We reflect more on the day, we talk about the strangeness of our generation being the first for centuries that has not been tested by war. Of course we're grateful for this, but wonder if anything is lost in not having been through this kind of process. Over grappas we plan our route on to Sofia tomorrow. Kay is tired and heads back to the *gasthaus*, J. and I find another bar for a late drink, and wish that we'd built in a rest day tomorrow, so we could have a bit of time to digest before moving on.

10 July 1999, Weimar to Sofia

We manage to connect with our train to Sofia at the railway junction town of Jena this morning. There is some concern from the stationmaster that this international train may not stop here. We point to our *Thomas Cook European Train Timetable*, wanting reassurance, but he makes an exasperated sound which we take as meaning that we should not trust its pages. But, in the end, our Hellas Express does decide to make a halt here and we clamber on gratefully with our rucksacks.

By the evening we're rattling through Hungary, by midnight we'll be crossing the border with Serbia. It will be strange going through Novi Sad in the early hours, where Kay and I have friends. No doubt it's these associations that start us talking in the restaurant car tonight, over some beers. We're reflecting on the walk yesterday and have gone back to the Steiner piece that began this chapter, the proximity of what he calls 'Central European humanism' to the barbarism of the concentration camps. Kay recalls my shock at discovering that half the attendees of the Wannsee Conference had doctorates; but should that really be such a surprise? *Come on, they were doctors of law, doctors of theology! Surely subjects that should have human rights and ethics at their heart?* Not necessarily. *Well, what about the wider culture of questioning that surely has been a part of academia since the beginning? The influence of Greek philosophy, especially the concept of Platonic thought and Socratic questioning?* J. then joins in by reflecting that there are other, more authoritarian traditions in education as well – not sure how much emphasis on questioning there was in the Prussian education system in the nineteenth century. Or, for that matter, in his own education in the 1970s.

The wider issue, though, is that the links between authoritarian power and the intellectual are closer than we often imagine. Primo Levi writes of this proximity in his essay on Jean Améry, 'The Intellectual in Auschwitz'. He speaks of a collusion that Améry rightly identifies, and then continues:

> By his very nature the intellectual . . . tends to become an accomplice to Power, and therefore approves of it. He tends to follow in Hegel's footsteps, and deify the state, any state; the sole fact of its existing justifies its existence. The chronicle of Hitlerian Germany teems with cases that confirm this tendency: to it have yielded, confirming it, the philosopher Heidegger, Sartre's mentor; the physicist Stark, a Nobel Prize winner, Cardinal Faulhaber, the highest Catholic authority in Germany, and innumerable others.

The Irish writer Fintan O'Toole goes even further: 'It is not just that the creative people are ultimately powerless against guns and prison camps, that the cultured person is at the mercy of the ignorant killer. It is something much worse: that the cultured person and the ignorant killer have often been one and the same.'

And of course, as we edge closer to the border with Serbia tonight, it is impossible not to think about the central role played by that published poet Dr Karadžić, in the catastrophe of the Yugoslavian war over the last decade. And indeed, the responsibility of the prolific writer Dobrica Ćosić, infamous for co-ordinating the 1986 memorandum published by the Serbian Academy of Sciences and Arts which claimed the Serbs had always been a persecuted nation and proposed 'the integrity of the Serb people' to be the central aim of future policy. The historian Noel Malcolm, in *Kosovo: A Short History*, describes the significance of this memorandum – it was 'in retrospect . . . a virtual manifesto for the Greater Serbian policies' pursued by Belgrade in the 1990s'. And going back even further, how can we quantify the damage done by the 750 Serbian academics who signed the notorious supporting statement that helped to establish Slobodan Milosevic as a serious political force in the 1980s?

Strikingly similar collusions – between the educated and the perpetrators of genocide – can be seen in the context of what happened in Rwanda in 1994. Fergal Keane makes this point in *Season of Blood*:

> In my journey through Rwanda I encountered many of the killers: the genocide was a crime of mass complicity, one could hardly avoid meeting people who had been involved. They stood at every roadblock, at every army encampment . . . A few gave the appearance of being truly psychopathic individuals. The mass of others were ragged and illiterate peasants easily roused to hatred of the Tutsis. Perhaps the most sinister people I met were the educated political elite, men and women of charm and sophistication who spoke flawless French and could engage in long, philosophical debates about the nature of war and democracy.

Philip Gourevitch, in *We Wish to Inform You That Tomorrow We Will Be Killed with Our Families*, describes how many of the impulses for the 1994 Rwandan genocide can be traced back to the publication in 1957 by nine Hutu intellectuals of what became known as the 'Hutu Manifesto'. He also quotes a lawyer from Kigali saying:

> The peasants who were paid or forced to kill were looking up to people of higher socio-economic standing to see how to behave. So the people of influence or the big financiers, are often the big men in the genocide. They may think that they didn't kill because they didn't take life with their own hands, but the people were looking to them for their orders.

The educated, the white collar, the desk killers. But I'm not sure we're much further on in trying to identify *exactly* what it was in European humanism that led not only to the extermination camps, but also to the earlier mindset of genocidal colonialism that Lindqvist sketches so vividly in *Exterminate All the Brutes*. Or indeed, to look beyond Europe, at the Hutu genocide of the Tutsis, for example. What impulse, what energy, propelled all of these initiatives forwards? A desire for racial purity? A quest for some perverted sense of 'perfectibility'? Lindqvist cites the supposedly 'liberal' philosopher Herbert Spencer's views on progress in the mid-nineteenth century and the perceived need for racial purity, and emphasises that such views were by no means extreme for the period:

> He writes in *Social Statics* . . . that imperialism has served civilisation by clearing the inferior races off the earth. 'The forces which are working out the great scheme of perfect happiness, taking no account of incidental suffering, exterminate such sections of mankind as stand in their way . . . Be he human or be he brute – the hindrance must be got rid of.'

And we should also remember the philosopher Eduard von Hartmann's advice not to prolong 'the death struggles of savages who are on the verge of extinction', and how 'the true philanthropist' should actually help with accelerating this process.

These statements embody, with a shocking clarity, the exterminist impulses within 'civilisation'. They seem to support Adorno's
contention (citing Freud) that 'civilisation itself produces anti-
civilisation and increasingly reinforces it . . . If barbarism itself is
inscribed within the principle of civilisation, then there is something desperate in the attempt to rise up against it.'

And, more and more, I now find myself moving away from
Steiner's idea of the 'proximity' between civilisation and barbarism, and reflecting that these two conditions may in fact be a
single condition – just as, in the seventeenth century, the coffee
houses of London (and all the fine talk of civilisation within them)
were built on the foundations of the slave trade and the Atlantic
Triangle. And if we think our current societies are so much better
– that we have moved on from such civil barbarism – let us look at
a single example from our times. Our governments now employ
lawyers to work out (on our behalf) the precise extent of how
far a man or a woman can be tortured (on our behalf) and what
method of torture may be employed (on our behalf), not using the
word 'torture' once.

These highly educated men and women are all around us.

'He thought of how the world organises its own affairs so that civilisation every day commits crimes for which any individual would be imprisoned for life. And how people accept this, either by ignoring it and calling it current affairs or politics or wars, or by making a space that has nothing to do with civilisation and calling that space their private life.'

Richard Flanagan, *The Narrow Road to the Deep North*

17

The Lawyers of Washington

In 2005 several documents were, for a short time, put into the public domain.[*] And in this narrow window I downloaded the documents on which this chapter is based. The memoranda – at least the four I've been able to read in detail, others were heavily redacted – were sent by two lawyers working in the office of the US Attorney General to John Rizzo, principal counsel for the CIA between August 2002 and May 2005. Over 124 pages, they detail the internal debates between senior legal officials in the Bush administration as to exactly what constitutes 'torture', what 'enhanced interrogation techniques' might be permissible, as well as philosophical discussions relating to the subjectivity of 'pain' and the meaning of 'severe mental pain and suffering'. The legal advice these men offered later shaped the treatment of suspects at the Guantánamo and Abu Ghraib detention centres.

This is one of the men involved:

---

[*] Having subsequently been removed from Internet search engines, these original documents are currently viewable at: www.therenditionproject.org.uk/documents /torture-docs.html.

Jay Bybee studied economics at Brigham Young University, graduating in 1977, subsequently gaining his law-school qualification from the J. Reuben Clark Law School at BYU. He began working in the US Department of Justice in 1984, rising to become Assistant Attorney General, leading the Office of Legal Counsel in 2001. He married Dianna Greer, a teacher, in 1986, and they had four children, Scott, David, Alyssa and Ryan. He is active in the Church of Jesus Christ of Latter-day Saints, more commonly known as the Mormons. Between 1973 and 1975 he volunteered on a mission for the Church in Santiago, Chile – his time there coinciding precisely with the American-backed coup that destroyed Allende and ushered in the early years of Pinochet's military dictatorship. Today he works as a judge on the Ninth Circuit Court of Appeals.

And this is the other man:

Steven Bradbury gained his first degree, in English, from Stanford in 1980, going on to further studies at the University of Michigan Law School, where he gained his graduate degree in 1988. He worked primarily in private law practice until joining the Office of Legal Counsel in 2004, where he was appointed Principal Deputy Assistant Attorney General. He is married to Hilde Kahn, they have three children, James, William and Susanna. Steven and Hilde are listed as having donated more than $5,000 to the Thomas Jefferson High School for Sciences and Technology, Fairfax, Virginia, fundraising campaign in 2013. Today Bradbury is General Counsel for the U.S. Department of Agriculture.

*

To spend a couple of hours reading these memoranda is to feel degraded. To feel ashamed of what our societies are capable of. Torture has been in the world for as long as human beings have existed. In early years, even before a word to describe what it was, men would have used violence against each other to get what they wanted. Brutal? Absolutely. More shocking than anything other animals do to each other? Undoubtedly so. But not as appalling as the perversion of a profession that should exist to uphold the rule of law. Not as disgraceful as the cold and clinical exchange of memoranda written by highly educated men, designed to enable suspects (who have never been charged with an offence, nor put before any court) to be tortured by the American government. As you read these documents your mind may return to the senior lawyers we met in Berlin, discussing how to organise the Holocaust by 'legal means'. There is also a very precise link between the language used to refer to torture in Nazi Germany, and the language used to refer to torture by the American government today. In 1936, Heinrich Müller of the Gestapo (who we last met at the Wannsee Conference) gained authorisation to implement 'intensified interrogations'*; in 2005, Steven Bradbury of the Attorney General's office advised on 'enhanced interrogation technique(s)'.†

The following extracts have been taken from four of the memoranda sent between August 2002 and May 2005. Not a word has been changed.

Memo 1: Top Secret [document blacked out – redacted in parts]
Date: August 1st, 2002
From: Jay S. Bybee, Assistant Attorney General
To: John Rizzo, Acting General Counsel of the Central Intelligence Agency
Subject: Interrogation of al Qaeda Operative

You wish to move the interrogations into what you have described as an 'increased pressure phase.' As part of this increased pressure phase Zubaydah will have contact only with a new interrogation specialist whom he has not met previously, and the Survival, Evasion, Resistance, Escape ('SERE') training psychologist who has been involved with the interrogations since they began. This phase will likely last no more than several days but could last up to thirty days. In this phase, you would like to employ ten techniques that you believe will dislocate his expectations regarding the treatment he believes he will receive and encourage him to disclose the crucial information mentioned above. These ten techniques are: (1) attention grasp, (2) walling, (3) facial hold, (4) facial slap (insult slap), (5) cramped confinement, (6) wall standing, (7) stress positions, (8) sleep deprivation, (9) insects placed in a confinement box, and (10) the waterboard. You have informed us that the use of these techniques would be on

---

* From *The Participants: The Men of the Wannsee Conference* by Hans-Christian Jasch and Christoph Kreutzmüller (eds.).

† Steven Bradbury, 'Memorandum for John A. Rizzo', 10 May 2005, p. 10.

*an as-needed basis and that not all of these techniques will nec-
essarily be used. The interrogation team would use these techniques in some combination to convince Zubaydah that the only
way he can influence his surrounding environment is through
cooperation. You have, however, informed us that you expect
these techniques to be used in some sort of escalating fashion,
culminating with the waterboard, though not necessarily ending
with this technique.*

Later in the memo he analyses the legal meaning of 'severe pain or
suffering' and explains that 'in order for pain or suffering to rise
to the level of torture the statute requires that it be severe'. Having
gone through all ten 'techniques' outlined above, he concludes that
'none of the proposed techniques inflicts such pain.' He describes
waterboarding like this:

*As we understand it, when the waterboard is used, the subject's
body responds as if the subject were drowning – even though the
subject may be well aware that he is in fact not drowning. You
have informed us that this procedure does not inflict actual physical harm. Thus, although the subject may experience the fear
or panic associated with the feeling of drowning, the waterboard
does not inflict physical pain. As we explained in the Section
2340A Memorandum, 'pain and suffering' as used in Section
2340 is best understood as a single concept, not distinct concepts of 'pain' as distinguished from 'suffering.' See Section 2340A
Memorandum at 6 n.3. The waterboard, which inflicts no pain
or actual harm whatsoever, does not, in our view inflict 'severe
pain or suffering.' Even if one were to parse the statute more finely
to attempt to treat 'suffering' as a distinct concept, the waterboard
could not be said to inflict severe suffering. The waterboard is
simply a controlled acute episode, lacking the connotation of a
protracted period of time generally given to suffering.*

A little later in the memo, Bybee discusses the issue of mental harm
caused by waterboarding:

Although the waterboard constitutes a threat of imminent death, prolonged mental harm must nonetheless result to violate the statutory prohibition on infliction of severe mental pain or suffering. See Section 2340A Memorandum at 7. We have previously concluded that prolonged mental harm is mental harm of some lasting duration, e.g., mental harm lasting months or years. See id. Prolonged mental harm is not simply the stress experienced in, for example, an interrogation by state police. See id. Based on your research into the use of these methods at the SERE school and consultation with others with expertise in the field of psychology and interrogation, you do not anticipate that any prolonged mental harm would result from the use of the waterboard . . . In the absence of prolonged mental harm, no severe mental pain or suffering would have been inflicted, and the use of these procedures would not constitute torture within the meaning of the statute.

Bybee notes that the CIA have consulted interrogation experts, mental health experts and psychologists and a 'comprehensive psychological profile of Zubaydah has been created' to determine if the 'use of the procedures' will result in prolonged mental harm. He concludes:

Reliance on this information about Zubaydah and about the effect of the use of these techniques more generally demonstrates the presence of a good faith belief that no prolonged mental harm will result from using these methods in the interrogation of Zubaydah. Moreover, we think that this represents not only an honest belief but also a reasonable belief based on the information that you have supplied to us. Thus, we believe that the specific intent to inflict prolonged mental [sic] is not present, and consequently, there is no specific intent to inflict severe mental pain or suffering. Accordingly, we conclude that on the facts in this case the use of these methods separately or a course of conduct would not violate Section 2340A.

There are three terms that stand out to me here – 'a good faith belief', 'an honest belief' and 'a reasonable belief'. As if, by using additional adjectives, justification can be found for views that have no faith, no honesty and no reasonableness.

*

Memos 2/3: Top Secret [document blacked out – redacted in parts]
Date: May 10th 2005, 17:50
From: Steven G. Bradbury, Principal Deputy Assistant Attorney General
To: John A. Rizzo, Senior Deputy General Counsel for the Central Intelligence Agency
Subject: Combined Use of Certain Techniques in the Interrogation of High Value al Qaeda Detainees.

These two memoranda, sent on the same afternoon from 'site 15 DOJ' by Steven Bradbury and constituting a single communication of sixty-six pages, carry on the theme of Bybee's previous memo, but go into far greater detail about the 'techniques' involved and the extent to which they comply with US law. He particularly focusses on how the combination of different interrogation procedures might potentially go over into the legal definition of torture; he is also keen for all participating CIA personnel, particularly interrogators and members of the CIA's Office of Medical Services (OMS), to be made aware of the care needed in this area. He starts by detailing the first stages in the treatment of detainees:

According to the Background Paper, before being flown to the site of interrogation, a detainee is given a medical examination. He then is 'securely shackled and is deprived of sight and sound through the use of blindfolds, earmuffs, and hoods' during the flight. Id at 2. An on-board medical officer monitors his condition. Security personnel also monitor the detainee for signs of distress. Upon arrival at the site, the detainee 'finds himself in complete control of Americans' and is subjected to 'precise, quiet, and almost clinical' procedures designed to underscore 'the enormity and suddenness of the change in environment, the uncertainty about what will happen next, and the potential dread [a detainee] may have of US custody.' Id. His head and face are shaved; his physical condition is documented through photographs taken while he is nude; and he is given medical and psychological interviews to assess his condition and to make sure there are no contraindications to the use of any particular interrogation techniques.

He also explains that the detention conditions at all CIA facilities include the use of 'white noise' and constant light:

Although we do not address the lawfulness of using white noise (not to exceed 79 decibels) and constant light, we note that according to materials you have furnished to us, (1) the Occupational Safety and Health Administration has determined that there is no risk of permanent hearing loss from continuous, 24-hour per day exposure of noise up to 82 decibels, and (2) detainees typically adapt fairly quickly to the constant light and it does not interfere unduly with their ability to sleep. See fax for Dan Levin, Acting Assistant Attorney General, Office of Legal Counsel, [document blacked out – redacted here] (Jan 4, 2005)

On the use of waterboarding, he specifies the time limits in relation to use of this 'technique' – only on five days within any thirty-day period, no more than two 'sessions' within a twenty-four-hour period, 'with a "session" defined to mean the time that the detainee is strapped to the waterboard and that no session may last more than two hours'. The maximum length of application of water is forty seconds. Later, he states: 'We also understand that the waterboard is not physically painful.' As with Bybee's comment earlier, at this point even the gentlest pacifist might want to see Bradbury experiencing this for himself, and also exposure to eighty-two-decibel noise for twenty-four hours.

Memorandum 3, sent at the same time, goes into greater detail still. We learn about the use of a further technique – 'water dousing' and the need for a medical officer to be present to monitor the detainee for 'signs of hypothermia'. Here too there are lists of dos and don'ts:

> For water temperature of 41°F, total duration of exposure may not exceed 20 minutes without drying and rewarming.
> For water temperature of 50°F, total duration of exposure may not exceed 40 minutes without drying and rewarming.
> For water temperature of 59°F, total duration of exposure may not exceed 60 minutes without drying and rewarming.

Technique number two is the use of enforced nudity:

> 2: Nudity. This technique is used to cause psychological discomfort, particularly if a detainee, for cultural or other reasons, is especially modest. When the technique is employed, clothing can be provided as an instant reward for cooperation. During and between interrogation sessions, a detainee may be kept nude provided that ambient temperatures and the health of the detainee permit. For this technique to be employed, ambient temperature must be at least 68F. No sexual abuse or threats of sexual abuse are permitted . . . We understand that interrogators 'are trained to avoid sexual innuendo or any acts of implicit or explicit sexual degradation.' Nevertheless, interrogators can exploit the detainee's fear of being seen naked. In addition, female officers involved in the interrogation process may see the detainees naked; and for purposes of our analysis, we will assume that detainees subjected to nudity as an interrogation technique are aware that they may be seen naked by females.

We learn that technique number 12 is sleep deprivation, and that 'the longest period of time for which any detainee has been deprived of sleep by the CIA is 180 hours'. This is how it works:

> 12. Sleep deprivation (more than 48 hours). This technique subjects a detainee to an extended period without sleep. You have informed us that the primary purpose of this technique is to weaken the subject and wear down his resistance.

The primary method of sleep deprivation involves the use of shackling to keep the detainee awake. In this method, the detainee is standing and is handcuffed, and the handcuffs are attached by a length of chain to the ceiling. The detainee's hands are shackled in front of his body, so that the detainee has approximately a two to three foot diameter of movement. The detainee's feet are shackled to a bolt in the floor. Due care is taken to ensure that the shackles are neither too loose nor too tight for physical safety. We understand from discussions with OMS that the shackling does not result in any significant physical pain for the subject. The detainee's hands are generally between the level of his heart and his chin. In some cases, the detainee's hands may be raised above the level of his head, but only for a period of up to two hours. All of the detainee's weight is borne by his legs and feet during standing sleep deprivation.

. . . We understand that a detainee undergoing sleep deprivation is generally fed by hand by CIA personnel so that he need not be unshackled; however, 'if progress is made during interrogation, the interrogators may unshackle the detainee and let him feed himself as a positive incentive,' October 12 [document blacked out – redacted here] Letter at 4.

If the detainee is clothed, he wears an adult diaper under his pants. Detainees subject to sleep deprivation who are also subject to nudity as a separate interrogation technique will at times be nude and wearing a diaper. If the detainee is wearing a diaper, it is checked regularly and changed as necessary. The use of the diaper is for sanitary and health purposes of the detainee; it is not used for the purpose of humiliating the detainee, and it is not considered to be an interrogation technique.

Towards the middle of this document, the lawyer, having drawn on many academic references, notes that 'drawing distinctions among gradations of pain is obviously not an easy task, especially given the lack of any precise, objective scientific criteria for measuring pain', and 'pain is a complex, subjective, perceptual phenomenon with a number of dimensions – intensity, quality, time course, impact and personal meaning – that are uniquely experienced by each individual and thus, can only be assessed indirectly'. There follow pages of attempts to then define 'severe mental pain or suffering' and the question of how 'prolonged mental harm' can be proved. The role of OMS personnel is emphasised strongly, and the presence of these medical personnel at the torture of men is portayed as showing their duty 'to prevent severe physical or mental pain or suffering'. Bradbury, unsurprisingly, concludes by saying: 'Although extended sleep deprivation and use of the waterboard present more substantial questions in certain respects under the statute and the use of the waterboard raises the most substantial issue – none of these specific techniques, considered individually, would violate the prohibition in sections 2340–2340A.'

*

Memo 4: Top Secret [document blacked out – redacted in parts]
Date: May 30th 2005
From: Steven G. Bradbury, Principal Deputy Assistant Attorney General
To: John A. Rizzo, Senior Deputy General Counsel for the Central Intelligence Agency
Subject: Application of United States Obligations Under Article 16 of the Convention Against Torture to Certain Techniques that May Be Used in the Interrogation of High Value al Qaeda Detainees.

This memorandum begins with a brazen exercise in legal cynicism. Bradbury describes the territorial reach of Article 16 of the United Nations Convention Against Torture and Other Cruel, Inhuman or Degrading Treatment or Punishment, of which the US is a signatory:

By its terms, Article 16 is limited to conduct within 'territory under [United States] jurisdiction.' We conclude that territory

871

under United States jurisdiction includes, at most, areas over which the United States exercises at least de facto authority as the government. Based on CIA assurances, we understand that the interrogations do not take place in any such areas. We therefore conclude that Article 16 is inapplicable to the CIA's interrogation practices and that those practices thus cannot violate Article 16.

However, Bradbury wants to explore whether if Article 16 *did* apply to the interrogation techniques used by the CIA, would these then be open to a challenge from the Supreme Court on the grounds of executive conduct which 'shocks the conscience'. This phrase is jarring in the context of these memoranda because, momentarily, it alludes to the existence of a world beyond the CIA. He then goes through pages of descriptions of the torturing of detainees, and how, in all cases, these 'enhanced techniques' have been justified by the 'significant information' that has emerged from those tortured.

Page after page then follow of legal argument about the precise meaning of the term 'territory under its jurisdiction', and how Guantanamo Bay may be exempted from this phrase. By page 27 of this document we return to an exploration of what government conduct that 'shocks the conscience' would actually mean. There are 'relatively few cases' in which the Supreme Court has analysed this, so little in the way of legal precedent exists. Bradbury then itemises the ways the CIA interrogation programme could be challenged:

- *We first consider whether the CIA interrogation program involves conduct that is 'constitutionally arbitrary'. 'We conclude that it does not'.*
- *We next address whether, considered in light of 'an understanding of traditional executive behavior, of contemporary practice, and of the standards of blame generally applied to them' use of the enhanced interrogation techniques constitutes government behavior that 'is so egregious, so outrageous, that it may fairly be said to shock the contemporary conscience.'*

This matter is more complicated to give a clear answer on. Bradbury later explains that: 'Each year in the State Department's Country Reports on Human Rights Practices, the United States condemns coercive interrogation techniques and other practices employed by other countries.' He then notes, rather worryingly: 'Certain of the techniques the United States has condemned appear to bear some resemblance to some of the CIA interrogation techniques.'

He then lists these as 'psychological torture', 'nudity, water dousing, sleep deprivation'. But he concludes this section by saying 'we do not believe that the reports provide evidence that the CIA interrogation program "shocks the contemporary conscience"'.

There's also a revealing footnote here, where Bradbury admits the hypocrisy at the heart of US policy:

> We recognize that as a matter of diplomacy, the United States may for various reasons call other nations to account for practices that may in some respects resemble conduct in which the United States might in some circumstances engage, covertly or otherwise.

Bradbury concludes this forty-page memorandum by stating:

> Based on CIA assurances, we understand that the CIA interrogation program is not conducted in the United States or 'territory under [United States] jurisdiction,' and that it is not authorized for use against United States persons. Accordingly, we conclude that the program does not implicate Article 16. We also conclude that the CIA interrogation program, subject to its careful screening, limits and medical monitoring, would not violate the substantive standards applicable to the United States under Article 16 even if those standards extended to the CIA interrogation program. Given the paucity of relevant precedent and the subjective nature of the inquiry, however, we cannot predict with confidence whether a court would agree with this conclusion, though, for the reasons explained, the question is unlikely to be subject to judicial inquiry.

Please let us know if we may be of further assistance.
Steven G. Bradbury
Principal Deputy Assistant Attorney General

*

Transactions. Rooms in Washington, DC. Insistent bleeping of phones. Men and women in smart greys and blues. Deadlines. More rooms in Langley, Virginia. Pinging of incoming email. People staring at screens. Urgency of requests. Needed by end of day. More calls. Sign off needed. 'Nice work people, nice job!'

Seven thousand miles away. US base in Afghanistan. Man, early thirties, suspect. Brought in, bloodied. Follow procedure. Commander informed. Plane readied. Man hooded, cuffed. Arrives in a country not under any legal jurisdiction. CIA base. White noise (not exceeding eighty-two decibels). Medical staff present. Enhanced interrogation can proceed. Everyone to their places. Terror can begin.

*

How rare it is that such memoranda ever see the light of day. Yet we can be sure that armies of lawyers and consultants and officials are generating communications similar to these on most, if not all, days of the year. The final act of violence may, sometimes, be witnessed, even condemned – but the bureaucrat or lawyer who created the supposed legitimacy for the subsequent action (via documents like we've seen above) is almost never seen. And we do not, yet, have the civic and judicial structures to hold such officials to account – let alone the moral frameworks in place that would enable individuals to understand the lethality of their responsibility. If you happened to meet either Mr Bybee or Mr Bradbury on the streets of Washington, and challenged them about their daily acts of desk killing, both would probably make some reference to the 'need to defend our civilised world from terrorists and enemies of freedom'. In exactly the way that our doctors of Wannsee felt they were upholding civilised German purity, and in exactly the way that nineteenth-century colonialists felt that exterminating the 'savages' was critical for the survival of their societies.

At least, this would be their public defence of what they do. I wonder whether, sometimes after they get home, there might be just a scintilla of disturbance, somewhere deep down? The faintest echo of something once heard at law school decades ago, that, for some reason, surfaces again tonight. Remember? It was some writer over from England, guy with a white beard, what did he say? Something about war? It had a certain succinct force . . . oh yes, that was it – 'Terrorism is the war of the poor, and war is the terrorism of the rich.'

*

'I would like my headstone to read, He always tried to do the right thing.'

Jay Bybee, quoted in *Time*, 28 April 2009, 'Jay Bybee: The Man Behind Waterboarding'

A Note on Fritz Haber, Clara Immerwahr, Hermann Haber and Claire Haber

Fritz Haber (1868–1934) was a Nobel Prize-winning German chemist, who invented the process by which ammonia is synthesised from nitrogen and hydrogen. He was also a pivotal figure in the development of the group of companies which became IG Farben in 1925. But earlier on, during the First World War in 1915, Haber had been working for BASF, and pioneered the production of the first poison gases to be used as a weapon of war – chlorine and phosgene gases. These were first used against French troops at Ypres on 22 April 1915, in an experimental attack in which thousands of soldiers were killed.

Haber at this time was married to Clara Immerwahr, from a Jewish family in Poland, where she had become the first woman to attain a PhD in chemistry at the University of Breslau. She and Haber married in 1901, had a son, Hermann, and settled in Germany. Despite her great intelligence and strong early feminist views, the pressures of German society meant that she only had limited scope to continue her research; she spent much of her time supporting her husband's burgeoning career, and translating his publications into English. However, all this time her activism in women's rights and pacifism was growing, and she became more and more aware of the limitations of her life, writing this to a friend:

> It has always been my attitude that a life has only been worth living if one has made full use of all one's abilities and tried to live out every kind of experience human life has to offer. It was under that impulse, among other things, that I decided to get married . . . The lift I got from it was very brief . . . and the main reasons for that was Fritz's oppressive way of putting himself first in our home and marriage, so that a less ruthlessly self-assertive personality was simply destroyed.

With the outbreak of the First World War, their lives and beliefs diverged even more strongly. Haber became a staunch supporter of the German military, while Clara's pacifism became even more pronounced. Haber was one of the principal movers behind the 'Fulda manifesto', published in October 1914, which declared to the world: 'Were it not for German militarism . . . German civilisation would long ago have been destroyed . . . The German army and the German people are one.' The final straw for Clara was Haber's critical role in developing poison gases to be used on the front line in Flanders. Shortly after his return from overseeing the first use of chlorine gas, at Ypres in April 1915 – a gas which killed by essentially burning through the throat and lungs of the soldiers who inhaled it – matters came to an equally violent conclusion in the family. On the night of 1 May 1915, following another row with Haber, Clara walked into their garden and shot herself in the heart with his service revolver. She was not killed straight away, and was found by her young son, Hermann, who had heard the shots, and then watched his mother die in his arms. Within days Haber left for the Eastern Front to oversee the first use of gas against the Russian army. In the course of the war 92,000 soldiers were killed and over a million injured by the use of Haber's poison gases.

*

Hermann Haber committed suicide in New York in 1946. Three years later, Hermann's daughter, Claire Haber (born in the same house where Clara had shot herself), was working as a scientist in Chicago, attempting to develop an antidote to the effects of chlorine gas poisoning, pioneered by her grandfather. She was told that this work had to be curtailed, as all scientific efforts were now to be put into the atomic bomb programme. Distraught hearing this news, she killed herself in Chicago in 1949, by swallowing cyanide.

Neither Clara, nor Hermann, nor Claire left suicide notes. Yet it is difficult to look at their lives, and deaths, without seeing the shadow of Fritz Haber – the father of chemical warfare – looming over all of them. Poignantly, the violence that Fritz Haber unleashed ultimately claimed the lives of his wife and children too. Susan Griffin, as we've seen, has written powerfully about the way that the violence and trauma of war is often passed down through families, through the generations, and so the damage done is never limited to the initial perpetrator of violence. This is borne out in the case of the Haber family. And in the cases of innumerable other families where extreme levels of violence and trauma have been transmitted, directly or indirectly, from the parents to the children.

*

As well as trying to contemplate the terror experienced by those prisoners subjected to the torture legitimised by Jay Bybee's and Steven Bradbury's memoranda, I also find myself thinking about the families of those two lawyers. Aren't they also victims here? I wonder what the Bradbury family think of their father's legal work. When the memoranda came into the public domain, were they angry? Did they confront him? Or did they try to pretend that nothing had happened?

Jay Bybee has stated publicly – as if expecting sympathy – that he 'regrets . . . the notoriety that this (case) has brought me. It has imposed enormous pressures on me both professionally and personally. It has had an impact on my family.' He doesn't go into details, but I would like to understand the effects that his words, when they became public in 2005, actually had on his young family. How could a man whose job was to uphold the law have contributed to legitimising the practice of torture? Would you ever be able to trust a man again who writes that it is not anticipated *'that any prolonged mental harm would result from the use of the waterboard.'** ? *And that because 'no severe mental pain or suffering would have been inflicted . . . the use of these procedures would not constitute torture within the meaning of the statute.'* If your father had written such words, would you ever be able to look him in the eye again?

PART SEVEN

Time and Love; Memory and Looking

18

Past Continuous

I trace the gradual lengthening of winter days, after the turning of the year, as I once traced the hair on your sleeping head. Gently. Not wanting to wake you in the night. Or stop the simple miracle of our breathing together. My finger lifts a single, coal-black curl away from your eyelid. Then, only millimetres from your skin, I trace a line down your nose, almost brushing your lips (fractionally parted, as if in concentration), down to your stubbled chin. Wondering if you will wake. If your dreaming state can feel my wandering finger, so near. Each breath in the dead of night a pulse of warmth. Us together. Brief travellers on this earth. I can feel the blood moving inside you, see the twitch of the artery in your neck, feel your heart beat. *Corazón*. The word you wouldn't translate. Blushing, turning away from me, your face to the sun.

And now you're sleeping on the other side of our turning world – summer to my winter. I'm back by the western sea. Trilling of curlew, urgent lapping of water. I sit on a fallen willow trunk, listening to the wash of the tide, reaching higher and higher over these mudflats. Each day now three or four minutes longer. Even in the middle of February the sense of spring, coiled and ready to sing, is tangible. Unstoppable. A tang in the air, a fractional lightening of green in the hedges. A mile away, on the other side of the bay, I watch a tractor moving patiently in the dusk, flashing yellow lights along the lane that leads back to the village. From there another pool of headlights moving. I guess they'll find each other at the corner by the farm. The lights momentarily pause as they meet, then move on again, resuming their journeys, lights searching out again, spooling into the darkness.

But you're with me again, in spirit, as vividly as this dusk. You were with me on waking, I think you visited me in the night, came into my dreams. I know one day we will be together again. Are. Were. Will be. But today these tenses are all one. Meaningless to separate. Thinking and writing about atrocities makes it even more urgent to love. And in my mind, inhabited for years by words and images that attack the human spirit, there are also the faces of all those I've ever loved, their voices, their laughter, their touch.

All that we carry inside us. Our pasts not past at all.

*

Is there any relationship between writing and happiness? Or is the opposite true? I know of very few writers, either living or dead, who could be described as being genuinely happy for much of their existence. Though perhaps the same could be said of everyone. After all, happiness is an elusive state for most of us. But the difference between writers and others, it seems to me, lies in the repeated activity of trying to fix in words emotional states which, by definition, defy the permanence of words. So writers, at least those skilled enough to have humility, are always coming up against the reality of their failure. Are always aware of the *provisional* nature of what they've written, the way their words slide away from their subjects, ending up somewhere unintended, only occasionally, perhaps, capturing some inner truth. So the majority of time is spent in states of differing levels of frustration; a restlessness that knows the destination is always just out of sight, just around the next corner – but, in reality, unreachable.

The sedentary nature of the writing life also doesn't seem to contribute much to happiness either. Staring at a screen most days, you might as well be in an office, the only difference being the scope for limitless procrastination at home. Then, forcing yourself out for a walk in the last of the light, you're confronted by other people who seem to have busy lives, places to go to, tangible objectives to achieve. You find yourself thinking: 'God, what a relief it must be to have a job that has a beginning, a middle and an end! Something tangible like delivering packages in a van. Or repairing broken pipes. Selling shoes. Anything that means at the end of the day you can shut up your shop, go home and not think about work until the next day . . .'. And then the writer returns home, and is confronted by the paltry amount of text generated in the course of a day's 'work' – and the spiral of self-loathing only increases . . .

I wonder what Epicurus, that great thinker on the question of happiness, would have thought of writers and their solitary pursuits today? He identified three factors as being significant influences on people's abilities to find contentment – freedom from authority, a community of friends, and time spent reflecting on life with others. On the first, writers might score relatively highly, for the generally high levels of autonomy they have around their work; but on the second and third, I'm sure Epicurus would have found the focus on *individual* creativity, above everything else, to be quite misconceived.

I'm also intrigued by the question of writing about the subject of happiness. While all of us could immediately name numerous novels, songs or plays which have suffering at their centre – after all, this is the essence of tragedy, the foundation of most literature – I'm certain that if we were asked to think of writing that portrays happiness in a vivid way then most of us would struggle to identify even half a dozen books where this state is written about convincingly. There seem to be two possible explanations for this: either that it is exceptionally difficult to capture a state which is essentially ephemeral; or that we as readers bring to such descriptions a strong degree of scepticism, no doubt partly based on our own experiences of such states. And this scepticism works against any writer's attempt to communicate happiness or joy.

There might also be a third explanation. At times in my own life when I've been either wildly happy, or in love (or, just occasionally, when these two states have coincided), I simply stop writing, because I'm too busy living. Fortunately or unfortunately, these states are by their very nature temporary – a matter of weeks sometimes, a few months at most. My last period of extended, total happiness tiptoed up on me two years ago, and for six months I wrote almost nothing.

Actually, that's not entirely true. I couldn't write prose. It was as if the reflective, circumlocutory nature of prose, the way of developing ideas over several pages, was quite unsuited to the momentary imperative of absolute happiness. Released from anxieties and fears, I only wanted to live in the sensual world, to still the analytical inner voices into temporary submission. And so, in these months, writing as a daily act went out of the window. But I couldn't give it up completely, I'd find myself, rather furtively, scribbling down a few words on a café tablecloth or the back of a cigarette packet. In the gaps. I'd hesitate to call such random groupings of words 'poems', but they had the urgency of the poetic. The desire to capture rapidly – what poetry uniquely can achieve. I actually became quite judgemental of my former self, and the way writers prioritise words and control over the living experience. If you were happy and well adjusted, would you want to spend day after day inside, staring at a screen? Given the choice between doing your 2,000 words for the day or an afternoon of fucking, what would you choose?

During this period I spent a surprising amount of time in Shepherd's Bush (I know it sounds strange, but please bear with me). The need to be in Shepherd's Bush was tied up with wanting to be with somebody I'd met. Felipe was Spanish, tall, with dark, curly hair and very brown eyes with long, sensuous eyelashes, and looked disarmingly like one of El Greco's portraits of young men, the same nobility in the face. Even the five-minute walk down the Uxbridge Road, not one of London's loveliest streets, became a passage of beauty because it was the way to him. Each charmless off-licence became transfigured, in a kind of reverse stations of the cross, into beacons of hope that edged me nearer towards seeing that loved face again. Each vandalised bus shelter brought me closer to shared desire.

Looking back on that time now, it does seem just like the song says – 'Sundown, yellow moon, I replay the past. / I know every scene by heart, they all went by so fast.' I can remember making him laugh, a shake of that head, eyes dancing delightedly as I tried to learn phrases in Spanish on that bench in Bedford Square – '*Relájate! Tenemos todo el tiempo del mundo . . .*' Hmmm, not sure about that one. Or driving back from the Lake District through the night and having a violent argument about the merits, or otherwise, of Patti Smith, so much so that I almost went into the back of a lorry. Almost every part of London still has associations from those four months. The alleyway next to the Riverside Studios going down to the Thames, where we'd rush out between films to kiss – and where we saw a shooting star; the corner of the Strand and Waterloo Bridge, which I'll never be able to look at without inwardly blushing. And that stretch of pavement outside the King's Head on Upper Street where it all began.

There is a great paradox, however, both about being happy, and trying to live in the present moment. As soon as they become conscious states, it's all over. And maybe this is the reason why we should stop writing – the primitive impulse that says 'don't kill it through consciousness'. I remember seeing *Jules et Jim* as a student. Yes, there were charming and funny parts to the film but overall I was pretty traumatised. It seemed to me a statement about the inability of lovers to make choices, the way love ends up torturing all who fall under its spell. But one line still haunts me, spoken by the narrator, which I remember as: 'Happiness came and went without anybody noticing.' That had the feel of truth. A state that can only be recognised when it's no longer there.

In the intensity of our growing love I also felt peculiarly connected to death. Part of it was that understandable sense of 'God, be careful how you cross the road – it would be terrible to die now when life is so amazing . . .' But there was something else at work as well. And this I did try to express at the time, in a letter to a friend in Canada:

> Paradoxically, in the first days of a new love, we are more closely connected to death than at any other time in our lives. The exquisite pain of this state consists of the certainty that this sense of mad burning and blossoming is finite. It will end. Whether in a week, or after sixty years, whether in the death of oneself or the other, whether in the fading of the love or the lover. So, contained within the coming of love, is death. Certain as ash after fire.

Strange to reread that and remember it was written at a time of great joy. And then, to see in a notebook, that on the same day I'd written this list:

> I want to see the Bosphorus with you,
> I want to explore every crevice and hair of your body,
> I want to show you the Salvator Rosa in the National Gallery,
> I want you to teach me Spanish,
> I want you to take me to your special mountain in Asturias,
> I want you to tell me why you love Victor Hugo,
> I want us to go to Mangal in the early hours, ravenous for lamb, after fucking the night away,
> I want to sleep out on the Heath with you under the summer stars . . .

Love and Death. The impossibility of anything lasting. The wilder the expectations, the more dizzying the ending.

Even today, writing this, I can hear two powerful voices pulling me in entirely opposite directions. One of these is saying, *Immerse yourself in the reality of that time. Try to express – as honestly as you can – the experience. The feelings of those months. After all, it's one of the hardest things you can ever try to communicate, especially as a man.* The other voice, more parental, protective, whispers, *Are you insane? You know that re-entering this territory can be toxic. Remember how it ended. Do you want to open up all that pain again?* The vast majority of the time I listen to this sensible voice; the notebooks and photographs from that time remain on a high shelf at home, pregnant with joy and pain, unlooked at from one year to the next.

But today I'm not there, I'm in the west, I'm released by the sea and the scudding clouds and the ravens on the cliffs croaking wildly. I'm roaring into the wind, feeling I exist as a body as well as a mind. Wanting to be released from these years of research into violence and horror and death. Write about the absolute opposite now. Write not him but you. Write about love. Write about tenderness, about hope. About beginnings.

*

Four moments.

The first evening. We meet outside the theatre, you'd just seen *Festen*. Both of us nervous but pretending not to be. The King's Head very crowded, but we talk, your serious face, fringed with dark, wiry hair, leaning towards mine intently as we talk about family, growing up gay and Catholic, our younger sisters and how protective we still feel. London as a home for millions of escapees, some fleeing persecution, most fleeing the stultifying conformity of conservative backgrounds. The astonishing freedom that you felt as soon as you arrived here. A place where you could be yourself. For the first time. And, as you talk, an energy between us, chemical, charged. The certainty of attraction. We're listening to each other, but also hearing another language altogether . . . Now you're describing the contrast with all the hiding you had to do at home, all the repression. And I'm talking about the willed ignorance of the Suffolk young farmers I grew up with, the narrowness of the Catholic school in Ipswich. You talk about Gigon. Terrible struggles with your father. Intense homophobia at school. Then our first feelings of attraction for boys. But, in those cultures, shameful, so immediately repressed. And we share how both of us later learned of boys in our classes who'd killed themselves – unable to reconcile their sexuality with their religion.

We also discover that we both went through a 'heterosexual phase', but giggled that this is probably quite normal for most young people, experimenting with the opposite sex, trying out the word 'bisexual' for a time. How dated that seems now . . . With immaculate timing, 'There Is a Light That Never Goes Out' now starts to reverberate around the pub, you frown and say something disparaging about The Smiths. I'm rather shocked, and you grudgingly admit that this song is 'OK', and your face cracks into a wicked, teasing smile . . . When the pub closes we continue talking animatedly on the pavement outside. But now it's time for us to part, and I'm suddenly indecisive, wistful, and sad about the age gap between us:

'Well, Felipe, I've had a really lovely evening . . . Isn't life weird sometimes? I, I was just thinking . . .' I look across and your eyes encourage me to go on: 'Well, if only you were a few years older and I was a few years younger . . .'

You look startled. 'Is it a problem for you? Really?!'

'Well, I mean . . . Isn't it for you?'

'Not at all. Dan, I'm really shocked – you, of all people! That's so *conservative!*'

'So, you mean, you'd like to . . . ?'

'Yes, absolutely!'

*

Our second meeting. The following day is the start of the Easter weekend, you're in Edinburgh, I'm in Suffolk. We're talking every day, aching to see each other again. Easter Monday, you're back in London, going to the ballet that night, but I've borrowed a car, and persuade you to 'meet me halfway'. Chelmsford station, from this day on, will never be the same again. In the drab car park, next to the bus station, completely oblivious to gaggles of teenage school-kids, we kiss with a wild hunger, darting tongues, rooting, branching, searching. Feeling every part of our bodies alive now. Wanting more, wanting it all, but also savouring this stage, which we know is very short, and very tender . . . We drive east, talking non-stop, laughing. As I change gear your hand finds mine, and stays there. You ask about my text yesterday, 'everything very beautiful here – carpets of flowers, april sunshine, baby lambs gambolling . . . missing you. come down tomorrow, it's only an hour from liverpool street.' You want to know what 'gambolling' means, and I smile, describing the combination of little leaps in the air and rushing around. 'Gam-boll-ing,' you roll the sounds around your mouth, as if tasting the word, 'yes, I like it!'

We drive to Bradwell, I want to show you the tiny chapel. But you just want to kiss again – deeply, thirstily, like a wanderer at an oasis in the desert. Walking down the track, hand in hand, we stop at a gate to watch the lambs, and, as if on queue, they start to gambol. You find this incredibly funny, and soon we're both doubled up. Inside the chapel you tell me of a very religious year you had at the convent when you were fifteen years old, going to Mass daily. But later you began to find Catholicism far too controlling, too judge-mental. Two butterflies flap at the little window high up the wall. We walk down to the mudflats, soon finding beds of seashells, bleached in the sun. We lie down. Utterly blue sky above us. Time then becomes suspended. We are in another space, so absorbed in the moment that hours pass but we have no consciousness of time. Lying curled next to each other, gazing into the other, the strangeness of eyes up so close, kissing, whispering questions and answers, kissing again, unbuttoning, tickling, nibbling, biting. Lips, necks, stubbled cheeks . . . At one point you stop, look rather serious and say: 'Dan, there's something I have to tell you. I probably should have told you before.' I freeze, scanning my mind rapidly for possible confessions. 'What is it?' I ask nervously. 'Well, it's quite embarrassing for me to tell you . . . You see, erm . . . I'm not much of an intellectual. I hardly read at all.' And then you crack the widest smile, and I punch you playfully on the shoulder. 'You fucker! You really had me worried!' Soon you're resting your head on my chest, and I can feel both of us slipping into sleep, hands entwined, I see your fine head rising and falling on my chest as your eyelids close.

When I return to consciousness, it comes with a surge of joy. A kind I haven't felt for a long time. I reach out for your hair, unable to believe in your corporeality. You turn towards me, half sleeping, half waking, and I feel the tenderest brush of your eyelashes against my cheek. The tiniest touch, yet enough to overpower me. You open your eyes, and then point at something in the sky, questioning. I follow your finger. High above us, we're astonished to see a small white bird hovering. Immediately above us. Five minutes, six minutes, maybe more. We cannot speak. Reduced to the awed sounds that children make. I've never seen anything like it, before, or since.

You stroke my cheek, ending at my lips again, and whisper: 'I want to stay like this for ever. It's like a miracle.'

'Not like a miracle. It is a miracle.'

*

Third moment. Six weeks on. The middle of May, my birthday, and a more significant one than usual. Happiness and joy. Has anyone ever really been able to differentiate these two close friends? For me happiness is a purring, rumbling state, and joy is a burst – rapid, glorious, transient. Joy can enter into times of happiness, making delirious raids that intensify this state; but happiness has no effect on joy. It is not needed.

In moments close to death, we are told that images of your life flash before you. As if, in those seconds, memories of all that you have lived, loved, suffered are telescoped into some kind of meaning. If this is so, then for me the weekend of my fortieth birthday will surely be one of those reappearing memories. Ageing is a process of disbelief and coming to terms with absurdity; I don't think I've ever met someone who feels their biological age. I certainly have never achieved this state. But this doesn't make ageing any easier. So I hadn't been looking forward to entering my fifth decade; it had crept up on me in a slightly shocking way. That realisation that, however you might feel, the world outside no longer regards you as young. Then, six weeks before, the night at the King's Head happened which transformed so much. Now there is another to help me navigate this rite of passage.

On the eve of my birthday we have a drink at our favourite pub in Hackney. I'm feeling strange, wobbly about the 'end of my youth'. I manage to express this, and you're lovely about it, saying that everything's in the mind, and that I'm just as young as you are in so many ways. Then you quote that wonderful Dylan line, 'But I was so much older then, I'm younger than that now'. I feel a lifting. Yes, you're right. I *was* older in my twenties, so much more puritanical and judgemental. Political purity seemed the most important thing when I was young. Now often I see, in any unbending political position, only the seeds of authoritarianism. So much to be done. So much to change. But let's start with the human, the fallible. You agree passionately, that's where all activism should start – with listening, with recognising the simultaneous imperatives – of raging against injustice, and loving each other. Then we head home. We're almost back at the flat, at the top of my steps, and, as if to prove what you've just said, we start kissing animalistically there. We're tearing at each other's clothes, no time to close the front door properly, we're soon fucking wildly in the hall.

A pause. We agree we won't turn the lights on for a while, so I get some wood and we make a fire, watching the twigs catch and the flames leap, and you say you want to give me the first of my presents now. I unwrap a fine, two-volume edition of *Les Misérables*, in which you've written this dedication:

The title doesn't make reference to your birthday, so don't worry! I was surprised when you told me you hadn't read this book, it's my favourite. I really admire the main character – very stoical (you see I *am* learning more advanced words!!). Please read pages 61–2, it's the most powerful piece of writing I've ever seen. You're in your best moment now, so enjoy it to the maximum. Forty makes you look wonderful. All my love and kisses xxx F.

I'm overcome, tears rolling down my face, Thank you, darling, my *corazón*. You holding me so tight now, and soon we're fucking again, watching our shadows in the firelight on the walls . . . Then, afterwards, our breathing slowing, and now completely together, you on top of me, only our seed between us (7 billion spermatozoa, apparently,[*] or rather 14 billion, with no place to go – truly we contain multitudes). Heart to heart, feeling our blood, one pulse now. We drift into rest, fingers entwined, only the twitching of the fire and our breathing now, slower and slower.

Later we fall ravenously on the roast lamb (gambolling is all very well, but roasted with garlic and rosemary is better, we agree), and at two minutes to midnight we go into the garden with a bottle of Malbec and wait for the bells to ring. And, as my birthday comes into being, and my thirties fade, we kiss again, with a tenderness that brings me to tears, a surging joy. The twelfth chime reverberates through the darkness and I feel alive, more alive than I've felt for years. What an astonishing way to begin the next stage of my life . . . As we go to sleep that night, I whisper in your ear: 'Why can't it always be like this?' And you smile, with a hint of melancholy, and say, 'Because we're human beings.'

I spend the afternoon of my birthday writing in the garden – the last part of the synopsis of this book (an early draft), for a liter-

---

[*] I'm not certain this figure is reliable – it comes, if that's the right word to use, from Paul Auster – but I've never been sure whether it's based on something scientific, or something more personal: 'each ejaculation contains several billion sperm cells – or roughly the same number as there are people in the world' (from *The Invention of Solitude*).

892

ary agent. I send it through, and he rings me back. He says how excited he is at the prospect of the work, and how I need to start preparing for the next phase of my life, as a writer. In the evening a gathering of all my closest friends at a restaurant in Spitalfields. I'm in irrepressible form tonight, and I've decided people should drink with no inhibitions, so I'm paying for all the wine. Drink as much as you like, and not the cheapest bottles please! Earthy, rooted food, simple but delicious pairings – asparagus and bacon, rabbit and mustard, octopus, smoked eel. And terrific, zingy vodka sorbets to finish. I'm extremely moved, especially when J. gives me a long rectangular package. I open it and it's a framed set of three photographs of us over the three decades of our friendship. I look up and you've got tears in your eyes as well. You love the evening, and meeting my friends, almost as much as I do; you say we all have a lust for life, and you're right.

The next three days are dreamlike. On the Friday evening we drive up to Suffolk, fifteen of us, cars and vans laden with food and drink. We get to the place at the end of the world, and spill out in the night, into different cottages. The bigger one has no electricity and is still lit by gaslight, which gives a softer, glowing light to the next days . . . Saturday, the grey skies clear to blue. Other friends arrive, and then all of my family from the other side of Suffolk – my mother bringing a dozen lobsters and crabs from West Mersea, my sister two exquisite chocolate, rum and almond cakes, with honeysuckle twined around the tops. My four nephews and nieces dart around with the other children they've just met, climbing onto the roof and searching in the shingle for stones and objects to create decorations for the table we're preparing. The bath is converted into a temporary fridge, with dozens of bottles of wine and beer. The kitchen is a hive of activity with friends finishing their various contributions, involving mushrooms and marsala, chicken livers and prosciutto.

We move all the tables outside onto the shingle, overlooking the sea, and create a single long table with twenty-five assorted chairs. The feast begins. A heat haze hovers over the sea. Every now and then sails and masts of boats going up the River Alde to our left, but only the tops visible behind the banks of shingle, which gives them a magical quality, drifting across our horizon as we savour the tastes of bubbly and shellfish. Nothing rushed today, as the hours of the feast continue . . . In the time between courses, the children race down to the sea, returning with dead crabs and orange stones they'd like to be amber. Talk and laughter bubbles around the table in waves. The time of presents and speeches. At one point I'm blindfolded and presented with a huge and heavy box. Suppressed giggles of all those in on the joke. I take my blind-fold off, and peel off the tape – the box bursts open, and my seven-year-old nephew emerges with a scream of delight! And then, of course, all the other children want to repeat this game . . . Again! Again!! At one point our eyes meet, dancing happiness. I squeeze your hand. Candles on the cakes, everyone singing. And later, in the early-evening sun, people drift down to the water in twos and threes, and sit on the shingle bank with bottles of wine. All of us in a kindled state of oneness with the world . . . How many days like this in a life?

*

Fourth moment. Three weeks on. The end of June. Just back from our weekend in the Lake District. In your small room, high up in the house in Shepherd's Bush. Very late, after fucking, we sit in bed, looking out at clouds of summer rain under the sodium street lights. You're talking softly, about our lovemaking, and how respon-sive we are to each other, how it feels we've been together for ever. Distill this moment. Keep it with you always.

The next morning we have to leave early. The rain is still teem-ing down. We kiss goodbye at the bus stop in Uxbridge Road and I hurry on towards the Tube. And then I realise I don't want to hurry. I'll change my plans for this morning. My left shoe is leak-ing as well, so I'm not enjoying walking in the rain. I'll go to that Lebanese café on the corner that I've passed so many times. I have an exceptionally strong coffee. And then waiting for the rain to stop, I start to write on a paper napkin, trying to find words for what happened in the night. Some of the only words written in this period.

Naked in the dark,
sitting together
in the upstairs window,
gazing out onto squalls of June rain
at 2 a.m.

The odd siren reaches us from the Uxbridge Road,
but mostly we hear each other breathe.
You say
It's as if we've skipped two seasons
and are already in November,
as if we've known each other for almost a year,
instead of two months.
Our hands find each other now
with the ease of
leaves unfolding in the morning sun,
fingers interlock without us noticing.

I've sat on Alpine ridges and watched choughs surf the air,
and seen the sun disappear behind Big Sur,
Yet Collingbourne Road at 2 a.m. –
This moment,
our bodies barely visible,
our voices hardly more than a whisper –
has more power.

Outside, through the curious, pollarded limes
wild wind driving rain,
And you, driving out my fear
relentlessly,
stroking the hairs on my arm
in the half-light.
I see my self
again,

and the hope takes the breath from my body
to yours.

*

Three months later you have your crisis. Then we have ours. Given how rapidly and how deeply our love has grown I'm bewildered at the lack of resilience now. You return to Spain. I return to my writing. It's over.

*

We all carry within ourselves a world made up of all that we have seen and loved. And it is to this world that we return incessantly.

And now, two years on, I'm back in the little cottage by the sea, where we had my birthday weekend. I'm sleeping again in that creaking bed, remembering the way you had to cover my mouth when you fucked me, because of my friends sleeping in the next room. And the charged eroticism of your strong hand across my face, preventing my gasps from spilling into the air. The return to places of greatest happiness. Now pregnant with pain. The working of memory. The ghost of voices, laughter, celebrations. Now winter, solitude, an empty window. All saying – this is how life is. Get used to it. Why do you ever think that such states can continue? The childish absurdity of believing that happiness can be a permanent condition. By its very nature it can never be. Even the urge towards it is suspect.

But, in a similar way, the impulse towards wanting to separate ourselves from the past is also absurd: 'The past is another country', 'Don't look back', 'Don't dwell on the past'. The number of clichés grows in direct proportion to the falsity of the 'common sense' that is propagated. In reality, the past is in us continually. Past and present are entirely conjoined, inseparable. I think Dennis Potter once said something about this – how the past is like a horse running alongside us all the time. Yes, absolutely. Past and present in a single tense.

I have loved.
You have felt.
She has lost.
We have hoped.
You have suffered.
They have survived.

Pascal understood this perhaps more than most. He wanted to live with his past so much that he actually sewed it into the clothes that he wore. For him the moment of greatest joy in his life came in the form of an overwhelming spiritual epiphany which lasted for two hours on 23 November 1654. He wanted this experience to live with him ever after, and so he stitched this moment into the lining of his jacket, that way it would always be part of him. Words that became 'The Memorial':

The year of grace 1654
Monday, 23 November, feast of St Clement, Pope and Martyr,
    and of others in the Martyrology.
Eve of St Chrysogonus, Martyr and others.
From about half past ten in the evening until half past
    midnight,
Fire.

God of Abraham, God of Isaac, God of Jacob,
not of philosophers and scholars.
Certainty. Certainty. Heartfelt. Joy. Peace.
God of Jesus Christ. . .
My God and your God.
Your God will be my God.
The world forgotten, and everything except God . . .
Greatness of the human soul . . .
Joy, joy, joy, tears of joy . . .

Jesus Christ.

Jesus Christ.

I have cut myself off from him, shunned him, denied him, crucified him.

Let me never be cut off from him! . . .

Sweet and total renunciation.

Total submission to Jesus Christ and my director.

Everlasting joy in return for one day's effort on earth.

I will not forget thy word.

Amen.

And, as Pascal with his epiphany, so all of us, with all that we carry. Memories that burn themselves into the present, stitched into our neural pathways. Experiences can never be taken from us. And, in this way, any time of love is in us always. Any experience of truth is never lost.

*

To record or to live? Or to try to do both simultaneously? Writing and living at the same time is not a very easy combination. Since the age of twenty-one I've kept a journal. I wouldn't like to use the word 'obsessively' with its pejorative connotations, but seriously, yes, I take it seriously. These journals are the same A4, hard-cover, blank-page Chartwell books (each 180 pages); I'm currently on number 134, which at approximately 90,000 words a journal comes to a little over 12 million words so far. For the last twenty-five years, they have been receivers of anything and everything – ideas for writing, psychological reflections on people in my life, overheard conversations on buses, occasional newspaper articles, snatches of dreams, records of work meetings, maps of walks completed, drawings, notes from books read, things that have outraged me or inspired me or made me laugh, and, inevitably, a lot of extremely personal reflections. In some ways it's like leading two lives – the one you live and the one you then reflect on – and the record. As the writer Eduardo Galeano has defined it – '*Recordar*: To remember; from the Latin *recordis*, to pass back through the heart'.

I don't write the journal every day but usually once a week or once a fortnight I'll sit down for a couple of hours and try and catch up with myself. In extremely busy periods this can stretch to only once a month or two, which can become quite disturbing because I then feel disconnected from myself, and almost unable to live any more life, until I've caught up with where I am. And then you can get the self-defeating situation of having to devote whole days to catching up. This does not feel good, and of course makes a mockery of any talk of living in the present. I have no doubt that a therapist would have a field day with this, but it's one way of getting through life. *Whatever gets you through the night,* as somebody once sang. And, in very difficult times, writing has, together with love and friendship, been my way of surviving.

So the six-month gap in my journals represents a significant challenge for me. And the irony that one of the happiest times in my life has almost no words to accompany it – this is not easy for me to accept. Though I do have photographs, scraps of thoughts, and, rather strangely, every single text message we ever exchanged. In fact, towards the end of our relationship, in an act of digital archaeology, I actually transcribed all the texts sent and received between us, as if by doing this I could recapture those moments, live them again. Despite this lack of writing I am surprised I am now able to recall, extremely vividly, so much of what happened in those months. Perhaps because of the sequence of events that stays in the mind, perhaps because the relationship itself seemed to have such a clear narrative arc. Or maybe because these experiences have lived with me since – as I said, they are still present for me.

Only once in the last twenty-five years have I lost a journal, but that once was traumatic enough. It was in a bag of mine, along with my wallet, stolen from a car parked in a service station on the M4 on the way back from Wales. From time to time I still dream of recovering that journal. It had notes on Gitta Sereny's book on Albert Speer – forty to forty-five page of reflections, as I recall. It also had a draft of a lecture I was about to give in Dortmund, and the beginning of a short story. Even to this day I cannot travel on the M4 past Delamere Services without shuddering. I was later told by the police that somebody had tried to use my bank cards in Newport, so I'm afraid that town in south Wales has always been under a cloud since then. I didn't mind about the wallet or the cards, but couldn't they have left the journal?

Anyway, my point, as you'll see, is not a complicated one. *How* the past is documented, to a great extent, determines how it is remembered. If I hadn't gone to that café on that wet morning in June, I wouldn't have written those words, and so I probably wouldn't have been able to recall, certainly not in such detail, those moments in the still of the night. Inevitably this begs many further questions, such as the selectivity of memory, or the inevitable way that words first simplify, and then begin to replace, the actual lived experience. And here there is a difference between the oral and the written use of words. If, for example, you've ever tried to recount a story from your own childhood you will be aware of how, even if you've repeated these story several times over the years, it never comes out quite the same. A detail about the weather on the day of the bee sting, or the friend you were with when you got cut off by the tide, these will be different every time you tell the story, possibly reflecting your mood or who you're telling the story to. Maybe only subtly so, but it will be different.

Contrast this fluid truth with the unbending fixity of the written word, which Socrates distrusted so much and compared to 'glass shards' which he believed would disable people's memories. Ironically, we only know about this view of Socrates' because Plato wrote down his thoughts later on – in the dialogue between Socrates and Phaedrus: 'for this discovery of yours [writing] will create forgetfulness in the learners' souls, because they will not use their memories; they will trust to the external written characters and not remember for themselves.'

But perhaps Socrates places too much trust in people's power of memory, with or without the written word. We can all think of examples in our own lives of sharing memories with those closest to us, and being shocked when the other's memory of an important day or event differs dramatically from our own vivid recollection. And we also know that memory can be a fickle, capricious companion, sometimes tripping us up, sometimes giving us only a glimpse of the past. If you keep a journal, one of the most disorientating aspects is to revisit a day in your life ten or twenty years ago, and find that significant details are quite different from your memory of them. Perhaps there's an inherent frustration with trying to remember anything from the past in detail. Maybe there's always the sense, the suspicion, that some of the truly important aspects remain, tantalisingly, just out of view. Even on our deathbeds, the blurred periphery of the vision is what we will be seeing, rather than the reality. In a similar way, on waking, we often remember the prosaic part of the dream, but sense an astonishing beauty or uplifting revelation, just beyond the reach of our memories.

This doesn't mean that reading other people's accounts of their lives, their pasts, is necessarily frustrating. On the contrary. But it does mean that although we might feel there's a remarkable truth to D. H. Lawrence's depiction of childhood, or his relationship with his mother in *Sons and Lovers*, for example, or Gorky's description of his grandparents in *My Childhood* – when Lawrence or Gorky themselves reread what they had written, they would have been aware of the partial nature of what they had captured. They would both have understood that there is no writing about memory without vast simplification.

The narrative arcs of our lives are never simple, and rarely arcs at all. They never travel in one direction, despite the human urge to tell ourselves that there are definable 'phases' and 'cycles' in our existences. We need to make sense of our lives, to see beginnings and endings, but the reality is always different. The vast simplifications of the stories we create – the 'epiphany' experienced or the 'closure' achieved. Does talking about 'the end' of a relationship even have a meaning? As if we're finishing a meal or a book. Often our thoughts and feelings for the other inhabit us for many years in an extraordinarily intimate way – long after we're supposed to have stopped thinking about them. The way past lovers often make their way into our dreams. The absurd idea that you ever 'get over' the death of someone you've loved. If this were true, then how to explain, years later, finding yourself in a café suddenly ambushed by the music they loved, weeping, seeing their face again?

*

And then, finally, there are some things that simply defy being written about. Not because they are invisible, or partially seen, but because they are central to our identities. If we wrote about them we would not only reveal vulnerabilities in ourselves that are kept in the most remote place inside us, but we would also be in danger of tempting the fates. Think about the love of a parent for their child, the child for their parent. An intensity of love unlike any other. A love that enables and disables simultaneously. That stays, however much it changes its form, for as long as you live.

Perhaps such love can only be written about in retrospect. As if a forcefield of energy surrounds it, when the parent is still alive, making such communication impossible. After the parent has gone, words can try to find the force of this love. And, very occasionally, words can (if only for a moment) reach into this place. This is the writer Jonathan Franzen opening the fridge in his mother's house, in the last days of her life:

> For the week or so before she was hospitalized, my mother couldn't keep any food down, and by the time I arrived her refrigerator was empty of almost everything but ancient condiments and delicacies. On the top shelf there was just a quart of skim milk, a tiny can of green peas with a square of foil on top, and, next to this can, a dish containing a single bite of peas. I was ambushed and nearly destroyed by this dish of peas. I was forced to imagine my mother

alone in the house and willing herself to eat a bite of something, anything, a bite of peas, and finding herself unable
to. With her usual frugality and optimism, she'd put both
the can and the dish in the refrigerator, in case her appetite
returned.

And this is the film director and poet Pier Paolo Pasolini writing to
his mother:

> Only you in all the world know what my / heart always held,
> before any other love. / So I must tell you something terri-
> ble to know: / from within your kindness my anguish grew. /
> You're irreplaceable. And because you are, / the life you gave
> me is condemned to loneliness. / And I don't want to be alone.
> I have an infinite hunger for love, love of bodies without souls.
> For the soul is inside you, it is you, but / you're my mother and
> your love's my slavery . . .

Sons. Mothers. Still one of the hardest of all bonds to write
about. And a hole in this book. My mother, a presence who
hovers over almost everything I've written about. Yet, almost
invisible in these pages. Corinne, the sun in my universe for
more than forty years. Giver of life. Giver of love. Giver of hope.
The person I have loved more than any other. And who I have
worried about more than any other. Even as I write these words
I am aware of the danger of expressing such thoughts. We're all
supposed to outgrow the love of our parents, and the love for
our parents, but I don't care. I've got to a point in my life where
I think love, wherever it's found, in all its forms – love of partners, love of friends, love of family – needs to be celebrated. No,
more than celebrated – how weak that word sounds – it needs
to be glorified. No, more than that too. I simply feel in awe of
this love.

The meaning of home. Coming home. Walking down the path, the
sound of the heavy wooden door opening, smell of woodsmoke,
Corinne getting up from her chair to greet me. That face. That

smile. Hands extending, reaching out to embrace. *Hello, love!* Here, together, now. Never taken for granted. And after supper, we sit facing each other, the table of books and papers between us, in the autumn and winter the fire burning in the hearth. A cat often on our laps. And we talk. We talk the world right. We talk for hours – feelings, politics, books. But that's equivalent to saying that rain reaches the ocean by 'river, estuary, sea'. It captures none of the movement, the lithe energy of streams of thoughts and words intertwining. Your hand periodically reaching for a Silk Cut, the blue smoke coiling above you in unruly haloes. Me sipping red wine. How often I have thought about trying to capture these times. But soon realising that it would be as elusive as trying to bottle the light from the stars. Trying to trap the essence of happiness itself.

Once I wrote about us. Only once did I capture something of this love. It was late. You'd gone to bed. I was in the bathroom, and through the wall I could hear your deep breathing as you slept. I then imagined a future time when that sound would no longer be in the world. And what that would feel like. And how impossible it is to express the love that connects us. This short piece still haunts me. I remember showing it to you, and the expression on your face as you read it, the way you squeezed my hand afterwards.

Maddeningly, I cannot find this writing any more. Occasionally I search through old journals, boxes of papers, hoping to stumble across it with a stab of delight and recognition, but it hasn't happened yet. The tantalising nature of a lost piece of writing. Another voice, of course, tells me that if I did find it again, this piece could only disappoint. That, over the years of being lost, it has grown in its beauty and poignancy, to impossible levels of emotional power which the original piece could never have possessed. I guess all writers have similar stories about their lost pieces of work – the ones that got away . . .

*

I look back on these pages a couple of days after having written them. Truly wild weather now, rain battering the cottage in sheets, the wind ripping the leaves from the trees. Two further thoughts come to mind; maybe you've got there before me? If our past is always with us, then it follows that our past suffering and pain is carried with us too. This can be seen at its starkest with people who've survived traumatic experiences such as torture (as we've seen with Jean Améry, for example), but all of us know there are experiences lodged in our minds that we wish we could forget. Batteries of pain that we try to keep at a distance. Often inexplicable, sometimes not. Death, loss, the end of love. As integral to life as birth, growth and the beginning of love. But I feel now that all of these experiences need to be accepted, as part of our present realities, not ushered away into a neglected corner marked 'the past'.

The other thought is perhaps a more disconcerting one. If we accept that the vast majority of the people I've been discussing in these books, involved with different kinds of desk killing, are not a different species from you and I. If we accept that only a very small percentage of these people could be termed 'sociopaths' or 'psychopaths' (i.e. people incapable of feeling empathy or love, in the common meaning of these terms), then it follows that the overwhelming majority of desk killers have also experienced the intense rush of joy that comes with new love, the paralysing beauty of watching your lover sleeping, the grief that comes when love ends.

Do we really believe this, though? Can we allow ourselves to think of the joy that Adolf Eichmann felt at the birth of his first child? Or the wild love that Albert Speer experienced for the first time late in his life? Or the intense happiness that Steven Bradbury and his wife experienced on their wedding day? Because the harrowing reality is *not* that the desk killers do not feel love, empathy, pain, grief and all the other intense emotions that are part of the human experience – it is that they have found a way to be selective in their humanity. They can stroke their child's sleeping face in the night, and in the morning send the email that kills people they have never met.

'They've taken out insurance against pity . . .'

Leo Tolstoy, *Resurrection*

19

The Wood Pigeons and the Train

If we simplify so much when remembering our own pasts, then what does this tell us about the writing of history – our collective past? Not for the first time I wonder how we have been taught to see, or not to see; how we have been trained to look at only certain aspects of the past. I sense that so much of what we are taught to regard as 'significant' or 'central' is often no more than the accretions of hundreds of years of repetition, a million examination paper questions and answers. And conversely, many astonishing realities lie just out of sight, or sometimes surprisingly manage to sneak into our peripheral vision. For instance, many years ago now, this two-inch paragraph appeared before my eyes, buried at the bottom of page 17 of the *Observer* newspaper. One of those items considered of only limited importance, and covered in single paragraphs in the 'In Brief' section:

Europe's biggest insurance company, Allianz, insured SS companies and barracks in Auschwitz, Cracow and other concentration camps during the Second World War, according to documents found by the German news magazine *Der Spiegel*. It was one of a number of German insurance companies that profited from victims and perpetrators alike by earning money on the insurance of deported Jews and the policies for forced labour companies run by the SS.

'We certainly came seriously close to the Holocaust . . . however, the SS would also have been capable of continuing their criminal activities without Allianz,' admitted Herbert Hansmeyer, a board member.

Allianz insured SS weapons factories and prisoners' barracks, material stores and vehicles in the concentration camps from 1940 to 1945. Representatives regularly inspected the factory halls. Allianz is being sued in New York by nine Holocaust survivors who claim that it profited from Jewish life insurance policies during the war.

An incredible reality that I'd never even considered – Auschwitz and all the concentration camps had been insured! And the insurance company profited from both sides, having policies for both the SS and the Jews. Could there be a more vivid example of the 'banality of evil' than the knowledge that Allianz's 'representatives regularly inspected the factory halls' during the years of extermination? This knowledge makes me want to ask other questions about the realities of the past. About the staggering cynicism of corporations only interested in their financial return. And about the connection between the Allianz of today – the largest insurance company in the world, in fact the largest financial services corporation on the planet, with total assets (in 2017) of €901.3 billion – and the Allianz of 1943 – the company that insured the extermination camps.

Today if you stopped people in the street and asked them about Allianz, they might tell you that they are a major sponsor of Formula One motor racing, or that the Allianz Arena is home to German football's most famous club – Bayern Munich. They also sponsor golf, tennis and rugby across the world. If you look at their Wikipedia entry you'll find twenty-nine lines on the company's varied sponsorship activities, compared to just eighteen lines on Allianz's 'Nazi-era activities and litigation'. But even here you will struggle to find more than the sketchiest summary of what these 'activities' were – few facts about the collusion of Allianz and Nazism.

Kurt Schmitt, chief executive of Allianz, in black SS uniform, standing immediately behind Hitler, giving the Nazi salute, 1 May 1934.

The fact that Allianz's chief executive, Kurt Schmitt, had been an early supporter of the Nazis, attending the dinner for Hitler at Goering's Berlin villa* in February 1933 which raised over 2 million DM for the subsequent election campaign.

The fact that Schmitt, while continuing on Allianz's board of directors, also became Hitler's Reich economy minister on 29 June 1933, serving until January 1935.

The fact that Schmitt not only joined the Nazi Party but also became a member of the SS, and the '*Freundeskreis Reichsführer SS*', a group which donated around 1 million DM a year to Himmler.

---

* See Book One, Chapter Ten, 'The Invisible Corporation'.

The fact that Allianz's director general, Eduard Hilgard, was also head of the *Reichsgruppe Versicherung* (the Reich Association for Private Insurance), which worked to support the Nazi government and ensure that German insurance companies maximised profits between 1933 and 1945.

The fact that Hilgard, following Kristallnacht in November 1938, created a policy which blocked insurance payments to Jewish claimants for their destroyed property, and instead diverted these payments to the Nazi state responsible for the terror.

The fact that Allianz played a key role in financing the Nazi government, and used its position to become the leading insurer in all occupied countries.

The fact that Allianz insured not only the property, but also the personnel of Nazi concentration camps and extermination camps, including the IG Farben staff at Auschwitz, and those involved directly in the implementaion of the Holocaust. Allianz inspectors were fully aware of the operations carried out at the camps, and continued to take payments for insurance policies throughout the war years.

Where today are the profits gained from these policies? Are they in the fabric of the headquarters building at Fritz-Schäffer-Strasse

I always think it is interesting to consider how these companies present themselves in recent advertisements when compared to their historical record.

911

in Munich?* Or in the salaries paid to its senior executives? Or can we see the result of the financial bonanza of the 1930s and 40s in the fact that eighty years later the company is operating in over seventy countries in the world and has a current annual revenue of €126.1 billion? Remember those words of Balzac, 'The secret of great wealth is a forgotten crime.'

*

Allianz is only one example of a corporation which made significant profits during the Third Reich. A myriad of German companies, and some international ones too, also benefited greatly from the twelve years of Nazi government. Let's look for a moment at a single sector of the economy – that of banking and insurance. I recently learnt that Deutsche Bank, today one of the most powerful banks in Europe, established its position primarily in the twelve years of Nazism, when it quadrupled its wealth. Significant contributions to the bank's early success was capital created from Aryanisations and forced purchases of Jewish companies. Hitler's government built Auschwitz and IG Farben built the Buna plant

---

* An interesting choice of address for Allianz – in a street named after a Bavarian politician known for his antisemitic speeches in the 1920s.

at Monowitz with huge loans from Deutsche Bank. They were also the chosen bankers for the Gestapo. Yet how visible are these historical truths today?

And what about Deutsche Bank's 'sister' company, Dresdner Bank?* They too took a leading role in the Aryanisation of Jewish property and businesses. I learnt more from another (remarkably short) article in February 2006, this time buried deep within the *Financial Times*:

> Dresdner Bank controlled a company that built Nazi concentration camps, funded the SS and was intimately connected to the economic infrastructure of Hitler's Germany. Those are the broad conclusions of a 2,374 page analysis of Dresdner's Nazi past, commissioned by the German bank, which was released last week. Dresdner, now part of the Allianz insurance group, owned 26 per cent of Huta, the construction company that built parts of the Auschwitz camp. There were also close connections between Dresdner directors and IG Farben, the company that made the gas for Jewish extermination camps.
> Patrick Jenkins, Frankfurt

I am intrigued by that reference to 'a 2,374 page analysis' and what it tells us about visibility or invisibility. We have this vast analysis and yet the journalist, quite understandably, refers only to the 'broad conclusions' of the report. From the bank's perspective, the sheer length of such a publication goes a long way to ensuring it will hardly be read at all. Or only by a handful of historians. And yet they would be very keen that the fact there are 2,374 pages is reported, as this demonstrates how thoroughly the bank has 'come to terms with its difficult past'. They would also no doubt be delighted that reference to such a report is then buried in a couple of column inches deep inside the financial pages of the newspapers.

---

* In 2002 Dresdner Bank became a subsidiary of Allianz, and in May 2009 it was legally merged with Commerzbank, and ceased to trade as a separate entity.

The sheer scale of complicity of banking and insurance companies with Nazi Germany defies the imagination. Between 1997 and 2001 it emerged that companies throughout Europe were incriminated. At first the charges were laid against Deutsche Bank, Dresdner Bank and Commerzbank in Germany for their roles in the Holocaust – an $18 billion lawsuit was issued against Deutsche and Dresdner banks alone in July 1998. This lawsuit partly concerned the fact that both banks had bought huge quantities of gold from the Reichsbank during the war, some of which had come directly from the concentration camps and extermination camps – melted down often from the teeth of those murdered in the gas chambers, extracted by special squads of the *Sonderkommando* with pliers. A spokesman for the bank said that it 'deeply regrets any injustices' and that Deutsche Bank were in contact with the World Jewish Congress on this question.

And then the ripples spread wider. It soon became apparent that many of Europe's most well-known banks had also tried to profit from the Holocaust:

- The Swiss government and the two major Swiss banks UBS and Credit Suisse were forced to pay out $1.25 billion in 1998 in compensation for their roles in looting Jewish bank accounts and assets in the war.[*]
- Creditanstalt and its parent company Bank Austria were also both involved in the illegal sale of Jewish assets. Compensation of $40 million was agreed in 1999.
- Seven French banks were sued in 1998 for seizing the accounts of Jewish clients killed in the Holocaust, and subsequently not returning these assets to any surviving relatives. These banks were Banque Paribas, Crédit Lyonnais, Société Générale, Crédit Commercial de France, Crédit Agricole, Banque Française du Commerce Extérieur and Banque Nationale de Paris. In January 2001 these banks agreed to

---

[*] See Book One, Chapter Three.

pay an undisclosed 'substantial, multimillion-dollar sum' into a compensation fund for relatives of these victims.

- Barclays Bank also settled this case for compensation, as part of the above lawsuit, and agreed to pay $3.6 million to relatives of victims (whose accounts Barclays had appropriated in France) in December 1998.

Then, in 1999, attention switched to the international insurance industry, and all the companies in this sector which had profited from the Holocaust and not accepted their responsibility up to this point. The year before, in August, the International Commission on Holocaust-Era Insurance Claims (ICHEIC) had been established, a group comprising the six European insurance companies most heavily involved in compensation claims – Allianz from Germany, Generali of Italy, AXA of France and Winterthur and Zurich from Switzerland – Basler from Germany later withdrew from ICHEIC. These companies, together with the Claims Conference (co-ordinating ongoing German compensation for the Holocaust), the World Jewish Restitution Organisation and the Israeli government, formed the commission, which was chaired by former US Secretary of State Lawrence Eagleburger. Between 2000 and 2007 the insurance companies paid $550 million into the ICHEIC compensation fund, and $300.1 million was paid out in claims in the same period. This is the breakdown of payments into the fund by the culpable insurance companies across Europe:

- German Insurance Association: $350 million (comprising Allianz and sixty-nine smaller insurance companies)
- Generali: $100 million
- Winterthur and Zurich companies: $25 million
- Austrian General Settlement Fund: $25 million
- Others (including Dutch and Belgian companies): $50 million

There were only two other implicated insurance companies who refused to join the ICHEIC process – one of these was Munich Re and the other was the British insurer Prudential. Prudential had controlled 7 per cent of the Polish insurance market at the outbreak of war, and held $21 million of dormant policies from Jewish clients at the end of the war. Because of their failure to co-operate with ICHEIC, Eagleburger called on the 2001 proposed merger between Prudential and American General to be blocked, which it was, after an international boycott caused serious financial damage to the company. Elan Steinberg of the World Jewish Congress said that 'we consider Prudential's response not simply inadequate, but frankly insulting'.

The most remarkable aspect of all this is that it had taken fifty-five years from the end of the war for these financial corporations to be held accountable. It is striking that thousands of individual Nazis were tried in the immediate post-war period, yet it took more than half a century for companies who had not only co-operated with Nazism but actually contributed to the Holocaust, to face a legal reckoning. This raises critical questions about comparable justice, and why it is so much harder to bring corporate perpetrators to court, and their boards of directors, than individuals. I also found it telling that the overwhelming media focus was on the legal aspects of the compensation claims, the amounts of money involved and the impact on the banks and insurers – for instance, delays to potential mergers. In all the news coverage between 1998 and 2001 we gained very little insight into the methods by which these corporations colluded, the details of how they had co-operated with the Nazis, nor the human cost in terms of their victims.

Perhaps there is a truth, hard for us to look at, in those supposedly insignificant insurance clerks making their inspections at Auschwitz. If we can move beyond the repeated images, the visual clichés of history, we might be able to see the truth – 'somewhere as yet undiscovered', as Sebald puts it. We've been staring at the monstrous images of those railway lines curling under that sinis-

916

ter arch at Birkenau, and those foul words in iron over that gate at Auschwitz – 'Arbeit Macht Frei' – for so long. But if we could release ourselves for a moment from those known images we might find something else – terrifying, rarely glimpsed, but another reality: the totally amoral exterminism of the bureaucrat, the blind annihilating greed of a corporation. Maybe, if we look up from the pages of history books for a moment, we will be able to see more. A single page from the *Financial Times* might convey a darker truth. The bastions of German finance – Deutsche Bank, Dresdner Bank, Allianz – all together, still powerful at the beginning of our century – all of them critical pillars of support for Nazism:

- Dresdner Bank, the bank that pioneered Aryanisation.
- Deutsche Bank, the bank whose loans built extermination camps.
- Allianz, the company which insured those camps.

Today, two of these three companies – which Hitler and Himmler relied on so strongly – are still major global players, without ever having undergone a proper reckoning with their pasts.

*

At the opening of the Imperial War Museum's permanent Holocaust Exhibition in June 2000, walking into a small, square room I saw something I had never seen before. It wasn't the most dramatic of exhibits, there was nothing graphic or overtly shocking about what was on these two walls, yet, in my eyes, it was the most remarkable display in that exceptional exhibition. There were two walls of the most intricate diagrams and webs of interconnectivity, attempting to convey something hugely complex – how all the numerous state institutions and agencies of Nazi Germany interacted to organise the Holocaust. I could hear the spirit of Raul Hilberg, the greatest historian of the Shoah, cheering from the other side of the Atlantic, because this was one of the challenges he always set himself, and his readers – to look at the structures and the details of history, to reconstruct, painstakingly, the precise interrelationships between the agencies and institutions that enabled the extermination to happen. As human beings, we have a tendency to prioritise the stories of individuals over the narratives of systems. This is entirely understandable, as it is vastly easier to encompass the meaning of a single life than to try to comprehend how institutions, how whole systems work. Yet, by focussing mainly on the biographical, we blur the wider reality.

Being in that exhibition room made me think about how the Holocaust has been represented to us over the last seventy years or so – particularly in the balance beween focussing on individual lives, of the survivors and perpetrators, and focussing on the numerous institutions and agencies which enabled the extermination to take place.

The years immediately after the war were dominated by the Nuremberg Trials and accounts of some of the key protagonists on both sides, but perhaps the most significant single book (certainly in terms of impact) was the publication in the Netherlands in 1947 of *Het Achterhuis: Dagboekbrieven 14 Juni 1942 – 1 Augustus 1944* ('The Annex: Diary Notes 14 June 1942 – 1 August 1944'), which on its publication in English five years later immediately became a global phenomenon as *Anne Frank: The Diary of a Young Girl* – this teenage girl's testimony gave a human face to the enormity of the genocide for the first time. One Dutch historian remarked that 'this apparently inconsequential diary by a child . . . embodies all the hideousness of fascism, more so than all the evidence of Nuremberg put together'.

In 1953 a law was passed in the Israeli Knesset establishing Yad Vashem,[*] 'the Martyrs' and Heroes' Remembrance Authority', which would become the world's first designated museum and memorial to the Shoah (the Hebrew word for 'catastrophe', 'calamity'), as the Jewish genocide was then officially called. Two years before, the government in Israel had initiated the original Yom Hazikaron la

---

* Yad Vashem was built on Mount Herzl in west Jerusalem between 1954 and 1957, when it was opened to the public for the first time.

Shoah Ve-Mered Hagetaot ('Holocaust and Ghetto Revolt Memorial Day'), later shortened to Yom HaShoah – the national day of remembrance of the Shoah. 1953 was also the year that Gerard Reitlinger's *The Final Solution: The Attempt to Exterminate the Jews of Europe 1939–1945* was published – the most significant work on the extermination written since the end of the war. 1956 saw the release of Alan Resnais' groundbreaking film *Night and Fog*, which made a great impression on audiences around the world. The late 1950s witnessed two publications of survivors' testimonies, both of which were to become internationally known. In 1958, Elie Wiesel's *La Nuit* came out, and the English edition *Night* followed in 1960. However, it took years for this work to be recognised; by 1963 it had sold just 3,000 copies. A very different fate awaited a book by a Viennese psychiatrist, Viktor Frankl, originally published in German in 1946 as *Trotzdem Ja Zum Leben Sagen: Ein Psychologe erlebt das Konzentrationslager* ('Nevertheless, Say Yes to Life: A Psychologist Experiences a Concentration Camp'). When it was translated into English and published by Beacon Press in 1959, with the much snappier title *Man's Search for Meaning*, it rapidly became a global bestseller.

1960 was the year that William Shirer's *The Rise and Fall of the Third Reich* was published, selling 2 million copies in hardback and paperback in the US, and reaching an even wider audience through magazine serialisation and later television adaptation. It is interesting to note that Shirer (reflecting wider society at this time) did not use the term 'the Holocaust' in this book to refer to the extermination of the Jews – instead he used the phrase 'the final solution'. But it wasn't until Raul Hilberg's monumental opus *The Destruction of the European Jews* came out in 1961 that the world had a definitive work of history which attempted a truly systemic analysis of the genocide. Although this was hugely influential among historians, the detail and length of the book (in three volumes – totalling over 1,300 pages) militated against a mass audience.

However, the televising of Eichmann's trial in the same year, and Hannah Arendt's brilliant study of that event and its wider meaning

– *Eichmann in Jerusalem: A Report on the Banality of Evil* (1963) – brought knowledge of the genocide to a far wider audience. It also refocussed attention on the perpetrators, but unlike Nuremberg, which had put the infamous Nazi leaders in the spotlight, Eichmann's trial explored the lethality of what could be termed 'the cogs in the machine', the armies of lower-ranking functionaries, bureaucrats and planners, all needed to enable the 'final solution' to be carried out.

Concurrent with this trial, and directly influenced by it, Stanley Milgram began the famous experiments into ordinary people's obedience to authority, which gave a strong, contemporary resonance to the way that people judged the Holocaust and particularly its perpetrators – bureaucrats in suits and ties could murder as easily as SS men with skulls on their uniforms. 1961 should be seen as a watershed year in how our societies began to change in relationship to the question of the Holocaust, for, in addition to the above developments, it was also the year that the greatest of all survivors' accounts suddenly found a large readership. Just as Eichmann's trial began, Primo Levi's *If This Is a Man* was finally translated into German and French, and began to sell in great quantities – fifteen years after Levi had written it, and fourteen years after its publication (with a print run of only 2,500 copies) by the small Italian press De Silva, the failure of which had led Levi to turn his back on writing, and return to his life as an industrial chemist.

The early and mid-1960s saw an enormous upsurge of interest in what was increasingly becoming known as 'the Holocaust', witnessed by a renewed desire to bring perpetrators to justice – evidenced by a series of new trials in Germany, such as the Auschwitz trials in Frankfurt, which which took place between December 1963 and August 1965, and the first Treblinka trial in Düsseldorf between October 1964 and September 1965. Simon Wiesenthal had been working since the end of the war attempting to locate Nazi perpetrators and bring them to justice, and in 1961 he was able to establish the Documentation Centre of the Association of Jewish Victims of the Nazi Regime in Vienna, which gave him greater resources. In France, at the same time, Beate and Serge

Klarsfeld also began to campaign for Nazi and Vichy perpetrators to be brought to justice.

Albert Speer's release from Spandau prison in 1966 and the publication of his *Inside the Third Reich* in 1970 generated huge media coverage, and put the spotlight back on the Nazi leadership. A quieter, though equally significant, development of the 1960s was that this was the decade that survivors of the Holocaust began to find their voices. Or rather, as we've already seen in Primo Levi's case, these voices finally started to find publishers and a receptive audience – another example being Jean Améry's searing work *At the Mind's Limits: Contemplations by a Survivor on Auschwitz and Its Realities*, published in 1966. Yad Vashem had recorded only seventeen survivor memoirs published up until 1960; ten years later this figure had leapt to 267 published testimonies.

The 1960s and early 1970s were also the decades which saw a dramatic increase in both the quantity and quality of historians' analyses of the Holocaust; this was the era when notable works were published by Yehuda Bauer, Martin Broszat, Saul Friedländer, Hans Mommsen and Lucy Dawidowicz among others. It is also intriguing at this time to see a move towards more focussed studies on specific institutions in relation to the Holocaust – for instance, Friedländer publishing his work on the Catholic Church in the war years, *Pie XII et le IIIe Reich, Documents* in 1964, Mommsen writing about *The Civil Service in the Third Reich* in 1966, and Broszat and Helmut Krausnick writing a pioneering study of the SS – *Anatomy of the SS State* – in 1970. George Steiner also published two extraordinary and influential collections of essays around this time – *Language and Silence* (1967) and *In Bluebeard's Castle* (1971) – which looked at the wider cultural implications of the Holocaust, taking up Adorno's famous question of whether there could be poetry after Auschwitz.[*] By the late 1960s, 'the Holocaust' had begun to estab-

---

[*] This is often misquoted as 'No poetry after Auschwitz' – what Adorno actually wrote, in 1949, was '*nach Auschwitz ein Gedicht zu schreiben, ist barbarisch*' ('to write a poem after Auschwitz is barbaric').

lish itself as the most widely used term to refer to the genocide, as can be seen in the title of Nora Levin's book published in 1968 – *The Holocaust: The Destruction of European Jewry, 1933–1945* – and a *New York Times* article by Eliot Fremont-Smith from the same year called 'Books of the Times: Moral Trauma and the Holocaust'.

Over the last forty years there has been an exponential growth in the cultural visibility of the Holocaust, across all media – so much so, that to attempt to track the key works out of thousands of books and articles and films is almost impossible.* But one striking development over the last decades has been the way that representations through television and film have brought it into the cultural mainstream, in a way that simply wasn't the case in the 1950s and 60s – a transition that has taken us from the pages of history books to the local multiplex. And though many were, rightly, critical of the historical inaccuracies of the 1978 TV series *Holocaust* starring Meryl Streep, the impact of such a series – especially in America and Germany – was considerable. In a similar way, with all its limitations the film of *Schindler's List* fifteen years later also brought a younger, mass audience to the subject for the first time. And for anyone who felt film treatments of the subject were inherently problematic, in 1985 Claude Lanzmann's monumental *Shoah* was released, bringing together interviews with survivors, perpetrators and witnesses in a way that had never been done before, and has never been done since.

The 1990s and 2000s witnessed what could be called the 'institutionalising' of the Holocaust, particularly through education programmes and memorialisation. In 1994, the Shoah Foundation was established by Steven Spielberg to document all possible survivor testimony on film before it was too late – 52,000 video testimonies with survivors were recorded between 1994 and 1999. The vast growth in interest of the previous decades became formalised through the establishment of many new museums focussing on the Holocaust throughout the world, the following list of which are just a sample of the most significant:

---

* Nevertheless I have attempted a (very subjective) summary of key Holocaust works in this period – see the chapter notes.

1992: the Sydney Jewish Museum opens in Australia

1993: Yad Vashem establishes its International School for Holocaust Studies

1993: the United States Holocuast Memorial Museum opens in Washington, DC

1996: the Jewish Museum of Deportation and Resistance opens in Mechelen, Belgium (later renamed the Kazerne Dossin)

1999: the Cape Town Holocaust Centre opens in South Africa

2000: the Imperial War Museum opens its permanent Holocaust Exhibition in London

2000: the Judenplatz Holocaust Memorial (the powerful work *Nameless Library* designed by Rachel Whiteread) is unveiled in Vienna

2001: the Jewish Museum in Berlin (strikingly conceived and designed by Daniel Libeskind) is inaugurated

2004: the Holocaust Memorial Centre opens in Budapest, Hungary

2005: the Memorial to the Murdered Jews of Europe, on a four-and-a-half-acre site in the heart of Berlin, opens to the public; the Memorial de la Shoah opens in Paris

2006: the University of Southern California is the new host of the Shoah Foundation Institute for Visual History and Education

2012: the Memorial at Drancy is opened in Paris

2013: the Museum of the History of Polish Jews opens in Warsaw

A similar process can be seen in academic studies. In addition to the educational courses and research established by Yad Vashem and the US Holocaust Memorial Musuem, Professor Martin Gilbert began a groundbreaking MA in Holocaust Studies at University College London in 2000. And important other initiatives were established – the Polish Centre for Holocaust Research in 2003, in Warsaw, and the Vienna Wiesenthal Institute for Holocaust Studies in Austria, in 2009. Many universities now offer degrees and postgraduate degrees, and schools around the world have made the Holocaust a central component of history curricula.

And as the twentieth century ended, calls for 'Holocaust Memorial Days' were widely accepted, with many countries adopting 27 January – the day Auschwitz was liberated by the Soviet army – as the day of remembrance; Britain marking its first Holocaust Memorial Day in 2001. For survivors who had lived through the late 1940s and 50s feeling as if the world had forgotten their appalling suffering, it must have been bizarre, to say the least, to watch presidents and prime ministers now queuing up to pay their respects. And for some, this new era of mass interest in the Holocaust was too much. In 2000 Norman Finkelstein published his critique, attacking what he called *The Holocaust Industry*, the way in which the American Jewish establishment and others had, in his view, exploited the suffering of Holocaust victims for political and financial ends – particularly an unconditional support for the state of Israel, regardless of its dubious human rights record.

But the aspect of 1990s historiography that was most fascinating from my perspective was the growing interest in the role of corporations in the Holocaust. Up until this decade, any focus on this aspect had predominantly looked at German manufacturing and chemical corporations, notably IG Farben, Degussa, Volkswagen, Daimler-Benz, BMW, Siemens, Krupp, Thyssen – all known as users of slave labour in the war years. But now three new developments occurred.

Firstly, as the slave labourers who'd survived the war years reached old age, their understandable indignation at never having received proper compensation from these pillars of German industry increased. Demands for reparation grew, aided by detailed new historical studies – for instance, Peter Hayes' authoritative work, *Industry and Ideology: IG Farben in the Nazi Era* (1987), Hans Mommsen and Manfred Grieger's *Volkswagen and Its Workers During the Third Reich* (1996) and Neil Gregor's *Daimler-Benz in the Third Reich* (1998). As a result of this growing groundswell of pressure, in 2000 the German government and German industry established a 10 billion DM fund, 'Remembrance, Responsibility and the Future', to compensate former slave labourers.

Secondly, in the wake of the German state and industries starting to accept their responsibility, more information emerged in the late 1990s about the role of German banks and insurers in the pillaging of Jewish assets (as we've seen earlier in this chapter), and so the focus shifted from the victims of slave labour (heavy industry – construction, steel, armaments, vehicles, etc.) to the victims of service industries (the financial sector, banking and insurance). From the brutality of slave labour to the lethality of paper.

And finally, we see a growing understanding of the part that international corporations played in the Holocaust – the significant responsibility of Swiss banks, the role of Austrian, Italian and French banks and insurers, and then, in 1998, the news emerged that Ford were going to be prosecuted for the fact that its subsidiary factory in Cologne had manufactured trucks for the Nazi war effort, and profited from the use of slave labour.

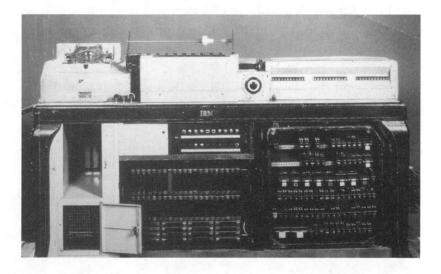

In 2001 Edwin Black published his explosive work *IBM and the Holocaust: The Strategic Alliance between Nazi Germany and America's Most Powerful Corporation*, which showed that IBM's Hollerith machine, created by their German subsidiary company Dehomag, had played a central role in Nazi Germany's ability to gather information on

Jews, Roma, Sinti and political opponents – information-gathering which had directly aided the organisation of the Holocaust, as we've seen in looking at the Wannsee Conference. On a more personal level, IBM's president, Thomas Watson, admired Hitler and fascist Germany greatly, writing of his 'highest esteem' for the Führer. And the sentiments were reciprocated by Hitler, when they met in Berlin in 1937 on the occasion of Watson being awarded the Order of the German Eagle in recognition of the company's exceptional service to Nazi Germany.

The publication of Black's book in 2001 played a contributory role in two legal actions against IBM, in 2001 and 2004, and an eventual payment of $3 million by IBM's German division into a German fund for Holocaust survivors.

*

Why had it taken more than fifty years for such a work to emerge? To get from *The Diary of Anne Frank* to *IBM and the Holocaust*? To move from focussing on individual perpetrators like Himmler to judging the responsibility of entire sectors of business such as banking? Much can be explained by the human tendency to see events through the prism of a person's life. But perhaps there is also something in the scale of research needed when looking into entire corporations, whole sectors of industry, which defeats not only our imaginations, but our best intentions and efforts.

Let's return to the questions raised by that little room in the Imperial War Museum's Holocaust exhibition. I know we are still not yet able to understand the totality of how the Holocaust happened. I'm not even sure if we are yet able to formulate the right questions about the labyrinthine interrelations between the German state and industry, between all the different sectors of that society. Reading Raul Hilberg's *Perpetrators, Victims, Bystanders*, published in 1992, I sense that he also shared this frustration, and that he didn't feel that the strong foundations he had laid in *The Destruction of the European Jews* thirty years before had really been built upon in a substantive way.

I can still remember reading *Perpetrators, Victims, Bystanders* in the Wiener Library and coming across Hilberg's challenge to all of us, to think more systemically about the Holocaust. He emphasises that 'all components of German organised life were drawn into this undertaking. Every agency was a contributor; every specialisation was utilised; and every stratum of society was represented in the envelopment of the victims.' Then, over several pages, he lists all the institutions of government, Civil Service, business, the military and the judiciary that were necessary to co-ordinate the Holocaust:

Reich Chancellery: Co-ordination of laws and decrees

Interior Ministry: Definition of the term 'Jew'; prohibition of mixed marriages; decrees for compulsory names; dismissals from the Civil Service; deprivation of property

Churches: Supply of proof of non-Jewish descent

Justice Ministry: Elimination of Jewish lawyers; inheritance questions; divorce questions; regulation of names of enterprises

Party Boycott Committee: Boycott of Jewish enterprises

Party Chancellery: Participation of decisions involving the status of Jews

Reich Chamber of Culture: Dismissals of musicians, artists and journalists and barring of writers

Education Ministry: Elimination of Jewish students, professors and researchers

Propaganda Ministry: Suggestions to the press

Economics Ministry: Regulation for the acquisition of Jewish firms

Dresdner Bank and Other Banking Concerns: Intermediaries in takeovers of Jewish firms

Various Firms in Retailing, Wholesaling, Manufacturing, and Construction: Acquisitions of Jewish firms; dismissals of Jewish employees; utilisation of Jewish forced labour in cities, ghettoes and camps; contracting for measures of destruction such as supply of poison gas

Finance Ministry: Discriminatory taxes; blocked funds; confiscation of personal belongings; special budgetary allocations, such as clearing Warsaw Ghetto ruins

Foreign Office: Negotiations for deportations of Jews in foreign countries and of foreign Jews in the Reich

Transport Ministry: Transports to ghettoes and camps; utilisation of forced Jewish labour; acquisitions of Jewish personal property

Armed Forces: Logistic support of killing operations in the occupied USSR; direct killings in Serbia and the occupied USSR; ghettoisation in the occupied USSR; discriminatory measures and deportations from France, Belgium, and Greece; regulation of forced Jewish labour in armament plants; employment of forced Jewish labour by army offices; transport questions

Municipal Authorities in the Greater German Reich: Movement and housing restrictions

Protektorat Administration in Bohemia and Moravia: Anti-Jewish measures patterned on those of the Reich

General Government in Occupied Central Poland: Confiscations; ghettoisation; forced labour; starvation measures; preparations for deportations

Ministry for Eastern Occupied Territories: Anti-Jewish measures patterned on those of the Reich

Reichskommissariat of the Netherlands: Anti-Jewish measures patterned on those of the Reich

Führer Chancellery: Staffing of the Belzec, Sobibor and Treblinka death camps

Reich Security Main Office: Marking of Jews in the Reich; supervision of the Jewish communities; in the Reich and Protektorat; *Einsatzgruppen* killings in the occupied USSR; preparations of European-wide deportations

Main Office Order Police: Guarding of ghettoes, trains and camps; participation in round-ups and shootings

Economic-Administrative Main Office: Administration of Auschwitz and Majdanek (Lublin)

Higher SS and Police Leaders in Occupied Poland: Deportations to death camps; administration of the Chelmno (Kulmhof), Belzec, Sobibor, and Treblinka death camps

Higher SS and Police Leaders in Occupied USSR: Shootings

All of these agencies combined to create the most systematic and industrialised act of mass murder ever carried out; each of these organisations' contributions were essential to the process; hundreds of thousands of men and women, from Germany and occupied countries, took part in this process. Simply by reading this list, you will understand the absurdity of any suggestion that the organisation of the Holocaust was only known about by a centralised cadre

929

of senior Nazi officials. But Hilberg's wider intent here is for us to begin to think about how all of these agencies worked together, how their decisions interlinked. In fact, the challenge has become even more complex since Hilberg published this list in 1992, because, as we've just seen, the 1990s and early 2000s unearthed numerous levels of corporate complicity in the Holocaust, not known before. So, how are we to go about this challenge – of trying to understand the Holocaust in its systemic entirety?

*

There have been moments in researching and writing this work when I've been overwhelmed by the impossibility of this task. When I've sensed that to cover even a small proportion of the activities of a corporation like IG Farben would require an army of researchers. Or to understand, in its totality, the workings of a single company like Shell today would need years of additional work. There have been times when the sheer volume of available material becomes absurd, even paralysing. Last summer, when I returned from investigating the Auschwitz archives, my single (part-time) research assistant called me to the Wiener Library, having located the transcripts of the IG Farben trial which took place in Nuremberg from 1947 to 1948. At least he thought they were the transcripts – there were two volumes, each of around 800 pages, printed on thin paper in discouragingly small print. But, examining these further, it soon became apparent that these were merely selected extracts from the trial. The full transcripts ran to some 12,000 pages and were only available on microfiche at the Public Records Office in Kew. Just to deal fully with this single strand of research, and all the associated lanes and avenues that the court transcripts would then lead you down – only one of maybe forty or fifty extremely important strands of research into corporations and the Holocaust – would take perhaps six months of full-time study. I left the Wiener Library that afternoon with my head spinning. If I had half a dozen researchers for a year! . . . or maybe I could do it with five? But who would ever be able to fund such a level of enquiry?

However, it is not only a question of volume of material. I sometimes doubt whether our brains are wired to be able to grapple with the real meaning of power, the abstractions of vast economic and political forces. We may rationally be able to take in information, but can we actually understand the meaning and the wider implications of that information? As an example, in 2017 the NGO Global Justice Now published this information about the top hundred economies in the world, noting that sixty-nine of these – shown in capital letters in the table – weren't countries, but corporations:

Top 100 Countries/CORPORATIONS

	Country/CORPORATION	Revenue US$bn			Country/CORPORATION	Revenue US$bn
1	United States	3,336		51	I & C BANK OF CHINA	153
2	China	2,591		52	AXA	149
3	Japan	1,678		53	TOTAL	149
4	Germany	1,598		54	PING AN INSURANCE	145
5	France	1,446		55	HONDA MOTOR	139
6	United Kingdom	984		56	CHINA CONSTRUCTION BANK	139
7	Italy	884		57	TRAFIGURA GROUP	136
8	Brazil	819		58	CHEVRON	135
9	Canada	624		59	CARDINAL HEALTH	130
10	WALMART	500		60	COSTCO	129
11	Spain	492		61	SAIC MOTOR	129
12	Australia	461		62	VERIZON	126
13	STATE GRID	349		63	ALLIANZ	124
14	Netherlands	345		64	Argentina	123
15	SINOPEC GROUP	327		65	KROGER	123
16	CHINA NATIONAL PETROLEUM	326		66	AGRICULTURAL BANK OF CHINA	122
17	South Korea	318		67	GENERAL ELECTRIC	122
18	ROYAL DUTCH SHELL	312		68	CHINA LIFE INSURANCE	120
19	Mexico	293		69	WALGREENS BOOTS ALLIANCE	118
20	Sweden	275		70	BNP PARIBAS	117
21	TOYOTA MOTOR	265		71	JAPAN POST HOLDINGS	117
22	VOLKSWAGEN	260		72	BANK OF CHINA	115
23	Russia	254		73	JP MORGAN CHASE & CO.	114
24	Belgium	250		74	FANNIE MAE	112
25	BP	245		75	GAZPROM	112
26	EXXON MOBIL	244		76	PRUDENTIAL	111
27	BERKSHIRE HATHAWAY	242		77	BMW GROUP	111
28	India	229		78	ALPHABET	111
29	APPLE	229		79	CHINA MOBILE COMMUNICATIONS	110
30	Switzerland	224		80	NISSAN MOTOR	108
31	Norway	214		81	NIPPON TELEGRAPH & TELEPHONE	107
32	SAMSUNG ELECTRONICS	212		82	CHINA RAILWAY ENGINEERING	103
33	McKESSON	208		83	HOME DEPOT	101
34	GLENCORE	205		84	CHINA RAILWAY CONSTRUCTION	101
35	UNITED HEALTH GROUP	201		85	ASSICURAZIONI GENERALI	101
36	Austria	195		86	BANK OF AMERICA	100
37	Saudi Arabia	186		87	EXPRESS SCRIPTS HOLDING	100
38	DAIMLER	185		88	WELLS FARGO	98
39	CVS HEALTH	184		89	Greece	95
40	AMAZON.COM	178		90	LUKOIL	94
41	Turkey	174		91	BOEING	93
42	Indonesia	174		92	DONGFENG MOTOR	93
43	Denmark	173		93	Taiwan	93
44	EXOR GROUP	162		94	Portugal	93
45	AT&T	161		95	Israel	92
46	GENERAL MOTORS	157		96	South Africa	92
47	FORD	157		97	SIEMENS	92
48	CHINA STATE CONSTRUCTION	156		98	PHILLIPS 66	92
49	HON HAI PRECISION INDUSTRY	155		99	CARREFOUR	91
50	AMERISOURCE-BERGEN	153		100	NESTLE	91

We may, rationally, be able to accept that Shell has a larger revenue base than the state of Mexico, or that Volkswagen's income is greater than India's, or that BP's annual financial revenue exceeds that of Russia – but can we understand the political meaning represented by these figures? Our societies still talk in terms of 'democracies' and 'elections' as if these are where power is located, yet for the last decades power has moved inexorably away from nation states to the free market rampant – from governments and politicians to armies of totally unelected, and unaccountable, men and women. And how many of us could state, with any certainty, that we know the precise place where the nation state ends and the corporation begins? In a 'public private partnership', for example? Or even a transcontinental oil pipeline? The corporations' power and the national governments' power become entirely blurred. Corporations may talk about autonomy and independence from governments, yet, when they fail, they expect to be rescued, just as the banks were in 2008. How they elude the grasp of responsibility. How they bleed almost invisibly into the fabric of our societies. Can we see the wood for the trees?

*

I was turning such thoughts over and over in my mind yesterday morning when I heard the post arrive – a letter from J. on my doormat. A rarity these days to receive a handwritten letter from a friend. I take it out into the garden with my coffee. I read that his father's been ill, and J. regrets the fact they never went on the walk through the Peloponnese that they'd often talked about doing, and now it's too late. Then J. goes on to describe the Kent marshes, close to where he lives, and how glorious they are at this time of year, with the spring just taking hold. He writes that he's been observing wood pigeons near the local railway, and, in particular, this curious display of behaviour:

Watching two wood pigeons courting (or are they disputing territory?). In full spring plumage – rich grey on the back of their necks, pinky white under the tail feathers, precise white bars on the nape. They work their way back and forth along the blue, iron rail at the top of the footbridge over the railway line. Back and forth – silhouetted against a bright blue sky like two people doing a tug-of-war or two men fencing . . . At one point one of them tips right down, bill almost to the ground, tail thrust up high in the air, accompanied by a deep growling coo. At regular junctures they flap up, cross over, swap places and land again. One always looking away from me, the other always facing towards me. The fact that they swap places suggests that they're courting. Far off I hear the train's horn blow. Will they fly off as the train arrives I wonder? Intriguingly when the train passes right under them and comes to a halt, they take no notice and carry on engrossed in their ritual. However, when a young man climbs the footbridge stairs and begins to cross the bridge, they suddenly fly off and away.

Perhaps the train was too large for them to 'see' as a threat at all? Whereas the man is recognisable. Just as the Aboriginals couldn't 'see' Captain Cook's ship when it arrived in what was to become Botany Bay. Too big a threat to 'see'.

I put the letter down, and look out over the garden. Could that be the answer? *'Too big to see'*? Is it possible that transnational corporations are simply too vast to perceive? That we glimpse the man, but cannot see the train? And, in a similar way, could this be why the Holocaust still defies our imaginations? Why the totality of this event has eluded the grasp of even the greatest historians over the last seventy years?

PART EIGHT

Opening the Prisons in Our Minds

20

The Architect in Prison – a Different Man?

Albert Speer arrived at Spandau prison, together with Hess, Dönitz, Raeder, Schirach, Funk and Neurath, on 18 July 1947 after a flight from Nuremberg that must have seemed like a dream after almost two years of confinement in the courthouse there. He describes it like this:

> Villages and small towns lay peacefully beneath us, seemingly intact. The fields were planted, and the forests, in spite of all the rumours, had not been cut down. Because life had stood still around me during the recent past, I had lost awareness of the fact that it was going on outside. A moving train, a tugboat on the Elbe, a smoking factory chimney gave me little thrills. We circled for perhaps half an hour over the buildings and ruins of Berlin . . . I was able to make out the East–West Axis, which I had completed for Hitler's fiftieth birthday . . . and . . . the Chancellery I had designed. It was still there, although damaged by several direct hits . . . The Grunewald and the Havel lakes were untouched and beautiful as ever.

Inside the prison, on the western fringes of the city, the seven men are brought down to earth. They are given inmates' clothing from Nazi concentration camps and Speer becomes 'Prisoner Number Five'. After an initial sense of relief to be away from Nuremberg and the oppressive associations, he is assailed by depression in these first weeks, as the reality of the next twenty years in this place begins to sink in.

Three months later, on Saturday 11 October, Speer meets this man for the first time – Pastor Georges Casalis:

Vigorously intellectual, left-wing, generous, pipe-smoking, Casalis had enormous doubts about whether to accept the posting to Spandau. As well as his religious background, he'd spent four years active in the French Resistance, and realised that the work at Spandau would entail helping men 'who were at the very least responsible for the death of an untold number of my very special friends, the friends of my war. They had not only died, many of them had been betrayed, tortured, put to death in unspeakable pain.' Only after discussing the matter for a long time with his wife Dorothée, and also with his mentor, the great Swiss theologian Karl Barth, was he persuaded to accept the job.

At the initial religious service, by candlelight, organised in a larger prison cell, Speer tells us that Casalis on that first day takes as the subject for his sermon 'The lepers of Israel were cut off from the community of the people by a host of legal prohibitions; these were as insurmountable as a prison wall.' Some of Speer's fellow prisoners are outraged by the implied comparison, but Speer disagrees, accepting Casalis' words as a challenge. He later tells him: 'don't spare our feelings, don't [be] careful or protective of us. You are exactly on course, exactly what is needed.'

Speer knows immediately he will be challenged by Casalis, because after the service he tells Speer that he holds him more responsible, more blameworthy than all of the other prisoners, because he was the most intelligent. He had been responsible for extending a war in which millions had died, including many of Casalis' own friends. Speer thanks him for his honesty, and then tells him he has a question to ask, which, given his usual emotional reserve, seems quite exceptional:

> I'll be as honest in return . . . I've been sentenced to twenty years, and I consider it just. I want to use this time that has . . . been given to me. What I want to ask you is: 'Would you help me become a different man?'*

---

* The actual phrase in German which Speer used was 'anderer Mensch', which carries a deeper meaning than 'different man'. Dorothée Casalis explained that Georges felt Speer's question implied a kind of rebirth.

Casalis, speaking years later, said that Speer was at this time, 'under the extraordinary cool he affected, the most guilt-ridden, the most tortured man I had ever known'. And, of course, to a religious man there must have been a significant challenge in that reality. Casalis agrees to help Speer, and, over the next three years, they work together in a way that is perhaps difficult for us to understand today. He later uses a strange, and remarkable, phrase to describe the process he encouraged Speer to go through – it had been 'a continuity of reflection, of studying, of opening his mind and spirit to suffering'.

Beyond all the public position-taking, beyond all the vanities of leadership, beyond self-justifications, beyond the ego. Stripping back to the essence of the human being. A man alone. Fear, doubt, suffering. Casalis was asking Speer to make Lear's journey to the heath, but in a totally intentional way; and in stripping away all the rank, the pomp, the arrogance of power, to try to connect with his own self, and most importantly, to connect to others who had suffered – 'to expose thyself to feel what wretches feel' – 'poor naked wretches . . . that bide the pelting of this pitiless storm'. And, remarkably, for the first time in his life Speer begins to open as a person. A tree now transplanted to different soil, tentatively beginning to grow towards the light. There is the quality of a miracle in this process; as Speer later says to his daughter Hilde, arguing about whether God can ever be approached with rationality: 'How do you explain . . . the fern I planted by mistake upside-down? It turned itself round, to grow straight up, bypassing its own root. I know you can find reasons: the nature of growth . . . whatever. Of course one can always say so, but if you are honest you have to admit that these are miracles, which become more mysterious the more you ponder them.'

Casalis first of all emphasises that he wants Speer to 'expand his thinking into realms he had not yet entered'; he tells him he needs to read Karl Barth's *Kirchliche Dogmatik* ('Church Dogmatics'). The next week he starts on this work – 9,000 pages, thirty-seven volumes. He reads it in its entirety over the next months, then discusses the thoughts and questions that come out of it in detail with Casalis at their weekly meetings. Speer has never experienced anything like this – deeply intellectual enquiry on an ongoing basis. The process of continually looking inwards, reflecting, questioning, doubting, challenging – the polar opposite of the blind faith that fascism had demanded. As Speer begins to trust this process more and more, Casalis sees significant changes take place in Speer as he learns 'to use spoken language to search for inner meanings and thereby let go some of the iron self-control imposed upon him, by himself, as well as others, since early childhood'. This process led him 'to discover hitherto unsuspected imaginative freedoms'.

We can glimpse aspects of these moral and emotional shifts in Speer's own words from *Spandau: The Secret Diaries* during the years Casalis is chaplain at the prison (1947–50). To put these into context, we need to remember Speer (at least up until this time) regarded himself as intensely reserved, often completely unable to connect with people on an emotional level. Those who worked with him during the war and before also remember a man known for his 'personal detachment'; 'he didn't see when people were troubled . . . I think he would have been glad to have this capacity to see . . . but he didn't have [it] . . . He was the world's most inhibited man' – the judgement of somebody who knew him better than almost anybody else: Annemarie Kempf, his private secretary. She relates Speer one day marvelling at Hitler's ability to be 'amazingly personal' – people sitting next to him would come away feeling he had really wanted to know about them. '"I'm really not good at that, am I?" he said, and I said, "No, you aren't."'

But, within weeks of Casalis' arrival, Speer writes of a new meditation exercise he's attempting:

> Lying in the dark I try to enter into the closest possible contact with my family and my friends by imagining each of them in detail: their walks, their voices, the characteristic movements of their hands, the way they tilt their heads when reading. I am afraid that otherwise they will slip away from me. I also

imagine that perhaps I can establish a kind of telepathic connection with them by this means. Moreover there must be people who think of me with pity or sympathy, though I do not even know them. Night after night therefore, I concentrate on one of these . . . thinking of an individual, trying to say a few words to a particular person . . . [this] invariably ends with my feeling a strong craving for a better world. Then time stretches out immeasurably. Frequently I fall asleep without having come to an end. But almost always I achieve a state of inner harmony that is akin to a trance.

An astonishing act of emotional and spiritual imagination for this man, who had said: 'I loathe peddling my feelings – they belong to one's inner self.' Yet here he is journeying into new territories, guided by Casalis.

For most of his adult life Speer had had little time (literally and figuratively) for reading fiction – the ultimate empathetic experience which cannot work unless you put yourself in another's shoes. Yet soon he's deep into *A Farewell to Arms* and revelling in it: 'something new, strange and fascinating to me. I know nothing like it.' Encouraged by Casalis, he immerses himself in wider reading – not just fiction (Zola, Dostoevsky, Tolstoy), but theology, philosophy, drama, history, psychology and even poetry. Gradually Speer grows to love books, as he reveals:

By now what has become most important to me is the world of books. Machiavelli in exile, shunned by friends, literally invited his books to be his guests. He dressed ceremonially for his evening intercourse with them, lit candles. I cannot do that obviously. But when the bolt at the cell door is slid shut at six o'clock in the evening, I am content. I know that for four hours I can remain alone with my books.

At their weekly discussions, Casalis repeatedly emphasises three things: the need to go beyond the world of facts, superficial intelligence and logic; the way that reading deeply and writing can lead to reflective breakthroughs (or 'grace', as it might be termed); and, through these approaches, Speer may then come to a real, inner, understanding of his guilt. Casalis could see that Speer had exceptional abilities, but he was also perceptive enough to see that it was precisely these abilities that were the obstacle to his real moral and intellectual development – because often this meant he was happy to stay within the areas he felt confident in (analytical thought, logic, systems). 'His thinking – as well as I fear, his actions – had become facile. What he needed to do . . . to become the "different man" he wanted to be, was to give up everything that was easy. For Speer, who I suspect was the most determined of men at whatever he undertook, the quasi-monastic life of Spandau was ideally suited for such an endeavour.'

Prompted by this impulse to go beyond his world of architecture and mathematics and problem-solving, in early 1948 Speer begins to think about writing seriously for the first time – 'liberation by writing things down', as he notes in the *Diaries* (a phrase that could have come straight from Casalis' mouth); the seeds are sown for the work that eventually evolves into *Inside the Third Reich*. He's daunted by the task, doubts whether he has the abilities to write such a work, wonders whether his memory is good enough or if he's 'seeing the past as if it were already behind a veil'. But finally he realises he is the only person left who was close to Hitler, who can write with authority about those catastrophic years.

Religious faith remains an enigma for Speer. We learn that Casalis has given him Barth's *Epistle to the Romans*, which he finds extremely difficult:

> As I understand him, the Christian commandments represent virtually infinite values, which even a saint can only approximate . . . every human being inevitably sins. I must confess that for pages at a time I could scarcely grasp Barth's thought. After the services today I said to Casalis that faith seems to me like a tremendous mountain range. Tempting from a distance, when you try to climb it you run into ravines, perpendicular

walls, and stretches of glacier. Most climbers are forced to turn back; some plunge to destruction; but almost nobody reaches the peak. Yet the world from on top must offer a wonderfully novel and clear view.

Towards the end of 1949 we can see a further development in Speer – a growing desire to look inside himself, even at a subconscious level – something the Speer of the earlier years would have scorned. Casalis encourages him to write down his dreams:

> Dream in the afternoon: my wife and I are quarrelling. Angrily, she walks some distance away from me in the garden. I follow her. Suddenly only her eyes are there. They are full of tears. Then I hear her voice saying she loves me. I look steadily into her eyes; then I embrace her firmly. I wake up and realise that I have wept for the first time since my father's death.

Some days later, in November 1949, we see a concerted period of inner reflection. Speer thinks about the deeper reasons for his reserved attitude towards others, and considers his associate's remark years before that he was 'Hitler's unrequited love'. He remembers his aloofness, his shyness with Hitler, and then in a startlingly honest admission says that 'Probably I would have liked to show Hitler my total veneration; but I was never able to express feelings freely. I could not even in this case, although quite often it seemed to me that he stood high above all the people I knew, probably even above my father, whom I truly revered.' We learn (improbably) that he's been reading Oscar Wilde's *The Picture of Dorian Gray*, and this again triggers a way of reassessing his relationship with Hitler; he quotes pointedly from the book: 'To influence a person is to give him one's own soul. He does not think his natural thoughts or burn with his natural passions. His virtues are not real to him. His sins, if there are such things as sins, are borrowed.'

But almost immediately Speer can see that this is too easy an excuse. And then makes an astute parallel with Gray: 'the dandy reserved his good looks by the portrait's taking over all the ugly features. Suppose I am now transferring all my moral ugliness to my autobiographical likeness? Would that be a way to escape alive?' Two days later, on 22 November, he is still wrestling with himself, and particularly the question of to what extent Hitler seduced him into architectural grandiosity or whether this urge was always there within him. And then in a passage that would have delighted Casalis (had he been able to read it at the time), Speer says this:

> Without the experiences and insights I acquired as a result of those years with him [Hitler], would I ever have learned that all historical grandeur means less than a modest gesture of humaneness; that all the national honour of which we dreamed is insignificant compared to simple readiness to help others? *How strangely I find my viewpoints shifting* [my emphasis].

And, throughout all of this time, in their conversations Casalis and Speer repeatedly returned to the questions of guilt and responsibility, and wider ethical issues, growing in Speer ever since his knowledge of Himmler's speech in Posen,* which had increased intensely through the process of the Nuremberg Trial and the documentary evidence shown and the testimony of Holocaust survivors. Casalis describes Speer's 'inner torture' in this regard:

> During those years, his reading, his studies, his thoughts originated in and were dominated by his very profound sense of guilt which was entirely centred on the murder of the Jews – to such a degree, indeed, that he seemed oblivious to Hitler's many other crimes.

But getting Speer to articulate the precise nature of his guilt was always going to be more difficult. At Nuremberg he'd accepted a form of collective responsibility for the crimes of Nazism, but he'd been extremely careful to avoid the word 'guilt' (which entails

---

* We will return to this defining moment in Book Four, 'The Architect in London: Last Trip'.

knowledge). Even with Casalis, whom he came to trust greatly, he found it hard to express more than a generalised sense of guilt. Through all the discussions with Casalis he evolved what could be seen as a nuanced ethical position – a position which meant he could, just about, live with himself. And Casalis, though I'm sure harbouring doubts about the abstract nature of such expressed guilt, did not see it as his role to push further – as he said:

> Of course when we talked, there were untold questions I wanted to ask him, but I couldn't; contrary to historians or psychiatrists, a pastor's task is not to probe or to interrogate men, but to help them live. A pastor cannot request self-revelation; he can only, if it occurs by the other's initiative, accept and respond to it.

Years later, Dorothée explained more about her husband's nuanced attitude towards Speer, and the guilt he carried inside – which Casalis described as being 'so enormous that it was unmanageable' when they first met at Spandau:

> Georges said that if Speer had admitted all he had known it would have killed him. And Georges would say: 'He lied to me about facts, that's clear – and I didn't always notice – or only afterwards. But he never lied to me about himself, his inner life and his progress and his questioning. Because he probably thought that I could help him go forward.'

The position Speer eventually adopted in relation to his own guilt, through all the discussions with Casalis, can best be understood in the letter he wrote to his daughter Hilde in May 1953 which we encountered at the end of Chapter Ten. When I first read this, I found Speer's apparent acceptance of guilt very persuasive. However, having learnt more about Speer now, when I reread his words they become more morally evasive. By *seeming* to accept a greater responsibility, isn't he, in reality, distancing himself from the tangible guilt of knowledge?

To reassure you however, of the dreadful things, I knew nothing ... Even so ... I ask myself what, given my lofty position, I could have found out had I wanted to . . . perhaps not everything, but certainly a great deal ... I saw my fate, if you like as God's judgement – not for having infringed any laws (for my transgressions in that sense were comparatively minimal) but for the deeper guilt of having so readily and unthinkingly gone along.

Speer also wrote to Hilde, emphasising (in a way completely traceable to Casalis' influence) the distinction between knowledge and feeling:

I have read and thought so much by now, and I suppose the *knowledge* I gain will remain with me later. I only hope though that I won't lose the *feeling* of faith once I'm back in ordinary life . . . As you see, it is ethics which particularly interest me . . . I read again and again what Jaspers said: 'Evil will rule unless I confront it at all times in myself and others.'

This, more metaphysical, question – of the nature of evil – was one that Speer wrestled with repeatedly in these years, and, perhaps unsurprisingly, never resolved. After all, it's an issue that has defeated many far greater minds than Speer's. Years later, when he is talking to Gitta Sereny, he returns to this question, remembering his father's extreme physical reaction when Speer first introduced him to Hitler (his face went pale, his body shuddered, he couldn't speak). He had instinctively felt something, a madness or an evil there. Speer related how he and Casalis 'talked about it many times. You know, the origin and nature of evil . . . I still don't know how to handle it.'

*

This defining period in Speer's life ended abruptly with Casalis' departure from Spandau on 1 June 1950. He and his wife Dorothée had been feeling increasingly uncomfortable living 'the extraordinarily privileged life as "occupiers" in Berlin'. So they accepted an invitation to move to posts in Strasbourg, where Casalis studied for his doctorate in theology. Speer later reflected that Casalis had been 'the most important person in my life, entirely unique', 'he was my conscience, that conscience which I continually manage to diminish and repress by superficial overuse'. He hoped he'd be able to continue on the moral journey with the strength that Casalis had given him, but within a few weeks he realised this wasn't possible, and this triggered a period of crisis – two years of intense depression and apathy. As he later wrote to Hilde: 'I had to face the fact that I am very dependent on external influences. If I have a Casalis I can manage. But without such a catalyst I fall apart: all my good intentions evaporate'. For his part, Casalis later regretted that he had left at this point, feeling that, had he stayed longer, Speer might have made greater progress towards fully understanding his guilt. He also underestimated the relationship he'd developed with 'Prisoner Number Five' and the consequent sense of devastating loss that Speer felt on his departure:

> Yes, I did feel I knew him very well indeed by the time I left
> . . . well enough that I should have realised that it was wrong
> of me to leave. Because of him, I should have stayed another
> three or four years.

Once he'd emerged from his deep depression, Speer only got through these next years by working intensely on creating a garden out of the wilderness at the back of the prison. He had begun this project soon after arriving at Spandau, but in 1951 and 1952 he threw himself into the work to such an extent that by June 1953 he'd planted a hundred chestnut trees, fifty hazels, a hundred lilac bushes and 800 strawberry plants, as well as creating an orchard of dozens of apple and plum trees, starting a vegetable garden and creating pretty paths through the little park, bordered by flowers. In parallel with this garden project, he continued his reading programme (1,500 books completed by 1956), alternating between architecture, novels and travel books and more demanding works on philosophy and theology. Lifted by a new sense of purpose, with the success of his garden, in early 1953 Speer begins to write the book that eventually became *Inside the Third Reich* and completes the first draft by January 1954 – a remarkable feat given that the whole work had to be written completely in secret (because of regular cell observations) on scraps of paper and then smuggled out with the help of a sympathetic prison guard.

*

On 20 September 1954 he begins a project, obsessive yet inspired, which was to occupy him right up until his release twelve years later – his 'Walk Around the World'. From his diary of 30 September 1954 we learn:

> I have begun, along with the garden work, to walk the distance from Berlin to Heidelberg – 626 kilometres! For that purpose I have marked out a circular course in the garden. Lacking a tape measure, I measured my shoe, paced off the distance step by step, and multiplied by the number of paces. Placing one foot ahead of the other 870 times, thirty-one centimetres a step, yields 270 metres for a round.[*]

In this way – by doing around twenty-six circuits of the garden each time – he aims to complete seven kilometres a day, and so forty-nine kilometres a week. By 19 March 1955 he has completed this journey to Heidelberg (delayed somewhat by a swollen knee, he's taken considerably longer than the planned eighty-nine days to do this walk), and now he decides he's going to continue on, first to Munich, then down to Rome, on to Sicily, and from here further eastwards, towards Asia. Over the months and years, by scouring atlases and maps and reading the most detailed accounts of travel books and guides, this walk in his mind becomes a won-

---

[*] Given Speer's love of mathematics and precision, I'm a little shocked, checking his calculations, to discover an error in these figures – 870 of his steps do not equal 270 metres but only 269.7 metres. Over a year this miscalculation gives a 109.5-metre differential, and over the twelve years of Speer's remaining imprisonment, it gives a 1.314 km differential.

derfully rich experience. He is helped on his way by his friend and former colleague Rudolf Wolters, who, through their correspondence, lives the walk with him, sometimes telling him of places he knows. When Speer reaches Siberia, Wolters writes to him: 'I am well acquainted with the Altai. It is the huge mountain chain near Novosibirsk where I spent a year. A famous mountain excursion is the Bjelucha,* the goal of all Siberian climbers, as is the Elbrus in the Caucasus. Will you have time to climb them?'

For a man often spoken of as lacking in imagination, this becomes an astonishingly vivid experience. Take this, for example, from August 1955:

> Shimmering heat waves over the *puszta* as I covered the stretch from Budapest to Belgrade, a few kilometres away from the Danube. The roads were sandy, there was seldom even a single shade tree, and the flies were a plague. From the nearby Havel I heard the sound of tugs, which I transformed into ships on the Danube. I plucked a stem of lemon balm from our herb bed and crushed the leaves between my fingers. The strong odour intensified the illusion of foreign places, tramping the roads, and freedom.

A few years later, Speer seems almost reconciled to the fact that any dreams of early release are now fading. He has achieved a kind of peace at Spandau, his 'Trappist existence', where, by the early 1960s, he's only speaking for five minutes a day or so. On 7 May 1960 he watches five hawks practising their diving in the garden:

> Finally a young pigeon came and perched on the lowest branch of the walnut tree, under which Hess and I had already been sitting for an hour in silence. Into the stillness Hess said, with almost a touch of embarrassment, 'Like paradise.' . . . Perhaps this was what life was like in the monasteries of the

---

* Wolters presumably means Mount Belukha here – the highest peak in the Altai.

Middle Ages? Isolation not only from people, but also from the bustle of the world. Sitting on the garden bench today, for a moment I saw myself as a monk, and the prison yard as a cloister garden. It seemed to me that my family alone still links me to the outside. Concern with everything else that makes up the world is more and more dropping away from me, and the idea of spending the rest of my days here is no longer frightening. On the contrary there is great peacefulness in the thought.

But the outside world cannot be kept out. In May 1960, Speer, like many others, is riveted by the capture of Adolf Eichmann in Argentina and his upcoming trial in Israel, and notes that the world's attention is now focussed again on the crimes of the Third Reich. In this context, 'the desire for release strikes me as almost absurd'. He again ponders how he and others could really have thought Hitler's antisemitism was 'a somewhat vulgar incidental, a hangover from his days in Vienna . . . moreover, the antisemitic slogans also seemed to me a tactical device for whipping up the instincts of the masses. I never thought them really important . . . Yet, hatred of the Jews was Hitler's central conviction.' He then considers the fact he became Hitler's architect – that is 'excusable'. He can even 'justify' serving as his armaments minister:

I can even conceive of a position from which a case could be made for the use of millions of prisoners of war and forced labourers in industry – even though I have never taken that position. But I have absolutely nothing to say when a name like Eichmann's is mentioned. I shall never be able to get over having served a leading position in a regime whose true energies were devoted to an extermination programme.

By 24 February 1963, more than eight years after starting the Walk Around the World, Speer is almost at Alaska:

In the immediate vicinity of Bering Strait, still craggy, hilly country, endless view of treeless, rocky landscape, as rough as the storms that prevail in the region. Sometimes I see creeping past me one of those Arctic foxes whose habits I have recently looked into. But I have also encountered fur seals and the Kamchatka beaver known as *kalan*. Bering Strait is seventy-two kilometres wide and frozen until the middle of March. Ever since I heard this from Bray [a prison guard], who comes from Alaska, I raised my weekly stint from fifty to sixty kilometres, for if I arrive in time I might be able to cross Bering Strait. I would presumably be the first central European to reach America on foot.

There's something of remarkable beauty in this. As an expression of the ability of the human mind to conjure light from darkness, it seems to be almost unparalleled. A Zen-like patience, the placing of one foot in front of another, whether in sun or in snow. And the ability to summon wild animals into your mind, and to see ice and crags and trees. An act of creativity of stunning scope. And to have the contemplative energy to do this over years and years and years . . . Is it wrong to feel a kind of admiration for the Albert Speer who walked in the garden, as he walked through his mind?

And then, an extraordinary detail, which demonstrates Speer's degree of self-containment. He's walking with Hess around the path. He tells him he's almost reached Alaska. Hess looks baffled. Speer then reminds him of how, in September 1954, more than eight years before, on the day he started the Walk, Hess advised him to count the circuits using beans from the garden, transferring them from one pocket to the other:

'Right now . . . we are in the middle of the seventy-eight thousand, five hundred and fourteenth round, and there in the mist we can see Bering Strait.'

Hess abruptly stopped. His face now took on a really concerned expression. 'You mean to say you've kept that up all this time?' he asked. 'Including leap years, up to today exactly eight years, five months and ten days . . . Up to this point I have covered twenty-one thousand, two hundred and one kilometres.'

Hess is astonished, and then – in a comical example of the pot calling the kettle black – looks rather pained, and asks Speer: 'Doesn't all this worry you? You know, it really is a kind of mania.' Yet his Walk Around the World was, in addition to being beneficial exercise, probably the single most important reason why Speer retained his sanity in these last twelve years of imprisonment.

*

This is Speer's entry for 9 March 1963:

Today I reckoned out that if I make my twenty-one-year imprisonment equal to a year, I would today have arrived at 27 October. If I equate it with the twenty-four hours of one day, 11.1 seconds pass every day. It is now only eight seconds beyond 7.58 p.m. That is, the day has already gone by, but the evening and the night still lie before me.

Is there something here – in fact in the whole enterprise of the Walk – that goes beyond a playful love of mathematics? Which is numerically obsessive? When relations with other human beings are so challenging, is there a sense of safety in numbers? Finding a kind of sanctuary in the discipline of counting and walking? Returning to something from childhood that had provided him with enormous pleasure and reassurance. As he had explained to Gitta Sereny, talking about his childhood: 'I loved mathematics . . . I can't describe to you how much or why I loved it. But becoming a mathematician was all I had ever thought of. It did everything for me that was . . . well . . . joy. It was my way . . . of experiencing triumph.'

As the year of his release grows nearer, he realises it's extremely unlikely he will be able to complete his circumnavigation of the world, but still he walks further and further each day:

> 21 December 1964: Today I passed Seattle on the West Coast of the United States. In sixty days, despite cold and high winds, I have covered 560 kilometres. Recently I broke my day's record and in five hours and forty minutes covered twenty-eight kilometres. By now my tramping has infected several of the guards. Some days four or five persons can be seen on the track, with determined looks on their faces. 'I'll tell you the difference between you and me,' Hess said to me today. 'Your follies are contagious.'

But again, just a couple of weeks later in January 1965, news from the outside presses in, and Speer begins to feel fearful about his release in this new climate:

> the newspapers are full of the Auschwitz trial, and I have the impression that the past . . . is once more being revived. Suddenly I feel something akin to fear of the world out there, which I no longer know and which is beginning to rediscover, with so much new passion, the things that have been slowly fading for me since Nuremberg, by dint of my conscious acceptance of atonement. And suddenly Spandau seems not so much the place of my imprisonment as of my protection.

He then expresses confusion, noting since the war the crimes of the supposedly 'good' side in the war – the French in Algeria, the Americans in Vietnam, the Russians in Hungary, and says:

> How much more difficult it has become to accept within oneself the guilty verdict pronounced by those judges. Moreover, the many years of brooding, of dialogues with myself, have dissipated my former guilt feelings. For at bottom every confrontation with one's guilt is probably an unconfessed search

for justification . . . And now this trial! I must seize upon what is being written in the newspapers about Auschwitz now as a kind of support. That can help me restore the lost meaning of these Spandau years, and at the same time help me recover moral clarity.

A fortnight before his release Speer tallies up his kilometre totals for each year of the Walk Around the World – 'the only tangible result of the Spandau years', as he expresses it rather curiously, 'there is nothing left but statistics, production figures':

1954–5	2,367 kilometres
1955–6	3,326
1956–7	3,868
1957–8	2,865
1958–9	2,168
1959–60	1,633
1960–1	1,832
1961–2	1,954
1962–3	2,664
1963–4	2,794
1964–5	3,258
1965–6	3,087
Total	31,816

Even on his last day in Spandau, 30 September 1966, he's still calculating the precise distance he's travelled: 'Since I drew up those statistics I have tramped an additional 114 kilometres. In a moment I am going into the garden and will cover another ten kilometres, so that I shall be ending my walking tour at kilometre 31,936' (amidst the excitement of the last day, Speer, uncharacteristically, miscalculates – the ten additional kilometres he walked subsequently took the total to 31,940 kilometres). Anyway, by this final stage, Speer is in deepest Mexico, and so informs us that 'At 11 p.m. a telegram is to be sent to my old friend which he should receive around midnight:

"PLEASE PICK ME UP THIRTY-FIVE KILOMETRES SOUTH OF GUADALAJARA, MEXICO. HOLZWEGE".*

A black Mercedes, courtesy of the industrialist Ernst Mommsen, is waiting for Speer, with his lawyer Flaschner and his wife, Margret. On the stroke of midnight the gates of Spandau swing open, and Speer's twenty years are over, in a blaze of flashbulbs and television spotlights. They drive the short distance to the ornate Hotel Gerhus in Grunewald, where they spend the night and where Speer gives the first of the numerous press conferences he was to hold after his release. The next day, Speer and Margret drive to a remote house in Schleswig-Holstein, where they spend a fortnight with the rest of the family. Although everyone tries hard, Speer feels a 'sense of awkwardness' and then makes this extremely revealing comment, which later appears on the last page of the *Diaries*:

> I think as I write this a few days later, that I should not attribute the sense of awkwardness to Spandau. It is even possible that the stiffness with which we sat facing each other in the visiting room is the kind of contact that accords with my nature. Hasn't there always been a sort of wall between me and others? Has not all casualness been only a strategy to make that wall invisible? . . . My whole life, in fact, appears to me strangely alienated. Architecture I loved, and I hoped to make my name live on in history by building. But my real work consisted in the organisation of an enormous system of technology.

*

And what became of his friendship with Casalis, whom Speer had called 'the most important person in my life'? After his release, Casalis came to feel that from a spiritual point of view there had only been a regression in Speer from the man he'd known in prison.

---

* 'Holzwege' was the pseudonym used by Speer in his clandestine correspondence, taken from the title of a book by Heidegger; the word has a double meaning – 'wood roads' or 'wrong ways'.

956

The man who had journeyed, by the time Casalis left Spandau in 1950, from being 'the most tortured man I'd ever known to the most repentant'. After Speer's release they met on only four occasions – extremely surprising given the glowing words that he had used about Casalis. But perhaps explained by Speer's delight in his public celebrity on his release (abhorrent to Casalis), and his sense of male pride. Casalis describes the penultimate time they were together, driving Speer in his little Citroën 2CV to Lille:

> We continued our Spandau conversations, but obviously from a different position. In Spandau he was the prisoner, living what he called then his 'sixteenth-century life' . . . His talks with me then were very central to all of this, and yes, I could see that they started something in and for him, and created in him a new dimension, a new space. But in the very public existence of his post-publication life, someone like me was . . . marginal . . . You know it is very difficult, very complicated for people who have received help from someone at a moment of great need, to return to such a person, to turn back to such a person. It is not that it is difficult to acknowledge what has been done for them. The real difficulty is to go on knowing someone who, at a time of crisis, has got to know you so deeply.

We know from Dorothée Casalis that there was one further meeting between Speer and Casalis after his release from Spandau. And her account of this particular evening demonstrates that Speer continued to feel riven by guilt even after he was a free man again:

> Speer continued to be troubled, tortured by the Jewish question. He asked Georges whether he could introduce him to friends who had lost relatives during the war and the occupation – that is Jewish men and women. Georges hesitated and then he contacted two sisters who had lost several members of their family in Auschwitz and elsewhere. They spent an evening which was both extraordinary and terrible with these two women, and their husbands who let it all out – their

hatred, their violence, their grief in the face of the irrecoverable. And he [Speer] took it all, and said: 'I have to hear this. I must not protect myself. That's how it is.' A few times Speer said 'I was responsible.' I don't know if he was able to say 'I was guilty', but *responsible* at least. Yes, he felt that very strongly that evening.

*

Reading between the lines. Always necessary, but acutely so in Speer's case. We have seen the remarkable developments that took place in him during the years that Casalis was chaplain at Spandau, the vast majority of which must be attributable to his exceptional guidance of Speer; we have also heard Speer's own praise for the pastor. His influence in these years was profound. Yet it is still an unsettling experience to go back to Speer's actual words from the *Diaries* and then to contrast these with the words he uses with Gitta Sereny in the interviews for her book. Like Sereny (given Speer's eulogistic comments about Casalis and the critical role he played during these years), I was also astonished not to find his name even mentioned in the index of the *Diaries*. And in the body of the text, between October 1947 and June 1950, Casalis is mentioned on only seven occasions:

11 October 1947 (Casalis' first service)
18 October 1947 (Speer's fellow prisoners complain about the previous week's sermon)
26 October 1947 (Casalis preaches that he is 'the greatest sinner among us')
15 May 1948 (Speer asks Casalis to postpone his wife's first visit)
5 February 1949 (Speer and Casalis discuss the nature of religious faith)
14 February 1949 (Casalis arranges for Speer's cousin, Hildebrecht Hommel, to visit him – his first personal visit in Spandau)
1 June 1950 (Speer describes Casalis' departure)

But even this final mention of the pastor in the *Diaries* is curiously formal, with no hint of the intensity of their relationship, their weekly discussions or the programme of intellectual and spiritual development which Casalis had taken Speer through:

> Chaplain Casalis, who has cared for us for three years, is going to Strasbourg. His sermons have taught me the meaning of faith. He tolerates no half measures and is effective because of his total commitment. Perhaps in the future too, his influence will help me through these Spandau years. In order to keep from losing my composure during his last sermon, I tried translating his words into French. Afterwards we were able to sit down together for half an hour because no Russian was present. Deeply moved, in bidding him goodbye I said with full conviction, 'May God preserve your strength.'

When Sereny challenges Speer about the omission of Casalis from the index of the *Diaries* (but not the book – as she appears to imply), and asks him why he hadn't written about their relationship, Speer shrugs: 'I'm not sure; perhaps it was too important, or perhaps . . . because I failed him.' Or perhaps it was more a question of the male pride that Casalis had recognised. No doubt when these diaries were first published in Germany in 1975 Speer wanted to let it appear that he had completed his journey alone. And acknowledging Casalis' formative role, at least in Speer's eyes, would have meant diminishing his own sense of personal achievement, of having come through the test of twenty years of imprisonment.

Whatever the realities of the relationship between these two men, there are some fascinating differences between the verbal account that Casalis gives to Sereny and the written version of Speer's in the *Diaries*, especially relating to the early days of Casalis' ministry at the prison. Speer, as we've seen, states that Casalis' sermon on his first day – 11 October 1947 – centres around the isolating treatment of lepers in the Holy Land, and that the other prisoners are deeply offended by this, and make a formal protest before the following week's service on 18 October, when he writes that: 'Raeder officially protested to Chaplain Casalis, in the name of five of his fellow prisoners' (not including Speer) 'because the chaplain had referred to them as lepers'.

But in Casalis' account given to Sereny, the first services 'passed tranquilly enough', and it is only 'on the *sixth* Saturday [my emphasis]' that he 'very nearly came a cropper when he chose as his subject Jesus's healing of the leper'. After this the prisoners leave in silence, refusing to shake hands with Casalis as they usually did. The following week, according to Casalis, 'Raeder stood up *at the end of the sermon* [my emphasis] . . . and said "Last week . . . you deeply offended us. It is entirely impermissible to address us as lepers."' The week after, both Casalis' account and Speer's written account tally in agreeing that the sermon is based on Jesus telling the Pharisees 'it is not the healthy who need a doctor, but the sick. I have not come to call the righteous, but sinners to repentance'. But Speer then simplifies, and in so doing irons out Casalis' nuanced and humane position. He says, baldly, that Casalis 'took occasion to say that he is the greatest sinner among us; all the churchgoers were gratified'. However, Casalis remembers breaking off from his sermon to suggest that they must not take the words from the Bible literally, as they are parables which each person needs to interpret the meaning of themselves. He then tells them:

> In my own interpretation of the parables, to me the first sinner and first sick person is always myself. We are together in this experiment here, in this attempt at finding common ground between you and your inner selves, between you and me, and between the things Jesus said and what you can accept or find in them. I am in that no different from you. I search.

Why spend time going through the details of these differing accounts? Couldn't some of this simply be attributable to inevitably diverging memories of the same events? Maybe so, but it is also worth considering that Speer deliberately conflated two events that happened six weeks apart – meeting Casalis for the first time and Casalis' sermon about the lepers that caused offence.

Why would he do this? Because by emphasising the furore over the sermon, he wouldn't have to confront the memory of himself, at the most difficult time in his life, talking to Casalis after that first service – one of the most significant conversations of Speer's life. And, astoundingly, completely omitted from his account in the *Diaries*. By doing this he wouldn't have to confront the memory of Casalis telling him he considered he was more blameworthy than any of the others in the Nazi leadership. And he wouldn't have to confront the memory of that vulnerable, broken man asking Casalis for help – the most important eight words that Speer ever spoke to another human being:

'Would you help me become a different man?'

21

Searching for Antigone in Ashford, and for Languages That Do Not Yet Exist . . .

Summer 2013, Pembrokeshire

In the house next door, a man who I have never met is dying. He is known around here as 'The Professor'. At the front of his house the riotous little garden of palm trees, clematis, roses and apple trees has grown out of control during his long illness. There seem to be no relatives, but every couple of days I catch sight of a young nurse negotiating the steep steps from the lane behind down to the house. Occasionally there's a light on upstairs, and you can see what appear to be glass jars and funnels from an old medical laboratory in the window. There's a winding path that runs between the little garden and the sea wall, so I often walk past the house on my way to the village. Each time I walk past the front door and windows I wonder if a face will appear, I ready myself for a wave or a smile, but there's never a sign of movement. A neighbour tells me that she's seen him, 'poor man', but then she stops herself. He knows he's going to die soon, but he's got strong religious faith and he seems remarkably calm. She described the way that he's had the bed moved downstairs to the front room, so that he can hear the sea better. Behind the bed is a large wooden crucifix, she tells me, and in front a mirror – so that he can face himself and the cross together. Looking at his future, on this earth and beyond.

In a society that doesn't quite know what to do with dying and death, here is this man not raging against his approaching end, but rather opening the door to it, welcoming it into the house, being with it, as he listens to the sound of the summer tides.

*

This thought takes me back about ten years, to a journey in France with J. I remember being in a 2CV, me in the passenger seat, and J. behind, we were being driven to Geneva by our friend Johann from his village in the mountains. He had a rather terrifying way of driving, with his face almost touching the steering wheel. As if he was fiercely concentrating on every foot of the road (perhaps a style learnt from his motorcycling, where such alert attention is critical all the time). The fierceness of his concentration made me concerned to ask him anything, in case it took his attention away from the road. We had been talking about a French philosopher, whose work and life had strongly affected both of us – Simone Weil. I had remembered a line of hers that stunned me when I first came across it, a line of such simplicity and such wonder: '*La croyance à l'existence d'autres êtres humains comme tels est amour*' ('The belief in the existence of other human beings – such a thing is love'). Yes, to *truly* believe in the existence of others! Not just when you wake in the night and see the breathing body next to you rise and fall. Not just when you hear your children playing in the other room. Not just when you ring your friends up, or see them. But the idea of the film of another person's life continuing when you're not there. As vividly as your own life . . .

And then Johann told us this story. He'd been visiting a Polish friend earlier that summer. His friend worked as a forester and they were walking one day in the woods near his house, and they came across a grave at the side of a track – a single grave on its own. There was a simple cross and some fresh flowers and that was all.

Johann asked who was buried there. Nobody knows exactly, his forester friend explained, he was a German soldier who was killed in that place by partisans in the war. Johann looked shocked that, given the intense enmity between the Germans and the Poles, this soldier had been buried and his grave was still tended with flowers. His friend looked at him sharply, disturbed by Johann's comment, and said simply:

'But here a man died.'

*

Late summer is here. The dominant colour now is the burnt rust of dying bracken on the cliff paths. The steep banks that burst with the pinks of campion and the purples of toadflax earlier in the year are now a bleached green. The manic skittishness of swallows in the skies has been replaced by raggledy rooks and ravens, hurling themselves giddily into the gusting squalls coming off the sea. The pontoon is gone, now there is only one solitary wooden boat bobbing in the bay. The knots of summer visitors and children with shrimping nets are preparing to return home, and back to school.

Today Simone Weil is in my mind again. I am sure that Casalis must have known her work well. Those words he uses about Speer –

asking him to *open his mind and spirit to suffering* – these are words that could have come directly from Weil. So much of her writing returns to the sense of human meaning that stems from understanding the suffering of others – 'It was other people's pain that moved her, not her own', as one biographer says. For her, empathy was not an abstract question, or something to aspire to, it was simply a part of her daily existence – 'no border could contain her empathy for the plight of others, from soldiers on the front lines to enemies subjected to harsh treaties'.

At the heart of Weil's thought is the link between empathy and suffering. The highest human capacity, 'almost a miracle', as she puts it, is connecting to the being of others – being which is inseparable from suffering, and suffering which is inseparable from life. But this, she concedes, is extraordinarily difficult to do. It is hard enough for the person suffering to express what they are feeling, but it is virtually impossible for another to really *hear* those words, and understand the sufferer's actual condition. So this, in turn, can create a terrible cycle:

> To listen to someone is to put yourself in their place while they are speaking. To put yourself in the place of someone whose soul is corroded by affliction . . . is to annihilate yourself.* It is more difficult than suicide would be for a happy child. Therefore the afflicted are not listened to. They are like someone whose tongue has been cut out and who occasionally forgets the fact. When they move their lips no ear perceives any sound. And they themselves soon sink into impotence in the use of language, because of the certainty of not being heard.

But, despite the enormous challenges inherent in communication, Weil believed that it is in the continual *attempt* to connect with

---

* This phrase does not carry a negative meaning for Weil – quite the opposite. In the same essay she explains: 'The only way into truth is through one's own annihilation.' She felt that this was the necessary prerequisite for passing to a stage of attention which can then really listen to truth and affliction – 'the name of this intense, pure, disinterested, gratuitous, generous attention is love'.

others that we experience our own humanity most fully. Though even then this experience is rarely more than fragmentary, and always a temporary condition. Like many of the most ethical people who have ever lived, she had little time for organised religion, for the conformity of churches and bishops. But she said this about the figure of Christ:

> Compassion for the afflicted is an impossibility. When it is really found (as in the life of Christ) we have a more astounding miracle than walking on the water . . . or even raising the dead.

That is part of what moves me about Casalis and Speer in Spandau. This is why I keep returning to what happened between those two men in those years. The attempt to find compassion in that place. The attempt of that reserved, awkward, middle-aged man to be emotionally raw, to go to territories inside that he had never gone to. And Casalis' compassion (literally 'suffering with' – from the Latin *com* + *pati*), and his choice to be with Speer in that place. Both of these men fallible, both of them cracked vessels. Mostly stumbling, occasionally glimpsing something that might be truth. Speer (before he met Casalis) one of the most utterly unempathetic men it would have been possible to meet, the icy, polar opposite of Simone Weil. Yet, in those years, something opens in him. The miracle that empathy might be able to be learnt, even at a late stage in life. An empathy with roots. Where other people's suffering – even if only for a moment – becomes as real as your own.

*

To find empathy inside the walls of a prison may seem strange at first. But perhaps it is not too much of a stretch to sense a link between the conceptual prison cells that exist in our minds, and the actual prison cells that few of us ever see. And also the way that all of us, at times, feel the walls that separate us from others, and wish we could break free. This may also explain the reason why literature and film and poetry go back again and again to the subject. The human being *in extremis*, the human being deprived of freedom, of love. We put ourselves in that situation, in that cell, and ask how, or if, we would survive. This is surely what is so moving about the poetry of Nâzim Hikmet and Yannis Ritsos, or the writing of Victor Serge or Antonio Gramsci. Not only to have come through many years of imprisonment, but to have alchemised their experiences into the essence of the human condition so that, with words, they escape the walls which contained them.

Hikmet, eight years into a sentence in Bursa prison, writes to his wife, Piraye, in September 1945 without a trace of self-pity, despite his political imprisonment and appalling treatment:

> How beautiful to think of you:
> amid news of death and victory,
> in prison,
> when I'm past forty . . .
> How beautiful to think of you:
> your hand resting on blue cloth,
> your hair grave and soft
> like my beloved Istanbul earth . . .
> How beautiful to think of you,
> to write about you,
> to sit back in prison and remember you . . .
> And jumping right up
> and grabbing the iron bars at my window,
> I must shout out the things I write for you
> To the milk-white blue of freedom . . .

Victor Serge describes how joy can pierce even the darkest cell, writing of his five years in a brutal French jail between 1912 and 1917:

> On the ceiling, in a corner, around ten in the morning, a rec-
> tangle of sunlight appears: a few square inches. The cell and its
> inmate are instantly transformed . . . the presence of this warm
> light . . . creates an inexpressible emotion. Your step quickens,

your back straightens, the day takes on a brighter aspect . . . Among those who succeed in resisting madness, their intense inner life brings them to a higher conception of life, to a deeper consciousness of the *self*, its value, its strength. A victory over jail is a great victory. At certain moments you feel astonishingly *free*. You sense that if this torture has not broken you, nothing will ever be able to break you.

He also takes inspiration from how the anarchist thinker Peter Kropotkin had survived his years in prison in St Petersburg. Having no pen or paper, every day, in his head – to keep his sanity – he edited a newspaper 'methodically, with the greatest seriousness; lead article, bulletins, features, scientific and artistic columns, society items . . . in this manner he mentally wrote thousands of articles'. Serge does a similar daily exercise, classifying and going over his own stock of knowledge, memories and ideas. He, like Speer, begins to 'understand the value of "retreats" as they were practised in past centuries in the Catholic world . . . Contemplation brings about a re-examination of all your values, an auditing of all of your accounts with yourself and with the universe. Introspection opens up the endless vistas of the inner life'.

Both Hikmet and Serge place a great emphasis on the ability of the human being to be free in their minds, even when imprisoned. Yet in our world today, it seems that we are dealing with the exact converse of this – that many people now feel imprisoned in their minds, even when free. That in fact our societies are becoming more and more adept at creating walls and barriers in our minds. And that the technologies which so many felt would bring the greatest freedoms are actually chaining us to addicted patterns of behaviour and shackling our abilities to deal with each other's humanity face to face. For all the horror of physical imprisonment, I find myself agreeing with Hikmet when he says:

They've taken us prisoner,
they've locked us up:
me inside the walls.

You outside.
But that's nothing.
The worst
is when people – knowingly or not –
carry prison inside themselves . . .

In a remarkable essay from 2004, 'A Master of Pitilessness?', John Berger revisits the work of Francis Bacon, and admits that for the previous fifty years he'd been wrong about this painter. For all this time he'd considered Bacon primarily as an artist who 'painted in order to shock . . . and such a motive, [he had believed], would wear thin with time'. But at an exhibition in Paris he realises that Bacon's vision had always been of 'a pitiless world', and in this regard, he'd been many years ahead of his time. But it is not the depiction of pain and torture that makes the work original; it is the fact that in Bacon's paintings the subject suffers alone – 'there are no witnesses and there is no grief'. I would go further, and say that in much of Bacon's work it seems as though the spaces his subjects inhabit are claustrophobic, hermetically sealed rooms, totally separated from any idea of a wider world. These are places of utter isolation, where people scream in padded cells and know that nobody will come, not even their torturers.

Later in the essay, Berger, prophetically, wrote this:

> The present period of history is one of the Wall. When the Berlin one fell, the prepared plans to build walls everywhere were unrolled. Concrete, bureaucratic, surveillance, security, racist, zone walls. Everywhere the walls separate the desperate poor from those who hope to stay relatively rich . . . On the one side: every armament conceivable, the dream of no-body-bag wars, the media, plenty, hygiene, many passwords to glamour. On the other: stones, short supplies, feuds, the violence of revenge, rampant illness, an acceptance of death and an ongoing preoccupation with surviving one more night – or perhaps one more week – together. The choice of meaning in

the world today is here between the two sides of the wall. The wall is also inside each one of us.

A multiplicity of walls – physical but also virtual. The way that technology now has enabled us, as never before, to communicate – but also the way that screens have now begun to distance us, separate us from the human voice, the face of pain and love, physical touch, the bodies of others. Bacon's dystopian world now edging closer. The illusion of connection, yet the reality of isolation. The prisons we all make in our minds. In darker moments I wonder whether we actually prefer exisiting within the walls we've built rather than living between the earth and the sky.

Weil is obsessed by the notion of the wall as well – the image recurs in her work. And the way that human beings imprison themselves – many don't recognise that they're in prison, but the wiser ones realise they are captives. With a great deal of work, and suffering, one day the questioning man

> will wake up on the other side of the wall. Perhaps he is still in a prison, although a larger one. No matter, he has found the key; he knows the secret which breaks down every wall. He has passed beyond what men call intelligence, into the beginning of wisdom.

She is also fascinated by reversing our perceptions of the world around us, delighting in paradox, finding limitations in the supposed 'freedoms' which our societies offer, and liberation in confinement. Sometimes, as here in *Gravity and Grace*, she, like a magician, allows us to see both sides simultaneously: 'The world is the closed door. It is a barrier. And at the same time it is the way through. Two prisoners whose cells adjoin communicate with each other by knocking on the wall. The wall is the thing which separates them but it is also their means of communication . . . Every separation is a link.'

*

So what, ultimately, are we to make of what happened between Speer and Casalis in those three years in Spandau? There is a danger in simplifying Speer's experience; it's tempting to see it as a wholly progressive arc of development. But, of course, the truth was far from that. However genuine Speer's attempts to become a different man were, however rigorously he applied himself to Casalis' programme of reading and discussion, there were always other forces, other instincts at work. Indeed, one of the fascinations of reading the *Diaries* is to witness a kind of ontological struggle raging inside Speer in this period. A large part of him relishing the challenge, and the toughness of the monastic regime Casalis has set in motion, but another part still dreaming of grandiosity and power in the outside world.

Only weeks after meeting his new mentor he is still describing in the *Diaries* how hard it is to relinquish his 'dreams of having a place in the history of architecture' and boasting of how he'd planned 'the biggest domed hall in the world' and repeating Hitler's words to his wife: 'I am assigning tasks to your husband that have not been given for four thousand years. He will erect buildings for eternity!' In the spring of 1948, when he's deep in his reading of the theologian Karl Barth, he's also recalling excitedly in his diary memories of grand meetings with Hitler and Winifred Wagner (the composer's daughter-in-law), or Hitler's detailed appreciation of an ornate theatre in Augsburg. In late 1948, a year into the intense focus on his inner life – this supposedly reflective existence – he still confides to his diary breathlessly that his wife has just received a letter from Mrs Alfred Knopf, and notes with excitement that she's the wife of 'the well-known American publisher who has published the works of Thomas Mann in the United States' and that he eventually 'would like to bring out my memoirs'.

In the Saturday meetings with Casalis, Speer would be the deeply thoughtful man grappling with his inner guilt and discussing theology, completely accepting Weil's challenge 'to strip ourselves of the imaginary royalty of the world. Absolute solitude. Then we possess the truth of the world.' Yet, away from Casalis, it seems the

971

external world of pomp and material success still held enormous attractions for the imprisoned architect. Perhaps it is not surprising that he never told Casalis about his writing in these years (knowing how shocked he would be by some of the subject matter); and perhaps it is also not surprising that, after his release, Speer once again became so seduced by the world of fame and power – which Casalis saw, correctly, only as a kind of regression.

*

There is a tantalising aspect to how we evaluate words which actually get written down and published. The fixity of such a process gives a kind of elevated status, a sense that the words could last for years, on many occasions long after the death of their authors. Yet, in many cases, it is the spoken words between people that could tell us vastly more. How much more extraordinary than reading Speer's fragmented, and highly selective, account of his life in the *Diaries* would it be if we could listen to him and Casalis talking together on one of these Saturdays in the prison chapel. In a similar vein, how wonderful it would be to be able to capture the uncontainable flow of words spoken between friends who haven't seen each other for too long. Like clouds of birds and butterflies flying into the dazzling light so a single one can no longer be seen. And all that is conveyed in the hesitations, the way of rephrasing, the nods and murmurs of agreement, the shared laughter. Without Sereny talking to Casalis (and then, later, these conversations being transcribed), we would never have learnt about many of the most important aspects of Speer's life.

This raises deeper questions about what is valued and given status in our societies. The way that we have habitually overvalued the written, and undervalued the spoken, just as Socrates predicted; the way we have, for hundreds of years, in a similar way, glorified the quantifiable *product* at the expense of the unquantifiable *process*. To give just a single example – read virtually any obituary today, and you will see an absurdly narrow way of looking at the world. In a page about the woman or man in question, there will be whole paragraphs listing all of their publications, their books, their external world 'achievements'; almost nothing on their humanity – nothing on the nature of their happiness or their struggles with depression or their experimental sexuality or their capacity for friendships or the unorthodox nature of their family relationships. And at the end, that ridiculously limited coda – 'He is survived by his wife and two children.'

In a similar way, I know that some of the most important work being done in the world today is invisible to many of us. Because we have not yet developed a language for valuing processes rather than products. For the last fifteen years, for example, Donald Reeves, formerly rector of St James's Church, Piccadilly, and his partner, Peter Pelz, have been working intensively in Bosnia, Serbia, Kosovo and the Republika Srpska. Their peace-building initiatives, grouped under the banner 'The Soul of Europe', have all been rooted in creating safe spaces where people from different ethnicities and political backgrounds can come together and start to talk to each other. This has often involved perpetrators, and relatives of perpetrators, sitting down next to survivors, and relatives of survivors, of the worst European atrocities since the Second World War. One of their guiding maxims is that 'Change happens when those who do not usually speak are heard by those who do not usually listen.'

I will never forget the experience of sitting in an orchard in Prijedor in July 2005 – the scene of some of the most barbaric acts of the Bosnian War a decade earlier – with a dozen young women and men, some teenagers, some in their early twenties. Their fathers, mothers, grandfathers and grandmothers had been directly involved in the massacres and torture; some had killed and tortured, some had been killed and tortured. Yet here they were ten years later, young Bosnian Muslims and Serbs, sitting together in a circle, under the apple trees, and listening to each other. Talking together about how they could build a memorial to the dead of Omarska.* In this still extremely divided society, Reeves and Pelz

---

* Explored in Book Three.

always try to work in an even-handed way – they have developed strong reconciliation processes which have enabled the rebuilding of the Ferhadija Mosque in Banja Luka to take place, and they are also creating an initiative that will help to protect the position of the Serbian Orthodox minority in Kosovo. This is some of the most important work on healing and reconciliation going on anywhere in our continent – yet, when they try to get their projects supported by funders, they are repeatedly told: 'your deliverables are not there', they need to demonstrate 'quantifiable partnership models'.

The language for the work they (and other pioneers around the world) are doing does not yet exist.

*

In August I travelled with two friends, Stefan and Alice, and Alice's two children, to try and find the grave of Simone Weil. The only information I had was that she had died in 1943, at a sanatorium in Ashford, Kent, but I wasn't aware she had been buried in the town until finding a photograph of her gravestone in a recent biography. I'd assumed that she would have been interred in France, her body repatriated after the war. But then, when you learn more about her attitude to her native country, you realise that France would not necessarily have welcomed back such a 'troublesome daughter', even after death. After all, this was the woman, vehemently anti-nationalist, always appalled at French colonialism, who infamously, perhaps even magnificently, wrote this comment in her journal on the day the Nazis thundered into Paris, and she could hear the Panzers rumbling down the Champs-Élysées:

This is a great day for the people of Indo-China.

Meaning that the terror the French, as colonial masters, had inflicted on Indo-China (Vietnam, Laos and Cambodia) for generations surely was now going to end. And indeed, Weil's comment was absolutely prescient. The forces of liberation in Indo-China became unstoppable, and the supposedly 'invulnerable' French forces, weakened irreparably by their humiliation in the Second World War, were eventually

974

defeated in Indo-China. This short sentence – that for Weil's detractors has been used (or rather abused) as an indication of her 'self-hatred', as a Jew, as a Frenchwoman – actually reveals itself to be one of the most powerful statements in the history of anti-colonialism. There is always a wider context, if we should choose to see it. And, on top of the geopolitical thrust of this statement, Weil is also challenging us to stop thinking that our own suffering and problems are all that matters, encouraging us to look beyond the narrow worlds that most of us inhabit. Colonial liberation starts with liberating ourselves from self-absorption. Being able to hear and see others for the first time.

I pick Stefan up at Dartford station, and we drive south and rendezvous with the others at Tonbridge. None of us know Kent well, and we're surprised at how shabby and run-down the town looks – boarded-up shops, broken bus shelters, a long way from our mental image of the affluent 'Garden of England'. We drive a couple of miles east to the village of Tudeley, and pull up outside All Saints' Church. It looks like a simple medieval church from the outside – rather squat, with a square tower and short spire – yet contained within is a breathtaking artwork, unique in the world. But before we enter, we walk to a tiny graveyard only a few hundred yards from the church, but hidden down a lane. The gate is locked, so we have to make our way over a fence at the back. A single oak dominates the little cemetery, perhaps a dozen graves spread out beneath its branches – the resting place of the d'Avigdor-Goldsmid family. Although Jewish cemeteries are common in our cities, it's less usual to find such places in the middle of the English countryside.

The gravestones are beautifully designed with fine lettering and decoration. The one I'm looking for has a line from a Shakespeare sonnet carved across the top – 'Summer's lease hath all too short a date' – and the name of the young woman commemorated – Sarah d'Avigdor-Goldsmid, and her dates, 1942–63 – with the simple inscription 'Lost at sea'. Her brief life is the reason why the artwork exists in the church. We are struck by another inscription, for an older relative, Osmond Elim d'Avigdor Goldsmidt, 1877–1940, who was president of the Board of Deputies of British Jews: 'A Life

975

Remarkable for Sincerity, Force of Character, Devotion to the Welfare of Others and Kindness to All'. On our way out we are fascinated to find another, smaller headstone, in a little enclosure all on its own, behind yew hedges. Clearly not somebody from the family, but obviously loved by them. But this grave seems quite mysterious, the life only hinted at by the four words given (two different names), and no dates at all: 'Mahmoud Bouchtet (Jon Carteret)'.

We have a picnic nearby, under willow trees, and I go through the little I know about Sarah's short life and death. She'd grown up nearby, at Somerhill House, a Jacobean stately home near Tonbridge – her father was Jewish, Sir Henry d'Avigdor-Goldsmid, and her mother, Lady Rosemary, was Anglican. Sarah was brought up Anglican too, both she and her mother worshipping at All Saints' in Tudeley. Sarah and Rosemary were very interested in modern art, and in 1961, at an exhibition in Paris, both had been electrified by seeing Marc Chagall's stained-glass windows, created for a synagogue in Jerusalem – Sarah called them 'jewels of translucent fire'. On 19 September 1963, tragedy struck the family. Sarah had been out for a day's sailing off the coast near Rye, with her boyfriend, David Winn, and Patrick Pakenham, the son of Lord Longford. In the evening, after a fine late summer's day, a sudden storm materialised, capsizing their boat, and throwing the three of them into the sea. They were a couple of miles from shore, and night was falling. They tried desperately to right the boat, but all their efforts failed, and first David and then Sarah slipped into the sea. Patrick, a stronger swimmer, managed to make it back to the shore, but by the time he had alerted help, his companions had drowned.

Over the following year or so, Sarah's mother, through her connections with the art world, invited Chagall to create a window in Sarah's memory at the church in Tudeley. The artist by this stage was an old man, very reluctant to take on new commissions, especially in a country he hardly knew, but Rosemary was persuasive, and Chagall appreciated the fact the family were Jewish and Christian (connecting to his own universalist beliefs), and so eventually he accepted the commission to design the east window at All Saints'. Four years after Sarah's death, in December 1967, Chagall came to Tudeley for the dedication of the extraordinary memorial window. When the eighty-year-old artist saw how brilliantly his design worked in the little church he was extremely moved, and declared, '*C'est magnifique! Je les ferai tous!*' – and, over the next eighteen years, true to his word, Chagall designed eleven further windows, the last being installed in 1985 – the year he died at the age of ninety-seven. Tudeley is the only church in the world to have all its windows designed by Chagall.

We walk up to the church, and just before we get there, as if by fate, the sun re-emerges from clouds, and so the moment we walk in, the late-afternoon light dapples and dances a flood of myriad blues and greens and yellows from the windows. It's an overwhelming sensory experience. We gaze at the east window, and the image of Sarah in a sea of indigo, and then a ladder leading up to an illuminated Christ with arms outstretched from the Cross . . . There are other windows with angels, horses and trees, birds, flowers and butterflies, exquisite paintings in light. The stone floor shimmers as we move across the nave, and the blues give way to honeyed golds and ochres. But the afternoon is fading now into early evening and Simone Weil is calling us to continue our journey eastwards.

We drive for an hour or so, down dipping Kentish lanes, tree tunnels. Squalls of August rains after the heat of the day. The talk now moves on to Germany, Alice is describing a conference there, high up in the mountains. A meeting of counsellors of refugee children that she'd been asked to speak at because of her writing. She was deeply troubled by how disturbed these counsellors seemed to be themselves, and so unaware of their inability to look at their own histories. A sense of burial of trauma, of denial. And yet they couldn't see how this must affect their work with the children. We're now on a B-road to Ashford, following a lorry, but I feel no impatience driving today. The rain intensifies. We talk about how the older generations of Germans – those who were young adults in the war years – dealt with the catastrophe that Nazism represented. Or in some cases didn't. I tell the story of Christian, the little boy growing up in the ruins just after the war, hiding behind the door, watching his parents singing Nazi songs with their friends. Just the sound of the windscreen wipers now. And a question in our minds of how many other children felt betrayed by their parents in these years. Stefan remembers how haunted he was, a long time ago, seeing Rossellini's devastating *Germany, Year Zero*, ending with the young boy's suicide among the ruins of post-war Berlin. Past Sissinghurst, edge of Ashford approaching. We're sweeping round on the ring road, DIY warehouses, ugly travel lodges. When we reach the end, we're amused to see the local authority has named this grim stretch of dual carriageway 'Simone Weil Avenue'.

From all my digging on Weil in Ashford I've managed to discover only sparse details. I know that she died in the Grosvenor Sanatorium, after being transferred there from the Middlesex Hospital in mid-August 1943. She'd been in London for just eight months, a mainly unhappy experience for her. Frail and passionate, she had repeatedly badgered the commanders at the Free French headquarters to allow her to parachute behind enemy lines to join the Resistance. Or to be part of a squadron of 'suicide nurses' who would tend to the injured and dying in the occupied territories, and prove to the Nazis that 'the French too could laugh in the face of death'. Hardly surprisingly, her entreaties were not taken very seriously. She did write, with an irony that would not have escaped her, *The Need for Roots* in London; she also developed a real affection for British culture, especially Shakespeare and pubs.

But her determination to continue a kind of starvation diet that she had started long before, in solidarity with all of those suffering under occupation – combined with her heavy smoking – led to her collapsing in April 1943. Her doctors at the Middlesex Hospital identified TB but also told her that rest and a proper diet would save her. They didn't understand who they were dealing with, though, as these two concepts were anathema to Weil. Later, they called her 'the worst patient we have ever encountered'. By the time she was transferred to the Grosvenor Sanatorium the TB had radically worsened and there was nothing more that could be done. On seeing her new accommodation in the sanatorium she simply said: 'What a beautiful room in which to die.'

I had only a single photograph of Grosvenor Hall for us to go on – the house which had housed the former tuberculosis sanatorium between 1913 and 1955. And the fact that the hall was located in Kennington, a district on the northern fringe of Ashford.

We drive up a gentle hill, through this suburb, hoping for some clue, some sign of this building. But soon we're emerging from the town, out into fields again. I turn the car round. By now Alice's children are tiring and the quest to stumble upon the old sanatorium seems a bridge too far. Resigned to this, we stop at a pub by a roundabout on the edge of Ashford, a large Victorian pile, have coffee and cake to boost our energy levels. Suddenly I look up at the inn, its high gables and its extension at the back. Could it possibly be the place? Stefan and I compare the little photograph with the building in front of us. There is a striking structural similiarity, though the chimneys seem slightly different. I go inside again and ask the landlord. No, he doesn't know anything about a sanatorium – as far as he knows this place has always been a hotel or an inn. But he gives me directions to Bybrook cemetery, where I know Weil is buried. In the gents, Stefan and I are chatting about our search when a guy emerges from a cubicle and says, 'I reckon the place you're after used to be the police training college – I think it was called Grosvenor Hall. It's just down the hill, near the cemetery.' We're wryly amused at the breakthroughs that can occur in unlikely places, and head back to the car, keen to tell Alice of our discovery. With our potential lead we drive back down the hill in much better spirits.

At the bottom of the hill we turn off, following Bybrook Road, and almost immediately there's another turn and a sign, 'Grosvenor Hall Outdoor Adventure Centre'. Yes, it must be here, surely! We drive up a long track, winding through pines and avenues of poplars. There are high fences, with barbed wire at the top, curious for such a place. Maybe left over from the police college days? Not a single other car or person around. We come round a bend, and finally, there it is in front of us at last – Grosvenor Hall, with its distinctive pointed gables and intricate chimneys, the place where Simone Weil died.

979

Some of the trees on the left of the photograph are still there. We try to imagine the landscape through her eyes, the countryside she saw from her window. The last of this place. The earth she inhabited so uneasily. The poplars would have grown since her time, but the oak and the beech she would have seen from her window, albeit as younger trees. Mid-August 1943. The war raging on, but the tide turning now. Hamburg still smouldering from the single night of bombing which had ended 42,000 lives. The Battle of Kursk on the Eastern Front and now the Soviet army about to liberate Kharkov. American troops landing in Sicily. But Speer, in his office in Berlin, more preoccupied with the American raid on Schweinfurt on 17 August and the disruption to armaments production . . .

And here in Kent the wheat almost ready for harvest, the orchards growing heavy with their fruit. The recovering TB patients walking around the grounds, planning concert parties in the evenings – Joan, Rusty, Irene, Betty, Joyce, Olive, Doris, Bobby, Trudy, Daphne, Agnes, Sheila, Winnie, Mary. All preparing their songs. And the thirty-four-year-old Simone in her room, thinking back on her life, watching the clouds move eastwards, back towards the country of her birth . . . The clouds with no limits. Able to fly over lands occupied, cities bombed. Beyond the railways and the extermination camps. Weil had not been surprised to learn about the mass murder of the Jews, having spent her life trying to understand the extreme barbarities of the world; in fact, she used the word 'holocaust' long before others, asking a friend, 'How do we condemn a holocaust if we have not condemned all past holocausts?'

We turn back down the track. Just the hum of the car's engine. Sun coming through, the early-evening light dappling the leaves above. The last of summer. The cemetery is much easier to find; we park by the gates, and walk through the neat paths, formed in rectangles under cherry trees. We pass a strange collection of graves – little, vibrantly coloured windmills whirling, dolls, teddy bears, and realise with a shudder that these must be children's graves. We arrive at the western edge of the cemetery, and it's almost as if I've been here before, I have such a strong sense of where the grave will be. We walk to the base of half a dozen tall pine trees and there, exactly as I'd imagined, is Simone Weil's grave. Edged by orange and pink flowers, a simple grey tablet, with the stark inscription:

SIMONE WEIL
3 fevrier 1909
24 aout 1943

Some wisps of dead flowers laid at one corner. But we're pleased to see that people still come here. There's another flecked grey tablet of stone that's been placed at the foot of her grave, with words carved in black letters, but it's very faded, only some of them are still legible, so it's a struggle to read:

MEMBER [?] OF PROVISIONAL FRENCH
GOVERNMENT IN LONDON
BUT DEVELOPED [?] TUBERCULOSIS
GROSVENOR
SANATORIUM ASHFORD
WRITINGS
FOREMOST
MODERN PHILOSOPHERS

We're intrigued at the grave next to hers, extremely close. Stephen Maynard, died in 1948, and Ethel Mary Maynard. The proximity suggests some connection with Weil. Stefan then reads the inscription which says: 'Don't look for flaws as you go through life; and even if you find them, it is wise and kind to be somewhat blind, and look for the virtues behind them.' Now that nobody's speaking I become aware of the constant, low rumble of the motorway a couple of hundred yards beyond the trees, down in the valley. Before we leave, knowing our friend Johann's strong connection with Weil's work, I read aloud his short meditation 'A Girl Like Antigone' – visiting her room in Paris, the table at which she wrote, the window overlooking the Jardin de Luxembourg and the city beyond:

> The room is long and narrow like the table. When she sat behind it, the door was on her left. The door gives on to a corridor: opposite was her father's consulting room. When she walked down the corridor towards the front door she would have passed the waiting room on her left. The sick, or those who feared they were sick, were immediately outside her door. She could have heard her father saying goodbye to each patient and greeting the next one: *Bonjour Madame*, sit down and tell me how you are . . .
>
> I sat at her table and read a poem which had marked a turning point in her life. In her hieroglyphic handwriting she had copied out the poem in English and learnt it by heart. At moments when she was overcome by despair or the pain of a migraine behind her eyes, she used to recite it out loud, like a prayer. On one such occasion, whilst reading it, she felt the physical presence of Christ and was astonished . . . Fifty years later, as I read the sonnet by George Herbert, the poem became a place, a dwelling. There was nobody in it. Inside it was shaped like a stone beehive. There are tombs and shelters like this in the Sahara. I have read many poems in my life but I had never before *visited* one. The words were the stones of a habitation which surrounded me.
>
> In the street below, above the entrance to the apartment block (today you need to tap a code to get in), there is a plaque

which reads: 'Simone Weil, philosopher, lived here between 1926 and 1942'.

As we walk back to the car, Alice says that she still finds something very disturbing about the almost wilful act of her death. At the height of the war when so many millions had little choice about dying, the way that Weil embraced death seems bewilderingly wasteful. The voluntary extinguishing of a life and a remarkable mind that could have contributed so much after the war.[*]

*

We head south, out of Ashford, soon onto the straight roads through the marshes that lead to Dungeness and the late film director Derek Jarman's old cottage – the last stop on our journey today. We wonder how much of Weil's iconic status today is tied up with her early death. But surely, I say, more is to do with her profound understanding of empathy, her instinctive identification with the suffering of others? Coming even before her own pain. Isn't that what resonates with our world today? Alice questions whether Weil's empathy with others was really as profound as it seems to us now: perhaps her instinctive compassion for others was not as unique as we think? After all, isn't this what most parents feel for their children as an almost automatic response? And we don't consider this something remarkable. Although maybe we should. Because the fact that such love can then go further, into the wider world, opens up transformatory possibilities. I'm sure this is true, but I'm still intrigued by a tantalising quality in Weil's life and thought that is difficult to put into words, and perhaps takes us beyond our use of the word 'empathy' – it's her ability to connect in an intuitive way with people beyond her family and friends. People she had never met. The suffering of the stranger, the pain of those colonised by her country thousands of miles away. She felt these realities not in an abstract way, but as an entirely visceral lived experience.

_____

[*] See chapter notes for further thoughts.

Triggered by this thought, I start to tell Alice and Stefan about Casalis' years with Speer in Spandau – and the compassion he showed, not only to a stranger but actually an enemy – and his entreaty to him 'to open his mind and spirit to suffering', and the transformatory impact this had on Speer. Perhaps part of my fascination with this lies in the Catholicism I was brought up with. It's hard to talk about such things, especially since I rejected this religion a long time ago. I don't find the words coming fluently, but I want to try to express something which, at root, may be a mystery. Signs to Lydd and New Romney ahead, we turn left to Dungeness. Perhaps it's to do with becoming more secure in our own values as we get older, and then maybe it's possible to see elements of real good, or even beauty, in something we have previously rejected. 'The end of all our exploring will be to arrive where we started and know the place for the first time.' At this point we then can approach that belief, or that idea, as if never encountered before, and be startled by its force. Like walking by a river that you know, in a different season, and suddenly seeing a salmon leap.

The concept of sacrificing something in yourself for another human being. Or even sacrificing your own life for another. These concepts seem miraculous. Because they run against so much that our society now teaches, from the extreme materialism of twenty-first-century capitalism to biological notions of selfish genes. I wonder what happens in such moments of sacrifice, both in the receiver and the giver. Is this connected in some way with the word 'redemption'? I'm surprised to hear myself using this word – a word used meaninglessly by priests decades ago to justify a fairy tale. But I feel like reclaiming it now, in humanist terms, and accepting that there *is* something redemptive in helping others beyond limits, beyond suffering.

We're driving now towards a sky mackerelled with greys and pinks, the power station at Dungeness now visible on the horizon. What I'm attempting to describe, and what moves me about Weil and Casalis, has nothing to do with altruism, nothing to do with 'saintliness'. I don't have much time for either. I don't accept those narratives. Actually, I've always found something repellent in the aura that attaches itself to supposedly 'saintly' people. The problem here lies in the self-consciousness of the seemingly good act. Whereas what I find compelling is the *instinctive* act of care for another, which could be called compassion. Yes, this is found between parents and children, between partners, between doctors and patients, yet it is even more extraordinary when it goes beyond the realm of family or professional relationships. Compassion for the stranger may be extremely rare, almost miraculous, as Weil puts it, but it does exist. And its existence breathes hope into the world.

Here Primo Levi again comes to mind. And particularly what he began to write when he returned to Italy after the war. He described the experience of starting 'The Story of Ten Days' as being 'like a flood which has been dammed and suddenly rushes forth'. It forms the last chapter of *If This Is a Man*, and yet it was the piece which he wrote first. Reflecting on this chapter later in a letter to Charles Conreau, one of the men who had survived Buna-Monowitz with him, Levi wrote about 'those ten incredibly intense days we lived together . . . our finest hour'.

Levi had finally reached his home in Turin on 19 October 1945, after a four-month odyssey across eastern Europe, and in January 1946 began working at DUCO (a paint and explosives factory, a subsidiary of Nobel-Montecatini), outside the city at Avigliana. Here, during the working week – because of limited transport in those post-war days and to save the costs of commuting between Turin and the factory – Levi was offered a room in the Casa Scapoli, a kind of workers' hostel, which gave him a magnificent panorama over the Susa valley to the mountains beyond. For the first time in many years he had his own space, and a sense of safety. Yet inside he was consumed by what he had experienced, and the overwhelming need, like Odysseus, to tell his account of what had happened to him, and many others.

By February, we know that he'd started to record 'pell-mell, thoughts and events, conversations, things heard and seen at the camp, on the back of train tickets, scraps of paper, flattened cigarette packets – anything he could find'. This frantic note-taking continued Levi's personal exorcism, but it was all in preparation for something extraordinary. 'Probably if I'd not written my book, I'd have remained one of the damned of the earth,' he remarked later. He wrote feverishly in the Casa Scapoli throughout spring and summer 1946, typing late into the night, and sometimes even racing back in his half-hour lunch break to complete something. He hardly socialised at all during this period, all his energies that weren't used up by his chemical work went into the developing book. By December the manuscript was completed. He wrote to a friend, the survivor Jean Samuel, 'I've worked on this book with love and rage.'

At the beginning of the chapter, Levi tells us that he'd come down with scarlet fever on 11 January 1945, at the height of the Polish winter, as the Russian guns get closer to Auschwitz. He's admitted to the *Infektionsabteilung* (the infectious-diseases room within the infirmary compound); there are twelve other men there, suffering from scarlet fever, diphtheria, typhus and other illnesses. He writes that he 'enjoyed four peaceful days. Outside it was snowing and very cold, but the room was heated. I was given strong doses of sulpha drugs.' He then learns from a barber that the whole camp is about to be evacuated, including all the patients able to walk. His friend Alberto, who has meant everything to Levi, comes to the window of the room to say goodbye. 'All the healthy prisoners ... left during the night of 18 January 1945. They must have been about twenty thousand, coming from different camps. Almost in their entirety they vanished during the evacuation march: Alberto was among them. Perhaps someone will write their story one day.' The following day all of the remaining Germans and SS in the camp leave, but the heating plant is abandoned too and, with the temperature outside minus five, heat becomes the overwhelming priority.

On 19 January Levi and the two Frenchmen with scarlet fever – Charles and Arthur (both from the Vosges, the former a teacher, the latter a peasant) – get up at dawn to try to find a stove, some fuel, and food. Despite their physical weakness they find a heavy iron stove and some potatoes and wheel them back across the camp in a wheelbarrow; the place now resembles some post-apocalyptic hell with skeletal prisoners crawling over the camp searching for food, fouling the snow. The three return to the *Infektionsabteilung* hut, exhausted from their efforts, and full of urgency to get the stove working. Levi then writes this, which expresses in more tangible words some of the abstracted concepts relating to compassion and redemption that we've been wrestling with today:

> We all three had our hands paralysed while the icy metal stuck to the skin of our fingers, but it was vitally urgent to set it up to warm ourselves and to boil the potatoes. We had found wood and coal as well as embers from the burnt huts. When the broken window was repaired and the stove began to spread its heat, something seemed to relax in everyone, and at that moment Towarowski (a Franco-Pole of twenty-three, typhus) proposed to the others that each of them offer a slice of bread to us three who had been working. And so it was agreed.
>
> Only a day before a similar event would have been inconceivable. The law of the *Lager* said: 'eat your own bread, and if you can, that of your neighbour', and left no room for gratitude ... It was the first human gesture that occurred among us. I believe that that moment can be dated as the beginning of the change by which we who had not died slowly changed from *Häftlinge* to men again.

In the next days, Charles and Levi find frozen turnips and some salt, they also collect wood, and snow for water. Arthur organises the stove, cleans the room and looks after the patients. They take it in turns to empty the lavatory bucket in a cesspool outside. They begin to explore the abandoned SS camp, just outside the fence; here they find frozen soup, vodka, medicines and eiderdowns which they take back to the hut, narrowly avoiding a group of SS officers, who half an hour later kill eighteen Frenchmen they catch in the abandoned dining hall. On the night of 22 January, Lakmaker, a seventeen-year-old Dutch Jew, in a terrible state, falls out of his bed, trying to reach the bucket. Levi then describes what they do – in the context of their illness and exhaustion these actions seem astounding and miraculous in their humanity:

> Charles climbed down from his bed and dressed in silence. While I held the lamp, he cut all the dirty patches from the straw mattress and the blankets with a knife. He lifted Lakmaker from the ground with the tenderness of a mother, cleaned him as best as possible with straw taken from the mattress and lifted him into the remade bed in the only position in which the unfortunate fellow could lie. He scraped the floor with a scrap of tinplate, diluted a little chloramines and finally spread disinfectant over everything, including himself. I judged his self-sacrifice by the tiredness which I would have had to overcome in myself to do what he had done.

Over the next days they find more potatoes, buried in two long ditches just outside the camp. Levi tries to get medical help for one of the men suffering from diphtheria. Outside their hut 'the pile of corpses in front of our window had by now overflowed out of the ditch'; they are acutely aware of the appalling conditions in the tuberculosis and dysentery wards next door, where Levi describes terrifying scenes. On 25 January the Hungarian chemist, Somogyi, suffering from scarlet fever and typhus, speaks for the first time in five days: 'I have a ration of bread under the sack. Divide it among you three. I shall not be eating anymore.' For the rest of that day and the next he falls into a delirium, murmuring '*Jawohl*' with every breath, thousands of times. Levi here writes:

> I never understood so clearly as at that moment how laborious is the death of a man. Outside the great silence continued. The number of ravens had increased considerably and everybody knew why. Only at distant intervals did the dialogue of the artillery wake up. We all said to each other that the Russians would arrive soon, at once; we all proclaimed it, we were all sure of it, but at the bottom nobody believed it.

Levi, Charles and Arthur talk around the stove and share stories and memories. 'I felt ourselves become men once again. We could speak of everything.' On the night of the 26th Somogyi finally dies; with his last gasp of life he throws himself from his bed.

27 January. Dawn. On the floor, the shameful wreck of skin and bones, the Somogyi thing . . . There are more urgent tasks: we cannot wash ourselves, so that we dare not touch him until we have cooked and eaten . . . The living are more demanding; the dead can wait. We began to work as on every day.

The Russians arrived while Charles and I were carrying Somogyi a little distance outside. He was very light. We overturned the stretcher on the grey snow. Charles took off his beret.

This is where *If This Is a Man* ends, and the point at which *The Truce* begins, with the arrival of the Russian army:

There were four young soldiers on horseback, who advanced along the road that marked the limits of the camp, cautiously holding their Sten guns. When they reached the barbed wire, they stopped to look, exchanging a few timid words, and throwing strangely embarrassed glances at the sprawling bodies, at the battered huts and at us few still alive.

To us they seemed wonderfully concrete and real, perched on their enormous horses, between the grey of the snow and the grey of the sky, immobile beneath the gusts of damp wind which threatened a thaw . . .

They did not greet us, nor did they smile; they seemed oppressed not only by compassion but by a confused restraint, which sealed their lips and bound their eyes to the funereal scene. It was that shame we knew so well, the shame . . . that the just man experiences at another man's crime: the feeling of guilt that such a crime should exist.

It is this concrete image I return to again and again. The collision of worlds. The living, the barely living and the dead. The young Russians. Levi and Charles. Somogyi. And, each year, at the end of January, I reread these passages, to spend time with these men again. These words recorded many years ago. *Recordar*, from the Latin *recordis*, to pass back through the heart. Which is all that we can do.

*

Our journey is almost over. We can sense the coast and the sea get-ting closer, and the skies getting vaster. Dungeness power station now looms in the distance, silhouetted by a vermillion blaze of sky behind, with the pylons strung out across the marshes.

We drive down the track and stop outside Derek Jarman's last sanc-tuary, 'Prospect Cottage', which he stumbled across in the late 1980s when filming the suitably titled *The Last of England*:

> Between the tumbledown shacks succulent sea kale sprouts like wreaths from the stones; broom blown flat by the wind hugs the ground. Not much grows in this stony ground and what does is blown into sinister druidical shapes like the ancient holly woods, watered by the salt spray that the wind whips from the waves . . . We knock at the door of Prospect Cottage, a tiny wooden fisherman's house displaying a 'For Sale' notice, which tosses and turns in the gale. The view is shingle and sea, no fence or garden to cut it off. From the back a wide empty expanse of scrubland with the nuclear power station . . . Dungeness was so silent. Only the sound of the wind. 'Does the wind ever stop?' I asked the sweet lady who owned the house. 'Sometimes,' she replied.

Even in the dusk, illuminated by the car's headlights, we can see the last miracle that Jarman created – the garden which he conjured from the shingle. Circles of bushes and sea holly, obelisks of drift-wood, banks of wild poppies shaking in the evening breeze.

As we crunch over the shingle beach looking towards the lights of Hythe and Dymchurch, I tell Alice and Stefan about the filming of *The Garden* here, and the incredible impact that work made on me as a young man in the late 1980s – the combination of rage and beauty – 'I walk in this garden / Holding the hands of dead friends / Old age came quickly for my frosted generation / Cold, cold, cold they died so silently / Did the forgotten gen-erations scream? / Or go full of resignation / Quietly protesting innocence / Cold, cold, cold they died so silently.' My God, how

990

we could do with his spirit in our times now – kicking against the pricks and outraging public decency and castigating intolerance and prejudice. A few months after the film came out, I found myself sitting alone in the tiny upstairs room at Maison Bertaux in Greek Street, Soho (where, at that time, it was still quiet enough to go and write). I was so absorbed with my journal that I didn't notice that anyone had come up the stairs, but when I looked up a few minutes later, I saw Jarman at the next table, also alone, also scribbling away in a little sketchbook. We then carried on writing and drawing, but on my way out a little while later, I paused by his table and said: 'Thank you for *The Garden* and *Sebastiane* – they meant so much to me.' He smiled, rather shyly I thought, 'Thank you. That's very kind of you!' and bobbed his head in a courtly bow as I left.

We drive on down the track to the lighthouse at the end. Alice and the children are bewitched by the landscape, 'outpost territory', as Alice calls it, this bizarre conjunction of the power station and the little wooden shacks below. Stefan tells us that Jarman is buried in Old Romney churchyard, and that he remembers coming down here a week after Jarman died and posting a poem he'd written through the letter box of Prospect Cottage. We drive back to the pub on the main road, and order fish and chips and ice cream, a partial reward for the children's exceptional patience today. We're not sure most young teenagers would have put up with our visits to graves and churches, our talk of trauma and suffering and death. But they seem fine about it, teasing Alice, saying, 'Oh, with Mum we're used to doing things like this!' 'What, even on your summer holidays?' – a question which provokes a few raised eyebrows and some more gentle laughter. Over generous plates of haddock and chips we talk about books from our childhood that have stayed with us – John Burningham's work, especially *Borka*, and Philippa Pearce's *Tom's Midnight Garden*, and then I'm amazed to discover that Alice and the children also knew, and loved, Hilda Lewis' *The Ship That Flew*. We talk about the power of that particular story, and the impact it had had on all of us; I'd had no idea that it was even still in print.

It's a warm evening, gentle summer breeze, none of us are in a rush to travel back, so afterwards we walk across the shingle to the water, which seems to be retreating. 'The sea is calm tonight. / The tide is full…' But no moon yet. I've never really agreed with Matthew Arnold about the 'melancholy' that he hears in the 'long, withdrawing roar, / Retreating, to the breath / Of the night-wind, down the vast edges drear / And naked shingles of the world.' That sound of the sea repeatedly drawing back the shingle on a beach, for me, is a sound of absolute equanimity. It always stills troubled spirits, and reassures utterly.

As the children search for unusual pebbles, Alice asks me about the seeds of all of this work, and where the original impetus had come from. I tell her about an inspiring young tutor at university, who I only got to meet in my final year. He'd told me that the Tragedy paper in part two of the tripos could be interpreted in many ways, not just the traditional Greek or Shakespearean form. For instance, did I know the work of Primo Levi or Jean Améry? Or that a remarkable book, *The Chronicle of the Lodz Ghetto*, had just been translated into English for the first time? 'Here, you can borrow it; let me know what you think next week. If you're interested I can draw up a reading list…' Then, a year later, the sheer, overwhelming power of seeing *Shoah* for the first time. Another decade on, the moment of revelation, reading Sereny's remarkable work on Speer.

But I've only realised recently that, however important all of these stimuli were, they would only have seeded if the soil had been there in the first place. And that soil was Mark, my father, and the devastating experience in Korea that he could never find the words to describe. And the way his silence haunted me as a child, sensing the suffering he would never speak about. The healing that lies beyond the reach of a child. The wound that never completely left the body. Yet his silence still communicated to me, as powerfully as a letter opened after death. Urging me to do the searching that he could never do, into the minds of those who cause violence, into unspoken histories and places of darkness. All that he spent the rest of his life running from, I would spend most of my life running towards.

I've never spoken to Alice about my father before. She's very shocked to hear about his death, killed in the fire on the fields where he'd grown up. Fifty-three years old. Stefan is looking at the sea ahead, reflective; his mother also died shockingly young. All that comes with us. The baggage we always carry. I hear myself saying something I've never articulated before, wondering if there's a relationship between my father not publishing and the strange feelings I have about finishing this work. I know it sounds curious, but, in a way, the act of publishing seems like a kind of disloyalty to Mark. And, inevitably, when I think of his rich and remarkable mind, his knowledge of so many worlds that I will never inhabit, it makes it harder to see my own work clearly, it makes me doubt. Alice and Stefan disagree passionately, saying it's precisely these kind of tensions that are critical to anything worthwhile – the internal dialogues we all have with our parents, alive or dead. But they're both sure that my father would be happy that I am moving into territory which he could never reach himself. I turn to look at the lapping waves in the moonlight, seeing them distorted now, through blurred eyes. The children are skimming flat stones, trying to get them to leap from one wave to the next.

Before we walk back to the car, Alice stoops down and collects two pebbles and gives them to us: 'Lucky stones for you both!' Driving back now, the pools of the headlights reaching into the night, we talk of primal memories of childhood, of being in the back of the car at night, being enfolded in that world. The warmth of the cocoon against the blackness beyond. Drifting in and out of sleep. Voices murmuring from the front. Alice is now recounting how her father would take her and her brothers on wild weekend trips from the city. Sometimes they'd head off on Friday evening straight after school, he'd meet them at the gates with no warning, and they'd all just pile into the car – Alice's older brothers never let her sit by the windows, so she'd always be in the middle – and then out into the Ontario night. They'd drive for hours, then pitch their tents, carry on the next day, just exploring, continuing through the weekend, finding new valleys and waterfalls and mountains.

There's very little traffic on the B-roads tonight. Only a few miles from Ashford now, where I'm going to drop everyone off to get their train back to London. The sense of the evening coming to a close, the melancholic pull of late August and the end of holidays. We're now discussing how talking in cars at night is different in texture from any other kind of talking. Especially on long journeys when it's just the driver and the passenger, the intense intimacy, the confessional energy of both people just focussed on the pools of light in front of the car and the words of the other. Inspired by this thought, Alice then wonders if this could be represented in film – two old friends who haven't seen each other for years, driving through the night and talking. And the film would be only this – the journey at night with just the two voices. And the sound of listening. And gears humming, and occasional windscreen wipers flapping. And all we'd see was the unspooling road ahead and glimpses of trees and buildings caught in the headlights. And the sound of friendship in the dark. The love between two people talking with no boundaries.

While Alice and I enthuse about this idea, Stefan, in the passenger seat next to me, is writing in the dark. I can hear the soft scraping of pen on paper. It's from film reviewing, he explains, you learn to scribble notes in the dark. But doesn't he find later that these are often impossible to decipher? Yes, all the time. He'd had one a couple of days ago which baffled him – it looked like he'd written 'Abigail – reverse – lawyers crossing' – not *one word* of which made any sense at all! So much for memory, if we can't even remember what the aides-memoires were supposed to mean . . . I tell the others about my grandmother, and that baffling euphemism we heard as children, that she'd 'lost her memory'. We're on a long, straight road now, ahead of us the glow of Ashford becoming visible. Alice is speaking of her father, and the Alzheimer's which also claimed him in the decade before he died. Towards the end, most of the time he didn't know who she was, but there were occasional moments of lucidity. Moments when a memory or a piece of music would get through, and she'd find him sitting in a chair weeping. The journeying and the exploring almost over.

The man who had once given them life, driven them through the night and into the morning.

*

We say our goodbyes outside the floodlit concrete concourse of Ashford International station, which looks like it's pretending to be the entrance to an airport rather than a railway station. I still have another three hours to drive tonight, to get back to the fisherman's cottage on the Suffolk coast where I'm staying for the next few days – the place where I began writing more than seven years ago, in the grip of winter. I look at my road atlas, sadly there seems to be no real alternative to the motorway up to the Dartford Crossing and beyond. I need more air to keep me awake, so put the window down as I drive away, and see the lights of Ashford International receding in my mirror.

Onto the motorway slip road, only a stone's throw from where we'd been earlier in the day, by Weil's grave, just beyond the line of poplars. But now dealing with a very different world, as I edge onto the motorway. Past eleven o'clock, but I'm shocked by the volume of traffic, and the stupid, aggressive driving, tailgating, overtaking on the wrong side. Impossible to find a greater contrast with the calmness of our day. I suddenly sense my exhaustion, a combination of having been up since six o'clock this morning, and the intensity of what we've experienced today. Dangerous to drive in this state, I'm finding it really hard to deal with the constant stream of lorries and cars. I pull over into the slow lane to avoid having to make decisions. Past Maidstone, Chatham, down into the valley of the Medway and up again, sensing the pull of London's orbit now, and the M25 just ahead. My eyes are so heavy, I'm having to slap my face to stay awake. I put on music, loud as possible, see if this will help. A lorry brakes, suddenly, in front of me, I slam on my brakes and only avoid hitting the back of the lorry by a matter of feet.

I know I need to get off the motorway. I take the next exit, and find a garage. I get a strong coffee from the machine, know the caffeine will take twenty minutes to start working, so put my seat back and try to sleep. I'm out like a light. When I wake half an hour later I feel revived. I flick through my shoebox of CDs on the passenger seat beside me, and pull out a few that will be my fellow travellers for the next couple of hours. Then back on the road, M25, Dartford Crossing, through the marshlands of southern Essex, then signs to the A12. The road emptying as I drive away from London, which is a great relief. There's a new one out in a series of Dylan bootlegs, most of the tracks are familiar, but suddenly I'm arrested by something I've never heard before – a mesmerising, rolling drum and bass, whiplash intensity and his voice coming in with hypnotic power and urgency, 'I was think-ing of a ser-ies of dreams, / where noth-ing comes up to the top, / every-thing stays down where it's woun-ded, / and comes to a permanent stoppp . . .' Thrilling to hear this song for the first time tonight, and also synchronistic, because it's an amazing piece to drive to, especially on long, straight roads like tonight, where you can put the car into fifth gear, and watch the speedometer dial move round to 80, 85, 90, the pounding energy of the music fusing with the road. As I drive north and east, I play this track again and again, in fact it takes me all the way from the A12 junction at Brentwood to Ipswich – at least an hour, so I must have played it a dozen times. Getting something new on each hearing. Being taken home by a series of dreams . . .

Over the Orwell Bridge, the last stretch finally, the curve round, then off on the road to Woodbridge. One forty-five now, very good progress. I stop for petrol at the twenty-four-hour garage. Shell, but there's no other choice. It always leaves a bitter taste to pay any money to this company, though as I fill up I reflect that if you wanted to come up with the definitive oxymoron, it would have to be 'ethical oil company', so I'm not certain any of the others are much better. I go into the shop, surprised it's still open, usually after midnight you have to pay through the 'night window'. The young guy on the till asks me if I have a Shell loyalty card. Normally I'd just let this go, but I don't tonight. After all, it's late, and there are no other people around. I ask the guy whether he thinks it's possible to be loyal to a corporation? He laughs, 'No, of course not! It's just the bullshit we have to ask everybody.' As I drive off, I see him picking up a book, illuminated in his nocturnal kiosk.

The dual carriageway comes to an end. I turn off onto a smaller road, trying to make sense of the day.

The white lines finally fade. A long, straight stretch through woods of pine and silver birch. Through a last village. And then the little road, barely signed at all. The road where you never meet another vehicle. Driving in a trance now, slowed to twenty, fifteen miles per hour. A tunnel of trees. Right-angle bend sweeps round. The telegraph pole where the barn owl was. To the left, a final sway the other way, out into the open again, over a small, white bridge. Tall reeds now on both sides. And finally the road becomes a track, and the track ends at the blackness of the sea. As the engine fades the certainty of that soft roar of waves and wind. And a flickering understanding that the end and the beginning are the same.

An almost full moon to the south, scudding silver cloud coming in from the sea. I crunch through the shingle to the front door of the cottage. 2.30 a.m., nineteen hours after I left here this morning. But, before I go inside, there's something I want to do – I walk the hundred yards or so down to the sea, and look south, trying to connect the waters of Suffolk with the waters of Kent, wondering how long it would take a piece of driftwood to travel the distance. And at that moment I feel in my pocket, and pull out the pebble Alice gave me a few hours ago. I kneel down by the shore, and pick up another one of a similar size, to accompany hers. They chink together in my pocket as I walk back to the cottage over the shingle, picking my way through the sea holly.

*

Postscript: 2019

Years on, I'm back in the west, with the cliffs and the ravens. Night has come. Authoritarianism is on the march again. Extreme nationalism and the viciousness of intolerance is suddenly everywhere. This time it will not return in the shape of killers in black uniforms, but in the anonymous tapping of algorithms into keyboards, and digital surveillance on a scale that none of us can imagine.

I'm still writing, past midnight, at my window in Wales, overlooking an inky high tide, shaping these strange arcs and lines onto a white page. I don't know what they can do. Words in the dark. But I still have hope. On the table in front of me are two pebbles – one grey, pockmarked with white scars, the other reddish but also with white marks.

I cannot now remember which comes from where. The grey one rests firmly on the wood of the table, the reddish one, more rounded, rocks gently as I push them together. Shingle from the east coast years ago. Carriers from another place and time. Touching the stones, I think about how far we have come. And how far we have to go.

I. You. We.

to be continued . . .

Notes

'*Once we accept, for a single hour . . .*' The Tolstoy quotation is taken from *Resurrection*, Part II, Chapter 40. (I've elided two sections of text from the chapter here – I hope Tolstoy's ghost is not offended by my editing).

'*In a dark time the eye begins to see . . .*' is from Theodore Roethke's poem 'In A Dark Time'.

Book One

Preface:
First Day, White Page

5 *Walter Stier, the railway official who timetabled the trains to Treblinka, insists again, 'I just sat at my desk . . . I was just a desk man.'* This is from Claude Lanzmann's film *Shoah* – the wording is directly transcribed from the original English subtitles of the film. The exchange between Lanzmann and Stier is as follows:

> 'Did you know that Treblinka meant extermination?'
> 'Of course not!'
> 'You didn't know?'
> 'Good God no! How could we know? I never went to Treblinka. I never left Krakow, Warsaw, I just sat at my desk.'
> 'You were a desk man?'
> 'I was a desk man, just a desk man.'

The words Lanzmann and Stier use here in German are '*schreibtisch mann*' (accurately translated as 'desk man'). However, in the official text of the film, published in 1995, there are many discrepancies – sometimes minor, sometimes not – between the original wording and the official text (for instance, the above exchange is changed to: 'I *stayed in* Krakow, in Warsaw, *glued* to my desk . . . I was *strictly a bureaucrat!*'). In my view, the original subtitles are both more literal, and more accurate, than the subsequent text version, and so throughout this work, when I quote from *Shoah* I use the original wording from the film subtitles.

Chapter One:
Explorations: Maps and the Curiosity of a Child's Mind

10 '*man is most nearly himself when he achieves the seriousness of a child at play.*' I came across this quotation from Heraclitus reading the introduction to the *Redstone Diary 2018*, the theme of which was 'Play'. I later found that Nietzsche had borrowed Heraclitus's concept in *Beyond Good and Evil*, Part 4, where he writes: 'Human maturity . . . means rediscovering the seriousness we had towards play when we were children.'

10 Perhaps another reason why the act of walking is so alluring in our societies is that it is one of the few activities that cannot really be commodified; you can spend hours walking in cities or countryside without spending any money at all. And, in a world where the insatiability of capitalism and the frenzied buying and selling of everything seems to increase exponentially, walking, in this way, becomes an almost invisible act of resistance.

11 These lines of John Clare's are all from 'The Moors' – a poem written in response to the 1809 Parliament 'Act for Inclosing Lands in the Parishes of Maxey and Helpstone, in the County of Northamptonshire'.

12 '*Who possesses this landscape? / The man who bought it or / I who am possessed by it? . . .*' from 'A Man in Assynt' by Norman MacCaig.

13 Today the former clinic is a pizza place, one of those bizarre London transmutations – from VD to Venezianas. The only tricky

period came when my friend suggested his Czech girlfriend could move in too, not fully appreciating the diplomatic sensitivity of Russo-Czech relations. Those couple of months pushed the notion of the 'one-bedroom flat' to its limits, though it did enable me to record a message on our answerphone which began: 'Welcome to the Centre for Anglo-Slavonic Research Studies, please leave a message after the beep . . .'

17 In the years since I first noticed these words on the steps at Tottenham Court Road underground station, the steel and name plates have now been superseded in the redevelopment of this station, so you will search in vain to find these traces of 'permanence' at Tottenham Court Road, though I've noticed recently that these nameplates still exist at other stations on the underground.

18 The wording of this memorandum is exactly the wording of the English subtitles when *Shoah* was first released in 1986, and the wording subsequently broadcast on Channel 4. This differs, in certain details, from the text of *Shoah*, published as a book in 1995 (see earlier note). Both of these versions differ considerably from the actual wording of the memorandum – as I explain in Chapter Five.

20 It's easy to forget how iconic the *A-Z* once was – a book containing maps of all the streets in London, designed with grid references so you could effortlessly find any street in the city, however small. In pre-app days it was simply an essential companion for anyone who lived and worked in London (not only for cabbies).

21 I only realised re-reading *Borka* recently after many years that (as children often do, subconsciously) I'd changed Borka's gender to my own, so total was my identification with this goose that didn't quite seem to fit in.

Chapter Two:
Gitta Sereny, Albert Speer and the Desk Killer

27 *I had made a contribution in which I described the research . . .*

The initial research for *I You We Them* began in 1996, when I was a co-director of the political arts organisation Platform, and lasted almost a decade. It is not possible here to summarise ten years' work, but the main phases in how the research eventually evolved into what you are now reading were as follows:

- 1996–2003: Early research and development of the '*killing us softly*' lecture performances.

As part of Platform's ambitious, ten-year project, '90% Crude' – an attempt to analyse the social and environmental impacts of transnational corporations, with specific reference to the oil industry – I began to focus on how individuals who worked for such corporations were able to reconcile their own ethics and beliefs with the sometimes devastating impacts of their companies' work. In the late 1990s I read widely in the field of perpetrator psychology, helped greatly by the staff and archive of the Wiener Library in London. I also began to research corporate collusion in the Holocaust – the numerous companies and businesses that worked so closely with the Nazi regime and the SS. In 1999 I decided to create a series of 'lecture-performances' to bring my research on 'desk killers' (both in history and today) to live audiences. These events also included film excerpts, images of walks at sites of genocide, passages of music and poetry, and discussion with those attending. Between 1999 and 2003 there were eight performances of *killing us softly* at Platform's space near Tower Bridge. The last event took place just before the outbreak of the Iraq War, at the end of March 2003.

- 2003–2004: Development of *The Desk Killer* into a book proposal, and the second research phase.

It became clear that although the live events had helped to evolve the work significantly, it was now time to find a new form. I began to work on the challenge of how to convert a scripted, live event into the very different form of a book, provisionally titled *The Desk Killer*. During the winter 2003–2004 I also undertook an important research trip to Berlin and Poland, visiting some of the key sites

I'd been researching – the villa of the Wannsee Conference, the Buna-Monowitz complex at Oswiecim (Auschwitz) and Chelmno, where the Saurer *gaswagen* were used.

- 2005: The third research phase, supported by the Lannan Foundation.

In early 2005, with the support of a major grant from the Lannan Foundation in New Mexico, I was able to employ a part-time researcher to help with the growing scope of the developing book, and one area in particular – IG Farben's vast synthetic fuels and rubber plant in Auschwitz, run in collaboration with the SS and the slave labour they provided from the neighbouring Monowitz concentration camp in the town. I also made another research trip – to Bosnia (to try and investigate Kurt Waldheim's wartime role there), and to Belgrade (to investigate the use of the Saurer *gaswagen* at the Semlin camp next to the River Sava). This research trip concluded with a return visit to Oswiecim, and several days working in the archives there, with the director, Dr Piotr Setkiewicz, learning more about the IG Farben complex and their cooperation with the SS, and many other companies who were also closely involved with the network of concentration camps and labour camps in Auschwitz and the surrounding area.

- 2006: The first writing phase.

In January 2006, still supported by the Lannan grant, I was able to take a six-month sabbatical from Platform, and our work on the 'Remember Saro-Wiwa' initiative – a campaign to create a memorial to the murdered Nigerian writer and activist Ken Saro-Wiwa and his eight colleagues – to begin the writing of The Desk Killer at a cottage on the Suffolk coast, which is where this book begins.

32 *'In this trial, we shall also encounter a new kind of killer . . .'* Hausner's opening speech quotations taken from the Eichmann trial transcripts, 17 April 1961. I find it intriguing, given Arendt's subsequent, vituperative criticism of Hausner, to read these words

and realise how much they echo some of her own later thoughts and analysis of Eichmann's pioneering form of white-collar genocide.

35 The advert for UAV Operator – UAE National Executive Solutions, Abu Dhabi, UAE was online at https://www.gulftalent.com/uae/jobs/uav-operator-uae-national-62963 (complete with the original spelling mistake – arial instead of aerial).

Chapter Three:
How We Look at History: A Moment at Liverpool Street Station

47 My account of the Meili affair has drawn primarily on Meili's testimony to the US Senate on 6 May 1997, and the transcript of this hearing – 'Hearing on Shredding of Holocaust Era Documents', and also on an *LA Times* article of 4 March 2001 ('Swiss bank whistleblower pays a high price'), and a *Guardian* piece on whistleblowers, 22 November 2014 ('"There were hundreds of us crying out for help": the afterlife of the whistleblower'). The settlement of UBS and the Swiss banks for collaboration with Nazism is informed by Mario König's report for the Bergier Commission, *Interhandel: The Swiss Holding of IG Farben and its Metamorphoses – An Affair About Property and Interests (1910–1999)*, Stuart Eizenstat's book *Imperfect Justice*, *The American Jewish Year Book 1998* edited by Daniel Singer, and *Swiss Banks and Jewish Souls* by Gregg Rickman.

52 The Swiss banks described as '*pro-fascist financial operators*' by Walter Sholes, US counsel in Basel during the war – quoted in *Nazi Gold* by Tom Bower.

Chapter Four:
Journeys with J.

57 'We take almost all the decisive steps in our lives as a result of slight inner adjustments of which we are barely conscious' from *Austerlitz* by Sebald.

59 One memory from my year on CUSU in 1983 stays with me, and is perhaps worth recounting. The Federation of Conservative Students were in their deeply offensive, extreme-Thatcherite heyday, aided by the far-right Monday Club – and, at an NUS conference I attended at Warwick University, many of them (including, I recall, the current Speaker of the House of Commons – who was then secretary of the Monday Club's 'Immigration and Repatriation Committee' – and several other future Tory MPs and ministers), proudly sported badges reading 'Hang Nelson Mandela'.

61 The Bishopsgate Institute in London has recently acquired the Platform archive, which is publicly accessible. I recently spent a very nostalgic couple of hours going through some of the earliest files of material from the Cambridge and Addenbrooke's campaign days, finding notes that J. and I had written, and publicity materials typed on my old Olympia typewriter.

Other figures in Platform's early days, many of who became artists and activists in their own right subsequently, were Paula Webb, Ravi Mirchandani, Rod Bolt and David Evans; Richard Fredman, Ingrid Simler, John Parry and Abigail Morris (the Corn Exchange project); Anna Wright, Wesley Stace, Mel Steel, Graham Burns and Mark Whelan ('Addenbrooke's Blues').

63 'The being together of two human beings . . .' Rilke, from 'On Being With Others' in Letters on Life.

63 'Let's be alone together . . .' Leonard Cohen, 'Waiting for the Miracle'.

70 At the end of our Ottoneum performance we chalked two sentences (translated into German) on vertical blackboards:
'The silence of the earth is our blindness'
'The silence of our country is your deafness'

And then we wrote our '6 Questions for FIU Kassel from FIU. London' (again translated):

1. Why does the Free International University have so little curiosity about other countries?

2. Why do you not debate the question of Power, Wealth and Class?
3. How much is the FIU really involved in its locality in Kassel?
4. When does theoretical discussion become accompanied by practical action?
5. With regard to ecological crisis, how far does your theory of self-responsibility go?
6. By refusing to listen to any criticism of its founder, will the FIU become ossified – like a church in which only the faithful talk to each other?

73 *'Here tulips bloom as they are told; / Unkempt about those hedges blows / An English unofficial rose . . .'* from 'The Old Vicarage, Grantchester' by Rupert Brooke (written in Berlin in 1912).

77 The Canadian sprinter was Ben Johnson. The new world record time set on 30 August 1987, that we saw in the bar in Twiste, was not 9.85 seconds, as I thought at the time – but (as my very conscientious copy-editor informs me) 9.83 seconds. However, Johnson subsequently admitted to steroid use between 1981 and 1988, and so this world record time was struck out of the official records by the IAAF Council in September 1989.

82 *'I see that I must give . . .'* The last line of *Fugitive Pieces* by Anne Michaels.

Chapter Five:
The Town of Organised Forgetting

83 *Shoah* was finally released in 1985, the premiere taking place in Paris in April 1985. The film was then shown, in different countries, over the next months – the first screening in America was in New York in October 1985, and in Britain in spring 1986. It was immediately acclaimed as a seminal work – called 'a sheer masterpiece' by Simone de Beauvoir and 'the greatest documentary about contemporary history ever made, bar none' by the great filmmaker Marcel Ophüls.

My journal from early 1987 records that on 2 and 3 January:

> [I] finally got to see the stunning *Shoah* – a ten hour film
> about the Holocaust – ('Shoah' = the Annihilation in Hebrew)
> at the Curzon. Remarkable for many reasons, but especially
> the lack of sentimentalizing or histrionics. Pared down to
> the bone, creating a rhythm of its own . . . No real dramatic
> climax, no need for it – it gave you room, it never bored.
> Until at the end . . . I wanted more. I could have watched for
> another twenty, thirty hours. It took Lanzmann eleven years
> to make – eleven years and hundreds of hours of film, some-
> how got down to nine and a half. How? The dedication of
> that – the nightmarishness of the task. Images now burned
> into my mind . . .

86 The full memorandum – 'II D 3 a (9) NI. 214/42 G.R.S. Berlin,
5th June 1942 Technical adjustments to special vans at present in
service and to those that are in production' – is reproduced in *Nazi
Mass Murder: A Documentary History of the Use of Poison Gas*,
edited by Kogon, Langbein and Ruckerl, Yale University Press,
1993.

87 Section 2 of the memorandum is extremely convoluted and
has caused a certain amount of confusion among translators:

The original German of this part of the memo is as follows:
> 2.) Die Beschickung der Wagen beträgt normalerweise 9 – 10
> pro m2. Bei den großräumigen Saurer-Spezialwagen ist eine
> Ausnutzung in dieser Form nicht möglich, weil dadurch zwar
> keine Überlastung eintritt, jedoch die Geländegängigkeit sehr
> herabgemindert wird.

Lanzmann's version in *Shoah* translates this as:
> The normal load is nine per square metre. In Saurer vehicles,
> which are very spacious, maximum use of space is impossible,
> not because of any overload but because loading to full capac-
> ity would affect the vehicle's stability.

The translation included in the Yale University Press work *Nazi Mass Murder* (ed. Kogon, Langbein and Ruckerl) is:

2.) The normal capacity of the vans is nine to ten per square metre. The capacity of the larger special Saurer vans is not so great. The problem is not one of overloading but of off-road manoeuverability on all terrains, which is severely diminished in this van.

90 Other trucks, including Opel Blitz, Renault, Dodge, Diamond and Magirus were used as *gaswagen* as well, though Saurers were the main lorries used.

Chapter Six:
Saurer: A Coda – 'The blind spot in the writing of history'

Material in this chapter is taken from the Bergier commission (final report) – available online at www.uek.ch/en/ and also the *Independent*'s obituary of Bergier (19 January 2010) and the *Telegraph*'s obituary (4 November 2009).

117 The information on China's use of execution vans comes from Amnesty International – 'Execution Vans, Organ Harvesting – Business as Usual in China' (19 February 2009). The *Irish Times* article (also 19 February 2009) is by Clifford Coonan in Beijing – 'Killing Vans Make Process Easier for China's Authorities'.

Chapter Seven:
Interlude in Which We Meet a Figure We Will Be Returning to . . .
The Architect in London; First Trip

Information about Speer's first trip to London, in summer 1936, is taken from his autobiography, *Inside the Third Reich*, Chapter Eight. Speer makes a curious error here, suggesting that Ribbentrop wanted the improvements to the German Embassy to be finished 'in time for the coronation of George VI in the spring of 1937' – yet, when Speer visited London in summer 1936, Edward VIII was king, and so it was *his* coronation which was scheduled for spring 1937, not George VI's. (Though, of course, Edward VIII's coronation never took place because of his abdication in December 1936.)

118 Material relating to Hitler giving Speer his own jacket at the Reich Chancellery is from *Albert Speer: His Battle with Truth*, Chapter Three, 'Dizzy With Excitement', by Sereny.

Chapter Eight:
'Lord take my soul, but the struggle continues'

Most of the Ken Saro-Wiwa quotations in this chapter are taken from a transcription I made of his final interview, 'Without Walls: Ken Saro-Wiwa, The Hanged Man; Nigeria's Shame', produced by Bandung, broadcast by Channel 4, November 1995.

127 The term 'the Black Holocaust' has been widely used to describe the genocide of millions of African men, women and children, killed during 400 years of slavery and the slave trade. It is also the title of a book – *The Black Holocaust for Beginners*, published by Writers & Readers, in 1995, by the American academic and activist S. E. Anderson.

135 *'Troops entered towns and villages shooting at random, as villagers fled to the surrounding bush . . .'* This witness testimony of the ISTF raids on Ogoniland appeared in the Human Rights Watch report 'The Ogoni Crisis: A Case-Study of Military Repression in Southeastern Nigeria', published in 1995.

137 The British barrister Michael Birnbaum, QC, published his powerful report *Nigeria: Fundamental Rights Denied, Report of the Trial of Ken Saro-Wiwa and Others* in June 1995. He had been an observer for part of the trial and his report found that 'the trial is fundamentally flawed and there is grave reason to fear that its continuation will represent a gross injustice and an abuse of human rights'.

138 Following the executions of the Ogoni Nine, Nelson Mandela launched a scathing attack on Nigeria and Abacha, calling for immediate sanctions, saying:

'What we are now proposing are short and sharp measures which will produce the results Nigerians and the world desire. We are dealing with an illegitimate, barbaric, arrogant, military dictatorship which has murdered activists, using a kangaroo court and using false evidence,' he told the newspaper . . . Mr Mandela also lashed out at the Shell petroleum company for its decision to go ahead with a $4bn (pounds 2.5bn) gas project in Nigeria, despite worldwide calls for the project to be shelved. He said he told Shell executives in Johannesburg last week that South Africa expected the company to suspend the project as a mark of protest.

'And when they hesitated to do so, I warned them that we are going to take action against them in this country, because we can't allow people to think in terms of their gains when the very lives of human beings are involved. That is the extent to which I have gone in this regard.' Mr Mandela has threatened to call for a boycott of Shell in South Africa. Following the meeting, Shell South Africa placed full-page advertisements in the South African press, defending its human-rights record in Nigeria.' (From the *Independent*, 'Mandela Guns for Nigerian Dictator', 27 November 1995.)

138 Birnbaum published a further report on the tribunal and verdicts in December 1995, called *A Travesty of Law and Justice: An Analysis of the Judgement in the Case of Ken Saro-Wiwa and Others*, published by Article 19 in December 1995. Birnbaum's conclusion was that 'The judgement of the Tribunal is not merely wrong, illogical or perverse. It is downright dishonest. The Tribunal consistently advanced arguments which no experienced lawyer could possibly believe to be logical or just. I believe that the Tribunal first decided on its verdict and then sought for arguments to justify them. No barrel was too deep to be scraped.'

145 *'I'm in good spirits . . . There's no doubt that my idea will succeed in time, but I'll have to bear the pain of the moment . . .'* This letter to

William Boyd is also published as the end of the preface in *A Year and a Day*.

It's clear that Ken Saro-Wiwa thought a lot about his possible death in the years before he was killed. There is a remarkable stoicism and clear-sightedness about the potential risks of his activism. His father, known as Pa Wiwa, recounted this story before he died in 2005, to another activist, Ike Okonta:

> He told me of the morning, now so long ago when Ken came to him and sought his permission to lead the Ogoni to freedom from the tyranny of Shell and the Nigerian state. 'It was a difficult decision for me to make,' Pa Wiwa told me.
>
> 'I asked my son, who will bury me after they have killed you? I asked him this question three times. But he was still determined to do something to save our people. In the end, I gave him my blessing.' (Quoted in *The Next Gulf*, by Rowell, Marriott and Stockman.)

It is also striking that – on two occasions – in his fiction writing Saro-Wiwa has protagonists facing execution the next day. In 'Africa Kills Her Sun', a satirical short story about the systemic nature of corruption in Nigeria, published in 1989, Bana the main character faces death by firing squad in the morning, together with two colleagues. He writes a last letter to his childhood girlfriend and tells her 'what is going to happen later this morning is welcome relief from burdens too heavy to bear. It's . . . you the living who are in prison . . . your happiness is the happiness of ignorance.' In *Lemona's Tale*, a novella published posthumously in 1996, a former prostitute recounts the story of her life to a special visitor, the day before she is going to be hanged. Although the story has simplistic and melodramatic aspects, it is a remarkable exercise in empathetic imagination, and an extremely sympathetic portrait of a woman's growing politicisation in a highly patriarchal society such as Nigeria. At one point she observes: 'And that was my problem wasn't it? Everything was happening to me. I did not happen to anything or anyone. Each time I tried to happen, disaster resulted.'

150 The John Berger quotation *'the powerful fear art . . .'* is from his short, and extraordinarily powerful, essay 'Miners', from the collection *Keeping a Rendezvous*.

Chapter Nine:
From a Desk in Waterloo to a Cell in Port Harcourt

153 The poem with the refrain *'And yet you will weep and know why'* is Gerard Manley Hopkins' 'Spring and Fall'.

155 *'It is not our business to try and influence a trial . . . Our business is to continue the business of petroleum.'* This comment by Brian Anderson, Shell Nigeria managing director, is from Reuters, London (Paul Harris, London Newsroom), reporting Shell's AGM on 15 May 1996: 'Royal Dutch Shell said on Wednesday that it would not intervene in the case of 19 Ogoni activists jailed . . . in Nigeria . . . Shell Nigeria managing director Brian Anderson told the firm's annual meeting that intervention was not the firm's role.'

Chapter Ten:
The Invisible Corporation

159 The excerpts taken from Moody-Stuart's legal deposition are verbatim quotations from the transcript – between pages 106 and 135 – of the 'Deposition Upon Oral Examination of Sir Mark Moody-Stuart, KCMG, on Thursday, April 15, 2004, commencing at 9.35 am, taken at the offices of: Leigh Day & Co. Solicitors, 25 St John's Lane London EC1M 4LB England, Reported by: Thelma Harries, MBIVR, ACR'.

168 *'I WOULD SHOOT ALL IDLERS . . .'* from Deterding's autobiography, *An International Oilman*.

Material in this chapter on Deterding's and Shell's links to Nazism, and the corporate funding of Nazism more generally, comes from *The Most Powerful Man in the World: The Life of Sir Henri Deterding* by Glyn Roberts, *Doing Business with the Nazis: Britain's Economic and Financial Relations with Germany 1931–1936* by Neil Forbes, *Company Man* by Anthony Sampson, *Tycoons and Tyrants* by Louis Lochner, *Who Financed Hitler* by James Pool, *Hitler – A Study in Tyranny* by Alan Bullock, *Montagu Norman: A Biography* by John Hargrave, *Germany Puts the Clock Back* by Edgar Mowrer, *A Century of War: Anglo-American Oil Politics and the New World Order* by William Engdahl, *Wall Street and the Rise of Hitler* by Antony C. Sutton, *Shell Shock: The Secrets and Spin of an Oil Giant* by Ian Cummins and John Beasant, *Hitler's Fortune* by Cris Whetton and the post-war *Affidavit of Georg von Schnitzler, Member of the Board of Directors of I.G. Farben, 10. November 1945, Regarding a Meeting of Industrialists with Hitler in February 1933, at which Schacht Proposed the Raising of an Election Fund* – as well as other articles and miscellaneous research from my wide reading in this area. Many newspaper accounts from the 1930s are also a critical source of material, as referenced in the chapter itself.

On the corporate funding of Nazism I've also drawn upon Adam Tooze's *The Wages of Destruction: The Making and Breaking of the Nazi Economy*. Regarding the significance of the 20 February 1933 meeting, Tooze writes: 'The meeting of 20 February and its aftermath are the most notorious instances of the willingness of German big business to assist Hitler in establishing his dictatorial regime. The evidence cannot be dodged.'

For a – very limited – view of Shell's corporate relationship with Nazi Germany it is also instructive to read the official history of the company – *From Challenger to Joint Industry Leader, 1890–1939: A History of Royal Dutch Shell*, by Jan Luiten van Zanden and Joost Jonker.

183 From contemporaneous notes of my interview with Ella Deterding, 20 September 2004.

188 Ella referred to Deterding's estate in Mecklenburg as 'Dobina' (it was officially called Dobbin, but the children referred to it as 'Dobina').

Chapter Eleven:
A Hillside in Grosseto; A Dream of My Father

203 The RSA trip to China took place in May 2006, and was organised by Michaela Crimmin, who was then the director of the RSA's Art and Ecology programme.

207 *Wogan* was a BBC TV chat show with the eponymous Terry Wogan presenting. It does seem utterly bizarre that a supposedly experimental theatre group like Complicité should have been on such a mainstream programme, but my memory of this event is quite vivid, because of what followed.

How People in Organisations Can Kill: The First Factor
214 The interview with Gwen Adshead was *Desert Island Discs*, BBC Radio 4, 11 July 2010. Although extremely sympathetic to Dr Adshead and her colleagues and what they are attempting to achieve in their work, I also wondered what the relatives of the Broadmoor patients' victims might have felt listening to this programme, and whether they had received correspondingly world-class therapeutic care to help them in their grieving after their partner, their child, their parent had been killed. What is the balance between care for the perpetrators of terrible acts and care for the survivors? Both groups surely are 'survivors of a disaster'?

217 Regarding Tom Segev's comment about the way that each task Stangl performed prepared him psychologically for the next (from *Soldiers of Evil: The Commandants of the Nazi Concentration Camps*), I have often wondered whether those in authority in the 'euthanasia' and extermination programmes – like Eicke and Wirth – in the process of training their men for mass killing, had access to medical science and particularly psychologists.

Chapter Twelve:
A Pool in East London

226 I think this article ('101 Solutions to All Your Problems') was by Michael Ventura, but it could have been James Hillman.

228 I still keep a record of every swim – the lengths and time taken. If I manage to shave ten or fifteen seconds off a previous time, this is a cause of significant satisfaction, though, as I get older, the reverse is more likely. I do realise there is something slightly obsessive about this. All this counting! And not just in the pool; I realise, writing this today, that I'm also a slave to my numerical ordering when shaving – counting out the number of splashes of hot water on my face needed before I can start to shave – a minimum of twenty-eight splashes for two days' stubble. But, oh, to be released from such counting would be such a liberation. And, to be honest, from time to time, I really do wonder what it's all about? When you step back and think about life, whether you've done thirty-two or thirty-six lengths seems utterly meaningless in the wider scheme of things. And I'm not even sure if all of this manic activity *is* so healthy anyway. I sometimes think there's a significant chance that swimming, in the way I do, might kill me – that I'll overdo it some evening, trying to shave two seconds off my fastest time, and my final view of life will be the ceiling of the pool, with one of those attendants hunched over, slapping my face. And then I imagine the grim humour of my friends – 'God, all that talk about fitness and swimming, and look what got him in the end! And here we are still on the booze and fags . . .'

229 Another example of the strange thoughts that often come while swimming. Recently, as I was doing my thirty-two lengths – and I have absolutely no idea why – I suddenly began thinking about shoes and feet in films, and their relationship to death. And how significant such representations can be, yet how I've never heard anyone talk about this:

- The last sequence in *Theorem*, as the wealthy industrialist strips off at Milan's fascist railway station. It's filmed from above, so we see a belt, trousers fall around his ankles, and then his two bare feet walking through the parting crowd. And then his scream, running through a volcanic landscape as the *St Matthew Passion* builds. This has haunted me since I first saw it at a university film club.

- The scene in *Crimes and Misdemeanours* when we first see the hitman who's going to get rid of Anjelica Huston (the mistress who's become too much of a problem for ophthalmologist Martin Landau). We see the killer get out of an unremarkable jeep, and then we get a glimpse, perhaps no more than a second or two, of his shoes. They look comfortable, middle-aged, Hush Puppies or something similar, with a cushioned sole. So different from what we think a 'killer' would wear, and all the more disturbing for that reason.

- Towards the end of *Dead Poets Society*, just before the pretty, shy boy (who's been told by his authoritarian father that he cannot do any more acting, and moreover is being moved to a military school) – before he kills himself, we see his naked feet moving through the house at night. And immediately afterwards we see his father lining his slippers up under the bed, with mathematical precision. An image of such sterility, implying that every aspect of life can be regimented and ordered. These cold slippers a representation of death in life. The force that will kill his own son.

234 The Stuart Hall/Bill Schwarz conversation was subsequently published in the jounal *Soundings* and is available online at: https://www.lwbooks.co.uk/sites/default/files/s37_15hall_schwarz.pdf.

How People in Organisations Can Kill: The Second Factor
238 The quotation from Richard Baer of witnessing a little girl *'flaming like a torch . . .'* I believe came from a publication I was researching in the Wiener Library in the late 1990s. I know it is an exact quotation, because I've recorded it in speech marks in my notes, but I have been unable to confirm the precise source, and would welcome verification.

244 'History walks on two feet'. A friend sent me this quotation, by Karl Marx, some years ago (also quoted in an article on the Slate website by Fred Kaplan, 'Learning from Bush's Mistakes', 27 September 2007).

Chapter Thirteen:
The Doctors of Wannsee Meet in a Villa by the Lake

252 'the strongest, most explicit and most widespread protest movement against any policy since the beginning of the Third Reich' from Richard Evans, The Third Reich at War.

252 Although Hitler formally suspended the T4 programme at the end of August 1941, this did not mean an end to killings at the six psychiatric hospitals. Aktion 14f13 had been established by Himmler and Bouhler in April 1941, to deal with concentration-camp prisoners who were too ill to work, or regarded as 'excess ballast'. From April 1941, panels of doctors would travel to concentration camps to select prisoners for 'elimination'. The T4 centres would then be used to carry out the killings of those selected – in summer 1941, 450 prisoners from Buchenwald and 575 prisoners from Auschwitz were gassed at Sonnenstein, and 1,000 prisoners from Mauthausen were gassed at Hartheim; in autumn 1941, 3,000 prisoners from Dachau were also gassed at Hartheim; in spring 1942, 1,600 women from Ravensbruck were selected and gassed at Bernburg.

Because of this continuation of 'euthanasia' killings, and also the fact that recent archival research in former East German archives has uncovered that far greater numbers were killed than originally estimated, the total number of victims between 1939 and 1945 is now thought to be between 275,000 and 300,000 (approximately 200,000 of these within Germany and Austria, and another 100,000 in occupied territories).

252 The figure of 7 per cent of doctors being members of the SS is from Alessandra Colaianni's article 'A long shadow: Nazi doctors,

moral vulnerability and contemporary medical culture', published in the *Journal of Medical Ethics*, 2012.

255 'Peep show format. Snuff films. Naked women led to execution. *People are being shot . . .*' from Gourevitch's article in the *Guardian*, 'Nightmare on 15th Street', 4 December 1999.

259 The Foreign Office files were actually deposited in four different castles – Schloss Falkenstein, Schloss Degenerhausen, Burg Falkenstein and Schloss Stolberg.

281 The interview with 'Christian' is from my contemporaneous notes.

286 The image from *'The Good Old Days': The Holocaust as Seen by Its Perpetrators and Bystanders* (ed. Klee, Dressen & Riess) comes in the section on 'Execution as popular entertainment' and is titled 'The Twelve Toppers and a Little Hat: A "Troop Welfare Kamerad" reports'.

288 Enzenberger's comment – *'Any cretin can throw a bomb. It is 1,000 times more difficult to defuse one'* – is from an essay in *Granta*, Christmas 1989.

300 I was so struck by the similarity in Levi's and Arendt's views of the perpetrators, expressed in these quotations, that I became curious about whether they may have corresponded during the 1960s. I did ask Jerome Kohn (Arendt's colleague and literary executor), but he wasn't aware of any direct contact between them.

305 Some of the background detail on Heydrich in Prague is informed by Callum Macdonald's *The Killing of SS Obergruppenführer Reinhard Heydrich*. Other details in this section are from *The Wannsee Conference and the Genocide of the European Jews*, published by the House of the Wannsee Conference Memorial and Education Site, *The Participants* (ed. Jasch and Kreuzmuller), *The Villa, the Lake, the Meeting* (Roseman), *Eichmann in Jerusalem* (Arendt), and my own research at the Wiener Library archives in London.

316 After the war, Dr Korherr was not prosecuted for his role in providing detailed information on Jewish populations across Europe for Eichmann, Heydrich and Himmler. He later worked

for the Federal Ministry of Finance in West Germany, and died in 1989, at the age of eighty-six.

326 Eichmann quote *'these gentlemen . . . sat together, and in very blunt words they referred to the matter . . .'* from Chapter Five, *The Villa, the Lake, the Meeting* by Mark Roseman.

335 *'Without a doubt, the laws and decrees drafted or approved by Stuckart himself were a cornerstone of the plan to almost completely exterminate Jews . . .'* from *The Participants* (ed. Jasch and Kreutzmuller).

337 I met Lanzmann in Cambridge, in March 2000, when he was presenting a screening of his recently released film, *A Visitor from the Living* – a remarkable interview with Maurice Roussel, a senior member of the Swiss Red Cross team which inspected Theresienstadt in 1944, and passed it as a fit and proper detention camp. After the screening, Lanzmann invited myself, J. and the academics who'd hosted the event to supper. We ended up in the basement of a rather noisy Turkish restaurant in Bridge Street, where we talked for an hour or so – about the Saurer memorandum (and the filming of that section of *Shoah*), about the Walter Stier interview, and about the Wannsee Conference, and the extremity of psychological compartmentalisation necessary to write such documents, and about the fact that such patterns of thought are absolutely present in our world, in the behaviour of 'desk killers' in our corporations and governments. Lanzmann was extremely interested in the research that I had then just started, and said that he'd be happy to show me other material in Paris he'd filmed for *Shoah*, which related to the kind of '*Schreibtischtaeter*' mentality I was investigating.

Our conversation was interrupted by something so bizarre it would have fitted neatly into a Coen brothers film. We were just discussing the precise details of the development of the *gaswagen*, when a half-naked woman, dressed in Anatolian colours, emerged into the basement with performers playing thunderous traditional music, and began to dance on our table! Far from being fazed by such an interruption, Lanzmann fished around in his wallet to give the dancer a tip, before continuing our discussion.

343 Hausner's speech from the Eichmann trial transcripts, 17 April 1961, and also quoted in Arendt, *Eichmann in Jerusalem*.

Chapter Fourteen:
Carpathian Days

354 *'Explicit recipes for being human'* is what Geoffrey Grigson wrote about W.H. Auden's best poetry, in his contribution to *W.H. Auden: A Tribute* (edited by Stephen Spender) published in 1975: 'If we follow him round, as he celebrates, investigates, discards, adds, re-attempts, we find in him explicit recipes for being human.'

354 In Ian Thomson's biography of Levi, *Primo Levi*, he notes that there were no fewer than 37 other people named Levi who travelled in Primo Levi's convoy to Auschwitz (although 161 of the 650 transported that day cannot be identified by name).

361 Izbica, sometimes also referred to as Izbica-Lubelska, is situated approximately 30 km north of Belzec, and was used as a 'transit ghetto' for Jews heading to Belzec. When the ghetto was full, fields close to the village, next to the railway tracks, were used as a kind of improvised camp, but without any buildings. The two SS men who ran the camp, Kurt Engel and Ludwig Klem, both in their twenties, were known as 'the lords of life and death'. Gilbert estimates that between 40,000 and 50,000 Jews were brought here between March 1942 and March 1943 – a supposed staging post between Theresienstadt and Belzec, though many thousands died here at Izbica.

372 Klemperer quotation from *LTI – Lingua Tertii Imperii* (1947), published in English as *The Language of the Third Reich*.

Chapter Fifteen:
Walking into Whiteness

374 *'I climbed down on the platform to stretch my legs . . .'* Levi quotation from *The Truce*, Chapter Three.

376 Not to discount Semprún's concept of a societal 'ability to listen', but it is also worth noting that there may have been particular reasons and circumstances that enabled people to start listening to Levi on the subject of the camps – the publications of his book, and Semprún's, in early spring 1961, came between the arrest of Richard Baer, the last commandant of Auschwitz, found working as a forester near Hamburg in December 1960, and the beginning of the trial of Adolf Eichmann in Tel Aviv in April 1961. So, for the first time since the Nuremberg Trials in 1945/46 there was a substantial, global focus on the Holocaust and its perpetrators.

It is also fascinating to realise that Raul Hilberg's magisterial *The Destruction of the European Jews* had a similarly tortuous journey to publication during this same period – only finally seeing the light of day in 1961 with its publication by the small press Quadrangle Books, after several years of rejections from the major publishing houses. And there's an equally complex narrative for Elie Wiesel's work coming into the world as well – *Night* was originally published in Yiddish, in Argentina, as *Un di velt hot geshvign* ('And the World Remained Silent') in 1956. It wasn't until 1960 that it gained an American publisher, Hill and Wang, and even then, the book initially had only very modest sales.

381 '*All at once the crowd fell silent . . .*' Filip Muller's testimony comes from *Eyewitness Auschwitz: Three Years in the Gas Chambers*, first published by Chicago/ Ivan R. Dee in 1979, reprinted in 1999 (Ivan R. Dee in association with the United States Holocaust Memorial Museum). Muller was also one of Lanzmann's interviewees, and gives an almost identical account of this episode in *Shoah* (1985).

394 A further reflection on '*Hier ist kein warum*' (Here there is no why). I have a profound admiration for Claude Lanzmann's work, above all for *Shoah*, yet I disagree with him on one, centrally important, point. He has repeatedly written and spoken of his 'war against the question "why?" in relation to the Holocaust – i.e. that it is an obscenity to attempt to explain *why* it happened, and that we should only ask the question *how* it happened. This dogmatic assertion also explains his disdain for the work of Hannah Arendt, Gitta Sereny

and others who have done so much to investigate the background and mentality of the perpetrators of the Holocaust. It seems to me, in his authoritarian refusal to allow the question 'why?', Lanzmann places himself dangerously close to the same nihilistic position as the SS guard at Monowitz who snatches the icicle from Levi's hand.

**Chapter Sixteen:
The Patience of a Hand and a Pencil**

402 Information on the destruction of the Jewish communities north-east of Lodz – Zgierz, Orzoków, Łęczyca, Dąbie – is from Martin Gilbert's *Holocaust Journey*.

419 Zdzisław's information about Mordechai Zurawski is correct. I later find out that he was a member of the last *Sonderkommando* at Chelmno, who escaped as the camp was being liquidated in January 1945. Altogether, between December 1941 and January 1945, there were only nine survivors of Chelmno – all from the *Sonderkommandos,* apart from Simon Srebnik. As well as Srebnik and Zurawski (survivors from January 1945), seven others managed to escape during winter 1941/42 – Mordechai Podchlebnik, Yakov Grojanowski, Milnak Meyer, Abraham Tauber, Abram Roj, Yitzhak Justman and Chaim Widawski. After the war, Srebnik, Podchelbnik and Zurawski testified at the Chelmno trials, and also at Eichmann's trial in Jerusalem in 1961. Claude Lanzmann managed to locate Srebnik and Podchlebnik in Israel when he was filming *Shoah*, and their testimony is among the most remarkable in the film. However, Lanzmann was wrong to claim, as he does in the opening sequence of the film, that 'only two came out alive' from Chelmno.

421 Yakov Grojanowski's testimony is taken from *The Holocaust* by Martin Gilbert, Chapter 16, 'Eye-witness to Mass Murder'. Today we know that 'Yakov Grojanowski' was a pseudonym, and Grojanowski was actually Szlama Ber Winer. After telling Rabbi Szulman in Grabow what was happening at Chelmno, Winer eventually got to Warsaw, where, in the ghetto, he also told his account to the historian Emanuel Ringelblum. This verbal report was then

transcribed in detail and distributed in Polish and German. Later, Winer reached Zamość, but towards the end of April 1942 he was captured and deported to Belzec, where he was murdered.

422 Franz Schalling's account – *'Our guard post was in front of the castle . . .'* from *Shoah.*

423 Mahmens Goldmann's account, *'When they arrived at the Schloss they [the Jews of Kłodawa] were at first treated most politely . . .'* is also from *The Holocaust* by Gilbert. Goldmann survived by hiding in a small room (just outside the warm 'reception room' in the *Schloss*, where he and his fellow Jews had undressed). But, after twenty-four hours' hiding, the cold became intense, he tried to leave the hiding place and was caught (on 12 January) and imprisoned along with the *Sonderkommando* at the *Schloss.* That night he told them what he'd witnessed; the following day Goldmann was taken to Rzuchów forest, along with his fellows in the *Sonderkommando,* but he was shot in a mass grave before the day's work began.

425 The figure of 360,000 killed at Chelmno derives from an early post-war estimate from Judge Bednarz of the Lodz District Court, who was one of the first to examine the mass murders which had taken place at Chelmno, as part of the Central Commission for Investigation of German Crimes in Poland. This is now considered an overestimate; however, there are still widely differing estimates of numbers killed at this site. These range from 152,000 dead (Raul Hilberg's figure) to 'more than 152,000' (Christopher Browning's estimate) to 160,000–170,000 dead (Chełmno Muzeum of Martyrdom figures) to 320,000 dead (Wiener Library for the Study of the Holocaust and Genocide and Yad Vashem figures).

434 *'There was a room – if I remember correctly – perhaps five times as large as this one . . .'* From testimony of Eichmann at his trial in 1961, quoted in Martin Gilbert's *The Holocaust*, Chapter Seventeen. Arendt also quotes this testimony in *Eichmann in Jerusalem,* but with some textual differences, possibly attributable to Arendt translating directly from Eichmann's German in court.

Book Two

Preface:
To the West

447 I've often wondered what would have happened in 2003 if Clare Short (then Secretary of State for International Development) had resigned on the same day as Robin Cook, on 17 March 2003. Would other cabinet ministers then have followed their lead? Might this have triggered a change of mind in the Labour government about the advisability of going to war in Iraq? And if Britain hadn't supported that disastrous and illegal war, would other countries have followed suit?

457 On the day I signed the contract for the book, in the publisher's airy, white offices in an unfamiliar part of west London, I began a new notebook, or rather a log book, as I thought of it, a diurnal companion on this odyssey of mine. One small page for each day that passes. So, for each day I had to account to that little book, and therefore to myself, for what I'd done to get this work closer to completion. Primarily in terms of writing and editing, but also ideas, books and articles read, fragments of research carried out. This sounds as if it might have been a dour and puritanical exercise, but actually it was quite the opposite. The pages were in blocks of vivid colours, so I'd spend a month in deepest pink, followed by weeks of warm terracotta, then the zing and cool of palest green. All with their own energy. And the reassurance of knowing that all thoughts, all quotations, anything crucial, would be somewhere in these pages . . .

459 *Perpetrators, Victims, Bystanders* is also the title of a book published by the pioneering, and peerless, historian of the Holocaust Raul Hilberg in 1992.

Chapter One:
A Hand in the Desert

468 'Who's *not* in the room?' is a question that I first came across learning about the work of the great feminist writer and educa-

tionalist bell hooks. It goes to the heart of how, even in supposedly 'progressive' activist circles, there is often much unconscious bias and self-selection – and that so many people whose voices need to be heard have enormous challenges just making it 'into the room' where the discussion is taking place.

469 *I have never before witnessed a camera used with such tenderness* . . . But Guzmán's tender treatment of his interviewees in *Nostalgia for the Light* can also be seen in his brilliant film *The Pinochet Case* (2001).

474 The Kissinger quote, *'Please, spare us your political science lectures!'*, I came across in Ken Loach's searing short-film contribution to *11'09'01 September 11* – the collection of eleven short films (of eleven minutes each) addressing the anniversary of the 11 September 2001 attacks in America.

Chapter Two:
The Use and Abuse of Words: Jan Karski and Albert Speer

The quotations in this chapter are mainly taken from Karski's wartime memoir, *Story of a Secret State*, originally published by Houghton Mifflin in 1944, today republished by Penguin Classics. Other quotations and material are from *Karski: How One Man Tried to Stop the Holocaust* by E. Thomas Wood and Stanislaw Jankowski, and my own transcription of Karski's interview in *Shoah*.

The material on Speer in this chapter is taken from *Albert Speer: His Battle with Truth* by Gitta Sereny, *Inside the Third Reich* by Speer, *The Spandau Diaries* by Speer and *The Last Days of Hitler* by Hugh Trevor-Roper.

481 *'There is nothing a man will not do to another; nothing a man will not do for another.'* From *Fugitive Pieces* by Anne Michaels.

498 *Albert Speer: His Battle with Truth* is a work of exceptional insight and power. When I read it for the first time in 1996 it had a

tremendous impact on the ideas I was then beginning to develop. I was struck by the way analytical rigour was combined with a compassion for humanity in her work. And that these forces were not regarded as threats to the other, mutually exclusive, but rather they acted together in a creative tension that gave a unique power to her writing. I'm aware that some historians are critical of her, for getting too close to her subject. This reveals more about the territoriality of historians than anything else, no doubt extremely envious of the unprecedented access that Speer gave Sereny. It also neglects the fact that she had written, eleven years earlier, what is widely regarded as the greatest work ever on perpetrator psychology – her devastating and terrifying book *Into That Darkness*, on Franz Stangl, commandant of Treblinka.

Chapter Three:
My Father and His Silence

513 *'I think we ought to read only the kind of books that wound and stab us . . .'* is from Kafka's letter to Oskar Pollak, 27 January 1904.

515 *'It was that shame we knew so well, the shame that drowned us after the selections . . .'* from the opening of *The Truce* by Primo Levi.

516 *'trying to look into the black sun which is the Holocaust'* – Claude Lanzmann interviewed by Ron Rosenbaum, *Explaining Hitler: The Search for the Origins of His Evil*.

Chapter Four:
The Silences of Societies in the Face of Atrocity:
Germany, France, America, Britain

518 *'I had grown up with the feeling that something was being kept from me . . .'* is from Sebald, *On the Natural History of Destruction*, 'Air War and Literature: Zurich Letters', part III.

518 The Kiefer quote, *'We had no information about the Third Reich when I was in school . . .'* I found in the Royal Academy catalogue of the

'Anselm Kiefer' exhibition in 2014 (I believe the original source was from an interview with the radio journalist Tim Marlow, in 2007).

521 *'Have you ever seen a map of London?. . .'* Hitler quoted by Speer, *Inside the Third Reich*, Chapter Twenty.

521 The casualty figures for Bomber Command (55,573 dead) are taken from the Royal Air Force Bomber Command Memorial in Green Park and also *Among the Dead Cities: Is the Targeting of Civilians in War Ever Justified?* by A. C. Grayling; the casualty figures for the Hamburg firebombing (42,500 civilians killed, and 37,000 injured) are from the definitive work on the subject – the four-volume *Strategic Air Offensive Against Germany 1939–1945* by Charles Webster and Noble Frankland.

524 *'The Germans have cut themselves off from half of their culture; they have disabled themselves . . .'* Kiefer interview with Jean-Marc Terrasse, 2011, quoted in Royal Academy catalogue, 2014.

525 *'The human condition is Auschwitz, and the principle of Auschwitz finds its perpetuation in our understanding of science and political systems . . .'* Beuys quoted in *Joseph Beuys* by Caroline Tisdall.

534 *'During the Thanksgiving holiday a few weeks ago, I took a walk with some friends and family in a national park . . .'* is from Arundhati Roy's *The Ordinary Person's Guide to Empire*, 'The Loneliness of Noam Chomsky'.

Chapter Five:
Vernichtung

In this chapter I've drawn principally upon material from *Exterminate All the Brutes* by Sven Lindqvist, *Rivers of Blood, Rivers of Gold* by Mark Cocker and, most of all, from *The Kaiser's Holocaust* by David Olusoga and Casper Erichsen. I have enormous admiration for the work of all these writers, but this chapter owes a substantial debt to Olusoga and Erichsen's brilliant research, which forms the backbone of what I've written here.

557 *'The most righteous of all wars is a war with savages . . .'* Theodore Roosevelt quoted in 'Theodore Roosevelt, Geopolitics, and Cosmopolitan Ideals' by Greg Russell, *Review of International Studies*, Vol. 32, No. 3 (July 2006).

594 *'The* Mischlinge *concept provided the lawyers and civil servants with both a conceptual framework and quasi-legal terminology . . .'* is from *The Kaiser's Holocaust* by David Olusoga and Casper Erichsen.

Chapter Six:
A Coda: The Power of History and the Burning of Books

601 *'where they have burned books, they will end in burning human beings too.'* Heine's famous words come from his 1821 play *Almansor* – 'Dort, wo man Bücher verbrennt, verbrennt man am Ende auch Menschen.'

601 *'You do well in this midnight hour to commit to the flames the evil spirit of the past.'* The Goebbels quotation is from *The Holocaust: An Encyclopedia and Document Collection*, edited by Paul R. Bartrop and Michael Dickerman.

604 *'If there is anything we must change it is the past . . .'* is from the poem 'Correspondences' by Anne Michaels.

Chapter Seven:
A Question from Günter Grass

605 The George Steiner quotations are from his essay 'Dying Is an Art' in *Language and Silence*.

611 My nieces' experience of history at school, together with Moni Mohsin's and Mukulika Banerjee's comments, lead me to think that very little has changed over recent generations, and that the teaching of British history is still clearly regarded as a 'hot potato' by education authorities and the state. There must have been decisions taken at government level which determined that learning about shame-

ful aspects of Britain's past would not be 'beneficial' for children in the late twentieth century and early twenty-first, nor helpful to our wider society. I feel this is a shocking dereliction of responsibility, by successive governments, but it is also a failure of our wider civil society that there has never been sufficient pressure to address this issue – because the narrative a country tells itself about its past is an extremely powerful phenomenon, for good or ill. It can try to liberate the generations that follow (look at Canada's processes for a new understanding of its First Peoples, or the way that the Truth and Reconcilation methodology made such an impact on post-apartheid South Africa); it can also stunt the development of an entire society. To give a single example: some years ago, in the pre-Internet age, I was trying to find out more about Britain's involvement in Tasmania and the extermination of the indigenous people there. I found my copy of the *History Today Companion to British History* and turned to the relevant page. The entire entry on 'Tasmania' was only twenty-nine words, and only *twelve* words referred to the genocide – less than half a sentence: 'The early years were marked by determined destruction of the Aboriginal population; prosperity from wheat-growing was followed by severe depression, saved after the 1880s by mining and forestry.' You'll also notice that there's no reference to who were the agents of this destruction – the government of Great Britain, and the white settlers of Tasmania.

Chapter Eight:
Crow-hunting in Tasmania

This chapter draws primarily on Mark Cocker's account of 'The British in Tasmania' from his exceptional work *Rivers of Blood, Rivers of Gold*, first published in 1998, so the quotations are from this book unless otherwise specified.

621 *Robert Hughes recounts a bushranger called Carrot...* (from *The Fatal Shore*).

628 There is ongoing debate about whether or not Truganini was 'the last pure Tasmanian' and also the status of a mixed community of

Aboriginal women who had been living with European sealers on the Bass Strait islands, and who did survive. At Cape Barren these numbered thirty-two adults and fifty-two children. And their descendents have grown. By 1976, 2,942 declared themselves Aboriginal, and by the 1990s, this figure had increased further to over 8,500.

Chapter Nine:
The British Famine – 'Slaughters done in Ireland by mere official red tape'

630 Many of the famine statistics on this page, and other data and material in this chapter, have been taken from the definitive publication of the event – *The Atlas of the Great Irish Famine*, edited by William J. Smyth, John Crowley and Mike Murphy (Cork Univeristy Press/New York University Press, 2012).

630 'in a matter of 72 to 96 hours, the better part of the 1846 crop was obliterated . . .' from *The Graves Are Walking: The Great Famine and the Saga of the Irish People*, by John Kelly, 2012.

636 'Russell, Wood and Trevelyan were highly conscientious men . . .' I found this quotation of A. J. P. Taylor's in *The Great Irish Potato Famine* by James Donnelly, 2001.

636 'Trevelyan sent his subordinates to Ireland equipped with Adam Smith's writings . . .' from *The Economist*, 12 December 2012 – a review of *The Graves Are Walking: The Great Famine and the Saga of the Irish People* by John Kelly.

637 The information on the Gregory clause and the resulting land clearances is taken from the work of Peter Gray, Colm Tóibín, Canon John O'Rourke and James Donnelly.

As well as Tim Pat Coogan's *The Famine Plot: England's Role in Ireland's Greatest Tragedy*, Michael de Nie (*The Eternal Paddy: Irish Identity and the British Press*) and Edward Lengel (*The Irish Through British Eyes*) have also looked in detail at how British racism towards the Irish laid the foundations for the lack of intervention during the Famine.

640 '*Her work is readable – something which later historians of the Famine have tried hard not to be . . .*' Colm Tóibín's assessment of Cecil Woodham-Smith's *The Great Hunger: Ireland 1845–49* appears in *The Irish Famine: A Documentary* (Tóibín and Ferriter).

649 In 1995, Cathal Póirtéir published *Famine Echoes* about the work of the Irish Folklore Commission in the 1930s and 1940s – the majority of the accounts of the Famine in this book are oral histories recounted by children and grandchildren of Famine survivors, some gathered by the IFC in 1935, some from a questionnaire sent out by the IFC in 1945; but virtually all of these testimonies were from people born in the 1860s, 1870s, 1880s – i.e. the children and grandchildren of those who actually experienced the Famine directly – so we still have this challenge of being distanced from the event itself, by one or two generations.

653 With regard to the Famine, there are some curious gaps in some of the greatest modern Irish writers' work – Joyce wrote almost nothing about it, Yeats only attempted fragments, for instance these lines, in his verse play *The Countess Cathleen*, put into the mouth of Teig, a fourteen-year-old boy:

> They say now that the land is famine struck
> The graves are walking . . .
> Two nights ago, at Carrick-orus
> A herdsman met a man who had no mouth,
> Nor eyes, nor ears; his face a wall of flesh;
> He saw him plainly by the light of the moon,
> What is the good of praying?

653 In response to Colm Tóibín's 'Erasures', David Craig made this important contribution, in a letter to the *LRB*, 20 August 1998:

> As I read Colm Tóibín's enthralling piece about the history of the Great Hunger in Ireland (*LRB*, 30 July), and noted his wish for the 'living, speaking voice' and 'the perspective of those who were not administrators or politicians or land-

lords', I began to think that at any moment he would make use of Thomas Gallagher's *Paddy's Lament: Ireland 1846–47*, which teems with such material. Gallagher, an American writer whose father had emigrated from County Roscommon, was able to get close to the Famine itself and the ways in which people suffered, retaliated and escaped, because he used, in addition to a great many contemporary newspapers and official records, the 2600 pages of transcribed interviews, conducted in 1955, with people 'old enough to remember their parents' stories of the famine'. These are stored in the Irish Folklore Department at University College, Dublin. From them, via Gallagher, we can learn how the first smell of the potato rot, like 'the bilge water of a ship', stole over the countryside and made the dogs howl. (I heard on Barra how the same thing happened in the same year in the Scottish Hebrides.) The fog that was common during that damp July is still called the 'potato fog'. Starvation soon followed, people began to fight for turnip cuttings, pick up fish offal with their toes in fish markets, and gather nettles from graveyards to make broth. They died exhausted, their 'entire alimentary canals, from mouth to anus . . . completely empty', or their intestines destroyed by gangrene so that their 'stools would resemble water in which raw meat had been washed' . . . Gallagher's work should be seen as central to the history of the Hunger.'

658 The Communist Manifesto, *which was first published in London on 21 February 1848* . . . It was printed by Jacob Burghard of Bishopsgate, owner of a print shop at 46 Liverpool Street, on behalf of the German Workers' Educational Association – and the initial print run was set at a very modest 1,000 copies. The first English translation was made by Helen Macfarlane, and published, in four sections, in the Chartist journal *The Red Republican* in November 1850.

663 I explore the specific type of behaviour which Trevelyan exhibits on his visit to Dublin – the inability to face the human beings

affected by his policies – in much greater detail in Book Four: 'How People in Organisations Kill: Looking Away or Not Seeing in the First Place.'

664 *'Remoteness from the suffering, he once stated, kept his judgement more acute than that of his administrators actually working among the people affected.'* This quotation about Trevelyan is taken from The History Place website.

664 My point about changing the language from 'the Irish Famine' to 'the British Famine' is not restricted to one of semantics, or even historical accuracy. It goes to the heart of British identity, and how utterly selective we have been in the creation of our national narrative. You could ask a hundred people on the streets of any city in Britain (with the possible exceptions of Glasgow, Liverpool and Manchester), and perhaps less than half a dozen would know about the Famine, and Britain's central role in creating it. This is hardly surprising as, again, you will struggle to find a single mention of the Famine in any British history school syllabus. Hundreds of books have been written about how the history of the Famine has been represented in Ireland over the last 170 years, but I've not read a *single* article about how the Famine is represented in *British* history, and in our wider culture. It is simply not part of our national narrative. And such a gaping omission is shameful.

664 For people seeking short, but informative, overviews of the British Famine in Ireland, and its historiography, two of the most useful are: 'Charles Trevelyan, John Mitchel and the Historiography of the Great Famine' by Christophe Gillissen, published in *Revue Française de Civilisation Britannique*, 2014, and 'The Irish Famine: A Historiographical Review' by Lori Henderson, 2005.

'What at one time one refuses to see never vanishes but returns again and again, in many forms.' 'Whenever a secret is kept it will make its way, like an object lighter than water and meant to float, to the surface.' Both quotations are from *A Chorus of Stones* by Susan Griffin (the first from the end of Chapter One, 'Denial', the second from Chapter Three, 'Exile').

Chapter Ten:
Moments of Seismic Shift: 7 December 1970, Warsaw; 2 June
2005, Belgrade; 14 August 2004, Okakarara; 14 July 2016,
Berlin

674 *'I could still apprehend the dying away of my native tongue . . .'*
from *Austerlitz* by W. G. Sebald.

678 The official text of Wieczorek-Zeul's statement, taken from the
German Embassy's website in Namibia, is copied below. Note: the title
of this speech does not refer to 'genocide' but to 'the 100th anniversary of the suppression of the Herero uprising' (http://www.windhuk
.diplo.de/Vertretung/windhuk/en/03__Topics/03__Politics/Com
memorative__Years__2004__2005/speech-2004-08-14-bmz.html).

> Speech by Federal Minister Heidemarie Wieczorek-Zeul at
> the commemorations of the 100th anniversary of the suppres-
> sion of the Herero uprising, Okakarara, on 14 August 2004:
> It is an honour to have been invited to take part in your
> commemorations here today. I would like to thank you for
> giving me, as the German Minister for Economic Coopera-
> tion and Development and as a representative of the German
> government and the German parliament, this opportunity to
> speak to you. Yet I am also here to listen to you.
> Today, I want to acknowledge the violence inflicted by the
> German colonial powers on your ancestors, particularly the
> Herero and the Nama. I am painfully aware of the atrocities
> committed: in the late 19th century, the German colonial
> powers drove the people from their land. When the Herero,
> when your ancestors, resisted, General von Trotha's troops
> embarked on a war of extermination against them and the
> Nama. In his infamous order General Trotha commanded
> that every Herero be shot – with no mercy shown even to
> women and children. After the battle of Waterberg in 1904,
> the survivors were forced into the Omaheke desert, where
> they were denied any access to water sources and were left
> to die of thirst and starvation. Following the uprisings, the

surviving Herero, Nama and Damara were interned in camps and put to forced labour of such brutality that many did not survive.

We pay tribute to those brave women and men, particularly from the Herero and the Nama, who fought and suffered so that their children and their children's children could live in freedom. I remember with great respect your ancestors who died fighting against their German oppressors. Even at that time, back in 1904, there were also Germans who opposed and spoke out against this war of oppression. One of them was August Bebel, the chairman of the same political party of which I am a member. In the German parliament, Bebel condemned the oppression of the Herero in the strongest terms and honoured their uprising as a just struggle for liberation. I am proud of that today.

A century ago, the oppressors – blinded by colonialist fervour – became agents of violence, discrimination, racism and annihilation in Germany's name. The atrocities committed at that time would today be termed genocide – and nowadays a General von Trotha would be prosecuted and convicted.

We Germans accept our historical and moral responsibility and the guilt incurred by Germans at that time. And so, in the words of the Lord's Prayer that we share, I ask you to forgive us our trespasses . . .'

685 *My Nazi Legacy,* directed by David Evans, was released in 2015, and shown on BBC Four as part of its *Storyville* strand on 30 March 2016. It follows the human rights lawyer Philippe Sands, Niklas Frank and Horst von Wächter, as they travel to sites of Nazi atrocities in eastern Europe.

686 *'Every man shares the responsibility and the guilt of the society to which he belongs'* is from a letter written by Henrik Ibsen to the German publisher and translator Ludwig Passarge, 16 June 1890, in response to questions Passarge had raised about *Peer Gynt* (which he had just translated into German).

Chapter Eleven:
Power and the Hurricane

692 *'for, in the hour of his death, he, like all men, cried out for his mother.'* I would be very grateful if any reader could help me trace this line – I'm sure it's not a figment of my imagination, but I've been unable to trace it!

699 'Homeland' was commissioned by the London International Festival of Theatre in 1993. The first phase took place over two weeks in June 1993, and involved taking a lorry-installation across London, to different sites connected to the countries which provided the raw materials for London's electricity: not only the company headquarters involved in the production of energy – British Coal (coal), General Electric (light bulbs) and Rio Tinto Zinc (copper) – but also the communities of the countries of extraction. So we spent days in Golborne Road, outside Café Lisboa and Café Oporto, working with the Portuguese community in London, then moved to the Anglo-Hungarian Society and Hungarian churches at different sites, and we ended outside the London Welsh Centre in Grays Inn Road. The rear doors of the lorry opened to reveal a complex installation mapping the journey of the invisible 'ghost of electricity' into London, and we then worked with our passer-by audience, and asked people to trace their 'animal territories' of belonging onto giant maps of London, and draw intimate representations of their sense of belonging, which then were added to the installation. And people also recorded their conversations about their map and drawing, which could then be listened to by others. By the end of the project, there were nearly 300 jewel-like images of belonging fluttering on the walls inside the lorry. One woman said it was 'like seeing people's souls displayed'.

712 *'Many of these people never had a chance to be . . .'* Dennis Potter's words from his interview with Michael Parkinson for *Desert Island Discs*, first broadcast on 21 February 1988.

Chapter Twelve:
The Architect on Trial

725 Speer's interview comes in the BBC documentary *Albert Speer: The Nazi Who Said Sorry,* directed by Martin Davidson, first broadcast on BBC2, 2 May 1996.

726 Robert Jackson's comments on Sauckel and Speer are from the transcripts of the Nuremberg Trial Proceedings, day 187 (Friday, 26 July 1946). These transcripts are also available online at the Yale Law School website – http://avalon.law.yale.edu/imt/02-27-46.asp.

726 Speer being *'almost disappointed – he'd brought himself to expect this [the death penalty] in a "euphoria of guilt"...'* Sereny's comment is also taken from the BBC documentary *Albert Speer: The Nazi Who Said Sorry.*

728 Samuel Rajzman's testimony at Nuremberg is from the transcripts of the Nuremberg Trial Proceedings, day 69 (Wednesday, 27 February 1946).

Chapter Thirteen:
Room 519: Into This Darkness

736 I should emphasise that I was extremely surprised that none of the figures we approached to take part in the 'Ethical Compartmentalisation in Business Leadership' interviews questioned us in detail about our political views, or the work of Platform. I'd made a point of being very open about this, but even so, I would have expected greater scrutiny. Perhaps the title of the research was actually cleverer than I had realised – both hitting the right kind of academic note, while also subtly flattering the prospective interviewees.

739 One of the strangest aspects of having worked on a project over many years is that, at times, you re-read earlier drafts and are struck by how dramatically things have changed. The most savage irony of all though hit home today – 9 November 2016, the day after the American presidential election – as I'm editing this chapter (which

was originally written in the heyday and optimism of Obama's first term). Today a man who ran his campaign by making the most racist and xenophobic generalisations about minorities has just been elected President. Doesn't Obama's argument about 'the arc of history bending towards justice' now seem very fragile indeed?

742 'cherish the questions themselves, like closed rooms and like books written in a very strange tongue, live everything, live the questions now.' is from Letters to a Young Poet by Rainer Maria Rilke.

744 Although I have changed names and, in some cases, the gender of interviewees, all the words quoted are taken verbatim from the transcripts of these interviews. The companies the individuals worked for have not been changed.

754 John Browne's justification for BP staying in apartheid South Africa – 'BP of course stayed in South Africa during a very tough time during apartheid . . .' – from the BBC Reith Lectures 2000, 'Respect for the Earth'.

754 Lord Salisbury's phrase about bringing 'English civilisation . . . [to] the dark places of the earth' comes in a speech to the British Parliament in 1900 concerning the activities of the Royal Niger Company (quoted in A Swamp Full of Dollars: Pipelines and Paramilitaries at Nigeria's Oil Frontier by Michael Peel).

How People in Organisations Can Kill: A Further Four Factors
756 "When I was on a trip once, years later in Brazil . . ." Stangl account from Into That Darkness by Gitta Sereny.

756 Einsatzgruppen language taken from The Einsatzgruppen Reports, ed. Arad, Krakowski and Spector.

757 Sir Timothy Garden, article in Guardian, 18 March 2003, 'Bigger, better bangs: new weapons on trial'

762 Description of the capabilities of the MQ-9 Reaper drone quoted in Drones – the Physical and Psychological Implications of a Global Theatre of War, report by Medact, 2012.

762 Stephen Sackur's interviews with drone operators in Nevada was for the programme *Drone Wars*, broadcast on BBC Radio 4 on 25 September 2011.

769 Speer on Hitler's attitude to violence, '*As a rule he avoided not only physical, but indeed visual contact, with violence . . .*' quoted in *Albert Speer: His Battle With Truth* by Gitta Sereny.

769 '*With the killing of Jews I had nothing to do . . .*' and '*During the trial, he showed unmistakable signs of sincere outrage . . .*' Both quotes relating to Eichmann taken from Arendt, *Eichmann in Jerusalem*.

769 '*Stangl, insisiting that he had never shot into a crowd of people . . .*' from Sereny, *Into That Darkness*.

771 '*Eichmann said . . . after much delay and a great deal of discussion. . .*' Wisliceny's testimony is taken from *Interrogations: The Nazi Elite in Allied Hands, 1945* by Richard Overy – 'Document 11 The Führer Order [Dieter Wisliceny]'.

772 Ohlendorf's testimony at his trial is taken from *The Holocaust: An Encyclopedia and Document Collection*, ed. Paul R. Bartrop and Michael Dickerman.

772 Milgram's experiment, 'Obedience to Authority: An Experimental View', has understandably received an enormous amount of attention ever since the results were first published in 1963. However, in recent years criticisms regarding the ethics of how the experiment was conducted have increased, particularly in regard to the amount of information given to the volunteers before the experiment, and the stress that some of them experienced being pressurised to administer what they believed were electric shocks. My own view regarding such criticisms is that the value of the research gained was so important that the methodology of the experiments was justified. It should be stressed that the volunteers were debriefed at the end of the experiment, told of the real purpose of the research, and assured that they had not given any electric shocks in reality.

But if the volunteers had been told at the outset that the shocks weren't real, or that the 'learner' in the other room was only an actor who was part of the experiment, the research would have had no value at all. This for me has always been the glaring weakness at the heart of Philip Zimbardo's 'Stanford Prison Experiment' in 1971, when college student volunteers were allocated 'roles' as 'prisoners' or 'prison guards'. All participants were essentially involved in a piece of role-play from the outset, everyone knowing that the conditions were only simulated, and far from real world. However disturbing some of the subsequent behaviour was, there was never an underpinning of reality to the research, as there was with Milgram's experiments.

Chapter Fourteen:
The Oilman and the Broken Wing

785 'Oil exploitation has turned Ogoni into a waste land . . .' Ken Saro-Wiwa, from *A Month and a Day* taken from his address to UNPO in Geneva, summer 1992.

786 'To the eyes of a miser a guinea is far more beautiful than the sun . . .' from William Blake's letter to Dr Trusler, 23 August 1799.

Chapter Fifteen:
A Painting in The Hague; A Farmhouse in Suffolk; A Stadium in Somalia

792 'the merry dance of death and trade' is from *Heart of Darkness* by Joseph Conrad.

802 The USS investment figures were from the 'Trustees Annual Report' for the year ended 31 March 1998. But in 2013 the figures were still substantial – a total of £694 million invested by USS in BP and Shell together (figure from the *Times Higher Education* website, 16 January 2014, 'USS' Largest Investments in Companies 2013' by Holly Else).

802 'The secret of great wealth is a forgotten crime' from Le Père Goriot by Honoré de Balzac.

802 'In a world filled with such inequalities . . .' from On the Edge of the New Century by Eric Hobsbawm.

806 'The moral "authority" of the face of the other is felt in my "infinite responsibility" for the other . . .' is from Entre Nous: Essays on Thinking of the Other by Emmanuel Levinas.

807 'It is in the glance, in the eyes' is from a lecture delivered by Hannah Arendt at the New School, New York in 1974 (cited in The Survivor by Terrence Des Pres).

810 I was very shocked to discover, some years ago, that The Portage to San Cristóbal of A.H. is no longer in print. It was only available as a 'print on demand' book from the University of Chicago Press

Chapter Sixteen:
A Walk from Goethe's Gartenhaus to the Gates of Buchenwald: 10,166 Steps

The books referenced in this section are among the most important works on the relationship between humanity and inhumanity ever published, and should be required reading for any person curious about the interrelationship between 'civilisation' and barbarism.

George Steiner:
  Language and Silence
  In Bluebeard's Castle
  The Portage to San Cristóbal of A.H.

Jorge Semprún:
  Literature or Life

Jean Améry:
  At the Mind's Limits

Sven Lindqvist:
Exterminate All the Brutes

Primo Levi:
If This Is a Man
The Drowned and the Saved

At times when I'm reading these writers I feel exhilarated, catching echoes and traces of thoughts I've had before, and sometimes wanting to go further; at other times I feel clumsy, almost shy, as if I have little of worth to say in their presence; little that they haven't already thought or written. But then, they, in their time, would probably have felt the same.

I sometimes imagine what it would have been like to have brought these five writers and thinkers together, to have walked with them on a summer's day, to have listened to these five voices, playing off each other. But, in the absence of this possibility, I have tried to bring them together in the pages of this chapter.

834 Weimar was also the place where Bach began writing his sonatas and partitas for solo violin, including the astonishing Partita No. 2 in D minor, which Brahms said contained 'a whole world of the deepest thoughts' and Yehudi Menuhin believed was simply 'the greatest structure for solo violin that exists'.

837 *'In living nature nothing happens that is not in connection with the whole . . .'* 'Der Versuch als Vermittler von Objekt und Subjekt' ('The Experiment as Mediator of Object and Subject') by Johann Wolfgang von Goethe.

849 The *'mortality among them was extraordinarily high'* quote about the Dora works is from *Inside the Third Reich* by Albert Speer.

853 Levi's comment on wanting the sequel to *The Drowned and the Saved* to be an investigation into *'the German industries (BASF, Siemens, Bayer) involved in the Nazi camps'* is from Ian Thomson's biography *Primo Levi* ('In London 1986'). The material on Levi's post-war dealings with IG Farben companies comes from the same

biography: *'Levi went out of his way to ruffle sensitivities at Bayer...'* from the chapter 'Journeys into Germany 1954–61'.

859 *'civilisation itself produces anti-civilisation and increasingly reinforces it . . .'* from the opening of 'Education After Auschwitz' by Theodor Adorno.

Chapter Seventeen:
The Lawyers of Washington

876 *'It has always been my attitude that a life has only been worth living...'* Clara Immerwahr's letter was written in 1909 to her friend Richard Abegg (quoted in *Hitler's Scientists* by John Cornwell, also the source of the Fulda manifesto quotation: *'Were it not for German militarism... German civilisation would long ago have been destroyed...'*).

875 *'Terrorism is the war of the poor, and war is the terrorism of the rich.'* I believe this is a quotation credited to Peter Ustinov.

876 The story of Fritz Haber, Clara Immerwahr and Claire Haber has recently been made into a play, *The Forbidden Zone*, by Katie Mitchell and Duncan Macmillan, performed in Salzburg and London in 2014–15.

Chapter Eighteen:
Past Continuous

885 *'Happiness came and went without anybody noticing.'* I've just checked the screenplay of *Jules et Jim* and, as so often with seemingly vivid memories, mine seems to be unreliable. The nearest I found were these words: 'We were happy a while but happiness didn't become a part of us.' (Though I prefer my remembered version to the original . . .)

896 *'We all carry within ourselves a world made up of all that we have seen and loved . . .'* from *Voyage en Italie* (1803–04) by François-René de Chateaubriand.

900 *'for this discovery of yours [writing] will create forgetfulness in the learners' souls . . .'* from *Phaedrus* by Plato, written in 360 B.C.

901 There are certain things in life with beginnings, middles and endings. And in fact, I love such activities. But they are few in number and perhaps not connected to the greater existential questions. Or maybe they are? Over the years I've come to see washing up as a therapeutic, almost a spiritual exercise. It has a kind of beauty, partly because it has that rare thing – a beginning, a middle and an end. A daily act of renewal. Of turning a pile of dirty, encrusted plates and bowls and cups into gleaming, steaming china again. Switching the radio on. Doing the glasses first, plates and cutlery in the middle, anything oily at the very end. Go slowly, don't hurry these Zen moments. Really focus totally on this particular cup in front of you. And finally, the inexplicable sense of satisfaction watching the dirty water and bubbles spiralling away . . .

Sport too, I now understand, also has a similar quality, which perhaps explains the time lavished by so many people on playing, or watching, sports. Football, for instance: the absolute perfection of limitation, only three results possible – win, draw, lose. In the muddied, grey messiness of our compromised lives, the liberation that comes from such clarity!

902 *'For the week or so before she was hospitalized, my mother couldn't keep any food down . . .'* is from 'Meet Me in St Louis' by Jonathan Franzen, *New Yorker*, 24 December 2001.

903 *'Only you in all the world know what my heart always held, before any other love . . .'* is from 'Prayer to My Mother' by Pier Paolo Pasolini.

Chapter Nineteen:
The Wood Pigeons and the Train

907 *'They've taken out insurance against pity . . .'* from *Resurrection* by Leo Tolstoy.

910 The historic material on Schmitt and Allianz's close links to Nazism from various sources, including findings from the main

study on this subject, Gerald Feldman's *Die Allianz und die deutsche Versicherungswirtschaft 1933–1945* (Allianz and the German Insurance Business, 1933–1945), published in 2001.

918 The praise for Anne Frank's diary (*'this apparently inconsequential diary by a child . . . embodies all the hideousness of fascism, more so than all the evidence of Nuremberg put together'*) comes from the Dutch historian Jan Romein, who had read the first manuscript of the diary, before it was published. His comment came in an article called 'Children's Voice' in the newspaper *Het Parool*, 3 April 1946.

922 Here, for what it's worth, is my attempt to summarise a chronology of some of the most significant books published on the Holocaust, Nazi Germany and related areas in my lifetime (and some which have had the deepest impact on me), and certain other events connected to this historiography over the last fifty years or so. I am aware that any such list is, by its very nature, highly personal and idiosyncratic. But here it is anyway, and I've no doubt that many will agree that these were – and are – landmark works.

1970: Albert Speer's *Inside the Third Reich* is published in English (after coming out as *Erinnerungen* (Memories) in Germany the year before.

1971: Professor Erich Goldhagen publishes *Albert Speer, Himmler, and the Secrecy of the Final Solution in Midstream*.

1973: Joachim Fest's massive biography *Hitler* is published in German to critical acclaim. It is the first major work on Hitler since Alan Bullock's influential 1952 opus *Hitler: A Study in Tyranny*.

1974: Gitta Sereny publishes *Into That Darkness: From Mercy Killing to Mass Murder*, a study of Franz Stangl, the commandant of Treblinka – probably the greatest single work ever published on the psychology of a 'genocidaire'.

1975: Speer's *Spandauer Tagebücher* is published in Germany and becomes a bestseller. It's translated into English and published the following year as *Spandau: The Secret Diaries*.

1975: Primo Levi publishes his brilliant *Il sistema periodico* (ten years later published in English as *The Periodic Table*).

1976: Terrence Des Pres' work *The Survivor: An Anatomy of Life in the Death Camps* comes out – a vital and harrowing book (which should be far more widely known than it is today).

1979: Filip Müller, one of the very few survivors of the Birkenau *Sonderkommandos*, publishes his searing memoir *Eyewitness Auschwitz – Three Years in the Gas Chambers*.

1980: The historian Walter Laqueur publishes *The Terrible Secret: Suppression of the Truth about Hitler's Final Solution*.

1981: The British historian Tim Mason writes an essay, 'Intention and Explanation: A Current Controversy about the Interpretation of National Socialism', in which he coins the terms 'Intentionist' and 'Functionalist' to describe two strands of historiography regarding the Holocaust – intentionists (later renamed 'intentionalists') being those who believe that the Holocaust was all planned and ordered from the very top of the Nazi state, i.e. Hitler; functionalists being those who believe that no such 'master plan' existed, and that much of the Holocaust was organised, and improvised, by agencies and lower-ranked figures in the bureaucracy of Nazi Germany.

1985: Claude Lanzmann's monumental film *Shoah* is released – the result of more than a decade's work. The film-maker Marcel Ophüls calls it 'the greatest documentary about contemporary history ever made'.

1986: Primo Levi, in the year before his death, publishes the most important collection of essays ever written on the Holocaust, *The Drowned and the Saved*.

1986: The beginning of the 'Historikerstreit' (the 'Historians' Argument') in Germany, with right-wing historians, led by Ernst Nolte, arguing that the Holocaust should not be seen as a unique event, and nor should the German people bear any unique guilt for the extermination. Nolte also attempted to draw an equivalence between crimes committed under German Nazism and Soviet Communism. Unsurprisingly, with the philosopher Jürgen Habermas and most German historians including Broszat and Mommsen, and the vast majority of international historians ranked against him, Nolte and his supporters lost this argument comprehensively.

1986: Martin Gilbert's *The Holocaust* is published – a very useful overall account of the Shoah (and under 1,000 pages too).

1987: Peter Hayes's *Industry and Ideology: IG Farben in the Nazi Era* is published.

1988: Steve Reich's *Different Trains* is composed (the Kronos Quartet's recording in 1990 winning a Grammy Award).

1989: The sociologist and philosopher Zygmunt Bauman publishes *Modernity and the Holocaust*, which attempts to see the Holocaust in a wider context – looking beyond ideology at how modern constructs of bureaucratisation and rationalisation made the extermination possible.

1989: Danuta Czech's *Auschwitz Chronicle* is published.

1991: *The Good Old Days – The Holocaust as Seen by Its Perpetrators and Bystanders* (ed. Klee, Dressen and Reiss) is published in English – a riveting collection of eyewitness documentation of the Holocaust.

1991: Alan Bullock publishes *Hitler and Stalin: Parallel Lives*.

1991: Art Spiegelman's *Maus*, a graphic novel, is published to great acclaim, and later wins a Pulitzer Prize.

1992: Christopher Browning publishes his groundbreaking work *Ordinary Men: Reserve Police Battalion 101 and the Final Solution in Poland* – a detailed study showing that a culture of terrifying obedience to authority, more than blood lust or violent antisemitism, was responsible for much of the mass killing in the Holocaust.

1992: Susan Griffin's brilliant *A Chorus of Stones: The Private Life of War* is published – an extraordinary interweaving of memoir and history.

1992: Sven Lindqvist's book *Utrota varenda jävel* is published in English as *Exterminate All the Brutes* – and makes a powerful argument that the Holocaust had its roots in earlier European colonial genocides.

1994: Between April and July, 800,000 people, around 70 per cent of the total Tutsi population, are killed in the Rwandan genocide.

1994: Jorge Semprún's *L'Écriture ou la vie* is published in French (English edition, *Literature or Life* in 1997).

1994: Götz Aly, Peter Chroust and Christian Pross publish *Cleansing the Fatherland: Nazi Medicine and Racial Hygiene* – a brilliant study of the T4 'euthanasia' programme and the corruption of the German medical establishment under Nazism.

1995: In July, Europe experiences its worst atrocity since the Second World War, when over 8,000 Bosnian Muslims are massacred at Srebrenica by the Bosnian Serb army under General Mladić.

1995: Gitta Sereny's monumental work *Albert Speer: His Battle with Truth* is published, the most revealing book ever written on Speer.

1995: Bernard Schlink's *The Reader* is published in Germany, and two years later, in English (and eventually translated into forty-five languages).

1996: W. G. Sebald's *The Emigrants* is published in English, the first of an incomparable series of books looking at the legacy of the Holocaust.

1996: Daniel Goldhagen's *Hitler's Willing Executioners: Ordinary Germans and the Holocaust* is published, to some controversy. Goldhagen, like Browning, shines a light on the perpetrators – but, unlike Browning, he argues that an 'eliminationist antisemitism' of a specifically German type played a critical role in the Holocaust.

1996: Mommsen and Grieger pubish *Volkswagen and Its Workers during the Third Reich*.

1997: Martin Gilbert's *Holocaust Journey* is published – a diary of a 1996 journey across Europe and sites connected to the genocide, made with his University College London Holocaust Studies MA students the year before.

1997: Laurence Ree's much praised *The Nazis: A Warning from History* is broadcast by the BBC in six episodes.

1998: W. G. Sebald's *The Rings of Saturn* is published in English.

1998: The first volume of Ian Kershaw's definitive biography is published – *'Hitler 1889–1936: Hubris.*

1998: Philip Gourevitch's brilliant work about the Rwandan genocide, *We Wish to Inform You That Tomorrow We Will Be Killed with Our Families* is published.

1998: Mark Mazower's *Dark Continent: Europe's Twentieth Century* is published.

1999: W. G. Sebald's *Luftkrieg und Literatur* ('Air War and Literature') is published in Germany (in 2003 in English as *The Natural History of Destruction*) – essays on the way post-war German culture dealt with the traumas of the Second World War.

2000: The Holocaust denier David Irving sues the writer Deborah Lipstadt and Penguin Books for libel, but he loses the trial at the High Court in London comprehensively, the judgement declaring him to be an 'active Holocaust denier . . . anti-semitic and racist'.

2000: Norman Finkelstein publishes his critique *The Holocaust Industry*.

2000: Ian Kershaw publishes the second volume of his biography – *Hitler 1936–1945: Nemesis*.

2001: Edwin Black's *IBM and the Holocaust: The Strategic Alliance between Nazi Germany and America's Most Powerful Corporation* is published.

2001: The historian Jan Gross publishes *Neighbors: The Destruction of the Jewish Community in Jedwabne, Poland*, igniting a renewed debate about antisemitism in Poland, and Polish involvement in the Holocaust.

2001: Peter Longerich's *The Unwritten Order* is published, focussing on Hitler's role in planning the Holocaust.

2001: Joachim Fest's *Speer: The Final Verdict* is published in English.

2001: Rachel Seiffert's *The Dark Room* is published.

2001: Sebald's final masterpiece, *Austerlitz*, is published to international acclaim, only a month before he is killed in a car accident in Norfolk.

2002: Jonathan Safran Foer's *Everything is Illuminated* is published.

2002: Ian Thomson publishes his definitive biography *Primo Levi*.

2002: Roman Polanski's film *The Pianist* (based on the Warsaw Ghetto memoirs of Władysław Szpilman) comes out to great critical praise.

2003–2008: Richard Evans' definitive trilogy on *The Third Reich* is published – *The Coming of the Third Reich* (2003), *The Third Reich in Power 1933–1939* (2005), *The Third Reich at War* (2008).

2005: Laurence Rees's *Auschwitz: The Nazis and the 'Final Solution'* is published, with an accompanying BBC television series.

2006: Adam Tooze's *The Wages of Destruction: The Making and Breaking of the Nazi Economy* is published.

2006: Jonathan Littell's *Les Bienveillantes* (*The Kindly Ones*) is published in France, and three years later in English.

2006: Robert Chandler's new English translation of Vassily Grossman's *Life and Fate* is published to great acclaim. New editions of *Everything Flows* and *The Road* follow in 2010.

2010: David Olusoga and Casper Erichsen's critical work on the first German genocide, in South-West Africa, is published – *The Kaiser's Holocaust: Germany's Forgotten Genocide*.

2011: Jan Karski's wartime memoir, *Story of a Secret State*, is republished by Penguin Classics.

2013: Otto Dov Kulka's work *Landscapes of the Metropolis of Death: Reflections on Memory and Imagination* is published internationally to universal praise.

2015: László Nemes' mesmerising film *Son of Saul*, about the Birkenau *Sonderkommando*, is released to enormous critical acclaim.

2015: Historian Timothy Snyder publishes *Black Earth: The Holocaust as History and Warning*.

2016: Lawyer Philippe Sands publishes *East West Street*, a profound meditation on his family and the Holocaust, and the two men who coined the terms 'genocide' and 'crimes against humanity' – Rafael Lemkin and Hersch Lauterpacht.

928 Raul Hilberg's list is at the beginning of the chapter 'The Establishment' in *Perpetrators, Victims, Bystanders*.

Chapter Twenty:
The Architect in Prison – a Different Man?

The majority of Speer quotations in this chapter are taken from three works: *Albert Speer: His Battle with Truth* by Gitta Sereny, and *Inside the Third Reich* and *Spandau: The Secret Diaries,* both by Albert Speer. Casalis' quotations are all from *Albert Speer: His Battle with Truth.*

939 Dorothée Casalis' words are from her interview in the BBC documentary *Albert Speer: The Nazi Who Said Sorry.*

958 Regarding Casalis' omission from the index of the *Diaries,* and downplaying of his role in Speer's life, perhaps there was a less generous impulse involved here? Maybe the wound of Casalis leaving, and Speer's profound sense of abandonment afterwards, never really left him? And so, retrospectively, Speer felt reluctant to give him the credit he deserved.

There is another possible explanation. Speer was always something of a chameleon, mirroring back what he felt his audience wanted to hear, subtly changing emphases where necessary. Maybe, knowing Gitta Sereny's fascination in psychological analysis and morality, and knowing of her affection for Casalis, he told her what she wanted to hear? Slightly exaggerating the role Casalis had played. (The only problem with this hypothesis is that we know that Speer had written to his daughter Hilde several times regarding the centrality of Casalis in his life's journey – unless here, too, he was attempting to tell her what he felt she wanted to hear.)

Chapter Twenty-one:
Searching for Antigone in Ashford, and for Languages That Do Not Yet Exist . . .

The Simone Weil quotations in this chapter are from 'La Personnalité humaine, le juste et l'injuste', *Gravity and Grace* and *Waiting for God.*

965 'It was other people's pain that moved her, not her own' is from *Simone Weil* by Palle Yourgrau, Chapter One.

967 'How beautiful to think of you: / amid news of death and victory, / in prison . . .' is from '9–10 pm' by Nâzim Hickmet.

967 'On the ceiling, in a corner, around ten in the morning, a rectangle of sunlight appears . . .' and the other quotations are from *Men in Prison* by Victor Serge.

981 'How do we condemn a holocaust if we have not condemned all past holocausts?' Weil's question was to her friend Maurice Schumann (quoted in *Simone Weil*, Chapter Eight, by Palle Yourgrau).

982 The George Herbert poem which Simone Weil loved more than any other was 'Love' (1633):

> Love bade me welcome. Yet my soul drew back
> > Guilty of dust and sin.
> But quick-eyed Love, observing me grow slack
> > From my first entrance in,
> Drew nearer to me, sweetly questioning,
> > If I lacked any thing.
>
> A guest, I answered, worthy to be here:
> > Love said, You shall be he.
> I the unkind, ungrateful? Ah my dear,
> > I cannot look on thee.
> Love took my hand, and smiling did reply,
> > Who made the eyes but I?
>
> Truth Lord, but I have marred them: let my shame
> > Go where it doth deserve.
> And know you not, says Love, who bore the blame?
> > My dear, then I will serve.
> You must sit down, says Love, and taste my meat:
> > So I did sit and eat.

983 *As we walk back to the car, Alice says that she still finds something very disturbing about the almost wilful act of her death* . . . I agree strongly with Alice's comment about Weil's death, and there are other aspects of Weil's life and work which I find problematic too – I think there was something missing in her activism, and all her writing about injustice: and that is rage. A real, determined fury to change the world, not just reflect on it, however exceptional many of her insights were. She certainly didn't follow Marx's advice – 'The philosophers have only interpreted the world in various ways; the point, however, is to change it'. I also find that, at certain times, her identification with suffering, and affliction, can become so extreme that it can tip over into a kind of masochistic self-indulgence, a wallowing in shame and humiliation. I think you have to be in the right mood to read Weil – it's like tuning into a radio frequency that's very hard to find. She makes you work harder than many other writers and philosophers, but the rewards are great –her insights can be astonishing.

984 *'The end of all our exploring will be to arrive where we started and know the place for the first time'* from 'Little Gidding', *Four Quartets* by T. S. Eliot.

985 Most of the material and quotations about the writing of 'The Story of the Ten Days' are from Thomson's *Primo Levi*.

990 Derek Jarman's account of finding 'Prospect Cottage' is from *Kicking Against the Pricks*.

992 My tutor in my final year at Cambridge was Stewart Eames. I thank him for helping to start my journey on the long road I've travelled for the last thirty years.

994 *Alice then wonders if this could be represented in film – two old friends who haven't seen each other for years, driving through the night and talking* . . . I should say here that the previous evening the three of us had been talking about *My Dinner with Andre* – that strange and beautiful film by Louis Malle, which involves a similar scenario – the meeting of two old friends (Wally Shawn and Andre Gregory, playing themselves), who haven't seen each other for years, meeting at a restaurant in Manhattan.

Companions to *I You We Them*

In place of the traditional bibliography I would like to celebrate in particular eighteen companions to *I You We Them*. These are writers, critics, artists, activists and film-makers whose creativity has been inspirational over many years. All are artists and thinkers that you can build a lifelong relationship with – who are fearless in the risks they take, and are always trying to look beyond the limits of the world view they inherited. All have created astounding individual works, yet their lives reach beyond the span of their art, because their work is indivisible from their humanity.

Jean Améry
Hannah Arendt
Susan Griffin
Raul Hilberg
Derek Jarman
Jan Karski
Claude Lanzmann
Primo Levi
Sven Lindqvist
David Olusoga and Casper Erichsen
Arundhati Roy
Ken Saro-Wiwa
W. G. Sebald

Jorge Semprún
Gitta Sereny
George Steiner
Simone Weil

Jean Améry (1912–1978)

Writer and philosopher. Active in the anti-Nazi Resistance movement in Belgium in World War II, he was captured in 1943, tortured, and later deported to Auschwitz (Buna-Monowitz, where
Primo Levi was a fellow prisoner), Buchenwald and Bergen-Belsen.
In 1966 he published *At the Mind's Limits: Contemplations by a
Survivor on Auschwitz and Its Realities* – one of the most remarkable meditations ever written on the meaning that lies behind the
word 'survival'. Reflecting on his own torture by the Gestapo he
wrote: 'Whoever was tortured, stays tortured. Torture is ineradica-
bly burned into him, even when no clinical traces can be detected'.
In the last decade of his life he published two other highly regarded
works – *On Aging* and *On Suicide: A Discourse on Voluntary Death*.
Primo Levi's final collection of essays, *The Drowned and the Saved*,
contains a compelling chapter, 'The Intellectual in Auschwitz', that
centres on Améry's life and thought, though Levi acknowledges that
Améry's view of humanity was ultimately bleaker than his own.

Hannah Arendt (1906–1975)

Writer and political philosopher. Forced to leave Germany in 1933,
she eventually made her way to the United States, where she settled
in 1941. The two works which established her reputation as one of
the leading thinkers of her day were *The Origins of Totalitarianism* (1951) and *The Human Condition* (1958). Following Adolf
Eichmann's trial in Israel, she also wrote a groundbreaking study
of this archetypal 'desk killer', investigating his psychology and the
inter-relationship between bureaucracy and genocide in his 'career'
– *Eichmann in Jerusalem: A Report on the Banality of Evil*. Her
work was fearless, 'thinking without a banister' as she put it; she
would never compromise on her fundamental beliefs, however
difficult this was for others, or for herself – '*Fiat veritas, et pereat*

mundus' was her intellectual credo: Let truth be told – though the world may perish.

Susan Griffin (1943–)

Writer and activist. She grew up in California, becoming a passionate ecologist early in life, inspired by the landscape of the High Sierras and the Pacific coast. She has described her work as 'drawing connections between the destruction of nature, the diminishment of women and racism, and tracing the causes of war to denial in both private and public life'. Regarded as a pioneer of ecofeminism – her book *Women and Nature* (1978) became a key work in this field. Among her prolific output of writing – plays, poetry and essays – perhaps one work stands out. *A Chorus of Stones: The Private Life of* War (1993) is an astonishing book which interweaves political and historical analysis with the intimacy of personal testimony. It focuses on violence, trauma and silence, and how denial runs though individual lives, families and societies. 'We forget that we are history . . . I was born and brought up in a nation that participated in the bombing of Dresden, and in the civilisation that planned the extermination of a whole people'.

Raul Hilberg (1926–2007)

Historian. Forced to flee Vienna in 1939, Hilberg and his family settled in New York. After army service in World War II he studied political science at Columbia University, and became engrossed by the subject that became known as 'the Holocaust' (though he himself never liked this term) – particularly the role of the perpetrators. This was the subject of his doctoral thesis, which, after many subsequent years of research, was finally published in 1961 (in three volumes) as *The Destruction of the European Jews*. More than any other historian before, or since, Hilberg's work sets out in painstaking detail the process of *how* the Holocaust happened – the precise role of each cog in the machine of extermination, the numerous agencies involved, the names of the perpetrators, including the armies of invisible bureaucrats and desk killers, who played such a central role in the genocide.

Derek Jarman (1942–1994)

Filmmaker, artist, writer and activist. After studying fine art at the Slade in London, he originally worked in stage design, moving to filmmaking in the 1970s. *Sebastiane, The Angelic Conversation, The Garden* and *Blue* are all works of staggering originality and power, combining visual beauty with radical representations of gay sexuality and anger at social injustice. He was also a fine writer, his vivid journals published as *Modern Nature* and *Kicking the Pricks*, a visual artist and, in the last years of his life, he created a remarkable garden in the shingle surrounding his cottage at Dungeness in Kent. But his outspoken activism and campaigning, as an HIV positive gay man living in times of extreme homophobia, was a constant throughout his life – an inspirational example to so many at the time, and to generations who have followed.

Jan Karski (1914–2000)

Polish resistance fighter and academic. Working as a talented young diplomat, with a master's in law and diplomatic science, Karski's life changed forever with the outbreak of World War II. He became a key figure in the Polish underground resistance, demonstrating remarkable courage on many missions. In summer 1942 he's smuggled into the Warsaw Ghetto and the Izbica transit camp, where he witnesses first-hand the genocide of the Jews; when he finally manages to get to Britain (and later America) he attempts to 'shake the conscience of the world' by relating the reality of what he's seen, so that action can be taken. But, despite meetings with the most senior government officials, including President Roosevelt himself, no military action is forthcoming. After the war he became a professor of history at Georgetown University. Later on, he contributed to Lanzmann's film *Shoah*, which ends with his unforgettable testimony.

Claude Lanzmann (1925–2018)

Filmmaker, journalist and anti-colonial activist. He joined the French Resistance as an eighteen year old, leading a Communist cell. After the war he studied philosophy in Germany, but also began working as a journalist. In the early 1950s he became a close friend of Jean-Paul Sartre, and a partner of Simone de Beauvoir, and edited Sartre's journal *Les Temps Modernes* for many years. He was also a committed activist, particularly against France's colonial war in Algeria; he became very close to the revolutionary thinker Frantz Fanon in 1961, and helped to promote his work in France. In the 1970s he moved into documentary filmmaking – his greatest achievement unquestionably being the film *Shoah* – a nine-and-a-half-hour work of mesmerising power, consisting of interviews with survivors, perpetrators and witnesses of the Holocaust – which Lanzmann created between 1974 and 1985.

Primo Levi (1919–1987)

Writer and chemist. Grew up in Torino, where he studied chemistry at university. In 1943 Levi joined a small group of Italian partisans, working against German forces in the mountains, but they were captured, and Levi was sent to the camp at Fossoli and then on to Auschwitz in early 1944. He spent a year there, working as a slave labourer at Monowitz-Buna, an experience he wrote about immediately after the war in his searing masterpiece, *If This Is a Man* – which took many years to find a global readership. His chemist's precision combined with the deepest understanding of humanity and morality created an incomparable body of work, including *The Periodic Table* (1975) and *The Drowned and the Saved* (1986). It has been said of Levi, rightly I think, that he is one of the very few writers 'with whom it is possible to sustain a lasting friendship . . . [who] offers us explicit recipes for being human'.

Sven Lindqvist (1932–2019)

Writer and traveller, born in Stockholm in 1932. He travelled extensively through Asia, Africa and Latin America, and was the author of over thirty books, including *Exterminate All the Brutes* (Granta, 1998), *A History of Bombing* (Granta, 2001), *Desert Divers* (Granta, 2002), *Bench Press* (Granta, 2003), *Terra Nullius: A Journey Through No One's Land* (Granta, 2007), *Saharan Journey*

(Granta, 2012) and *The Myth of Wu Tao-tzu* (Granta, 2012). I can still recall the visceral impact of reading *Exterminate All the Brutes* for the first time – a terrifying journey into the psychology of European colonisation of Africa. And most of Lindqvist's powerful argument that 'Europe's destruction of the "inferior races" of four continents prepared the ground for Hitler's destruction of six million Jews in Europe'. Indeed Hitler explicitly regarded such genocides as providing a kind of blueprint for his own ambitions: 'What Hitler wished to create when he sought *Lebensraum* in the East was a continental equivalent of the British Empire. It was in the British and other Western European peoples that he found the models . . .'

David Olusoga (1970–) and Casper Erichsen (1973–)

Pioneering historians who co-authored *The Kaiser's Holocaust*, published in 2010, the definitive work on Germany's 'forgotten genocide' – that of the Herero and Nama peoples in Namibia in the first years of the twentieth century. Erichsen grew up in Denmark, but has spent much of the last two decades based in Namibia, researching this genocide. He is currently a special advisor for IPPF and lives in London. Olusoga was born in Nigeria and grew up in Britain. As well as his highly regarded books of history, including *Black and British: A Forgotten History* (2016), he is an acclaimed broadcaster, responsible for the groundbreaking, BAFTA award-winning BBC series *Britain's Forgotten Slave Owners* (2015) – made in partnership with the Legacies of British Slave-ownership project, based at University College London.

Arundhati Roy (1961–)

Writer and activist. She grew up in Kerala, India, and originally studied architecture at university, before working in film and television. In 1997 she published her first novel, *The God of Small Things*, which immediately reached a global audience. Following this success she's devoted much of her time to activism, becoming a powerful critic of nationalism, neo-imperialism and globalisation. She has published brilliant collections of essays, including

The Ordinary Person's Guide to Empire (2004), which focussed on the legacy of the 11 September 2001 attacks and the invasion of Iraq, and *Listening to Grasshoppers: Field Notes on Democracy* (2009), which analysed the disturbing nationalistic forces at play behind India's growing economic power. Her long-awaited second novel, *The Ministry of Utmost Happiness*, was published in 2017, and a collection of non-fiction, *My Seditious Heart*, was published in 2019. She sees all of her writing as being about 'the relationship between power and powerlessness', saying that 'fiction dances out of me [but] non-fiction is wrenched out by the aching, broken world I wake up to every morning'.

Ken Saro-Wiwa (1941–1995)

Writer and activist. He grew up in Ogoniland, in southern Nigeria, and studied English at the University of Ibaden, before starting to teach at Lagos University. In the late 1960s and early 1970s he took jobs in local government, before establishing himself as a successful businessman. But his real passion was writing, and by the 1980s he was able to focus on this full-time, creating a highly successful television series, *Basi & Co.*, and publishing his satirical masterpiece, *Sozaboy: A Novel in Rotten English*, in 1985. From 1990 onwards Saro-Wiwa's life became dominated by his activism, as he saw his Ogoni homeland becoming more and more devastated by the environmental impacts of the oil industry, particularly Shell and Chevron. He became the charismatic leader of the Movement for the Survival of the Ogoni People (MOSOP), and rapidly built a highly effective, non-violent campaign, which soon gathered global support, writing vividly about this process in *A Month and a Day*. In 1994 he was arrested on trumped-up charges of murder, and, following a show trial, on 10 November 1995, he and eight fellow Ogoni activists were executed in Port Harcourt. His view of what writing and art could achieve is inspirational: 'It's not . . . an ego trip, it is serious, it is politics, it is economics, it's everything, and art in that instance becomes so meaningful, both to the artist and to the consumers of that art.'

W. G. Sebald (1944–2001)

Writer and academic. Born in a small Bavarian village towards the end of World War II, Sebald studied English and German literature in Germany and Switzerland, before taking a lectureship at the University of Manchester in 1966. In 1970 he completed his PhD at the University of East Anglia, where he worked for the rest of his life, becoming professor of European literature and establishing the British Centre for Literary Translation. He began to publish outside academia relatively late – his first novel, *Vertigo*, only being published in 1990. *The Emigrants* (1992) and *The Rings of Saturn* (1995) rapidly consolidated his growing reputation – his writing being utterly distinctive and uncompromisingly out-of-step with modern life. Extraordinarily empathetic portraits of individuals left behind by the march of 'progress', culminating in his greatest work, *Austerlitz,* published in 2001 – an astounding meditation on time, memory loss and the Holocaust, seen through the eyes of a *Kindertransport* survivor.

Jorge Semprún (1923–2011)

Writer and screenwriter. Born in Spain, but after Franco came to power his family moved to the Netherlands and then France, where Semprún began studying at the Sorbonne in 1939. Following the Nazi occupation, Semprún joined the Communist Party and became active in the Resistance. In 1943 he was captured by the Gestapo and sent to Buchenwald concentration camp. After the war he returned to France, working for two decades as an organiser for the exiled Communist Party of Spain, serving on the executive committee. He also wrote his first book, *Le grand voyage* (eventually published in 1963), a fictionalised portayal of his experience in Buchenwald, In the late 1960s, following his expulsion from the Party for not following 'the party line', he began to concentrate more on his writing, not only novels but also screenwriting including two films with the director Costa-Gavras , *Z* (1969) and *The Confession* (1970). After serving as Minister of Culture in the Socialist government of Felipe González in the late 1980s, in 1994 he published his greatest work, *Literature or Life* – a gripping account of not only his time at Buchenwald but the legacy of those years in his life afterwards.

Gitta Sereny (1921–2012)

Writer. She grew up in Vienna, but moved to France after the Nazi takeover of Austria in 1938. After the war she worked with the United Nations refugee programme, trying to reunite children who had been separated from their families under Nazism. In 1949 she settled in London and began her career as an investigative journalist, particularly for *The Sunday Times* and the *Telegraph*; much of her work focussed on vulnerable children and the social services. But her most important work – all of which involved trying to understand what lies behind the lazy label of 'evil' – was yet to come. She spent weeks interviewing Franz Stangl, the commandant of Treblinka, and this eventually became *Into That Darkness,* published in 1974 – probably the greatest ever study of the mind of a mass murderer. Her meticulous interviewing technique and combination of exceptional empathy and unsparing judgement is also evident in her other master work – *Albert Speer: His Battle with Truth* (1995) – which managed to go far deeper than any historian or biographer before or since, in understanding how such a 'civilised' and educated man could have become a centrally important figure in the regime of Nazi Germany.

George Steiner (1929–)

Writer, critic, philosopher, academic and polymath. From a Viennese Jewish family, Steiner grew up in Paris, but in 1940, with the Nazi occupation of France imminent, his family were forced to relocate again, this time to New York. He studied literature, as well as mathematics and physics at Chicago, Harvard and Oxford University. After periods as an academic in the United States and Austria, he became a founding fellow of Churchill College, Cambridge in 1961, before becoming professor of English and comparative literature at the University of Geneva in 1974, a post he held for twenty years. In addition to being an inspirational teacher, he has published prolifically throughout his life, works on a dizzying range of subjects, though he has also stated 'my whole life has been about death, remembering and the Holocaust'. To select just three of the most outstanding works – *Language and Silence* (1967) is a brilliant collection of essays on literature and the Holocaust, *In Bluebeard's Castle* (1971) raised profound questions about the proximity of civilisation and barbarism, and *The Portage to San Cristobal of A.H.* (1981) is a vivid novel which imagines Israeli agents in 1977 finding an elderly and feeble Adolf Hitler deep in the Amazonian rainforest. It divided its critics, as Steiner often has, but it contains extraordinary passages relating to the Holocaust, the origins of antisemitism and the power of language, and its abuse.

Simone Weil (1909–1943)

Writer, philosopher and activist. Born in Paris, she grew up in a secular Jewish family, and became drawn to philosophy from an early age. After studying at the École Normale Supérieure, she became a teacher, but also began to be drawn to political activism, particularly around workers' rights. As a young woman she was strongly influenced by Marxism and anarchism, and was also an ardent pacifist, though later she grew more critical of Marxism. In 1934, she took a year's leave from her teaching job so that she could work in a Renault factory on the production line; she felt this was the only way of overcoming her bourgeois background and being able to empathise fully with workers. Although she'd always kept a journal, she also began to write essays on labour issues and reflections on war for anarchist journals and political publications, but her work was not known beyond circles of radical politics. In the late 1930s she began to experience intense religious revelations, and her focus began to shift away from activism and more towards spirituality. In 1942 she left occupied France with her family, first for the United States, but then moving to Britain, where she hoped to work for the French government-in-exile, and volunteer for Resistance activities back in France. However, her health began to deteriorate badly in 1943, just as she was writing her book *The Need for Roots* and her extraordinary essay *La personalité humaine, le juste et l'injuste*, and she died in the Grosvenor Hall sanatorium in Ashford,

Kent in August 1943. The majority of Weil's work, selected from her journals and notebooks, was published posthumously, *Gravity and Grace* in 1947, *The Need for Roots* (1949) and *Waiting on God* (1950), with her reputation growing greatly in the decades that followed, Camus calling her 'the only great spirit of our time'. Her writing defies easy classification, but, at its best, has a laser-like clarity and power – '*La croyance à l'existence d'autres êtres humains comme tels est amour*' ('The belief in the existence of other human beings – such a thing is love') or '*L'attention est la forme la plus rare et la plus pure de la générosité*' ('Attention is the rarest and purest form of generosity').

Appreciation and Gratitude

The word 'Acknowledgements', which traditionally appears at the end of publications, has always seemed to me a very limited word to use as a way of thanking the many people behind the creation and production of any book. And in the case of a sequence of books, which has taken more than two decades to come into the world, people certainly need to be thanked fully rather than simply acknowledged. And because I believe that the dead are always with us, I think that they should be thanked as well – so I make no distinction in this appreciation as to whether people are physically alive or alive in spirit.

*

First of all my deepest thanks to my family and friends, who have given me so much love and support over the many years this work has taken. Thank you to Corinne, Mark, Meg and family, Adam and family, and my nieces and nephews, Anna, Ben, Isabelle and Jacob. And thank you so much to my long-suffering friends, who have endured the numerous ups and downs of this epic journey with humour, conviviality and large quantities of alcohol – James, Em, John, Ann, Mark, Colette, Luca, Emma, Graham, Nicki, Diane, Gareth, Martin, Nick, Helen, Pete, Claire, Denis, Sue, David, Alan, Donald and Peter. I feel very lucky to have you all in my life. And

1069

in Hackney, thank you to the families of foxes – several generations now – who have shared the wildness of my garden, and are the real spirit of this place.

Much gratitude and appreciation to all at Platform – the genesis of *I You We Them* were those exhilarating years from 1996 onwards, when we were all working so closely together on researching the culture and power of transnational corporations, particularly the oil industry, and coming up with the most innovative ways of highlighting the corporate psychology, and consequent environmental devastation and human rights abuses caused. The ideas and energy that emerged from that little workspace by the Thames at 7 Horsleydown Lane – the performances, guided walks, commuter newspapers, meetings, boat discussions, memorials, books, university courses – were years ahead of their time. Thank you to James Marriott, Greg Muttitt, Jane Trowell, John Jordan, Emma McFarland, Diane Wittner, Emma Sangster, Anna Wright, Rosey Hurst, Nick Robins and Wallace Heim for sharing those times and giving so much. And also special appreciation to Andy Rowell and Cindy Baxter, who helped start our ten-year voyage on the *90% CRUDE* project.

The *Remember Saro-Wiwa* campaign, for all its challenges, was the most important work we ever did. Thank you to all at Platform and Maria Saro-Wiwa, Ken Wiwa, David A. Bailey, Anita and Gordon Roddick, Sokari Douglas Camp, Lorne Stockman, Ben Amunwa, Nick McCarthy, Eno Osua, Lazarus Tamana, Terry Ndee, Diana Morant, Kadija Sesay, Simon Murray, Nii Ayikwei Parkes, Beth Hamer, Tim Sowula, Jo Hurst-Croft, Michelle Akande, Lola Young, John Sauven, Eric Soul, Nneka, Gus Casely Hayford, Yinka Shonibare, Ruth Borthwick, Wole Soyinka, Alice Oswald, Lemn Sissay, Helon Habila, Buchi Emecheta, Linton Kwesi Johnson, William Boyd and Angela Davis for helping to make the Living Memorial, and all the associated work and publications, an inspiring reality.

*

The *killing us softly* events, which took place at Platform between December 1999 and March 2003, were critical in developing many of the initial themes and ideas for the books that have followed. Warmest appreciation to James, Jane and Emma (Platform) and Kate O'Connor and Ute Spittler (for the music and production of these events) and to all seventy-two individuals who came to these performances, and contributed their thoughts afterwards (Heike Roms, Nick Stewart, Jane Rendell, Malcolm Miles, Jock Encombe, Claire Gordon, Derek Wax, Sara Boas, Tim Nunn, Bill Hewitt, Patrick Field, Carla Drahorad, Tim Fairs and Sue Palmer – my gratitude for your strong engagement with the work and your additional ideas and support). My deep appreciation to Pete Harrison, not only for friendship and support on this project, but also for all the work at the Wiener Library and British Library in 2005, helping with the research on IG Farben at Buna-Monowitz and also the Austrian lawyer (an archetypal desk killer), who eventually became secretary-general of the United Nations (and who we'll meet in Book Three) . . .

Nothing in the arts is possible without proper funding, so here my strong appreciation goes to: the Lannan Foundation (in particular Patrick Lannan and Jaune Evans) for supporting vital research work, two trips to Poland and Bosnia, and my early writing time; the Ashden Trust (who supported the original *killing us softly* events); Arts Council England, the Network for Social Change (in particular Anne Robbins and Mark Brown), the Authors' Foundation, Society of Authors and the Barry Amiel and Norman Melburn Trust – all for supporting my writing time. And also huge gratitude to those who've helped financially on an individual level in the final stages of editing, when my publishing advances had dwindled to almost nothing. And lastly on funding, a special word of appreciation to Lloyds Bank – who mis-sold me so many loans over the years that the compensation they eventually had to pay supported another year of my writing time!

The places where I've written have played such an important role in the work that has emerged, so many thanks to all those who have lent me houses, cottages and cabins to write in: Rosie Thompson for the fisherman's cabin at Shingle Street – where the odyssey began all those years ago overlooking the 'German Ocean'; Holly Aylett and Peter Chappell, for use of the house in Pembrokeshire – which contributed greatly to the flow of creativity between 2011 and 2013; (also to Ali and Martin, Sean and Wendy for good times there, and Marion for the Boat House); Kate Wells and the Hughes family for use of Carreg y Ro Bach in 2013 and 2014 – a wonderful and nostalgic return to Traeth Bach after so many years away. Also my thanks to Teresa Elwes (for Aldeburgh), Andrew Kotting (for St. Leonards) and Jay Griffiths (for enabling me to use that magical log cabin in the Welsh beech woods).

*

The next part – concerning the sixteen-year journey from the final *killing us softly* event (in March 2003) to the publication of this first book (in 2019) – can only really be related as a narrative, with all its twists and turns, and lessons learned along the way, so I will try to summarise the main chapters in the story here:

The evolution of this work from a live event to a sequence of books began with John Berger's passionate response to the *killing us softly* event in March 2003, after which he urged me to consider how the spoken words of the event might become words on a page. And the weeks which followed, including time at John's house in Paris, were critical in giving me direction towards making this transition. I can still remember sitting under an apple tree in blossom, in John's garden in Antony, and him saying to me: *'Well, you've got so much material there already! I mean, what, it might take another six months? A year?'* Over the course of the next fourteen years, we'd occasionally recall this moment and laugh uproariously, before John would say: *'But it's not about the length of the journey is it? No! It's about everything you've experienced along the way – just like the Cavafy poem, "Ithaka"!*

Along the long, and sometimes rocky, path I was lucky enough to experience several happenings, which in retrospect seem like miracles. In January 2005 I received a phone call, out of the blue, from Patrick Lannan, the founder of the Lannan Foundation in America. Patrick told me he'd just heard about my work on the 'desk killer', which seemed to him of critical importance, so what did I need to complete the research and the writing? Six weeks later, aided by the redoubtable Jaune Evans, then executive director at the Foundation, I received a major grant, giving me funding for more than a year – enabling me to undertake two further research trips, employ a part-time researcher and take a six-month sabbatical from Platform – which gave me the space I needed to start the process of writing. A lesson here – sometimes the answer comes from a direction you're not even looking in.

There followed a frenetically busy period at Platform (the period when we were working intensively on the *Remember Saro-Wiwa* campaign), and so inevitably I had to put the book on the back-burner for a couple of years. The second miracle occurred in summer 2010. And again, it came at a moment when the project needed it most. I received an email quite unexpectedly from Philip Gwyn Jones, then executive publisher at Granta and Portobello Books, saying that he'd been looking at maps, planning a family holiday through northern Switzerland, and this had triggered a memory. He'd heard some time before about the research I'd done into the Swiss company that manufactured the *gaswagen* used in the Holocaust, and thought I was developing a book proposal. Did I have a publisher? Would I like to have lunch and update him on the work? This led to the book (then titled *The Desk Killer*) being commissioned in 2011, and an extremely creative working relationship followed. For the first time in my life, I was able to write full-time with no distractions, and the combination of Philip's strong commitment and gentle encouragement together with my exhilaration at having discovered a rhythm of writing in Wales created a remarkable flow of work between 2011 and 2013, and laid the foundations for the four books of *I You We Them*.

This period ended abruptly in May 2013 in a very difficult period at Granta, when most of the senior editorial staff, including Philip, left the company. At this point, because I'd lost my commissioning editor, I decided that I now really needed to guide *I You We Them* to a new home. I embarked on a search for an agent who would be able to help me through this challenging territory and also be a powerful advocate for the work. Over these months I had fruitful meetings with David Grossman, Victoria Hobbs and Peter Straus among others. (Peter, thank you for suggesting that *I You We Them* should be published as four books – I appreciated your ambition!) Thanks also to Hisham Matar for suggestions and facilitating some of these meetings. And to Robert Macfarlane for further, extremely helpful, advice at this time.

My third great stroke of luck came in September 2013 when the agent Jessica Woollard replied to an exploratory email with enormous excitement. A couple of days later, when she'd read all four books, she rang me from India and we spoke for more than an hour. I knew instinctively that I had found the agent I'd been searching for, somebody who could be a passionate advocate for the work. What I didn't know then was that I'd also found a brilliantly perceptive reader and editor, and a person of immense integrity and kindness, who would become a dear friend.

In early 2014 we worked intensively on the manuscript, and by the spring Jessica started to arrange meetings with prospective publishers. On a sunny day in March, at a café outside the British Museum, Tom Avery, senior editor at Heinemann, arrived on his bike, smiling, but looking at me rather nervously, as if I might bolt off at any moment. He was effusive about the manuscript, and we talked animatedly for the next hours, ending up in a nearby pub. By the time he left I had a strong intuition that I'd found my new publisher. Within weeks the deal was agreed, and we began to work energetically on how these four books could best be edited and published.

Tom's remarkable energy and total belief in the project over the last five years has been exceptional. He was undaunted by the considerable length of the original manuscript, and has always had an extraordinary ability to see the wider 'architecture' of the whole work in his head, and make striking suggestions about re-positioning chapters, or proposing where new pieces of writing would help the reader. Other editors may have baulked at the prospect of my adding to the original manuscript – by, for example, writing additional sections on Hannah Arendt and Adolf Eichmann for Book Four. But Tom recognised the essential place of such pieces in the work, and was extremely encouraging about my taking time to write them. There have been several moments, over the last years of working together, when I felt that he knew my manuscript better than I knew it myself – a slightly unnerving experience for any writer, but rather wonderful at the same time. I'm not sure that either of us understood quite what a massive undertaking it would be for me to finally relinquish more than two decades of research and thought, and move to the finality of a finished text. Perhaps I'd always been influenced subconsciously by one of Thomas Mann's more cheery reflections?: *'When the house is finished, death comes'.* And so, maybe understandably, I'd wanted to put this point off for as long as possible . . .

In February 2015, in the middle of the iciest east coast winter for years, I travelled to New York to meet Ileene Smith, executive editor at Farrar, Straus and Giroux, to discuss their interest in publishing the American edition of *I You We Them*. Again, the first meeting was a conversation – in Ileene's apartment, high above the streets of Manhattan. And again, just as with Jessica, and just as with Tom, I knew almost immediately that we would be able to work well together. She told me that all editors rely on a 'sixth sense', and she'd known as soon as she'd started reading the manuscript that FSG must publish this book, which combined the urgency of the subject matter with a voice that was able to interweave historical and political themes with such personal and intimate material.

With these two foundations now in place (financial security from the two publishing contracts and feeling supported by this dynamic triangle of agent and editors), there then followed a period of time that writers can only dream of – three uninterrupted years of thought and creativity. By 2015 I was living mainly in Wales, on

Pen Llŷn, having found a house overlooking the mountains and the sea, close to where RS Thomas wrote his last poems. I could now focus totally on editing the books, and finally bringing two decades of work to fruition. Over the next three years, Tom and I (helped greatly by Ileene's incisive suggestions), worked assiduously on re-shaping the whole work, and editing Books One and Two into the volume that you have in your hands. By the end of 2018 the writing was finished.*

*

In early 2019 attention turned to finalising the images and maps. Special thanks here must go to James Norton – who arrived in January like an angel of mercy to help with sourcing many of the photographs and images needed. He could have been daunted, as I was, at the prospect of organising so many images – photographing documents, finding better quality images in archives, contacting copyright-holders – but all was done in a spirit of Zen-like calm. Thank you also to James Marriott for helping me conceptualise how the text and images could work together more effectively. Thanks also to Emma Sangster and Abiy and the team at Kodak Express, Mornington Crescent for work on digitising my slide images from 15 years ago. A chance meeting with the brilliant Joff Winterhart led to the fox-tracks map at the beginning of Book One – thanks so much for that, and for musical inspiration too! And in the last weeks, Darren Bennett at DKB Creative, deepest gratitude for your masterly work on the maps – I loved discussing these with you (and our football chat too – fingers still crossed for both of our teams) . . .

*

There are many others I would also like to thank – friends and colleagues who have contributed so much. Donald Reeves and Peter

---

* Although Edward Said certainly would not agree with this premise – 'Texts are not finished objects', as he wrote in *Culture and Imperialism*.

Pelz – your work at St James's Piccadilly was something very special; but your work with the Soul of Europe, supposedly in your 'retirement', on peace and reconciliation in the Balkans – in Bosnia, Serbia, Republika Srpska and Kosovo – has been inspirational to so many, a beacon of light in the darkness. Your friendship has meant an enormous amount and taught me so much.

Alan Boldon, Sue Palmer, David Williams and Alan Read – who I originally met through teaching work at Dartington College (when Dartington was still concerned with education) – all four passionately committed educators who I've learned a great deal from over the years. (And also thanks to Michaela Crimmin, Scott Lash, Jeremy Deller and Alan B. for those conversations at the back of the bus on the RSA trip to China many years ago. I can still remember them vividly . . .)

Nicki Jackowska, John Fennelly and Emma McFarland, thank you so much for your engagement with many issues connected to my writing life over the last years – from musing over the question of titles and subtitles, to helping me navigate the unfamiliar waters of interactions with agents and publishing companies. Your guidance and advice has been invaluable.

Dr Chris Seeley and Dr Vicki Culpin (of Ashridge Business School) and Dr Kate Mackenzie Davey (of Birkbeck College, University of London) – my appreciation for invitations to speak to students at Ashridge, and also for the important work we initiated together on the research project 'Ethical Compartmentalisation in Business Leadership'.

My gratitude also for your inspiration, support and friendship to all the following: Firstly to my beloved aunt and uncle, Eleanor and Casimir Hollack (Fif and Casey), who after sixty-two years of marriage, died only seventeen days apart, in October 2018. Despite the great sadness, it also seemed fitting to be working on the very last parts of this book, while clearing out your beautiful flat (full of books and memories) in west London. Also my love, gratitude and respect to Diane Wittner, Jon Acheson, Gabriel and Baird (my

'Baltimore family'), Lucy Fairley (activist extraordinaire and friend to the most vulnerable in our society), Stuart Eames (for opening my mind to the literature of the Holocaust all those years ago in Cambridge), Nella Bielski (happy memories of 'Hotel Spinoza'), Jerome Kohn (thank you for wonderful conversations and reflections on Hannah Arendt), Ben Barkow and Colin Clarke (and all the past and present Wiener Library staff – thank you for all your archival assistance over so many years), John Parry, Liz Anklow and family (for all the New Jersey times), Nigel Beanland and Lucy Johnson (for exceptional insight and support), Kevin Kemp and Ken ('The Buddhas of Victoria Park'), Marcelo Bielsa (for re-igniting my passion for The Beautiful Game – here's to next season!), and to Leonard Cohen and Bob Dylan for being the inexhaustible musical companions of my life – the Schubert and Beethoven of our times. And my warmest appreciation and respect for you and your work also to Melissa Benn and Paul Gordon, Mike Dibb and Cheli Duran, Catherine and Erich Fried, Bill Hewitt, Luke Holland, Hannah Hurtzig, Miche Fabre-Lewin, Peter Kennard, Jelena Mackin, Louis Charalambous, Yves Froidevaux, Colin Spencer, Stephen Watts, Jean McCrindle, Andrea Zimmerman, Grant Gee, Harriet and Colin Ward, Lucy Neal, Julia Rowntree and Rose Fenton. And thank you to all the students, teachers and staff I ever worked with at Peter Street – some incredible times in that old corner of Soho . . .

I would also like to thank Andy Rowell (for fearless journalism, especially on Nigeria, Ken Saro-Wiwa and the Ogoni struggle for self determination, and for wise advice), Sheila O'Donnell in California (for help with research into one of the desk killers), Alex Wade at Reviewed & Cleared – regardless of later challenges I appreciated the legal expertise you provided to try and allow a strongly political work to come into the world with its voice intact. My gratitude also to my scrupulous copy editor David Milner (any errors that may still remain are certainly not yours), and to Declan Ryan for helping to resolve a technical challenge at just the right time. Finally thanks to Alice Howe and all of the foreign rights team at David Higham Associates.

I also think it's important to recognise the role that anger can play in spurring creativity on – and also in activism more generally. (I remember Anita Roddick once saying that the secret of successful activism and a fulfilling life was anger and the best quality tomatoes.) I'd like to thank all those who have doubted this work over the last two decades, or put obstacles in my way – you've only succeeded in strengthening my resolve! I would also like to credit the role of all the corporations and governments who continue to treat people with contempt, and who in their headlong rush to free-marketise the entire planet, believe that we will forget their crimes. They have only redoubled my determination to finish this work. They will never understand those words of Anne Michaels – 'History is amoral: events occurred. But memory is moral.'

*

In Wales thank you to Angus and Jenny for *Fron Oleu*, which gave me a breathtaking introduction to Pen Llŷn (and for the loan of all the furniture too!), and to Martin (for other help with the move), and thank you to Judith and Raymond for activism and good company, to David, Sara, Helen and all at Browsers Bookshop, Porthmadog, for keeping me supplied with pens, books and maps, to Dafydd and all at Felin Uchaf for inspiration and making the *Gwlad beirdd a chantorion* a living reality, to Gary at Efail Rhos garage (for working miracles with my ancient car), to John in Llanbedrog (for helping to keep my 2005 laptop going), to the late-night Spar in Abersoch (for keeping me in smokes and beer), and to Llinos for teaching me Welsh (yes I know – it's a work in progress) . . .

My deep gratitude to the place of the waters, which has given me so much inspiration over the last few years, and also to the ravens of Carn Fadryn, the choughs on Cilan, the hares of Ystum-cegid, the peregrines at Pen y Cil, the ospreys on the Glaslyn, the bursts of blackthorn blossom in early spring, the swallows dipping down the path to Porth Ysgo, the hills of purple heather and deep yellow gorse in summer, the churches at Llanfaelrhys, Llandudwen and Llangwnnadl and all the lanes and tracks and paths I've walked these last years, my companions through many dusks.

*

And always in my heart – AV, JJC and AP – the loves of my life, моя прелесть, *corazón, amante*. For all the joys we've shared, and all that's still to come . . .

*

Then hovering in the background for the last two decades, like a benevolent spirit, an artistic and political phenomenon, a one-man festival of ideas – my deepest gratitude to the irrepressible Gareth Evans. Bringing together the worlds of film, community activism, psychogeography, bookshops, music, performance, city walks, poetry, political protest and literary happenings. Organising extraordinary events on shoestrings and generosity of spirit, linking people from different backgrounds who'd never normally connect, making things happen, all the time. Who else, when you meet, would hand over bags of proof copies of critical texts on Chile and flyers about stopping the sell-off of public housing in Harringay and programmes of all-night Jarman screenings in east London dives? – all of them 'essential!', 'crucial!' 'must-see!'. Where Peter Brook created his Empty Space, you Gareth have created a Gathering Space. And our culture would be so much poorer without it . . . Deep gratitude for all, and for too many links, recommendations, books, inspirations to list here – but I wanted to thank you for one particular stage in the book's development, which was invaluable for me. There was a difficult year, riddled with challenges for both of us, but I remember the exhilaration of the late-night sessions we had in your tiny kitchen at Beaumont Court. I would return from a week's writing in Wales, another chapter drafted, and then round to yours, and I'd read what I'd just written, and you'd listen, making notes, and then we'd talk into the early hours, often into the dawn with only the sound of blackbirds from the Upper Clapton Road drifting up to that little room. A sense of intense connection at that time and place. And I'd always leave buoyed up, always inspired, always reinvigorated . . .

*

And finally, the two people who have been my constant companions through the formidable mountains of this quest – my inspirational friends and guides in this writing labour for more than fifteen years – one of you at each shoulder as I researched and wrote – John Berger and Anne Michaels. Your words have created entire worlds. I will never be able to express how much your sustained support, passion and encouragement meant to me. You both gave me courage which I didn't know I possessed, a fierce determination in the face of great challenges, and an absolute belief in the beauty and importance of the work. You both lifted me with this belief; your faith meant that I could withstand any blow of fate, any setback. It meant the world to me. You have carried me through.

Permissions Acknowledgements

Please see notes and 'Companions' for further source information.

Extracts from *At the Mind's Limit* by Jean Améry reproduced by kind permission of Indiana University Press.

Extracts from *Letters On Life* by Rainer Maria Rilke, translated by Ulrich Baer, published by Everyman Editions, Penguin Random House.

Extracts from 'That the Science of Cartography is Limited' by Eavan Boland taken from *Collected Poems*, published by Carcanet,

Quotations from *Drowning by Bullets*, a film by Philip Brooks and Alan Hayling, first broadcast on 13 July 1992.

Lyrics from 'If You See Her, Say Hello', 'Masters of War', 'Ballad of a Thin Man', 'Just Like Tom Thumb's Blues' and 'My Back Pages' by Bob Dylan, reproduced by kind permission of Special Rider.

Extracts from 'Famine, a Sequence' by Desmond Egan, in *Famine* (1998; 2012; 2018), published by Goldsmith Press Ltd, Newbridge.

Extracts taken from *Pedagogy of the Oppressed* by Paulo Freire, translated by Myra Ramos and published by Bloomsbury Continuum.

PERMISSIONS ACKNOWLEDGEMENTS

Extracts from 'The Scar' by John Hewitt are taken from *Selected Poems*, eds. Michael Longley and Frank Ormsby (Blackstaff Press, 2007), and reproduced by permission of Blackstaff Press on behalf of the Estate of John Hewitt.

Extracts from Nâzim Hikmet's poetry taken from *Beyond the Walls*, translated by Talât Sait Halman, Richard McKane and Ruth Christie, and published by Anvil Press, an imprint of Carcanet.

Extracts from 'La plegaria a un labrador' by Victor Jara taken from *His Hands Were Gentle*, translated by Adrian Mitchell and published by Smokestack Books.

Extracts from 'My Dark Fathers' by Brendan Kennelly, taken from *The Essential Brendan Kennelly*, and reproduced by kind permission of Bloodaxe Books.

Extracts from *The Nazi Doctors: Medical Killing and the Psychology of Genocide* by Robert Jay Lifton, published by Basic Books.

'You took away all the oceans and all the room' by Osip Mandelstam, taken from *Selected Poems*, translated by Clarence Brown and W. S. Merwin, published by New York Review of Books Classics.

Extracts from 'On a Single Day' by Christy Moore: https://www.christymoore.com.

Extracts from *Eyewitness Auschwitz: Three Years in the Gas Chambers* by Filip Muller, reproduced by permission of Taylor and Francis Group Ltd.

Extract from 'For Ken Saro-Wiwa' by Ben Okri, reproduced by kind permission of the author.

Extracts from 'My Sister's Song' by Yannis Ritsos, taken from *Selected Poems 1935–1989*, published by The Hellenic College Press.

Illustration Credits

Ken Saro-Wiwa	*Times Newspapers/ Shutterstock*
Meeting of RSW at Platform	*Emma Sangster*
Remember Saro-Wiwa bus memorial	*Platform collection*
Mark Moody-Stuart	*Gianluigi Guercia/AFP/ Getty Images*
Shell Centre, London	*Wikimedia Commons 2004. Przemyslaw 'BlueShade' Idzkiewicz. Used under license: CC-BY-SA 1.0*
Old Shell HQ, St Helen's Place, London	*James Norton*
Henri Deterding	*Public domain via Wikimedia Commons*
Map of Berlin (overview)	*Darren Bennett*
Spanish Embassy, Berlin	*Wikimedia Commons 2008. Sargoth. Used under license: CC-BY-SA 3.0*
Map of Berlin Day One Walk	*Darren Bennett*
T4 building, Tiergartenstrasse	*Landesarchiv Berlin*
Heydrich letter	*Public domain*
Georg Leibbrandt	*Ullstein Bild/Getty Images*
Wilhelm Stuckart	*Ullstein Bild/Getty Images*
Josef Bühler	*Public domain via Wikimedia Commons*
Karl Eberhard Schöngarth	*Public domain via Wikimedia Commons*
Alfred Meyer	*Ullstein Bild/Getty Images*
Rudolf Lange	*Bundesarchiv*
Roland Freisler	*Ullstein Bild/Getty Images*
Gerhard Klopfer	*Bundesarchiv*
Friedrich Kritzinger	*Public domain via Wikimedia Commons*
Erich Neumann	*Ullstein Bild/Getty Images*
Martin Luther	*Ullstein Bild/Getty Images*
Map of Berlin Day Two Walk: (1)	*Darren Bennett*
Map of Berlin Day Two Walk: (2)	*Darren Bennett*
Foreign Ministry, Berlin	*Wikimedia Commons. Bundesarchiv. Used under license: CC-BY-SA 3.0*

Führer Chancellery, Berlin	*Wikimedia Commons. Bundesarchiv. Used under license: CC-BY-SA 3.0*
Site of former Fuhrer Chancellery, Berlin	*Author photograph*
Former German rail headquarters, Berlin	*Author photograph*
Former office of Adolf Eichmann, Berlin	*Public domain*
Former office of Adolf Eichmann, Berlin	*Ullstein Bild/TopFoto*
Grünewald station	*Author photograph*
Grünewald railway sleeper (one)	*Author photograph*
Grünewald railway sleeper (two)	*Author photograph*
Kinderzenen – Träumerei score by Schumann	*Public domain*
Diagram of Wannsee participants	*Darren Bennett*
Wannsee Conference minutes page 1	*Public domain*
Wannsee Conference minutes page 2	*Public domain*
Wannsee Conference minutes page 3	*Public domain*
Wannsee Conference minutes page 4	*Public domain*
Wannsee Conference minutes page 5	*Public domain*
Wannsee Conference minutes page 6	*Public domain*
Wannsee Conference minutes page 7	*Public domain*
Wannsee Conference minutes page 8	*Public domain*
Wannsee Conference minutes page 9	*Public domain*
Wannsee Conference minutes page 10	*Public domain*
Wannsee Conference minutes page 14	*Public domain*
Wannsee Conference minutes page 15	*Public domain*
The Wannsee Conference villa	*Author photograph*
Wannsee lake	*Author photograph*
The meeting room at the Haus der Wannseekonferenz	*Wikimedia Commons 2017. Kjetil Ree. Used under license: CC-BY-SA 3.0*
Student group at the Haus der Wannseekonferenz	*Wikimedia Commons 2016. Dr. Avishai Teicher. Used under license: CC-BY-SA 4.0*
Carpathians walk	*Author photograph*
Carpathians tree	*Author photograph*
Trzbinia station	*Author photograph*
Oswiecim bridge	*Author photograph*
Oswiecim flats	*Author photograph*
Oswiecim chemical workers estate	*Author photograph*

Oswiecim outskirts with trees	*Author photograph*
Oswiecim pipes next to chemical plant	*Author photograph*
Buna today	*Author photograph*
Oswiecim sign	*Author photograph*
Monowice sign	*Author photograph*
Map of Oswiecim/ Auschwitz	*Darren Bennett*
Monowice hamlet	*Author photograph*
Map of Chelmno	*Darren Bennett*
Zawadki house	*Author photograph*
Zawadki trees at site of mill building	*Author photograph*
Inside Krystof's taxi	*Author photograp*
Chelmno museum	*Author photograph*
Zdzisław Lorek and J. at Chelmno	*Author photograph*
Chelmno church	*Author photograph*
Chelmno grave	*Author photograph*
360 in the snow	*Author photograph*
Chelmno walk 1	*Author photograph*
Chelmno walk 2	*Author photograph*
Chelmno walk 3	*Author photograph*
Chelmno walk 4	*Author photograph*
Chelmno walk 5	*Author photograph*
Chelmno walk 6	*Author photograph*
Chelmno walk 7	*Author photograph*
Chelmno Waldlager	*Author photograph*
Lidice school class, 1942	*© Hulton-Deutsch Collection/Corbis/Getty Images*
Book Two:	
Jan Karski	*Wikimedia Commons 2011. Lilly M. Used under license: CC-BY-SA 3.0*
Albert Speer on plane	*Ullstein Bild/Getty Images*
Speer with children	*Public domain*
Mark in Germany	*Author collection*
Mark and author as boy	*Author collection*
Mark in Korea	*Author collection*
Plaque on Pont Saint-Michel, Paris	*Public domain*
Map of Namibia	*Darren Bennett*
Extermination order by von Trotha	*Public domain*

The Rider statue, Windhoek	*Wikimedia Commons 2004. Harald Süpfle. Used under license: CC-BY-SA 2.5*
Karl Dove	*Public domain*
Paul Rohrbach	*Public domain*
Eugen Fischer	*Ullstein Bild/Getty Images*
Captain Cook, from *The Story of Captain Cook* by L. du Garde Peach/ John Kenney	*Penguin Random House*
Governor Sir George Arthur	*Public domain via Wikimedia Commons*
Truganini	*Public domain via Wikimedia Commons*
Sir Charles Trevelyan	*Universal History Archive/ Getty Images*
Karl Marx	*Roger Viollet/Getty Images*
Willy Brandt in Warsaw, December 1970	*Getty Images*
Heidemarie Wieczorek-Zeul and Namibian officials, Namibia, 2004	*Public domain*
Turkish migrant worker in Germany, 1973, from *A Seventh Man* by Berger/ Mohr	*© Jean Mohr, Musée de l'Elysee, Lausanne*
The Anatomy Lesson of Dr Tulp, Rembrandt van Rijn, 1632	*Public domain via Wikimedia Commons*
Self-Portrait with Velvet Beret, Rembrandt van Rijn	*Public domain via Wikimedia Commons*
Farmhouse in Suffolk	*Author photograph*
Will of Sir Herbert Waterhouse	*Author collection*
Map of Weimar/ Buchenwald walk	*Darren Bennett*
Goethe's Gartenhaus, Weimar	*Wikimedia Commons 2014. Dr. Bernd Gross. Used under license: CC-BY-SA 3.0*
Weimar to Buchenwald walk 1	*Author photograph*
Weimar to Buchenwald walk 2	*Author photograph*
Weimar to Buchenwald walk 3	*Author photograph*
Weimar to Buchenwald walk 4	*Author photograph*
Weimar to Buchenwald walk 5	*Author photograph*
Weimar to Buchenwald walk 6	*Author photograph*
The gates of Buchenwald	*Author photograph*

Jay Bybee	*Public domain via Wikimedia Commons*
Steven Bradbury	*Public domain via Wikimedia Commons*
Kurt Schmitt of Allianz saluting behind Adolf Hitler, 1 May 1934	*Bayerische Staatsbibliothek, München/Bildarchiv*
Allianz advertisement	*Public domain*
Deutsche Bank advertisement	*Public domain*
Thomas Watson and Adolf Hitler	*Public domain*
Hollerith machine	*Public domain*
Table of the top 100 countries and corporations	*Public domain (but based on Global Justice Now's original table)*
Spandau Prison	*Public domain*
Georges Casalis	*© Société de l'Histoire du Protestantisme Français.*
Simone Weil	*Public domain via Wikimedia Commons*
Grosvenor Hall, Ashford	*Kingswood Learning & Leisure Group*